The International Business Environment

Global and Local Marketplaces in a Changing World

Second Edition

Janet Morrison

palgrave
macmillan

First published 2002
Second edition published 2006 by
PALGRAVE MACMILLAN
Houndmills, Basingstoke, Hampshire RG21 6XS and
175 Fifth Avenue, New York, N.Y. 10010
Companies and representatives throughout the world

PALGRAVE MACMILLAN is the global academic imprint of the Palgrave Macmillan division of St. Martin's Press, LLC and of Palgrave Macmillan Ltd. Macmillan® is a registered trademark in the United States, United Kingdom and other countries. Palgrave is a registered trademark in the European Union and other countries.

ISBN-13: 978–1–4039–3691–2
ISBN-10: 1–4039–3691–9

This book is printed on paper suitable for recycling and made from fully managed and sustained forest sources. Logging, pulping and manufac-turing processes are expected to conform to the environmental regula-tions of the country of origin.

A catalogue record for this book is available from the British Library.

A catalog record for this book is available from the Library of Congress.

Library of Congres Catalog Card Number: 2005056112

10 9 8 7 6 5 4
15 14 13 12 11 10 09 08

Printed and bound in China

Contents

List of figures	x
List of tables	xii
List of case studies	xiii
List of maps	xiv
Preface to the second edition	xv
Acknowledgements	xvi
List of acronyms	xvii
Maps	xviii

Introduction	xxiii
Themes and plan of the book	xxiv
Part 1: The business in its environment	xxv
Part 2: Dimensions of the international environment	xxv
Part 3: Global forces	xxv
Part 4: Issues and challenges	xxvi
Features	xxvi

Part 1 The Business in its Environment	1
1 The internal business environment	3
Introduction	4
What is business?	5
MINIFILE Amazon.com	7
Classification of businesses	7
Forms of business ownership	7
Classification of businesses by size	11
MINIFILE Picsel technologies	12
Business organization	13
Functional approach	13
Divisional structure	14
Matrix structure	16

Organizations and change: business strategy	18
Hierarchies and networks	21
Corporate governance	23
Governance structures	23
Governance issues in the contemporary environment	28
Tools for formulating business strategy	30
PEST analysis	30
SWOT analysis	31
Conclusions	33
Review questions	34
Assignments	34
Further reading	35

2 Functional dimensions which shape the organization and its strategy	36
Introduction	37
Operations	38
Operations strategy and performance	41
Operations in the international environment	43
Marketing	43
The marketing concept	44
Elements of marketing	45
Marketing in the international environment	48
Human resource management	51
Elements of HRM	52
HRM in the international environment	54
Accounting and finance	56
Elements of management accounting and financial reporting	56
Accounting and finance in the international environment	58
Innovation	59
New product development	60
Innovation strategy	61

Conclusions   63
Review questions   63
Assignments   64
Further reading   64

3   The national economic environment   65
    Introduction   66
    The macroeconomic environment: flows of
        economic resources   66
    Gross national income and gross domestic product   67
    Industrial structure   70
    Inflation and unemployment   71
        Inflation   71
        Unemployment   74
    Balance of payments   75
    Economic growth   76
    The business cycle   79
    The role of governance in the economy   81
        Institutional framework of economic policy   81
        Fiscal policy   82
        Monetary pollicy   85
    European Monetary Union (EMU)   86
    MINIFILE Maastricht convergence criteria   87
    Conclusions   91
    Review questions   92
    Assignments   92
    Further reading   92

4   Major economic systems   93
    Introduction   94
    Overview of world economic systems   94
    Capitalism: elements of the market economy   95
    MINIFILE The United States economy   95
        Freedom of enterprise   95
        Competitive markets: supply and demand   97
    MINIFILE The British economy   101
        Private property   101
    Market structures   102
        Porter's five-forces model   103
        Monopoly and oligopoly   105
        Competition policy   106
    Social market capitalism   109
    MINIFILE The French economy   109
    MINIFILE The German economy   111
    Asian capitalism   112
        Japan   112
    MINIFILE The Japanese economy   113

    The late industrializing economies of Asia   113
    MINIFILE The two Koreas   114
        An Asian model of capitalism?   116
    The planned economy   117
        The Soviet Union   117
        From state plan to market: the example
            of China   117
    MINIFILE The Chinese economy   118
    Transition economies in Central and Eastern Europe   119
        The transition process   121
        Impact of EU enlargement on European
            economies   123
    Divergence and regionalization   126
    Conclusions   127
    Review questions   128
    Assignments   128
    Further reading   129
    End of Part 1 case study   130

Part 2 Dimensions of the International
Environment   135

5   The global economy and globalization
    processes   137
    Introduction   138
    Globalization   138
    Internationalization vs. globalization: the role
        of FDI   140
    Transnational or multinational corporations   141
    The growth of TNCs as drivers of the global
        economy   144
    International business in the context of
        postwar shifts in international power   145
    Trends in globalization processes   148
    Globalization of the firm   152
    Industrial production: the legacy of Fordism   154
    Post-Fordist organizations   156
    MINIFILE Kaizen   157
    Organizational changes and TNCs   158
    Global and local markets   159
    Transnationality of the firm   161
    The globalization debate   163
    Conclusions   164
    Review questions   165
    Assignments   165
    Further reading   165

6   The cultural environment: diversity and
    globalization   167
    Introduction   168
    What is culture and how is it relevant to business? 168
    National cultures   172
    Languages   174
        Linguistic diversity   175
        English: the global language?   178
    Religions   179
        Christianity   181
    MINIFILE The megachurch as big business   182
        Islam   182
        Asian religions   186
    Western values and Asian values: the debate   187
    Multicultural societies   189
    Cultural theories   191
    Organizational culture   195
    Culture change   198
    Cultural globalization: myth or reality?   199
        Role of the media in cultural globalization   199
    MINIFILE Multilingual websites   200
        Global culture and national culture   201
    Conclusions   201
    Review questions   202
    Assignments   203
    Further reading   203

7   Society and business   204
    Introduction   205
    Types of society: the development of modern
        industrial societies   206
    Stratification in societies   208
        Rigid social stratification   208
        Social class   209
        Changes in capitalist society   210
    Changing populations   212
        Ageing societies and implications for business   213
        International migration   217
        Recent patterns of migration   218
    Urbanism   221
        Urbanization in Western economies   222
        Urbanization in the developing world   224
    Labour relations   225
    Gender and work   227
    Families   230
    Conclusions   232
    Review questions   233

    Assignments   233
    Further reading   233

8   The changing political environment:
    national, regional and international forces   234
    Introduction   235
    The political sphere and civil society: how political
        factors affect business   235
    Nation-states and political framework   237
        Territoriality and the state   238
        Sovereignty   240
        Political risk and national security   242
    MINIFILE NATO   243
    Sources of authority in the state   246
    Democracy and authoritarianism contrasted   247
    Democratic government: the criteria   248
    Unitary and federal states   250
    Legislative assemblies   252
    Elections   253
    MINIFILE The referendum in democratic systems   255
    Political parties   256
    Systems of government: presidential, parliamentary
        and 'hybrid' systems   259
    Transitional democracies   262
        Regional divergence in democratic transition   263
        Transitional democracies and international
            business   266
    Global politics   266
        The United Nations   267
    MINIFILE Charter of the United Nations   267
        The European Union   269
    Conclusions   273
    Review questions   274
    Assignments   274
    Further reading   274

9   The international legal environment of
    business: moving towards harmonization   275
    Introduction   276
    How legal systems affect business   277
    National legal systems   280
        Civil law tradition   282
        Common law tradition   284
        Non-Western legal systems   285
    Legal framework of the European Union   286
    International business transactions   289
        International codification   289

Cultural factors in international contracts   290
Resolution of disputes in international business   291
   Contractual disputes   291
   Negligence and product liability   293
MINIFILE Global companies under fire   295
Crime, corruption and law   298
The growing impact of international law on business   299
   Treaties and conventions   300
   Settlement of disputes in international law   300
Human rights   301
MINIFILE Implications for business of the Human Rights Act 1998   304
Conclusions   305
Review questions   306
Assignments   306
Further reading   306
End of Part 2 case study   307

Part 3 Global Forces   311

10 World trade and the international competitive environment   313
Introduction   314
International trade theories   316
   The theory of comparative advantage   316
   Newer trade theories   318
   Porter's theory of competitive advantage   318
MINIFILE Global competitiveness rankings   322
   Product life cycle theory   323
Trade policy and national priorities   324
   Promoting industrialization   325
   Protecting employment   325
   Protecting consumers   326
   Promoting national interests   326
Tools of governmental trade policy   327
International regulation of trade   330
   GATT principles   331
   WTO and the regulation of world trade   332
Trade liberalization: the Doha Round   334
   Labour standards and environmental protection   335
   International competition policy   336
Regionalism   337
   The European Union   340
   NAFTA   341
   Regionalism in Asia   343
Developing countries and world trade   344

Globalization and the world trading system   346
Conclusions   347
Review questions   347
Assignments   348
Further reading   348

11 Technology and innovation   349
Introduction   350
Concepts and processes   351
Technological innovation theories   353
   Schumpeter's industrial waves theory   353
   Product life cycle theory reconsidered   355
National innovation systems   357
   Education and training   358
   Science and technology capabilities   359
   Industrial structure   360
   Science and technology strengths and weaknesses   361
   Interactions within the innovation system   361
   Some conclusions on national innovation systems   362
Patents and innovation   364
MINIFILE Where would we be without...?   365
   What is a patentable invention?   365
   Patent rights   366
   The Trade-related Aspects of Intellectual Property agreement   369
Technology transfer   370
   Channels for international technology transfer   370
   Technology diffusion and innovation   372
Information and communications technology (ICT)   373
   The technology revolution   373
   The internet and e-commerce   375
Biotechnology   380
Globalization and technological innovation   383
Conclusions   383
Review questions   384
Assignments   385
Further reading   385

12 International financial markets   386
Introduction   387
International capital markets   387
   Stock exchanges   388
MINIFILE The UK Financial Services Authority   391
   Bond markets   391
Development of the international monetary system   392
   The gold standard   393

The Bretton Woods agreement   393

Foreign exchange in the contemporary environment 395
  Exchange rate systems   395
  Money markets   396

The International Monetary Fund (IMF) and the
  World Bank   397

The Asian financial crisis   401
  Genesis of the crisis   401
  Aftermath of the crisis   402

Global markets for corporate control   406
  Mergers and acquisitions   406
  Trends in cross-border mergers   407

Regulation and TNCs   411

The global financial environment and developing
  countries   412

Conclusions   414

Review questions   414

Assignments   415

Further reading   415

End of Part 3 case study   416

Part 4 Issues and Challenges   **421**

**13 Environmental challenges: global and
local perspectives**   **423**

Introduction   424

Environmental degradation   425

Climate change   427

Transboundary pollution and implications for
  energy policies   431

International legal frameworks   433

MINIFILE The Rio Declaration on Environment
and Development, 1992   434

Challenges of environmental protection for business 435
  Sustainable development in the business
    context   435
  Environmental management   437

EU initiatives on the environment   439

MINIFILE Protecting the environment: the
UK Budget 2000   441

Green consumerism   442

Environmental protection and changing values   443

Conclusions   444

Review questions   446

Assignments   446

Further reading   446

**14 Global challenges and the responsible
business**   **447**

Introduction   448

Global and national environments: an overview   448

Change in the business environment   449

Left behind? The least developed nations   451
  Poverty: its many dimensions   452
  Development prospects for Africa   457

Social responsibility of the firm   460
  Theories of corporate social responsibility   463
  Raising corporate standards   466
  Reaching for international standards   467

Challenges of the new information age   468

Globalization and national diversity: the way ahead 470

Conclusions   471

Review questions   472

Assignments   472

Further reading   473

End of Part 4 case study   474

Glossary   479

References   494

Index   506

List of figures

1.1 The business organization in its environment 4

1.2 Contrasting perceptions of self-employment 8

1.3 Percentage of enterprises, employment and turnover in micro, small, medium and large firms in the UK, at the start of 2002 12

1.4 Organization based on functional departments 14

1.5 The multidivisional structure 15

1.6 The global matrix 16

1.7 Corporate governance structure typical of an American or UK company 24

1.8 Shareholder and stakeholder perspectives on corporate governance 29

1.9 PEST analysis in the international business environment 31

1.10 SWOT analysis 32

1.11 SWOT analysis for a business selling wine online 32

2.1 Business functions in the organizational environment 37

2.2 The transformation process 38

2.3 Brand share of the US passenger car market 46

2.4 Marketing mix 47

2.5 Consumer perceptions of brand portfolios as healthy 50

2.6 Strategic HRM 54

2.7 The digital photography revolution 59

3.1 Circular flows of income in the economy 67

3.2 Changes in GNI in selected economies 1998–2002 68

3.3 Employment by industry in the UK, 2004 71

3.4 UK current account 2001–3 76

3.5 Trends in world GDP growth 77

3.6 Breakdown of UK government spending 83

3.7 Government budget balance as percentage of GDP 85

4.1 Total entrepreneurial activity by country 96

4.2 Supply and demand: the determination of equilibrium price 98

4.3 Porter's five forces model: forces driving industry competition 103

4.4 Accession 10 states as a percentage of the European Union's population 124

4.5 Accession 10 states as a percentage of European Union GDP 124

4.6 Share of agriculture as a percentage of employment in 10 new EU member and 3 applicant countries 126

5.1 World inflows of foreign direct investment 149

5.2 Comparisons in ownership of FDI outward stock 149

5.3 National regulatory changes, 1992–2002 150

5.4 Internationalizing production by the TNC 153

6.1 Online language populations 179

6.2 World Christianity by denomination 181

7.1 World population in 2003 212

7.2 World population estimates for 2050 213

7.3a Proportion of total population aged 0–14 and 60 and over, for more developed regions 213

7.3b Proportion of total population aged 0–14 and 60 and over, for less developed regions 214

7.4 Ageing populations 215

7.5 Migration 2000–2050: major sending and receiving countries of migrants 218

7.6 Flows of remittances to home countries 219

7.7 Remittances as percentage of GDP 219

7.8 Projected growth in urban populations, 2003–2030 222

7.9 Trade union density in the UK 226

7.10 Women in the workforce 227

7.11 Women's average hourly pay as a percentage of men's, for UK full-time employees 228

8.1 United Nations member states 238
8.2 US military spending compared to the rest of the world 243
8.3a The German general election 2002: percentage of the vote 254
8.3b The German general election 2002: composition of the Bundestag 255
8.4 Shifting priorities of voters 259
8.5 Parties' share of votes in UK general election, 2005 261
8.6 Parties' share of seats in House of Commons after UK general election, 2005 261
8.7 Freedom survey among the world's independent states 263
8.8 Voter turnout in European Parliament elections 272

9.1 The three interlocking spheres of the international legal environment 276
9.2 County Court claims in England and Wales 280
9.3 Businesses' lack of confidence in courts 281
9.4 Cost of the tort system as percentage of GDP 294
9.5 Firms reporting bribes: regional variations 298
9.6 Breakdown of counterfeit goods seized in the EU, 2003 299

10.1 Shares of merchandise exports of the major exporting regions 314
10.2a World merchandise trade: leading exporters 315
10.2b World merchandise trade: leading importers 315
10.3 Porter's diamond: the determinants of national advantage 319
10.4 International product life cycle 324
10.5 Agricultural subsidies in selected economies 329
10.6 Export flows within and between major regions (merchandise flows) 337
10.7 Increase in numbers of regional trade agreements notified to GATT/WTO, 1950–2002 338
10.8 Shares of world merchandise exports by region 345

11.1 The innovation process for intellectual property 351
11.2 Student performance in science in selected OECD countries 358
11.3 University graduates with science and engineering degrees 359
11.4 Expenditure on R&D in selected OECD countries 360
11.5 R&D expenditure as a percentage of GDP 360

11.6a PCT applications from the three top-ranking countries 369
11.6b PCT applications from other key countries 369
11.7 Growth in EU internet use by individuals and enterprises 375
11.8 Internet usage by individuals, compared according to educational level 375
11.9 Breakdown of global internet use by region 376
11.10 Online retail sales in Europe, 2004 377

12.1 European IPOs, 1997 to June 2004 388
12.2 The FTSE all-world index 389
12.3 Number of shares listed on major stock exchanges 390
12.4 Corporate bond issues in the US, 2000 to June 2004 392
12.5 Dollar fluctuation against Western European and Asian currencies 395
12.6 Exchange rates of Asian currencies against the US dollar 402
12.7 Foreign bank lending and FDI flows for Indonesia and five Asian economies 403
12.8 Cross-border mergers and acquisitions by economy of purchaser 408

13.1 Greenhouse gas emissions per capita 427
13.2 Percentage share of world greenhouse gas emissions 427
13.3 Gap between emissions in 2000 and Kyoto targets 429
13.4 World coal consumption by region 432
13.5 Share of nuclear power in electricity generation 433
13.6 UK greenhouse gas emissions in 1990 and projections for 2010 440

14.1 GDP per capita in the poorest and richest countries 452
14.2 People living on less than US$1 per day 453
14.3 OECD agricultural subsidies in perspective 458
14.4 US and EU agricultural subsidies contrasted with development aid 458
14.5 Carroll's pyramid of corporate social responsibility 464
14.6 Prevalence of internet use in different regions 469

List of tables

3.1 Size of the economy in selected countries 69

3.2 International comparisons of unemployment, 2004 74

3.3 Corporation tax rates in selected countries 84

4.1 Productivity gains in formerly nationalized industries 108

4.2 Economic profiles of the European Union's 10 new member states acceding in 2004 125

4.3 Economic indicators for selected transition economies in the wider Europe 126

5.1 Globalization: two schools of thought 139

5.2 The world's top ten non-financial TNCs by foreign assets, 2002 145

5.3 The world's top TNCs by degree of transnationality, 2002 162

6.1 The world's top ten languages 175

6.2 Web content by language 179

6.3 Growth of major world religions 180

6.4 Ranks of selected countries on four dimensions of national culture, based on research by Hofstede 193

6.5 Growth in television ownership 199

7.1 UK socioeconomic classification scheme 209

7.2 Population in major areas of the world, 1950, 2000 and 2003 212

7.3 Distribution of the world's population in urban and rural areas 222

7.4 The world's ten largest cities 224

8.1 Military commitment in selected states 242

8.2 Women in national legislatures in selected EU countries 253

8.3 Summary of systems of government 262

8.4 The Council and Parliament of the European Union 271

9.1 Summary of major areas of law affecting business and relevant authorities 277

9.2 Outline of civil law and criminal law 278

9.3 Legal protection of foreign investors in China 279

9.4 Selected civil law and common law countries 282

9.5 Summary of civil law and common law traditions 285

10.1 Regional trade groupings 339

11.1 Declining costs of transport and communications 350

11.2 Summary of long waves of technical change 354

11.3 Patent applications to the European Patent Office 368

11.4 PCs and internet users across the world 374

12.1 Global acquisitions, 1999–2000 408

14.1 Global and national environments 449

14.2 Rich countries' policies towards the least-developed countries 459

14.3 Economic activity of children in different regions, 2000 466

List of case studies

1.1 Has restructuring paid off at Procter & Gamble? 17

1.2 Honda and the US motorcycle market 19

1.3 Disney Corporation: it all started with a mouse 26

2.1 Ryanair and the revolution in low-cost air travel 39

2.2 Nike becomes a fan of football 48

2.3 The Apple iPod sets the standard 60

3.1 The ups and downs of manufacturing in Wales 73

3.2 Is Germany back on track for economic growth? 78

3.3 Sweden says 'no' to the euro 87

4.1 Changing global demand for mobile phones 99

4.2 Microsoft takes on the antitrust authorities 106

4.3 National champions in France 110

4.4 IKEA branches out in Russia 119

End of Part 1: A bright future for Coca-Cola? 130

5.1 FDI bonanza in China 142

5.2 Formula for FDI success in the Czech Republic 146

5.3 Finding the right strategy for setting up shop in Japan 160

6.1 Image change at McDonald's 170

6.2 Winning over Hispanic consumers in the US 176

6.3 Islam under strain in Saudi Arabia 184

6.4 Can DaimlerChrysler turn an amalgam of corporate cultures to its advantage? 196

7.1 New era of the flexible friend in Asia 206

7.2 The growing power of the older consumer 216

7.3 Call centre jobs migrate to India 229

8.1 Testing times for democracy in Nigeria 239

8.2 Challenging times for Spain's politicians 250

8.3 The voices of Indian democracy 257

8.4 Costa Rican democracy reaps FDI rewards 264

9.1 Legal reforms win business in Turkey 283

9.2 Legal battle between Tesco and Levi Strauss 287

9.3 Asbestos: liability goes global 296

9.4 Firestone recalls 6.5 million tyres 297

End of Part 2: Fiat: Italian champion struggles to compete globally 307

10.1 The impact of oil in world trade 316

10.2 Two cheers for Australia's wine exporters 320

10.3 Trade war averted over steel tariffs 332

10.4 Brazil's trading relations: signalling shifts in global trade 342

11.1 Sony aims to keep a step ahead 356

11.2 New start for South Korea's GM Daewoo 362

11.3 Feeling lucky with Google 378

11.4 Food for thought in the debate on genetically modified organisms 381

12.1 Argentina tests international financial institutions 398

12.2 The lessons of financial crisis in Indonesia 403

12.3 Vodafone's takeover of Mannesmann: a turning point for European takeovers? 409

End of Part 3: GE seeks growth in a globalized environment 416

13.1 Global water resources become precarious 430

13.2 Ecover cleans up with green consumers 439

14.1 The worldwide garment industry: winners and losers 455

14.2 Vibrant coffee culture contrasts with woes for producers 461

End of Part 4: GlaxoSmithKline and what the world expects from a big pharmaceutical company 474

List of maps

Africa and the Middle East	xviii
Asia and Australasia	xix
South America	xx
North America	xxi
Europe	xxii

Preface to the second edition

This second edition aspires to meet the same needs of readers as the first edition and improve on that effort in ways readers will find helpful and informative. The aim remains to provide an introductory text for business and management students on a range of undergraduate and postgraduate courses. The most obvious changes from the first edition are that the book has grown in size and is now organized into four major parts. In addition to the short case studies in each chapter, there are now longer case studies at the end of each part, which bring together the themes of the relevant chapters and invite critical analysis. The former Chapter 12, on global changes and challenges, has now expanded into two chapters, which form Part 4, in recognition of the growing importance of environmental and ethical issues.

As in the first edition, I have attempted to clarify basic concepts for readers with little or no background in business studies. To this end, an additional chapter, Chapter 2, on functional dimensions, has been included, bearing in mind the needs of readers who are unfamiliar with these specialist areas. I have also been aware of the need to offer space for critical reflection on the many broad issues that arise. Hence, an additional feature of this edition is the inclusion of 'Critical perspectives', which invite thought and discussion. All other features have been retained and updated. As well as updating data, I have tried to highlight changes and trends which, while not readily measurable in quantitative terms, are, nonetheless, re-shaping the ways in which we perceive the world. As with the first edition, I have endeavoured to present the material clearly, offering balanced comment and interesting case examples with which the reader can engage.

The book's perspective remains thoroughly international, in both approach and case study examples. Students and teachers who have let me know their thoughts on the first edition have expressed appreciation of this approach. I am grateful for their comments and I hope this new edition meets with their approval.

I owe thanks to the reviewers of both the first edition and the draft of the second, who provided much insight through their comments, which I have aimed to take into account.

JANET MORRISON

Acknowledgements

I would like to thank Ian Morrison and Ursula Gavin. Without their help and encouragement, this book would not have been written.

Every effort has been made to trace all the copyright-holders, but if any have been inadvertently overlooked the publishers will be pleased to make the necessary arrangements at the first opportunity.

List of acronyms

AIDS/HIV	acquired immunodeficiency syndrome/ human immunodeficiency virus
APEC	Asia-Pacific Economic Cooperation Group
ASEAN	Association of Southeast Asian Nations
B2B	business-to-business
B2C	business-to-consumer
BSE	bovine spongiform encephalopathy
CAD	computer-aided design
CEO	chief executive officer
CISG	Convention on Contracts for the International Sale of Goods
CPI	consumer price index
DEFRA	Department for Environment, Food and Rural Affairs (UK)
ECHR	European Convention on Human Rights
ECJ	European Court of Justice
ECB	European Central Bank
EMU	European Monetary Union
EPC	European Patent Convention
EPO	European Patent Office
ERM	exchange rate mechanism
EU	European Union
FDI	foreign direct investment
FSA	Financial Services Authority (UK)
GATT	General Agreement on Tariffs and Trade
GDP	gross domestic product
GM	genetically modified
GNI	gross national income
HIPCs	heavily indebted poor countries
HRM	human resource management
ICC	International Criminal Court
ICJ	International Court of Justice
ICT	information and communication technology
IMF	International Monetary Fund
IT	information technology
ILO	International Labour Organization
IP	intellectual property

IPO	initial public offering
ISO	International Organization for Standardization
LBO	leveraged buy-out
LDCs	least developed countries
M&A	merger and acquisition
MEA	multilateral environmental agreement
NAFTA	North American Free Trade Agreement
NATO	North Atlantic Treaty Organization
NIEs	newly industrialized economies
NGO	non-governmental organization
OECD	Organization for Economic Co-operation and Development
OPEC	Organization of Petroleum Exporting Countries
PCT	Patent Co-operation Treaty
PPP	purchasing power parity
PR	proportional representation
QMV	qualified majority voting
RTA	regional trade agreement
RPI	Retail Price Index
R&D	research and development
SME	small to medium-size enterprise
SOE	state-owned enterprise
TNC	transnational corporation
TRIPs	Trade-related Aspects of Intellectual Property
UK	United Kingdom
UN	United Nations
UNCITRAL	United Nations Commission on International Trade Law
UNCTAD	United Nations Conference on Trade and Development
UNEP	United Nations Environment Programme
UNIDROIT	United Nations International Institute for the Unification of Private International Law
US/USA	United States of America
VERs	voluntary export restraints
WIPO	World Intellectual Property Organization
WTO	World Trade Organization

Maps

Africa and the Middle East

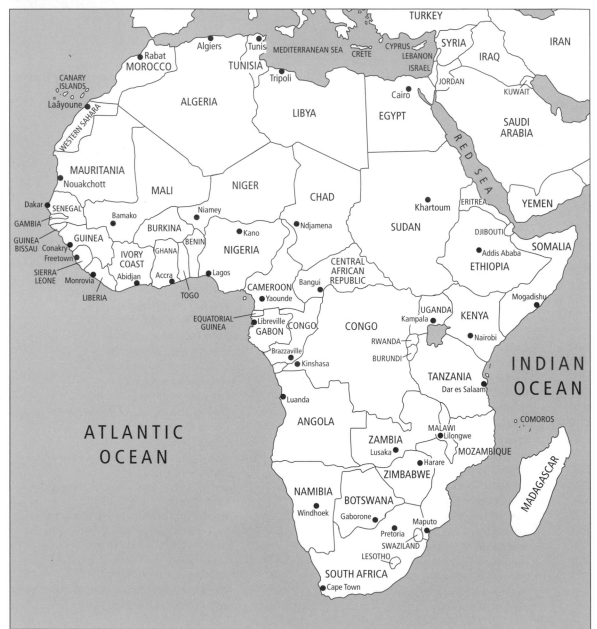

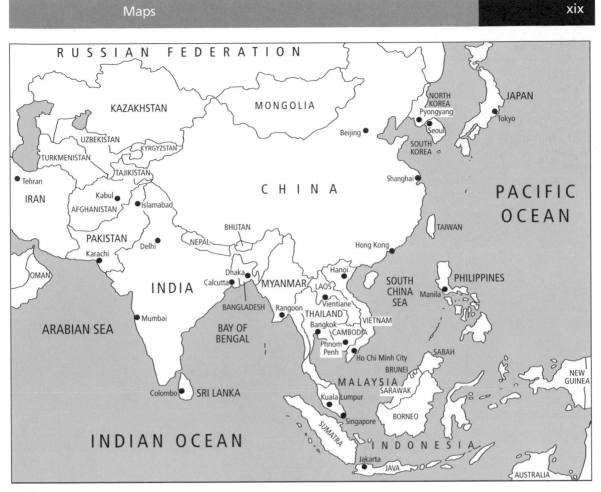

Asia

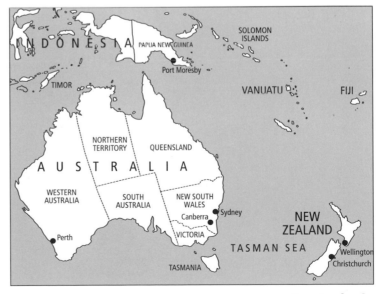

Australasia

South America

North America

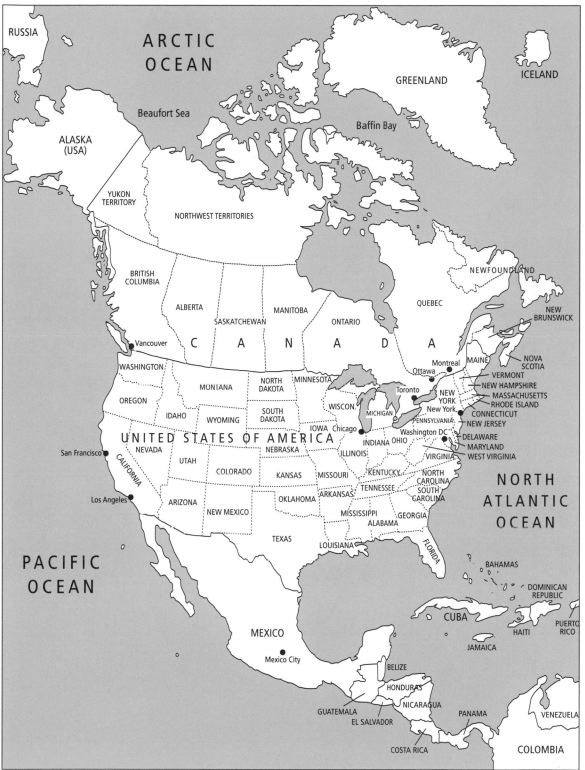

RUSSIA

ARCTIC OCEAN

GREENLAND

ICELAND

Beaufort Sea

Baffin Bay

ALASKA (USA)

YUKON TERRITORY

NORTHWEST TERRITORIES

BRITISH COLUMBIA

NEWFOUNDLAND

ALBERTA

SASKATCHEWAN

MANITOBA

ONTARIO

QUEBEC

C A N A D A

Vancouver

NEW BRUNSWICK

WASHINGTON

MONTANA

NORTH DAKOTA

MINNESOTA

Montreal

MAINE

NOVA SCOTIA

Ottawa

VERMONT

OREGON

IDAHO

WYOMING

SOUTH DAKOTA

WISCON.

Toronto

NEW HAMPSHIRE

MASSACHUSETTS

RHODE ISLAND

MICHIGAN

NEW YORK

New York

CONNECTICUT

NEW JERSEY

San Francisco

CALIFORNIA

NEVADA

UTAH

IOWA

Chicago

PENNSYLVANIA

UNITED STATES OF AMERICA

INDIANA

OHIO

Washington DC

DELAWARE

MARYLAND

COLORADO

NEBRASKA

ILLINOIS

VIRGINIA

WEST VIRGINIA

NORTH ATLANTIC OCEAN

Los Angeles

ARIZONA

NEW MEXICO

KANSAS

MISSOURI

KENTUCKY

TENNESSEE

NORTH CAROLINA

SOUTH CAROLINA

OKLAHOMA

ARKANSAS

MISSISSIPPI

ALABAMA

GEORGIA

TEXAS

LOUISIANA

FLORIDA

PACIFIC OCEAN

BAHAMAS

DOMINICAN REPUBLIC

MEXICO

CUBA

PUERTO RICO

HAITI

JAMAICA

Mexico City

BELIZE

HONDURAS

GUATEMALA

NICARAGUA

EL SALVADOR

PANAMA

VENEZUELA

COSTA RICA

COLOMBIA

Europe

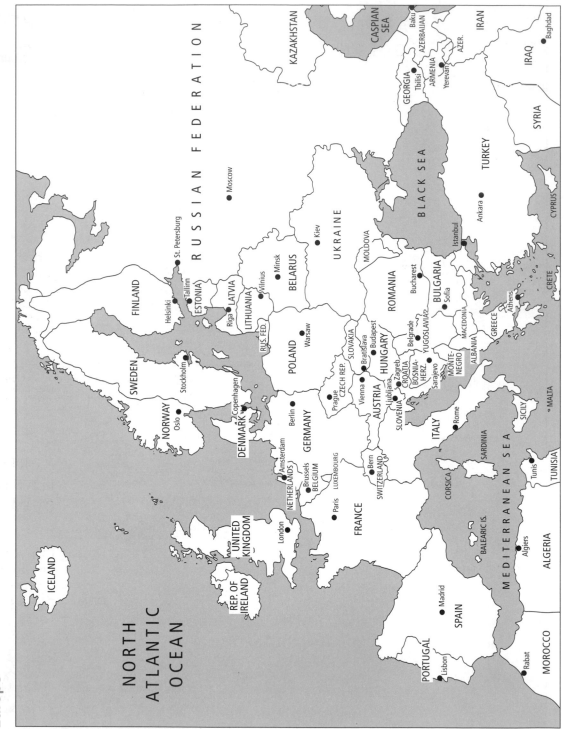

Introduction

While the study of business activities from an academic point of view goes back many years, the notion of business studies as a coherent set of disciplines comprising whole degree courses is relatively new, having blossomed only in the past three decades. In that relatively short time, however, our views of how to approach business studies, both in the structured academic setting and the world of business generally, have changed dramatically, in two major ways. First, it used to be customary to look on the business organization itself as taking centre stage and see the environment as being of less importance, simply 'background', and not directly relevant to the operations of business. This attitude has now given way to an approach which encompasses the business in its environment seen as an entirety, recognizing that there are no strict boundaries between the organization and its environment. The relationship is one of dynamic interaction: as social influences, for example, shape business activities, so businesses bring about changes in the society in which they operate. Indeed, our notion of the environment itself has broadened to encompass international forces. Secondly, the main focus of business studies has traditionally been national business life, bringing in the international dimension only as an 'added-on' dimension. This view, too, is no longer tenable. As business has become increasingly globalized, the distinction between home country and international environment has become blurred. The international dimension has moved from the periphery to the centre. For business managers, as for students of business, a recognition of the new centrality of the international sphere presents a more complex and challenging environmental perspective, opening up broader horizons and presenting far greater opportunities in the wider global economy.

In this, the second edition of this book, the international perspective remains the focus. While, again, readers will find that many core concepts and principles are explained in the context of the UK environment, equal attention is given to other geographic regions and the interrelationships between regions and national economies. The major developed economies, including the US and Japan, as well as the transition economies of Central and Eastern Europe and Asia are covered. The growing importance of China has warranted extensive discussion. The deepening integration of other developing countries in the world economy, with their divergent perspectives on international business, is also covered.

Much is now made of the opportunities – and risks – presented by the new economy, the high-tech world of global companies whose lifeblood is the internet, and who inhabit the borderless 'invisible continent'. But all companies, even virtual ones, still depend on business structures, employees and customers in the context of national environments, each with its own particular social and institutional makeup. This book takes a genuinely multidisciplinary approach, giving weight to all aspects of the business environment. These include: economic structures, social relations, cultural values, political institutions, technological development, and the global financial and competitive environments. The aim is to look at each sphere from the business point of view and to highlight the interactions between spheres in the international arena. Clearly, formal international links are an important consideration, but so too are the growing informal relations between businesses, greatly enhanced by the growing use of the internet.

Given such a broad expanse of subject matter, this book can aspire only to give an introduction to each subject area. That said, the underlying premise is that an introduction to the basic concepts, principles and frameworks that shape each subject area will be of primary help to the reader in gaining an understanding of the processes at work. Business examples and applications are integrated into the text, providing a balance between theory and practice. The reader will then be able to build on this foundation as specialist knowledge of other disciplines is assimilated. The book focuses on key themes which provide an underpinning for the varied content of each chapter, enabling the reader to develop an overview of the forces driving the global economy.

Themes and plan of the book

A departure from the first edition is the division of the book into four parts, with integrative case studies at the close of each part. It is hoped that grouping chapters under broad headings will make the subject matter more manageable. In addition, the separate parts should afford a sharper focus on the major themes. These themes, which form integrative links between the different aspects of the environment, are:

● *Globalization*, or the deepening global integration between businesses, governments and societies. The business environment has undergone rapid change in the past two decades, largely thanks to the advances of computing and information technology. These changes have impacted not just in the technological environment, but across the environmental spectrum, most particularly in the financial and competitive environments.
● *Diversity* among national societies, groups, regions and organizations, which interact with the forces of globalization. The tensions between global forces and local diversity impact on virtually every business, whether its managers are fully aware of the wider picture or not! Understanding the underlying currents helps considerably in determining appropriate business responses.

The following is a brief summary of the four parts of the book, indicating how the chapters contribute to each part's overall themes.

Part 1: The business in its environment

This part comprises four chapters. Chapter 1 provides an introduction to the business organization, outlining key concepts and organizational structures. The chapter stresses the interactions between internal and external environments in an introduction to business strategy, which includes PEST and SWOT analyses. Chapter 2 analyses the separate functions which characterize any business, linking them to organizational and strategic considerations. Chapters 3 and 4 consider the national economic environment, focusing on the interactions between the organization and the immediate local and national environment, which is likely to have the most profound influence on the firm in its formative stages. Divergent pathways of economic development across the globe are considered in Chapter 4, highlighting economic liberalization and opening markets as a broad trend in the global economy. The closing case study, Coca-Cola, brings together the themes developed in the four chapters, contrasting the company's global brand strategies with diverging consumer markets.

Part 2: Dimensions of the international environment

This part comprises five chapters. Chapter 5 introduces the major theme of globalization and its impacts. It stresses that globalization is not one but many processes, which proceed in different ways and at different speeds in different regions of the world. This theme is explored in the other chapters in this part. Chapter 6 looks at the cultural environment, examining the role of values and norms of behaviour as they inform both organizations and societies. Similarly, Chapter 7, on the social environment, looks at ways in which divergent societies and cultural groups have changed through the forces of industrialization, urbanization and economic development. Long familiar to those in advanced economies, these processes are now bringing about radical changes in many developing and transitional economies. Similarly, the political environment, the subject of Chapter 8, is undergoing radical changes in many countries and having a profound impact on international business. Chapter 9 examines the legal environment. It builds on the institutional and social aspects of national environments discussed in the previous three chapters, and explores the growth of international legal frameworks as they impact on international businesses. These themes are brought together in the closing case study on Fiat.

Part 3: Global forces

There are three chapters in this part. Chapter 10 presents an overall view of the global competitive environment, including world trade. Theories of international trade and competitive advantage are examined in relation to corporate strategies. As well as world trading patterns, the impact of regionalism on trade and the competitive environment is assessed. The subject of Chapter 11 is technology and innovation, one of the acknowledged leading sources of competitive advantage. Innovation and technological capacities are explored at both the national and international level, highlighting trends towards the integration of R&D into international networks. Perhaps one of the chief international dimensions in which globalization is reshaping competitive capacities is the financial environment, which is the subject of Chapter 12. The international institutional framework is explained, along with analytical concepts for understanding global capital flows as they affect transnational business operations across the globe. From the firm's perspective, the strategic area of mergers and acquisitions is explored in the international context. The closing case study, on General Electric (GE), brings together these themes, illustrating GE's changing strategies and structures in the global competitive environment.

Part 4:
Issues and
challenges

The last part consists of two chapters which focus on the challenges facing businesses in the global ecological environment and the societies in which they operate. Chapter 13 is devoted to the natural environment. As processes such as industrialization and the extraction of natural resources have taken their toll on the environment, businesses now recognize their responsibilities for examining their operations in order to reduce environmental degradation. Research on the damaging effects of climate change has lent impetus to governmental and international attempts to reduce emissions; businesses globally are playing crucial roles in these initiatives. A strategic focus on environmental impact is part of an overall approach to social responsibility, which is the subject of Chapter 14. Here, discussion turns to the ways in which businesses are increasingly called on to address the broader social issues beyond their traditional economic role. Social issues have become particularly acute in the developing world, where governments, international organizations and businesses are all engaged. The broader role of the responsible business is highlighted in theories of corporate social responsibility (CSR) and stakeholder management. These themes are integrated in the case study which closes the last part of the book, on the global pharmaceutical company, GlaxoSmithKline.

Each of the four parts is preceded by an introduction, which gives a more detailed account of the chapters.

Features

The book is designed to present the content in an easily accessible manner, with a number of aids for the reader. A new feature of this edition is the **Critical perspectives** box, described below. While ideally one would begin with Chapter 1 and read each successive chapter in order, the book has been designed so that any chapter can be read alone, and the reader will be aided by suitable references to earlier relevant chapters given in brackets. The content of each chapter is divided into sections and subsections, which are outlined at the start of the chapter, and also appear in the Contents. Each chapter also outlines **Learning objectives** at the beginning, to clarify the particular outcomes which the reader can expect from the chapter. **Conclusions** at the end of each chapter provide a concise list of important points by way of summary.

The list that follows outlines other aids that have been included:

- Key concepts, key terms, principles and organizations appear in **bold letters** when used for the first time. They are defined in a **Glossary** at the end.
- References are given in brackets in the text, for example (Smith, 1991). The **References** section at the end of the book is a list of all references in the main text. References within case studies are given at the end of each case study. For newspaper reports, the name of the paper and publication date are given in brackets in the text, as in (*Financial Times*, 6 November 1999).

- **Summary points** boxes appear throughout each chapter. These are not a substitute for reading the section! They should help to consolidate the main points.
- Boxes labelled **Minifile** contain extended examples of particular points, to complement the main text.
- Several short **Case studies** are given in every chapter. These appear in boxes at appropriate points in the text. Each case study consists of a business application of an issue which arises in the international environment. They feature all types of businesses and all areas of the globe. Each case study has case questions at the end, which can be a basis of group discussion or a short assignment.
- **Web alert** boxes appear throughout the text. These refer the reader to websites for additional information, which in turn often contain links to related sites. Every effort has been made to ensure that these addresses are accurate, but websites are constantly changing and do sometimes move house. The Web alert boxes will provide a starting point for further exploration of the topics. They offer a variety of sources, including public information services, governmental offices, non-governmental organizations and companies themselves. A word of caution is, however, in order. Every organization has its own perspective and values, which its website is designed to present to a wider public. While providing helpful information, its interpretation of that information is likely to reflect its own perspective, and may well downplay or leave out aspects of the organization which are less than flattering. A balanced picture is probably best obtained by checking out a number of sources. An unfortunate trend for the student is that many databases provided by public authorities and research bodies, which, while available on the web, are available only on payment of a subscription (sometimes considerable). These bodies do usually provide summary information freely, and universities may pay subscriptions on behalf of their students, to acquire access to an entire database. (The data in this text derives entirely from freely available sources, at the time of access.)
- Suggestions for **Further reading** are given at the end of each chapter. These include a variety of sources. Some are specialized textbooks on the subject for more in-depth study. Others are expositions by well-known authorities in the field, whose works are seen as 'landmark' books or articles. Others are compendiums of articles by a number of scholars, whose journal articles are often difficult to track down in isolation.

Other learning aids are listed below:

- Besides the questions at the end of each case study, a number of **Review questions** are given at the end of each chapter. These are either for self-study or discussion, to check that you have grasped the main points and issues in the chapter.
- Two **Assignments** are given after each set of review questions. These are broader in scope than the review questions. They require some independent research and considered critical analysis of the issues.
- A new feature in this second edition is the inclusion of **Critical perspectives** boxes on relevant topics as they arise. An excerpt is quoted from a leading authority, followed by questions for thought and discussion. Some of these authors present

strong views with which you may well disagree. These passages are intended to be thought-provoking, inviting you to look at different lines of reasoning and form your own assessments of their validity.

● The book contains a number of **maps** for reference. Developing an understanding of the geographical location of nations and regions may seem incidental, but is immensely useful in understanding the substantive issues discussed in the text.

The study of the international business environment has never been more interesting or more challenging. While no one can purport to have all the answers, it is hoped that this book at least points readers on a sound path to understanding the ever-changing world of international business. The advice of Confucius, some 2400 years ago, is still appropriate:

Extend your learning and hold fast to your purpose; question closely and meditate on things at hand: there you will find the fullness of your humanity.

Confucius, *The Analects*
(trans. Simon Leys)

Part 1

The Business in its Environment

1 The internal business environment 3

2 Functional dimensions which shape the organization and its strategy 36

3 The national economic environment 65

4 Major economic systems 93

End of Part 1 case study 130

Every business begins with an idea of a product or service that people will need and be willing to buy. Turning that idea into an economic activity, that will both satisfy the needs of some groups of consumers and generate profits for the owners, is the starting point of Part 1. Most businesses involve a number of people working together. Even in the early stages, therefore, they can be said to have some kind of organization, albeit a rudimentary one, such as two people in partnership. This organizational background is the focus of Chapter 1, which goes on to look at how complex organizations develop and form strategies. The organizational theme is continued in Chapter 2, with an examination of the various functions which business enterprises entail. As will be seen, developing a strategic approach for the long haul involves coordination and balance between these functions.

The most immediate environmental factors which impinge on, and interact with, a business are its local and national environments. These form the bases of Chapters 3 and 4. In Chapter 3, the essential characteristics of a national economic system are examined, while in Chapter 4, different types of national economic systems are discussed, with an eye on how they facilitate enterprises. Case studies in these chapters present examples of businesses which have succeeded (and also some which have struggled) in differing national environments. While the great variety of economic systems across the world is a striking feature, it is also striking to see how businesses adapt in different environments. The final case study in Part 1, on Coca-Cola, brings together these themes. Coca-Cola as a business has faced challenges in terms of its organization, its responsiveness to customers' needs and its operations in different countries. This case is also an appropriate introduction to the dimensions of the international environment explored in Part 2.

1 The internal business environment

Outline of chapter

- ■ Introduction
- ■ What is business?
- ■ Classification of businesses
  - • Forms of business ownership
  - • Classification of businesses by size
- ■ Business organization
  - • Functional approach
  - • Divisional structure
  - • Matrix structure
- ■ Organizations and change: business strategy
- ■ Hierarchies and networks
- ■ Corporate governance
  - • Governance structures
  - • Governance issues in the contemporary environment
- ■ Tools for formulating business strategy
  - • PEST analysis
  - • SWOT analysis
- ■ Conclusions

Learning objectives

1. To identify key elements of the internal and external aspects of the business environment and their dynamic interaction.
2. To recognize different types of business ownership and different designs of business structure and their implications for how businesses are run.
3. To appreciate the many dimensions of strategic change in organizations, in the context of the changing international environment.
4. To understand the principles underlying corporate governance and their implications for diverse governance structures and practices.
5. To use simple strategic planning tools, including PEST and SWOT analysis.

Introduction

Business takes place the world over, in a huge diversity of societies and between widely varying organizations. The business environment has become more complex, with expanding and deepening ties between societies and between the many organizations within those societies. Moreover, many large organizations now see themselves as truly global in scope, not rooted in any one society. The business environment may be visualized in terms of layers, beginning with the immediate internal environment within the organization, and moving outwards to the external environment surrounding the business and influencing its organization and operations (see Figure 1.1). The external environment includes an array of dimensions, including economic, political, legal and technological factors. While only a few decades ago these external aspects were seen as centring on the home country of the business, the environmental horizon of business has now widened to take in a host of international forces, which interact with national and local factors.

Tensions exist between an organization and the external forces that impact on it, from local through to international, and these tensions are reflected in its internal environment. This chapter sets the scene by focusing on the essential elements of the internal environment, beginning with the ways in which different types of organization are formed and structured. Business organization, processes and strategy change over time, responding to changing circumstances in both the internal and external environments. This chapter covers a wide range of organizations. When we think of international business, we tend to think of large multinationals, but most of the world's businesses are very much smaller, and, increasingly, these smaller firms are becoming international in their outlook. A large American corporation such as IBM

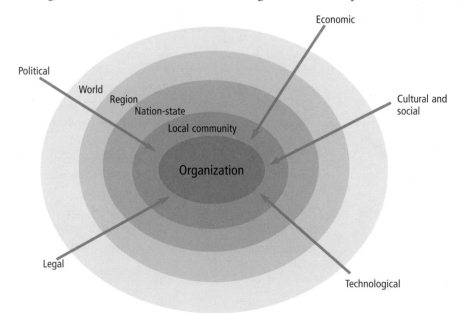

Figure 1.1 **The business organization in its environment**

may seem to have very little in common with a family-run firm in Hong Kong. Yet both face challenges common to businesses over the centuries, such as how to achieve a smooth-running and efficient organization and how to satisfy the needs of customers. Their responses may be different, but both will be addressing universal issues, each in its own way.

What is business?

Business refers to the vast array of economic activity, in which goods and services are supplied in exchange for some payment, usually money. It includes buying and selling, manufacturing products, extracting natural resources and farming. While the word covers business activities in general, as in the term, 'the business community', it is also used in relation to individual businesses. Businesses generally aim to make a profit, but there are also numerous not-for-profit enterprises in every society, such as charities and educational bodies. While we tend to think of business-people as private individuals, governments often engage in business activities, which are directed towards benefiting society. Business has been around a long time. Ancient societies grew prosperous largely because of thriving business activity, extending to trade with other countries (Landes, 1998). The urge to do business also seems to be universal, taking place in all societies, even in communist societies which do not officially recognize private enterprise. When we look at the variety of products and services that are taken for granted in modern consumer societies, such as motorcars, convenience food, fashion and entertainment, we can see that all have arisen through business activities.

Typically, business begins in a small way, nurtured by a talented and enthusiastic founder, the entrepreneur, who commits his or her own funds as well as energy to the enterprise. The **entrepreneur** is:

> one who creates a new business in the face of risk and uncertainty for the purpose of achieving profit and growth by identifying opportunities and assembling the necessary resources to capitalize on them. (Zimmerer and Scarborough, 1998, p. 3)

While many fall by the wayside, some go on to develop into the large enterprises that we are familiar with today. McDonald's, the fast-food restaurant, for example, started life as a single hamburger outlet in the US, in 1955, and has grown into a global company with thousands of restaurants in 120 countries. Like other successful companies, it has evolved as an organization, becoming more complex as it has grown. A large proportion of its restaurants, mainly those in the US, are run as franchises (described later in this chapter), by which individual entrepreneurs own the business and operate it under an agreement with McDonald's.

International business refers to business activities that straddle two or more countries. Businesses are increasingly looking beyond the bounds of their home country for new opportunities. A company may begin by selling its products or purchasing raw materials abroad, and go on to producing its products abroad. Or, as in the case of McDonald's, it may open restaurants abroad. Nowadays, thanks to advances in communication technology and transport, it is easier for companies to expand a variety of business activities across national borders. However, 'going global' adds considerably to the complexity of the organization (Bartlett and Ghoshal, 1998). The domestic business does not simply grow bigger, but international activities add a new dimension, which will be reflected in the organization of the company, and how it is run. When a company expands to the extent that a large portion of its business is outside its home country, it becomes a global business. (These points will be discussed in Chapter 5.) Its shareholders, too, may be dispersed across the globe. McDonald's now derives over half its profits from outside the US, and indeed, its growth overseas is stronger than its growth at home. Amazon.com was one of the earliest internet retailers. Largely due to the perseverance and vision of its enthusiastic founder Jeff Bezos, it was able to weather the collapse in dot.com businesses in 1999 (see minifile). His innovative internet retailing model was designed for US consumers, but has evolved as the business has become internationalized.

Some businesses are conceived as international in scope at the time of their founding. Referred to as 'born-globals', these firms have become more common in the areas of information technology (Knight and Cavusgil, 2004). In contrast to the more traditional pattern of becoming established at national level before expanding internationally, these firms' managers think from the outset in terms of international resources and international markets. Picsel Technologies, described in the second minifile, is an example of a born-global enterprise. Note that it is highly entrepreneurial and innovative – characteristics that it shares with other firms of this type.

WEB ALERT!　For entrepreneurship, look at the following websites:

http://entrepreneurship.mit.edu
http://www.entreworld.com
http://www.gemconsortium.org
The UK Small Business Service, run by the Department of Trade and Industry, is at http://www.sbs.gov.uk

Business, whether national or international, consists of a number of different activities or functions. The main functions are operations, human resource management (HRM), accounting, marketing, and research and development (R&D). Each function plays a crucial part in the process of designing and producing products which meet the needs of customers, for prices they are willing to pay. In a small business, workers may well turn their hand to several different functions, while in larger organizations, there is a group of specialized workers for each function. Although they may be seen as separate specialist activities, the ability to coordinate them effectively in pursuit of the business's overall goals is a key to business success. Functions are examined in detail in the next chapter. The functional approach to organizational structures is introduced later in this chapter.

Minifile

AMAZON.COM

1994: Founder, Jeff Bezos starts Amazon.com with $10,000; borrows $44,000

1995: Founder's father and mother invest $245,000

1995–6: Business 'angels' invest nearly $100,000

1996 (May): Founder's family invest $20,000

1996 (June): Two venture capital funds invest $8 million

1997: Initial public offering: 3 million shares offered to the public, raising $49.1 million

2002: Amazon makes its first quarterly profit

Amazon.com grew from a start-up online bookseller to one of the largest retailers on the Web in just four years. Its growth and the innovations it brought to online retailing were largely down to its charismatic founder, Jeff Bezos. In its first two years, Amazon.com was mainly kept in the Bezos family. This changed dramatically with the arrival on the scene of venture capitalists, companies which specialize in spotting 'rising stars', providing funds on a much larger scale, and taking them to the public offering stage.

Bezos's vision was that Amazon.com would be not just a bookseller, but at the centre of e-shopping. He linked up with several other companies, to sell toys, sportswear, pet supplies and electrical goods. Still, the company made losses in 1999, as costs soared more rapidly than sales. The year 2002 marked a turning point, as the company reported its first quarterly profit. Its international sales grew as internet use became more widespread. In Japan, it registered 2 million users from 2000 to 2003, making changes in its US model to adapt to the Japanese market. For example, it allowed Japanese customers to pay cash on delivery, as credit cards are less widely used in Japan than in the US. Sales of electronics and other goods now account for more than a quarter of the company's worldwide sales, which were worth $6.9 billion in 2004. As Amazon has turned itself into more of a general online retailer, it is facing serious competition from Wal-Mart and other bricks-and-mortar rivals, who are now increasingly attracting online customers. Nonetheless, Jeff Bezos retains his characteristic optimism that Amazon is leading the way in customer service. He says that his aim is for people to think of Amazon as 'earth's most customer-centric company' (Birchall, 20 May 2005).

Sources: Brooker, K., 'Amazon vs. Everybody', *Fortune*, **44**(9), 8 November 1999; Mayer, C., 'Developing the rules for corporate governance', *Mastering Management*, Part 6, Financial Times Publishing, 6 November 2000; Buckley, N., 'Amazon.com figures beat expectations', *Financial Times*, 23 July 2003; Rahman, B., 'Amazon predicts Japan will be second market', *Financial Times*, 2 July 2003; Birchall, J., 'Amazon battles to sell its expansion into retail jungle', *Financial Times*, 20 May 2005.

Classification of businesses

Businesses may be classified according to their form of ownership and also by size. The two variables are related, in that businesses of sole traders tend to be small, while company structures are more suited to large organizations. We look at each type of classification in turn.

Forms of business ownership

Three basic forms of ownership in most countries are: sole trader, partnership and limited company.

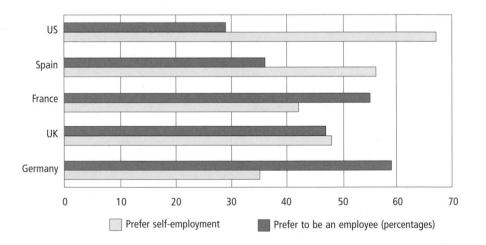

Sole trader

The simplest type of business is the **sole trader**, or self-employed person. For the sole trader, such as a small shopkeeper or small farmer, the business is highly personal, and responsibility for its success or failure rests on his or her shoulders. When the shopkeeper buys goods for the shop, or the farmer buys seed, the bill falls to be paid by him or her personally. The sole trader typically owns the building and equipment used by the business. As the business is personal to its owner, it may end when the owner retires, unless there is another family member or purchaser to carry it on. If the business fails, the personal wealth of its owner can be used to cover the business's debts, and, on the worst scenario, the owner's resources could be wiped out, in order to pay the business debts. This risk is known as 'unlimited liability', and is one of the major drawbacks of being in business as a sole trader. Thus, many sole traders decide to convert their businesses into limited companies, also motivated by the more advantageous tax position of limited companies over sole traders.

Monitoring the extent of self-employment in a country or region provides an indication of entrepreneurial activity in the society. Self-employment differs from country to country, between age groups and between the sexes. In general, men are far more likely to be self-employed than women. While there are examples of successful entrepreneurs in their twenties, the peak ages for self-employment are between 36 and 45, when people are more likely to have accumulated sufficient resources to start up a business. In 2002, about 11 per cent of workers in the UK were self-employed (Weir, 2003). Self-employment is higher in Turkey and Greece, where farming is more prevalent, as farmers are more likely to be self-employed than workers in manufacturing and service industries. Research commissioned by the European Commission indicates that, while many of us find the idea of self-employment appealing, we are put off by the risk involved (Gallup Europe, 2002). As Figure 1.2 shows, when respondents were asked whether they would prefer to be an employee or self-employed, 67 per cent in the US were more inclined towards self-employment, while the percentage is much lower in European countries. In

Figure 1.2 **Contrasting perceptions of self-employment**
Source: Gallup Europe (2002), 'Entrepreneurship', Eurobarometer 134, at http://www.eosgallupeurope.com.

Germany, in particular, the risk of failure loomed large in people's minds, as only 35 per cent preferred self-employment, while 59 per cent preferred to be employed.

For individual entrepreneurs, the franchise provides a less risky route to starting a business. The **franchise** agreement allows a businessperson to trade under the name of an established brand, backed by an established organization (the 'franchisor'), while retaining ownership of the business. Under the agreement, the business owner ('franchisee') pays fees to the franchisor organization for the right to sell its products or services. The franchisee does not have the freedom over the business that an independent owner would have, but stands a greater chance of success due to the strength of the established business 'formula' of the brand. Besides McDonald's, Burger King and other fast-food chains, there are numerous other goods and services providers, such as car rental companies, which have grown through the use of franchising.

Partnership

The **partnership** as a form of business involves two or more people carrying on a business in common, with a view to profit (Morse, 1991). A partnership may be any type of business, but has commonly been adopted by professional people such as accountants and lawyers. The partnership is called a 'firm', although this term is now used generally to refer to a company, not just a partnership. The partnership as a form is midway between the sole trader and company. Partners share the firm's profits and are all liable for its debts. While a limited partnership is possible, most partners, like the sole trader, have unlimited liability for the debts of the business. Partnership therefore rests heavily on personal trust between partners. The partnership is not a separate entity in the eyes of the law, but the partners can be sued (that is, face court proceedings) in the firm's name. To overcome the problems of unlimited liability that can arise when professional people are sued, firms take out considerable insurance cover.

Partnership is also used to describe a variety of relationships between two businesses, or between a government agency and a business. For example, a joint venture between two companies in different countries (which will be discussed in Chapter 5) may be referred to as a partnership, the basis of which is cooperation to achieve a common goal. Partnerships in this broader sense may include a variety of both formal and informal alliances between organizations.

Company

The company is the preferred form for businesses when they grow beyond a size that can be managed personally by a sole trader. The **company**, also called a corporation, is a legal entity separate from the members, or shareholders, who constitute it. Thus, the organization takes on a more impersonal character than the family business. The company is said to have 'perpetual succession', which means that it continues in existence, although its members may come and go over time (Morse, 1995, p. 5). As the company has a separate existence as a legal person, it involves greater dependence on formal documents. While there are several types of company, most companies are formed by registration, which is the filing of prescribed documents with the relevant government authority (Companies House in the UK, for example). In the US, companies register in one of the 50 states. When companies fail, they do not simply die; they must go through a legal procedure of 'winding up'.

From the point of view of a growing business, the advantage of converting into a company is that of attaining limited liability, which derives from the separate corporate status which the company enjoys. This means that the shareholder is liable only up to the amount of the face value of the shares acquired. Unlike the business owned personally by the sole trader, the company is legally owned by its **shareholders**, known as stockholders in many countries, including the US. A **share** in a company is a type of personal property, and the whole of a company's shares are its share capital, also known as **equity**.

Companies may be divided into private companies and public companies. Private companies are not allowed to offer shares to the public, whereas public companies do, although they need only offer a portion of their shares, such as 25 per cent. The private company is usually small, often with only a few shareholders who are family members. The public company is a much larger organization, and, when its shares are traded publicly on stock exchanges, it is likely to attract more public interest. Vodafone and Tesco are public companies, but there are some examples of high-profile private companies, such as the Virgin group of companies. In contrast, one of America's largest private companies, Cargill, a farm machinery company, is not widely known and sees its position as a private company as contributing to its low profile. In the UK, a public company has 'plc' after its name, to distinguish it from private companies, which are simply 'limited'.

WEB ALERT!

Companies House is at http://www.companieshouse.gov.uk
The website of the Virgin Group is http://www.Virgin.com
Cargill's website is at http://www.cargill.com

State-owned enterprises

State-owned enterprises (SOEs) differ from those owned by private individuals, in that they are owned and run, in effect, as limbs of government, often providing services for the public generally. They are often referred to as 'nationalized industries', like Petroleos de Venezuela, the Venezuelan state-owned oil company. These enterprises are thus in the 'public sector', while 'private sector' refers to businesses owned by private citizens. State-controlled enterprises have played an important part in economic activity in many countries, and they vary in their organization and business orientation. While they have had a reputation as sluggish and inefficient, a trend from the 1980s onwards has been for nationalized industries to be 'privatized', that is, converted into public limited companies, offering a portion of shares to the public. In many cases, the state retains a significant proportion. These privatized companies have become fitter and more responsive to consumers than they were as nationalized industries, and have also branched out into world markets. In Europe, the telecommunications industry and utilities, such as gas, water and electricity, have been privatized in this way. (Privatization is examined in more detail in Chapter 4.) Global companies which still have significant stakes owned by the state include the car maker, Renault in France and the telecommunications company, Deutsche Telekom in Germany, in which the state is the largest shareholder.

Types of business ownership

- **Sole trader** – Business under the ownership and control of an individual, often extending to family members; depends on personal control and becomes harder to manage as the business grows. Example: small craft shop.
- **Partnership** – Two or more people in business together, sharing the profits; depends on trust between the partners. Example: professionals such as accountants or lawyers.
- **Private limited company** – formation of a separate legal entity, the company, through registration and filing of documents (Memorandum of Association and Articles of Association in the UK); not allowed to offer shares to the public. Example: Virgin Atlantic.
- **Public limited company (plc)** – Limited company which is registered as a plc and offers shares to the public. Example: Marks & Spencer plc.
- **State-owned enterprise (SOE)** – an entity owned and controlled by government, such as a nationalized industry; known as a public sector enterprise. Example: Petroleos de Venezuela, the state-owned oil company. Privatization is the process of selling these enterprises to private investors, although the state often retains a large stake. Example: British Telecom.

Classification of businesses by size

The size of a business may be determined by a variety of criteria, including number of employees, turnover and market share (Buckley, 1999). However, these criteria are interpreted differently in different national and regional contexts, largely reflecting the size of the economy. While in some contexts 499 employees is used as the upper limit for a medium-size business, in many others, an upper limit of 249 is used. A commonly used classification based on number of employees is given below:

- Micro: 0–9 employees
- Small: 10–49 employees
- Medium: 50–249 employees
- Large: 250 or more employees.

However defined, **small-to-medium size enterprises (SMEs)** provide an important source of employment and economic activity in all countries. They account for roughly 60–70 per cent of employment in OECD countries, and 30 per cent of world exports of manufactures (UNIDO, 2000). SMEs range from informal 'micro-enterprises' to firms working at the forefront of advanced technology. Picsel, featured in the minifile, is an example of the latter. SMEs such as Picsel are more innovative and flexible than large organizations and are often able to specialize in 'niche' markets. Increasingly, these opportunities have become international in scope, facilitated by advances in information and communications technology (Buckley, 1999; Gankema et al., 2000). Picsel, for example, successfully sought both financial backing and markets in Asia in the very early stages of development of its new technology.

Figure 1.3 gives a breakdown of the UK's 1,167,000 employers in 2002. It shows that 82.8 per cent are micro-enterprises, which, combined with small enterprises, amount to 97 per cent of all UK enterprises. However, large enterprises account for about half of all UK employment in terms of numbers employed and turnover.

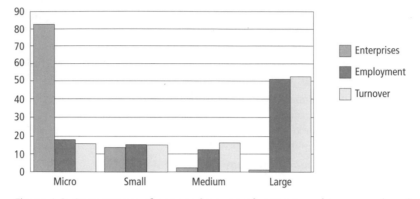

Figure 1.3 **Percentage of enterprises, employment and turnover in micro, small, medium and large firms in the UK, at the start of 2002**
Source: ONS (2004) *Small and Medium-sized Enterprises Statistics 2002*, at http://www.statistics.gov.uk.

Minifile

PICSEL TECHNOLOGIES

Picsel exemplifies a blend of entrepreneurship and innovation which has been highly successful in the rapidly changing area of computer software technology. Founded in Glasgow in 1998, the company provides multimedia software for use in mobile phones, personal digital assistants (PDAs), and other small-screen devices. Since then, it has grown from a start-up business with little more than ideas for new software products to a company with a £17 million turnover in 2005, supplying software to some of the world's biggest electronics brands, including Sony, Panasonic and Samsung. The company now has offices in California, Japan, China and Malaysia. Picsel's software, which can be embedded in a variety of mobile devices, allows users to easily access most types of content, regardless of format, changing between them with the greatest of ease.

The company's success is due to its two founders, Imran Khan, now CEO, the entrepreneurial mastermind, and Majid Anwar, the chief scientist, who developed the innovative software. Their strategy for selling the company's products and raising funding has been a major factor in their rapid growth. The two decided that the Asian market would be more promising for innovations in small-screen

devices. In 1999, they visited Japan to present their software to major manufacturers, even though its development at that time was at an early stage. Through an approach that they admit was akin to 'brinkmanship', they managed to reach agreements with Sony, NEC and Samsung. In 2001 they secured a £7.7 million investment from Softbank and Bank of Boston. This was followed in 2002, with a second round of funding from Japanese investors, who were investing in a UK company for the first time. Investors see bright prospects for growth, with the many new developments in small-screen devices and growing consumer appetite for all forms of electronic content.

Imran Khan says of their success: 'the essence of where we are is an undying faith in our technology and a belief that we will succeed. We're great salespeople also – perhaps it's part Pakistani DNA and part Scottish DNA – a combination of hard work and innovation from the Scottish side, and the entrepreneurial energy from the eastern side' (Nicholson, 2004).

Sources: Nicholson, M., 'How to make it big on the small screen' *Financial Times*, 20 January 2004; 'Picsel's £7m backing' *Daily Telegraph*, 20 May 2004; Bolger, A., 'Lining up the next development stage', *Financial Times*, 16 February 2005; Picsel website at www.picsel.com.

Business organization

An organization may be defined as 'two or more people who work together in a structured way to achieve a specific goal or set of goals' (Stoner and Freeman, 1992, p. 4). This broad definition encompasses many types of organization. It includes, for example, police forces, hospitals and schools, as well as the many types of business enterprises that make up modern consumer society. An organization run for profit aims to offer products or services that customers are willing to buy, at prices they are willing to pay. Physical resources, including plant, machinery and offices must be organized, and functions such as finance, purchasing and marketing must be coordinated, to enable the entire enterprise to function smoothly as a unit.

While every organization wishes to make the most of its expertise and resources, there is no one type of organization which can be said to be an ideal model that suits all businesses. There is a large body of organization theory, which studies 'the structure, functioning and performance of organizations and the behaviour of groups and individuals within them' (Pugh, 1997, p. xii). Structure has been defined as 'the design of organization through which the enterprise is administered' (Chandler, 1990, p. 14). It includes both formal and informal lines of authority. Organizational structures can be divided into three broad categories. The first is organization based simply on function. The second is the divisional structure, based on products, brands or regions. Thirdly, there is the organizational structure based on a matrix, the aim of which is to bring together the benefits of the other types. We look at each in turn.

Functional approach

In the functional approach to organization, business functions determine organizational structure. The importance of particular functions depends in part on the type of business. Product design and production, along with research and development, feature mainly in manufacturing firms, whereas all firms have need of finance, HRM and marketing functions. The main functions, which appear in Figure 1.4, are set out below:

- *Finance and accounting* – Control over the revenues and outgoings of the business, aiming to balance the books and generate sufficient profits for the future health of the firm. This function is far more complex in large public companies than in SMEs.
- *HRM* – Formerly known as 'personnel management', HRM focuses on all aspects of the management of people in the organization, including recruiting, training and rewarding the workforce.
- *Marketing* – This focuses on satisfying the needs and expectations of customers. Marketing covers a range of related functions, including advertising, pricing and distribution of goods.
- *Product design* – Product designers, mainly in manufacturing companies, are specialist engineers, who develop new products and improve existing products, from the beginnings of a single 'prototype', through to testing and revision of the design before large-scale production can begin.

● *R&D* – The scientific and technical research which underlies new products. Without an R&D focus, companies risk falling behind competitors in innovative new products.

● *Production and operations* – Focuses on the operational processes by which products are manufactured, such as assembly lines. Production increasingly relies on sophisticated machinery and computerized systems. Quality, safety and efficiency are major concerns of production engineers and managers.

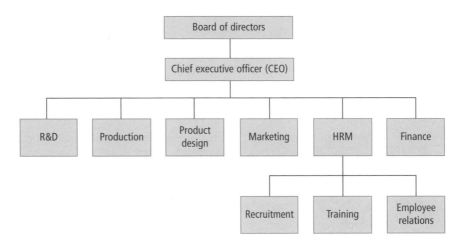

Figure 1.4 **Organization based on functional departments**

The functional organizational approach is depicted in Figure 1.4. There is a risk in this type of structure that each functional department will become inward-looking and lose sight of organizational goals. Within the formal structure, the functional specialists must be coordinated into a smooth-running whole. Central management and, in particular, its chief executive officer (CEO) is at the pinnacle of the organization. The CEO is therefore crucial in coordinating the departments. Management is the:

> process of planning, organizing, leading and controlling the work of organization members, and of using all available organizational resources to reach stated organizational goals. (Stoner and Freeman, 1992, p. 4)

The larger the company, the more cumbersome this structure becomes. For large companies, which produce a number of products in different regions of the world, this structure has given way to the more decentralized divisional structure.

Divisional structure

When a company has grown to the extent that it has a number of successful products in different regions, it may structure the organization into business units or divisions, which may be based on product, brand or geographical region (see Figure 1.5). Known as the multidivisional structure, this has been one of the major structural innovations of modern corporations, seeking to solve the problems of how to decentralize a large company, while still maintaining overall coordination of the parts. A full account of its development is given in Alfred Chandler's *Strategy and Structure* (1990). In it he recounts the experiences of General Motors (GM) and the American chemical corporation Du Pont, which adopted the multidivisional structure in the early 1900s. The principle is that each division is headed by a division manager who has responsibility for managing the division as a profit centre in its own right. The division itself may be a separate company, known as a 'subsidiary' company, whose major shareholder is the 'parent' company. The company's executives at head office concentrate on the broader corporate aims, leaving the divisions considerable independence. The head office will have centralized functional departments, such as finance, for the group as a whole. A divisional structure based on *product divisions* has been adopted by a number of global companies, including General Electric (GE), British Telecom (BT) and Ericsson. An advantage of this approach, in theory, is the ability to coordinate activities to produce and market a particular line worldwide, but a drawback tends to be that its standardized approach overlooks differences in national markets (Birkinshaw, 2000). The Fiat case study at the end of Part 1 and the GE case study at the end of Part 3 provide contrasting examples of the way this type of structure works in reality. Both cases highlight the difficulties of coordination in practice and problems with underperforming units in highly competitive markets.

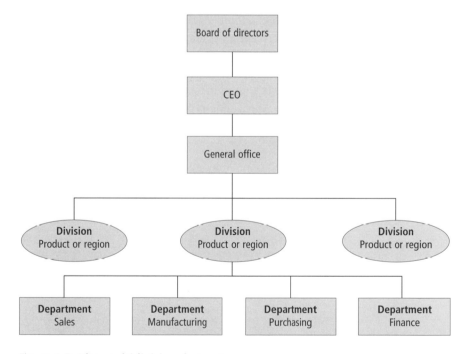

Figure 1.5 **The multidivisional structure**

The *area division* is a way of addressing different regional conditions. In this type of organization structure, country or regional managers preside over area divisions, and are responsible for all the company's activities in that area. The area may be, for example, Asia Pacific, in which case the area manager has charge of operations in that area, including control over resources. A main advantage of the area division structure is that is able to respond to regional needs. It also lends itself to decentralization, that is, the delegating of decision-making down to the divisions. Many global companies, including Nestlé and Unilever, have been organized in this way, although they have found it difficult to achieve economies of scale in development and production (Birkinshaw, 2000). They have tended to move towards global product divisions or a combination of geographical regions plus product divisions, as Unilever has done.

The **holding company** may also be said to be based on divisions, in that a parent company is the owner of a diverse array of subsidiary companies. However, unlike the multidivisional companies described above, the holding company exerts little control over the separate companies and provides few general functions for the group as a whole. The companies within the group operate, in effect, as independent organizations.

Matrix structure

The **matrix structure** is a way of structuring the organization to incorporate the benefits of other types of structure, such as the functional organization, product divisions and area divisions. It involves two lines of management, as indicated in Figure 1.6. The product manager must coordinate with the area manager for the launch of a new product in that region. In theory, this allows the company to respond to local trends and also derive the benefits of globally coordinated product management. In practice, however, it is difficult to reconcile these different lines of authority, and the system can lead to deadlock in decision-making (Bartlett and Ghoshal, 1990). Thus, although the matrix should theoretically provide flexibility, it can lead to inefficiency. Some companies adopt a compromise, using product divisions, but adding country

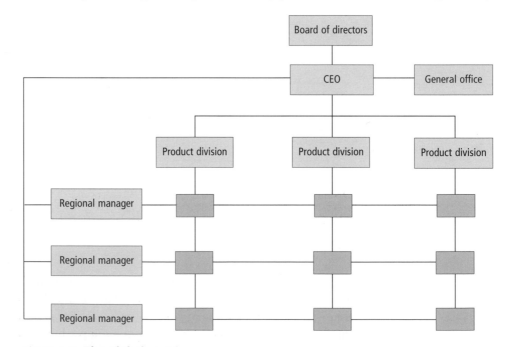

Figure 1.6 **The global matrix**

management where it is specifically needed, for example in developing countries such as China (Birkinshaw, 2000). In the early 1990s, the Swiss–Swedish electrical engineering company, ABB, put in place a matrix structure, but changed to a divisional structure based on products and technologies in 1998. In 2001, the company underwent a further restructuring, in which the divisions were replaced by four 'consumer segments', aimed at developing a greater customer orientation.

Case study 1.1 Has restructuring paid off at Procter & Gamble?

Procter & Gamble (P&G), formed by William Procter and James Gamble in Cincinnati in 1837, is one of the oldest global companies. Its famous brands include Tide, Pringles and Crest. For much of its history, the company has been innovative in producing new consumer products and new marketing techniques, such as the soap opera. However, despite its record of reliable profit growth, by the 1990s P&G had become weighed down by bureaucratic hierarchy. According to Richard Tomkins: 'the company became formula-driven, risk-averse and inbred. Even the smallest decisions had to be referred to senior management. Individuality was frowned upon: employees learnt how to write memos, how to speak and how to think' (*Financial Times*, 12 June 2000). Times became harder for the well-known brands, which were losing sales to copycat products and supermarket own brands. The big supermarket chains, such as Wal-Mart, grew more powerful and were able to demand lower prices from manufacturers.

In a restructuring in 1990, P&G's chief executive closed 30 plants worldwide, cutting 13,000 jobs. This move brought down prices, but damaged employee morale and adversely affected product innovation. In 1999, a new chief executive, Durk Jager, took radical measures to dismantle the company's multilayered bureaucracy. Aiming to recreate entrepreneurial spirit, he took power away from country-based divisions and created global product managers, with greater control over their budgets. But the change from country-based divisions to product divisions proved expensive, and the costs did not translate immediately into greater sales. Further, the radical changes had a disorienting effect on employees. It has been estimated that of P&G's 200–300 top managers, only 20 per cent were left doing the same job they had done 18 months previously.

Arguably, Jager did what was necessary to drag the company into the twenty-first century, but shareholders expected a speedy recovery, which was not forthcoming. After only 18 months in office, in which three profits warnings had to be issued, he was forced to go. By 2002, recovery seemed to be on track, under a new chief executive, A. G. Lafley, who took over in 2000. Lafley continued Jager's strategy, putting faith in the global business units to generate innovation. At the same time, he has focused on the company's leading brands which are its main earners.

Acquisitions have strengthened P&G's competitive position in global markets. Clairol, the hair products company, was acquired in 2001 for $4.5 billion, followed in 2003 by the acquisition of Wella, the hair care group. These two big acquisitions in the hair and beauty sector shifted the balance in the company's portfolio. The health and beauty care businesses are now driving growth: the beauty care brands enjoyed a 41 per cent increase in volume of sales in 2004. The acquisition of Gillette in 2005 further strengthened the group's presence in health and beauty products, adding Gillette's razor and hair care products to the group's portfolio. Gillette's tradition of innovation is also a major attraction for Lafley. He says: 'Fundamentally you have to ask yourself whether you are inherently a commodity business or an innovation business. What we've tried to do is accelerate innovation from within' (Grant, 4 February 2005). The combined focus on innovation and major brands has contributed to a resurgence in growth, built on the ambitious restructuring carried out by Jager.

Sources: Tomkins, R., 'Revenge of the Proctoids', *Financial Times*, 12 June 2000; 'Durk's dismissal', *Financial Times*, 12 June 2000; Jones, A., 'Consumed by the consumer', *Financial Times*, 23 May 2001; Buckley, N. 'Reconditioned P&G is continuing to shine', *Financial Times*, 30 October 2002; Buckley, N., 'Change of focus boosts P&G', *Financial*
Times, 3 August 2004; Roberts, D., and Grant, J., 'P&G looks to gain strength through unity', *Financial Times*, 31 January 2005; Grant, J., '"We can build a juggernaut" – P&G and Gillette lead the way through a new retail landscape', *Financial Times*, 5 February 2005.

Case questions

In what ways did Procter & Gamble's organizational culture and structure need to be changed?

How has Jager's strategy now been vindicated?

WEB ALERT!

Procter & Gamble's website is http://www.pg.com

Organizations and change: business strategy

No two organizations, even two with similar outward structures, will be run in exactly the same way. Differences in behaviour, values and overall atmosphere are part of a business's organizational culture, and are particularly evident in situations of turbulence and uncertainty. Some businesses become set in their ways, assuming that structures and processes which served well in the past will continue to do so into the future. In a competitive environment, they are likely to lose out to more efficient and innovative rivals. Forward-looking organizations look for ways to reform their structures and improve communications within the organization and with its customers. Change may be radical or it may be gradual, that is, introduced incrementally, step by step. If an organization has been 'drifting' for a number of years, then looming crisis may dictate that it needs a radical shake-up involving restructuring. Changes need not involve entire restructuring, but involve a redefinition of the aims of the company within the existing structures. It is easier to change structures than to change organizational culture, which represents engrained ways of doing things. A takeover may be the catalyst of radical change in structure and processes. Or, if one division is underperforming, a merger with another division may be advisable. The timing of change and decisions as to whether it should be revolutionary or incremental are issues of strategy.

Strategy is often thought of simply as planning, but in fact it is much broader in scope. It encompasses not just physical changes such as shutting down a division, but also changes of corporate focus and attitudes on the part of the workforce. Chandler defined strategy as:

the determination of the basic long-term goals and objectives of an enterprise, and the adoption of courses of action and the allocation of resources necessary for carrying out these goals. (Chandler, 1990, p. 13)

Chandler believed that structure follows strategy. His reasoning was that if a company sees new opportunities created by the changing environment, say by technological change, it alters its strategy and then changes its structure accordingly. This approach views strategy as a 'top-down' process. However, in a rapidly changing environment, strategies may emerge as events unfold. Strategy is often a combination of 'deliberate' strategy, that which has been originally intended, and 'emergent' strategy, which has arisen from events not part of the intended strategy (Mintzberg, 2000). In this way, some large organizations, such as ICI, found that strategy emerged slowly, as changes in beliefs and structure became settled (Pettigrew, 1997). Case study 1.2 on Honda's success in America shows the importance of accident and good luck in shaping strategy.

Awareness of changes taking place in the environment and new opportunities is captured in the concept of **strategic thinking**, which can be defined as bringing together all the information available from those within the organization and converting that knowledge into a vision of the aims the business should pursue. As Mintzberg explains:

> in the case of emergent strategy, because big strategies can grow from little ideas (initiatives), and in strange places, not to mention at unexpected times, almost anyone in the organization can prove to be a strategist. (Mintzberg, 2000, p. 26)

Experience suggests, therefore, that strategy is more diffuse and complex than the idea of planning suggests. The flexible organization with open communication, able to adapt its strategy to the changing environment, is more likely to spot and exploit new opportunities than one with a rigid structure.

Case study 1.2 Honda and the US motorcycle market

It had been accepted that Honda's penetration of the US motorcycle market had been based on a deliberate strategy to target the bottom end of the US market, with the 50cc Supercub. However, research by Richard Pascale in 1984 revealed a different story. He found from speaking to Honda's executives that they were confident that the Honda 50 was a brilliant design, but they had had difficulties in raising production capacity in Japan. When they went to the US in 1959, they set themselves a target of exporting just 6000 machines per year for several years, leaving the actual timescale unspecified. They reckoned on 25 per cent of each of their four products: the 50cc Supercub, and the 125cc, 250cc and 305cc machines.

The dramatic success of the 50cc came about through 'accident, good luck and the Honda US executives' willingness to respond to events and learn from the market' (Barwise, 1997). They concentrated first on selling the larger bikes, as they thought they were more suitable for the US market, where everything was bigger and more luxurious. However, these machines started to break down, as they were being driven harder and longer than in Japan. The Honda executives themselves used the Honda 50s to ride around Los Angeles on errands. They attracted attention, including a call from a Sears buyer. While they were apprehensive that the small bikes would dent the macho image of their machines, they felt compelled to sell them when their bigger bikes were struggling. Surprisingly, the retailers buying the Honda 50 were not motorcycle dealers, but sporting goods stores.

Honda enjoyed an initial design advantage in Japan, along with an efficient production line. But its seemingly unplanned success in the US demonstrates that successful strategy may emerge, rather than be the result of deliberate strategy. For Honda, successful strategy was a combination of opportunism and design.

Kay concludes that the the lesson of Honda is: 'that a business with a distinctive capability that

develops innovative products to exploit that capability and recognizes the appropriate distribution channels for such innovations can take the world by storm' (Kay, 2004).

Sources: Barwise, P. (1997) 'Strategic investment decisions and emergent strategy', *Mastering Management*, Part 15, Financial Times/Pitman, pp. 562–71; Pascale, R.T., 'Perspectives on strategy: the real story behind Honda's success', *California Management Review*, Spring 1984, pp. 47–72; Kay, J., 'Driving through the spin on Honda's success', *Financial Times*, 16 November 2004.

Case question

What do we learn about emergent strategy from Honda's success with the Honda 50 in the US?

WEB ALERT! ·

Honda's main website is http://www.honda.com

Its motorcycle website is http://powersports.honda.com

SUMMARY POINTS

Varying approaches to strategy

The **planning approach** holds that:

● strategy formation should be a controlled and conscious formalized process

● responsibility for the overall process rests with the chief executive in principle, although responsibility for its execution rests with staff planners in practice

● detailed strategic plans that result from this process are then implemented.

The **emergent strategy approach** holds that:

● strategy is a combination of intended and unintended. Some intended strategy is not realized. The part that is realized is deliberate strategy

● much realized strategy emerges from events that were not part of the intended strategy. This is emergent strategy.

Sources: Mintzberg, H. (2000) *The Rise and Fall of Strategy*, London, Pearson Education; Barwise, P. (1997) 'Strategic investment decisions and emergent strategy' *Mastering Management*, Financial Times/Pitman, pp. 562–71.

CRITICAL PERSPECTIVES

Strategic change

The reason so few firms sustain their position is that change is extraordinarily painful and difficult for any successful organization. Complacency is much more natural. The past strategy becomes ingrained in organizational routines. Information that would modify or challenge it is not sought or filtered out. The past strategy takes on an aura of invincibility and becomes rooted in company culture. Suggesting change is tantamount to disloyalty. Successful companies often seek predictability and stability. They become preoccupied with defending what they have, and any change is tempered by the concern that there is much to lose … Few companies make significant improvements and strategy changes voluntarily; most are forced to. The pressure to change is more often environmental than internal. (Porter, 1998b, p. 52)

■   Think of some actual companies that have fallen into the situation described by Porter. Did they successfully change strategy, and, if so, how?

Hierarchies and networks

Whatever their structure, large companies, in order to manage their growing complexities, tend to become hierarchical. A hierarchy essentially differentiates people in terms of power in a vertical fashion. Those at the top are the chief decision-makers in the organization, whereas those at the bottom, who carry out the routine activities of the business, have little decision-making power. There may be many layers of management and supervision in between. Each worker in the hierarchy has a definite position, with lines of authority above and below, in a system known as bureaucracy. When we think of bureaucracies, we think of the benefits of efficiency, with each task fitting into an overall whole, as in an assembly line. But we also tend to think of bureaucracies as inflexible and dependent on procedural formalities. They function best in unchanging environments, but in the context of a rapidly changing competitive environment, companies are shifting away from the bureaucratic model in order to introduce more flexibility and more open communication and quicker responses to customer needs.

One of the obvious reforms of bureaucratic structures is to reduce the number of layers, or flatten the structure. The structure may be flattened by reducing layers in the middle if there are too many layers of middle management. Or the power to take decisions may be decentralized to lower levels, through empowerment, one of the major developments in HRM thinking. Empowerment holds that employees at all levels in the organization are 'responsible for their own actions, and should be given authority to make decisions about their work' (Peiperi, 1997). The rationale behind empowerment is that those at the lower levels have considerable knowledge of operational matters, and so are able to respond more quickly. Recent theory stresses that one of the organization's major assets is knowledge, which is dispersed throughout its structure. Managers therefore need to look for ways to allow this knowledge to be tapped and channelled, for example into new products or new ways of doing things. It is increasingly recognized that products are not the sole preserve of product engineers, but involve cross-functional cooperation. Empowerment also allows the formation of cross-functional links.

At the organizational level, empowerment ties in with the **network organization** (Jackson and Schuler, 2000). The network organization does not really represent a new type of structure, but a new way of looking at the lines of communication and informal links within the preceding structural frameworks. **Networking** is 'the informal overlay that cuts across whatever formal structure is chosen' (Birkinshaw, 2000, p. 4). Thus project teams may be drawn from different functional groups or different area divisions. It may speed up decision-making, which in any large organization tends to become sluggish and slow. Positional structure still exists, but project activities which cross structural boundaries bring the flexibility needed for dynamic processes (Fukuyama, 1999). The tools for networking are enhanced by the use of email communications, which can cut across divisional boundaries. A project team can thus be assembled from various locations across the globe. Network organizations are also more likely to develop links with other organizations, creating networks across organizational boundaries (Jackson and Schuler, 2000). It is often said that networks rely on 'social capital', that is, shared norms and relationships of trust, rather than formal authority structures.

SUMMARY POINTS

!!!

Hierarchies vs. networks

- **Hierarchies** are based on formal rules and lines of authority in centralized bureaucratic structures. There is little delegation from the centre. This type of organization becomes inflexible, unable to respond to a changing environment.

- The **network organization** relies on shared norms and values, rather than formal rules. Networks allow information to flow freely within the organization. Informal, self-directed groups of workers provide a more flexible means of coordination within the organization than formal hierarchies.

CRITICAL PERSPECTIVES

Empowerment

We believe that empowerment without a *shared sense of direction* can lead to anarchy. While bureaucracy can strangle initiative and progress, so too can a large number of empowered but unaligned individuals who are working at cross-purposes … The notion of a shared direction, what we call a 'strategic intent', reconciles the needs of individual freedom and concerted, coordinated effort …

Employees want a sense of direction just as much as they want freedom of empowerment. (Hamel and Prahalad, 1994, p. 319)

In this passage, Hamel and Prahalad point out the negative side of empowerment. How valid are their comments?

Corporate governance

Corporate governance refers to the structures and processes by which ultimate control and decision-making in the company are exercised. The word 'governance' stems from analogy with a political system, in which those in positions of authority are held accountable to the citizenry. In a company, directors and managers are accountable to the shareholders as owners. These structures and processes reflect broader perspectives on the company's role in society, however, which have come to be highlighted in the wider debate on corporate governance in recent years. This section, therefore, examines the systems first, and then explores the wider issues.

Governance structures

A typical structure of a public company in the US or UK is set out in Figure 1.7. Ultimate responsibility for the company's activities lies with the **directors**, who collectively constitute a board of directors, elected by the company's shareholders at their annual general meeting (AGM). The AGM affords an opportunity for shareholders to question directors on company policies and performance. Corporate governance differs from business to business, and is influenced by national economic, social, cultural and legal environments. In Germany and other European countries, a two-tier board of directors is the norm. A supervisory board holds the ultimate authority for major decisions, while a management board is the 'engine of management' (Charkham, 1994). While the single board in the Anglo-American type of structure is based on the principle of representing shareholders' interests, the supervisory board in the German system encompasses not just shareholder interests, but also includes employee and trade union representatives. This point will be developed further in the next section.

The OECD's *Principles of Corporate Governance* state that there is no single model that suits all companies (OECD, 2004, p. 13). However, there are general principles generally recognized as good practice. These are set out in the summary box below. Directors may be active managers in the company (called 'executive' directors in the US) or independent ('non-executive') directors. It is generally thought that a 'balanced' board, consisting of both executive and independent directors, representing both insider and outsider perspectives, represents best practice. A proportion of independent directors is usually recommended in national codes of corporate governance and in the OECD's *Principles of Corporate Governance*. Also recommended as good practice is the separation of the roles of chairman and CEO, whereby the chairman is independent of the CEO. However, many companies, particularly American ones, combine the roles in a single person. This practice can be seen in a number of the case studies in this book, for example those on GE, Nike and Apple Computers. Case study 1.3 on the Disney Corporation highlights this issue, along with a number of other current governance issues, including independent directors and responsiveness to shareholders.

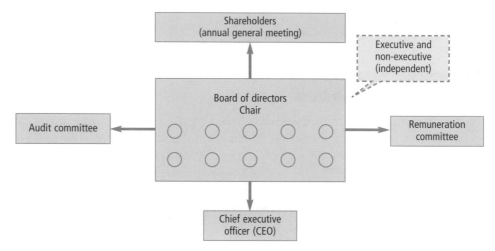

Figure 1.7 **Corporate governance structure typical of an American or UK company**

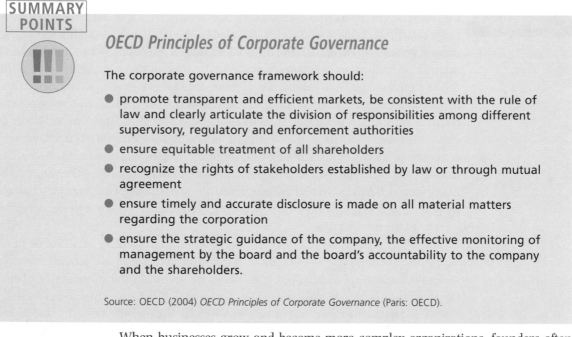

SUMMARY POINTS

OECD Principles of Corporate Governance

The corporate governance framework should:

● promote transparent and efficient markets, be consistent with the rule of law and clearly articulate the division of responsibilities among different supervisory, regulatory and enforcement authorities

● ensure equitable treatment of all shareholders

● recognize the rights of stakeholders established by law or through mutual agreement

● ensure timely and accurate disclosure is made on all material matters regarding the corporation

● ensure the strategic guidance of the company, the effective monitoring of management by the board and the board's accountability to the company and the shareholders.

Source: OECD (2004) *OECD Principles of Corporate Governance* (Paris: OECD).

When businesses grow and become more complex organizations, founders often come to the realization that they need to bring in professional managers, even though this entails reducing their control of the organization. Founder owners may also see their ownership stake reduced if the organization becomes a public company, as outside investors become shareholders. A divide thus develops between ownership and control, in that outside shareholders gain increasing ownership stakes, while control tends to shift to professional managers, as occurred in the Disney Corporation. This phenomenon was first examined by Berle and Means in their seminal work in the 1930s (Berle and Means, 1932). Companies adopted the practice of issuing shares and share options to managers as part of their remuneration, to align their interests with the owners. Some companies adopt a system of different classes of shares, often aimed at maintaining family control, so that some shares may have little or no voting power. In Ford Motor Company, for example, the Ford family own 3.9 per cent of the stock, but control 40 per cent of the votes. While we might think it odd that investors would buy non-voting shares, they have usually been content to see share values rising and reap the profits when they come to sell their shares. Falling stock markets, however, from 2000 onwards, have led to shareholders becoming more aware of their voice – or lack of it – in corporate affairs, and to directors being reminded that they are ultimately accountable to shareholders as owners. Recent years have therefore seen a rise in shareholder activism, as the Disney case study shows, driven to a significant degree by financial institutions, such as pension funds, that hold large stakes in public companies. There are diverse perspectives on shareholder activism. On the one hand, advocates point to shareholder democracy as a healthy development, while, on the other, directors complain that shareholders tend to have a short-term perspective, making it difficult for managers to focus on long-term value. The P&G case study illustrates this dilemma.

WEB ALERT!

The OECD has a comprehensive website on corporate governance at http://www.oecd.org. *Corporate Governance Principles* may be found here, as well as *Guidelines for Multinational Enterprises*

The European Commission's website on corporate governance is http://europa.eu.int/comm./internal_market/company/index

There are also a number of websites which take the shareholder perspective. In the UK, the Pensions Investment Research Consultants (PIRC) is at http://www.pirc.co.uk. The California Public Employees Retirement System (CalPERS), the highly active investors, at http://www.calpers.ca.gov

Another investor-oriented website, designed for both individual and institutional investors, is at http://www.corpgov.net

All directors, whether executive or non-executive, are responsible for oversight of the company's activities. While they oversee corporate strategy, they are also responsible for seeing that the company meets financial reporting requirements. Corruption scandals involving Enron, the energy trading company, in the US in 2001, and Parmalat, the Italian dairy company in 2003, have raised awareness of corporate governance issues, including the need for transparent processes of accountability, to maintain public confidence in corporations. Enron had a corporate governance system which looked admirable on paper. However, its senior executives were able to steer the company towards their own goals, and the bodies which should have provided a check on their actions (such as the board and auditors) failed to do so. Board members, although formally independent, all had financial ties with the company, and failed to exert control on senior executives. While Enron directors amassed personal fortunes, ordinary shareholders, many of them employees of the company, found their shares worthless when the company collapsed.

Enron and Parmalat, while both large organizations with many subsidiaries and affiliated companies, present contrasting governance perspectives. Enron was a management-dominated company, while Parmalat was founded as a family company, and its structures remained family-dominated, as is common in Italy (see the case study on Fiat at the end of Part 2). According to the OECD, more than 75 per cent of all registered companies in industrialized countries are family businesses (Becht et al., 2003). While most of these are SMEs, in many, including even large public companies, founders and family members retain large shareholdings and exert ultimate control. It has been estimated the one-third of the Fortune 500 largest companies in the US are family-controlled. Many European companies are also family-dominated: examples are the French car maker, PSA Peugeot-Citroën and the Italian car maker, Fiat. About 50–60 per cent of all employees in industrialized economies work for family companies (Becht et al., 2003). By contrast, in companies where there are widely diversified shareholders, who view their holdings simply as an investment, directors see maximization of shareholder value as their primary goal. This shareholder-centred view of corporate governance has been prominent in the US and UK.

Case study 1.3　Disney Corporation: it all started with a mouse

Walt Disney, the founder of the Walt Disney Company in 1923, is famously quoted as saying to his successors in the company: 'I only hope that we never lose sight of one thing – that it all started with a mouse.' The business was started by Walt Disney and his brother, who rented a small studio to produce animated films, introducing its most famous character, Mickey Mouse, in 1928. It was in animated films that the studio excelled, and on which its reputation and brand are based. The company has grown into a $28-billion-a-year media and entertainment empire, consisting of film studios, theme parks and resorts, a television network and consumer products divisions. Much of this development has taken place under the leadership of Michael Eisner, who took over as chief executive in 1984. He is credited with the huge expansion of the theme parks and resorts. However, from the late 1990s, the company's performance took a downturn (see figure). New competitors in the theme park business, combined with the

downturn in tourism following the World Trade Center attacks of 11 September 2001, affected theme park attendance. Wavering consumer confidence has affected the consumer products division, which needs new characters beyond Mickey Mouse – now in his seventies – to reinvigorate the Disney brand. The loss-making television network, ABC, having been a leading network in the 1970s and 80s, noted for nurturing creative ideas, fell behind the other major networks in the US. There has been a 'brain drain' of creative talent in the flagship animation division.

Eisner held combined roles of chairman and chief executive, while, in the vice-chairman's seat, was Roy Disney, nephew of the founder and still a substantial shareholder. The board consisted mainly of insiders and personal associates of Eisner. Roy Disney has been a leading critic of Eisner, and the corporate governance of the company generally, voicing concerns of many, including the institutional shareholders, who hold 30 per cent of Disney stock. They have criticized

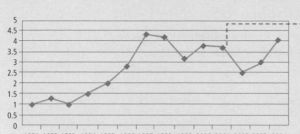

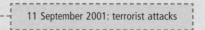

11 September 2001: terrorist attacks

**Disney's operating income
1991–2004 (estimate for 2004)**
Source: Burt, 8 November 2004.

Eisner's autocratic management style for destroying morale in the company. They also point to poor investment decisions which affected shareholder value.

From 2001, changes in corporate governance were made, to reflect recommended best practice. Enlargement of the board to thirteen members was followed by the introduction of more independent directors in 2004. The company announced that all but three directors are independent, and it has adopted a code of business ethics. These moves, however, did not dampen criticism of Eisner. In March 2004, he was forced to step down as chairman when 43 percent of the shareholders voted against his reappointment. Under pressure, the board then voted to split the roles of chairman and chief executive. This move, however, still did not placate the shareholders, particularly as the new chairman voted in, George Mitchell, was rejected by 24 per cent of the shareholders. Mitchell, former Senate majority leader in the US Congress, had been a director of companies associated with poor corporate governance, including Xerox, where accusations of manipulating financial results led to six officials paying $22 million in fines. CalPERS, the California public pension fund and a Disney shareholder, called for Mitchell's resignation.

Roy Disney resigned from the board in 2004, but as a substantial shareholder, he has been vocal in a 'Save Disney' campaign. Throughout the upheaval, Disney directors have been stalwart in their defence of Eisner's management. In 2004, he promised to increase profit growth by impressive figures of 30 per cent, and could point to the fact that core businesses were doing well: ABC was gaining ground on its rivals, and box office takings were rising. However, shareholders,

it has become apparent, are interested in more than just seeing rising share price. As one global corporate governance adviser has said of the directors: 'They're suddenly going to have to prove publicly they do pay attention to ownership issues. Whether the stock price is going up or down in the short term is not the issue at Disney. The issue is that too much power is accumulated in the hands of one individual' (Wine, 5 March 2004). The Disney board, packed as it was with friends and supporters of Eisner, offered little prospect of proper oversight. ABC's founder, reflecting on the current situation at Disney, has said: 'Good outside directors will always try to do what's good for the company. Management directors are always tempted to do what's good for themselves' (Parkes et al., 2002).

In 2005, the board announced that Eisner would step down as CEO, and that Robert Iger, chief operating officer (COO) and preferred candidate of Eisner, was the unanimous choice of the board for the post of CEO. Roy Disney and another former director, Stanley Gold, launched legal proceedings against the Disney directors, claiming that the choice of Iger was a foregone conclusion and that no proper selection process had taken place.

Sources: Parkes, C., Grimes, C. and Burt, T. 'The fairytale may end in tears as Eisner's Magic Kingdom shows signs of crumbling', *Financial Times*, 24 September 2002; Burt, T. 'Disney banks on its mouse to roar again', *Financial Times*, 15 November 2003; Burt, T. 'Disney in boardroom shake-up', *Financial Times*, 8 January 2004; Burt, T. and Parkes, C. 'A "resounding victory" for shareholders', *Financial Times*, 5 March 2004; Wine, R. 'Rise of the corporate crusaders', *Financial Times*, 5 March 2004; Burt, T., 'Calm amid the storm: despite a bruising year, Eisner remains sure of his strategy', *Financial Times*, 8 November 2004; Gapper, J., 'A tale of intrigue at the court of Disney's king', *Financial Times*, 28 February 2005; Parkes, C., 'Legal challenge to Disney board', *Financial Times*, 10 May 2005.

Case questions

**What were the corporate governance problems at Disney?
To what extent have they been solved?**

WEB ALERT!

Disney's corporate website is at http://corporate.disney.go.com

Disney's main website is http://disney.go.com

CRITICAL PERSPECTIVES

Corporate governance

An effective corporate governance system requires a system of checks and balances, assuring that the right questions get asked ("Do we need to revise our corporate strategy? Our asset mix? Our organizational structure? Our allocation of resources? How is the CEO doing? How is the board doing?") of the right people (those with the fewest conflicts of interest, and the authority to make the decisions and see they get implemented) … A corporate governance system that is not effective is one in which questions are raised too late, or not at all, or are decided by people who are unable to evaluate them properly. (Monks and Minow, 1996, p. 261)

■   What is meant by a system of checks and balances in the context of corporate governance? How does the presence of a majority of independent (non-executive) directors on the board ensure that effective checks and balances are carried out?

Governance issues in the contemporary environment

In addition to accountability to shareholders, corporate governance has taken on broader implications, as managers have become more aware of the interrelationships between the internal and external environment of the company. This broader concept is that of stakeholders. A **stakeholder** may be anyone, even the community generally, who has an interest in the company, direct or indirect. Besides shareholders, those with a *direct* affect on the company include employees, trade unions, customers (who may be businesses such as retailers), consumers (who purchase products from retailers) and suppliers. The company is likely to have contractual or other formal links with these groups, which represent coherent sets of interests (see Figure 1.8). In countries with a two-tier board structure, the position of employees is formally recognized, but this stakeholder model of governance is limited, in that it does not bring in other stakeholder groups besides employees. *Indirect* stakeholders, while they are affected by the company's operations, cover a range of broader societal interests which enjoy fewer direct channels of communication with managers. They include the local community, society generally and the ecological environment affected by the company's operations. These indirect stakeholders are shown as dotted lines in Figure 1.8. Often, especially in overseas operations, these stakeholders have little organizational capacity and few means to voice their concerns. Non-governmental organizations (NGOs) have stepped in to raise stakeholder issues in many cases, arguing that they fall within corporate responsibility. The extent of responsibility to both direct and indirect stakeholders has become a far-reaching issue, and is discussed further in Chapter 14.

The interests of some stakeholder groups may potentially conflict with others. For example, moving production to a cheaper location may please shareholders and customers, but harm employees who have lost jobs. Reconciling the interests of shareholders and other stakeholders has thus become an important consideration for corporate strategy.

Figure 1.8 **Shareholder and stakeholder perspectives on corporate governance**

SUMMARY POINTS

Contemporary corporate governance issues

Shareholder perspective:

- shareholder value is the primary aim of the company, in keeping with the role of shareholders as owners
- directors accountable to shareholders through board structure
- trend towards more active investors, as shareholders seek to promote active monitoring of directors and the voicing of shareholder concerns.

Stakeholder perspective:

- stakeholders represent a range of broader interests which impact directly or indirectly on the company

- in some countries, a two-tier board is established (for example Germany), and employees are represented on the supervisory board
- a broad view of stakeholder interests encompasses specific groups, such as employees, and more heterogeneous interests, such as society and community, affected by the company's operations.

Tools for formulating business strategy

Business strategy must take into account both the external and internal environment of the organization. Two traditional tools, PEST analysis and SWOT analysis are given below. While both tend to oversimplify the processes, they do serve to highlight major issues.

PEST analysis

Analysis of the external environment may be expressed by the acronym **PEST**, standing for political, economic, sociocultural, and technological factors. Also known as 'environmental scanning', the PEST analysis is a useful tool for monitoring and evaluating forces which affect the organization over the long term. Research has shown that environmental scanning is linked to company performance (Thomas et al., 1993). Below are the headings, with a few questions that arise under each one:

- *Political and legal environment* – Is the existing government a stable one, and what is the strength of any opposition to it? What constraints has the government imposed on business, or is it likely to impose in the future? In the European Union (EU), what forthcoming legislation, such as new law on mergers, is likely to affect the business?
- *Economic environment* – Is the economy growing, or is there a recession looming? Are wages and consumer spending rising? Which sectors of the economy are growing and which sectors are not? Which regions of the country are experiencing the best growth? Is there high unemployment?
- *Sociocultural environment* – Is the society culturally diverse? What are the educational levels of the population generally? To what extent do women have educational opportunities and play an active part in business life? What is the pattern of family life – is there a large proportion of single-parent families, or are extended families the norm?
- *Technological environment* – What is the level of technology education and training, which would influence the recruitment of skilled staff? Is technological innovation encouraged? What funding is available, from government and elsewhere, for technology development? How computer-literate is the society generally?

Answers to these – and many other – questions present an environmental profile of any society, which differentiate it from other societies, even those in the same geographic region. The PEST analysis is thus particularly useful for strategic managers in international businesses which operate in a number of different national environments. Figure 1.9 provides a summary of the key variables in the international environment.

Political-legal

- Political stability
- Form of government, for example democratic, authoritarian
- Level of freedoms, for example freedom of expression and association
- Incentives to foreign investors
- Competition law and policy
- Employment law

Economic

- Level of economic development
- Trends in GDP
- Rate of inflation
- Wage levels and level of unemployment
- Strength of currency and convertibility
- Rates of taxation

Sociocultural

- Growth rate of population, and age distribution of population
- Language(s)
- Main religious and cultural groupings
- Educational attainment levels
- Level of social cohesion
- Role of women

Technological

- Government spending on R&D
- Legal regime for patent protection
- Energy availability and costs
- Transport infrastructure and costs
- Innovation system, including availability of skilled workforce
- Level of technology transfer

Figure 1.9 **PEST analysis in the international business environment**

The PEST analysis, while helpful as a tool, clearly does not cover all relevant aspects of the business environment. Legal factors are commonly grouped with political factors, as in the summary above. By expanding the acronym to LE PEST C, we can include legal factors as a separate heading, followed by ecological factors. Lastly, the competitive environment is added, to provide the basis of more comprehensive environmental scanning. These headings form the framework for the chapters of this book, with the addition of a separate chapter on the financial environment. The ecological environment is dealt with in Chapter 13.

Clearly, if a business is considering expanding in its home market, it will already have a good deal of knowledge about each of these aspects of the environment. On the other hand, if it is considering expanding to Vietnam, for example, it will probably know little. The more knowledge it acquires, the better, in order to avoid making costly mistakes. When the firm has done its research on Vietnam, it must ask itself, why should this firm in particular do business there?

SWOT analysis

The **SWOT** analysis is a commonly used planning tool, which assesses the firm's strategic profile in terms of its strengths, weaknesses, opportunities and threats. Focusing on both internal and external environments, it serves to highlight a firm's distinctive competences, which will enable it to gain competitive advantage.

The SWOT analysis is usually expressed as a matrix: strengths and weaknesses in the top boxes relate to the company itself, while opportunities and threats, in the lower boxes, reflect relevant aspects of the external environment. These are set out in Figure 1.10.

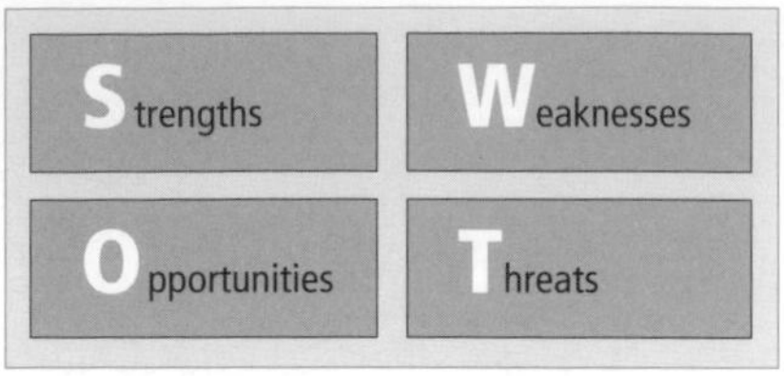

Figure 1.10 **SWOT analysis**

Some of the key issues which are addressed in a SWOT analysis are:

External environment – opportunities and threats:

- What are the main factors in the societal environment (political-legal, economic, sociocultural and technological)?
- What is the market strength of competitors?
- What new products or services, both those of the firm and its competitors, are in the pipeline?
- What is the level of consumer demand and can it be expected to remain stable?
- What is the likely threat of new entrants in the market for the firm's products?

Internal environment – strengths and weaknesses:

- Does the organization have a structure that helps it to achieve its objectives?
- Does it have clear marketing objectives and strategy?
- Does the organization use IT effectively in all aspects of its activities?
- Does its investment in R&D match or exceed that of competitors?
- Does the organization meet its financial objectives?
- To what extent does the firm have clear HRM objectives and strategies in areas such as employee motivation, staff turnover and provision of training?

Figure 1.11 sets out an example of a SWOT analysis for an online wine retailer, which runs no bricks-and-mortar outlets.

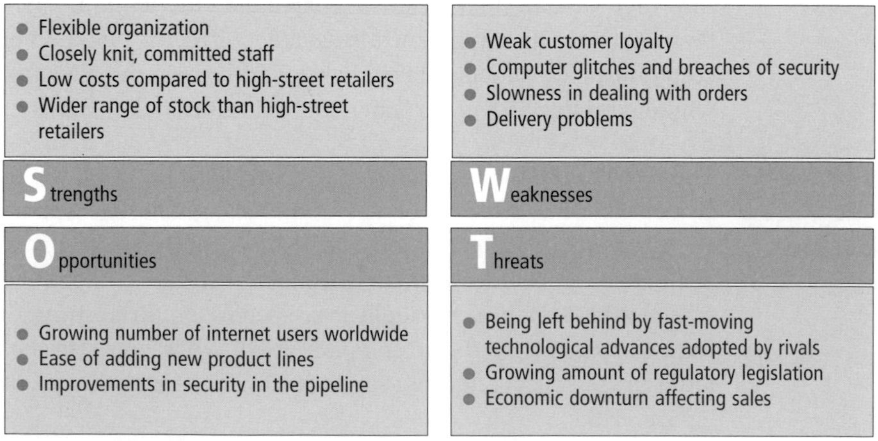

Figure 1.11 **SWOT analysis for a business selling wine online**

In this example, the SWOT analysis will be useful in formulating strategy to take advantage of opportunities, such as growing markets from new internet users. It will also help to minimize the effects of threats or anticipated threats. The SWOT analysis shows there are lingering doubts in the minds of many consumers about buying goods and services online, and many dot.com companies have struggled to build a customer base. It only takes one highly publicized security failure to damage consumer confidence. Consumers may also have more mundane worries, such as that of cases of wine being left on the doorstep when they are not at home. The online wine merchant must therefore endeavour to use the advantages of online selling, such as that of greater, more flexible product range, to compensate for the perceived drawbacks. Strategic options should therefore emerge in the SWOT analysis.

The SWOT analysis can be carried out in planning teams or by groups of executives (Piercy and Giles, 1989), and their impressions can be quite different. It has been found that higher level managers tend to take a broad overview, seeing organizational factors as strengths, while lower level ones single out marketing and financial factors (Mintzberg, 2000, p. 276). This suggests that people's views are influenced by their own position in the business, and the SWOT exercise can serve to widen the perspectives of participants in the planning process.

While this chapter has focused on the internal environment of the organization, it has emerged that key aspects such as structure, processes, change and strategy are tied in with many aspects of the external environment, so that change becomes an interactive process. It has also emerged that the activities of any organization consist of a number of different functions which form part of the interactive process. Each of the functional activities interacts with the external environment as well as with the other functions within the organization. Understanding these interactions is the subject of the next chapter.

Conclusions

1 Business covers a wide range of economic activity, including buying and selling goods, manufacturing products and providing services. International business refers to those activities between organizations in two or more countries.

2 Businesses may be sole traders, partnerships or companies. Typically, businesspeople set out as sole traders and convert the business to a limited company.

3 When they expand, businesses become more formally structured. Business organizations may be designed on a functional, multidivisional or matrix structure. No single structure can be said to suit all businesses.

4 Business strategy may evolve in many ways, emerging over time, rather than simply being the product of formal planning. Flexible organizations are more likely to be able to adapt strategy to the changing environment than rigid, hierarchical organizations.

5 While shareholder value is a key focus of company executives, companies have a broad range of other stakeholders, including employees, customers, and the community at large. The task of corporate governance, therefore, can often be seen as one involving balancing many stakeholder interests.

6 Two common tools used in formulating strategy are the PEST and SWOT analyses. Although they oversimplify complex processes, they serve to focus on key elements of strategic planning.

Review questions

1 What are the advantages and disadvantages of being a sole trader?

2 What are the aspects of the limited company which distinguish it from other types of business ownership?

3 Why are SMEs important to the economy?

4 Explain the reasons behind the adoption of a multidivisional structure for large companies.

5 What is a matrix structure? Assess its advantages and drawbacks in practice for the large organization.

6 What is meant by 'emergent strategy', and how does it differ from a strategic planning approach?

7 Contrast the bureaucratic organization with the network organization. Why is networking now seen as preferable from the organizational point of view, as well as from the perspective of individual employees?

8 How does corporate governance differ from the day-to-day management of a company?

9 Explain the shareholder and stakeholder perspectives on corporate governance.

10 What is the function of a PEST analysis?

Assignments

1 Assume that you are the CEO of a large international company in the media industry, which owns satellite television stations in Europe, Asia, and the Americas. Assess the advantages and disadvantages of different types of corporate structures for the company.

2 Construct a SWOT analysis for a small company which makes animated cartoons.

Further reading

Bartlett, C. and Ghoshal, S. (2002) *Managing across Borders: the Transnational Solution*, 2nd edn (Boston: Harvard Business School Press).

Brown, A. (1998) *Organisational Culture*, 2nd edn (London: Pitman).

Johnson, G., Scholes, K. and Whittington, R. (2004) *Exploring Corporate Strategy*, 7th edn (London: Pearson).

Kay, J. (2000) *Foundations of Corporate Success* (Oxford: Oxford University Press).

Mintzberg, H. (2000) *The Rise and Fall of Strategic Planning* (London: Financial Times/Prentice Hall).

Monks, R. and Minow, N. (2003) *Corporate Governance* (Oxford: Blackwell).

Mullins, L. (2004) *Management and Organizational Behaviour*, 7th edn (London: Financial Times/Prentice Hall).

Pugh, D.S. (ed.) (1995) *Organization Theory: Selected Readings*, 4th edn (London: Penguin Books).

Quinn, J., Mintzberg, H., James, R., Lampel, J. and Ghoshal, S. (eds) (2003) *The Strategy Process* (London: Financial Times/Prentice Hall).

Wheelen, T. and Hunger, J. (2002) *Strategic Management and Business Policy*, 8th edn (Upper Saddle River, NJ: Addison Wesley).

2 Functional dimensions which shape the organization and its strategy

Outline of chapter

- Introduction
- Operations
  - Operations strategy and performance
  - Operations in the international environment
- Marketing
  - The marketing concept
  - Elements of marketing
  - Marketing in the international environment
- Human resource management (HRM)
  - Elements of HRM
  - HRM in the international environment
- Accounting and finance
  - Elements of management accounting and financial reporting
  - Accounting and finance in the international environment
- Innovation
  - New product development
  - Innovation strategy
- Conclusions

Learning objectives

1 To acquire an overview of the essential business functions, in the context of organizational goals.

2 To gain an understanding of the elements of each functional area and how they combine to give a strategic focus for corporate decision-makers.

3 To appreciate the broad international context with which specific functional areas interact.

4 To gain a critical perspective on the ways in which functional specialisms differ from business to business, between different sectors and between manufacturing and service sectors.

Introduction

Every business, whether large or small, involves a number of different activities, or functions. A **function** is a type of activity that forms part of the overall process of providing a product for the consumer, from the design stage to the final point at which it reaches the customer. Business functions may be categorized broadly under the headings which appear in Figure 2.1. These broad functions were identified in the first chapter in the context of organizational structures. Each of these functional areas itself may be subdivided into further specialist elements, particularly evident in large, complex organizations. This chapter provides both an overview of each of the broad functions and a summary of the different activities which each comprises. For example, within the broad marketing function, we find market research and marketing communications, each of which is a specialized activity. Each subsection which follows will also highlight the ways in which business functions interact with the environment and the other functional areas. Understanding these dynamic relationships is key to successful strategy in the international environment. An important driver of strategy is innovation. While it may be viewed narrowly as a business function which concentrates on new product development, innovation, coupled with entrepreneurship, is now conceived more broadly as a strategic objective, to which all the functional activities contribute.

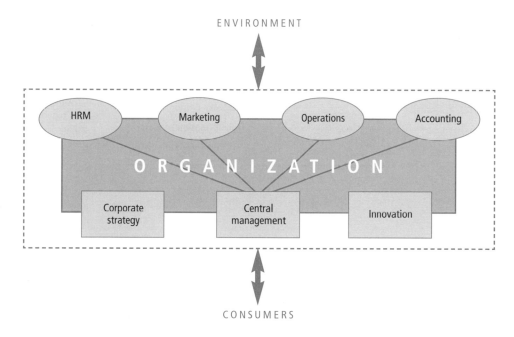

Figure 2.1 **Business functions in the organizational environment**

Operations

Operations comprises one of the broadest ranges of activities in the business organization. Production and manufacturing immediately come to mind as operations, but the provision of services is also reliant on the operations function. Operations can be defined broadly as the creation and provision of both goods and services to be offered to the consumer. Service operations have become increasingly important in international business, especially with advances in IT. A related development has been that the traditional distinctions between goods and services have become blurred. In fact, the notion of a 'pure' goods or service provider has given way to a more integrated view of operations as providing a blend of products and services (Slack et al., 2004, p. 16). Operations management may be divided into three distinctive groups of activity which relate to stages in the creation and delivery of the product. The first is product design and associated activities such as forecasting demand, equipment design, work design and location. The second is the operation of the system, which includes scheduling, quality control and cost control. Thirdly, there are supply chain management activities, which include purchasing, inventory control and distribution.

Operations are usually depicted as a system by which inputs such as resources are processed or transformed to produce outputs which are delivered to customers. This is known as the transformation process (Slack et al., 2004, p. 12), which is depicted in Figure 2.2.

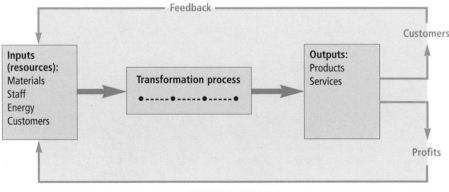

Figure 2.2　The transformation process

Inputs vary depending on the nature of the process. For a manufacturing process, the main inputs may be materials to be transformed, the operators and the machinery to carry out the process. The process is one of transforming materials to produce a tangible output, such as a digital camera, for the customer. For a service provider, the main input is likely to be customers themselves, and the processing of customers is the essence of the operation. For example, patients who enter a hospital to receive treatment are the inputs, and the output of the process is the patient who has been treated. Both types of operation rely on facilities and staff. Facilities include the buildings, equipment and technology to carry out processes, while the expertise of staff is crucial to carrying out the process. Although both types of process aim to satisfy customers, performance, outputs and how to measure customer satisfaction vary from operation to operation.

The manufactured product such as the camera is tangible, that is, we can see and touch it. It is relatively durable and the customer expects it to take photos over a long period. The service such as hospital treatment is not a product in the same sense. Its essence is the skilled treatment by medical staff and the output is that we recover from illness and feel healthy. These benefits are mainly intangible, in that they cannot be seen and touched like a physical product, but they are nonetheless real. Within these categories, there are wide variations stemming particularly from volume of output and the variety of output offered to the customer. The digital camera is a high-volume, mass-produced product, whereas a luxury yacht, also a tangible product, is likely to be produced by skilled craft workers, in small numbers and customized for particular customers. Services, too, vary widely. A low-cost airline aims to offer a standard product in high volume, whereas a tour operator may offer a customized holiday for the customer, consisting of air transport, hotel accommodation in multiple destinations, transport between locations and local excursions. One thing which stands out from these examples is the contrast between the high-volume operation producing a standardized product and the low-volume operation designed to meet the needs of individual customers. For each, the company's strategic objectives are paramount. This point is demonstrated in Case study 2.1 on Ryanair, a successful low-cost airline. Operations strategy, therefore, is vital to the company in achieving its corporate objectives.

Case study 2.1   Ryanair and the revolution in low-cost air travel

The low-cost airline, pioneered by Southwest Airlines in the US, offers the passenger a 'no-frills' service at a lower price than the traditional service with food and entertainment which has been the mainstay of the major airline companies. The two companies which have developed the low-cost model most successfully in Europe have been easyJet and Ryanair. Both have enjoyed phenomenal growth, building market share at the expense of the major flagship carriers such as British Airways (BA) and Lufthansa, in effect revolutionizing air travel within Europe. Low-cost travel now enjoys a market share of over 10 per cent of intra-European air travel. Of the two companies, Ryanair has been the more radical in its low-cost strategy, charging as little as under 10 euros for a flight. But how sustainable is this strategy in the long term?

Ryanair relies on high volume, filling as many seats as possible on each flight, and also adding capacity to its network, which it has rapidly built up. Michael O'Leary, the CEO of Ryanair, says: 'This is Tesco. How is Tesco cheaper compared with other stores? They buy more and sell it at low prices' (Felsted, 4 November 2003). Ryanair flew 11.3 million passengers in 2003, 45 per cent up on 2002. 'Load factor' is the number of seats sold as a proportion of those seats available on each flight. Ryanair's load factor fell from over 80 per cent in 2002 to 77 per cent in 2003 (which is still high for the industry), partly because of a 60 per cent increase in the number of seats available. O'Leary looks for every possible means of reducing costs in the operation. Almost all seats are booked via the internet, saving costs in administration. Aircraft are operated on tight schedules with quick turnaround times of only 25 minutes, allowing more flying time in a day than rival carriers: it can run two more flights a day than rivals such as BA. Ryanair pilots fly 887 hours a year, close to the legal limit of 900 hours, and more than the 780 hours a year flown by easyJet pilots. The company has invested in older aircraft, for which depreciation costs are less steep. With its ambitious expansion plans, it has ordered 102 new Boeing aircraft, which will entail significant depreciation costs. This is one of the factors which might affect future profits. On the other hand, the new aircraft have greater capacity and are more fuel-efficient. Despite its older planes, Ryanair's maintenance costs are lower than those of easyJet, and lower than would be expected by industry experts, but the company denies that safety is being compromised.

Ryanair's major cost savings have come from its use of secondary airports, where fees are lower than those of major hubs. It is estimated that its landing costs per passenger are only £4.90 out of an average fare of £33, compared with £10.75 per passenger out of an average EasyJet fare of £46, arriving at a major airport. Moreover, O'Leary has been successful in doing deals with these underused airports, including,

for example, provision of hotel accommodation for crews. However, this strategy suffered a setback with the European Commission ruling that such a deal with Charleroi airport in Belgium, which is state-owned, amounted to a state subsidy, which is disallowed under European law. While some observers saw this as a blow to the Ryanair business model, O'Leary shrugged off such comments as unfounded, confident that cheap airport deals are still possible.

For Ryanair, 2004 was a calmer year, with slower growth, in which capacity increased only 16 per cent and passenger volumes increased 19 per cent. Profit margins were down, from 28 per cent in 2003 to 22 per cent, as shown in the figure. Is this a sign that the boom days are over? Ryanair, registered in Dublin, pays corporation tax in Ireland, where the rate has dropped to 12.5 per cent. A less advantageous tax regime would affect its position and, in particular, any future tax on fuel. Environmentalists have singled out the high level of emissions from short-haul flights as a cause of global warming. Other costs, such as operating costs, rising oil prices and higher airport charges, are also under pressure. O'Leary remains upbeat about Ryanair's long-term future, while pointing to likely casualties among the many newer entrants into the low-cost sector.

Sources: Dombey, D., Doné, K., and Felsted, A., 'As regulators launch an inquiry into suspected illegal subsidies, is cheap air travel in Europe too good to last?', *Financial Times*, 12 December 2002; Felsted, A., '"Everyone is looking for the secret under the bed." Can Michael O'Leary sustain Ryanair's low-cost success?', *Financial Times*, 4 December 2003; Felsted, A., 'Budget airlines fly on a knife edge', *Financial Times*, 11 August 2002; Done, K., 'Ryanair talks of disaster, but the low-cost revolution flies on', *Financial Times*, 7 February 2004; Done, K., 'Ryanair suffers first net profit drop in 15 years', *Financial Times*, 2 June 2004.

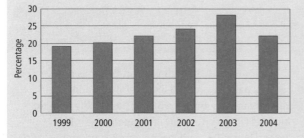

Ryanair's profit margins
Source: *Financial Times*, 2 June 2004.

Case questions

What are the essential elements of Ryanair's low-cost strategy?
What factors will affect its long-term sustainability?

WEB ALERT!

Ryanair's website is http://www.ryanair.com
easyJet's website is http://www.easyjet.com
Southwest, the pioneer low-cost airline, is at http://www.southwest.com

Operations strategy and performance

Operations strategy can be defined as 'the pattern of strategic decisions and actions which set the role, objectives and activities of the operation' (Slack et al., 2004, p. 67). All operations aim to produce a product to satisfy customers' expectations for a price they are willing to pay. The assumption is that the customer is willing to pay more for a high-quality product, and the focus on quality is the primary aim of some businesses. At the opposite extreme is the low-cost producer, whose primary aim is to reduce cost, increasing market share by charging less than competitors. Operations management generally seeks to both satisfy customers and utilize resources efficiently. Five performance objectives are generally recognized as making up operations strategy (Slack et al., 2004, p. 44). These are:

● *Quality* – Quality is not an absolute concept, but varies according to the type of product and customer expectations. For a manufactured product, such as a washing machine, quality would consist of its fitness for purpose, its reliability and durability. The customer is dissatisfied if it breaks down six months after purchase, but consumer expectations depend to a great extent on price: Miele, the German manufacturer, finds that customers are willing to pay a premium price for its high-quality machines, as they are designed to last many years. Service quality, too, depends on customer expectations. The customer who simply wishes to travel from A to B as cheaply as possible is satisfied with the no-frills service of the low-cost carrier, despite crowded check-in facilities, whereas the passenger who pays for an expensive flight expects smooth check-in with no wait, pleasant staff, high-quality meals and other amenities to make the flight an enjoyable experience.

● *Dependability* – The operation needs to produce the goods, services or information at the time promised to the customer, and, in the case of manufactured goods, in the right quantity and to the right specification. No operation can guarantee that there will never be any slippages. A firm may fail to make a delivery on time because a vital piece of machinery in the manufacturing process has broken down. For the operations manager, maintenance and repair arrangements need to be in place to minimize disruption. Such arrangements are cost-effective in the long term, as the disruption may potentially be costly in terms of emergency repairs and possible lost orders if customers are disappointed.

● *Speed* – In today's fast-moving business environment, it is important for the firm to be able to respond quickly to customers' requests for goods or services. Operations management, therefore, may hold the key to attracting customers and receiving future orders. Speed of response varies with the type of business. The manufacturer needs to meet orders quickly from stock, while the retail outlet needs to ensure that customers do not have to wait to be served. Similarly, a restaurant with slow and inefficient service is less likely to attract repeat visits from diners than one with quick service.

- *Flexibility* – Flexibility in operations refers to the ability to change in response to customers' needs. While consumers years ago were happy to accept the uniform, standardized product, modern consumers expect a diversity of product options, even on standard goods and services. Largely due to advances in computer technology, this is now possible through the approach known as 'mass customization', whereby mass-produced products can be customized to the individual customer's needs. Cars produced on the modern assembly line, for example, are likely each to incorporate preferences (such as colour, finish and features) of the customers who have ordered them. Flexibility also refers to the ability of the firm to respond to changes in volume requested and delivery dates. The firm that is able to respond quickly to an order for an increased quantity of goods is more likely to get repeat business than the firm which lacks this flexibility.

- *Cost* – Every organization must manage costs, but reducing costs is not a straightforwardly simple objective. A manufacturer may buy cheaper components for vehicles, but if they are inferior and have to be replaced, the costs could soar and much customer goodwill would be lost. The difficult task is to reduce the cost while achieving the level of quality that customers expect of the product. Some costs, such as those entailed in safety, are perceived as essential and reducing them may not be possible without compromising safety, although, as the case study on Ryanair highlighted, the company has been able to trim maintenance costs. In industries in which staff costs are a major component in overall costs, there may be little scope for reduction, but we have seen in recent years that for many operations, such as call centres, it is possible to move to low-cost locations, significantly reducing costs (see Case study 7.3). The other objectives in this section – quality, dependability, speed and flexibility – all have cost implications and the organization's overall strategy will prioritize one or more of these objectives over others.

SUMMARY POINTS

Operations strategy

The aim is to produce goods or services which satisfy customers' expectations, at a price they are willing to pay.

Performance objectives:

- **Quality** – level of quality expected by the customer for this type of product or service
- **Dependability** – meeting contractual terms for specification and delivery

- **Speed** – speed of response, which may be crucial in winning and retaining customers
- **Flexibility** – sensitivity to customers' needs and willingness to adapt products
- **Cost** – controlling costs while ensuring satisfaction of other performance objectives.

Operations in the international environment

Operations processes constantly interact with the environment and changes in the environment have direct – and sometimes dramatic – impact on costs. Inputs such as materials, energy, labour and finance are susceptible to fluctuations dependent on many factors. Steep rises in the price of oil in the 1970s caused a radical rethink of operations across the globe. Even a slight rise in the price of an essential resource may have repercussions leading to changes in sourcing or even redesign of the product. Rising labour costs in the advanced economies have led firms to seek low-cost locations, in some cases thousands of miles from customers. A growing phenomenon has been the international scope of operations, a theme which will be developed in the next chapter. While industries such as motor manufacturing were once predominantly national, they are now international in scope. Components may be sourced from different continents and must be available for assembly at the right time, in the correct quantity and of the right quality. Efficient coordination of production in this environment, therefore, has become highly complex and the importance of operations management is viewed as critical. Greater complexity and internationalization of processes have been facilitated by advances in computer and information technology. Technological innovation has altered operating processes and led to changes in the way that operations strategy is conceived. Computerized management information systems have enhanced the ability of all types of organizations to meet customers' needs more quickly and efficiently, even when customers are scattered across the globe.

WEB ALERT! Sources for operations management

The Technology and Operations Management (TOMI) portal run by Sussex University is at http://www.sussex.ac.uk/Users/dt31/TOMI

The homepage of the *Journal of Operations Management* is at http://www1.elsevier.com/homepage/sae/orms/jom

Marketing

The last section stressed the underlying importance of providing products that satisfy customers' needs at prices they are willing to pay. The success of the enterprise, therefore, whether large or small, depends on interaction with customers and responsiveness to their needs. This broad range of activities falls within the marketing function. The highly visible aspects of marketing, such as advertising which we encounter every day, tend to cause us to lose sight of the many other marketing activities, which include research, product design, price, distribution and consumer behaviour. Marketing can be defined as 'individual and organizational activities that facilitate and expedite satisfying exchange relationships in a dynamic environment through the creation, distribution, promotion and pricing of goods, services and ideas' (Dibb et al., 1997, p. 5). This definition highlights key aspects of marketing, which are examined in this section. First, it is an interactive process between the organization and consumers, which aims to satisfy their needs. This is embodied in the marketing concept. Second, it involves a range of distinctive activities, which are the elements of marketing. And, third, it takes place in a dynamic environment. These are examined in turn.

The marketing concept

The **marketing concept** rests on the belief that meeting the needs and wants of the consumer is central to the goals of the organization. Some companies have a 'product orientation', taking the approach that the aim of marketing is simply to promote the company's products. These companies concentrate their attention on product innovations and improvements, assuming that this approach will lead automatically to sales. A more recent approach may be described as one of 'marketing orientation', which places the satisfying of customers' needs as the primary aim of the organization. This view is expressed by Kotler et al., 2002, p. 15:

> The marketing concept holds that achieving organizational goals depends on determining the needs and wants of target markets and delivering the desired satisfactions more effectively and efficiently than competitors do.

The marketing orientation thus focuses primarily on the consumer rather than on the product. A core concept is the exchange transaction: a buyer offers payment, usually money, to a seller for the products desired. A group of buyers of a particular product forms a market. But buyers may buy a particular product, such as a car, for different reasons. While some will look mainly at performance and quality of manufacture, others will focus on external or internal appearance. Some will focus on safety features while others look mainly at durability. Some consumers need a car simply to travel to and from their workplace, while others are looking for a vehicle with large carrying capacity for long trips. Finding out what specific groups of consumers want, designing products to satisfy them and keeping informed of changing consumer tastes are at the heart of the marketing concept.

SUMMARY POINTS

The marketing concept

- The marketing concept holds that satisfying the needs and wants of the consumer is central to the goals of the organization.
- Satisfying the needs of differing groups of consumers and responding to changing consumer tastes are inherent in the marketing concept.

Elements of marketing

Marketing can be divided into a number of elements which form the basis of marketing strategy. These include market research, segmentation and branding. The aim of market research is to gather and analyse information from consumers. Most obviously, their likes and dislikes of existing product offerings are valuable, and also it is vital to find out their views on possible new products. Market research also uncovers much information about consumers themselves, including employment, lifestyle and leisure activities. This information is often collected by specialist market research firms. Through market research, organizations are able to judge which new products are likely to succeed and which consumers are likely to buy them. Marketers are thus able to target particular products and particular groups of consumers, through the processes of market segmentation and product differentiation.

Consumer needs and wants in today's world are diverse and a standard product is unlikely to satisfy all consumers in all locations. Segmentation and product differentiation are therefore increasingly important elements of marketing. **Segmentation** may be defined as:

> dividing a market into distinct groups of buyers with different needs, characteristics or behaviour, who might require separate products or marketing mixes. (Kotler et al., 2002, p. 314)

Segments may be based on gender, age, geographical location, cultural background and lifestyle (for example urban or rural), or a combination of these characteristics. A company may offer a small range of products to a small number of clearly defined market segments. Makers of luxury goods fall into this category. Other companies offer a wide range of products to many different segments. The major car manufacturers, Ford and General Motors (GM), are examples. They produce a huge range of models, from the basic small car to the luxury saloon. Ford's market researchers have recently focused on the mid-size saloon, which accounts for 18 per cent of the market and is one of the most competitive segments (Grant and McIntosh, 2004). They found that consumers of these vehicles expect them to be equipped with many features common in the sports utility vehicle (SUV), such as plenty of cupholders and extra storage space. Accordingly, Ford's new saloon model features eight cupholders and a boot capable of holding eight sets of golf clubs!

Differentiation is also achieved by branding, discussed below. Finally, there are companies which produce a standard product for a mass market. Coca-Cola is an example, but this global company is increasingly sensitive to differing segments. It has increased its portfolio of products beyond its best-known product, Coke, and adapts advertising and marketing to suit local markets. The in-depth case study at the end of Part 1 details Coca-Cola's changing strategy in response to changing markets.

CRITICAL PERSPECTIVES

The customer-led company

The goal is not simply to be led by customers' expressed needs; responsiveness is not enough. The objective is to amaze customers by anticipating and fulfilling their unarticulated needs. To do this, a company must gain deep insights into potential classes of customer benefits … The goal is thus to be broadly *benefits driven* – constantly searching for, investing in, and mastering the technology that will bring unanticipated benefits to humankind. (Hamel and Prahalad, 1994, pp. 320–1)

- In this excerpt, what is the difference between a product and a consumer benefit?
- Think of some examples of new products which fulfil unarticulated needs, thus creating demand.

Brand refers to the visual identity of a product or company. It may be a name or logo, which is known as a trademark. With the rise in media output and increasing access to global media by consumers in all countries, branding has become central to marketing strategy. Establishing a strong brand image, which the consumer associates with quality and reliability, has helped Japanese car manufacturers to increase market share in the US. As Figure 2.3 shows, American brands have lost ground to Japanese brands. In response, American manufacturers have promised new models, greater choice and improved quality, to match Japanese rivals. A company is likely to have its corporate logo as a brand and, in addition, separate brands on particular products which are targeted at different market segments (Aaker, 2004). As suggested above, car manufacturers like GM, produce different brands for different markets, for example, the Opel for the European markets. Alternatively, a company may choose to market all its products under its corporate brand, such as Nike. Some companies have excelled in branding at both corporate and product levels. For example, Microsoft is now one of the world's most familiar brands, but Windows, the operating system, is also a strong brand.

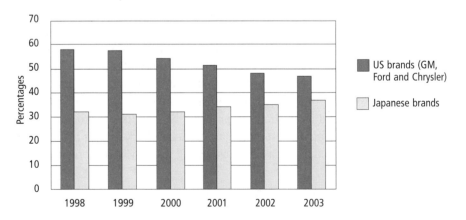

Figure 2.3 **Brand share of the US passenger car market**
Source: *Financial Times*, 5 January 2004.

In marketing literature, it is common to speak of the 'marketing mix', which consists of product, price, promotion and place (known as the four Ps). The marketing mix may be defined as 'the combination of the 4Ps that creates an integrated and consistent offering to potential customers that satisfies their needs and wants' (Brassington and Pettitt, 2003, p. 1105). The *product* may be goods, services, information or, commonly, a blend of these. The *price* reflects the company's differentiated product lines. In addition, the company may well price the same product differently in different markets, based on a range of factors, including cost of production, level of local average incomes and consumer spending habits. However, using the internet, consumers are able to compare prices between markets and so companies are finding it more difficult to maintain price differences. The common currency, the euro, across the eurozone countries has also made it easier for customers to compare prices.

Place refers to the processes which link together to deliver the product to the targeted consumers. These include distribution networks, transport, wholesalers and retailers. These processes have been transformed by technological advances. As indicated in Chapter 1, networks are now international in scope, and the internet has facilitated the growth in e-commerce and internet marketing. *Promotion*, too, has been revolutionized by internet developments. Promotion refers to all the means whereby the company communicates with consumers, encouraging them to buy the product. It encompasses advertising, sales promotions (such as coupons for discounts on future purchases), direct marketing (such as selling from its website) and sponsorship (such as sponsoring a sporting event which is broadcast to a large audience). To spread awareness of products and brands, companies rely heavily on promotional activities and some have huge advertising budgets. Marketing strategists stress, however, that elements of the marketing mix must be effectively coordinated to reach the targeted consumers and satisfy their needs. Money spent on advertising is wasted, for example, if the product is unavailable or does not meet consumer expectations for quality and performance. Moreover, advertising which causes negative reactions in local cultural contexts may damage the company's reputation as well as lose it sales.

Figure 2.4 **Marketing mix**

Marketing activities interact with all aspects of the organization's environment. This section will highlight some of the most important interactions. Consumer needs and wants, which are central to marketing, are shaped in the cultural and social environment of each market. Language, religion, values about family life and norms of social behaviour are all aspects of culture which must be taken into account. Furthermore, preferences in food and drink and other aspects of lifestyle may differ from market to market. Understanding local cultures will help to target products to the needs of particular consumers and formulate a marketing strategy to which the targeted customers respond positively. McDonald's now sells a variety of products to cater for local tastes in its restaurants, in addition to the Big Mac. Market research provides relevant information about consumer lifestyles which also reflects the economic environment. In China's rapidly growing economy, the car is fast replacing the bicycle as the preferred means of transport. Car sales doubled from 2.1 million in 2000 to 4.2 million 2003, making it the world's third largest car market and a target for foreign manufacturers, who see Chinese expansion as offsetting sluggish sales in established markets. Through its joint ventures, Volkswagen claims 30 per cent of the Chinese market and increased its sales in China 40 per cent from 2002 to 2003. The company is likely to focus expansion plans in this market rather than in markets where consumer spending is weak. Case study 2.2 on Nike illustrates the process of refocusing the brand onto football in international markets, marking a shift from the focus on athletic shoes, on which the brand was established in the American market.

Case study 2.2 Nike becomes a fan of football

Nike built its iconic brand on its reputation for high-quality athletic footwear, incorporating innovative features, for which consumers were willing to pay premium prices. The Air Jordan is an example, with its bubble soles, fashion appeal and sports star endorsement of Michael Jordan in 1985. A bright young prospect at the time, he went on to become the most famous basketball player ever. Nike credits this endorsement as having opened up a new market of young, urban, male consumers (Garrahan, 5 August 2003). The appeal of Air Jordans, now in their eighteenth model, is fading, as consumers are choosing between performance and fashion in trainers, with the 'retro' trainer gaining in popularity. While Nike accounts for 39 per cent of the market in branded athletic shoes, this share has slumped from 48 per cent in 1997, in a market which is now more fragmented. Performance brands, such as New Balance, have prospered, and

other brands, such as Puma, have gravitated more to the fashion trainer. Nike should be a strong presence in both these segments, but it is wary of the fashion route, as fashions are notoriously ephemeral and demand cannot be predicted. Its signing of the basketball star Le Bron James for an estimated $90 million, in 2003, was a way of renewing its established strength in basketball.

Looking to expand in international markets, Nike concluded that football had the greatest market potential. The catalyst, as its CEO explains, was the 1994 World Cup in the US: 'Up until the 1994 World Cup the US was the centre of this company's universe ... We came to the realization that we could only become so big in the US and if we wanted to be taken seriously on a global scale, football had to be a priority' (Garrahan, 5 August 2003). Its football division has now become the driver of non-US sales. It concluded sponsorship deals with the Brazil national team and Manchester United, the latter a 13-year £303 million kit deal reached in 2002. It has also made sponsorship deals with Ronaldo (Real Madrid and Brazil) Luis Figo (Real Madrid and Portugal) and Wayne Rooney (Manchester United and England). For the first time in 2003, Nike generated more revenue from overseas markets than it did in its home market. It also overtook Adidas, with $10 billion in revenues. A further milestone occurred in 2004, when Nike overtook Adidas in European market share, accounting for 34 per cent of the football-related footwear market, compared to the 30.2 per cent share of Adidas, which has traditionally dominated European football.

Nike is aware that celebrity sponsorship does not translate automatically into sales. It stresses: 'We have to deliver a product that captivates the consumer. And then we have to market it so that it is special.' At the same time, the Nike brand has been extended to many sports and events, including the Olympics, golf and professional cycling (it sponsored Lance Armstrong, 7-times winner of the Tour de France). Is it spreading itself too thinly? Its CEO says: 'We have to keep renewing and refreshing what Nike stands for' (Garrahan, 5 Aug 2003).

Sources: Gapper, J., 'The big bucks that keep Nike in the big league', *Financial Times*, 4 November 2003; Garrahan, M., 'The fabulous football money machine', *Financial Times*, 26 April 2003; Garrahan, M., 'How to keep doing it all over the world', *Financial Times*, 5 August 2003; Garrahan, M., 'Nike scores on the football pitch', *Financial Times*, 19 August 2004; Garrahan, M., 'Nike overtakes Adidas in football field', *Financial Times*, 19 August 2004.

Case questions

Why did Nike shift its focus to football?

What lessons does the case study highlight for other companies wishing to expand in international markets?

WEB ALERT!

Marketing resources may be found at http://www.marketingsource.com/articles

There are many academic journals in marketing, notably the *Journal of Marketing*, published by the American Marketing Association (AMA), and the *European Journal of Marketing*, published by the European Marketing Academy. Journals on specific areas of marketing include the *Journal of Consumer Behaviour* and the *International Journal of Market Research*. Links to these and many other marketing journals may be found on the AMA website, at http://www.marketingpower.com/live/content

A marketing website which includes both practitioner and academic sources is http://www.marketingprofs.com

Nike's homepage is http://www.nike.com

Nike's football homepage is http://www.nikefootball.com

Marketing must also take account of the legal and political environment. National regulatory frameworks govern many aspects of the goods and services themselves. Governments see their role as protecting the public interest. For example, a company offering investment products must adhere to the legal requirements of financial regulators, which in the UK is the Financial Services Authority (FSA). Dealings with customers are regulated under consumer protection legislation, which provides that goods must be safe, of satisfactory quality and fit for purpose. Communication with customers is also a sensitive issue, as technology makes it possible to store and transmit huge amounts of personal data about customers. Legislation on data protection at a national level is now coordinated through international agreement, which aims to control the use of personal data in e-commerce.

WEB ALERT!

Issues of fair trade, consumer safety and quality standards are overseen in the UK by the Office of Fair Trading at http://www.oft.gov.uk

Trading Standards Central is at http://www.tradingstandards.net/

The National Consumer Council is at http://www.ncc.org.uk. Information on various aspects of consumer protection, including data protection, is at http://www.ncc.org.uk/dataprotection

Finally, companies face the more nebulous issues of the ethical environment. Targeting the advertising of products such as carbonated drinks or high-fat foods at young people is legal, but many consider it unethical, as these products are unhealthy. Krispy Kreme Donuts, for example, has recognized that it has a tricky task marketing an inherently unhealthy product. Its CEO says:

> We're pretty transparent about what we are. People don't come to us for nutrition. It's all a question of balance – we're an affordable indulgence. (Liu, 2004)

Still, the company is considering sugar-free, low-calorie doughnuts. In 2004, Coca-Cola decided to remove its vending machines from schools in response to health-conscious consumers. As Figure 2.5 shows, such concerns appear to be justified, as most consumers perceive Coca-Cola's key brands as unhealthy. While this move reflects ethical considerations, it also responds to consumer desires. Kotler has introduced the

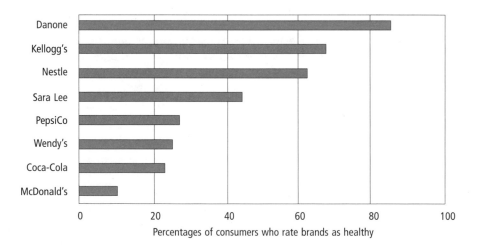

Figure 2.5 **Consumer perceptions of brand portfolios as healthy**
Source: *Financial Times*, 31 August 2004.

'societal marketing concept', shifting from the pure marketing concept, which focuses on the individual consumer's wants and needs, to the broader concept of the long-term well-being of society. (Kotler et al., 2002, p. 17) The societal marketing concept seeks to balance short-term factors, such as satisfying consumer wants and maximizing company profits, with long-term factors, such as environmental concerns and consumer health. With its range of healthy products, Danone is well placed to benefit from growing numbers of health-conscious consumers.

Human resource management

The focus of **human resource management (HRM)** is the people who make up the organization and concerns the relations between employees and the organization. Until the 1980s, this function was known as the 'personnel' function, which took a rather mechanistic approach to relations between employers and employees. It tended to emphasize the employment contract as defining the legal rights and duties of employers and employees, and, in practice, the focus was on a rather narrow range of employment issues, such as recruitment, job descriptions and training. Relations were likely to be confrontational, and trade unions played an important role in collective bargaining (see Chapter 7 for a discussion of the role of trade unions). Rethinking in the 1980s led to a broader view of the function as integrated into the organization's overall strategy and covering a wider range of issues. This approach came to be called the 'HRM model'.

In this more recent thinking, HRM has a more strategic focus, involving employees in the overall objectives of the organization and, it is anticipated, building a sense of commitment on the part of employees to the employer. Underlying this view is the belief 'that the aim is not merely to seek compliance with rules and regulations from employees, but to strive for the much more ambitious objective of commitment' (Storey, 1995, p. 5). The emphasis, according to Storey, is less on rules and procedure and more on the management of culture in the organization:

> Human resource management is a distinctive approach to employment management which seeks to achieve competitive advantage through strategic deployment of a highly committed and capable workforce, using an integrated array of cultural, structural and personnel techniques. (Storey, 1995, p. 5)

This newer approach stresses flexibility in employment relations, with the aim of linking individual capabilities and values with organizational goals. The goal is to achieve better performance from the firm's perspective and greater job satisfaction from the employee's perspective. Of course, traditional personnel activities still have a role to play, but they become part of the wider organizational picture.

WEB ALERT!

HRM resources can be found at http://hrmguide.net.hrm/. This site has links to sources on many HR and work-related topics

In the UK, the Chartered Institute of Personnel and Development (CIPD) offers links to many HR topics at http://www.cipd.co.uk

Whatever the theoretical perspective, HRM is about managing people. While large organizations have specialist departments and formal procedures, these are the exception in business generally. For smaller businesses, personnel functions are part of general administration rather than jobs for specialists and there may be little formal procedure. Nonetheless, the essential elements of personnel management can be identified. Elements highlighted here are recruitment and selection, reward management, HR development and employee relations.

Recruitment and selection are critical for both the organization and the prospective employee. It is now recognized that psychological factors play a part in the motivation and commitment of employees and these are now a part of this process, in addition to the traditional formal qualifications and experience (Bratton and Gold, 2003, p. 222). Every organization, large or small, wishes to recruit the 'right' people for the job and employers increasingly look at 'competences', which relate to behaviour patterns relevant to the job.

Reward systems are another important aspect of HRM, stemming from the essential contractual nature of the employment relationship, which is an exchange transaction between employer and employee in which the employer pays an agreed remuneration for work carried out by the employee. There is now considerable diversity in reward systems: salaries, commission, bonus arrangements, benefits in kind (as opposed to monetary payment) and performance-related pay are various alternatives. Money compensation is at the core of reward systems, but other types of non-monetary benefits may form part of the reward 'package'. There are divergent views on how the reward system should be designed and to what extent it should be based on monetary reward. Rewards may be linked to distinct elements of performance, but the emphasis on performance and variability of reward which follows may affect the overall motivation of employees and undermine commitment to organizational goals (Bratton and Gold, 2003, p. 293). In the design of reward systems, HR managers must take account of the need for equity between workers and transparency in the arrangements. Benefits other than monetary compensation may include benefits such as the company car, health insurance or childcare. It should be remembered that the motivation and reward of employees are influenced by culture and may differ according to enterprise structures in different societies (Whitley, 1999). Monetary compensation based on formal contractual relations, while predominant in Western contexts, is less important in Asian contexts, where informal and personal relations are stressed.

SUMMARY POINTS

How employees are rewarded

Employees are rewarded through a combination of direct pay and other benefits, which vary greatly from one organization to another:

Direct monetary rewards:

● basic wage or salary, plus overtime pay at an agreed rate

- performance-related pay, which varies according to individual or team performance
- commission – pay according to individual transactions carried out for the organization; acts as a financial incentive.

Other types of reward:

- benefits in kind, such as subsidized accommodation, company car
- health insurance, particularly important in the US
- childcare
- pension scheme.

HR development is an increasingly important element of HRM. Formerly, training was seen in rather narrow terms as skills relevant to particular jobs. Development now takes a broader view of the individual employee's needs in terms of learning and personal development. Indeed, there is much literature on the notion of 'organizational learning', stressing the fact that learning in both individual and organizational contexts is necessary for coping with change (Hamel and Prahalad, 1994). In the rapidly changing environment, technological advances in particular have brought about radical changes in the nature of work. The employee whose skills have become outdated faces possible redundancy without retraining. From the organizational perspective, new developments in products and processes imply putting in place new technology, for which learning and retraining play an important role.

Employee relations have in the past been equated with 'industrial' or 'labour' relations, suggesting that trade union representation and collective bargaining are at its core. Now, the term is more broadly interpreted as encompassing both individual and collective relations between employers and employees. It covers formal ties such as contractual employment terms, but also informal ties through day-to-day communication, which are seen as influential in building employee commitment and strengthening organizational culture (Marchington, 1995). While there is clearly the need for organizational rules and disciplinary procedures, consultation with employees and employee participation in decision-making are more likely to build trust between management and employees than management emphasis on control mechanisms. This is particularly the case in the newer, knowledge-based types of work, where employees and managers share expertise.

Strategic HRM links the elements of HRM in the pursuit of corporate goals, as illustrated in Figure 2.6. This strategic focus is based not simply on employee compliance with the rule-based elements of the employment relationship, but on an embeddedness in the organizational culture. As Figure 2.6 shows, HRM is influenced by aspects of the external environment. Those highlighted include the impact of the social and cultural environment on employee goals and organizational culture; the impact of the economic environment on reward systems; and the impact of the political and legal environment on employee relations. These environmental contexts differ from country to country and international HRM increasingly highlights this diversity.

Figure 2.6 **Strategic HRM**

SUMMARY POINTS

Elements of HRM

- **Recruitment and selection** – competences as well as qualifications and skills.
- **Reward management** – monetary and non-monetary rewards.
- **HR development** – learning in the broad organizational context.
- **Employee relations** – individual and collective relations between employer and employees, both formal and informal.

HRM in the international environment

Legal requirements touch on almost every aspect of relations between employers and employees. Employment legislation and policies differ from country to country, reflecting governments' perceptions of their social and economic roles. Laws typically spell out duties which businesses within their territory must adhere to, so that workers are not exploited by employers or subjected to unsafe working conditions. There are laws governing working conditions, health and safety at work, hours of work, the wages employers are compelled to pay and even paid holidays. In addition, there are laws covering the collective aspect of employment, including laws on trade unions and labour relations. Importantly, too, there are laws prohibiting discrimination at work, including race, sex and religious discrimination. It must be said, however, that, in some countries, worker protection is much weaker than in others, and, in addition, enforcement of the law differs from country to country. This patchwork of legal frameworks has become a prominent feature of the international HRM landscape. Lax regulation in some countries may constitute an attraction for businesses which operate internationally, as costs are likely to be lower than those in more regulated environments; however, consumers are likely to react negatively to products produced in poor conditions or by exploitative practices (see Chapter 14).

CRITICAL PERSPECTIVES

Strategic HRM

Companies that focus on product design and innovation or on customer-focused or customized solutions require different workforce strategies. For example, product-based companies need to foster innovation and risk-taking among certain employees. Staffing, reward and development practices to do this will differ from practices needed to support customer services or process improvement. (Dreher, 2003, p. 27)

How will the elements of HRM highlighted in this excerpt differ between a young, high-tech company and a bank, for example? Think of other contrasting organizations in which strategic HRM is adapted to organizational goals.

Changes in the nature of work have impacted dramatically on management practices. Personnel management is associated with the large, bureaucratic organizations which characterized industrial development in advanced Western economies. From the 1970s onwards, changes in technology led to changes in work and organizational structures. More flexible organizations called for more flexible employment patterns, often in networks, which in many cases crossed national borders. HRM reflected these changes, moving away from formal structures and processes to focus more on values, communication and broader corporate goals. At the same time, there emerged a growing awareness of the impact of sociocultural diversity on HRM in different locations.

Industrial development in Japan after World War II drew international attention to the ways in which Asian management differed from Western counterparts. In particular, differing perspectives on the role of the company in society and the place of individuals within the more group-oriented organizational settings typical in Japan offered alternative models built on notions of reward and commitment which stressed relational ties rather than individual achievement. But could innovations such teamworking and quality management systems, for which Japanese manufacturing companies have become famous, be transferred successfully to other cultural environments? The answer seems to be a partial yes, in that there are examples in Western environments where elements such as work teams have been successfully introduced (Bratton and Gold, 2003, p. 131). Generally, however, there is no one best HRM model, and managing people cannot be separated from the sociocultural environment of the organization. A trend seen in Japan's recent period of economic stagnation is the introduction of market-based incentives characteristic of more individualist cultural environments. (These are discussed more fully in Chapter 6.)

HRM in the international environment

- Impact of technology on work and communications.
- Flexible employment patterns.
- Networking and working in teams, including cross-border interaction.
- Impact of social and cultural diversity on HR practices.
- Changing legal environment, affecting, for example, labour relations, health and safety, employment protection and non-discrimination in the workplace.

Accounting and finance

The centrality of accounting as a function of business has been recognized for centuries, wherever economic activity has flourished. Accounting records were kept in the societies of the ancient world, Egypt and China, while modern book-keeping dates from the medieval period (Glynn et al., 1998, p. 1). In its long history and diverse environments, however, accounting has taken many different forms, in keeping with the needs of organizations in the societies in which they are located. Where state ownership predominates, for example, systems differ markedly from countries with predominantly market economies. Trends have been towards more market-oriented systems and the growing internationalization of business. Attention has focused on differing approaches among countries, raising issues of possible harmonization between systems. Accounting and finance cover three main functions which are related to each other. First, financial management concerns the processes by which the company raises funds to do what it wishes to do. Companies commonly raise capital by inviting investors to become shareholders in the company, as seen in Chapter 1 (equity financing), or by borrowing, often from banks (debt financing). Second, management accounting is the process by which the company decision-makers direct and control funds to achieve the goals of the enterprise, and third, financial reporting concerns the provision of financial information about the company to a range of interested parties, including shareholders, regulatory authorities and the investing public.

Elements of management accounting and financial reporting

Management accounting is closely linked with other functions of the business. It involves planning how funds will be used and controlling the process. **Management accounting** provides valuable information for decision-makers on the costs of labour, materials, energy and services that the firm requires. It links with operations and HRM. There are five key elements of management accounting:

- Budgeting – a budget quantitatively assesses how the allocation of resources will be linked to performance. Budgeting is a process which impacts on all aspects of an organization and can be a cause of friction, as views differ on spending priorities.

- Cost accounting – involves detailed analysis of all the firm's direct and indirect costs and is important in decisions on the pricing of the firm's products.
- Investment appraisal – an essential activity which can affect the long-term health of the company, as it looks at investment alternatives among which judgments must be made, such as acquiring another firm or entering a new market.
- Cash flow management – this is crucial, as the firm needs to balance outflows against money coming in, and have sufficient cash to meet any unforeseen expenditure. It must invest in the means to generate future profits, such as new plant and machinery, but risks having cash flow problems if revenues fall short of expectations.
- Strategy formation – decision-making relies heavily on the information provided on costs of possible investments (including, for example, expansion or acquisition) or proceeds of possible sales (including sale of a production unit or brand).

SUMMARY POINTS

Elements in management accounting

- **Budgeting** – allocation of resources.
- **Cost accounting** – analysis of firm's direct and indirect costs.
- **Investment appraisal** – assessment of investment alternatives.
- **Cash flow management** – balance of outflows and inflows.
- **Corporate strategy** – analysis of cost implications of proposed strategic changes.

Financial reporting requirements differ according to the regulatory framework in force in the particular country, which provides differing disclosure requirements depending on the status, size and complexity of the company. At a minimum, companies are generally required to produce a profit and loss account, a balance sheet, a directors' report and an auditor's report. The **profit and loss account** gives details of income and expenditure of the company for a set period, while the **balance sheet** gives a picture of the company's financial position in terms of its assets and liabilities. Financial information is a key indicator of the health of the company, and, in the case of public companies, is publicly available. The **auditor** is an independent professional appointed by the company to prepare the financial report. The auditor, usually a firm of accountants, owes a duty to the company to present an accurate picture, and should any misreporting or possible misuse of funds come to light, they are legally obliged to query it. Following corporate scandals, including Enron in the US and Parmalat in Europe, auditors have become more aware of their responsibilities to ensure objective and transparent financial reports. In the case of Enron, Arthur Andersen – until then one of the world's largest and most prestigious auditing firms – was so entangled in the fraud of the Enron directors, that it collapsed.

WEB ALERT!

An array of accounting resources may be found at
http://www.accountingweb.co.uk/expert_guides/standards

The UK Chartered Institute of Management Accountants (CIMA) is at
http://www.cimaglobal.com

The Financial Reporting Council is at http://www.asb.org.uk

The International Accounting Standards Board is found at http://www.iasb.org,
while its overview of international financial reporting standards is at
http://www.iasb.org/standards/index/asp

**Accounting
and finance
in the
international
environment**

The legal environment defines the standards and practices within which accounting activities take place. Accounting practices differ from country to country and financial reporting varies accordingly. The extent of disclosure required by law is high in some countries, whereas in others there is less transparency. Legal provisions and their enforcement are influenced by other dimensions of the business environment, including sociocultural values and political institutions. Generally, in open market economies where there is widespread share ownership, as in the US, there are pressures for stringent disclosure rules and transparency, while in countries where share ownership is more concentrated, and the market for ownership and control is weaker, the levels of transparency required by law are lower. Germany and Japan are examples of the latter, although recent trends in both are towards market reforms. Of the cases mentioned above, Enron was an American company with dispersed share ownership, while Parmalat was an Italian, family-dominated company. Yet both were found to have histories of corruption, extending to webs of subsidiaries and affiliates worldwide. The damage inflicted on investor confidence in the US was considerable and legislation (the Sarbanes-Oxley Act of 2002), which strengthened financial reporting regulation, was soon passed by the US Congress.

Harmonization of accounting standards within the EU is taking place, emphasizing the need for greater transparency and consistency across the many different systems which have developed in differing European countries. This task faced new challenges with the addition of ten new EU member states in 2004, most of which are relatively new market economies which emerged post-1990 from the break-up of the Soviet Union. More far reachingly, increasing economic integration in international business has led to moves towards internationally recognized accounting standards. One result was the setting up by the EU of the International Accounting Standards Committee (IASC) in 1973 to oversee moves towards standardization. International accounting standards issued by the IASC are gradually becoming more widely recognized and are also advocated by the European Commission. While both EU and IASC developments bring undoubted benefits for cross-border businesses and investors, at the informal level, norms of behaviour and individual ethical standards still play important roles and these evolve more slowly.

Innovation

Every business seeks to offer goods or services which better meet the needs of consumers than those of rival firms. Achieving this aim depends in large measure on its capacity to develop new products and improve existing ones. These activities fall under the broad function of innovation. Innovation as a business function may be concentrated in a new product development unit in the organization. However, innovation includes a wide range of other developments in addition to new products. These include:

● improvements in processes
● new methods in administration and control
● new approaches to marketing
● new developments in distribution and delivery of the product.

The success of iPod, discussed in Case study 2.3, is an example of technological innovation which focuses on the means by which customers buy music. Innovation brings together a number of the functions discussed so far in this chapter, providing a strategic focus. It is closely linked with marketing, as information on consumers and their needs is vital if new products are to be successful. It is also linked with operations, as new products may require new machinery and new processes. In turn, when changing work methods and new technology are envisaged, HRM implications must be considered. Kodak, the photographic company, had a 68 per cent share of the US conventional photographic market, but with the rise in digital technology, it had to cut 12,000–15,000 jobs worldwide, amounting to a fifth of its workforce, in order to adapt to the boom in digital photography, which has completely reshaped the photographic industry, as Figure 2.7 indicates. Finally, any innovation involves a commitment of financial resources and the firm relies on management accountants to provide the necessary information on costs and forecasts of returns.

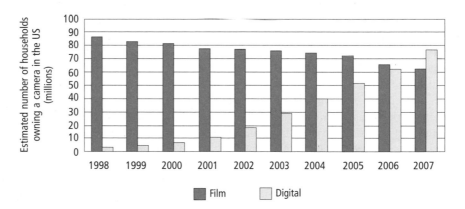

Figure 2.7 **The digital photography revolution**
Source: *Financial Times*, 23 January 2004.

New product development

Innovation relies on bringing together different types of research and utilizing this knowledge to design new products. In some industries, research has a scientific focus, and this is often what is envisaged as research and development (R&D). (Key concepts and processes in technological innovation are discussed in greater detail in Chapter 11.) In some industries, such as the pharmaceutical industry, scientific research is the key to new products, whereas in other industries, such as the automotive industry, R&D is likely to be more focused on technology and engineering. In all these industries, leading companies invest large sums in R&D, often relying on specialist R&D carried out by affiliated companies. To be commercially viable, the 'development' dimension of R&D is crucial. The new product must be tested, usually through a prototype, to determine whether it can be industrially produced, while incorporating necessary quality and safety standards. At the same time, design from an aesthetic perspective must be considered. Design may be an important factor in the consumer's decision to purchase, and design-conscious consumers may well have different preferences in different markets.

Innovation in non-manufacturing industries relies on technological developments and creativity. In media and creative industries, innovation is equally vital, but relies less on structured departments than on individuals and teams dedicated to new product development. The array of new formats, offering many new ways of delivering content to the consumer, has revolutionized these businesses. For example, downloading music from the internet was an innovation which has had widespread implications across the music industry, as Case study 2.3 shows.

Case study 2.3 The Apple iPod sets the standard

Apple Computers modestly informs visitors to its website: 'Apple ignited the personal computer revolution in the 1970s with the Apple II and reinvented the personal computer in the 1980s with the Macintosh' (London, 2004). Yet its share of the PC market has dwindled to a meagre 3.5 per cent. Even loyal fans of Apple question whether the company can escape its apparent destiny of forever being a niche player. The company has a history of creating, in the words of Steve Jobs, its founder and CEO, 'insanely great' products, but it has struggled to hold its market against rival products based on Intel chips and Microsoft software (London, 2004). Its latest creation is the iPod miniature music player. The consumer downloads music tracks from Apple's online iTunes Music Service for 99 cents each. This arrangement is the result of Jobs having concluded deals with the major music companies which own the copyrights for about 70 per cent of all legal online music.

The iPod has taken the world by storm. Launched in 2002, two million iPods were sold in its first two years. Moreover, the cheap legal downloading has been a boost to the music industry, which has been concerned about how to combat the rise of online music piracy. A year after the launch, market research showed that customers were buying a broader range of music, much of it they would not otherwise have bought. The music industry has rested on the sale of albums, typically containing 16 or more tracks, but CD sales have been slumping, largely because of piracy. The new legal online music, including iTunes and subscription services, is singles-driven, but seems not to have damaged CD sales, which saw healthy rises in sales between 2003 and 2004. As the figure shows, global music sales grew in this period, a rise which has been attributed largely to the popularity of legitimate online music.

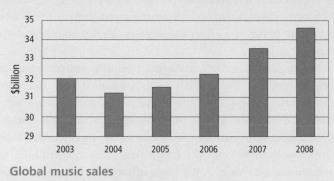

Global music sales
Source: *Financial Times*, 30 July 2004.

In 2004, Apple did a deal to allow Hewlett-Packard to resell the iPod music player under the HP label, and HP would install the iTunes software on its PCs. This deal marks a major departure for Apple, which has traditionally avoided cooperative agreement with rivals. Is iPod becoming the industry standard? The opportunity exists for iPod to become the leading platform in digital music, but the company would have to break with tradition, licensing its technology to rivals, to allow development of new products which use the new platform. Industry strategists question whether Apple's strong corporate culture would allow it to take such a step. Meanwhile, it has accused RealNetworks of 'hacking' into iPod's technology, to allow downloads from RealNetworks' music store to play on an iPod. Apple's old foe Microsoft has also introduced an online music store. With the online music business still in its infancy, Apple's 70 per cent of online music sales and 25–30 per cent share of the global digital music player market will be under pressure.

Sources: Healey, J., and Leeds, J., 'Music labels jumping to a brand new beat', *Financial Times*, 4 May 2004; London, S., 'Product to platform: the iPod's big play', *Financial Times*, 19 January 2004; Morrison, S., 'Apple's iPod agreement is showstopper', *Financial Times*, 11 January 2004; Taylor, P., 'Apple "stunned" by rival's software "hack"', *Financial Times*, 30 July 2004; Burt, T., 'Music industry loses the blues', *Financial Times*, 30 July 2004; Morrison, S., 'Microsoft to enter online music battle', *Financial Times*, 30 July 2004.

Case questions

How is the miniature music player, in combination with online music, transforming the way people listen to music?

What are the probabilities of Apple's iPod and iTunes staying ahead of their rivals?

Innovation strategy

The role of innovation has been highlighted as a driver of strategy. Successful individual entrepreneurs combine creative thinking and commitment with a willingness to take risks in turning their ideas into tangible, commercial successes. While entrepreneurship is associated with successful individual entrepreneurs, the vision and determination of the entrepreneur are qualities which all businesses value. Translating this determination and vision, in the context of a larger company with an established organizational culture, is one of the major challenges faced by firms as they mature. Large companies, concerned that innovation may be stifled by bureaucracy, may benefit from the adaptation of entrepreneurial qualities in the organization, known as 'corporate entrepreneurship'. Corporate entrepreneurship aims to create and build a corporate culture and learning environment more akin to the start-up company, while benefiting from the organizational stability of the large established company.

For a firm to sustain strategic innovation, its organizational culture must be attuned to changing consumer needs and it must have the skilled staff to exploit new opportunities. Hamel and Prahalad (1994) stress the importance of a company's core *competences* to capture future opportunities. The firm's competences represent a broader notion than just the skills of its staff or the expertise of its R&D researchers: competences involve all the firm's resources and are built up over time through organizational learning. For a large organization, these competences cross the boundaries between different business units and may bring in different functional areas. Hamel and Prahalad see core competences as the gateways to future markets, fostering, for example, families of new products. They distinguish between the firm's competences and its 'endowments', such as its brands, assets and patents. Endowments inherited from the past will not sustain profitability in the future. Patents may be superseded by a rival's newer technology and brands may lose their sparkle with consumers. They cite the example of Intel, which relies on intellectual property (IP) and semiconductor design, two key endowments. As new innovations reshape microprocessor technology, it must meet the challenges through its design, manufacturing and distribution competences (Hamel and Prahalad, 1994, p. 231). The case study on Nike illustrated how its strategic refocusing has built on its core competences, which are design, innovative products, sports star endorsement and merchandising.

CRITICAL PERSPECTIVES

Where does innovation come from?

If companies can't depend on the lightning bolt of sudden inspiration or serendipitous discovery, then what? An innovative environment can be consciously created – if a company is willing to abandon old rules, shed old habits, and upend cherished conventions … In any company, a hierarchy of organization dominates a hierarchy of ideas. The antidote: To encourage innovation, unlock ideas from across the company. Bring together a cross-section of employees at all levels to share the new perspectives that may just contain the kernel of a bold new idea. Realize that every company promotes success as defined by today's reigning strategy; the question is how to promote new ideas that may have nothing to do with that strategy – or may even cut against it. (Hamel and Skarzynski, 2001)

In this excerpt, the authors are suggesting how an innovative environment involving all the staff can be created in an existing company. What are the implications of their recommendations for the specialist functional areas discussed in this chapter?

Conclusions

1 Business functions perform specialist activities necessary in order for the organization to achieve its overall goals.

2 Operations concerns the way the organization produces and delivers products – goods or services – which serve consumers' needs. Operations may be depicted as a transformation system, by which inputs or resources are processed to produce outputs which are delivered to customers.

3 The marketing concept rests on the belief that meeting the needs and wants of the consumer is central to the goals of the organization. Through segmentation, consumers may be divided into different groups with distinctive needs. Satisfying each group depends on elements of the marketing mix. Marketing in the international arena must take account of differing social and cultural environments.

4 HRM concerns the relations between the organization and the people who work for it. While in the past the focus was on formal aspects of these relations, the more recent approach sees them in the context of overall organizational goals and culture.

5 Accounting and finance, central to the organization's success, are linked with other functions of the organization. Management accounting provides valuable information for decision-makers on the costs of resources. Financial reporting presents a profile of the organization's financial position, essential for those within the company, and, in the case of public companies, the investing public.

6 The capacity to innovate, creating new products and services, as well as new ways of providing existing products, is crucial for competitive success and therefore central to strategy. All the functional areas contribute to innovative capabilities.

Review questions

1 What specific activities fall within operations management? How do they differ between manufacturing and services sectors?

2 What are the five performance objectives in operations strategy, and how are they interrelated?

3 What is the marketing concept and how does a marketing orientation differ from a product-driven approach?

4 What is segmentation in marketing and why is it taking on greater significance in international markets?

5 Assess the changes in approach of strategic HRM in contrast to traditional personnel management.

6   Which dimensions of the external environment impact directly on HRM in practice?

7   What is the role of management accounting in the organization? Assess its importance in strategy formation.

8   What are the aims of financial reporting? To what extent are the reforms and harmonization of standards restoring confidence following high-profile corporate scandals?

9   Start-up businesses are closely associated with innovation, but for large, established businesses, maintaining innovative initiatives can be elusive. What can these larger organizations do to remain innovative?

Assignments

1   Assume you have just taken over as the CEO of a company which sells general merchandise, mainly clothes and household furnishings, through retail outlets in out-of-town locations. In this highly competitive sector, your company has been losing market share to rivals, and the expectation is that you will turn round its performance. Explain what operations management issues you will address urgently and why they are critical in achieving your objectives. Remember that the investors are looking for a quick upturn in the business.

2   Applying the four Ps of the marketing mix, design a marketing strategy for a new brand of juice-based drink to be targeted at health-conscious consumers in the 20–35-year-old age group.

Further reading

Aaker, D. (2004) *Strategic Market Management*, 7th edn (London: John Wiley).

Brassington, F. and Pettitt, S. (2003) *Principles of Marketing*, 3rd edn (Harlow: Pearson Education).

Bratton, J. and Gold, J. (2003) *Human Resource Management*, 3rd edn (Basingstoke: Palgrave Macmillan).

Christensen, C. and Overdorf, M. (2001) *Innovation* (Boston, MA: Harvard Business School Press).

Elliott, B. and Elliott, J. (2003) *Financial Accounting and Reporting*, 8th edn (Harlow: Financial Times/Prentice Hall).

Glynn, J., Perrin, J. and Murphy, M. (1998) *Accounting for Managers*, 2nd edn (London: International Thomson Press).

Kotler, P., Armstrong, G., Saunders, J. and Wong, V. (2002) *Principles of Marketing*, 3rd European edn (Harlow: Pearson Education).

Slack, N., Chambers, S. and Johnson, R. (2004) *Operations Management*, 4th edn (Harlow: Financial Times/Prentice Hall).

3 The national economic environment

Outline of chapter

- ■ Introduction
- ■ The macroeconomic environment: flows of economic resources
- ■ Gross national income and gross domestic product
- ■ Industrial structure
- ■ Inflation and unemployment
  - • Inflation
  - • Unemployment
- ■ Balance of payments
- ■ Economic growth
- ■ The business cycle
- ■ The role of government in the economy
  - • Institutional framework of economic policy
  - • Fiscal policy
  - • Monetary policy
- ■ European Monetary Union (EMU)
- ■ Conclusions

Learning objectives

1 To define and apply the major concepts used to analyse the macroeconomic environment

2 To appreciate the aims and role of national economic policies

3 To understand the ways in which changes in national economies affect business planning and operations

Introduction

The economic activity of every nation-state makes up its national economy. There is considerable diversity among national economies, mainly because the world's nearly 200 nation-states differ widely in their size, geography, population, climate and natural resources. These differences have direct effects on the types and intensity of economic activity that are viable. For example, trade is traditionally more likely to prosper in a coastal state than in a landlocked one. States rich in natural resources, such as minerals and oil, have developed national economies built round these natural endowments, whereas labour-intensive manufacturing industries have gravitated to states with large populations offering abundant labour (a point which will be developed in Chapter 5). No country has unlimited resources. In each, the national economy represents the processes which determine how to allocate scarce resources so as to satisfy the needs and wants of those within its territory. The ways in which national economies exploit their differing natural endowments are influenced by a host of factors, including historical forces and the social and cultural norms of their peoples. This diversity will be explored in the next chapter, while this chapter will introduce the concepts by which all national economies may be analysed and compared with each other.

There are numerous economic 'players' in every society, including businesses, consumers and governments. Each has particular interests, often conflicting with those of other groups. Consumers would like lower prices, but, as employees, they also desire higher wages. Balancing the interests between groups in the economy is a complex process, in which government plays a key role, both directly and indirectly. Governments both take in and spend large sums of money, and they also act indirectly through policy formation, which is an important element in the nation's economic environment. National economic forces and government responses affect businesses in their planning in both the short and long term. Moreover, businesses are themselves major players in shaping the economic environment. This chapter will therefore explore the dynamic interactions which take place within the economy, highlighting the interests of groups in society and the importance of government policies and activities for business.

The macroeconomic environment: flows of economic resources

Economists study both the overall activity in the national economy and the economic activity which takes place between businesses and consumers. Macroeconomics is the study of national economies, while microeconomics refers to the study of economic activity at the level of individuals and firms. The two areas of economic study are related. A country's macroeconomic environment consists of its national output, employment levels and consumer prices generally. However, these data are compiled by aggregating data from individuals and firms, so that microeconomic analysis feeds into macroeconomic analysis and policy-making. As an example, microeconomic analysis may focus on motor vehicles in particular, including the market and prices, and this information forms part of the macroeconomic picture of total employment and prices in the economy as a whole.

Flows of economic resources in the economy can be depicted as a model based on circular flows. While this type of model is greatly oversimplified, it does serve to show the interaction between the main groups, businesses and consumers, as can be seen in Figure 3.1. Businesses provide employment and wages to households, while consumers spend earned income on goods and services. At the same time, both businesses and individuals pay taxes to government, which are used to fund public spending and social security. By increasing or decreasing public spending or altering the tax regime, it is therefore possible for government to influence spending by firms and consumers. For example, public spending on government projects will provide firms with more orders and greater need for workers. These workers will, in turn, purchase consumer goods. Therefore, the 'injection' of government funds will have had a general effect on the economy, referred to by economists as a 'multiplier' effect, because of its ripple effects across the economy. It should also be noticed that effects of international flows are taken into account in Figure 3.1. Consumers buy imported products, which is depicted as a 'leakage' from the circular flow. Similarly, when firms export products, the income that arises is an injection, as is overseas investment.

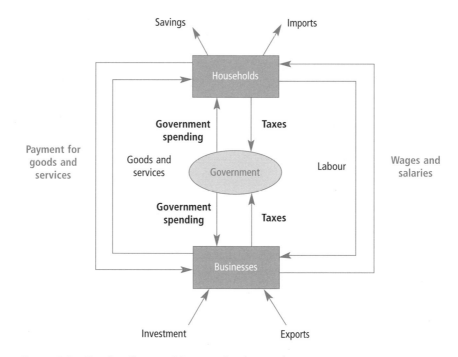

Figure 3.1 **Circular flows of income in the economy**

Gross national income and gross domestic product

The economy of a nation-state is capable of being measured in a number of ways. One of these is **gross national income (GNI)**, formerly called gross national product.

GNI represents the total income from all the final products and services produced by a national economy, including income that national residents earn from overseas investments, in a given year. It is the broadest measure of a nation's economic activity. It includes **gross domestic product (GDP)**, which represents the value of the total economic activity produced within a country in a single year, including both domestic and foreign producers. GDP and GNI vary enormously from one country to another. As can be seen in Figure 3.2, the US is by far the world's largest economy, with a GNI of over $10,000bn. in 2002, representing growth of 27.6 per cent between 1998 and 2002. The Chinese economy, however, grew by 30 per cent in the same period, while the German economy lost ground, contracting by nearly 12 per cent.

GDP or GNI per head (per capita) is calculated in order to facilitate comparisons between countries. The US, with a population of 288 million, has a GNI per head of $35,060 (see Table 3.1). By contrast, India, with a population of just over one billion, has a GNI of $501.5bn., about one-tenth that of the US, but its GNI per capita is only $480, about one-seventieth of the US. GNI per head represents an average figure. It does not take account of the distribution of wealth within the country. Some countries may have extremes of wealth between the rich and poor, while others with roughly the same GNI per head may be more egalitarian. India has a low GNI per head, but is nonetheless seen as a huge potential market because of its large middle class, an estimated 150 million consumers, wanting to buy products such as televisions and mobile phones that middle-class consumers all over the world desire. This information is valuable for companies whose marketing strategy is targeted at emerging markets.

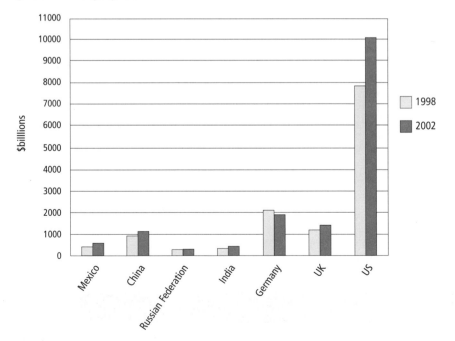

Figure 3.2 **Changes in GNI in selected economies 1998–2002**
Sources: World Bank, *World Development Reports* 1999–2000 and 2004 (Washington, DC: The World Bank).

GDP and GNI must be expressed in terms of a common currency, normally the US dollar. However, exchange rates vary: the dollar may be strong or weak against a particular national currency and this needs to be taken into account. Moreover, the cost of living varies from one country to another. The Indian equivalent of $480 will buy more of life's necessities in India than $480 would buy in the US. Hence, economists use the measure of **purchasing power parity (PPP)**. PPP estimates the number of units of the foreign currency which would be needed to buy goods or services equivalent to those which the US dollar would buy in the US. The advantage of using PPP estimates to measure GNI per capita is that they more accurately reflect relative living standards in different countries. In the list of selected countries in Table 3.1, note that in all but one, the cost of living is estimated to be lower than it is in the US, and therefore the GNI per capita, measured at PPP (the last column), is *higher* than the figure in the previous column. Measured at PPP, India's GNI per capita rises to $2,570, still only about one-fourteenth that of the US. In Japan, the cost of living is higher than in the US, and the figure in the last column is therefore *lower* than in the previous column.

Table 3.1 Size of the economy in selected countries

Economy		GNI, 2002 ($billions)	GNI per capita (dollars)	GNI per capita, measured at PPP (dollars)
The Americas	Argentina	154.1	4,060	9,930
	Brazil	497.4	2,850	7,250
	Chile	66.3	4,260	9,180
	Mexico	596.7	5,910	8,540
	United States	10,110.1	35,060	35,060
Europe	France	1,342.7	22,010	26,180
	Germany	1,870.4	22,670	26,220
	Greece	123.9	11,660	18,240
	Netherlands	386.8	23,960	27,470
	Poland	176.6	4,570	10,130
	Spain	594.1	14,430	20,460
	United Kingdom	1,486.2	25,250	25,870
Asia Pacific	Australia	386.6	19,740	26,960
	China	1,209.5	940	4,390
	India	501.5	480	2,570
	Indonesia	149.9	710	2,990
	Japan	4,265.6	35,550	26,070
Africa	Sierra Leone	0.7	140	490
	South Africa	113.5	2,600	9,870

Source: World Bank (2003) *World Development Report 2004* (Washington, DC: The World Bank), Table 1, p. 252.

WEB ALERT!

Up-to-date economic development indicators are published by the World Bank at http://www.worldbank.org/data/wdi2004/worldview.htm

Industrial structure

Economic activity may be divided into sectors. All economies change over time and looking at trends in the performance in different sectors provides useful indicators, especially relevant to the economy's need for specific types of employment. The sectors of the national economy are:

- *Primary sector* – refers to agriculture, fishing and the extraction of natural resources, such as oil and minerals.
- *Secondary sector* – refers to manufacturing industry, producing industrial products, and also processing primary commodities, such as food. Much of the food we eat is, in effect, industrially produced.
- *Tertiary sector* – refers to the service industries, including distribution, hotels and restaurants; transport and communications; finance and business services; public administration, education and health.

Historically, the major change that has taken place in terms of economic development has been industrialization, marking the transition from a mainly agricultural economy to an industrial one. This pattern of structural change can be shown by looking at the industrialized nations of Western Europe and the US. As industrialization progressed, the numbers employed in agriculture dwindled. These countries now have small percentages of their populations engaged in agriculture – under 5 per cent. Similarly, extractive industries, such as mining, have also declined. Coal mining, once the dominant industry in areas of England and Wales, has now all but disappeared. Manufacturing, usually looked on as the backbone of an industrial economy, has declined in importance, while there has been a surge in the service industries. As Figure 3.3 shows, 79 per cent of UK jobs are in services, while only 12 per cent are in manufacturing. Much manufacturing has been transformed by high-tech operations, which require fewer workers, while low-tech, labour-intensive industries have often relocated in developing countries, lured particularly by cheaper labour costs, as will be explored in Chapter 5. Case study 3.1 illustrates the problems and the opportunities facing manufacturing in Wales.

Looking at recent trends, computing and IT have transformed jobs in both services and manufacturing. In these high-tech areas, the US has played a dominant role, which enabled it to achieve sustained economic growth and low unemployment, as well as low inflation throughout the 1990s. However, economic conditions and competitive forces, both domestic and international, present a dynamic, changing scene, in which there can be no guarantees of indefinite prosperity. The signs of a slowdown in the US economy were apparent by the end of 2000, prompted, it was generally felt, by overinvestment in new technology industries. At the same time, growth in service sector jobs has been driven in large measure by greater demand for data-processing and telecommunications services, such as call centres. Many of these jobs are now being shifted to developing countries in a process known as 'outsourcing'. It is estimated that up to 5 per cent of all service sector jobs in industrialized countries could potentially relocate in developing countries (ILO, 2001a).

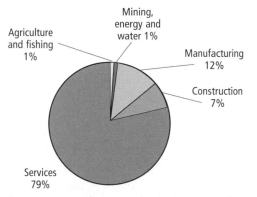

Figure 3.3 **Employment by industry in the UK, 2004**
Source: Office for National Statistics, *Labour Market Statistics*, May 2004 (London: ONS).

Inflation and unemployment

Inflation and unemployment are linked phenomena which affect all economies, varying in their severity and persistence between countries and regions. They directly affect businesses in terms of costs of raw materials, wages, prices of finished products and availability of labour. National policy-makers naturally seek to maintain price stability and low levels of unemployment. However, growing interdependence among economies limits their room for manoeuvre, while making national economies vulnerable to external forces.

Inflation

Inflation can be defined as the continuing general rise in prices in the economy. Its effect is to make the country's currency worth less. The opposite phenomenon is 'deflation', or a general fall in prices. Deflation is usually considered damaging, reflecting falling demand. Japan is the most notable example in the 1990s, where deflation accompanied economic recession. However, prices may fall due to improvements in productivity, as has been the case in China, where booming manufacturing has led export growth, as will be seen in Case study 5.1. The rate of inflation is expressed as a percentage rise or fall in prices with reference to a specific starting point in time. These rises and falls are tracked in the consumer price index for every country, usually making allowances for seasonal adjustments, such as seasonal variations in food prices. In the UK, the retail price index (RPI), representing a 'basket' of products and services purchased by the average consumer, has been the official measure since 1914, and, although this measure is being superseded by the newer European measure, it is useful to look at the background.

The RPI is calculated on a monthly basis, the composition of the basket having changed with changing lifestyles, for example foreign holidays were a later addition. Importantly, the RPI includes housing costs for owner-occupiers, and an alternative measure, the RPIX, was devised, which excluded mortgage payments and tended to show a lower rate of inflation. These measures have been officially superseded by a measure devised by the European Central Bank, the consumer price index (CPI), which was adopted by the Bank of England in December, 2003. The CPI, formerly called the harmonized index of consumer prices, enables comparisons between states in the eurozone. It is similar to the old RPIX, in that it excludes owner-occupier housing costs. As a result of the changeover to the CPI, the Bank of England's target inflation rate became 2 per cent, replacing the 2.5 per cent target under the RPI measure. The RPI, however, remains a highly respected measure and the UK Chancellor of the Exchequer has continued to use it for calculating index-linked benefits such as pensions.

Economists point to a number of causes of inflation. 'Demand-pull' and 'cost-push' arguments are two of the most commonly advanced causes. The demand-pull explanation holds that excess demand in the economy, which may be the result of cheap borrowing or tax cuts, encourages producers to raise prices, which lead to rises in wage demands as workers strive to maintain their standard of living. The cost-push argument holds that excessive costs drive up prices. As a significant element of costs is accounted for by wages, this theory becomes linked with the demand-pull argument. Rising wage costs tend to be passed on to consumers in the form of higher prices, thus creating what is known as the 'wage-price inflationary spiral'.

The damaging effects of high inflation can be far-reaching. A country's domestic producers will find their goods less competitive in global markets, and foreign investors may turn to countries where inflation is lower. High inflation tends to force up interest rates, to enable investors to achieve a real return on their investments. However, high interest rates may adversely affect growth rates, by reducing domestic demand. The importance of energy costs as a driver of inflation was highlighted in the oil price shocks of the 1970s, which quadrupled the price of oil. Resultant increases in energy and transport costs affected all industrial sectors and sent inflation soaring in developed economies. To bring down inflation, governments can resort to imposing controls on prices or wages, but these measures can be damaging. In particular, they can lead to rising unemployment, as employers cut back on costs. In an environment of relatively low inflation, monetary policy is therefore designed to prevent inflationary pressures arising.

SUMMARY POINTS

Inflation

- A continuing rise in prices, which in turn is likely to cause wage inflation, as workers strive to maintain their standard of living.
- It is expressed as an annual percentage rise in prices.
- Increasing costs (such as the price of energy) and increasing demand in the economy are two related causes.

Case study 3.1 The ups and downs of manufacturing in Wales

Just under 20 per cent of employee jobs in Wales are in manufacturing. This percentage is higher than that of the UK generally. However, manufacturing employment in Wales has diminished, along with manufacturing jobs generally in the UK. Wales has seen plants close and existing plants have contracted their workforce. At 7 per cent, Wales has a higher rate of unemployment than other parts of the UK except the northeast, and its GDP per head is about 80 per cent of the national average. Wales qualifies for economic support from the European Commission, to bring greater prosperity to the region.

Some manufacturing firms have managed to succeed, and even grow, in this difficult competitive environment. DBK Technitherm Ltd of Wales manufactures advanced technology heating systems used in a range of applications, including white goods such as tumble dryers and hot plates used in coffee machines. In 2004, it received two large contracts, leading the management to increase the workforce by a fifth, to 120 workers. But rising oil and steel prices and rising interest rates adding a 20 per cent rise in costs in one year, began to worry the managing director. The company has been warned by its major steel supplier, the Anglo-Dutch group Corus, that further rises are in the pipeline. Steel is a key material in much manufacturing and economic growth would be inconceivable without it. Surging demand for steel by the Chinese economy has led to rising global prices (see figure). For manufacturing businesses such as DBK, rising costs are eroding margins. The company could even be making a loss on some of its products. The managing director says: 'We are being squeezed from the top end by our customers in the white goods markets, who are seeing falling retail prices, and by the costs of components from our suppliers.' With retail prices low in white goods markets, 'it is difficult to get that price

increase on to the customer ... We are stuck in the middle' (Moules, 2004). Of course, rising steel and oil prices are affecting all businesses, wherever they are. Although the price of steel has doubled in three years, this level may fall as demand in China slows and its steel corporations, having grown rapidly in response to home demand, are now rethinking further expansion plans. However, apart from these cyclical factors, businesses in the EU are affected by employment protection legislation and high levels of taxation. In particular, the EU's Working Time Directive limits working hours that employees may work in a week to 40 hours. The effect may be to raise the wage bill considerably, adding to costs.

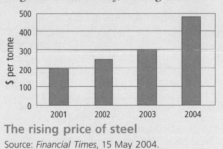

The rising price of steel
Source: *Financial Times*, 15 May 2004.

Of concern to the company, and other similar manufacturing businesses, is the fact that its products may become uncompetitive in international markets. Welsh governmental authorities are committed to keeping manufacturing as a significant share of employment in Wales. The success of technologically advanced manufacturers such as DBK Technitherm is indicative of levels of innovation and skills in component manufacturing, which will contribute to economic development.

Sources: Moules, J., 'Dearer oil, steel and money turn the screw on UK businesses', *Financial Times*, 15 May 2004; DBK Technitherm's website at http://www.dbktechnitherm.ltd.uk; Welsh European Funding Office website at http://wefo.wales.gov.uk

Case questions

What are the causes of DBK's financial strain, and to what extent are all manufacturing businesses affected by the same forces? What would be your advice to DBK management?

'Full employment', contrary to what it implies, is used by economists to refer to a country's natural rate of unemployment which exists in all societies. What we commonly refer to as **unemployment** reflects the percentage of people in the workforce who are willing to work but are without jobs. The internationally agreed definition is 'ILO unemployment', which consists of people who are:

● without a job, want a job, have actively sought work in the last four weeks and are available to start work in the next two weeks
● out of work, have found a job and are waiting to start it in the next two weeks.

During the years following the Great Depression of 1929, unemployment was very high, as was inflation. Along with inflation, unemployment again rose in the period following the oil shocks of the 1970s. While levels of unemployment have come down in most industrialized countries, they have been high in the countries of Central and Eastern Europe which are making the transition to market economies (see Chapter 4). Rates of unemployment in a range of countries appear in Table 3.2.

Table 3.2 International comparisons of unemployment, 2004

	ILO unemployment rate (%)
Czech Republic	8.4
France	9.4
Germany	9.3
Italy	8.5
Poland	19.0
Spain	11.1
UK	4.7
EU 25	9.0
EU 15	8.0
Japan	4.7
US	5.7

Note: EU 15 comprises member states before the 2004 enlargement (Germany, France, Ireland, Finland, Italy, Spain, Netherlands, Belgium, UK, Denmark, Sweden, Greece, Portugal, Austria, Luxembourg).
EU 25 comprises the EU 15 plus the 10 new members admitted in 2004 (Cyprus, Estonia, Poland, Czech Republic, Slovenia, Hungary, Slovakia, Latvia, Lithuania, Malta).
Source: Office for National Statistics, *Labour Market Statistics*, May 2004 (London: ONS)

Unemployment may be 'structural', meaning that jobs have been lost due to changing technology or industries relocating in other regions or other countries. Or it may be 'frictional', which refers to the usual turnover in the labour force, for example when people are out of work looking for new jobs. Long-term unemployment is a cause of concern to governments: social security payments will rise or, in countries which lack extensive state benefit schemes, the burden of individual hardship may fall on families. Moreover, social and political unrest can be triggered by problems associated with high unemployment. It should be borne in mind that overall rates of unemployment tell only part of the story. Almost all countries experience regional disparities in unemployment, differing rates between age groups and between men and women. The higher rate of unemployment in Wales was highlighted in Case study 3.1, for example. Governments therefore target policies to attract businesses to particular geographical areas and raise the skill levels of the workforce. In Britain, the more prosperous region of London and the southeast contrasts with the northern regions, where levels of unemployment are higher, creating the phenomenon known as the 'north-south divide'. Italy is another example of the north-south divide, between the prosperous north and poor south, although inflows of foreign investment into the south have helped to balance this picture.

Economic growth, inflation and unemployment are related, although among economists there are differing interpretations of the relationship. All countries wish to see sustained growth and a low level of unemployment. The risk is that when there is full employment, this will exert inflationary pressure. On the other hand, if there is high unemployment, growth may slow, as illustrated in Case study 3.2 on Germany.

WEB ALERT!

The homepage of the International Labour Organization (ILO) is http://www.ilo.org

SUMMARY POINTS

Unemployment

- The measure of the section of the population willing to work, but unable to find employment.
- It is expressed as a percentage of the total available labour force.
- Unemployment may rise if shifts in the industrial structure leave some workers without the skills needed for the jobs available.
- Other factors affecting unemployment are high wages and weak demand in the economy.

Balance of payments

The balance of payments refers to credit and debit transactions between a country's residents (including companies) and those of other countries. Transactions are divided into the current account and capital account. The current account is made up of trade in goods (the merchandise trade account), services (the services account), and profits and interest earned from overseas assets. The capital account includes transactions involving the sale and purchase of assets, such as investment in shares. If a country has a current account deficit, it imports more goods and services than it exports. If it has a current account surplus, it exports more than it imports. Governments grow concerned if there is a current account deficit and, in particular, a trade deficit, as it suggests that the country's companies are uncompetitive. As Figure 3.4 shows, the UK runs a continuing deficit on trade in goods and a surplus on trade in services, indicating relative success in exports of services, but weakness in manufacturing exports. Overall, the current account for 2003 was in deficit by £18.8bn. These figures, however, are dwarfed by the US current account deficit, which stood at $550bn. (£290bn., €440bn.) in 2003, the largest imbalance ever recorded. This represents 5 per cent of GDP, in contrast to the UK's current account deficit of 1.7 per cent of GDP. Between 1990 and 2003, US exports of goods and services grew at 5.7 per cent a year, whereas imports grew at nearly 9 per cent (*Financial Times*, 1 March 2004). By comparison, Asian economies generally run current account surpluses, reflecting their attractiveness to foreign investors.

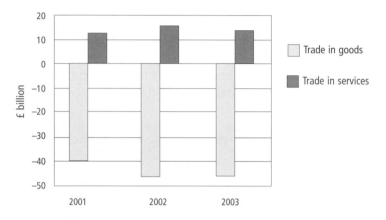

Figure 3.4 **UK current account 2001–3**
Source: Office for National Statistics, *Balance of Payments 2003* (London: ONS).

The balance of payments reflects demand both at home and abroad. It also reflects exchange rates (which will be discussed in Chapter 12) and the relative costs of domestic production. Governments can exert influence by varying the exchange rate, raising interests rates (to slow down growth) or imposing tariff barriers such as import duties and quotas. A number of Asian countries do not allow their currency to float freely. In particular, China, whose currency is pegged to the US dollar, has come under pressure to allow its currency to appreciate. Raising interest rates is a means of decreasing demand, but possibly deterring future investment. The world's main trading countries are now linked in regional and multilateral trade groupings which, as will be discussed later, have brought down trade barriers, so that governments are no longer able simply to restrict imports. Nor would they be advised to do so, because of the risk of retaliation by trading partners. In globally integrated production networks and markets, government objectives and the means of achieving them have therefore become complex calculations, involving a number of internal and external considerations.

Economic growth

Each country wishes to keep production up to its capacity, to achieve full employment and price stability. **Economic growth** refers to a country's increase in national income, reflecting expansion in the production of goods and services. Capital investment and technological innovation are important factors in theories of economic growth (Coates, 1999). A high growth rate in GDP is taken to indicate rising living standards, healthy capital investment and rising welfare provisions. However, the benefits of growth in the economy are often unevenly distributed. While growth provides the basis for national prosperity, it does not in itself guarantee improvements in well-being for the whole of society, especially in countries where there is rapid population growth, weak institutions or wide inequalities of income and opportunities between groups.

Growth is highest in periods of industrialization and investment, as experienced by European economies in the 1950s and 60s, and Japan in the 1970s and 80s. As Figure 3.5 shows, growth is very modest in the EU, well behind the growth rate of the US, while Japan appears to be recovering from its long recession. Germany's economy has been in the doldrums for three years, as discussed in Case study 3.2. As the largest economy in the EU, its faltering growth has been a cause for concern both at home and within the EU generally, as economic integration has grown among EU economies. The industrializing Southeast Asian countries experienced high rates of growth in the 1980s and 90s, but were struck by financial crisis in 1997, from which their economies have only slowly recovered. China enjoyed strong growth in the 1990s, but the rate of growth has steadied at around 8 per cent. Some economists fear that China, like other economies which have experienced rapid growth, may be heading for a reversal. Factors which might affect China's economic future are the rising costs of energy and raw materials and a weakening of demand for Chinese exports. China's leaders have set an official target growth rate of 7 per cent, which represents a cooling down, aiming especially to reduce capacity in the many remaining state-owned industries which are pollutant or unprofitable.

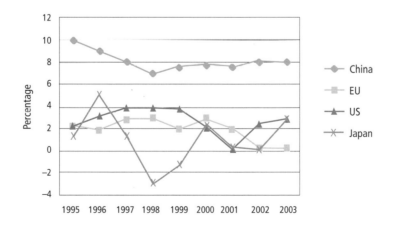

Figure 3.5 **Trends in world GDP growth**
Sources: *Financial Times*, 24 March 2004; The Economist (2003) *The World in 2004* (London: The Economist Group).

CRITICAL PERSPECTIVES

The rate of economic growth

For most of the past year, investors have based their trades on a belief in a 'Goldilocks' economy, in which growth was 'just right' – neither too fast, so as to cause inflation or higher interest rates, nor too slow, so as to prevent corporate profits from rising. Now investors seem to have switched fairy tales and are worrying about Cinderella's ugly sisters, in the form of higher inflation and slower growth. (Coggan, 2004)

These words were written of the US in 2004. Why would fast growth lead to inflation and why would investors be worried?

Case study 3.2 Is Germany back on track for economic growth?

While it was hoped that an upturn in the German economy would take place in the new millennium, optimism has been in short supply. The German economy has stagnated for three years. Its economic woes are highlighted by comparison with the UK growth rate, shown in the figure below. It was hoped that Germany, the EU's largest economy, would grow again in 2004, achieving a growth rate of 1.2 per cent, but growth prospects were slim.

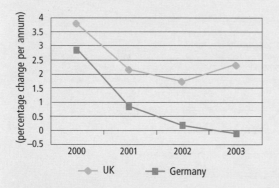

GDP growth per annum: comparison between Germany and the UK

Source: The Economist Intelligence Unit (2004) Economic data, at http://www.economist.co.uk

The unification of Germany in 1990, uniting the former Communist East Germany with the more economically advanced West Germany, provided a new sense of optimism among Germany's 82 million inhabitants, despite the huge amount of economic catching up that was entailed in rebuilding the economy of the former East Germany. Despite huge injections of resources, unemployment has remained high in the East, at around 15–20 per cent, contributing to an overall unemployment figure of 9 per cent in 2004. The German government has been committed to social welfare spending, which accounts for 50 per cent of government expenditure. It has incurred the wrath of the EU for its budget deficit, which, hovering around 4 per cent of GDP, risks breaching the eurozone's budgetary rules (see figure below). The bill for social benefits in Germany is higher than in France, Italy, the UK, Spain, the US or Japan. These costs, including social security, healthcare and pensions, contribute to Germany's position as having the highest labour costs in the world, second only to the Norwegians. Clearly, Germany is in need of more job creation; one economist has said: 'you are seven times more likely to lose your job in the US as in Germany but 10 times more likely to get a new one' (Benoit, 7 January 2004).

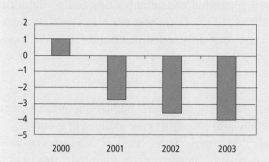

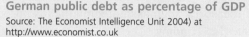

German public debt as percentage of GDP

Source: The Economist Intelligence Unit 2004) at
http://www.economist.co.uk

Nearly 70 per cent of workers are employed in Germany's approximately 3.3 million SMEs, making up the *Mittelstand*, which is considered the backbone of the economy. In manufacturing, large firms of over 500 employees make up only 1 per cent of the total, while firms with fewer that 250 employees account for 45 per cent of manufacturing employment. Insolvencies among SMEs have run at record levels, while a parallel concern has been the low level of private sector investment in the economy, which fell a total of 12 per cent from 2001 to 2003. At the same time, consumer spending was weak and the rate of savings went up, both recognized features of an economic downturn. In these circumstances, economists would advise a lowering of interest rates, but the European Central Bank's modest easing of interest rates in 2003 had little impact, and Germany as a eurozone economy is unable to act unilaterally. The government of Helmut Schröder in 2003 put forward a comprehensive package of reforms called Agenda 2010 consisting of more than a dozen pieces of legislation. These were in areas of social security reform, the health service and labour market reforms. Labour market reforms, aiming to bring about greater flexibility, were seen as key to the structural problems which have made German businesses uncompetitive. Of particular concern was the worry that jobs would migrate to the new EU member states to the East, where costs are lower. Compromises had to be made in order to get the unpopular measures through the legislature and reforms were less sweeping than originally envisaged.

Unemployment benefits have been reduced, as have pensions, both deeply unpopular reforms. A reduction in both income and corporation taxes, brought forward from 2005 to 2004, has been the only universally popular reform. To further encourage employers, protection against dismissal has been relaxed, and employer contributions to the health service have been reduced. The hope is for export-led growth to generate economic recovery. However, the government still faces a budget deficit in public finances and people have little appetite for further reforms which trim Germany's social welfare system.

Sources: Barber, T. 'Economic downturn originates from home', *Financial Times*, 18 January 2002; Simonian, H., 'Troubles plague the powerhouse of Europe', *Financial Times*, 25 November 2002; Benoit, B., 'Schröder's unfinished business: why the reforms agreed for Germany's ailing economy leave the job half-done', *Financial Times*, 7 January 2004; Munchau, W., 'Grounded: why Germany's once soaring economy is failing to take off', *Financial Times*, 1 April 2004; OECD (2002) *Small and Medium Enterprise Outlook* (Paris: OECD).

Case questions

What are the main aspects of Germany's economic woes?
Assess the government's success in tackling them.

The business cycle

All countries experience fluctuations in their economies, enjoying periods of prosperity followed by periods of downturn. Long cycles, or waves, can be distinguished from the pattern of shorter term fluctuations, often referred to as the business cycle.

The nature and causes of cycles have generated considerable debate and differing viewpoints among economists (Maddison, 1991). Long-wave analysis rests on theories of capitalist development and innovation (discussed in Chapter 11). We focus here on the shorter term fluctuations of the business cycle. The cycle can be divided into phases of prosperity, recession, depression and recovery:

- *Prosperity* – the expansive phase, in which total income is high and unemployment is low. Optimism pervades the economy and consumers are inclined to spend.
- *Recession* – the phase of economic downturn, when confidence is waning and unemployment is rising, as consumers and businesses spend less. In this period governments can take a number of measures, such as lightening the tax burden or reducing interest rates, to stimulate the economy.
- *Depression* – the phase when recession deepens to a near total lack of confidence in the economy, with high unemployment and weak consumer spending. Through policy adjustments, governments may be able to prevent recession from deteriorating into depression.
- *Recovery* – the phase of upturn from recession or depression, in which confidence is returning, unemployment is declining and consumers resume spending. Recovery, however, may be a false dawn if prosperity, which may seem just round the corner, does not materialize.

The worst depression of the twentieth century, the Great Depression of 1929, affected most countries of the world, lasting up to three years in the worst affected countries. Governments now take a stronger regulatory role than they did before the Second World War, and major bank failures, which were an aspect of the Great Depression, are now less likely (Maddison, 1991). Governments use monetary and fiscal policy to ward off the extremes of 'boom and bust' which are associated with the most severe swings of the business cycle. An interest rate cut is quicker to take effect than a reduction in taxes, but tax reductions provide a more direct boost to consumer spending. In the US in 2001, the reduction in interest rates was accompanied by an announcement by the newly elected President George W. Bush of back-dated tax cuts. It should be noted that as national economies have become interdependent, economic downturn in one country, especially the US, is likely to have widespread repercussions in the world economy. Regional economic integration has intensified this interdependence and left governments with less room to manoeuvre. Regional integration has been most advanced in the EU, where national policies have become intertwined with EU policies, as will be seen in the next section.

WEB ALERT!

Statistics for the European Union, covering a wide range of data, can be found at the Eurostat site, http://www.europa.eu.int/comm/eurostat/

UK economic data, including the latest economic indicators, are at the Treasury's website, http://www.hm-treasury.gov.uk

The OECD publishes its Economic Outlook twice a year, giving its economic analysis and trends for the major economies. The OECD Economic Outlook is at http://www.oecd.org

The role of governance in the economy

Governments seek policies which ensure economic growth, low inflation and low unemployment, but there is considerable divergence of opinion on the extent to which they should intervene or, alternatively, allow market forces to prevail. The role of government varies considerably between different types of economic system, which will be discussed in greater detail in Chapter 4. For present purposes, looking at economic systems in general, it is safe to say that most governments are now tending towards more market-oriented policies, with targeted intervention to maintain stability. **Fiscal policy** refers to the budgetary policies for balancing spending with taxation, while **monetary policy** refers to policies for determining the amount of money in supply, rates of interest and exchange rates.

Economic thinking has come a long way since Adam Smith, the classical economist, spoke of the 'invisible hand' of the market guiding the economic system in *The Wealth of Nations* (Smith [1776]1950). Governments and central banks now exert control through monetary and fiscal policies, but economists have long been divided on issues of economic policy. John Maynard Keynes, founder of the 'Keynesian' school, as it came to be known, was the major economic theorist to argue against pure market forces. He argued for 'demand management' through fiscal policy, such as cutting taxes or increasing public spending, to achieve full employment. His major work, *The General Theory of Employment, Interest and Money* (Keynes, 1936), dates from the interwar period, when, in the wake of the Depression, unemployment was a major problem. The other important school of thought is the 'monetarist' school, whose leading authority is Milton Friedman. Monetarists advocate the use of monetary policy to limit the supply of money. This philosophy dominated the government of former Prime Minister Margaret Thatcher in the UK, where it held the ascendancy during the 1970s and 80s, when inflation was a major problem. Economic thinking and research are constantly evolving between these two schools of thought, and this is reflected in more recent government policy, which looks both at inflation targets and the need for reducing unemployment. We look first at the institutional framework for the formulation of policies.

Institutional framework of economic policy

In most countries, governments are required to submit a national budget annually, setting out plans for public expenditure and the raising of money, which must be approved by the legislature. The Treasury is the government department responsible for overseeing spending policy and making budget recommendations to the government. The government minister responsible for delivering the budget in the UK is the Chancellor of the Exchequer, a powerful position in government. Numerous groups and interests look for favourable treatment in the budget, and chancellors, like finance ministers in all governments, are also subject to political pressures, such as the inevitable pressure to bring in tax cuts just before general elections. However, in most countries, while fiscal policy rests with governments, monetary policy has generally become the preserve of the central bank. The **central bank** is at the pinnacle of the country's financial system. It is responsible for issuing the country's notes and coins and implementing the government's monetary policy by, for example, setting interest rates. It is also the banker to the government and the lender of last resort. Most central banks are institutionally independent of government, to avoid undue political influence. In the US the central bank is the powerful and respected Federal Reserve. Alan Greenspan, its chairman through the 1990s, is revered as having been largely responsible for America's sustained economic boom.

In the UK, while the Bank of England is a limb of government, the independent Monetary Policy Committee (MPC) of the Bank advises the government on a regular basis, in order to ensure that policies are seen to be free of short-term political influence. In Germany, the Bundesbank gained a reputation as a strong, independent institution. As will be seen, an implication of European monetary union is that the European Central Bank has now taken on many of the powers of the national central banks in the EU states in the eurozone. At international level, the International Monetary Fund (IMF), which will be discussed in Chapter 12, has oversight of international exchange rate stability and has also considerably expanded its role into areas of economic policy once thought to be purely 'domestic' national policy. The institutional framework of economic policy has thus become more complex as globalization has impacted on national economies.

WEB ALERT!

The website of the European Central Bank is http://www.ecb.int/
Other central banks are:
UK: http://www.bankofengland.co.uk/
France: http://www.banque-france.fr/
Germany: http://www.bundesbank.de/
Ireland: http://www.centralbank.ie/
Spain: http://www.bde.es/
Italy: http://www.bancaditalia.it/

Fiscal policy

Government spending in the UK accounts for about 40 per cent of GDP. This public expenditure covers social security, health, education, defence, infrastructure and many other headings. The breakdown of public spending appears in Figure 3.6.

Governments must raise large sums of money in order to fund public spending. In terms of circular flow analysis, if the government reduces taxation or increases public spending, there will be increased demand for goods and services in the economy. Conversely, if taxation is increased or public spending reduced, this demand contracts, with a detrimental effect on businesses and possibly leading to a rise in unemployment. The fiscal framework in the UK is based on five central principles: transparency, stability, responsibility, fairness (including that between generations) and efficiency. Two fiscal rules exemplify these principles. The first is the 'golden rule', which holds that the government will borrow each year only to invest and not to fund current spending. The second, the 'sustainable investment' rule, stipulates that the public sector net debt will be held at a 'stable and prudent' level (HM Treasury, 2000).

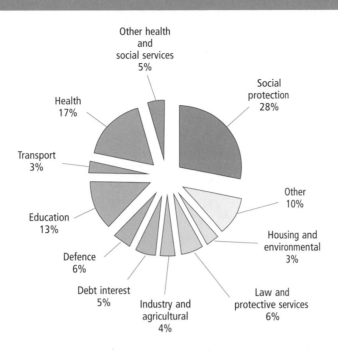

Figure 3.6 Breakdown of UK government spending
Source: HM Treasury, *Budget 2004* (London: Stationery Office).

Public spending is funded in the main from direct and indirect taxation, social security contributions and borrowing. Income tax and corporation tax are types of direct taxation, while VAT and petrol duty are indirect taxes. The balance between direct and indirect taxation varies between countries. In Britain, the government derives more revenue from indirect than direct taxes, whereas in many other EU countries, the reverse is true. Income tax, in contrast to indirect taxes, is a progressive tax, which means that the tax burden rises according to income. For businesses, tax considerations can be crucial when considering future investment. Tax concessions to corporate taxpayers or SMEs, for example, can encourage investment. Reduced rates of corporation tax for SMEs apply in a number of countries, as Table 3.3 shows. Of the countries listed, Ireland has the lowest rate, while Germany has the highest. In a survey of foreign pharmaceutical companies investing in Ireland, the low rate of corporation tax was found to be the most important motive (Bourke, 2000). Governments are aware that while a favourable tax regime helps to attract investors, 'footloose' investment may be lost to another country which offers a more favourable tax regime. Governments can thus use fiscal policies for particular objectives, such as to foster enterprise and innovation. An example is the R&D tax credit introduced in the UK in the 2000 budget. Across-the-board measures, such as a reduction in the rate of income tax, on the other hand, can ignite inflationary pressures.

Table 3.3 Corporation tax rates in selected countries (per cent)

	Basic rate	Reduced rate for SMEs (where applicable)
Germany	40*	n/a
France	33.3	25
Italy	37	n/a
Czech Republic	31	n/a
UK	30	10–20
Ireland	24	12.5
Australia	34	n/a
Japan	30	22
US	35	15

*Basic rate on retained profiits; 25 per cent on distributed profiits.
Source: OECD (2002) *Small and Medium Enterprise Outlook* (Paris: OECD), p. 45.

Governments enjoy a budget surplus when they receive more in revenue than they spend. 'Good housekeeping' principles would suggest that governments, like households, should not spend more than they take in. It is common, however, for governments to be in deficit, spending more than they receive in revenue. In the UK, the **public sector borrowing requirement (PSBR)** represents the deficit which exists – the extent that public spending exceeds receipts. The debt that accumulates over the years is known as the **national debt**. National debt, expressed as a percentage of GDP, can grow to large proportions, causing considerable problems for government finances and, in extreme cases, even the payment of interest becomes problematic. The convergence criteria for entering the EU's European Monetary Union (EMU), or Maastricht criteria, specify that the government deficit (PSBR) should be below 3 per cent of GDP and national debt should not exceed 60 per cent of GDP. UK national debt as a proportion of GDP declined for most of the postwar period, but rose again in the 1990s, peaking at 44 per cent in 1996–7. Since then, it has fallen to about 36 per cent of GDP. In 2001, the UK had a budget surplus of £17 billion (nearly 2 per cent of GDP). Since then, public spending has surged while government receipts have decreased, creating a swing into deficit, as Figure 3.7 shows. For 2003–4 there was a budget deficit of about the same amount, with a PSBR of £33.1bn., which is 3.4 per cent of GDP (HM Treasury, 2004b). Thus, while the UK falls within the Maastricht ceiling for national debt, it is hovering around the limit for public sector borrowing. From the national perspective, the fiscal rules established by the Chancellor have come under pressure. His hope in the 2004 budget was that an upswing in economic growth, along with controls in public spending, would reduce the deficit. The US budget deficit, also shown in Figure 3.7, is huge and certainly flies in the face of 'good housekeeping' principles. However, economic growth in the US is strong, estimated to be over 4 per cent in 2005. Nonetheless, economists stress the need for steps to reduce the federal budge deficit (Krugman, 2004).

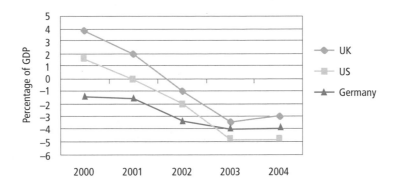

Figure 3.7 **Government budget balance as percentage of GDP**
Source: *Financial Times*, 9 June 2004.

Monetary policy

Monetary policy governs the quantity of money in circulation, the rate of interest and the exchange rate. It is important to remember that changes in one country have implications in other countries, particularly its neighbours and its trading partners. Money supply, interest rates and exchange rates are interrelated. For example, a reduction in interest rates designed to boost the economy will usually have the effect of reducing the value of the currency, as the foreign exchange dealers shift funds out of the country. If money supply is increased, exchange rates tend to fall.

Governments must decide whether to set 'targets' for each of these variables. *Money supply* denotes the availability of liquid assets in the economy. However, it can be defined in a number of ways. It can refer to just notes and coins (*narrow money*), or it can also include less liquid assets, such as bank accounts (*broad money*). In the UK, the Bank of England monitors money supply under the various definitions. But given the widespread use of credit, instead of notes and coins, for consumer and business spending, attempts to control money supply can be somewhat ineffective.

In the UK, the government sets an inflation target, leaving the Bank of England's MPC to set interest rates in order to meet the target. The Labour government which came into office in 1997 set a target of 2.5 per cent for the annual increase in the RPI excluding mortgage interest payments (RPIX). RPIX inflation remained below the target from April 1999, averaging 2.25 per cent. Falling import prices are partly responsible, contributing to competitive pressure on domestic producers and retailers. Inflation remained low in 1999 despite a doubling in the price of oil. However, services inflation presented a different picture, rising from 4.25 per cent to 5.5 per cent in 1999, reflecting growing demand and less competitive pressure in services. Household spending grew 4 per cent in 1999, driven by rising real incomes and falling unemployment. Interest rates fell from 7.5 per cent in mid-1998 to 5 per cent in summer 1999. From September 1999, the MPC raised interest rates by one percentage point, in a move aimed at slowing down household consumption. The strength of sterling contributed to keeping down the price of goods, along with the depreciation of the euro. In the eurozone, by contrast, goods inflation was pushed up by the euro's weakness.

How monetary and fiscal policies are formed

- **Monetary policy framework** – institutional framework governed by the central bank, which is responsible for monitoring and regulating money supply, exchange rate and interest rates. For eurozone states, the European Central Bank now controls monetary policy.

- **Fiscal policy framework** – government authorities, chiefly finance ministries, monitor and formulate policies for government spending and the raising of revenues, including taxation. Where governments are democratically elected, fiscal proposals must be presented in an annual budget and approved by the country's legislature.

CRITICAL PERSPECTIVES

Budget deficits in the US

Why ... do we face the prospect of huge deficits as far as the eye can see? Part of the answer is the surge in defence and homeland security spending. The main reason for deficits, however, is that revenues have plunged. Federal tax receipts as a share of national income are now at their lowest level since 1950 ... The decline in revenue has come almost entirely from taxes that are mostly paid by the richest 5 per cent of families: the personal income tax and the corporate profits tax ... This decline in tax collections from the wealthy is partly the result of the Bush tax cuts, which account for more than half of this year's projected deficit. But it also probably reflects an epidemic of tax avoidance and evasion. (Krugman, 2004, p. 456)

Should Mr Bush, the US president, be concerned about the budget deficit? What advice would you give him to reduce the deficit?

European Monetary Union (EMU)

For the member states of the EU, growing economic integration has brought about a diminishing of national economic autonomy. One of the pillars of the EU is the EMU, which now comprises 12 of the 25 member states of the EU. Proposals for the EMU were agreed under the Maastricht Treaty of 1992, to commence in 1999. The European Central Bank (ECB) was established, to have oversight of monetary policy for all members of EMU and, in particular, to set interest rates centrally. A common currency, the euro, was introduced on 1 January, 1999, while the coins and notes were introduced in 2002. Each government must meet the Maastricht criteria on convergence (see minifile).

Of the EU's 25 member states, 11 joined the eurozone at the outset. They are Belgium, Germany, France, Ireland, Italy, Luxembourg, the Netherlands, Austria,

Portugal, Spain and Finland. Greece was admitted in 2001. The Danish people voted against membership in a referendum in September 2000, the result of which was 53.1 per cent voting 'no' and 46.9 per cent voting 'yes' to the euro. The Danish vote sounded a note of caution to the British government, whose own plan for a referendum was set back. The 'no' vote of Sweden in September 2003 also highlighted difficulties in convincing a sceptical electorate of the benefits of the euro, as Case study 3.3 highlights. As in Denmark, the issue of the common currency has divided public opinion in Britain. Those in favour point to the convenience of the single currency, especially for businesses which regularly transact business in a number of European member states. They also note that some large companies already in Britain, or thinking of investing, are likely to migrate to the eurozone. Those against joining the euro point to the strength of sterling outside the eurozone and the erosion of national sovereignty which would be entailed. As the case study indicates, there is considerable doubt in the minds of voters on the wisdom of transferring economic policy-making to the EU. Nonetheless, the euro is spearheading greater economic integration across the EU, as transnational corporations with pan-European supply chains, such as Nissan and Toyota, now require suppliers to deal in euros, even in the UK and other states not in the eurozone.

Minifile

MAASTRICHT CONVERGENCE CRITERIA

The convergence criteria, which are listed below, provide five 'tests' for EU countries wishing to join the eurozone. However, they were not intended to be applied rigidly and initial applicant countries were given considerable leeway in the interpretation of these requirements. Notwithstanding, the governor of the ECB announced in 2000 that, in his view, Britain would not be able to sidestep the two-year requirement of the exchange rate mechanism (ERM) (*Financial Times*, 24 November, 2000). The five criteria are:

1 *Sustainability of public finances:* government deficit (PSBR) should not exceed 3 per cent of GDP.

2 *Public debt under control:* the ratio of national debt to GDP should not exceed 60 per cent, unless the ratio is sufficiently diminishing and approaching the value 'at a satisfactory pace'.

3 *Price stability:* inflation should not exceed that of the three best-performing countries by more than 1.5 per cent.

4 *Interest rate stability:* long-term interest rates should not exceed the three best-performing countries by more than 2 per cent.

5 *Exchange rate stability:* countries should observe 'normal' fluctuation margins within the ERM margins for two years, without devaluing against the currency of any other member state.

Source: *Economic and Monetary Union*, Financial Times Survey, 23 March, 1998.

Case study 3.3 Sweden says 'no' to the euro

On 14 September 2003, Swedish voters had the opportunity to vote on whether Sweden should join the eurozone. The vote was widely seen as a vote on the monetary, fiscal and structural policies of the eurozone's leaders. In the event, Sweden voted to stay out, by a margin of 56 per cent to 42 per cent, which amounted to a vote of no-confidence in the eurozone economy. The vote provided an opportunity for Swedes to assess their place in Europe, and also an indication of electoral sentiment for other EU member states not in the eurozone to analyse, particularly Denmark (which had rejected the euro in a referendum in 2001) and the UK (where a referendum is on hold).

Sweden only joined the EU in 1995, 22 years after Denmark. The vote to join the EU was the closest of any country which has had a vote on the issue, 53 to 47 per cent. Swedish public opinion has remained sceptical about the benefits of EU membership. One Swedish worker says: 'We have definitely not seen any benefits from being in the EU. We are a net contributor to its budget, but it is money we could have used better ourselves' (Brown-Humes, 7 August 2003). Sweden's economy is based on the the social market model, dating from the 1930s, which combines a welfare state with a market economy. Extensive welfare spending has led to some of the world's highest tax rates and a large public sector: more than 50 per cent of Swedes depend directly on the state for their income, either through public sector employment or benefits. Sweden has been described as a 'consensus-driven egalitarian society' (Brown-Humes, 30 August 2002). It has lower unemployment, lower inflation and higher growth than most other EU countries (see figure).

The 'yes' campaign, supported by the government, pointed to the fact that the eurozone accounts for 40 per cent of Swedish trade and that Swedish multinationals, such as Ericsson, Volvo and Scania, rely on exports. They argued that eurozone membership would increase trade, promote jobs and bring the benefits of lower interest rates, as Sweden's key interest rate was 2.75 per cent, compared with the ECB's 2 per cent. A consequence, they urged, would be lower costs of mortgages for householders.

For the 'no' side, however, there was the persuasive argument that the Swedish economy was performing rather well and a widespread fear that prices, far from going down, would be rounded up when converted to euros. Opponents

of the euro pointed to the fact that the three EU countries outside the eurozone were performing better than the 12 in the eurozone. In the end, government support for the euro seemed to crumble, as ministers went over to the 'no' side. Importantly, key trade unions supported the 'no' vote. Analysis of the results showed large majorities of 'no' voters among women, blue-collar and public sector workers and, perhaps surprisingly, 18–30-year-olds. Even Gothenburg, home to Volvo and other key exporters, voted 'no'. Most Swedes remained sceptical of the supposed benefits and opted for the system they knew. As the *Financial Times'* editorial commented after the vote: 'What is clear ... is that the benefits of joining will have to become more self-evident for electorates with a history of scepticism on EU matters to be convinced' (*Financial Times*, 15 September, 2003). This would include both Denmark and the UK. Perhaps ironically, the EU's ten newer members seem to be more eager to join the eurozone than the three more Euro-sceptic members of the EU 15.

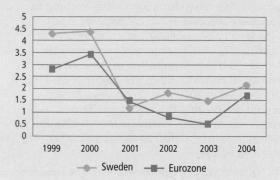

Comparison of Sweden's GDP growth with the Eurozone

Note: Annual percentage change; for 2003 and 2004, estimates based on preliminary data.
Source: Statitiska centrabyrån (Statistics Sweden) at http://scb.se

Sources: George, N. 'Swedes normal deference aside in favour of revolt', *Financial Times*, 16 September 2003; Brown-Humes, C. 'Sweden's ageing model' *Financial Times*, 30 August 2002; Brown-Humes, C. 'Sweden's euro choice: sceptical voters fear the consequences for a cherished welfare model and isolationist heritage', *Financial Times*, 7 August 2003; *Financial Times*, 'Sweden's no vote', 15 September 2003.

Case questions

What are the lessons for Sweden's political leaders, and for leaders of other EU countries contemplating eurozone entry, in the Swedish electorate's rejection of the euro?

In the UK, the Labour government, re-elected in May 2005, is committed to joining the eurozone, but stresses that the timing of Britain's entry will need to be carefully planned. Gordon Brown, the Chancellor of the Exchequer, is concerned that the ECB needs to become more open and accountable. He has set out five further tests, in addition to the formal convergence criteria, which must be satisfied before Britain can join the single currency. Unlike the formal criteria, which are quantitative, these tests are matters of judgement:

- Is there sustainable convergence between Britain's economic structures and those of the eurozone?
- Is there flexibility within the eurozone decision-making structures to cope with economic change?
- What is the impact of EMU on long-term investment prospects in the UK?
- What is the impact of EMU on the UK's financial services industry?
- What is the impact of EMU on the UK's growth and employment?

The chancellor's major concern is that entry into the eurozone would inevitably require a lowering of interest and exchange rates to eurozone levels, which could set off inflation and cause economic instability. Clearly, much depends on entering at the right exchange rate. When the government is confident that the five tests have been satisfied, the issue will be put to the electorate in a referendum.

The euro has not as yet led to convergence among the 11 original member states. Growth rates and inflation differ considerably. The EU's 10 new member states which joined in 2004 have turned their sights on joining the eurozone, which would create greater divergence. Fiscal policy, for the time being, remains a preserve of national governments, which are able to vary the tax burden on individuals and corporations in line with national goals. Governments in member states have set themselves a heavy agenda of structural reforms, to reduce taxation and public expenditure and deregulate product and labour markets. Programmes to reduce the tax burden in Germany and France are underway. The German government reduced the top rate of corporation tax from 55 per cent to 40 per cent. Reducing the corporate tax burden is arguably desirable in its own right, as part of a programme of business incentives. It may also be seen in the wider context of EU convergence, reflecting the influence of growing cross-border economic activity in the eurozone.

SUMMARY POINTS

European Monetary Union (EMU)

● The Treaty of European Union, which dates from 1992, laid the groundwork for the EMU, by authorizing the creation of the ECB.

● In 1998, governments of the 11 original members of the EMU, known as the 'eurozone', appointed a president and board to govern the ECB.

● In 1999, the process began of fixing the exchange rates of member states' currencies to the European currency, the euro.

● From 2001, Greece, having fulfilled the convergence criteria, was admitted to the eurozone.

● Euro banknotes were put into circulation on 1 January 2002.

The major disappointment in the euro's first two years was its dramatic slump in value. Launched at a value of US$1.17, it slumped to $0.84, losing a third of its value in its first 22 months. In September 2000, the ECB and other central banks coordinated a rescue operation to stop the downward spiral. Observers felt that the euro's weakness stemmed largely from the strength of the US economy, and that a slowdown in the US economy would prompt a recovery of the euro, luring investors to Europe. Structural reforms in eurozone economies, should aid the process, but progress is likely to be uneven, so long as these remain in the hands of the 11 national governments. The euro has risen in value, to over $1.20 in 2004, but now the weakness of the US dollar has been a major consideration. The UK economy, outside the eurozone, has enjoyed higher rates of growth than those in the eurozone. Although the European Commission has aspired to achieve a coordination of economic policies within member states – not simply those in the eurozone – as yet, economic goals and policies still diverge among the member states. As has been seen, national economies throughout Europe are shaped by elected governments, reflecting divergent social and cultural values, which influence economic activities. As a result, societies have evolved differing economic systems, which are further evolving in the context of regionalization and globalization, as will be explored in Chapter 4.

CRITICAL PERSPECTIVES

European economic integration and the single currency

On a purely economic level, most European leaders believe that a common currency will constitute a bulwark against inflation and currency manipulation ... On a psychological level, many have believed that once monetary unity was achieved, everything else would fall naturally into place and Europe would be able to deal with such serious common economic problems as low economic growth and chronic high unemployment. For these and similar political, economic, and psychological reasons, European leaders have expected that the success or failure of monetary unity would shape European integration. (Gilpin, 2000, p. 203)

◼ Has the eurozone so far delivered the benefits that Gilpin describes, and, if not, what are the reasons? What impact is enlargement having on further economic integration?

Conclusions

1   The macroeconomic environment can be depicted in terms of flows of resources, income, production and expenditure.

2   GNI and GDP are used to measure the size of national economies.

3   Economic activity may be divided into primary, secondary and tertiary sectors. The world's industrialized nations have seen a relative decline in manufacturing industries and an upsurge in service industries, especially those in the high-tech sector.

4   Controlling inflation and unemployment are major concerns of modern governments, in order to achieve sustained growth in the economy.

5   Balance of payments calculations are used to assess a country's trade with other countries. A trade deficit indicates that it imports more than it exports.

6   While the fluctuations of the business cycle affect all economies, governments use monetary and fiscal policies to avoid the damaging effects of severe swings.

7   Public spending and taxation are matters of governments' fiscal policy. Reducing taxation or increasing public spending are seen as ways of stimulating the economy.

8   Monetary policy usually rests with central banks. Altering interest and exchange rates are seen as tools for controlling inflation. Within the EMU (the eurozone), interest and exchange rates are determined by the ECB, while fiscal policies are still determined by national authorities.

9   Regional and global economic integration limits the room for manoeuvre once enjoyed by national governments over economic policies.

Review questions

1   In what ways is the circular flow diagram useful to show overall economic activity in the national economy?

2   How are GDP and GNI per capita used to compare countries and what are their limitations?

3   Describe the three sectors of the modern industrial economy. Which is growing the most rapidly and why?

4   Define inflation and explain what its damaging effects can be on a national economy.

5   What are the dimensions of unemployment which impact on different business locations, and what government policies can be used to deal with sectoral or regional unemployment?

6   Why is the balance of payments important to policy-makers, and why are governments concerned if there is a current account deficit?

7   What factors cause economic growth, and which countries at present show the strongest rates of growth?

8   Describe the stages of the business cycle. How do they impact on business activities?

9   In what ways do governments control monetary policy, and how has their room for manoeuvre become more limited with economic integration?

10 What are the implications of EMU? Is EMU bringing about convergence between member states?

Assignments

1   Looking at the key indicators of the macroeconomic environment, what policy instruments are available to national decision-makers, and to what extent are they now limited by factors beyond their borders?

2   Assess the major factors influencing economic growth, and give recommendations to policy-makers concerned to boost growth without fuelling inflation.

Further reading

De Grauwe, P. (2003) *Economics of Monetary Union*, 5th edn (Oxford: Oxford University Press)

Eijffinger, S. and deHaan, J. (2000) *European Monetary and Fiscal Policy* (Oxford: Oxford University Press)

Dunning, J. (ed.) (1997) *Governments, Globalization and International Business* (Oxford: Oxford University Press)

Maddison, A. (1991) *Dynamic Forces in Capitalist Development* (Oxford: Oxford University Press)

Maddison, A. (2001) *The World Economy: A Millennial Perspective* (Paris: OECD).

Parkin, M., Powell, M., Matthews, K., King, D. and Matthews, K.G.P. (2001) *Economics*, 5th edn (Harlow: Financial Times/Prentice Hall)

Piggott, J. and Cook, M. (2005) *International Business Economics* (Basingstoke: Palgrave Macmillan).

4 Major economic systems

Outline of chapter

- Introduction
- Overview of world economic systems
- Capitalism: elements of the market economy
  - Freedom of enterprise
  - Competitive markets: supply and demand
  - Private property
- Market structures
  - Porter's five forces model
  - Monopoly and oligopoly
  - Competition policy
- Social market capitalism
- Asian capitalism
  - Japan
  - The late industrializing economies of Asia
  - An Asian model of capitalism?
- The planned economy
  - The Soviet Union
  - From state plan to market: the example of China
- Transition economies in Central and Eastern Europe
  - The transition process
  - Impact of EU enlargement on European economies
- Divergence and regionalization
- Conclusions

Learning objectives

1 To identify the distinguishing features of different economic systems and how they impact on business structures and activities.

2 To appreciate the defining principles of capitalism, as exemplified in major Western economies.

3 To distinguish between different models of capitalist market economy and how they are evolving in the global environment.

4 To assess the strength and content of regionalization and economic integration in the context of national economic pathways.

Introduction

Each nation must come to terms with how to allocate scarce resources to satisfy the needs of those within its territory. This is the chief function of its economic system. Economic systems vary from society to society. The values and attitudes that a society attaches to the activities of production, such as work and wealth accumulation, are key to its economic system, as are the values that it holds about how wealth should be distributed. While there are recognized factors of production – made up of capital, labour and land – there are numerous ways in which their ownership and use may be organized. They range from total state ownership and control at one extreme to free-market capitalism at the other extreme. In practice, most systems fall somewhere between these two extremes. However, there are major differences in economic systems from society to society, which impact on business organization and operations. Moreover, economic systems are not static, but are influenced by changes in the national, regional and international environment.

A trend observable across all continents has been the shift towards more open markets and away from state ownership and control. This trend has brought greater opportunities for the expansion of business enterprises into wider markets globally. On the other hand, governmental regulation of enterprise has proliferated, adding to the complexity of business activities. The main aim of this chapter is to examine the main types of economic system, both in their 'ideal' forms and how they function in practice in major nation-states. The chapter looks at how national economies fit into broad categories, adapting systems in national environments. Trends in both developed and transitional economies are highlighted, as business organizations play key roles in the changing environment. Finally, we assess the impact of globalization and regionalization on the business environment.

Overview of world economic systems

The world's major economic systems are usually classified in rather a broadbrush manner as capitalism on the one hand and socialism on the other. This polarized view of economies probably fitted reality most accurately during the cold-war period, when economic systems were seen in the context of dominant ideologies – complete world pictures of societal structures and human values. The socialist states were the state-planned, collectivist economies, while the capitalist states were free-market economies. With the crumbling of the Soviet Union and market reforms taking place in the other major socialist power, China, this dualistic view has given way to a much more fragmented and diverse spectrum of contrasting economic systems. There are now hardly any avowedly socialist states left, and even they, notably North Korea and Cuba, have made tentative steps to open their economies. On the other hand, while all systems now seem to be some hue of capitalism, there are significant differences between them and the inclusion of social welfare elements indicates how capitalism as a model has evolved since its early days.

Capitalism: elements of the market economy

The force behind nineteenth-century industrialization in Europe and the US was capitalism. Capitalism rests on the principle that a market economy, in which ownership of production is in private hands, is preferable to a state-run economy, in which ownership and control of the means of production reside in the state. The underlying assumption of capitalism is that, through each individual's pursuit of self-interested economic activity, society as a whole benefits. This guiding principle is associated with capitalism in its purest form, or laissez-faire capitalism. The main examples of the *laissez-faire* model are Britain and the US, the countries in which capitalism as an economic system took shape (featured in the first two minifiles in this chapter). It comprises three key elements: freedom of enterprise, competitive markets and private property.

Minifile

THE UNITED STATES ECONOMY

GDP for 2003 (millions): $10,871,095

GDP per head, at PPP: $37,352

GDP growth rate, 2002–3: 3.1 per cent

Key points:

1 World's strongest economy, and foremost example of free-market capitalism

2 Consistently impressive growth rates in the 1990s, attributable to corporate restructuring, flexible working and innovations in IT

3 Dominant global position in IT and international finance

4 Social problems, such as persistent poverty and the provision of medical care for the poor and elderly, are continuing difficult issues for government

Sources of data: World Bank (2004) *World Development Indicators 2004*, at http://worldbank.org; Economist Intelligence Unit (2004) at http://www.economist.co.uk.

WEB ALERT!

Up-to-date US economic data is available from the Economic Statistics Briefing Room of the White House at http://www.whitehouse.gov/fsbe/esbr.html

The US Gateway to Government, providing links to all government departments, is at http://www.whitehouse.gov/WH/html/handbook.html

Freedom of enterprise

Freedom of enterprise is the right of all individuals in a society to pursue their own choice of business activity, in the place they wish to pursue it. Freedom of enterprise flourishes in an open society, in which individuals are free to compete in a marketplace and accumulate private wealth. Such an environment encourages entrepreneurial activity and it is usual for governments to put in place policies to encourage business creation (OECD, 2002). Levels of entrepreneurial activity differ markedly between countries, as Figure 4.1 shows. As one would expect, the US has a high level, but so, too, does China, where market reforms have led to economic growth. The high levels evident in some developing countries, such as Venezuela and Uganda, can be explained in part by 'necessity entrepreneurship' and also by the small base from which economic activity is growing. The high level of entrepreneurial activity in New Zealand, a high-income country, is due to large numbers of small businesses. In Japan, by contrast, just 3 per cent of the population were involved in starting up or managing a business under 42 months old. At the start of 2003, the Japanese government set up a scheme making it possible to start up a company for just one yen (Ibison, 2003). Disappointingly, only 178 one-yen companies were actually set up during the first year. On the other hand, new business formation in Japan rose by 8 per cent in 2003. It is recognized that environmental factors play a role in discouraging entrepreneurship in Japan, including a cultural aversion to risk-taking and difficulties in obtaining finance.

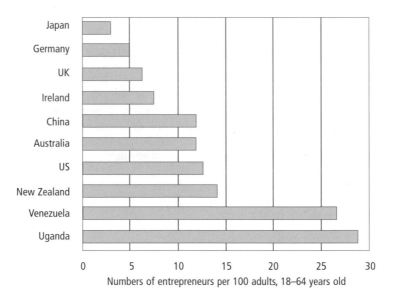

(Note that in this research entrepreneurs are defined as adults from 18 to 64 years old who are either in the start-up phase of a business or managing a new business less than 42 months old.)

Figure 4.1 **Total entrepreneurial activity by country**

Source: GEM Consortium (2004) *Global Entrepreneurship Monitor 2003*, at www.gemconsortium.org.

Governments play a balancing role between encouraging free enterprise and stifling it by overregulation. Individual entrepreneurs are less likely to flourish in an environment hemmed in by hundreds of bureaucratic regulations governing location and planning permissions, building requirements and employment regulations – all of which are referred to as 'red tape'. At the same time, transparent and fair regimes of business regulation are part of a system of free enterprise. A stable and impartial legal framework is an important prerequisite for free enterprise to flourish. If connections with government officials or the payment of bribes are necessary to carry on business, corruption sets in, inhibiting the operation of a free market.

As was seen in Chapter 3, authorities can facilitate business development in numerous ways, through incentives, 'enterprise zones' and advantageous tax regimes. The entrepreneurial environment in China presents a combination of these factors. On the one hand, bureaucratic regulation and the role of political authorities can prove frustrating, but, on the other hand, government policy has been to encourage entrepreneurial activity, which has blossomed since the early 1990s (Story, 2003). By the late 1990s, private enterprises had become the main source of new jobs in the Chinese economy, the bulk of these in services and the manufacture of consumer goods.

Other constraints on freedom of enterprise arise from the perceived need for regulation in the social, economic and natural environment. A factory may emit pollutants which ruin the agricultural crops in the adjacent field or even in a neighbouring country. Factory processes which are unsafe or employ child labourers may be economically efficient, but harmful to health and unethical. Human rights and protection of the natural environment have now become major concerns for both governments and businesses. The legal and ethical environment of business in most countries now curtails these practices.

Competitive markets: supply and demand

The essence of the market economy is competition, whereby businesses compete against each other in offering goods and services to the public. Entrepreneurs in a marketplace are competing for consumers' money, through supply and demand. Demand arises from the consumer and market demand represents the sum total of the demands of all the individual consumers. Supply originates with producers and market supply represents the total availability of the good in the market in a particular period, from all producers. Demand in this context means demand that is backed up by the ability to pay, under specific economic conditions, or 'effective demand'. It should therefore be distinguished from the needs and wants of consumers. A consumer may wish to have a luxury holiday or feels the need for one, but this wish will not be turned into demand unless matched by an ability to pay. Demand theory holds that if demand for the product is greater than supply, the price will rise and producers may be encouraged to produce more. If supply exceeds demand, the price will fall and producers will respond by producing less of the product.

The relationship between supply and demand determines the price of a good. The *equilibrium price* is that which is obtained when demand and supply are equally matched. In Figure 4.2, this is the point at which the demand and supply curves intersect. When the price is above the equilibrium price, supply is greater than demand, and therefore must fall. If the price is below the equilibrium price, demand is greater than supply and the price will rise. Thus the system adjusts to the wants of consumers. Figure 4.2 shows an increase in demand for a product from D to D_1, with supplies remaining constant. This increase, which could be caused by a number of factors, such as a change in consumer tastes favouring the product, will cause the price to rise, as the product is perceived to be in short supply. Producers will respond to the opportunity to sell more of the good, and new producers are likely to enter the market, thus increasing supply. A new equilibrium price, P_1, is reached, reflecting the new levels of both supply and demand at Q_1.

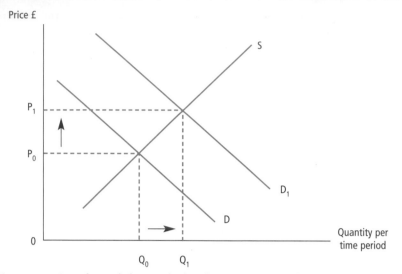

Figure 4.2 **Supply and demand: the determination of equilibrium price**

At any given time, producers are encouraged to allocate resources to producing the products in demand, as these will have higher prices and yield greater profit. The producers who are quicker to respond with new products to meet these shifts in consumer tastes are more likely to profit than slower rivals. Also important in markets is the cost of production, as the producers with higher costs and higher prices will be undercut by more efficient producers. The producer's profit depends on the difference between the selling price of the goods and the cost of their production. In Case study 4.1 on the demand for mobile phones, the huge investment in third-generation (3G) technology implies high prices, but there is doubt about the extent to which consumers will be willing to pay for 3G phones, both in terms of handsets and operators' charges. In addition, the necessary infrastructure to facilitate 3G has been built in the major urban areas, but has progressed rather more slowly in other areas, leaving gaps in coverage which might deter potential customers. On the other hand, there is growing demand in developing countries for low-end mobile phones. These are cheap to produce and price competitiveness is crucial. The profit on each phone sold is slim, however, and the producer relies on volume of sales to generate profits.

For business planning, it is important to be able to assess the level of demand for a product and the effect of price on the consumer's decision whether to purchase it. The responsiveness of one variable to another is known as **elasticity**. *Price elasticity* refers to the effect of price changes on the quantity demanded by consumers. The concept of price elasticity can be expressed as a formula:

$$\text{Price elasticity} = \frac{\%\ \text{change in quantity demanded}}{\%\ \text{change in price}}$$

If the percentage change in quantity is greater than the percentage change in price, then demand is relatively *elastic*, that is, sensitive to price changes. In this case, the price elasticity (E) is greater than one. However, if the percentage change in quantity demanded is less than the percentage change in price, demand is relatively *inelastic*, implying that it is not very sensitive to price changes. In this case, the value of price elasticity (E) is less than one. Clearly, goods such as necessities will have a low value of elasticity, in that a household will be compelled to buy them, whatever the price. On the other hand, for goods which are seen as luxuries, such as package holidays, an increase in price can sharply affect demand.

Demand is also influenced by changes in consumers' income, as an increase or decrease in income will affect the consumer's decision to purchase. This concept is known as *income elasticity*, expressed as the formula:

$$\text{Income elasticity} = \frac{\%\ \text{change in quantity demanded}}{\%\ \text{change in income}}$$

Goods may be classified as normal, superior or inferior, depending on consumer perceptions. For normal goods, such as household electrical appliances, an increase in income will lead to an increase in demand. For goods perceived as inferior, such as low-cost or low-quality food products, demand may decline as income increases and consumers turn to better quality, more expensive products. Consumer expectations and tastes change over time and vary from country to country. Calculating the elasticities of demand can help organizations in decision-making about particular markets, but it should be remembered that they hold for particular sets of conditions, which may change.

Case study 4.1   Changing global demand for mobile phones

The years 2000–2003 saw changes in demand for mobile phones which contained a mixture of gloom and optimism for handset manufacturers. On the gloomy front, global handset sales declined, with saturation in many Western markets – mobile phone penetration across Europe was over 70 per cent. Average selling prices also declined. Nokia of Finland, the leading manufacturer, which sells nearly two out of every five mobile phones made (see figure), saw falls in their average price from €144 to €135 in the course of 2003, triggering a drop of 15 per cent in its share price. Among consumers, there was scepticism about the benefits of the much-publicized introduction of revolutionary 3G phones, especially in light of the slow development of 3G networks. Questions over the safety of mobile phones were a concern, especially with their increasing use by children. While both handsets and masts emit radiation, research suggests that emissions from phones pose the greater risk, but the new 3G base stations have higher levels of emissions than their predecessors, which are subject to further research. Replacement phones represent the bulk of purchases in established markets, and consumers would need to be tempted to buy new phones amid generally sluggish consumer spending in European economies. The gradual introduction of new features and services, including colour screens and picture messaging – sometimes referred to as '2.5G' – seemed to be the best way to spur sustainable demand.

Optimistic notes became more confident, but they signalled changes occurring in global markets. While sales had been flat in established markets, sales in emerging markets, such as China, India, Russia and Brazil, had been forging ahead. Strong sales in China helped manufacturers Motorola of the US and Samsung of Korea to increase sales and global market share. In the second half of 2003, the global market grew by 16 per cent to 470 million handsets, and sales are expected to reach 750 million in 2005. Market shares of leading brands in 2004 are indicated in the figure. But will higher volumes translate into higher revenues? A cause of falling average prices globally is the growing proportion of phones sold in emerging markets, where prices are cheaper. Consumers now enjoy more choice than ever, in an increasingly segmented market. At the low end, handsets are becoming 'commoditized', where demand is for entry-level models, on which margins are low. This is the case in many developing countries, where landline infrastructure is poor and mobile infrastructure provides a substitute. At the higher end, mainly in developed countries, advanced handsets offer consumers features and functions, including camera phones, entertainment and business applications. The Asian manufacturers, with their strengths in consumer electronics, have been well placed to exploit new opportunities. Sony Ericsson is in a strong position to build on media expertise. Asian manufacturers' new upmarket handsets, with colour screens and polyphonic sound, have proved to be popular with consumers. In the UK, Samsung's market share rose from under 1 per cent to 10 per cent of the market in only one year, between 2001 and 2002.

Relations with telecommunications operators are an important element in the mobile phone market. Operators are keen to have their own brand on phones, and to feature models customized to offer their services. Operators are in a strong position to promote new models by offering subsidies to consumers who buy subscription packages. Does this imply that customer loyalty might lean more towards the operator than to the handset manufacturer? With links between operators, handset manufacturers and software companies, all hope to benefit. In the emerging 'smartphone' market, handphones are becoming multimedia devices, offering a range of functions, from gaming to music playing and digital cameras. Demand will depend heavily on whether the new services excite consumers, with prices to tempt them.

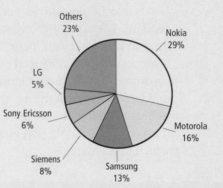

The global market for mobile handsets, 2004 (market share, 1st quarter)
Source: *Financial Times*, 9 June 2004.

Sources: Brown-Humes, C. 'Nokia message has a ring of confidence', *Financial Times*, 23 January 2004; Brown-Humes, C. 'Nokia warning hits hopes of recovery', *Financial Times*, 18 July 2003; Budden, R. 'Industry hopes new models will ring the changes', *Financial Times*, 18 September 2002; Harvey, F. 'Turning point the wireless world', *Financial Times*, 28 October 2003; Budden, R., 'Safety of mobile phones 'remains open to question'', *Financial Times*, 15 January 2004; Nuttall, C., 'Mobile sales to hit 600m this year', *Financial Times*, 9 June 2004.

Case questions

How is global demand for mobile phones changing?
What are the implications for handset manufacturers?

WEB ALERT!

Websites of mobile phone manufacturers are as follows:
www.nokia.com, www.samsung.com and www.sonyericsson.com

Minifile

THE BRITISH ECONOMY

GDP for 2003 (millions): $1,606,853

GDP per head (at PPP): $27,106

GDP rate of growth, 2002–3: 2.3 per cent

Key points:

1 Labour government under Prime Minister Tony Blair, elected in 1997 and re-elected in 2001 and 2005, has pursued a 'third way' agenda between market capitalism and social justice

2 Sustained economic growth, mainly in service sector

3 Health and education are main areas of government and public attention, with problems of quality and exclusion of most concern

4 Persistence of north-south divide, contrasting depressed northern areas with booming southeast

5 Welfare-to-work policy to encourage the unemployed back to work

6 Plans to join the eurozone, but no timetable

Sources of data: World Bank (2004) *World Development Indicators 2004*, at http://www.worldbank.org; Economist Intelligence Unit (2004) at http://economist.co.uk.

Private property

The third of the elements of capitalism is private ownership of property. Property includes capital, goods and the property that exists in a person's labour. Private ownership is linked to incentives in capitalism: the system aims to assure citizens that they personally will be the beneficiaries of their property and labour. On the other hand, wealth accumulation within capitalist systems has tended to concentrate in the hands of the few, producing a wide gap between rich and poor. The extreme inequalities of income distribution, which are inherent in the capitalist model, have led to government intervention to protect the weakest in society through a host of social welfare measures, such as income support and housing benefit. In the US and UK, these measures have been seen as a 'safety net', whereas in other countries, as discussed later in this chapter, they have taken on a much stronger role.

An area of private property which is growing in economic significance is intellectual property. **Intellectual property (IP)** refers to the 'products' of human ingenuity. It includes patents for new products or processes; copyright for written, musical and artistic works (which includes computer software); and trademarks for a company's logos. In common with other types of property, the inventor of a new product wishes to exploit it for gain and be assured that others will not steal the idea and set up in business producing an identical product. Patents also protect new technology. As capturing technological advances is crucial to competitive advantage, the monopoly granted by a patent may be worth a great deal of money in global markets. Internet technology, along with its many benefits, has made life easier for infringers, while firms are finding it difficult to protect their IP, especially across national borders (see Chapter 11).

CRITICAL PERSPECTIVES

Defining capitalism

Capitalism has always had three fundamental properties. First, it is a system of the private ownership of property. Second, economic activity is guided by price signals set in markets. And third, it expects and depends upon the motivation for action to be the quest for profit ... But I do not regard these attributes of capitalism as absolutes; property, prices and profits are not independent of social mores and preferences, history and politics. Private property-holders can have complete auton-omy ... over their property in some capitalist systems; in others they have to accept all manner of reciprocal obligations ... Equally, what is considered a reasonable profit ... varies significantly between capitalist economies. And no society allows all the inputs into the economic process to be completely commoditized, so that nothing matters but the logic of supply and demand. (Hutton, 2000, p. 12)

■   In this passage, Hutton puts forward qualifications to 'pure capitalism', but it might be argued that, if these defining characteristics are diluted, the system is not essentially capitalist. Do you agree or disagree and why?

Market structures

Economists analyse markets in terms of their degree of competition. At one end of the spectrum lies the ideal 'perfect competition' and at the opposite extreme exists monopoly. Under perfect competition, there are many buyers and sellers, none of whom is able to influence the price to a greater extent than the others. Players can come and go freely, as there are no barriers to entry or exit. In a monopoly, by con-trast, there is only one player and no competition at all, leaving the monopolist in a position to determine price and quantity. In reality, perfect competition hardly exists, and markets experience degrees of competition along the continuum from one extreme to the other. The emergence of monopolies and oligopolies has accompanied capitalist development and some of these concentrations of economic power are of global proportions. These forms of economic concentration are often formed by mergers of already powerful companies. They are generally viewed as damaging to consumer interests. As *The Economist* (11 September 1999) pointed out in its survey of the twentieth century, economic concentration presents a paradox of capitalism: the encouragement of individual enterprise is the incentive of capitalism, but business, if it grows too big, destroys incentives. Governments have thus evolved systems of regulation and competition policy.

Porter's five forces model

Michael Porter devised a model to explain the forces that determine the competitive intensity of an industry and thereby the profit potential for companies within the industry. He defines an industry as 'the group of firms producing products that are close substitutes for each other' (Porter, 1998a, p. 5). The five competitive forces are shown in Figure 4.3. The stronger these forces, the greater threat they pose, and the more constrained a company is in its ability to raise prices and increase profits in the short term. However, in the long term, a company may respond to strong competitive forces with strategies designed to alter the strength of particular forces to its advantage. As Porter says:

> The goal of competitive strategy for a business unit in an industry is to find a position in the industry where the company can best defend itself against these competitive forces or can influence them in its favour ... The key for developing strategy is to delve below the surface and analyse the sources of each. (Porter, 1998a, p. 4)

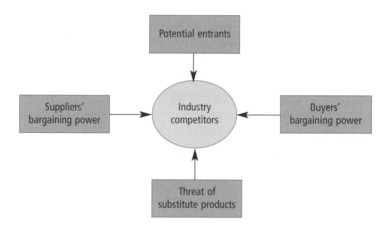

Figure 4.3 **Porter's five forces model: forces driving industry competition**
Source: Adapted from Porter, M. (1998) *Competitive Strategy: Techniques for Analysing Industries and Competitors* (London: Free Press).

Each of the five forces are examined in turn.

Potential entrants

New entrants offer an industry greater capacity and greater competition for market share, thus posing a threat to existing competitors. The extent of this threat depends on barriers to entry. If barriers are high, then the threat of new entrants is low. Sources of barriers to entry include:

- *Economies of scale*, whereby unit costs decline as the volume produced increases. New entrants may thus have to enter on a large scale or not at all. If they enter on a small scale, they face cost disadvantage.
- *Product differentiation*, which may be based on building brand identification over time, entailing substantial expenditure on advertising. For example, new entrants in the soap powder market, which is dominated by a few strong brands (such as Ariel and Persil), are faced by the huge potential costs of advertising and promotions to gain market share.

- *Capital requirements* – the necessity to make a huge capital investment deters new entrants. A new entrant in an industry which relies on high levels of expenditure on R&D, such as the pharmaceutical industry, will need a huge amount of capital to compete with the large companies.
- *Access to distribution channels* – the new entrant may have difficulty finding willing distributors. For example, the maker of a new food product may struggle to persuade supermarkets to stock it.

Intensity of rivalry among existing competitors

Competitors in markets are interdependent. Prices, advertising campaigns, promotions and customer warranties are monitored by competing firms, who then respond. The intensity of rivalry depends on several factors (Porter, 1998a, pp. 17–23). The following factors may be highlighted:

- *Numerous or equally balanced competitors* – where firms are numerous, companies tend not to keep a close eye on competitors' moves, but where they are more equally balanced, each tracks others' moves with a view to countering competitors' strategies.
- *Rate of industry growth* – where an industry is growing rapidly, there is plenty of opportunity for firms to expand. Where an industry is growing slowly, competition centres on gaining market share.
- *Product or service characteristics* – if a product is so basic as to be essentially the same, regardless of supplier, it resembles a commodity and the buyer's choice depends on price and services, where intense competition results. This point is highlighted in the case study on mobile phones.
- *Level of fixed costs* – where there are high fixed costs, there is pressure for companies to fill capacity, cutting prices in order at least to cover fixed costs. An example is the airline industry. Scheduled flights may fly at less than their capacity of passengers, and airline companies offer discounted fares through various outlets.
- *High exit barriers* – these are the 'economic, strategic and emotional factors' that keep a company in an industry (Porter, 1998a, p. 20). It may have invested in particular assets, for example, which would be difficult to sell or convert to other uses. Managers are inclined to carry on business so long as they are not making huge losses.

Pressure from substitute products

A substitute product is one that performs the same function as the industry's product. Substitute products may appear to be different – tea and coffee, for example, are quite different but serve the same function. Substitutes in effect place a ceiling on the prices that companies in the industry can charge. If the price of coffee rises steeply, consumers will be likely to switch to tea.

Bargaining power of buyers

Important buyer groups can be powerful in forcing down prices or bargaining for higher quality or better terms. They may be in a position to play off one producer against another. The buyers who are in the strongest positions are those who purchase a large proportion of the seller's output, or can change to alternative suppliers with ease, as the product is a standard one.

Bargaining power of suppliers

Key suppliers can threaten to raise prices or reduce quality. A supplier is in a powerful position if the supply industry is dominated by a few powerful companies (such as the petrol industry), or there are few available substitutes for its product (again, such as petrol).

Monopoly and oligopoly

Economic concentration in its extreme form is found in the monopoly. A monopoly exists if a single firm is the sole supplier in a market and new entrants are precluded. Such a situation may exist even in a market economy, where there is 'imperfect' competition. Some industries, such as public utilities, have been seen as natural monopolies, largely because of the scale economies to be gained, and are defended on the grounds that they are in the public interest. However, monopolies seldom operate in the consumer's interest. The monopolist is in a position to control supply and determine price, with no fear of being undercut by rivals or losing customers to producers offering an improved product. The monopolist may be inefficient as a producer, but has little incentive to streamline procedures or staffing levels. The monopolist thus faces no competitive pressure to offer the consumer a better product or a better deal. The pure monopoly is now becoming rare, as state-owned industries are being dismantled in most countries. More common are the industries dominated by a few powerful players.

An oligopoly exists when a few large producers dominate a market. The oligopolistic market is characterized by a lack of price competition, as firms are reluctant to increase or reduce prices for fear of sacrificing market share. These markets are also noted for large amounts of advertising and brands, which constitute non-price competition. The growth in transnational corporations (TNCs), along with trends towards industry consolidation, has produced numerous oligopolistic industries. They include oil, motor vehicles and soap powder, to name just a few. Some markets are dominated by just two producers. This market structure is known as a 'duopoly'. Prices and sales in an oligopolistic market are heavily influenced by the interplay between producers. To understand their strategies, economists often use *game theory*, which, as in ordinary everyday games, looks at the ways players seek to maximize their own positions in given situations (Parkin et al., 1997). As in ordinary games, too, there is the temptation to cheat. One common way is by collusion, which may be a price-fixing agreement or a carve-up of markets. When firms engage in such agreements systematically, a cartel is said to exist. The cartel is generally assumed to be anti-competitive and against the interests of the consumer.

WEB ALERT!

The UK government website on consumer affairs and competition policy is at http://www.dti.gov.uk/cacp, and provides links for UK, EU and international policy

The Competition Commission is at http://www.competition-commission.gov.uk/

The Competition Act 1998 is available at http://www.hmso.gov.uk/acts/acts1998/19980041.htm

For EU competition policy, see the European Commission website at http://europa.er.int/int/comm./competition

Competition policy

Most countries have enacted legislation to curtail monopolists (known as antitrust law in America) and anti-competitive practices, such as price-fixing agreements through cartels or informal groups of companies, aimed at controlling the market. The OECD sees 'hard core cartels' as a 'major public policy problem' for developing as well as developed countries, costing economies worldwide billions of dollars (*Financial Times*, 6 June 2000).

Competition law provides for notification and approval of mergers and takeovers. The UK has had legal mechanisms for the regulation of monopolies and restrictive trade practices since 1948, when the Monopolies and Mergers Commission was set up. With the Competition Act 1998, this area of the law is now being harmonized with EU law and a new Competition Commission has been set up. Under the new law, 'abuse of a dominant position' in the UK constitutes an infringement, in keeping with Article 82 of the Treaty of Amsterdam (which came into force in 1999). Agreements which 'prevent, restrict or distort' competition also constitute infringement (in accordance with Article 81 of the Treaty of Amsterdam), unless the agreement can be brought within one of the exemptions, the criteria generally being the potential benefit to consumers.

US antitrust law goes back even further, to the Sherman Act 1890, but cartels, holding companies and trusts, which had by then grown powerful, were not easily tamed. Moreover, the US courts have tended to tread lightly on big business (Kovacic and Shapiro, 2000). The US has more global companies by far than any other country and size is seen as an advantage in global competition. Still, there are examples where the federal authorities have brought high-profile antitrust cases, such as that against Microsoft. Featured in Case study 4.2, the case highlights the ambivalence of Americans to big business: Bill Gates is the epitome of the American dream on the one hand, but represents corporate might against the individual on the other.

The EU Commission has become increasingly influential in its role in regulating competition and is perceived as taking a harder line on large mergers than American authorities. For example, a proposed merger between GE and Honeywell in 2001 was cleared by US federal authorities, but rejected by the EU Commission, as it was felt that GE would gain an unfair advantage in the aircraft engine and avionics industries. More recently, the EU Competition commissioner has turned his attention to Microsoft, as Case study 4.2 examines.

WEB ALERT!

The OECD, known as the rich countries' 'club', now has 30 members. Its website is divided into a number of themes and provides a great deal of data and analysis. It is at http://www.oecd.org

Case study 4.2 Microsoft takes on the antitrust authorities

Microsoft was founded in 1975 by college dropout Bill Gates, when he was 20. At 44, and worth an estimated $85 billion, he stepped down as chairman and CEO. But when his successor took over, the company's fate seemed to be hanging in the balance. Antitrust actions against Microsoft's software empire, specifically for its 'tie-in' sales of applications and operating systems, began in 1990 and continued throughout the 1990s. In the 'browser wars' with its bitter rival Netscape Communications, Microsoft inserted contract clauses to prevent manufacturers of computers and internet services companies from distributing Netscape's browser software. Microsoft was alleged to have violated a court order issued in 1995. In 1997, The US Justice Department and 20 US states brought an action against the company for anti-competitive practices, which were designed to maintain a monopoly in its Windows operating systems and extend that monopoly to internet browsing software, by forcing PC manufacturers to install its internet browser, Explorer, as a condition of installing Windows. Although the court held that the company had used anti-competitive means to maintain its monopoly, by the integration of the two products, Windows and its browser software, the company was able to reach an agreement to alter its practices to satisfy the court.

Microsoft's antitrust problems were not over, however, as it faced legal action in Europe, where other rivals, mainly Sun Microsystems and RealNetworks, complained against the linking of Windows PC system to Microsoft software running on other devices and the practice of 'bundling' into Windows new software features, such as the online media player, which are offered as separate products by other companies. The European Commission ruled in 2004 that Microsoft was in abuse of a dominant market position, fining the company €497.3mn. ($613mn.) and ordering that it should offer an 'unbundled' version of Windows. The Competition Commissioner Mario Monti said: 'The Commission has taken a decision today which finds that Microsoft has abused its virtual monopoly power over the PC desktop market in Europe' (Dombey, 25 March 2004). The company's next step in its battle against the competition authorities

is appeal to the European Court of Justice, which could be a lengthy process. Meanwhile, other complaints against Microsoft have been filed in relation to the company's bundling of other products, including Instant Messenger, Outlook Express and Movie Player, onto Windows XP.

Added to worries about actions from regulators have been the technological and business challenges facing Microsoft. Lapses in security have caused embarrassment for the company, highlighting the vulnerability of Windows to virus attacks, which, given Windows' dominant position, have had far-reaching effects. Another challenge is the rise of the Linux open-source operating system, which is gaining in popularity in the server market, as a potential alternative to Windows. Advocates of open-source systems claim that, as well as financial savings, these systems are less prone to virus attacks. Finally, developments in mobile phone and home entertainment devices are moving the focus of attention away from the desktop PC. In these newer markets, competitors have forged ahead in Windows-free environments. What is more, Microsoft's aggressive tactics have ensured that it will meet with resistance in finding partners in these new areas. Microsoft has seen its strength over nearly three decades as relying on its ruthlessly aggressive corporate culture, but its battles with regulators, coupled with hostility from competitors and potential partners, may, ironically perhaps, dent its competitiveness in the rapidly changing environment.

Sources: Wolffe, R. and Kehoe, L. 'Operating error', *Financial Times*, 5 April 2000; Wolffe, R., 'Twin options suit Justice Department', *Financial Times*, 29 April 2000; Wolffe, R., 'Microsoft tries to update legal history', *Financial Times*, 20 July 2001; Waters, R. 'Microsoft versus Monti: how the challenges to the long reign of Windows are growing in Europe and beyond, *Financial Times*, 22 March 2004; Dombey, D., 'US giant seeks reason behind ruling', *Financial Times*, 25 March 2004; Blitz, R., 'The choice is all about the bottom line', *Financial Times*, 9 May 2005.

Case questions

What is the reasoning behind the judgments against Microsoft in both the US and EU?

How is the company affected by the shifting competitive environment?

Public utilities such as water, electricity supply, gas, postal services and telecommunications have long enjoyed monopoly status as nationalized industries in many countries. The process of transferring them from state ownership to private sector companies is **privatization**. Privatization aims to reduce the inefficient bureaucracies that characterize state enterprises, introducing governance arrangements which make managers responsible to directors, who, in turn, are accountable to shareholders in the newly formed companies. From the 1980s onwards, privatization of these state monopolies has been a continuing trend. In the UK, the process began in the 1980s. Ownership is transferred to a company, which then offers shares to the public. Typically, the state retains a large share, such as a 40 per cent stake or more. Productivity gains from two formerly nationalized industries are shown in Table 4.1. However, privatizations do not open the door directly to competition, as the new companies have customarily enjoyed privileged status in the early phase of their existence. In the UK, privatizations in the 1980s were accompanied by the establishment of independent regulatory, or 'watchdog', bodies to oversee the interests of consumers. In the 1990s markets began opening up and competition started to bite, offering consumer choice and product differentiation. While the opening of gas and electricity markets has taken place in most EU countries, agreement on overall targets has been a slow process, with France and Germany particularly cautious in respect of the liberalization of their energy markets. Following intense EU negotiations, the deadline of 2002 for the opening of markets for commercial users was put back to 2004, while for householders, the target date receded to 2007–2009. As Case study 4.3 shows, the processes of privatization and liberalization are linked, as both involve embracing market forces, whereby powerful state entities must undergo both structural and cultural changes which can cause deep upheaval.

Table 4.1 Productivity gains in formerly nationalized industries

	British Telecom	British Gas
Employees (1979)	233,400	101,800
Year of privatization	1984	1986
Employees post-privatization (1994)	165,700	79,400
Turnover pre-privatization (1992 prices)	£6.99 billion	£7.69 billion
Turnover post-privatization (1992 prices)	£13.68 billion	£10.39 billion
Productivity per person gain	180 per cent	71 per cent

Source: *Financial Times*, 23 March 2004.

Privatizations of telecommunications have created new global players, such as BT and Deutsche Telekom, which are themselves acquiring other telecommunications services through further privatizations. In this way, Deutsche Telekom has acquired considerable stakes in Central and Eastern Europe. These acquisitions are a logical response to the loss of the domestic monopoly, but, in addition, a major force at work is the need to maximize shareholder value, which is paramount for corporations in market economies.

SUMMARY POINTS

Laissez-faire capitalist model

- Entrepreneurial, individualistic culture.
- Limited government intervention in markets.
- Little state ownership.
- Social legislation as a safety net.
- Emphasis on shareholder value in corporate governance.

Social market capitalism

The concept of the welfare state dates from the aftermath of The Great Depression of 1929, when Western governments introduced systems of social security, unemployment benefit and other programmes now taken for granted. To many, mainly those on the political right, these measures are seen as an essential social safety net in the market economy, while to those more to the left, social justice is seen as a goal in itself. The social market model gives a social justice dimension to the capitalist model. Often called the *mixed economy*, its main features are state ownership in key sectors and extensive social welfare programmes which reduce the inequalities inherent in the pure capitalist model. State ownership and private ownership exist side by side. Major concerns such as heavy industry, banks, oil companies and airlines may be state-owned. Seen as national champions, they are naturally protected from takeover bids and, should they fall on hard times, can be helped out by the state. On the other hand, sustaining a large public sector and social programmes entails huge public expenditure, risking budget deficits. The majority shareholder in the privatized France Telecom is still the state, which provided €9bn. to prop up the company in 2003. As Case study 4.3 on French national champions illustrates, the state continues to play a major role in the economy, and privatizations, which are part of government policy, face difficulties in practice, particularly from employees and trade unions who see the privileged civil service status being eroded.

Minifile

THE FRENCH ECONOMY

GDP 2003 (millions): $1,632,119

GDP per head (at PPP): $27,327

GDP rate of growth 2002–3:   0.17 per cent

Key points:

1 French capitalism is characterized by state enterprises as national champions

2 Liberalization and diminishing role of the state in the 1990s, as evidenced in privatizations and international expansion of French firms

3 Tradition of extensive welfare state provisions and government subsidies

4 The introduction of the 35-hour week, accompanied by state subsidies to firms, is bringing about greater flexibility in employment, but has been opposed by the trade unions

Sources of data: World Bank (2004) *World Development Indicators 2004*, at http://www.worldbank.org; Economist Intelligence Unit (2004) at http://economist.com.

The social market model has evolved differently in the diverse societies in which it has been adopted. In Sweden the emphasis is on an extensive welfare state to reduce social inequalities (Pontusson, 1997). France and Germany (see minifiles) also have extensive social welfare policies, but they differ in the role played by the state in economic life. In France, the centralized state has created a more 'statist' model, while the German model is more 'corporatist', based on cooperation between the state, business and labour (Vitols, 2000). In Germany, co-determination is the principle by which workers are legally entitled to a say in company management. Germany is a more decentralized state than France. As such, it contrasts with the laissez-faire model of the US and the statist model in France (Streeck, 1997). Many tiers of government in Germany, however, have tended to create complex regulatory regimes for businesses to navigate through.

Case study 4.3 National champions in France

The strong role of the state in the French economy has been a feature of French capitalism. Large enterprises either wholly or partially owned by the state operate in numerous sectors. They cover a range of industries, including electricity, gas, telecommunications, railways, motorways and lotteries. Under pressure from the EU and other EU member states, a programme of privatization has been proceeding slowly, but has met stalwart resistance from employees and their trade union representatives, who see risks to jobs and conditions in further market reforms. Similarly, the liberalization of the electricity and gas markets, required by EU directives, has proceeded slowly and only to the minimum degree required by the legislation. While criticisms of the French government for its lukewarm embrace of market liberalization have mounted, so too have problems for the French finance ministry in controlling the growing budget deficit, as shown in the figure.

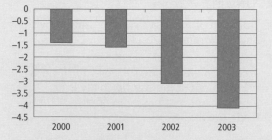

Budget deficit of France as percentage of GDP

Source: Economist Intelligence Unit (2004) at http://www.economist.com.

Nearly one in every four employees in France works in the public sector. Civil servant status brings them job security, generous pay and pension packages which private sector employees do not enjoy. As a consequence, wages and pensions of public sector employees account for almost half of government spending in France. Electricité de France (EDF), the state-owned power utility, would be the most significant privatization to date. However, plans to privatize it have been set back due to resistance from employees, including industrial action. Reform of EDF's pension system, agreed by the three major trade union federations in 2002, was surprisingly rejected by members in a ballot, revealing the depth of grassroots concerns over reform. Tentative steps were taken in 2004, when 30 per cent of the electricity market for non-residential users was first opened to competition. This means that businesses can now shop around for their electricity supply. Also in 2004, EDF, and Gaz de France were converted from state entities to companies. This latter move would pave the way for a percentage of their capital to be sold off to private shareholders, but a large sell-off is not envisaged. The finance minister said at the time: 'one could well imagine the state remaining a 100 per cent shareholder for years: nothing says the state needs to cede its stake' (Graham, 16 June 2004).

EDF has pursued an aggressively expansionist strategy in world energy markets, acquiring sizeable stakes in energy companies throughout Europe, as well as in Latin America and China.

Not surprisingly, it has faced criticism for taking advantage of liberalization in other markets, while its own dominant domestic position remains intact. For example, its purchase of 18 per cent of Italenergia of Italy attracted criticism in Italy and, because of the perceived French invasion, EDF's voting rights were reduced to two per cent.

For the French government, privatizations present opportunities to raise much-needed funds in the face of worrying budget deficits. France has exceeded the eurozone limit of 3 per cent of GDP for four years in a row, but the government has faced political pressure at home to maintain public spending at high levels, while being committed to reducing the tax burden. Meanwhile, sluggish economic growth is adding to the government's headaches. The case for privatization to bring about efficiency gains and raise funds would seem to be compelling, but the resistance of vested interests is likely to ensure that change is piecemeal rather than radical.

Sources: Mallet, V., 'France goes on sale', *Financial Times*, 18 June 2002; Mallet, V., 'EdF faces rough ride in power struggle, *Financial Times*, 19 June 2002; Johnson, J., 'Everyone talks of independent board members and shareholder activism but no one believes it', *Financial Times*, 24 April 2003; Graham, R., 'France puts off privatization of state utilities', *Financial Times*, 16 June 2004; Economist Intelligence Unit (2004) at http://www.economist.com

Case questions

What is the case for privatization in France?

What obstacles lie ahead for privatization plans in France?

In both France and Germany, deregulation and growing market orientation, often referred to as liberalization measures, have in recent years pushed back state regulation and introduced greater competitiveness (Vitols, 2000). In the process, French and German companies have become more active in overseas investment. The acquisition by Renault (40 per cent owned by the French government) of a 36.8 per cent stake in Nissan is an example, as is the acquisitions of water suppliers in many parts of the world by French utilities companies. Germany has had to overcome the problems of rebuilding in Eastern Germany after reunification, where unemployment and the need to modernize outdated industries have presented major challenges, highlighted in Case study 3.2. From the business perspective, corporate restructuring represents a shift towards shareholder value as a priority and a growing market for corporate control through takeovers and mergers.

Minifile

THE GERMAN ECONOMY

GDP 2003 (millions): $2,279,134

GDP per head (at PPP): $27,608

GDP rate of growth 2002–3:   –0.10 per cent

Key points:

1 High costs of social welfare programmes, particularly pensions and health, have been a source of concern

2 Deregulation in former state monopolies of telecommunications and electricity

3 Government policies to reform corporate taxation and reduce state subsidies aimed at fostering economic growth

4 Concern over high level of unemployment (9 per cent), as German companies shift production to new EU member states where costs are lower

Sources of data: World Bank (2004) *World Development Indicators 2004*, at http://www.worldbank.org; Economist Intelligence Unit (2004) at http://www.economist.com.

The social market model of capitalism

● Significant state involvement in economy.
● Bureaucratic regulation of business.
● Extensive social welfare programmes.
● Corporate governance based on social priorities, rather than shareholder value.
● Closed system of corporate control and little takeover market.

CRITICAL PERSPECTIVES

The future of the social market model

European nation-states developed a capacity to govern 'their' economies, applying public power to control economic activities and market outcomes in the 'public interest'. Especially where state interventionism coincided with democracy, or 'social democracy', that public interest was defined to include preservation of social cohesion through prevention of excessive inequality, provision of some degree of social security in the widest sense and generally protection of the citizenry from the worst uncertainties wrought upon them by the 'free play of market forces'. (Streeck, 1996, p. 300)

■ With growing economic integration across national boundaries, will this model of the social market inevitably lose out to the free-market model?

Asian capitalism

Economic activities in any country are embedded in the social and cultural experiences of its people. Industrialization and economic development in the nations of East and Southeast Asia are often grouped together as representing a distinctive model of Asian capitalism. Their development can be seen in three phases: first, Japan; secondly, the Asian 'tiger' economies; and, lastly, China. In looking at their capitalist development, their similarities – and differences – become apparent.

Japan Japan, like Germany, faced the task of rebuilding its industries after the Second World War. The state provided economic guidance and hence Japan is looked on as the 'developmental state' model (Johnson, 1982). The use of 'industrial policy', rather than outright state ownership, has been a chief feature of its economic development, relying on cooperation between the three centres of power – the bureaucracy, politicians and big businesses (see minifile). Business in Japan has traditionally been organized around groups of companies, or **keiretsu**, linked by cross-shareholdings and informal networks with suppliers and customers. The keiretsu, usually centred around a main bank, have served as a source of generous loans, but have also provided a bulwark against hostile takeovers and a deterrent to market entry by out-siders. The reliance on interlocking corporate structures as a source of economic dynamism has given rise to the notion of 'alliance capitalism', as a category to cover the range of economic systems in which inter-firm relations, rather than free-market exchange, predominate (Gerlach, 1991).

The Japanese view of the company stands out against its Western counterparts. The company is seen as a family and a focus of loyalty, rather than simply as a source of income. This outlook is often depicted as the Confucian work ethic, in which collective values and consensus, rather than individualism and self-interest, are the driving force. The guarantee of a job for life has been taken for granted by Japanese workers, a fact that has impeded efforts to restructure in the era of global competition. Restructuring and cost-cutting were imposed on the company from outside. From a position of economic powerhouse in the 1980s, the Japanese economy descended into stagnation in the 1990s. While the immediate cause was a collapse of the banking and financial system, the longer term causes lay with the failure of the system to adapt to global competition. The reluctance of the government to recognize the scale of the financial woes and of companies to downsize and restructure, even when making losses, has hampered recovery.

Minifile

THE JAPANESE ECONOMY

GDP for 2003 (millions): $3,582,515

GDP per head (at PPP): $28,162

GDP rate of growth 2002–3:   2.72 per cent

Key points:

1 State guidance and industrial policy led Japan's postwar economic 'miracle'

2 Collapse of the 'bubble' economy in 1990 left intractable problems of weak, debt-burdened banks, in need of restructuring

3 Closely knit keiretsu groups, which were the engine of economic growth, are now fragmenting in the face of market forces

4 Companies have been slow to restructure and reduce capacity, which are needed if competitiveness is to be restored

5 After two 'false dawns' indicating recovery from the recession of the 1990s, sustained recovery seemed to be in evidence in 2004

Sources of data: World Bank (2004) *World Development Indicators 2004*, at http://www.worldbank.org; Economist Intelligence Unit (2004) at http://www.economist.com.

The late industrializing economies of Asia

Japan served as an example to other Asian late industrializers. The East Asian countries of South Korea, Singapore, Taiwan and Hong Kong (now part of the People's Republic of China) became known as the 'Asian tigers', whose economies took off in the 1980s. They were followed by other Asian countries, the Philippines, Thailand, Indonesia and Malaysia. Last to join has been China, whose command economy has been much slower to welcome market reforms. In this section we identify key elements of Asian economic systems, assessing those features which have contributed to economic growth. The Asian economic 'miracle', as it was called, came to an abrupt halt in July 1997, with a series of financial crises (discussed in detail in Chapter 12).

The original tiger economies are all of Chinese cultural heritage, and the notion of the Confucian ethic underpinning their societies is perhaps the strongest feature they have in common. The Confucian priority given to the family and filial duty has provided a culture based on diligence and loyalty to the firm. The traditional Chinese family business has played a dominant part in the economic development of all these societies. Even so, the state has also played an important role. Taiwan, with its strong export-oriented economy, has had state-owned industries in key sectors, which account for one-third of its GDP, but is currently embarked on a privatization programme.

The city-state of Singapore has also adopted an approach of state intervention, but has refrained from state ownership, instead welcoming foreign direct investment (FDI). The city-state can claim 5000 international companies within its borders. Singaporeans have tolerated a high degree of state interference in business, but are reluctant to complain, as the government has provided a well-managed economy and prosperity. This is the basis of the 'social contract' between Singapores's government and its 3 million inhabitants. Following the Asian financial crises of 1997, they submitted to austerity measures, which reduced salaries; at the same time, families and firms shoulder many welfare burdens which are provided routinely by the state in most Western societies. A report in 1998 found that public spending on social welfare programmes amounts to just over 5 per cent of GDP in Singapore and Hong Kong; 10 per cent in South Korea and Taiwan; and about 15 per cent in Japan. By contrast, the figure is 25 per cent or more in Europe (London School of Economics, 1998).

South Korea's economic development owes its impetus to the large family-owned conglomerates, or **chaebol**, which expanded aggressively overseas during the 1980s. While these groups, including Daewoo, Hyundai and LG, are often compared with Japanese keiretsu, there are some basic differences. The chaebol are family-owned and controlled, not equity-based, as in Japan. Whereas the keiretsu is often based on a main bank, finance in Korea is provided by preferential bank loans, effectively guaranteed by the state. In the late 1990s, it emerged that the chaebols' overseas expansion had rested on unsound lending practices, in a web of implicit guarantees between the state, the banks and the business community. These relationships form the basis of what is called 'crony capitalism', in which personal connections carry more weight than objective business considerations. The build-up of bad loans was especially acute in the case of Daewoo, which has had to be broken up into its separate businesses. (This restructuring is the subject of Case study 11.2.) South Korea has received IMF loans to help to rebuild its economy, but, at the same time, the IMF imposed conditions for restructuring and opening markets which the nation has been slow to implement. (These are further discussed in Chapter 11.) Relations between South Korea and the Communist regime across the border in North Korea are only gradually thawing. Contacts are now cautiously being made, which could lead to an opening up of the North Korean economy. However, North Korea's military might and possible nuclear threat are obstacles to developing relations with other countries which could pave the way for economic development (see minifile).

Minifile

THE TWO KOREAS

Since the end of the Korean War in 1953, the line that has divided North and South Korea has separated two different worlds: the impoverished, isolationist and heavily militarized

Communist state to the north and the prosperous, democratic, tiger economy to the south. The two Koreas evoke the ideological divides of the cold war, and the military tension is marked by the continued presence of the American armed forces in South Korea. The South's living standards are ten times higher than those in the North, where famine was a major problem in the mid-1990s and, according to humanitarian aid workers, chronic poverty is still a problem.

South Korea has a population of 46.4 million and a GDP per capita of $17,000 (see table below). Its economy, however, suffered in the Asian financial crisis, and its recovery was hampered by slowness in corporate restructuring, as well as political instability. In a landmark meeting in 2000, an agreement between the leaders of the two Koreas was signed, in the hope of beginning a new era of cooperation under the banner of the 'sunshine policy'. The aims were to reduce the risk of military conflict and promote badly needed economic development in the North. As a result, Hyundai, the South Korean conglomerate, entered into contracts in the North. When it later emerged that North Korea had secretly been paid $100m. for its participation, the historic event, as well as Kim Dae-jung's reputation, rather lost their shine.

Comparisons between North and South Korea

	South Korea	North Korea
Population	46.4m.	22m.
GDP	$420bn.	$19.4bn.
GDP per capita (at PPP)	$17,000	$1,000
Military expenditure (as percentage of GDP)	3%	25%
Numbers in armed forces	0.67m.	1.1m.

Source: Kynge and Ward (2003).

Roh Moo-hyun, elected president of South Korea in 2002, was keen to pursue economic reform policies, but met resistance from conservative opponents in parliament. He found that tackling the power of the chaebol business groups aroused opposition, while South Korea's militant trade unions were also a source of instability. He also wished to improve relations with North Korea begun in the 2000 summit meeting. By then, however, North Korea's apparent restart of its nuclear programme led to renewed fears for national security, halting moves towards reconciliation. Roh managed to survive impeachment proceedings against him in parliament, and, re-elected in 2004, felt more confident in his policies for liberalizing the economy and possibly resuming relations with North Korea.

North Korea's population of 22 million has a GDP per capita estimated at about $1000 per person. The North Korean government has attempted to attract foreign investment in the country, but poor infrastructure, unreliable power supplies and a patchy transport network are major obstacles. World attention has focused on North Korea's military establishment and nuclear programme, which are potential threats to its neighbours in the region and world peace generally. North Korea's armed forces consist of over a million people (see table). About 17 per cent of economically active males are employed in the military and an estimated 25 per cent of GDP is military expenditure. Moreover, North Korea has amassed an arsenal of weapons, particularly missiles, including long-range ballistic missiles. It has withdrawn from the Nuclear Non-Proliferation Treaty and expelled UN nuclear inspectors. At the same time, it restarted a mothballed nuclear reactor, creating concern that it is developing nuclear bombs.

Sources: Struck, D., 'High Hopes Mark Talks Between Two Koreas', *Washington Post*, 14 June 2000; 'Kimraderie, at last', *The Economist*, 17 June 2000; Burton, J., 'South Korea faces up to huge financial cost of modernising the North', *Financial Times*, 16 June 2000; Kynge, J., and Ward, A., 'Back to the table: why Kim Jong-il's failing economy may be the key to halting his nuclear programme', *Financial Times*, 23 April 2003; Ward, A., 'Crunch time for South Korea: Roh's impeachment increases the risk of "five lost years" for a turbulent nation', *Financial Times*, 15 March 2004; Ward, A., 'Shadow across the sunshine', *Financial Times*, 19 June 2004.

Political instability is a major factor in the late industrializing states of Malaysia and Indonesia, where ethnic divisions are a source of social and political unrest. Both have traditions of authoritarian leadership, bolstered by military establishments. Both have relied on FDI as a driving force for economic growth. The Chinese have a strong economic presence in Indonesia: although they make up only 4 per cent of the population, they control more than 70 per cent of listed companies (Beeson, 2000). The toppling of President Suharto in 1998 brought to an end a 32-year reign, which saw impressive economic growth (averaging 4.6 per cent annually from 1965 onwards) and much improved infrastructure, education and economic prosperity for Indonesians. President Suharto was known as the 'Father of Development', but was also at the centre of a family business empire noted for its corruption. The overthrow of the Suharto regime left a void, and, although there is optimism that the new democratic system will bring the stability needed for economic growth, the future looks uncertain.

An Asian model of capitalism?

We now summarize and assess the extent to which the economic systems of Japan and Southeast Asia's newly industrialized countries present a new Asian model of capitalism. These economies present features in common, but also divergencies. All are mixed economies, combining market forces with state guidance. They differ considerably, however, in their perception of the role of the state, varying from a regulatory role, as in Japan, to a more interventionist role, as in Korea. While the Confucian ethic is often said to underpin the Asian model, this generalization also conceals a good deal of cultural diversity. Some countries are predominantly Muslim, while in the countries which do have a Confucian cultural heritage, Confucian values have evolved over time. The family firm as a focus of loyalty is much more prevalent in Taiwan and Korea than in Japan, where the company 'as community' has taken the place of the family. It has been suggested that the strongest thread running through Asian capitalism is its embeddedness in social and cultural experience, which emphasizes the collectivity rather than the individual. However, as global economic integration deepens, these economic systems are undertaking liberal reforms and opening markets. Stable democratic governments and greater transparency in regulatory regimes are seen as the way forward to stability and sustainable growth for Asian economies.

Lastly, China, the largest Asian country, is also undertaking market reforms, but still within the framework of the one-party state bequeathed by the Communist revolution. Before looking at the evolving Chinese economic system, we identify the main elements of the planned economy.

SUMMARY POINTS

The Asian model of capitalism

- Strong state intervention.
- Bureaucratic regulation of business.
- Corporate culture based on the company as family.
- Groups of companies, both formal and informal, which act as barriers to new entrants and barriers to takeovers.
- Weak welfare state provisions.

The planned economy

The **planned economy**, also known as the 'command economy', is based on total ownership and control by the state of the means of production. The economy is based on collectivism rather than individualism and private enterprise. Production is governed by state plans rather than supply and demand, and prices are set by the state. The aim is achieving targets rather than satisfying consumers' wants. Over-production, inefficiencies, and inflexibility are recurring problems in this type of system – a fact which goes some way to explaining why these systems in their pure form have not been successful in the long term. While their designers maintained a vision of socialism as the ideal society, in which all would be equal, the reality has been stark inequalities under Communist Party domination of the state. The two leading examples of Communist states have been the Soviet Union and China.

The Soviet Union

The Soviet Union (USSR, or Union of Soviet Socialist Republics) dates from 1918, with the overthrow of the Russian czar by the Russian revolutionaries, led by Lenin. Their Marxist-Leninist ideology imbued the economic development of the Soviet Union for 74 years. The first five-year plan dates from 1928, when agriculture was collectivized. The Soviet Union expanded, putting in place satellite regimes in Eastern and Central Europe, supported by Russian military might. While state planning brought industrialization and economic growth, its emphasis was on heavy industries, which were inefficient and highly pollutant, while it neglected consumer goods. The Soviet system simply could not keep pace with modern industries in market-based economies. Numerous liberalizing reforms were attempted, to restructure and introduce flexibility, but all failed in the end. Perestroika, 1987–9, introduced some freedom of contract between enterprises and some latitude for enterprises to decide what to produce, but these modest reforms were too little, too late. The breakaway of the satellite states started in 1989 and collapse of the Soviet Union itself finally came in 1991. With the dismantling of Communism, these independent states now have both democratic constitutions and transitional market economies in place.

From state plan to market: the example of China

While China is an ancient civilization, the current state of China (its full name is the People's Republic of China) dates only from the Communist revolution of 1949. Communist rule has changed considerably since then, as its ideological underpinning has evolved. The Maoism of the early years (based on the teachings of Mao Zedong) was in the vein of orthodox Marxism-Leninism. The period from 1958 to 1979 proved to be disastrous for China's people, millions of whom died from famine. Liberal economic reforms began only in 1979, under the leadership of Deng Xiaoping. Thereafter, China's economy grew dramatically, achieving 10 per cent average growth rates for the next two decades. The prosperity of its people has also grown, although there are wide variations between the rural standard of living and that enjoyed by the new urban dwellers.

China's leadership seems committed to economic reforms and is keen to open up the country to market forces. An indication is record levels of FDI flowing into the country, mainly through joint ventures with partners from Western economies: over $100 billion in FDI flowed into the country from 2002 to 2003 (this is the subject of Case study 5.1). In China's five special economic zones, which are the powerhouses of the economy, foreign investors enjoy incentives, such as a 15 per cent rate of corporation tax, in comparison to the 33 per cent rate paid by domestic companies. China's admission to the World Trade Organization (WTO) has committed the leadership to opening up the economy. Domestic demand is fuelling much of this growth, coming from China's growing numbers of urban middle-class consumers. Yet there are doubts casting shadows over China's continued economic growth. Chinese industrial demand has led to rises in prices of raw materials in world markets and also rises in energy prices. Experts fear problems associated with overinvestment and overcontrol in an environment which still lacks many of the regulatory mechanisms of market economies. Starting from zero in 1979, China's economy is now about 40 per cent privately owned and the percentage is continuously rising. Between 1998 and 2001 alone, the number of private businesses increased from 90,000 to 2.3 million (Kynge and McGregor, 2002).

Minifile

THE CHINESE ECONOMY

GDP 2003 (millions): $6,435,838

GDP per head (at PPP): $4,995

GDP rate of growth 2002–3:   8 per cent

Key points:

1 Rapid economic growth driven by export-led manufacturing, in which foreign investors and joint ventures play key roles

2 Divide between prosperous coastal areas, where industrialization and urbanization are concentrated, and inland rural areas, where unemployment is high

3 Economic reform policies and market liberalization since the 1980s, but political authority remains controlled by Communist Party structures

4 Growing consumer society, making China a huge potential market for consumer goods and services, particularly since China's entry into the WTO has brought down trade barriers

Source: World Bank (2004) *World Development Indicators 2004* at http://www.worldbank.org.

China's state-owned sector is rapidly contracting: the number of state-owned industrial enterprises fell from 102,300 in 1989 to 42,900 in 2002 (Kynge and McGregor, 2002). However, state-owned industries, despite their inefficiencies and damage to the environment, are difficult to shut down because of concern over unemployment and possible social unrest. A worrying aspect of China's economic development has been its unevenness: the prosperous coastal areas differ markedly from the vast, less-developed inland areas. Attracting FDI throughout China and promoting the non-state sector will play crucial roles in providing new employment.

By contrast, Central and Eastern Europe present a group of transition economies in which economic and political transformations are proceeding hand in hand.

CRITICAL PERSPECTIVES

Chinese economic development

Certainly, China's impressively rapid industrialization and extraordinary rise as an exporter support the contention that China is 'another Japan' or even a 'super Japan.' However, this characterization of Chinese economic development must be qualified in certain ways. For example, although China's trade surplus with the United States of $40 to $50 billion annually is approximately the same as Japan's, such export success does not make China an economic superpower. China's economic success has been heavily dependent on its access to foreign capital and technology, as well as on its access to the American market. (Gilpin, 2000, p. 283)

■   In what other ways is China's economic development following a different path from that of Japan?

Transition economies in Central and Eastern Europe

The Soviet bloc started to break up in 1989. East Germany was united with West Germany in 1990. In the early 1990s, the states of Hungary, Poland, Czechoslovakia Romania and Bulgaria became sovereign states. Further fragmentation resulted in the creation of separate Czech and Slovak Republics, as well as the separate Balkan republics of Slovenia, Croatia, Bosnia and the Yugoslav Federation. The Soviet Union itself broke up into 15 separate republics. The three Baltic republics – Estonia, Latvia and Lithuania – went their own way. Russia, which had been the largest of the Soviet republics, adopted a new constitution in 1993, but its economic and political transition has been less successful than that in the more peripheral parts of the Soviet empire. It is important to remember that the former Soviet republics had experienced the socialist planned economy since 1928, whereas the states of central Europe and the Baltic states were 'sovietized' only in 1948, and thus had recent memories of real independence and a market economy (Bradshaw, 1996). These states were therefore better placed to make the transition to market economies.

Case study 4.4   IKEA branches out in Russia

IKEA, the Swedish furniture retailer, has seized the opportunities presented by the emerging market economies in Central and Eastern Europe, steadily opening new stores in the region following the fall of the Berlin Wall. While its store locations in Poland, the Czech Republic and Hungary were in the more stable and successful transition economies, its foray into Russia presented greater risks. The attempted radical economic and political reforms in Russia in the 1990s had been traumatic, culminating in financial crisis in 1998. Since then, rebuilding and economic development have gradually got back on track. The economy grew 7.3 per cent in 2003, bringing cumulative annual growth to 38 per cent since the 1998 crisis (see figure). This impressive performance owes much to Russia's oil and gas revenues, but the government's policies have been aimed at developing a more diversified economy, including telecommunications, construction and retailing, which are stimulating domestic demand.

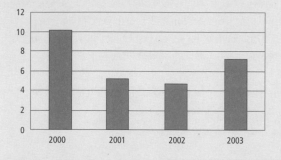

GDP growth in Russia
Source: Economist Intelligence Unit (2004) at http://www.economist.com.

When IKEA opened its second store in Moscow in 2001, it was inundated with 44,000 shoppers in just a few hours. While the company has prided itself on its classic Scandinavian-style furniture, it was overwhelmed with the response of the Moscow public. After all, Russians enjoy a far lower general standard of living than IKEA's typical middle-class customers – Russian GDP per capita was just $2,346, less than a tenth of that of Germany, its largest market, where it has 31 stores. IKEA has prided itself on its good design and low prices which the bulk of consumers could afford, but in Russia, surely only the elite could afford to shop there. IKEA's general director in Russia said: 'If we had relied on official statistics, we would never have believed that Russians would buy as much' (Brown-Humes, 17 May 2002). But consumer demand was growing and spending power was concentrated in Moscow, which, with a population of 10 million (approximately that of the Czech Republic) presented the opportunity for moving in ahead of other retailers.

Russia's economic transition, however, remains clouded by doubts about its long-term prospects. Market reforms are taking place, but the economy still suffers from corruption, lack of transparency and a weak legal system. Both foreign investors and Russian businesspeople have therefore been less than enthusiastic about investing in Russia. Flows of FDI were $1144m. in 2003 (UNCTAD, 2004), well below those of the Czech Republic. Moreover, extreme inequality and high levels of poverty remain. In an overall population of 144 million, 20 per cent are below the official poverty line of 50 per cent of median income. Worryingly, life expectancy actually went down in the 1990s: the probability of a Russian inhabitant not surviving to the age of 60 is 29 per cent, placing Russia alongside some of the world's poorest developing countries (UN, 2004). Sustained growth and stability offer some hope of improvement in the investment climate.

IKEA's business has been built on a philosophy based on the wish to improve the lives of ordinary people, including those who live in cramped conditions. For this reason, its founder says: 'I am much more eager to open stores in Russia than in Germany or the UK' (Brown-Humes, 12 August 2002). Accordingly, new stores in other Russian provinces are envisaged, as well as in Ukraine. The CEO says that, because IKEA is not a public company, it can afford to take a more long-term perspective (George, 28 September 2004). He also points to the benefits of becoming established in new markets before competitors move in: 'we believe very strongly that going early into these markets has some advantages ... One is that you can get hold of good locations at reasonable prices, and then international competition is not too heavy so you can establish brand recognition' (George, 28 September 2004).

Sources: Ostrovsky, 'Growth is strongest in nearly a century', *Financial Times*, 13 April 2004; Brown-Humes, 'Moscow crowds surprise retailer', *Financial Times*, 17 May 2002; Brown-Humes, C., 'The bolt that holds the IKEA empire together', *Financial Times*, 12 August 2002; George, N., 'IKEA continues to build on global success', *Financial Times*, 28 September 2004; United Nations (2004) *Human Development Report 2004* (Oxford: OUP); UNCTAD (2004) *World Investment Report 2004* (Geneva: UN).

Case questions

What were the reasons behind IKEA's expansion into Russia?
What are the risks and opportunities for doing business in Russia?

The transition process

A transition economy is one making the shift from one economic system to another, while 'reform' is a milder form of change, implying altering aspects of an existing system (Bradshaw, 1996). Reforms, such as limited privatization, had taken place to varying degrees throughout the Soviet empire in the 1980s, but they had not been sufficient to turn round these declining economies. The legacies of Communism left the newly created states with a host of problems which could not be wiped out overnight. All had weak economies which had been dependent on the Soviet Union. Their SOEs largely comprised out-of-date, inefficient heavy industries which polluted the environment. Like the Soviet Union, they produced insufficient consumer goods. The planned economy had fixed both prices and wages, leaving little scope for individual incentive. In Poland, the agricultural sector, which had been highly productive and a source of exports before the Second World War, deteriorated so badly under Communisim that food shortages led to riots in the early 1970s.

The conversion of a planned economy into a market economy can be carried out by 'shock therapy' or a gradualist approach. Shock therapy aims to set up market institutions in as short a time as possible, while gradualism involves dismantling Communism over a longer period of time. Shock therapy was the preferred approach in Poland, whereas Hungary adopted the more gradualist approach. Both countries had had recent experience of market economies. It is arguable that a combined approach could be the most effective: initial shock therapy, instituting irreversible institutional changes, followed by gradualist measures, such as piecemeal privatizations, to spread out the pain of laying off workers (Bradshaw, 1996). By contrast, shock therapy in Russia in 1992 was less successful, reflecting deep historical and cultural factors that have worked against a smooth transition.

SUMMARY POINTS

Transition economies of Central and Eastern Europe

● Privatization of former SOEs.

● Setting up of new legal and regulatory framework.

● Progress in overcoming problems of unemployment and inflation.

● Fragile democratic institutions.

● Increasing integration with Western European economic structures.

Whatever the pace of transition, four interrelated processes may be identified as keys to its success (Bradshaw, 1996). These are stabilization, liberalization, internationalization and privatization. We look at each in turn.

Stabilization

Inflation has been a major problem in Central and Eastern European economies. The lack of consumer goods available during Communist rule had resulted in a build-up of personal savings. When consumer goods became freely available, a boom in spending led to price rises, fuelling inflation. Controlling inflation required wage restraint and keeping the money supply under control. This was easier said than done, as demands on the state came from several directions at once: the unemployed, who were casualties of the new market forces; pensioners, whose savings had been wiped out; and agricultural workers who had grown dependent on subsidies. The Polish, Hungarian and Czech economies all declined in the early transitional period from 1989 to 1992, but their economies have recovered since then and unemployment and inflation have both gone down.

Liberalization

In the planned economy, wages and prices are determined by government. When state control was removed and prices were freed, the result was a price shock for consumers who were accustomed to paying prices for commodities which were less than world market levels. Price liberalization thus contributed to inflationary pressures. In the long term, there should be no place in a market economy for inefficient, uncompetitive state-run enterprises. However, in the shorter term, political pressures compelled governments to subsidize them, largely to keep unemployment under control. Liberalization was perceived as a threat to industrial and agricultural workers in particular. In Poland, for example, the movement to overthrow Soviet rule was led by the Solidarity trade union, supported by the Polish Catholic Church, both of which are still powerful and both of which are sceptical about liberal reform policies. Solidarity has been a key political player in coalition governments since the first free post-Communist elections in 1991.

International-ization

Crucial to the transition economies is their opening up to trade and investment. As privatization proceeds, the state withdraws from its direct role in trade, and takes on more of a regulatory role, as befits a market economy. The industries in post-Communist states were largely uncompetitive, and there has been political pressure to maintain a protectionist policy. Some feared that liberalization would open markets to a flood of imports, leading to a balance of payments crisis. As the 1990s progressed, however, liberalization has brought economic benefits. Trade and flows of FDI have grown, indicating the potential of these emerging markets and the perception that they have become politically stable. In the years leading up to EU accession, more than 70 per cent of the imports into the Czech Republic, Poland and Hungary were already coming from EU member states, while more than 60 per cent of their exports went to EU states. This economic integration was the strongest driving force behind EU accession.

Privatization

Privatization encompasses the conversion of state enterprises to privately owned and operated companies, and also the fostering of new start-up enterprises. SMEs were some of the earliest and easiest to privatize, as they could be taken over by their managers and workers. Medium and large-scale enterprises have been more difficult to privatize. They could be sold to their own managers, but those in the strongest position were the former Communists, and public opinion was hostile to the thought that these individuals would be the chief beneficiaries of privatization. Sales to foreign buyers also risked hostile public opinion. The 'leveraged' buy-out (LBO) by workers (financed by government loan) was a favoured method. The large-scale enterprises have been the most difficult and politically sensitive to privatize. Two methods have been to sell them or allow them to be taken over by joint ventures, bringing in a foreign investor, usually one based in a Western European country.

CRITICAL PERSPECTIVES

Post-Communist transition in Central and Eastern Europe

Eastern European governments may rightfully prefer the dynamism (and possibly disorder) of markets to the stagnation of central planning. It is only by adequate institutional design that markets deliver an acceptable mix between short-run efficiency, long-run innovation and a minimal degree of social justice. The need for Eastern Europe to invent new rules of the game and institutions along with markets is more and more recognized by experts. (Boyer, 1996, p. 108)

■   In which countries in the region has institutional design contributed positively to economic transition, and in which has the possible disorder of markets been more in evidence?

Impact of EU enlargement on European economies

Wide divergence exists among Central and Eastern European states, as well as between these states and the EU's 15 member states prior to the enlargement of 2004 (referred to here as the 'EU 15', they are Belgium, Germany, France, Denmark, Ireland, Italy, Luxembourg, the Netherlands, the UK, Austria, Greece, Portugal, Spain, Finland and Sweden). The EU sets three criteria for new members, as defined in the Copenhagen European Council (June 1993):

- The stability of democracy and institutional establishment of the rule of law and respect for human rights
- Functioning market economy, with mechanisms for coping with competitive pressure and market forces within the EU
- Adoption and application of the EU's existing rules and policies

The majority of the 10 new members are in Central Europe. The states of Poland, the Czech Republic, Hungary, Slovenia and the Slovak Republic were well on the way to building market economies and democratic systems. These countries were joined by the Baltic states of Estonia, Latvia and Lithuania, in the surge for EU membership. Finally, Malta and Cyprus became the last two countries for 2004 accession. It was hoped that accession of Cyprus would give impetus to reunification of the island, where the northern sector is Turkish controlled, but a reunification plan was rejected in 2003.

While democratic and market reforms had been progressing in the Central European states in the years following the fall of the Berlin Wall, the final criterion presented a considerable hurdle for government authorities in the aspiring states. Moreover, the road to accession was paved with intense negotiation between old and new members on a number of sensitive issues, including the EU budget, immigration and new governing structures of the EU's institutions. Constitutional and governance arrangements will be examined in Chapter 8, while this section focuses on economic issues.

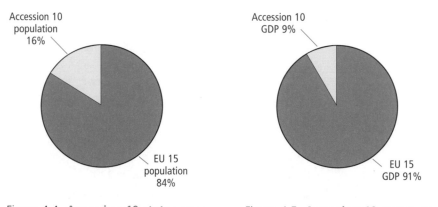

Figure 4.4 **Accession 10 states as a percentage of the European Union's population** (total = 453,900,000)
Source of data: World Bank (2004) *World Development Indicators 2004* at http://www.worldbank.org.

Figure 4.5 **Accession 10 states as a percentage of European Union GDP**
Source of data: World Bank (2004) *World Development Indicators 2004* at http://www.worldbank.org.

The new members add 74 million people to the EU's population, making up 16 per cent of the overall EU population, which now stands at about 454 million (see Figure 4.4.) The economies of the accession countries are generally poorer than the EU 15, as Figure 4.5 shows and their combined GDP forms less than 10 per cent of the EU total. As part of their entry arrangements, these nations were keen to secure advantageous terms for funding, particularly in light of their development needs. At the same time, poor regions in the EU 15, such as parts of Ireland and Portugal, feared that they would lose out, as funding priorities would shift to the poorer regions in the new member states. For these transition economies, major hurdles have been inflation, unemployment and the urgent need to modernize industries and infrastructure. Privatization and the opening of markets to competition have brought greater integration with Western European economies. As low-cost economies, they have attracted foreign investment, much of it from the more advanced EU 15 countries. (This is highlighted in Case study 5.2 on the Czech Republic.) As can be seen from Table 4.2, GDP per capita in the accession countries is well below that of the EU 15 countries. An effect of opening borders would be the possible migration of workers into the nearby EU 15 countries. As a consequence, a transition period of seven years was eventually agreed for opening borders, to allow controls on migration to be lifted gradually.

Table 4.2 Economic profiles of the European Union's 10 new member states acceding in 2004

Country	Population (millions) 2003	GDP per head (at PPP) 2003	Percentage of average GDP per head of EU 15	Unemployment (percentage) March 2004
Czech Republic	10.2	$16,448	62	8.4
Hungary	10.1	$15,870	60	6.0
Poland	38.2	$11,622	44	19.0
Slovenia	2.00	$19,330	73	6.5
Slovak Republic	5.40	$13,468	50	16.5
Estonia	1.40	$13,384	50	9.3
Lithuania	3.5	$11,250	42	11.5
Latvia	2.3	$9,981	38	10.7
Cyprus	0.8	$17,962	68	4.7
Malta	0.4	$17,716	67	9.0

Sources: World Bank (2004) *World Development Indicators 2004* at http://www.worldbank.org; Eurostat (2004) Eurostat news release, May 2004.

Agriculture has been one of the most difficult and sensitive issues on which agreement has had to be reached. As Figure 4.6 shows, agricultural employment is relatively high in the Central and Eastern European economies, where farm subsidies were the norm. Within the EU, states become part of the common agricultural policy (CAP). Of the new entrants, Poland in particular was concerned that rural inhabitants would get a poor deal when existing subsidies are phased out and CAP arrangements take their place. The arrangement reached provided that CAP funding for Poland's farmers would be phased in over a 10-year period, while EU rural development funding would be provided, to lessen the effects of perceived disadvantages in the transition period.

Prospects for further enlargement of the EU have now turned further afield, to other post-Communist economies of Eastern Europe and Turkey. The four countries whose admission is actively being considered are Croatia, Bulgaria, Romania and Turkey. The last three of these are poorer than the 10 countries which entered in 2004, as Table 4.3 indicates. Romania and Turkey have large populations, and their economies are over one-third agricultural (see Figure 4.6). The four countries have an aggregate population of over 105 million, which is more than 25 million more people than the total population of the 10 accession countries of 2004. Their plentiful supply of labour and low labour costs are therefore attracting foreign investors.

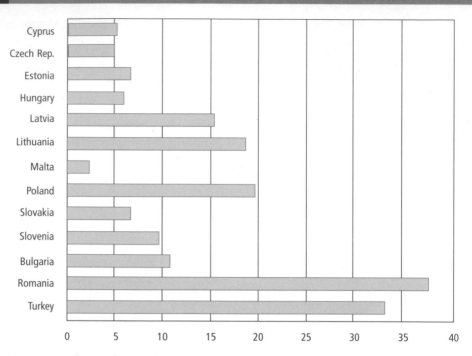

Figure 4.6 **Share of agriculture as a percentage of employment in 10 new EU member and 3 applicant countries (Bulgaria, Romania and Turkey)**

Source: European Commission (2003), *Continuing Enlargement Strategy Paper*, COM(2003)676 at http://europa.eu.int/scadplus.

Table 4.3 **Economic indicators for selected transition economies in the wider Europe**

Country	Population (millions) 2003	GDP per head, 2003 (at PPP)	Percentage of average GDP per head of EU 15
Bulgaria	8	$6,749	30
Croatia	4.4	$11,139	42
Romania	22.2	$7,221	27
Turkey	70.7	$6,749	25

Source: World Bank (2004) *World Development Indicators 2004* at http://www.worldbank.org.

Divergence and regionalization

Starting with the capitalist model of a market economy, we have seen a number of different interpretations evolve in different contexts. Greater integration between economies is taking place, particularly within the enlarged EU, but this is not to say that there is a clear picture emerging of a 'global model' of capitalism. Diversity has been especially obvious in two areas: the involvement of the state in the economy, and corporate ownership and control. State guidance of business is more active in some economies than in others. Corporate governance is more market-oriented towards shareholder value in the Anglo-American models than in either the Asian or the social-market models of Europe. However, there is also considerable divergence within each region, as national development paths within any region can differ considerably, despite sociocultural similarities between countries.

Nonetheless, regionalization has been taking place throughout the world. By regionalization, we mean growing economic links and cooperation within a geographic region, both on the part of businesses and governments. Countries within an indentifiable geographic area may have shared historical experiences, such as the need for Western European countries to rebuild after the Second World War. The end of the cold war, dominated as it was by the two power blocs, has seen the emergence of regional cooperation and integration. The trend is more advanced in some regions than in others: the EU is much more advanced than either the North America Free Trade Agreement (NAFTA) or the Asean Free Trade Area.

The EU is the most deeply integrated region. The extent to which it provides the basis of a definable regional capitalism is much debated. As has been seen, liberalization of the social market model is proceeding, with more opening of markets and greater labour flexibility. However, there is not as yet a consensus on the philosophy of the new European capitalism. For governments, the twin needs to attract transnational capital and compete in international markets are uppermost. On the other hand, many perceive an erosion of social protection and problems of growing inequalities, while others object to the giving up of monetary sovereignty. There remain national identities and interests, complicated by enlargement, which have entailed new European institutional arrangements (see Chapter 8). Moreover, at the corporate level, there is divergence on issues of corporate governance. The potential for conflict between shareholder interests and those of broader stakeholder groups adds to the complexities facing businesses with pan-European operations.

Conclusions

1   Economic systems range from the planned economy to capitalism, reflecting society's values regarding production and the accumulation of wealth.

2   Capitalism rests on three essential principles: free enterprise, competition and private property. While the US and UK have historically come closest to the laissez-faire model, state intervention and welfare state measures have become a feature of modern capitalist systems generally.

3   Economic concentration in the form of monopolies and cartels creates imperfect competition, and most states have antitrust and anti-competitive practices legislation for their control.

4   Social market capitalism, as exemplified by France and Germany, has relied on greater state ownership and more extensive social welfare programmes. The current trend in these systems, however, is towards liberalization of markets.

5   Asian capitalist models, including Japan, have also relied on strong state guidance. The Asian model, however, is underpinned with Confucian values of the strong family and the company itself as family.

6   The planned economy as a system is giving way to market forces, as exemplified by China, where privatization and foreign investment are rapidly transforming the economy.

7   While they have struggled to overcome the problems of restructuring outdated industries, the post-Communist transitional economies of Central and Eastern Europe have become increasingly integrated with advanced Western economies.

8   Economic integration between national economies has been facilitated by liberalization measures. At the same time, regionalization, most advanced in the EU, is becoming an increasingly important force in international business.

Review questions

1   What are the distinguishing characteristics of capitalism as an economic system?

2   Why are monopoly and oligopoly considered to be 'market imperfections'?

3   What is 'competition policy' and what role does it play in market economies?

4   Which countries are considered strongholds of the social market model of capitalism, and how are their economies evolving at present?

5   What are the specific strengths of the Asian model of capitalism? In the case of Japan, how did these strengths seem to translate into weaknesses in the 1990s?

6   What are the elements of the transition process towards a market economy in (a) China; and (b) the transition economies of Central and Eastern Europe?

7   What are the forces behind the growth in regionalization? How does the economic profile of the enlarged EU in 2004 differ from that of the EU 15?

Assignments

1   To what extent has the evolution of the capitalist market economy displayed divergence along regional lines?

2   Assess the ways in which opportunities and threats are emerging for businesses operating in the newly enlarged EU of 2004, giving specific examples.

Further reading

Amable, B. (2003) *The Diversity of Modern Capitalism* (Oxford: Oxford University Press).

Coates, D. (1999) *Models of Capitalism* (Cambridge: Polity Press).

Cook, M. and Farquharson, C. (1998) *Business Economics* (London: Pitman Publishing).

Gros, D. and Steinherr, A. (2004) *Economic Transition in Central and Eastern Europe: Planting the Seeds* (Cambridge: Cambridge University Press).

Hall, P. and Soskice, D. (2001) *Varieties of Capitalism: The Institutional Foundations of Comparative Advantage* (Oxford: Oxford University Press).

Landes, D. (1998) *The Wealth and Poverty of Nations* (London: W.W. Norton & Co.).

Mattli, W. (1999) *The Logic of Regional Integration: Europe and Beyond* (Cambridge: Cambridge University Press).

Schnitzer, M. (2000) *Comparative Economic Systems*, 8th edn (Cincinnati: South-Western Publishing).

Whitley, R. (1999) *Divergent Capitalisms* (Oxford: Oxford University Press).

END OF PART 1 CASE STUDY

A bright future for Coca-Cola?

Coca-Cola is one of the world's most widely recognized brands. The company even claims that Coke is the second most understood word on the planet after OK. Its most famous drink, 'classic' Coke, goes back over a hundred years, its image evoking the American lifestyle perhaps more strongly than any other product. The company expanded from its American roots following the Second World War, when 64 bottling plants, which were built round the world to supply US troops, became the infrastructure on which a global empire was built. A boom in sales followed, turning Coca-Cola into the world's most successful global brand. Its success was epitomized by a memorable advertisement in 1971, featuring a group of 500 young people, each holding a bottle of Coke, singing, 'I'd like to buy the world a Coke,' on a hilltop in Italy.

The classic carbonated soft drink is made up of carbonated water with added sugar and flavours. It is high in calories, low in nutrients and its caffeine content is significant, about half that of coffee. Nutritionists have long been concerned that soft drinks have replaced milk in the diets of many American children (Nestle, 2002). Between 1970 and 1997, the production of carbonated soft drinks in the US market increased from 22 to 41 gallons per person per year – providing every American adult, child and infant with 1.2 12-ounce soft drinks per day. Most notable was the increase in intake by children: from the early to mid-1990s, children aged 2–17 increased their daily soft drink intake from 7 ounces to 10 ounces. Coca-Cola, which enjoyed 44 per cent of the American market, was successful in negotiating lucrative 'pouring rights' contracts with school districts across America. These gave it exclusive rights to place vending machines in schools, usually for a 5- or 10-year period. They also provided much-needed funding for schools, which could be spent on books, computers, sports facilities and other needs that had been squeezed

in tight school budgets. School administrators received lump sums immediately, followed by further sums linked to sales. These contracts came in for criticism, however, on ethical and health grounds. Exposure to the single brand was designed to build brand loyalty for a generation of consumers who had a lifetime of drinking soft drinks ahead of them. From the health point of view, they encouraged consumption of sugar-based soft drinks, which, critics pointed out, contributed to cultivating unhealthy eating habits in children. Moreover, administrators were in the position of encouraging soft drink purchases in order to raise more money for the school. Other soft drink companies, perhaps expectedly, also objected to the pouring contracts as a restriction on their right to trade. Coca-Cola announced in 2001 that it would no longer require exclusivity in these contracts, and that the effect on sales would be minimal because school contracts accounted for only 1 per cent of its annual revenue. However, the health issues were indicative of changing consumer sentiment.

By the end of the 1990s, home sales were flagging and the future looked less bright for Coca-Cola. It has expanded internationally, selling 160 brands of soft drinks in 200 countries by 1999, but expansion in overseas markets was affected by the Asian financial crisis of 1997, followed by a general economic downturn. From 1999 to 2004 the share price fell 28 per cent, while that of its rival, PepsiCo, rose 74 per cent. Changing world markets and little scope for growth in carbonated soft drinks in its American heartland raised questions about the direction of the company and how it is run.

Today's consumers: what are they looking for?

Coca-Cola's strength has been in the carbonated soft drinks market, served by its flagship brand, Coke, and promoted by global advertising campaigns. This 'Coke-centric' strategy was slow to recognize the growing popularity of other drinks such as bottled water, fruit juices and sports drinks. Their popularity owes much to the perceptions of consumers that they were healthier and more beneficial than carbonated soft drinks. Coca-Cola has had success with Diet Coke, mainly in the US market, but rivals in the beverages industry were offering a broader range of products to appeal to health-conscious consumers long before Coca-Cola woke up to changing tastes. PepsiCo, for example, offered Gatorade, the sports drink, and Tropicana fruit juices, whose markets grew rapidly. As the first figure shows, in 1998, Coca-Cola had neither a bottled water nor a sports drink.

In 2000, Coke's CEO attempted to buy Quaker Oats, which owned the Gatorade brand, announcing that the company needed to become an 'all-beverage' company, but this proposal was vetoed by the board and Quaker Oats was bought by PepsiCo. PepsiCo had built up a snacks business by this time, having bought Frito-Lay, and the acquisition of Quaker's popular snack foods bolstered PepsiCo's position. By 2003, Coca-Cola's position had improved, as the second figure shows, having successfully launched a bottled water, Dasani, and a sports drink, Powerade. However, in 2004, non-carbonated beverages still accounted for only about 17 per cent of Coca-Cola's global volume, while Coke-branded drinks still make up 56 per cent of the company's total volume. The development of 'mid-calorie' colas, by both Coca-Cola and PepsiCo, is designed to attract the health-conscious consumer who prefers a cola drink. The planned launch in Europe of Dasani, a purified tap water, had to be postponed indefinitely following the discovery that the water contained illegal levels of bromate, a chemical that could increase the risk of cancer. This costly debacle echoed an earlier contamination scare and recall of Coke in Europe in 1999. The company later admitted that it had not managed this incident well, having first denied there was a problem. This setback was partly responsible for the departure of Chairman and

CEO Douglas Ivester in 1999, to be replaced by Douglas Daft. At the time, Daft had been leading the push into Asian markets, where future growth seemed to lie.

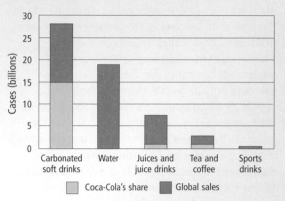

The global soft drinks industry by volume, 1998

Source: *Financial Times*, 10 March 2004.

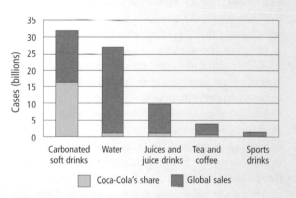

The global soft drinks industry by volume, 2003

Source: *Financial Times*, 10 March 2004.

Looking east for growth

A radical restructuring of the company took place under Daft. It had become overcentralized and slow to react to consumers. Decisions on local marketing, local communications and even which local charity to support had been taken in Atlanta, the corporate HQ. Coca-Cola's image had suffered as a result of the contamination scare. There were clashes with antitrust regulators in

Europe and Chile, which also damaged the company's reputation and its share price. Coca-Cola undertook a radical rethinking of its organization and its strategy. The company laid off 6000 workers (21 per cent of the workforce) in its Atlanta headquarters, giving more power to local managers. This strategy has been called a 'multilocal' strategy, more in keeping with the company's changing markets, as 70 per cent of sales are outside North America (see figure opposite). Local managers are now able to devise their own marketing strategies and choose the products from the Coke portfolio that are best suited to local tastes. Daft said: 'we do not do business in markets; we do business in societies ... In our recent past, we succeeded because we understood and appealed to global commonalities. In our future, we'll succeed because we will also understand an appeal to local differences. The 21st century demands nothing less' (Daft, *Financial Times*, 27 March, 2000). In particular, Daft played down Coca-Cola's American image, recognizing that the Coke brand attracts hostility in much of the world.

China and India have presented the largest potential markets, but also the greatest challenges in designing products to suit consumers and overcoming logistical problems. Coke now has a 50 per cent share of the carbonated drinks market in China's large cities, but reaching the rural areas, which are home to most of the population, has been a challenge. The design of the single-serving returnable glass bottle at an affordable price has been key to this market, as well as the Indian market, which presents similar problems. Here Coca-Cola reduced the size of bottles and packed them in smaller crates, making them easier for trucks to distribute to the outlets in rural India, which now number about a million. It benchmarked the price at an affordable Rs5, half the price of a conventional bottle. In addition, the Indian management ditched the company's global advertising campaign in favour of one featuring film stars from the Bombay film industry, known as 'Bollywood'. The advertising campaign also boasted of the Rs5 price, deterring retailers from overcharging. Coca-Cola's operations chief in

India has said: 'We were just not addressing the masses, and that was the problem' (Merchant, *Financial Times*, 18 June 2003).

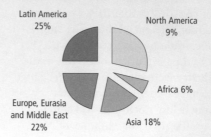

Coca-Cola's worldwide unit case volume
Source: *Coca-Cola Annual Report* 2003.

Uncertainty at the top

There were more job cuts in both North America and overseas locations in 2003, as Coca-Cola attempted to trim costs. A former employee filed lawsuits against the company, alleging misconduct, and federal authorities launched investigations into possible marketing malpractice. After five years at the helm, Douglas Daft announced his retirement in 2004, but there was no obvious successor, and the board launched a worldwide search for a new CEO, assisted by a firm of headhunters. To observers of the company, this situation seemed strange, as they expected succession issues to be resolved out of the glare of publicity. Coca-Cola's board is dominated by long-standing members with links to the company, akin to an 'old boys' club'. Particularly influential is its main shareholder, Warren Buffet, who owns 8.2 per cent of the shares. Shareholders at the company's AGM in 2004 expressed concern over the highly public selection process and also called for the roles of chairman and chief executive to be split, in accordance with best corporate governance practice. In terms of strategy, analysts question whether the board possibly needs reinvigorating. One analyst has said: 'This company is trying to adapt to a new era and look who's sitting on the board – successful older men in their seventies in charge of a company selling soda pop to teenagers' (Liu, 10 March 2004). They opted not for an outsider as the new CEO, but to bring back a former Coca-Cola executive, Neville Isdell, who had served the company for 38 years. He became the third CEO in seven years, and, as with his predecessors, expectations are that he will restore Coca-Cola's competitive position in global markets. However, as research suggests, the advent of a new CEO may be of more symbolic than real significance (Wiersema, 2002). It is the company's strategies and policies, many of which have evolved over a long period, that are the key to its future success in the changing environment. The challenge facing Coca-Cola is to adapt to changing consumer tastes in its many diverse markets, while maintaining financial performance which keeps shareholders happy.

Sources: Daft, D., 'Back to classic Coke,' *Financial Times*, 27 March 2000; Tomkins, R., 'Global chief thinks locally,' *Financial Times*, 1 August 2000; States, A., 'Message in a bottle,' *Financial Times Business*, 13 January, 2001; Liu, B., 'The Coca-Cola challenge: Douglas Daft's impending departure creates leadership doubts at the drinks giant', *Financial Times*, 10 March 2004; Merchant, K. 'Coca-Cola finds formula for India' *Financial Times*, 18 June 2003; McGregor, R., 'Coke explores the Chinese countryside' *Financial Times*, 26 February 2004; Buckley, N. 'Coke investors speak out', *Financial Times*, 22 April 2004; Wiersema, M. (2002) 'Holes at the top: Why CEO firings backfire' *Harvard Business Review*, **80**(12), pp. 70–7; Nestle, M. (2002) *Food Politics* (Berkeley: University of California Press).

End of Part 1 case questions

1 **What global changes are taking place in consumer markets for beverages?**

2 **How is Coca-Cola adapting to changing markets? If you were the new CEO at Coca-Cola, what recommendations would you make?**

3 **How is Coca-Cola's corporate governance criticized? What changes should be introduced?**

4 **What are the prospects for Coke as a global brand in future, and for global brands in general?**

Part 2

Dimensions of the International Environment

5   The global economy and globalization processes 137

6   The cultural environment: diversity and globalization 167

7   Society and business 204

8   The changing political environment: national, regional and international forces 234

9   The international legal environment of business: moving towards harmonization 275

End of Part 2 case study 307

Part 2 introduces and explores the two main themes of this book – globalization and national diversity. Chapter 5 defines globalization processes and looks at their impact on businesses, national economies and societies. These processes focus particularly on the transnational company (TNC) and foreign direct investment (FDI). Case studies illustrate the transformational aspects of FDI in specific national environments. Dimensions of the international environment are then discussed in greater depth in the four chapters which follow. In Chapter 6, on the cultural environment, we look at the key elements of culture, including language, religion and behaviour norms, that form the foundations of differences between societies. These values and norms influence the social institutions, political systems and legal frameworks which develop in different national environments. This cultural backdrop also influences a country's business organizations, including their structures, goals and international perspectives.

Society and business is the broad theme of Chapter 7, highlighting issues of demographic change, immigration, urbanization and changing family structures. While these are, in a sense, 'global' issues, they are also profoundly local: their impacts differ from society to society, presenting businesses with strategic challenges. Another challenge for businesses is the changing political environment (Chapter 8), which, in many instances, has facilitated market developments, but has also presented risks and instability. Indeed, the opportunities of opening markets have often emerged in unstable political climates. While we attempt to define specific political risks, we also attempt to take a long perspective on political changes in different societies – and on international relations between nations – to gain a greater understanding of underlying trends. Closely linked to political systems is the legal framework, which is the subject of Chapter 9. Here we see the variety of national legal systems in their regulation of business activities, and also growing interconnectedness of legal relations across national boundaries. This last topic recalls the theme of globalization, with which Part 2 began. The case study on Fiat which concludes this part highlights the various themes which have emerged, focusing on a tussle between national business culture and forces of globalization. The case study, therefore, also provides a prelude for Part 3, Global Forces.

5 The global economy and globalization processes

Outline of chapter

- Introduction
- Globalization
- Internationalization versus globalization: the role of FDI
- Transnational or multinational corporations
- The growth of TNCs as drivers of the global economy
- International business in the context of postwar shifts in international power
- Trends in globalization processes
- Globalization of the firm
- Industrial production: the legacy of Fordism
- Post-Fordist organizations
- Organizational changes and TNCs
- Global and local markets
- Transnationality of the firm
- The globalization debate
- Conclusions

Learning objectives

1. To gain an overview of the processes of globalization.
2. To appreciate the role played by transnational corporations in globalization processes.
3. To understand the changes in organizations and their strategies in global and local environments.
4. To gain a broad appreciation of the issues facing companies and societies generally in the changing global economy.

Introduction

The second half of the twentieth century saw processes of globalization impacting on people's lives across the world: from cosmopolitan urban centres to rural outposts; from advanced industrial complexes to craft workshops. Increasing interconnectedness and interdependence between people, organizations and governments has been facilitated by improvements in technology, especially in the spheres of communication and transport. Yet, while all would agree that the global economy is a reality, the extent of its reach and the depth of its penetration into social and economic life present different configurations in different parts of the world.

This chapter takes a broad overview of the world economy. It aims, first, to examine the forces of globalization in perspective, and, secondly, to assess changes that are taking place in the context of international business. Focus will inevitably fall on multinational corporations (MNCs), which have been the driving force behind globalization. Their global strategies, centred on overseas production, have been key factors in the interrelationships we now see between economic, political, social, cultural and technological environments in the global economy. This overview outlines the broad contours of these relationships, to be followed by more specific analysis of these environmental dimensions in succeeding chapters.

Globalization

'Globalization' is not a single, all-encompassing process sweeping the globe. The term more accurately describes a number of processes by which products, people, companies, money and information are able to move freely and quickly around the world, unimpeded by national borders or other territorial limitations. The pace and impact of change may differ from one sphere of activity to another. The use of the term began only in the 1960s and gained common currency only in the 1980s (Waters, 2001, p. 2). Globalization has brought about dramatic changes in the ways in which people live and work, opening up new opportunities but also creating new risks and uncertainties from forces which seem remote and unfathomable. A consumer in Europe may be affected by upheaval in the financial markets in Asia. A worker in an Asian factory may lose his or her job as a result of a decision taken in a company boardroom in Michigan. The worldwide repercussions of the Asian financial crisis of 1997 brought home to many the interconnectedness of financial markets, which has been one of the most spectacular examples of the effects of globalization. Interpretation of these trends, their impact on local communities and ultimate benefits or detriments are issues of extensive debate. Some commentators see the emergence of an era of the borderless global marketplace. This extreme view has been called *hyperglobalization* (Gray, 1998). While not subscribing to it himself, Gray summarizes this school of thought, which:

> envisions the global economy as inhabited by powerless nation-states and homeless corporations. As the powers of sovereign states wither, those of multinational corporations wax.

As national cultures become little more than consumer preferences, so companies become ever more cosmopolitan in their corporate cultures. (Gray, 1998, p. 67)

Table 5.1 Globalization: two schools of thought

	Hyperglobalists	Transformationalists
What's new?	A global age	Historically unprecedented levels of global interconnectedness
Dominant features	Global capitalism; global governance; global civil society	'Thick' (intensive and extensive) globalization
Power of national governments	Declining or eroding	Reconstituted, restructured
Conceptualization of globalization	As a reordering of the framework of human action	As a reordering of inter-regional relations and action at a distance
Historical trajectory	Global civilization	Indeterminate: global integration and fragmentation

Source: Adapted from Held, D., McGrew, A., Goldblatt, D. and Perraton, J. (1999) *Global Transformations: Politics, Economics and Culture* (Cambridge: Polity Press), p. 10.

In contrast to the hyperglobalization view, there is the less extreme *transformational* view, described by Held, as shown in Table 5.1. This view acknowledges globalization as a driving force reshaping modern societies, but takes a more tentative stance on its outcomes, which are transforming the economic, social and political environments in which we live. In this changing global order, shifting patterns are emerging in the functions and powers of companies and governments and through the emergence of other important forces, such as regionalism. It is argued that, as we live in a constantly changing environment, outcomes are uncertain and predictions of a world system are premature. This more cautious approach looks at globalization as a complex set of processes, often uneven, rather than a linear progression. It stresses that, while economic globalization has accelerated, local differences, often with deep social and cultural roots, have revealed underlying tensions in the international business environment. Its historical trajectory, shown in the last column of Table 5.1, may be characterized by both deepening integration *and* fragmentation. As the transformational view takes account of the underlying complexity of globalization processes, it has come to be widely recognized as a more valid approach than the hyperglobalization school of thought.

WEB ALERT!

The International Monetary Fund (IMF) offers data and analysis on a number of topics at http://www.imf.org. Included is the World Economic Outlook

The International Forum on Globalization is at http://www.ifg.org. There are many links to other organizations dealing with different dimensions of globalization

The World Bank also offers data and analysis of global economic prospects at http://www.worldbank.org

Internationalization vs. globalization: the role of FDI

In a sense, economic globalization has been happening for centuries. International trade was economically important long before industrialization transformed production methods and before modern technology transformed transport. Wealth generated by companies through international trade could be seen as contributing to the wealth of national economies of sovereign states (Hirst and Thompson, 1999). The growth of international trade relations, greatly enhanced by industrialization and improvements in transport in the late nineteenth century, has been described as a process of **internationalization** (Dicken, 2003). Production, companies and industry were still essentially based in national economies. National economies were to a considerable degree autonomous and economic policy issues, such as the imposition of tariffs, were matters for national governments to decide. Growth in world trade was a hallmark of internationalization in the period before 1914. The world before the First World War could accurately be described as a global market, reflecting flourishing international flows of goods, services, capital and people. However, the depth of economic integration has been described as 'shallow', characterized by arm's-length transactions between independent companies based in national economies (Dicken, 2003, p. 10). **Globalization**, by contrast, represents deeper integration, in that international interactions become qualitatively transformed from exchange transactions to long-term, multidimensional links.

At the heart of this deeper integration is **foreign direct investment (FDI)**. Companies may decide to invest in foreign firms in a number of ways. A *foreign portfolio investment* consists of buying shares (equity), usually under 10 per cent, in the foreign company as an investment only, with a view to relatively short-term gains. By contrast, the FDI investor aims to play a more direct role, with deeper involvement in the management of the company as a productive unit. That control can come through sufficient ownership of the foreign company's equity to give control (usually 30 per cent or more), or contractual, non-equity agreements that give control of the foreign affiliate company. These links, both equity and other alliances, affect both the *home* country (that of the investor) and the *host* country (that of the company invested in).

The growth in FDI has had a pervasive impact on international business. No longer could it be said that a company, its factories and the products it manufactures are necessarily the products of its home nation. Such is the geographical dispersal of production, that a 'German' car may actually be manufactured in South Carolina and a 'Japanese' car in the UK. If the majority of the parts that go into a car assembled at the Nissan plant in the UK are British, it would be logical to think of the car as British. Yet the company – and many of the companies supplying its components – is Japanese. With the acquisition by Renault, the French car manufacturer, of a 36.8 per cent share in Nissan in 1999, control effectively passed to Renault, reducing the influence of Japanese managers in Nissan. While consumers might still think in terms of 'Japanese' cars or 'German' cars as having distinctive national characteristics, the concept of national origin of many complex products such as motor vehicles would seem to have ceased to contain any real meaning in the global economy (Reich, 1991).

SUMMARY
POINTS

Internationalization versus globalization

- **Internationalization processes:** extensions of economic activities across national borders, growing *quantitatively*.
- **Globalization processes:** both geographical extensions of economic activity (as in internationalization) and the *qualitatively* different functional integration of internationally dispersed activities.

Source: Dicken, P. (2003) *Global Shift: Reshaping the Global Economic Map in the 21st Century*, 4th edn (London: Sage Publications.), p. 12.

CRITICAL PERSPECTIVES

Globalization

Globalization of industries decouples the firm from the factor endowment of a single nation. Raw materials, components, machinery, and many services are available globally on comparable terms. Transportation improvements have lowered the cost of exchanging factors or factor dependent goods among nations. Having a local steel industry, for example, is no longer an advantage in buying steel. It may well be a disadvantage if there are national policies or pressures that promote purchasing from high-cost domestic suppliers. (Porter, 1998b, pp. 14–15)

Think of some domestic industries with which you are familiar. What has been the effect of globalization, as described by Porter?

Transnational or multinational corporations

While 'multinational' suggests a very large, multidivisional company, the **transnational corporation (TNC)**, has been defined as 'a firm which has the power to coordinate and control operations in more than one country, even if it does not own them' (Dicken, 2003, p. 198). This definition emphasizes that scope, rather than sheer size, is critical. Dicken (2003, p. 198) highlights three characteristics of the TNC:

- its coordination and control of various stages of individual production chains within and between different countries
- its potential ability to take advantage of geographical differences in the distribution of factors of production (such as natural resources, capital, labour) and in state policies (such as taxes, trade barriers, subsidies and so on)
- its potential geographical flexibility – an ability to switch and reswitch its sources and operations between locations at an international level.

The growth of TNCs has coincided with industrialization and expansion of trade from the early nineteenth century to the present. TNCs now control a third of world output and about two-thirds of world trade. TNCs vary considerably in size and organizational structures. Advances in IT and communications have made it possible for SMEs to 'go global'. In Europe, about a third of all SMEs reported increased international business activity from 1996–2002 (OECD, 2002). Small and large firms alike have found that they must seek investment opportunities overseas to remain competitive. As a result, the number of TNCs has increased enormously: from the end of the 1960s to the end of the 1990s, the number of TNCs in the 15 most important developed countries had increased from 7000 to 40,000 (United Nations, 1999a). This growth reflects the growth in FDI worldwide.

Most TNCs start life as national companies and expand through internationalizing their operations. They may have a range of motives for doing so, depending on the advantages they hope to gain and the requirements of their particular industry. Proximity to natural resources may be paramount for extraction industries such as mining and oil. For manufacturing industries, availability of abundant low-cost labour may be paramount. This factor is paramount in flows of FDI to China, as Case Study 5.1 indicates. For many TNCs, the decision to locate in a particular country is guided by the existence of local and regional markets. The particular location can thus become an 'export platform'. Indeed, TNCs may acquire local companies to speed up the process of entering new markets. The TNC which has fashioned a global corporate strategy may thus divide operations between locations, depending on the particular advantages of each. The economic, political and cultural environment also play important roles. Government incentives to overseas investors can enhance the attractiveness of a location. FDI flows to Mexico, for example, increased steadily throughout the 1990s due to the availability of low-cost labour, proximity to the large American market and the incentives offered to foreign investors. However, they fell by nearly half from 2001 to 2002, largely because of the availability of cheaper labour elsewhere, particularly in China. Mexico has moved from labour-intensive manufacturing to more advanced manufacturing, reliant on IT and increased R&D capacity (United Nations, 2003, p. 59). However, as Case study 5.1 shows, China is also developing such capacities, highlighting the factors at work in corporate strategists' decisions regarding the location of their operations.

Case study 5.1   FDI bonanza in China

China has become the new workshop of the world, its factories churning out consumer goods for both domestic consumption and export. Its own growing middle class is a huge market in itself, but more important are growing export markets, in which Chinese production costs undercut virtually all rival locations.

Inflows of FDI reached a record $52.7bn. in 2002, followed by $53.5bn. in 2003. This has been a key factor in China's success and low-cost labour has been the chief attraction for foreign investors. The opening of the economy began in 1979, when China's Communist Party rulers introduced economic liberalization policies which were to gradually reduce state ownership and control. These reforms paved the way for outside investors to enter China through joint ventures with local companies. Foreign ownership restrictions have been further relaxed in recent years, and, combined with WTO membership in 2002, China's attraction for foreign investors has continued to rise. As the figure shows, inward FDI stock has rapidly risen from virtually nil in 1980 to 35.6 per cent of GDP in 2003. Labour costs have risen in other Southeast Asian economies, including Taiwan and South Korea, and these economies have consequently lost out to China as a manufacturing location, where the cost of unskilled labour undercuts all but Indonesia, Vietnam and Cambodia.

FDI has concentrated in the southern coastal area of the Pearl River delta, which has seen booming industrialization, made possible by a seemingly endless supplies of workers. In this area, approximately the size of Belgium, 30 million people work in manufacturing, producing a vast range of products from shoes to computers. The area is home to 800 shoe manufacturers. One of the largest, the Taiwanese company Pou Chen, employs a total of 110,000 workers, 80,000 in one factory, producing 100 million pairs of shoes a year for brands including Nike, Adidas, Timberland and Reebok. It is estimated that 80 per cent of the stock of FDI in China is held by overseas Chinese investors, mainly from Hong Kong, Taiwan and Singapore (Story, 2003). These investors have seized the opportunities presented by liberalization, and their Chinese cultural heritage gives them an advantage over other foreign investors.

Dr Martens, the British shoe manufacturer, concluded in 2003 that it could not compete unless it, too, shifted production to China. Dr Martens was paying workers $490 per week in its factory in the UK, where assembly of whole shoes was carried out by small groups of workers. By contrast, mass production techniques are used in the massive Pou Chen factories, where workers earn about $96 (£59; €89) a month for a 69-hour week.

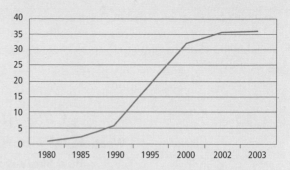

Inward FDI in China as a percentage of GDP
Source of data: United Nations, *World Investment Report 2004* (Geneva: UN), Annex table B.6.

High-tech industries are also flourishing. Flextronics, a Singapore-based electronics manufacturer, is a contract producer for Microsoft, Motorola, Dell and Sony Ericsson. The output of its factory near Zhuhai rose 500 per cent from 2001 to 2002. Ricoh, the Japanese electronics company, makes most of its photocopiers in the Shenzhen special economic zone, which claims to make 70 per cent of the world's photocopiers. While it used to make all its newer models in Japan, Ricoh now uses the Chinese factory to manufacture models only months after they begin production in Japan.

Whether FDI flows will continue to rise is a question which concerns both Chinese policy-makers and foreign investors. Labour costs are inevitably rising. More highly skilled work in technology-based industries lures workers away from the likes of the shoe factories, which find it hard to retain workers. A solution adopted by Pou Chen is to build factories further inland, where labour is in abundant supply. One manufacturer explains: 'If we run out of people, we just go deeper into China' (Roberts and Kynge, 2003). It is estimated that there is a pool of some 200 million rural inhabitants who are underemployed: while they are a source of labour for manufacturing expansion, they are also a potential source of social unrest, should economic growth falter. Jobs provided by the continued manufacturing boom would bring economic development to these poorer areas. On the other hand, China's economic liberalization has not been paralleled by political liberalization. The long-term economic prosperity of its people will require its political and social institutions to adapt to the rapidly changing environment.

Sources: Kynge, J. 'An industrial powerhouse emerges by the waterfront', *Financial Times*, 23 January 2003; Roberts, D. and Kynge, J. 'How cheap labour, foreign investment and rapid industrialization are creating a new workshop of the world', *Financial Times*, 4 February 2003; Story, J. (2003) *China: the Race to Market* (Harlow: FT Prentice Hall); United Nations (2004) *World Investment Report 2004* (Geneva: UN).

Case questions

What are the factors in China's FDI boom?
How likely is it to continue?

WEB ALERT!

Detailed information on FDI in China can be found on the website of the Ministry of Commerce of the People's Republic of China, at http://mofcom.gov.cn/column/fdi

Briefing on the national business environment in China can be found on the World Bank's website at http://www.worldbank.org/DoingBusiness/exploreEconomies/

The Office of the US Trade Representative, at http://www.ustr.gov, also provides briefing documents on national investment climate

The growth of TNCs as drivers of the global economy

The growth of international trade and transnational manufacturing in the late nineteenth and early twentieth centuries is linked to the growth in TNCs in the major industrial countries of the period. The large UK investors focused on primary products, including mineral extraction and agricultural commodities, during the period before 1914, making the UK the largest holder of foreign capital assets (Dunning, 1993a). The majority of these investments were in developing countries, mainly those under British colonial rule.

Taking advantage of advances in technology, US, British and other European companies invested in overseas production in areas such as machinery, textiles, food and chemicals. Many inventions, such as the steam engine, electric turbine and railway locomotive, originating in Britain, spread to Europe and the US. US companies were later to industrialize than their European counterparts and were better placed to take advantage of technological innovation, making use of electrical power and the internal combustion engine to transform factory production processes. Consumer goods of consistent quality could thus be produced for vastly expanded markets, allowing companies to benefit from economies of scale. By the end of the nineteenth century, Ford cars and Singer sewing machines were becoming global brands.

The effects of changes in both manufacturing and transport brought about dramatic changes in society. In America, a bare 8 per cent of workers were engaged in manufacturing in 1870, and only one in five lived in a city of 8000 or more inhabitants. By 1910, the percentage engaged in manufacturing had risen to one-third, and the percentage living in cities had risen to more than one-half (Reich, 1991). The population of Chicago, the crossroads of east-west commercial activities, grew from 109,260 in 1860 to a staggering 2.2 million in 1910. The large American conglomerates, such as US Steel, American Telephone & Telegraph, GE, Standard Oil, Ford and General Motors, date from this era. These giant companies, whose names are still familiar, exemplify the dominance of American companies in the world economy during the first half of the twentieth century. A look at the rankings (Table 5.2) of the ten largest TNCs in terms of foreign assets in 2002 shows that they are still mainly in the automobile, telecommunications and petroleum industries. American companies are no longer dominant, however, occupying four of the ten places, while prominent European companies, through recent international expansion, occupy five places.

Table 5.2 The world's top ten non-financial TNCs by foreign assets, 2002

Rank by foreign assets	Corporation	Country	Industry
1	General Electric	United States	Electrical & electronic equipment
2	Vodafone	United Kingdom	Telecommuncations
3	Ford Motor Company	United States	Motor vehicles
4	British Petroleum	United Kingdom	Petroleum
5	General Motors	United States	Motor vehicles
6	Royal Dutch/Shell	United Kingdom/Netherlands	Petroleum
7	Toyota Motor Corporation	Japan	Motor vehicles
8	TotalFinaElf	France	Petroleum
9	France Telecom	France	Telecommunications
10	ExxonMobil Corporation	United States	Petroleum

Source: United Nations, *World Investment Report 2004*, (Geneva: United Nations), Annex table A.I.3, p. 276.

International business in the context of postwar shifts in international power

The period following the Second World War brought changes in both the world economy and world political structures, which went hand in hand. The war had caused severe disruption, and even devastation, to much of the industrialized world, with the exception of America, whose large corporations were thus in a position to expand their already dominant position in the world economy. The destruction was worst in Germany and Japan, where the industrial base and infrastructure had to be rebuilt from scratch. Postwar economic development in both countries has been termed an 'economic miracle'. Major factors (which were examined in detail in Chapter 4) were the ability to exploit technological advances in production and information and the strong role of government in the development processes. The success of corporate rebuilding in both countries provided 'models' of economic development which drew world attention, as well as emulation. Moreover, the rapid internationalization of Japanese companies soon had an impact in key sectors such as the motor industry and electronics. Japanese companies targeted the American market, where their competitive strengths soon unsettled domestic producers. In 1960, Japan produced 165,000 automobiles; by 1991, the figure had risen to 13 million – a quarter of the world's output. In 1960, the US produced more than half the world's automobiles but, by 1991, its share had dropped to 18 per cent (Stutz and de Souza, 1998). In the space of less than three decades, the Japanese economy grew to become an economic superpower.

On the political front, the postwar world was dominated by the divide between the Western countries (which included Japan) and the Eastern bloc (which represented the Soviet Union and its satellite countries in Central and Eastern Europe). The East-West cold war has been depicted as one between rival civilizations: the one representing democracy, liberal values and the market economy; the other representing authoritarianism, Communist ideology and the state-planned economy. The cold war, with its ideological poles of freedom and authoritarianism, dominated international relations and also investment patterns, as economic power blocs developed in both East and West.

The disintegration of the Soviet Union in the early 1990s marked the end of the cold war, creating newly independent states in former Soviet territory and the satellite countries of Central and Eastern Europe. These nations represent enormous cultural and social diversity, suppressed under authoritarianism, but allowed to flourish with independence. They have instituted market reforms and set about dismantling state-owned industries through privatization. (These changes were discussed in Chapter 4.) At the same time they have designed new democratic political institutions. In the reinvigorated business climate, their new leaders have actively encouraged foreign investment. Foreign TNCs, for their part, have been attracted by cheap labour and prospects of expanding markets covering an area of roughly 400 million inhabitants. The prospect of EU membership for Eastern European countries and the Baltic states, with others to follow, served to enhance their appeal for foreign investors, as shown in Case Study 5.2 on the Czech Republic. In marked contrast to these success stories, the collapse of the Russian economy in the 1990s and the political disintegration of Yugoslavia into its separate national units represented the difficulties of transition. The decade following the end of the cold war, therefore, revealed the complexities of the political, cultural and social environment, but it has also shown the extent of global integration, in which local and national interests are increasingly bound up with the forces of globalization.

Case study 5.2 Formula for FDI success in the Czech Republic

Following a period of weak growth from 1997 to 1999, the Czech Republic has overtaken its Central and Eastern European neighbours in attracting FDI. From 2000, it has attracted the highest per capita inflows of the former Communist states in the region, and now has a larger stock of investment than Hungary, which was an early leader in attracting foreign investors. Of the two countries, whose economies are similar in size, the Czech Republic has surged ahead in attracting FDI (see figure). Historically, the Czechs are linked with brewing and Skoda cars, now owned by Volkswagen of Germany. But the country has moved on from its indigenous beer and engineering past. A major achievement was success in persuading the joint venture between Toyota and Citroen to invest €1.5bn. in a new car factory in Kolin in 2001, employing 3000 workers. Poland had hoped to be selected for this plant, pointing particularly to the fact that, with a population of 39 million, it is four times the size of either Hungary or the Czech Republic, and market size is an important factor for potential investors. However, the investment incentives and training grants offered by the Czech government were factors which swung the decision towards the Czech Republic.

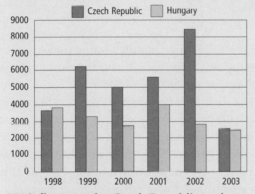

FDI inflows to the Czech Republic and Hungary (millions of dollars)
Source of data: United Nations (2004) *World Investment Report 2004* (Geneva: UN), Annex table B.1.

The turnaround in FDI has been largely a result of the policies of the Social Democrat government which took office in 1998. It put together a package of policies which, in addition to FDI incentives, included major privatizations of the banks, telecommunications and energy. It initiated subsidies to municipal authorities to build industrial parks. It created CzechInvest, an agency designed to be a 'one-stop shop' for foreign investors, to reduce bureaucracy and costs. The

Poles lamented the fact that, in stark contrast to the CzechInvest process, would-be investors in Poland face interrogation from three different ministries. No wonder, they say, Toyota and Citroen opted for the Czech Republic. The head of Poland's Chamber of Commerce lamented that, in Poland, to get a work permit requires filing 17 documents, a process which takes seven to eight weeks and costs the equivalent of €382.

The Czech Republic benefits from relatively low wages, one-fifth of those in Germany, but wages are rising, aided by EU membership in 2004. Foreign investors do not see the country simply as a low-cost location. It offers a central geographical position, good infrastructure, a technical skills base and a growing supplier network. It has attracted numerous investments in the electronics industry, including Matsushita's first television plant in Central Europe in 1996. The biggest greenfield investment has been that of Philips, the Dutch electronics group, and LG Electronics of South Korea, which opened a €200 million television tube plant in 2001. Such was the supply of skilled workers that 3000 people applied for the first 850 operations jobs in the factory.

CzechInvest has turned its focus from manufacturing to more diversified investment. It has offered incentives to companies investing in services, attracting IBM to build an expert solutions centre for handling customer information systems. It has also attracted Accenture, the consultancy, to invest in outsourcing of clients financing and accounting services. The agency is also planning to attract R&D activity linked with manufacturing, reasoning that, as wages rise and manufacturers are tempted to move operations further east, they will see the advantages of the research units and local suppliers and resist the temptation to move. CzechInvest sees that, in the future, the country's central position, good telecommunications system, technical and language skills will make it an attractive location for services. Its attractiveness was enhanced by EU membership in 2004. The Czech Republic, therefore, is in a position to gain from economic integration in the enlarged EU.

Sources: Anderson, R., 'Looking for jobs beyond the age of manufacturing', *Financial Times*, 12 December 2001; Wagstyl, S., 'Policy shift brings prosperity', *Financial Times*, 21 November 2002; Marsh, P., 'Czech Republic switches to the right mix for foreign investors', *Financial Times*, 21 May 2002; Reed, J., 'Poland in slow lane as Czechs win car plant', *Financial Times*, 26 February 2002.

Case questions

Why is the Czech Republic popular with foreign investors?

What risks and opportunities lie on the horizon in terms of future FDI flows?

WEB ALERT!

Information on FDI in the Czech Republic can be found at http://www.fdimagazine.com. Click on the Czech Republic

A policy brief on the Czech Republic can be found on the OECD's website at http://www.oecd.org

Background information is available on the EU's website at http://europa.eu.int/comm./enlargement/Czech/

Trends in globalization processes

The transformation from internationalization centred mainly around trade to globalization of production accelerated from the 1970s onwards. By far the most important player has been – and still is – the US. Yet, as the global economy has become more widely ramified, US companies have lost their former dominant position in outward FDI. US TNCs' share of global FDI stock dropped from nearly two-thirds in the early 1970s to one-third by 1990. Inward investment in the US, on the other hand, grew dramatically, from $13bn. in 1970 to $550.7bn. in 1994 (Stutz and deSouza, 1998). These figures represent an increase from 11 per cent of world totals in 1975 to 21 per cent by 1985. These inward investors were not just companies from Europe and Japan, but also from the newly industrialized economies of Southeast Asia, such as Korea's large industrial conglomerates, which have invested heavily in both Europe and the US.

Following a peak in 2000, FDI inflows have declined globally, as shown in Figure 5.1. This decline was largely caused by a slowing down in economic growth in most regions of the world, which, in turn, reflected difficulties at the corporate level, including weaker profits, falling share prices and slowness in carrying out necessary restructuring. The fall in FDI was unevenly distributed, however. In 2002, the developed economies suffered large declines, accounted for mainly by a decline of nearly 90 per cent in inflows to the US (United Nations, 2003). Flows to developed economies continued their decline in 2003. Flows to developing countries, however, rose by 9 per cent from 2002 to 2003 (United Nations, 2004). In the Asia Pacific region, consisting of 57 economies, flows to 31 declined in 2002, but China amassed record inflows of $53bn. Central and Eastern European countries also performed well, inflows rising by 15 per cent in 2002. Here, too, flows were uneven, with falling FDI in 10 out of the region's 19 economies. Factors at work in this region were the surge in investment in the Russian Federation and the prospects associated with EU enlargement (United Nations, 2003, pp. 8–10).

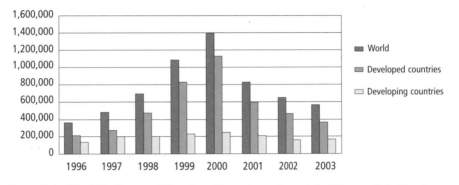

Figure 5.1 **World inflows of foreign direct investment (millions of dollars)**
Source: United Nations, *World Investment Report 2004* (Geneva: United Nations), Annex table B.1, p. 249.

It is generally true that the home countries of most outward investors are in the developed world, while developing countries are net recipients of foreign investment. Both outward and inward investment has been dominated by the **Triad blocs** (the US, EU countries and Japan): between 1985 and 2002, the triad countries accounted for about 80 per cent of outward stock and 50–60 per cent of inward stock (United Nations, 2003). The EU has taken over from the US as the largest source of outward FDI. Japan's outward stock remains about a tenth of that of the EU. In 1980, the US and EU were roughly equal in outward FDI stocks, but a gap opened up over the next two decades, as can be seen in Figure 5.2. In 2002, EU stock was more than twice that of the US. By contrast, FDI stock from developing countries was only 11 per cent of outward FDI stock in 1980, increasing to 12 per cent in 2002. A significant development has been the rise of South, East and Southeast Asia, in outward FDI stock. These countries overtook Japan in 1997, and in 2002 accounted for a proportion almost double that of Japan's outward FDI stock.

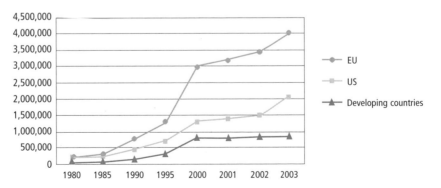

Figure 5.2 **Comparisons in ownership of FDI outward stock (millions of dollars)**
Source: United Nations, *World Investment Report 2004* (Geneva: United Nations), Annex table B.4, p. 382.

WEB ALERT!

Each year the United Nations Conference on Trade and Development (UNCTAD) publishes its World Investment Report. Highlights are available from http://www.unctac.org. UNCTAD also publishes a Trade and Investment Report annually, available via its website

The International Chamber of Commerce's world business organization is at http://www.iccwbo.org/

National governments in both developed and developing countries have made regulatory changes to attract investment. As Figure 5.3 shows, there has been a trend towards reducing regulatory controls, known as liberalization, which accelerated in 2001 and 2002, in response to the global downturn in FDI. Regulatory changes more favourable to FDI leapt from 147 in 2000 to 236 in 2002. This trend has been accompanied by trade liberalization. These measures have been complemented by international agreements, the most significant of which was the General Agreement on Tariffs and Trade (GATT), whereby many barriers to free trade have been dismantled (although many still remain in place). International regulation gained an institutional dimension with the setting up of the World Trade Organization (WTO), which superseded GATT in 1994. World trade and national competitiveness are discussed in detail in Chapter 10. Suffice it to say here that the establishment of an internationally recognized trade regime (whose membership had risen to 148 in 2004), together with machinery for the settlement of disputes, has been both an indicator of the impact of the global economy on national regimes and a basis for the further deepening of global networks.

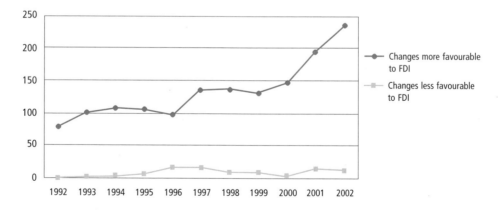

Figure 5.3 **National regulatory changes, 1992–2002 (number of regulatory changes introduced by countries)**
Source of data: United Nations, *World Investment Report 2003* (Geneva: United Nations) p. 21.

Amin and Thrift (1994, pp. 2–5), writing on globalization and regional development, identify seven factors that characterize the widening and deepening global economy. These are:

1 Increasing centrality of financial structure, and degree of power exerted by financial structures over businesses and national economies

2 Increasing importance of knowledge as a factor of production, whereby 'knowledge structure' is less and less tied to particular national or local business cultures

3 Transnationalization of technology, coupled with an enormous increase in the rapidity of redundancy of given technologies

4 Rise of global oligopolies, facilitated by accelerated technological change, the mobility of capital and advances in transport and communication

5 Rise of transnational economic diplomacy and the globalization of state power, with 'plural authority' structures replacing traditional power structures

6 Rise of global cultural flows and 'deterritorialized' signs, meanings and identities, while retaining cultural heterogeneity

7 Rise of new global geographies, with emphasis on the local within global networks.

As Amin and Thrift point out, there are numerous strands within each of the above factors, and each is the focus of research and debate on the precise nature and scope of the globalization trends. Detailed analysis of each of these spheres appears in the chapters which follow. Focus at present is on the seventh factor, the rise of new global geographies, which serves as a theme linking all seven factors.

Transnational corporations are able to shift production from one location to another with unprecedented ease. To meet the challenges of the changing competitive environment, the TNC views its operations from a global perspective in which strategy formulators seek to take advantage of the benefits offered by each specific geographic location. Sourcing components from widely dispersed locations has become a trend in evolving global strategy. It is estimated that a quarter to a third of world trade is intra-firm trade, that is, between affiliated companies of the same parent, which trade with each other across national borders.

Global networks now function at numerous geographical levels, from local through to transnational. The rise of regional groupings, such as the EU and NAFTA, have facilitated both regional trade and cross-border investment. Regionalism, which will be discussed in detail in Chapter 10, can be seen as a parallel trend to globalization in the global economy, linking neighbouring states, which often share historical and cultural links, as well as economic ties.

SUMMARY POINTS

!!!

Trends in globalization processes

- Increasing geographic 'scanning' ability of large TNCs.
- Increasing flows of FDI, encompassing a wider range of countries.
- Liberalization of regulatory controls on FDI by governments, including privatization.
- Growing international regulatory regimes, such as the WTO.
- Growth in regionalism, through organizations such as the EU.
- Inter-firm and intra-firm networks, extending from local to global.

Globalization can hardly be said to have yet produced a borderless 'deterritorialized' world. It would be more accurate to say that globalization represents a 'redefinition of places', in which 'the local meets the global' (Amin and Thrift, 1994, p. 10). Global networks traverse national boundaries, reaching down to the local level. The result has been greater interconnectedness and interdependencies between the various levels – transnational, regional, national and local. Firms – often in partnership – have played the key roles in these new networks. The remaining sections of this chapter look at globalization from the point of view of the firm.

Globalization of the firm

The question of why firms seeking foreign expansion locate in particular places and not in others has given rise to location theories based on costs of production and the markets for the firm's products (Dicken and Lloyd, 1990). Alfred Weber, an influential early theorist, devised a location theory based on the least-cost approach. A company, he argued, would choose a location which offers the lowest transport and labour costs. Further, he argued that costs are reduced by **industrial agglomeration**, which is the concentration of several producers in a single location. Proximity of suppliers and customers is a crucial factor, which supports the clustering of industries in particular locations.

Perhaps the most comprehensive theoretical attempt to explain FDI is John Dunning's 'eclectic' paradigm. It is also called the **OLI paradigm**, after the variables which, according to Dunning (1993a, pp. 76–9), affect a firm's decision to internationalize, namely advantages of ownership, location and internalization:

- *Ownership-specific advantages* – these include property rights over assets, broadly defined and including both tangible and intangible resources: capital, technology, labour, natural resources, know-how, organizational and entrepreneurial skills.
- *Location-specific advantages* – these include the cultural, political and social environment of the country: low labour costs, government incentives and the size and structure of markets.
- *Internalization advantages* – derived from the theory of the firm developed by economists, these look to the reduction of transaction costs through hierarchical organization as an alternative to reliance on market forces. A firm may thus acquire control of the supply of raw materials or components, achieving vertical integration which reduces costs.

The contribution of Dunning has been to offer a multidisciplinary theoretical framework highlighting the interrelatedness of the three variables. The decision to produce abroad depends on all three conditions being satisfied, but the configuration of the factors, and their importance relative to each other, will vary from one firm to another, and from situation to situation. The in-built flexibility of interpretation is one of the strong points of the framework as an analytical tool.

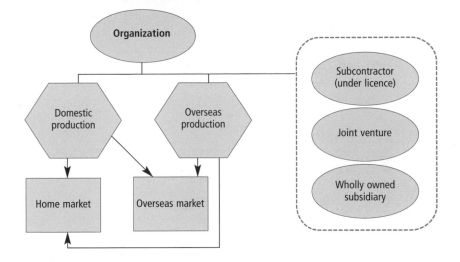

Figure 5.4 **Internationalizing production by the TNC**

A company currently operating in its domestic market may see continued growth as dependent on entering overseas markets. If it is a manufacturer, it may export its products initially using the services of an agent, and, depending on sales, seek a more long-term presence in the overseas market. As has been seen in the case studies on China and the Czech Republic, acquiring production capacity overseas may provide a platform for serving growing markets abroad, and may also lead to a concentration of production in a low-cost overseas location. If a company owns patents for its products or sells under its own brand name, it may give permission for a manufacturer abroad to produce the product under licence as shown in Figure 5.4. In this arrangement, the local company buys the right to use the trademark or process. It is possible for a company seeking overseas expansion by this means to exert a good deal of control through careful drafting of the licensing agreement, and, importantly, through the build-up of trust between the parties.

A company may gain more direct involvement in overseas production by means of a joint venture. The joint venture is an agreement between the overseas investor and a local partner to produce or sell a product or service. The direct setting up of a new facility by a foreign firm, such as a new plant on a greenfield site, may be highly risky in an unfamiliar location and the local partner's knowledge of the business environment is invaluable. Moreover, direct foreign ownership is prohibited in some countries and finding a local partner is a necessity. Until recently, this was the case in China, as the case study shows. From 2002, private and foreign investors have been allowed to acquire controlling stakes in domestic companies in China, including SOEs (United Nations, 2003). Even where not a legal requirement, the joint venture has become a popular option for foreign investors, as local firms possess inside knowledge of how to deal with authorities and suppliers. The joint venture may involve the formation of a new entity in which both partners acquire ownership. Typically, the local firm holds a 51 per cent stake and the foreign firm, 49 per cent. Nonetheless, the industry expertise of the foreign partner gives it the upper hand in management control of the operation. A good deal of trust between the partners is required to make a success of the joint venture, especially given the likely cultural differences between the partners (Hoon-Halbauer, 1999).

CRITICAL PERSPECTIVES

Internationalization of the firm

Rarely, in seeking to identify the reasons for business achievement, is one able to find a single common denominator. Sometimes excellence is primarily based on innovatory ingenuity; sometimes on the access to or control of key inputs or markets … sometimes on the diversity of operational experiences and capabilities; and sometimes on an unusual aptitude to manage both intra-and inter-firm relationships. But in most cases, success is founded on some amalgam of these … Call it what you will – for example a holistic and integrated approach to the creation and organization of business wealth – the success of the modern international corporation is increasingly determined by the ability to organize natural resources, information, money and people across national boundaries, both within and between organizations. (Dunning, 1993b, pp. 4–5)

■   How does Dunning's approach characterize the *global* firm, as opposed to the national firm seeking international expansion?

Industrial production: the legacy of Fordism

The changing nature of industrial operations, largely as a result of technological advances, has had a profound impact on manufacturing industries in particular. As industrialization took hold, the factory became the basic unit of production from the late nineteenth century onwards. The growth of the factory probably reached its zenith with Henry Ford. In Ford's River Rouge plant, which employed 35,000 people under one roof, coal and iron went in at one end and complete Ford cars rolled out the other. 'Fordism', as it has been called, encapsulates the characteristics of mass production. While at the lowest level it served to describe industrial mass production as practised in postwar America up to the early 1970s, Fordism came to be seen as a model of this type of system generally. Its characteristics are summarized in the box below.

Essentials of Fordism

- Large factories where there was mass production based on assembly line processes, operated by semi-skilled workers.
- Recognition of trade unions with industry-wide collective bargaining powers.
- Standardized products designed for mass markets, with long runs.
- Growth dependant on rising productivity based on economies of scale and growing demand generated by rising wages.
- Organization based on the large, multidivisional corporate structure, controlled from the centre.
- Production systems based on internalization of processes where economies of scale are achievable.
- Oligopolistic corporations controlling markets and leading to control of prices.

The postwar period from the early 1950s to the 1970s was one of almost continuous growth in the world's economies, none more so than the US, where burgeoning mass production was matched by mass consumption. In this 'golden age', America's large factories supplied an ever-increasing demand for consumer goods – automobiles, television sets, refrigerators. The numbers of automobiles on America's roads increased from 10 million in 1949 to 24 million by 1957, an increase of nearly two-and-a-half times in only eight years (Reich, 1991). The major corporations dominated the economy: about five hundred major corporations accounted for about half of the nation's industrial output and owned about three-quarters of the country's industrial assets. General Motors alone accounted for 3 per cent of the GNP in 1955, making it the world's largest manufacturing company. The expression, 'what is good for General Motors is good for the country', contained more than a grain of truth.

Then, in the 1970s, the boom faltered. A major factor was the fourfold increase in oil prices brought in by the Organization of Petroleum Exporting Countries (OPEC). But there were other factors too. Labour costs and wage settlements had been rising, as had costs of raw materials. Meanwhile, companies in other parts of the world were becoming more competitive, leading to demands for protectionism for US industries. The Bretton Woods international monetary system, designed in 1944 to keep national currencies in line with each other, disintegrated in 1971, when the US adopted a floating exchange rate. These events can be interpreted as simply part of the natural cycle of economic activity, which consists of long waves of boom followed by slump. On this interpretation, a slowdown was bound to follow the golden age. However, many commentators see deeper causes, largely stemming from the tendencies inherent in Fordism from the outset. Thus, explanations of the breakup of the Fordist system have become part of a larger debate on the development of modern capitalism in the context of globalization.

As a system producing high-volume, standardized products, Fordist production was inflexible and bureaucratic: the launch of a new product typically required several years' planning, entailing the complete alteration of production machinery. Bureaucratic hierarchies depended on detailed production manuals and job descriptions, leaving little scope for individual initiative, and also engendering boredom and minimal job satisfaction for those blue-collar workers doing monotonous, repetitive work. Labour relations with management were highly confrontational, based on a system of national collective bargaining. The success of the system depended on sustained consumer demand for the mass-produced goods it churned out. If consumer taste shifted to non-standard or customized products, or if consumer spending slumped, companies were left high and dry. Recession in the 1970s brought home the unpalatable truth that the large American companies had become uncompetitive globally.

Challenges from Japanese manufacturers, later to be joined by those from newly industrialized countries, highlighted what was called the crisis of Fordism and engendered a rethinking of industrial organization.

Post-Fordist organizations

It is generally agreed that Fordism, in its industrial, economic and political embodiments, represented the end of an era, but there is less consensus about the new era unfolding. The terms 'postindustrial' and 'postmodern' have been used to describe the **post-Fordist** era. Some scholars take the view that what followed Fordism has been a transitional phase, rather than a radical break with the past (Amin and Thrift, 1994, p. 2). There is agreement on some aspects of the post-Fordist industrial landscape, focusing on the increasing importance of technological advance and the need for flexibility in response to markets.

SUMMARY POINTS

Post-Fordist industry

- The increasing importance of technology and information systems in the new industrial 'paradigm'.
- Replacement of mass consumerism with recognition of a variety of consumer markets, in which choice, quality and product differentiation are paramount.
- Decentralization of management structures.
- Fragmentation of industrial complexes into smaller production units capable of flexible specialization.
- Shifting geographical centres of industries, with more localized clusters of firms.
- Organizational flexibility and decentralized management structures within the firm, recognizing the need for flexibility in the assigning and carrying out of tasks by management and workers.

The post-Fordist world is one in which diversity and specialization are replacing conformity and standardization. As a consequence, industries and firms may vary considerably in their organizational structures and corporate cultures. For example, industrial relations are influenced by the particular social and cultural environment in which a firm is located. Confrontational labour relations can be counterproductive, and there are numerous ways to achieve a more consensual approach to employee relations – some involving direct worker participation and some involving the mediation of trade unions. The 'Californian' model of an unstructured workplace, with no unions, flexible contracts and a strong corporate culture, suits Silicon Valley, but is not universally applicable. On the other hand, the Japanese model, which has been hugely successful, seems to present a hybrid of Fordist and post-Fordist characteristics.

The Japanese model has been called one of **flexible mass production** (Sabel, 1994, p. 122). The large Japanese manufacturing companies, such as Toyota, the leading car maker, allow for flexibility in production and organization within a hierarchical structure. While producing for mass markets, the system of centralized product development is nonetheless able to respond to changes in demand, making use of technology to reduce development time. New automated manufacturing equipment facilitates the rapid implementation of changes and variations in the product. This flexibility is reflected in a workforce trained to understand the entire process involved in the new technology, enabling workers to change tasks with ease and operate just-in-time delivery systems. High levels of knowledge and training are also essential to the Japanese philosophy of quality control, which emphasizes worker involvement and contribution (summed up in the concept of kaizen.) A consensus-based system of worker participation is a long way from the confrontational labour relations of classical mass production.

It has been argued that a culture of cooperation reflects a tendency towards collectivism in Japanese society generally, leaving open to question the transferability of these production systems into other cultural environments. Nonetheless, the Japanese model has been copied the world over, by Western companies as well as Japanese companies in their foreign transplants. Its attractiveness lies in the successful combination of goals which had been seen as mutually incompatible: price competitiveness through scale economies, responsiveness to changes in demand, emphasis on quality and more harmonious labour–management relations. This is highlighted by Sabel (1994, p. 137) who cited a dramatic case: at Freemont, California, Toyota and General Motors rebuilt an abandoned General Motors assembly plant, reorganized work according to Toyota's principles and rehired selected employees from the old facility – which had a history of bitter labour disputes – to operate the new one. The New United Motors Company became almost 50 per cent more efficient than the old General Motors plant on the same site, and also almost 50 per cent more efficient than comparable GM assembly plants which were modernized while Freemont was closed.

Minifile

KAIZEN

AB Electronics in Cardiff, a medium-size company, is one of many that have found dramatic increases in productivity as a result of kaizen training. The company, which makes car components such as wiper motors and heating controls, exports about half its annual output. Its managing director says: 'Despite the strength of sterling, we have been able to compete more effectively in global markets as a direct result of using kaizen principles.' The new approach involved dividing the workforce into multilevel teams, including staff from administration, production logistics and other departments. A team would be given a week to concentrate on a particular issue, for example the wastefulness of the product-labelling process. This is known as the 'kaizen blitz'. The team would then have authority to make changes, including buying new equipment. 'Kaizen has changed our company culture,' said the managing director, 'and is directly responsible for reducing scrap, improving quality and improving health and safety.'

The operations manager of another company, Avon Automotive, which has successfully used kaizen techniques, highlights three potential problems:

1 The deepest pitfall is to bite off more than you can chew. Tackle small elements of the business relating to specific processes.

2 Failure to sustain the changes made.

3 The most fundamental problem is reluctance by senior managers to devolve responsibility. Avon Automotive's operations manager says that 'when staff know they can question everything and are allowed by senior managers to make changes, they build a tremendous enthusiasm for their work and a commitment to improvement.'

Source: Smith, D.S., 'Kaizen: that's Japanese for helping Britain work better', *The Sunday Times*, 16 January, 2000.

A leading book on kaizen is *The Kaizen Blitz: Accelerating Breakthroughs in Productivity and Performance*, by A.C. Laraia, P. Moody, and R. Hall (John Wiley, 1999).

WEB ALERT!

The Kaizen Institute's website is at http://www.kaizen-institute.com/kzn.htm

The kaizen blitz was pioneered by the Association For Manufacturing Excellence, http://www.ame.org/

Organizational changes and TNCs

TNCs increasingly seek a greater variety of organizational forms for their international activities, which has accompanied the geographical dispersal of their operations. The proliferation of strategic alliances and other innovative types of cooperative alliance reflects the need for greater organizational flexibility in the complex international environment, as well as the perceived need to develop relational ties in the differing cultural environments of each location. Globalization and localization strategies are thus perceived as complementary, rather than contradictory.

Modern organizational forms for international companies have evolved in a number of ways. The firm may have multiple divisions which are subsidiary companies wholly owned by the parent company. Or, as is increasingly common, it may subcontract or outsource products and services. The subcontractor is legally an independent firm, who supplies goods or services on the basis of market exchange. Subcontractors in the manufacturing industries often build up informal, relational links with customers over time, even formalized by cross-shareholdings (especially common in Japan), but remain legally independent. Contrast their position with that of the subsidiary, which is owned by a parent company. For the TNC, acquisition of a subsidiary is, as we have seen, a means of internalization, circumventing the risks of the open market. By contrast, restructuring in the auto industry at the end of the 1990s saw a shift towards **externalization**, whereby the auto companies look beyond existing suppliers, seeking competitive terms from other suppliers in global marketplaces, aided by use of the internet. A result has been the 'freeing' of suppliers, who themselves are free to seek customers independently. General Motors spun off its components subsidiary, Delphi Automotive Systems in 1998. In just under a year Delphi had drummed up new non-GM business amounting to 60 per cent of its total business. Visteon, Ford's largest components subsidiary, was spun off in 2000, but has struggled to find non-Ford business and had to rescued by Ford with a $2.2bn. bailout in 2005. A restructuring is planned, which will see the replacement of its unionized workforce with one that is mainly non-unionized, in order to reduce costs.

In the new era of post-Fordist industrial restructuring, the global corporation has effectively 'localized' its strategy. The corporate strategies of the multinationals rely on their ability to coordinate production in their various geographical centres, seeking the greatest efficiency in each. The availability of abundant cheap labour in some countries and regions – in Asia and Latin America, for example – has given these locations favoured status, whereas economic development in less endowed parts of the world, such as Africa, has hardly progressed. FDI flows to China, Brazil and Mexico accounted for half of the total to all developing countries in 2002 (United Nations, 2003). China alone attracted nearly one-third of the total to all developing countries. FDI flows to the 49 least developed countries, on the other hand, account for only 3.2 per cent of flows to developing countries generally, and less than 1 per cent of world FDI flows (United Nations, 2003). Globalization, then, has favoured some cities and regions, but not others. An example is the thriving software industry which has grown up in India. A consequence has been rivalry between regions at sub-national level, to attract foreign investors.

Global and local markets

Improved transport and communications, especially the rise of e-commerce, have brought the notion of a global marketplace closer to reality. However, the spread of global markets does not necessarily imply a growing uniformity in consumer tastes and the melting away of national markets. Theorists of globalization in its extreme form, as described earlier in this chapter, predicted the fading away of local differences and diminution of local autonomy. Yet, global corporate strategy has moved away from the production of a standard product for all markets. A major theme of this book is the continuing diversity which persists *within* the global economy. TNCs have become sensitive to locational differences of all kinds: cultural values, religious values, political sensitivities, legal constraints, levels of technological development and many other aspects of the business environment. The internet has made it possible for companies to acquire more information about local markets all over the globe. The ability to respond and adapt to local differences and changing tastes has become an imperative for the global company in the new competitive environment. Adopting the right strategy for a local market is a key to long-term success, as Case study 5.3 shows.

Case study 5.3   Finding the right strategy for setting up shop in Japan

The world's largest grocery retailers have varied in their taste for international expansion and in their strategies. As the two figures show, Wal-Mart is by far the largest, but, mainly because of its vast domestic market in the US, has been tentative in looking to expand abroad, generating only just over 20 per cent of its sales outside its home market. Carrefour, by contrast, has been active in Asia, and Tesco, the UK's largest grocery retailer, has branched out, mainly in Eastern Europe and Asia. All these global retailers inevitably eye Japan, the world's second largest consumer market. However, Japan has proved to be a difficult market for outside retailers to penetrate. Its consumers are traditionally more concerned with the quality and presentation of products on offer than with low prices. Its complex distribution networks make it difficult for retailers to streamline the distribution chain. With their focus on discounting and bypassing interme-diaries to keep prices low, Western retailers find that the Japanese market requires adjustments to the strategies that have been successful in their home markets.

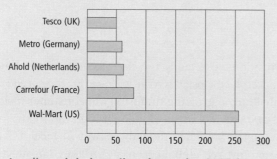

Leading global retailers (net sales 2003 in $billions)
Source: Voyle (2004).

Carrefour, the French hypermarket retailer, entered Japan in 2000, rolling out hypermarkets modelled on its French operation. It opened three stores in the first three months, but since then, expansion has stalled, as the company encountered pricing and branding problems. The Japanese found the low prices at Carrefour did not fit their image of a French brand as exclusive and expensive – French luxury brands such as Chanel have been highly successful in Japan. They expected French goods, but found Japanese groceries on offer. Carrefour's efforts to bypass the multilayered distribution systems were only partially successful: it managed to buy only about half its goods direct from the manufacturers.

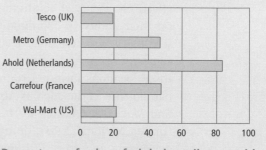

Percentage of sales of global retailers outside their home market
Source: Voyle (2004).

Wal-Mart, having seen Carrefour's difficulties, adopted a more cautious approach, seeking a Japanese partner with knowledge of local consumer tastes. Following six months of negotia-tions, it bought a 6 per cent stake in Seiyu, Japan's fourth largest supermarket group, in 2002. This partnership seemed to work smoothly, and it raised its stake to 34 percent of Seiyu six months later. Wal-Mart allowed the Japanese management to continue running the business and retained the Seiyu name on the stores. This strategy is similar to its market entry strategy in the UK, where it acquired Asda supermarkets.

Tesco, the largest UK retailer but with less international presence than Carrefour or Wal-Mart, also felt that expansion in Japan was imperative, but its choice of entry mode differed markedly from the other two. Although Tesco had entered other countries through its hypermarket model, it entered Japan by purchasing an entire chain of convenience stores in 2003. The chain, C Two, which has about 80 stores in the Tokyo area, had built its business on a combination of low prices and astute product procurement, features which Tesco found attractive. Called the 'third way' by some analysts, this mode of entry was seen as a lower risk and lower cost strategy than that of its larger rivals.

Carrefour, Wal-Mart and Tesco all felt the need to enter the Japanese market, but their strategies differ markedly. Of the three, Tesco's is perhaps the most cautious, reflecting a wariness of the retailing environment in Japan. One analyst has summed up the attractions and dangers of Japan

in a simple comparison: supermarket retailers see a market, which, given its large population of affluent consumers, looks guaranteed to be profitable, but 'they are all moths to the flame' (Voyle and Sanchanta, 2003).

Sources: Voyle, S. and Sanchanta, M., 'Tesco finds convenient way to enter Japan', *Financial Times*, 11 June 2003; Rahman, B., 'Retailers set sights on Japan', *Financial Times*, 13 December 2002; Nakamoto, M, and Sanchanta, M., 'Wal-Mart set for Japan challenge', *Financial Times*, 18 March 2002; Voyle, S. 'Tesco's tough act: with record profits, Britain's biggest retailer prepares for further challenges at home and abroad', *Financial Times*, 20 April 2004.

Case question

Assess which of the three market entry strategies has the greatest likelihood of success in Japan.

Transnationality of the firm

Corporations, like individuals, are influenced by their own national environment and culture, but to what extent do they transform themselves into truly global companies as they grow? There is a school of thought which holds that corporations, as they become global, become 'denationalized' (Reich, 1991; Ohmae, 1995). However, there is considerable research to suggest that, in their structures and behaviour, companies reflect their national origins and carry on doing so when they have become global enterprises (Dicken, 2003). Research by Pauly and Reich (1997) shows that national institutional and ideological frameworks form a 'permanent imprint' on multinationals based in the US, Germany, and Japan, the three home countries of 75 out of the world's top 100 multinationals. They conclude that there are enduring differences between the companies of these different nationalities, which determine their internal governance, financial structures, R&D strategy, investment and other strategic decisions.

Since 1990, UNCTAD has compiled a 'transnationality index' (TNI), composed of three ratios: foreign assets/total assets; foreign sales/total sales; and foreign employment/total employment. Overall transnationality of the world's top 100 TNCs grew from 51 per cent in 1990 to 55 per cent in 1997, but fell back to 52.6 per cent in 2001. The list of the top ten TNCs in terms of transnationality appears in Table 5.3. Only one is from the US, and many are from smaller countries. By contrast, the world's largest TNCs in terms of foreign assets, which appear in Table 5.2, are much less transnational: GE ranks 84, while General Motors ranks 95 in the TNI. While measurements such as these are limited as tools, they are indicative, along with results of other research, that the global company is still more myth than reality.

Table 5.3 The world's top TNCs by degree of transnationality, 2002

TNI Ranking	Ranking by foreign assets	Corporation	Country	Industry	Transnationality Index (%)
1	82	NTL Inc.	US	Telecommunications	99.1
2	58	Thomson Corp.	Canada	Printing and publishing	97.9
3	61	Holcim AG	Switzerland	Non-metallic mineral products	95.5
4	99	CRH Plc	Ireland	Lumber and building materials	94.7
5	35	ABB	Switzerland	Machinery and equipment	94.5
6	22	Roche Group	Switzerland	Pharmaceuticals	91.0
7	98	Interbrew SA	Belgium	Beverages	90.8
8	97	Publicis Groupe SA	France	Business services	90.7
9	21	News Corporation	Australia	Media	90.1
10	37	Philips Electronics	Netherlands	Electrical and electronic equipment	86.8

Source: United Nations, *World Investment Report 2004*, (Geneva: United Nations), Annex table A.I.3, pp. 276–8.

It might be expected that the trend towards localization should impact on TNCs, eventually weakening the home base bias and strengthening local links. However, the depth of local embeddedness can vary enormously, depending on central management decision-making and the degree of local autonomy of foreign units. Bartlett and Ghoshal (1998) envisage four TNC models:

1 The *multinational organization* – The large firm decentralizes its overseas operations, giving a high degree of autonomy to local units. While local responsiveness is achieved, fragmentation and lack of overall coordination are disadvantages.
2 The *international organization* – There is more control by the centre over the overseas units and more coordination from the company's headquarters. This model is conducive to exploiting firm-specific assets such as technology advances or market power, as exemplified by the large American companies.
3 The *classic global organization* – The parent company exerts tight control over overseas units, allowing little scope for local decision-making. The Japanese plants established in the US in the 1970s and 80s are examples of this model.
4 The *complex global organization* – This is emerging through the development of integrated global networks. The three other models represent a choice: either local autonomy or central control. By contrast, this model, which takes into account the more recent forms of strategic alliances, seems to combine the twin goals of localization and central coordination.

If a production unit is allowed to choose its own suppliers among local firms, then this externalization will allow it to develop its own relational ties with other firms in the area. Hence, networks grow up over time, and the firm becomes enmeshed in the local social, cultural and political environment. The growth of these 'industrial districts' benefits local firms and the local host economy. However, it need not follow that greater strategic involvement of subsidiaries at the local level will translate into strategic roles in the organization overall. The organization is ultimately looking to achieve global strategic objectives, which are served by weighing up the advantages of specific locations. As the growth of FDI in the global economy has demonstrated, a company may favour one location for the time being, but abandon it and relocate tomorrow, as costs and markets dictate. Even the capital investment associated with building new manufacturing units does not guarantee long-term commitment. In 1993, Hoover closed its vacuum cleaner factory in Dijon in France with the loss of 600 jobs. It then created 400 new jobs at its Scottish plant, where new working practices and wage structures would result in a reduction in costs by a quarter. The French government immediately protested at the apparent transfer of jobs from France to Scotland, but its protests were in vain.

The globalization debate

The overview of the processes of globalization outlined here shows TNCs as the drivers of the global economy, with freedom to move among the world's states and regions at will. Whether globalization is seen as essentially beneficial, increasing overall well-being or, at the other extreme, essentially unchecked power threatening well-being depends considerably on one's point of view. The low-skilled worker who has just lost a job due to cheap foreign competition is likely to feel a victim of globalization, while shareholders and directors in a successful global company will extol its benefits, as will countries whose economies grow as a result of foreign investment. For the opponents of globalization, the most worrying fact is that a company as a capitalist enterprise exists, first and foremost, to maximize its profits. While it does much that is good, such as providing employment, filling shops everywhere with high-quality goods and leading technological innovation which promotes well-being, it is also capable of much that is bad, such as damaging the environment, creating risks to human health and widening the gap between the world's haves and have-nots. As we have seen in this chapter, the benefits of globalization have not as yet trickled down to all the world's countries: on the contrary, economic growth has brought growing inequalities between nations.

One of the aspects of globalization that is particularly worrying to its sceptics is that large commercial organizations are perceived as unaccountable to wider society. How to devise governance mechanisms that reconcile corporate interests with society's broader interests is one of the major challenges facing the large TNCs. (This challenge is discussed in Part 4.)

Companies are becoming increasingly sensitive to the environments in which they operate. No doubt this stance partly reflects the perception that shareholder value is sensitive to human and environmental issues. In the world of instant communication, corporate disasters make news the world over. Global economic integration has transformed societies, but the process has revealed a multiplicity of divergent interests, values, and goals, not simply between countries but between groups and regions within societies. Understanding the changing dynamics of these interactions is a key to business success in the globalized environment.

CRITICAL PERSPECTIVES

Globalization's winners and losers

Globalization is associated with an evolving dynamic global structure of enablement and constraint. But it is also a highly stratified structure since globalization is profoundly uneven: it both reflects existing patterns of inequality and hierarchy while also generating new patterns of inclusion and exclusion, new winners and losers. (Held et al., 1999, p. 27)

■   Assess the unevenness of globalization, giving examples of winners and losers.

Conclusions

1   Through the processes of globalization, products, people, companies, money and information move freely across national borders. While international trade has been thriving for centuries, the deeper economic integration which defines globalization has taken off only since the end of the Second World War.

2   Facilitated, above all, by technological advances in communications and transport, globalization has brought about growing interconnectedness between people, organizations and governments in global networks.

3   The driving force behind the new global economy has been the TNCs, whose global strategies have rested primarily on FDI, which has played a transformative role, particularly evident in emerging economies around the world.

4   The globalization of production has brought about a renewed focus on the local within the global enterprise. TNCs, seeking location-specific advantages, while naturally drawn to cheap labour, increasingly recognize the significance of wider implications of local diversity in cultural, political, social and technological environments.

5   The Fordist mass production systems of the 1950s and 60s, producing standardized products for mass consumer markets, have given way to a variety of organizational changes, involving greater decentralization and localization. An aim of newer flexible specialization models is to be able to respond quickly and efficiently to the demands of changing markets.

6 The geographical dispersal of functions within the global company, combined with more flexible organizational structures, has led to a growth in strategic alliances between firms, local and global, blurring organizational boundaries.

7 The undoubted power of TNCs has been highlighted by their geographical scanning ability. The globalization debate has focused on questions of the accountability of TNCs, highlighting the multiplicity of interests and values that make up the international environment.

Review questions

1 How is globalization distinguishable from internationalization?

2 What are the leading schools of thought on the extent and depth of globalization?

3 What are the chief features of the TNC?

4 What is FDI? Give three of the reasons for FDI on the part of companies.

5 How have the postwar shifts in international power led to (a) growing FDI; and (b) changing patterns of FDI?

6 What is the role of national liberalization policies in attracting FDI?

7 What are the elements of Dunning's eclectic paradigm of FDI?

8 What were the advantages and drawbacks of Fordist production systems?

9 How do localization strategies fit into global strategies for the global company?

10 What are the broad contours of the controversy over the direction of globalization?

Assignments

1 Examine the major globalization processes at work in today's world economy, and assess their impact on the international business environment.

2 Assess the extent to which the FDI strategies of TNCs have generated a rethinking of organizational links across national borders, including greater localization within a global strategy.

Further reading

Dicken, P. (2003) *Global Shift: Reshaping the Global Economic Map of the 21st Century*, 4th edn (London: Sage).

Giddens, A. (2000) *Runaway World: How Globalization is Reshaping our Lives* (Andover: Routledge).

Held, D., McGrew, A., Goldblatt, D. and Perraton, J. (1999) *Global Transformations: Politics, Economics and Culture* (Cambridge: Polity Press).

Held, D. (ed.) (2000) *Globalizing World? Culture, Economics, Politics* (London: Routledge).

Hirst, P. and Thompson, G. (1999) *Globalization in Question*, 2nd edn (Cambridge: Polity Press).

Keane, J. (2003) *Global Civil Society?* (Cambridge: Cambridge University Press).

Reich, R. (1991) *The Work of Nations: Preparing Ourselves for 21st Century Capitalism* (London: Simon & Schuster).

Sklair, L. (2004) *Globalization: Capitalism and Its Alternatives* (Oxford: Oxford University Press).

Waters, M. (2001) *Globalization*, 2nd edn (London: Routledge).

Zysman, J. (1996) 'The Myth of a "Global" Economy: Enduring National Foundations and Emerging Regional Realities', *New Political Economy*, **1**(2), pp. 157–84.

6 The cultural environment: diversity and globalization

Outline of chapter

- ■ Introduction
- ■ What is culture and how is it relevant to business?
- ■ National cultures
- ■ Languages
  - • Linguistic diversity
  - • English: the global language?
- ■ Religions
  - • Christianity
  - • Islam
  - • Asian religions
- ■ Western values and Asian values: the debate
- ■ Multicultural societies
- ■ Culture theories
- ■ Organizational culture
- ■ Culture change
- ■ Cultural globalization: myth or reality?
  - • Role of the media in cultural globalization
  - • Global culture and national cultures
- ■ Conclusions

Learning objectives

1 To identify the dimensions of culture in society which impact on international business activities

2 To understand the origins of cultural diversity based on national and other collective cultural identities

3 To assess the importance of cultural values and expressions in the modern global environment

4 To appreciate the role of organizational culture in international enterprises

Introduction

The process of globalization has brought people from different parts of the globe and different cultural backgrounds into routine contact with each other and each other's cultures. But does greater interaction imply that people are drawing closer together and becoming more like each other? An international businessperson will argue on the basis of personal experience that negotiating a business deal in Morocco is very different from negotiating a similar deal in Japan or Germany. In each case, achieving a successful outcome, in both the initial agreement and the long-term business relationship, will depend on sensitivity to differences in languages, value systems and norms of behaviour between themselves and their hosts. In short, being attuned to cultural differences can directly affect the success or failure of the project.

This chapter has two broad aims. The first is to gain an understanding of the many dimensions of culture, and its importance in how business is transacted between people across the globe. The second aim is to examine the impact of globalization in the dynamic cultural environment. While there is abundant evidence, such as the explosive growth of internet use, which points to an emerging global culture, there is also considerable evidence that local cultural identities are not withering away, as some expected, but are adapting and persisting in the new global environment. The second aim, therefore, is to examine the interacting cultural dynamic between the global and the local. For international business, grasping this dynamic interaction is the key to 'riding the waves of culture' (Trompenaars, 1994). We begin by defining culture, looking at the dimensions of culture in society and the makeup of specific cultural identities among the world's peoples.

What is culture and how is it relevant to business?

Culture has been defined in many different ways, reflecting the variety of cultural phenomena that can be observed. Language, religious ritual and art are just a few examples of cultural symbols whose shared meanings form the unique fingerprint of a particular society. Culture can be broadly defined as, 'a learned, shared, compelling, interrelated set of symbols whose meanings provide a set of orientations for members of a society' (Terpstra and David, 1991, p. 6). Inevitably, we all view and interpret the world around us through a cultural 'filter' to some degree. **Ethnocentrism** denotes the inflexible approach of relating to the world only in terms of our own culture, while **polycentrism** is the approach of attempting to overcome our own cultural assumptions and develop an openness and understanding of other cultures. Successful international business relationships depend in large measure on developing a polycentric approach in situations where cross-cultural issues arise, such as joint ventures.

Culture includes the system of values and beliefs shared by the group and the norms of behaviour expected of group members. Values relate primarily to notions of good and evil, right and wrong. Values also include notions of the individual in relation to the group. An important distinguishing characteristic of particular Western value systems, for example, is the intrinsic value accorded to the individual. Where individualism is highly valued, the society's institutional and governance structures will seek to guarantee individual freedoms. The growth of democracy in countries with strong individualist cultures is no coincidence, but an outcome of value systems. By contrast, societies which place greater value on the collectivity, such as the family or the kinship group, are likely to develop institutional structures which are more paternalistic, that is, dominated by a father figure. These societies are likely to value group loyalty more highly than individual freedoms.

SUMMARY POINTS

What is culture?

Learned, shared, interrelated set of symbols which unite and identify members of a society.

Aspects of culture:

- Values and beliefs, including moral and religious beliefs
- Communication, including spoken and written language, and also body language
- Norms of behaviour, for example, associated with eating and drinking, dress
- Customs
- Art, music, dance, sport.

Norms relate to patterns and standards of behaviour. They shape what is considered normal and abnormal behaviour within a society. Norms include the role of the family, the upbringing of children, the role of women and the respect accorded to age. Norms often reflect values and, like values, can derive from religious beliefs and take on religious significance in many societies. Norms may also reflect customs which distinguish societies one from another. Manner of dress, food and the etiquette associated with eating and drinking are also obvious distinguishing features of a culture. For businesspeople in a foreign environment, an understanding of local culture is needed not just in the context of doing business, but in general social relations with hosts. Indeed, in Asian cultures, doing business is not confined merely to working hours, but blends into social occasions such as meals together. It is here that bonds of trust are built and where sensitivity to cultural values and norms can be critical.

Values and norms of behaviour are learned in the social context – we are not born with them. For this reason they are not fixed and static, but are capable of change. Societies may evolve over time, and individuals may change when they move to a new environment. Organizations, too, may change as they expand internationally. One of the themes of this chapter is the extent to which growth in interactions between cultures and growth of international markets and global brands, such as McDonald's and Nike, leads to a global or 'cosmopolitan' culture. The spread of Western cultural symbols, such as Levi jeans, Western pop music and fast food are often grouped together as trends towards the globalization of culture. However, they have not supplanted local cultural preferences. The Big Mac and Coca-Cola epitomize the uniform standard product for all markets. But in fact, McDonald's has long been sensitive to differing local tastes, offering the teriyaki burger in Japan, for example, although relying on their core brands as the mainstay of the business. Waning enthusiasm for hamburgers in their mature markets, however, has given impetus to a change of strategy. Coca-Cola, too, has revised its global strategy, offering different products to suit consumers in different markets, under a variety of brand names, as seen in the closing case study in Part 1. Similarly, entertainment and media industries, including music and film, present a mixed picture – the emergence of several global companies, but also much local output designed for local tastes.

Case study 6.1   Image change at McDonald's

The Big Mac is perhaps the foremost symbol of the globalization of fast food – universal, but distinctively American. The Big Mac was invented in 1958 and for the next three decades McDonald's restaurants were concentrated in America. In 1985, only 22 per cent of the company's 8900 restaurants were outside America. By 1995, this percentage had leapt to 38 per cent. A major breakthrough was the establishment of its restaurants in Russia, which has been so successful that it inspired a book, *To Russia with Fries*, penned by the founder of the McDonald's Russian operation. McDonald's now has 30,000 restaurants in 120 countries. The company has prided itself on its adaptations of its products to suit local preferences, for example the 'Maharaja Mac' in India, which is made of mutton, as Hindus consider cows sacred and do not eat beef. Similarly, Chinese McDonald's offer rice cakes with mushroom and ginger, which are more suited to Chinese tastes. Growth in China has been slow, but the company is hoping to increase the number of outlets in the country by 50 per cent to 1000 by the time of the Beijing Olympics in 2008.

Following stagnant sales in the US and negative publicity linking eating at McDonald's with obesity, the company is now undergoing a rethink of its strategy, particularly in the US and Europe. As the figure shows, the proportion of the population that is overweight has grown rapidly.

While lawsuits by two New York teenagers against the company failed to show that McDonald's caused their obesity, the negative publicity and possibility of further litigation have contributed to the rethink. A doctor who runs an obesity clinic in California has pointed to the cultural embeddedness of McDonald's, saying: 'People have no idea that if they eat a Big Mac, French fries and a soda, they've consumed nearly all their recommended calorie intake for the day' (Buckley, 12 July 2002). In 2005, the company launched new television advertisements in the US which show no burgers or fries, but, instead, feature a new image of Ronald McDonald playing soccer with children.

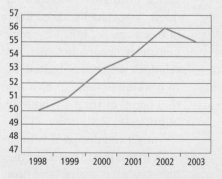

Note: Overweight is defined as having a BMI (body mass index) of 25 or more; BMI is defined as body weight in kilograms divided by height in metres squared (kg/m2).

Percentage of the US population overweight
Source: 'Spoilt for choice: A survey of food', *The Economist*, 13–19 December 2003.

Changing eating habits both in the US and other markets have seen health-conscious customers turn away from burgers and fries, to the more interesting and healthier offerings of the new 'quick casual' restaurants, which are winning customers from the traditional fast-food establishments. New menus at McDonald's feature main course salads, fresh fruit and mineral water. This trend might explain the slight drop in the percentage of overweight people in the US in 2003, as shown in the figure. Along with the new menus, McDonald's is revamping its restaurants, to complete its image change. Restaurants in France have been in the forefront of the revamping, bringing in comfortable seating, improved decor, and even iPod digital music players along the walls. This new look McDonald's is being rolled out across Europe, to be extended worldwide. However, these changes will be brought in only gradually, as the company is now focusing less on numbers of new openings and more on improving quality and service, to encourage customers to keep coming back to its existing restaurants. While they opened some 1000 new restaurants in 2002, in 2003 they opened just 360. An important consideration for McDonald's executives is that 70 per cent of its restaurants are franchises, run by individual owner-operators. Franchisees will have to find most of the extra money to carry out any revamp, and even though they can expect a boost in sales after the revamp, they may have little capital to spend if sales have been flat for some years.

The company's diversification in the 1990s into 'partner brands', including the Chipotle Mexican Grill and Donato's Pizzerias, praised at the time as a growth strategy to complement its mature hamburger business, is now seen as perhaps having diverted management attention away from the basics of the company's main business. Donato's was sold back to its former owner in 2003, and expansion of the other brands scaled down. It has kept a minority stake in Pret A Manger, which prides itself on fresh, high-quality sandwiches.

The 'back-to-basics' strategy is not necessarily a guarantee of success for McDonald's. Historically, the company has been more successful at growing the business by opening new restaurants than it has by getting more customers to come to existing restaurants more often. Designing new menus which suit local tastes is crucial, as is the look and feel of the new 'deplasticized' interiors. Much depends, however, on franchisees' willingness to buy into the new image.

Sources: Buckley, N. 'Eyes on the fries: will new products, restaurant refits and a marketing overhaul sustain the Golden Arches?', *Financial Times*, 29 August 2003; Griffith, V. and Buckley, N. 'The scary fat end of the wedge', *Financial Times*, 12 July 2002; Buckley, N., 'Hamburger focus for McDonald's', *Financial Times*, 16 December 2003; 'Spoilt for choice: a survey of food', *The Economist*, 13–19 December, 2003; Nestle, M. (2002) *Food Politics* (Berkeley, CA: University of California Press); Ward, A., 'Chips are down for Ronald as anti-obesity lobby swells', *Financial Times*, 8 February 2005; Grant, J., 'McDonald's to open China "drive-through"', *Financial Times*, 12 May 2005.

Case questions

How does the new strategy at McDonald's depart from the company's traditional strategy?

Is the new image likely to succeed?

WEB ALERT!

McDonald's website is at http://www.mcdonalds.com

Pret A Manger's website is at http://www.pret.com

CRITICAL PERSPECTIVES

Culture and markets

People point to McDonald's or Coca-Cola as examples of tastes, markets and hence cultures becoming similar everywhere. There are, indeed, many products and services becoming common to world markets. What is important to consider, however, is not what they are and where they are found physically, but what they mean to the people in each culture … The essence of culture is not what is visible on the surface. It is the shared ways groups of people understand and interpret the world. So the fact that we can all listen to Walkmans and eat hamburgers tells us that there are some novel products that can be sold on a universal message, but it does not tell us what eating hamburgers or listening to Walkmans means in different cultures. (Trompenaars, 1994, p. 3).

■ Is Trompenaars underestimating the impact of global products and brands in influencing cultural values? Think of some other examples that confirm his view. Are there also examples of products or brands indicative of a deeper globalization of culture, apparently contradicting his view?

National cultures

Research has shown that people have acquired their basic value systems by the age of ten (Hofstede, 1994). It is during these formative years that national culture exerts its strongest influence, through family and early schooling. Nations are distinguishable from each other by language, religion, ethnic or racial identity and, above all, by a shared cultural history. Together, these distinguishing characteristics blend into a national culture. National culture influences family life, education, organizational culture and economic and political structures. The sense of belonging to a nation is one of the most important focal points of cultural identity. In the course of time, myth mixes with historical events in the collective memory and the associated symbols serve as powerful emotive links between present and past and even the future.

The nation-state combines the concept of cultural bonds created by the nation with the territorial and organizational structures of the state. However, the world's peoples comprise many more nations than states and hence most states contain multiple cultural and national identities. Historically, nations have sought self-determination for their own people, through nationalist movements. New nation-states thus often represent the culmination of national aspirations and the mobilization of nationalist movements to attain independence from existing ruling regimes in which they feel their interests are not properly represented. Largely as a result of the break-up of colonial empires, the number of nation-states has grown dramatically since the end of the Second World War. However, many of these states have proved to be ill-fitting administrative containers for the multiple social and ethnic groups within their borders.

Growing cultural awareness has also brought into the international limelight tensions between national self-awareness and existing state institutions. We look at two contrasting examples of nationhood and cultural identity: first, Japan, an old state with a homogeneous culture, and, secondly, the new states of Eastern Europe, where heterogeneous cultures present challenges for nation-building as well as for constructing new institutions of state.

SUMMARY POINTS

Elements of national culture

- Common language, or dialect.
- Shared religious and moral values.
- National symbols and rituals, such as flags, national festivals, particular places and monuments.
- Shared history.
- Patterns of family life and family values.
- Roles of males and females.
- Attitudes to education.
- Relationship between the individual and group, including the work organization and the state.
- Ways of resolving conflicts.
- Geographic homeland.

Japan has been described as an 'ethnic state' (Smith, 1991, p. 105), in that it is one of the few countries that approach the ideal of the one-to-one fit between nation and state. This cultural unity stems partly from the Japanese language, which is unique to Japan, and the religion of Shinto, also exclusively Japanese, which reinforces national cohesion. A strong sense of national identity, coupled with group loyalty, was a major factor in Japan's impressive record of postwar reconstruction and economic development. Japan served as the first example that modern capitalism need not rest on accepted Western values of individualism, but can be built on an Asian value system. In the 1990s, however, as was seen in Chapter 4, Japan's cultural strengths seemed to have turned into weaknesses, inhibiting its businesses' ability to adapt to the changing global environment. Significantly, Nissan's regained competitiveness under Renault's control has been the outcome of restructuring imposed from outside traditional Japanese structures and values.

The nations of Central and Eastern Europe, by contrast, present a much less clearcut picture. The boundaries of the modern states of Europe have not been constant, but have been drawn to reflect the winners' and losers' positions in numerous wars and political battles fought out over territorial claims. Similarly, the rise and subsequent disintegration of empires have left their mark across the cultural landscape. The Soviet Union suppressed dozens of nationalities within an all-embracing Communist ideology. With its break-up, the peoples of Eastern Europe have rediscovered and asserted their national identity and cultural heritage. Cultural factors have played a part in the development paths of the independent nation-states which have emerged since the fall of the Berlin Wall in 1989. Poland, Hungary and the Czech Republic have built on a sense of community, with a single dominant language and constitutional safeguards for minority groups. By contrast, in Yugoslavia, a Balkan state, multiple nationalities which had been unified under authoritarian rule fragmented in the new state. The central governmental authority of the new Yugoslav federal state, in which the Serbs are the dominant group, was unable to maintain its legitimacy in the eyes of the different ethnic and religious groups. Croats, Bosnians, Slovenians and Macedonians have broken away to form separate states as homelands. The province of Kosovo, predominantly Muslim, which had been semi-self-governing within Yugoslavia, sought independence from the predominantly Orthodox Serbian establishment. Following the war in Kosovo in 1998, Kosovo's administration was taken over by UN and NATO authorities. The destructive forces of ethnic hostility in the Balkans illustrate the power of historical cultural forces in the modern world. The examples of Japan and Yugoslavia present dramatic contrasts: in the first, the sense of nationhood unified people in a sense of social purpose; in the second, it led to ethnic conflict, destabilizing society.

Just as new national cultural identities are emerging in the former Communist states, European integration is seeking to mould a new European sense of identity. Is European economic, social and political integration bringing about a sense of unified 'Europeanness' among the various populations of member states? Europe as a whole lacks the shared sense of culture, history, ethnicity and language that identify nations as enduring entities. As we have seen, a person may have multiple cultural identities. A Hispanic American, for example, has a dual identity, but both have relatively long histories and shared cultures. A European identity is more like a social construct, which would require 'mental reprogramming', to use to Hofstede's phrase (Hofstede, 1994, p. 4). In his view, such reprogramming is not possible, given the wide national cultural differences between European nations and their deep historical roots. Nonetheless, Europeans may feel national identity *plus* European identity, as has been found in the Eurobarometer surveys of public opinion conducted on behalf of the European Commission. Respondents were invited to place themselves in one of four categories in terms of identity: nationality alone; nationality and European; European and nationality; and European only. Forty-six per cent felt themselves to be 'nationality plus European' (Eurobarometer, 1998). The majority, however, identified themselves by their nationality only. This suggests that perceptions of European cultural identity have proceeded more slowly than economic and political integration.

Languages

Language is the basic means of communication between people, which facilitates social interaction and fosters a system of shared values and norms. Language is more than the vocabulary and grammar that make up written and spoken expression. Hall and Hall (1960) distinguish between 'low-context' and 'high-context' cultures . In a **low-context culture**, communication is clear and direct; speakers come straight to the point and say exactly what they mean. America is a good example of the low-context culture. In a **high-context culture**, much goes unsaid; depending on the relationship between the speakers, each is able to interpret body language and 'read between the lines'. In this type of culture, ambiguity is the norm and directness is avoided. Asian cultures fall into this type. For Americans, meeting people from high-context cultures can seem frustrating, as they are unsure where they stand, while their Asian counterparts are unsettled by their directness of approach, which may come across as insincerity.

In terms of numbers, the linguistic family of Chinese is spoken by the largest numbers of people, amounting to about 20 per cent of the world's population. Only about 5.4 per cent of the world's population have English as their native language, and they have been slightly overtaken in numbers by native Spanish speakers, as shown in Table 6.1.

Table 6.1 The world's top ten languages

Rank	Language	Population (in millions)
1	Chinese, Mandarin	885
2	Spanish	332
3	English	322
4	Bengali	189
5	Hindi	182
6	Portuguese	170
7	Russian	170
8	Japanese	125
9	German, Standard	98
10	Chinese, Wu	77

Note: Figures refer to first-language speakers in all countries, 1999.
Source: Summer Institute of Linguistics (2000) Ethnologue, at www.sil.org/ethnologue/.

WEB ALERT!

For foreign language and culture specific resources on the web, look at
http://www.ethnologue.com

For minority languages, the following websites contain hundreds of links:
http://www.123worldcom/languages
http://www.linguasphere.org/

Linguistic diversity

In most countries, one or more dominant languages exist alongside minority languages, which may be concentrated in specific geographical regions. Canada has two official languages, English and French, and the minority French speakers have a history of separatist activism. Switzerland, by contrast, has four official languages (German, French, Italian and Romansh) which co-exist in harmony.

Linguistic diversity within a state may arise in several different ways. First, a minority language may represent a native culture, such as the Indian nations which inhabited North and South America before the arrival of European settlers. The US, Australia and South Africa are all settler societies, where tensions erupted between the new arrivals and existing native cultures. These tensions are still observable today, as evidenced by the second-class citizen status of which native Americans complain.

Second, colonizing states introduced their own language into their colonies, using language as a tool of conquest. Thus, the language of Brazil is Portuguese, the language of the imperial power. The Western imperial powers of the sixteenth to the nineteenth centuries included the British, French, Dutch, Belgians, Spanish and Portuguese. All left their national languages in their colonies, where the colonial language became that of the elites, as well as that of government and administration. The many indigenous peoples spoke native languages, but struggled to maintain their cultures in the tide of colonialism. Today, most of South America is Spanish-speaking, and in recent years Spanish companies have expanded in the region, attracted by a perceived affinity with these markets derived from a common language. Large parts of Africa are French-speaking. African countries, such as Zaire and Nigeria, have a cultural heritage of tribal loyalties, fostered by many different languages. Depending on the context, the use of English can overcome the problems of intercultural communication. However, the choice of language is a matter of cultural sensitivity and outsiders risk offending their hosts if they make the wrong choice in the circumstances.

Third, immigration can create linguistic diversity. Immigrants are faced with the difficulties of assimilation in a new culture, or maintaining a separate identity. Where immigrants are concentrated geographically, they may form a subculture in which they speak their home language. An example of the effects of immigration can be seen in the increase in numbers of Hispanic people in America. Hispanics, who are people of Latin American origin whose first language is Spanish, made up 13.3 per cent of the US population in 2003, a proportion that grew 60 per cent in the 1990s (Therrien and Ramirez, 2000; Ramirez and de la Cruz, 2002). The US Census Bureau expects this proportion to reach 24.4 per cent by 2050 (Grimes, 2004). Their numbers are rapidly approaching 40 million, making them the equivalent of the world's fifth largest Spanish-speaking country. Case study 6.2 highlights the responses of businesses in tailoring products and advertising to this growing group of consumers.

Case study 6.2 Winning over Hispanic consumers in the US

Hispanic people in the US are a heterogeneous group numbering 37.4 million people, or more than one in eight of the total US population. Also referred to as Latinos, they may be of any race and have their roots in any of a number of countries in Central and South America, although about two-thirds are Mexican (see figure). US Census Bureau research indicates that they are generally less well off and less well educated than the non-Hispanic white inhabitants. They are geographically more concentrated (in the west and south), more likely to be under 18 and twice as likely to live in large households (five or more people). Like their numbers, their spending power is growing rapidly, and businesses are waking up to their particular needs. Simply translating information and advertising into Spanish is not enough to win them over. Consumer products, food and beverages were some of the earliest products to be targeted at Hispanic consumers. Häagen-Dazs created a new flavour for its Argentinian market, *dulce de leche*, which it brought to the US Hispanic market with great success in the 1990s. The flavour became one of the company's bestsellers. P&G has launched a laundry detergent designed specifically for Latino consumers, and relies on its multicultural marketing division for advertising. The company, like others, has found that outreach activities in the community, providing information for consumers, is helpful in this market, where the culture revolves around family bonds and activities.

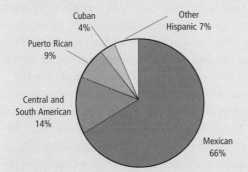

US Hispanics by origin, 2002

Source: US Census Bureau (2002) *Annual Demographic Supplement to the March 2002 Current Population Survey* (Washington, DC: US Census Bureau).

Evidence from research organizations indicates that businesses should not treat this as a one-size-fits-all market. Given that some 43 per cent were

born in the US, most Hispanics are either bi-lingual or mainly English-speaking. They tend to shift their language use for different types of product or service: they would deal with a travel agent in Spanish, but when buying a product such as a car or mobile phone, they prefer English. General Motors found it had difficulties reaching Hispanic consumers, losing out to other brands. It recast its television advertising campaigns to feature family themes, emotional appeal and vibrant colours, designed to tap into strong Hispanic values. Significantly, Hispanic TV audiences are likely to watch as a family and pay attention to TV advertisements, unlike those in many other places, who switch channels or leave the room during commercial breaks.

Banking would not appear to present obvious opportunities among Hispanic people, especially as recent immigrants have negative images of banks in their countries of origin. However, Mexicans send over $7bn. each year back home to Mexico. These funds, known as 'remittances', offer a business opportunity to banks. Bank of America introduced a product called SafeSend, facilitating the easy transfer of funds to Mexico. Citigroup also, introduced a scheme for sending remittances, launching it on Mothers' Day, which is a particularly important day for Mexicans. Mortgage lending has followed, as middle-class Hispanic families have become more affluent. A bonus is that, although they may be slow to buy new products or services, when they are won over, they tend to be loyal customers.

Sources: Ramirez, R. and de la Cruz, G.P., 'The Hispanic population in the United States: March 2002', *Current Population Reports*, No. P20-545, Washington, DC: US Census Bureau; Yeager, H. 'Chasing the Latino dollar', *Financial Times*, 23 August, 2002; Murray, S. 'The American dream gets a Latino beat', *Financial Times*, 25 March 2004; Authers, J. '*Se habla español* is no longer enough', *Financial Times*, 13 January 2004; Grimes, C., 'Big shift forecast in US ethnic make-up', *Financial Times*, 18 March 2004; Authers, J., 'Banks look to cash in on the flow of money to Mexico', *Financial Times*, 8 August 2002.

Case question

What are the distinguishing aspects of Hispanic culture which affect consumer behaviour?

The strength of language as a cultural force is shown by the policies of national governments. Almost all specify an official language of the state and control the use of other languages. Authorities seek to exert these controls in the school system, as well as in the national press and other media. Deliberate policies to foster the national language may serve two purposes: it can stifle splintering effects caused by the use of minority languages, and it can help to push back what is seen as the tide of English. Minority groups that promote a strong separate identity can be a destabilizing factor within societies. In both France and Spain, for example, promotion by the Basque people of their own cultural identity, coupled with demands for autonomy are a persistent feature. On the Spanish side of the border, these demands are only partially accommodated in Spain's system of 'autonomous regions', and militant Basques have often resorted to violence. The island of Corsica is part of France, but its separate identity and language, coupled with cultural and historical links with Italy have made it a thorn in the side of French governments. The Corsicans have a long history of separatist violence, which has discouraged potential investors. In 2001, the French national assembly passed a new law designed to devolve limited powers to a Corsican assembly in areas such as the environment, tourism and culture. It includes provision for the teaching of Corsican in schools, and has caused controversy among those who support a strong central administration and the supremacy of the French language (Graham, 2001).

English: the global language?

The importance of English as a global language extends far beyond the number of native speakers. English is the commonest language for the global media and the internet, and the commonest second language. For the many people who travel internationally, English is a recognized means of communication, often when neither of the parties speaks English as a first language. These globetrotters include not only businesspeople and diplomats, but tourists, sportspeople, academics and students. The English language in these contexts is an intercultural means of communicating. Businesspeople are likely to use English in their international business activities, but speak their own first language at home. By the same token, while Hindi is the official language of India, English as an associate national language facilitates communication between the many non-Hindi-speaking groups. India is one of the world's most multilingual countries, with 14 major languages and many more minor ones. English is spoken by about 50 per cent of India's population. Moreover, in the booming IT industry, the predominance of English language is proving a location advantage.

The internet is predominantly in English. Of the estimated total number of web-pages of 313 billion in 2004, 68.4 per cent are in English, as Table 6.2 shows. This does not mean, however, that the world's online population is made up of this large proportion of English speakers. Research indicates that there are large online populations in the major language groups, and that many people access the internet in two languages, commonly their first language and English. They are more likely to access the internet at home in their first language, in which they feel more comfortable (Global Reach, 2004). It is estimated, for example, that of the 204.3 million Americans online, only 177 million access the internet in English (Global Reach,

2004). In Figure 6.1, the 35.8 per cent of people accessing the internet in English includes those who go online in other languages as well. The implications for e-business and marketing are that communication in local languages is likely to reach more consumers than English-only websites.

Table 6.2 Web content by language

Language	Percentage of global web content
English	68.4
Japanese	5.9
German	5.8
Chinese	3.9
French	3.0
Spanish	2.4
Russian	1.9
Italian	1.6
Portuguese	1.4
Korean	1.3
Other	4.6

Source: Global Reach (2004) 'Global Internet Statistics (by Language)' at http://glreach.com/globstats/.

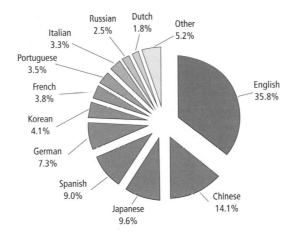

Figure 6.1 **Online language populations**
Source: Global Reach 2004.

Religions

The system of values and beliefs that characterizes a culture may be embodied in a particular religion. Research has identified over 15,000 distinct religions and religious movements among the world's population (Barrett, 1997). They range from simple folk religions to highly refined systems of beliefs, with set rituals, organized worship, sacred texts and a hierarchy of religious leaders. The major religions in terms of numbers of followers, Christianity and Islam, fall into this latter category. All religions call on their followers to believe in supernatural forces which affect their lives and to follow prescribed moral rules. As well as religious power, religion may exercise considerable secular and political power, and can form a major unifying force in society. Religious divides, both within states and between states, can also be a source of friction. Research suggests that a large proportion of terrorism stems from religious groups, many of these either independent or on the fringes of mainstream religions (Juergensmeyer, 2003).

Most of the world's states adhere in principle to the right of religious freedom, allowing multiple religions to worship freely. But in practice, there are exceptions, where the practice of particular religions is prohibited by state authorities. States may have a dominant or even an official religion, although most modern states follow the principle of separation of church and state. Religious affiliation may coincide with a sense of nationhood, as in Poland, where being a Pole and being Roman Catholic are integrally linked in the nation's sense of identity. The Church in Poland is still a potent force, but the government stepped back from a national Church in its new constitution in 1997, and opted instead for an expression of the importance of the Church in national life. In countries where religion is a major element of the cultural environment, sensitivity to local religious beliefs and practices is particularly important in building business relations.

The world's two major religions are Christianity and Islam (whose adherents are called Muslims). Both are monotheistic, that is, believing in one God, in contrast to a polytheistic religion such as Hinduism, in which there is a panoply of gods. Christianity and Islam are both proselytizing religions, which means that they deliberately aim to expand numbers and convert new followers. Since 1970, numbers of Muslims have grown more rapidly than numbers of Christians, as Table 6.3 indicates. The higher birth rate in predominantly Muslim countries is an important factor. The major religions which appear in Table 6.3 account for just over 70 per cent of the world's people, leaving some 15 per cent who are adherents of many other smaller religions, including indigenous religions of Africa and Asia. Africa and Asia, which have the largest Muslim populations, are now also home to more Christians than the traditional centres in Europe.

Table 6.3 Growth of major world religions

	1900		1970		1990		2000	
Christians	558.1	(34.5%)	1,236	(33.5%)	1,747	(33.2%)	1,999	(33.0%)
Muslims	199.9	(12.3%)	553.5	(15.0%)	962.3	(18.3%)	1,188	(19.6%)
Hindus	203.0	(12.5%)	462.5	(12.5%)	685.9	(13.0%)	811.3	(13.4%)
Buddhists	127.0	(7.8%)	233.4	(6.3%)	323.1	(6.1%)	359.9	(5.9%)
Jews	12.3	(0.8%)	14.7	(0.4%)	13.1	(0.3%)	14.4	(0.2%)
Non-religious	3.0	(0.2%)	532.0	(14.4%)	707.1	(13.4%)	768.1	(12.7%)

Note: Numbers in millions, followed by percentage of the world's population (in brackets).
Source: Barrett, D., Kurian, G. and Johnson, T. (eds) (2001) *World Christian Encyclopedia*, 2nd edn (New York: Oxford University Press).

Christianity

About 33 per cent of the world's population identifies with Christianity, as Table 6.3 shows. Through missionary activity, Christianity has spread from Europe and America to all parts of the globe. While all Christians believe in the divinity of Jesus Christ and regard the Bible as authoritative, differences of interpretation have emerged, to cause theological splits among Christians. The first of Christianity's major splits occurred in the eleventh century, between the Orthodox Church and the Roman Catholic Church. The Roman Catholics are now by far the more numerous, but followers of the Orthodox rites are still influential in many countries, such as Greece and Russia. The second major split in the Christian world occurred in the sixteenth century, when the Protestant Churches separated from Rome. Protestants went on to establish themselves throughout Europe and America, through different denominations, such as Methodists and Baptists. Protestantism is associated with the principle that individual salvation is achievable independently of the institutional Church. The position of the Pope and the sainthood are anathema to Protestants and have been the root cause of many religious conflicts, some with long and bitter histories. Recent trends in both Protestantism and Roman Catholicism have been the growth of more evangelical groups and growing numbers of followers outside traditional centres, in, for example, Latin America and Africa. Catholics in Latin America now make up nearly half the world's Catholics, and Latin America has also seen a dramatic rise in the numbers of Protestants, from just 2 million in 1960 to more that 60 million in 2003. Looking at Figure 6.2, it is noticeable that there has been an increase in the number of Christian groups who identify themselves as independent, many of which have broken away from the mainstream Christian denominations. Many, too, are specific to a single country or region, such as Latin America or Africa, indicating an increasing diversity within Christianity.

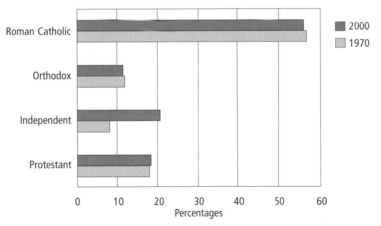

Figure 6.2 **World Christianity by denomination**
Source: Barrett, D., Kurian, G., and Johnson, T. (eds) (2001) *World Christian Encyclopedia*, 2nd edn (New York: Oxford University Press).

Strong religious allegiance, while it has a personal and private dimension, also has social and political implications. Social associations and political parties in many countries are commonly based on religious affiliations, and these form an essential dimension of the business environment. For example, the growth in membership and influence of large churches in parts of the US impacts on the social and cultural environment of the communities in which they are located (see minifile). If there is an established religion in a location, a business must take account of its wide ramifications, while in locations where there are multiple religions, a business as a good corporate citizen should not discriminate, for example, in employment conditions. See the summary at the end of this section for a list of the many ways in which religion impacts on business life.

Minifile

THE MEGACHURCH AS BIG BUSINESS

Lakewood Church in Texas attracts attendances of 25,000 for a service which features a 12-piece stage band, three large screens and professionally designed mood lighting. Clearly, this is no ordinary church – it is a 'megachurch'. The growth in megachurches, and their influence in parts of the US, has been a fairly recent phenomenon. Defined as a non-Catholic church with at least 2000 members, these very large churches have grown in number from just 10 in 1970 to 740 in 2003. Numbers of worshippers have also increased, some congregations numbering many thousands. It is estimated that combined membership totals nearly 4 million. While many are mainstream Protestant denominations, increasingly they see themselves as independent or 'nondenominational'. These churches bear little resemblance to the traditional picture of a community church – they are vast arenas, often part of a larger complex of buildings on a 'campus'. The complex may include an office block, private primary school, sports facilities and media centre. These complexes have become multimillion dollar businesses in effect, their pastors more like CEOs than traditional ministers.

The growth in megachurches provides an example of the use of media strategy and marketing principles to increase membership. They typically use television and radio broadcasts, organize entertainment, run websites and publish CDs and books. For example, Willow Creek Community Church has a staff of 500 employees, specializing in running conferences and seminars for teaching other churches how to market themselves. Scott Thumma, a specialist in research on religions, says: 'They're playing on a whole different understanding of religion; it's not something that looks like your parents' faith. They're tapping into the bigger is better, mall-like mentality of America' (Liu, 25 October 2003).

Sources: Liu, B. 'Churchgoers of America pray that bigger is better', *Financial Times*, 25 October 2003; Kroll, L., 'Megachurches, Megabusinesses', *Forbes*, 17 September 2003.

Islam

Muslims number over a billion globally, spread among many different countries, ranging from the Middle East and Africa to areas now part of Russia and extending as far as China and Malaysia in East Asia. They make up a majority of the population in over thirty countries and large minorities in others. Founded by the prophet Mohammed in the seventh century, Islam unites its followers through shared faith, shared ritual in everyday life and belief in the words of the Koran, the sacred book. There are two major branches of Islam, Sunni and Shi-ite. For the Muslim, religious ritual is part of everyday life, not confined to worship on a particular day of the week. While codes of conduct form part of the values of all religions, Islam is particularly endowed with formal prescriptive guidance in all aspects of life, including social relations, social behaviour, rules for the consumption of food and drink and the role and appearance of women in society. Religious leaders play an important guiding role and are influential particularly in education, as the case study on Saudi Arabia shows.

An enterprise culture is fostered in Muslim societies and economic development is promoted. However, it is forbidden to earn a profit based on the exploitation of others. Interests payments are seen as sinful, and therefore the common forms of financing used in Western countries violate Muslim law. Muslim banking has developed systems complying with Muslim law (see Chapter 9), and Western businesses are able to make financial arrangements which accommodate both sides. These arrangements show the adaptability of Muslim institutions to modern business conditions. Similarly, state courts have grown up in Muslim countries, where traditionally there were only religious courts. State courts can apply both religious law and Western-style commercial law, signifying an accommodation with Western legal forms. The issue of Westernization divides Muslims. 'Westernization' refers to a society's adoption of Western culture and values and is associated with processes of modernization, while 'Islamic fundamentalism' refers to maintenance of the supremacy of Islam in all aspects of society. Westernization has not been universally welcomed by Muslims, many of whom see their religious values being undermined in the process.

SUMMARY POINTS

Countries home to the major world religions

- **Predominantly Roman Catholic countries:** Italy, France, Spain, Poland, Mexico and other Central American countries, Brazil and other South American countries, Philippines.
- **Predominantly Protestant countries:** the UK, Germany, Norway, Sweden, Denmark, Finland, the US, Australia, South Africa.
- **Predominantly Eastern Orthodox countries:** Greece, Russia, Romania.
- **Predominantly Muslim countries:** Albania, Saudi Arabia, Egypt, Algeria, Tunisia, Morocco, Syria, Libya, Pakistan, Iran, Iraq, Indonesia.
- **Predominantly Hindu countries:** India, Nepal.

Oil-rich Iran experienced rapid modernization and industrialization under the Shah, who came to power in 1959. The Shah was a supporter of cultural Westernization, and had close ties with the US, which had a strategic interest in Iran's oil wealth. But not all Iranians benefited from the country's oil boom: the agricultural sector and non-oil-related industries suffered and the numbers of urban poor increased. The disaffected were successfully mobilized by the fundamentalist religious leader, Ayatollah Khomeini, who had lived in exile for most of the Shah's tenure. The Shah's regime was overthrown in 1979 and an Islamic regime of religious government took control. The Islamic revolution in Iran was the first in which a popular movement united by religious fundamentalism has overthrown an existing government. Iran's current government is cautiously embracing liberal economic reforms.

The process of modernization has brought urbanization, widespread literacy and education, greater communication with other cultures and also more exposure to the global media. Fundamentalists argue that Western materialism and liberal ethical values are adversely influencing young people especially, and in particular the urban young, who form the fastest growing section of Muslim societies. Women, too, have felt the conflict between Western and fundamentalist values. Westernization has brought women more opportunities for education and greater mobility than would be possible in the restrictive regime of traditional Muslim societies. The requirement for women to cover their hair and wear long clothing has also been relaxed in some Muslim societies. The tension which is evident between fundamentalism and Westernization in Muslim societies impacts on the business environment as shown in Case study 6.3. New, younger leaders in a number of Arab states – Morocco, Jordan, Syria and the United Arab Emirates – are gradually introducing social and economic reforms and also welcoming foreign investors.

Case study 6.3 Islam under strain in Saudi Arabia

The desert kingdom of Saudi Arabia presents many cultural contrasts. It is the birthplace of Islam and home to Islam's two most sacred cities, Mecca and Medina. Under its rulers, the royal House of Saud, the state is run according to the strict Wahhabi form of Sunni Islam. As the world's largest oil-exporting country, it has accumulated vast wealth from oil revenues, beginning at the time of the oil crises in the 1970s which saw soaring oil prices. Global and, in particular, American demand for oil has focused world attention on Saudi Arabia, its way of life and the prospects for its long-term stability. However, Saudi rulers face pressure from a number of sources. The Americans accuse Saudi Arabia of doing too little to combat terrorism, pointing to the fact that religious terrorist groups, particularly al-Qaeda, originated in Saudi Arabia. The Saudi government also faces pressure from the conservative religious establishment on which its legitimacy rests and, finally, from the growing voices for reform within the kingdom.

Oil wealth held much promise for the kingdom, funding education, health and other social welfare programmes for the country's rapidly growing population. At the same time, the wealth accumulated by the oil-rich elite funded a luxury lifestyle far removed from ordinary people. In recent years, state finances have become strained as they struggle to maintain welfare programmes. The ruling dynasty has been reluctant to

introduce market reforms in the economy, which remains state-dominated, and economic growth faltered as oil revenues fell back. Unemployment, estimated at 15 per cent, has become a growing problem, particularly among the young, and 62 per cent of the population are under 25. GDP per head peaked at $23,980 in 1977, and since then has fallen to just over half that figure, standing at $12,650 in 2002 (see figure). There are concerns that social unrest and instability may flourish in this environment, finding an outlet in religious radicalism. However, suggestions for reforms from well-meaning outsiders, urging the adoption of more modern, liberal values, have been resisted by the establishment.

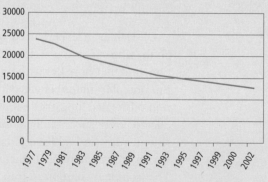

Declining GDP per capita in Saudi Arabia (dollars, at PPP)

Source: United Nations Development Programme (2004) *Human Development Report 2004* (New York: UNDP), Table 13.

Nevertheless, there are voices within Saudi Arabia urging reforms of the education system in particular and the role of women in society. Women are now better educated than previous generations and are less willing to accept their very limited rights in Saudi society. While literacy has reached high levels, the education system has aimed above all to imbue strict Islamic culture, with an emphasis on memorizing texts, leaving students poorly prepared for challenging employment. One Saudi executive has said: 'It's a one-way education, teachers lecture and students listen. They don't develop an inquisitive mind. They are not creative when put in the job market' (Khalaf, 20 November 2002). There is little scope for other subjects, such as foreign languages, which are seen as posing a threat to their own culture. One girl student who was disappointed at not being able to learn English has said: 'By learning English we open the door to different ideas, different ways of thinking and different ways of living. That, after all, is what education is about – or should be about' (Khalaf, 30 October 2002). It has been suggested by the United Nations Development Programme (2002) that a 'knowledge deficit' is holding back economic development in Arab countries generally, noting that highly qualified citizens often want to emigrate to the industrialized world.

Liberal intellectuals in Saudi Arabia, many of whom were educated abroad, advocate social reforms, democracy and a constitution, while Islamic reformists urge more limited reforms such as some power sharing. An additional consideration is that the kingdom has attracted many foreign workers and their families, now accounting for over a quarter of the population. The society has become more culturally diverse, and the economy now depends on their skills. King Abdullah has initiated a forum for discussion between Wahhabi clerics and both Sunni and Shia representatives, to bring about greater dialogue and perhaps signalling a moderation in the power of the Wahhabi clerics. Cultural changes seem inevitable. Reformists stress that the gradual change is the better pathway to preserving essential values and social stability, warning that inflexible resistance to the calls for change may lead to social upheaval.

Sources: Khalaf, R. 'Saudis start to question society that leaves women marginalized', *Financial Times*, 30 October 2002; Khalaf, R., 'Plenty of debate but little action', *Financial Times*, 20 November 2002; Khalaf, R. 'Inside the desert kingdom', *Financial Times*, 18 and 19 November, 2003; Righter, R. 'Poverty of knowledge amid the oil riches', *The Times*, 30 July 2002; Gardner, D. 'Chaos theory', *Financial Times*, 30 July 2004; United Nations Development Programme (2002) *Arab Human Development Report*(New York: UNDP); United Nations Development Programme (2004) *Human Development Report 2004* (New York: UNDP).

Case questions

What are the cultural challenges emerging in Saudi Arabia, and how do they impact beyond the country's borders?

WEB ALERT!

For information on the world's major religions, look at:
http://www.islam.org/
http://www1.christianity.net/
http://www.buddhanet.net
http://hindu.org
http://judaism.com/

Sites on comparative religion:
http://www.adherents.com
http://www.religioustolerance.org/worldrel.htm

Asian religions

Asia has been a rich source of some of the world's oldest religions. Among many others, Hinduism, Buddhism and Confucianism originated in Asia and still have millions of followers and they are briefly discussed.

Hinduism

Unlike either Christianity or Islam, **Hinduism** is polytheistic, its believers worshipping many different gods through many different rituals. The sheer diversity of Hinduism is a major feature, despite the fact that geographically Hindus are mostly concentrated in the Indian subcontinent. Hindus make up 80 per cent of the population of India. Hinduism is an ancient religion, older than all the other major world religions. Its followers do not revere a single founder, nor do they follow one sacred scripture. In keeping with its ancient origins, Hinduism resembles folk religion, associated with rural communities and accessible to illiterate as well as literate followers. An important social and economic aspect of Hinduism is the **caste system** of rigid social stratification. This system, while officially abolished in the modern state, is still a force in Indian society, as is Hinduism itself. India's government was led from 1998 to 2004 by the Hindu nationalist party, the Bharatiya Janata Party (BJP), which is based on an alliance of smaller Hindu groups. The party brought in liberal economic reforms designed to spearhead economic development. Its surprise defeat by the Congress Party in elections in 2004 has been interpreted as an indication that the benefits of development, while felt in the cities, had not reached the vast majority of poor Indians, mainly in the rural areas. (See Case study 8.3 on the impact of political change in India.)

Buddhism

Buddhism also originated in India, where it has some five million followers. Buddhism has also been an important religious influence in China and Japan. A feature of the Buddhist heritage in all these countries has been its assimilation with other religions: in Indian temples Buddhism and Hinduism mingle; in Japan, Buddhist temples and Shinto shrines rub shoulders. Buddhism does not recognize the many gods of Hinduism; nor does it subscribe to the caste system. The Buddha's teachings form the basis of the religion. They centre on the 'eightfold-path', whereby the individual goes through a series of rebirths before reaching nirvana. As the Buddha's teachings were never written down, Buddhism split into a number of different schools. The two major ones are the Hinayana, which subscribes to a more ascetic lifestyle and is followed mainly in Sri Lanka, Thailand and Burma; and the Mahayana, which is less austere and is followed in China and Japan. From this latter school arose Zen Buddhism, which became a quite distinctive sect, highly influential in the cultures of both China and Japan. Zen's attraction has been its simplicity and directness, with its emphasis on meditation and the rejection of dogmatic teaching. Some large Japanese companies send new employees for Zen training.

Confucianism

Confucianism is often considered the cornerstone of Asian values. Founded in the fifth century BC by the Chinese philosopher Confucius, Confucianism is more a set of moral precepts than a religion. Simon Leys, the modern translator of the *Analects of Confucius*, describes it as 'an affirmation of humanist ethics ... the spiritual cornerstone of the most populous and oldest living civilization on earth' (Leys, 1997, p. xvii). At the heart of Confucianism is the family and 'filial piety', the paramount value of family loyalty. The countries with a strong Confucian heritage – China, Korea and Japan – have in common the prevalence of family-based social organization. In China, Confucianism was rejected by the Communist revolution of 1949, but the recent opening up of China has led to a renewed interest in Confucius. Symposiums on Chinese cultural history in 1982 and 1986 were the first attempts to rediscover Confucian culture, as a prelude to blending the strengths of traditional Confucianism with the aims of modernization (Rozman, 1991). In this regard, the example of Japan stands out, for its success in adapting a Confucian cultural heritage to the needs of modernization.

SUMMARY POINTS

How religion impacts on business life

Religious beliefs and practices may have direct (and indirect) influence on many aspects of business life, including:

- Particular foods that are forbidden (for example beef for Hindus)
- Ban, or restrictions, on consumption of alcoholic drink
- Religious festivals, during which work may be forbidden or curtailed (for example Ramadan for Muslims)
- Requirements for daily prayers
- Weekly day of religious observance (for example Saturday for the Jewish faith)
- Clothing requirements (such as long clothing for women in Muslim societies)
- Requirement for women and men to be segregated in the work environment (Muslim societies)
- Restrictions on media, for example newspapers, magazines, television, deemed to conflict with established religion
- Restriction on business hours and trading hours, for example the ban on Sunday shopping in some countries
- Religious law (for example in Muslim countries).

WEB ALERT!

For websites on Asian business and culture, look at http://www.apmforum.com/default.htm. This is the site of the Asia Pacific Management Forum, which contains a wealth of information and links

Other relevant websites are:
http://www.china.biz.org/Asian_Business_Folder/Asian_Business.Culture
http://www.japanecho.com/

Western values and Asian values: the debate

The sociologist Max Weber (1930) devised the theory that the 'Protestant work ethic', an ethic of individual endeavour, contributed to the rise of an enterprise culture and accompanying economic development in countries where Protestantism was dominant, such as England and Germany in the nineteenth century. He saw a connection between hard work, frugality and wealth creation. Protestants worked hard, not simply to gain pleasure from material well-being, but out of a sense of religious duty which rejected worldly pleasure as a goal in itself. Frugality dictated that gains should be invested wisely, enabling enterprises to prosper in the long term. This outlook on economic activity, known as the 'spirit of capitalism', fostered economic development. Moreover, Protestantism emphasized the individual's direct relationship with God, in contrast to the Catholic Church, for which the intercession of intermediaries was crucial. The value system based on individualism formed a logical foundation for individual freedoms in society generally, entailing both economic and political freedoms. These freedoms are the basis of the Western value systems that underlie the market economy in its 'pure' model, as outlined in Chapter 4. However, as was also pointed out, market economies are emerging in a variety of cultural environments which do not fit the traditional liberal Western pattern. The most striking example is the success of Asian economic development.

Asian nations differ greatly in their religious and cultural backgrounds, so there is no one system which one can point to as representing 'Asian values'. Nonetheless, the term is frequently used in a comparative context, to highlight contrasts with Western values. The closest approximation to a common thread running through Asian value systems is Confucianism. The 'Confucian ethic' is usually depicted as a set of values in which loyalty, hierarchy, and obedience to superiors are paramount, and the individual is subordinate to the group. Chris Patten, the last governor of Hong Kong, before it ceased to be a British colony and reverted to Chinese sovereignty in 1997, cites three issues which lie at the heart of the Asian versus Western debate: they are 'social order, the family and education' (Patten, 1998). As he points out, however, while the family as a unit is stronger in Asian countries, the traditional picture of family life is changing, especially as women are increasingly going out to work. Greater mobility, urbanization and a sense of insecurity in a changing environment are impacting on Asian societies, in much the same ways as in other parts of the world. Lee Kwan Yew, the former prime minister of Singapore, who is credited with orchestrating Singapore's remarkable economic growth – 8.5 per cent per annum between 1966 and 1990 – has long upheld the uniqueness of Asian values. As the Asian economies mature, he recognizes, however, that change is taking place, saying in an interview with the *Financial Times* (10 October 2000):

> There will be significant modification of our original culture, but I do not see it being totally transformed. It is not possible. You can take a Chinese family and put it in the US and in two generations they may be completely Americanized, but you can't do that when you've got a large group influencing each other and sustaining the basic values they share.

CRITICAL PERSPECTIVES

A multicultural world

In the post-Cold War world, the most important distinctions among peoples are not ideological, political, or economic. They are cultural. Peoples and nations are attempting to answer the most basic question humans face: Who are we? And they are answering that question in the traditional way human beings have answered it, by reference to things that mean most to them. People define themselves in terms of ancestry, religion, language, history, values, customs, and institutions. They identify with cultural groups: tribes, ethnic groups, religious communities, nations, and, at the broadest level, civilizations … Non-Western societies, particularly in East Asia, are developing their economic wealth … As their power and self-confidence increase, non-Western societies increasingly assert their own cultural values and reject those 'imposed' on them by the West. (Huntington, 1996, p. 21)

- Critically analyse the two broad points made by Huntington: the first about culture generally and the second about the impact of Western culture.
- Look at examples of industrializing non-Western societies, such as China and Japan. Do they bear out Huntington's analysis?

Multicultural societies

Almost all modern societies are home to more than one ethnic or racial group. Ethnic groups may be indigenous, like the Indian tribes of North and South America who existed long before the European settlers arrived, or they may be migrants to the country. It is an unfortunate fact that ethnic, racial and religious conflicts occur in virtually every modern society. When they reach widespread proportions, beyond the powers of authorities to control, the instability which results can hugely disrupt all types of economic activity, including agriculture, manufacturing industries, commerce and tourism.

There are three broad approaches to ethnic minorities which are discernible within societies. The first approach is that of assimilation, in which the minority adapts to the values and norms of the majority. France has actively pursued this approach, offering citizens of former French colonies in the Caribbean and Africa a right to reside in France. By contrast, the UK policies on immigration and assimilation have been variable. In the 1950s and 60s, the UK welcomed immigrants from former colonies in the Indian subcontinent, Africa and the Caribbean. These groups form the bulk of Britain's ethnic minorities today, which are 7.9 per cent of the total population. More restrictive immigration laws from the 1970s onwards have greatly restricted the flow of immigrants. Britain, like most Western economies, sees immigration policy as a way of filling skills shortages, as in health services and information technology.

A second approach is that of the melting pot, in which waves of immigrants create a blend of many cultural values. The US is usually cited as the archetypal melting pot society. When we look more closely, however, the national 'mainstream' culture which emerged reflected the nineteenth and early twentieth-century European immigrants, while black native Americans suffered discrimination. It is against this historical backdrop that modern patterns of cultural pluralism have evolved in the US, superseding the melting pot model (Rex, 1996). The newer immigrants, such as Hispanic Americans, have tended to retain their cultural identities and close ties with their home countries, much facilitated by modern transport and advanced telecommunications – in contrast to immigrants of previous generations. Nearly 25 million Mexicans live and work in the US, mainly in states bordering on Mexico and in the southern sun belt. Their remittances to families and communities back in Mexico amounted to $7 billion a year, and were Mexico's third largest source of foreign exchange in 2000, following oil and tourism. (See Chapter 7 for a discussion of international migration generally.)

The third model is that of cultural pluralism. In this model, numerous subcultures are recognized but alongside a national identity which acts as a unifying bond. The UK government has recognized this approach in its White Paper on the integration of refugees, saying: 'Britain has become and benefited from being a multicultural society. Inclusion in our society does not mean that a refugee is required to assimilate' (Home Office, 1999). Recent British policy has been somewhere in the middle between assimilation and cultural pluralism, recognizing cultural diversity as an aspect of modern society (Rex, 1996; Statham, 1999). The US has evolved from a melting pot type of culture to a more culturally pluralistic one in recent years, as minority ethnic groups, both indigenous and immigrant, have been keen to assert a 'distinct but equal' status (Giddens, 1997, p. 236). The distinguished commentator Sheldon Wolin (1993, p. 479) has observed that this policy can lead to a 'limited sort of inclusion'. Cultural pluralism can lead to social tension, especially in societies where there are economic inequalities between groups, as well as geographic separation. In Indonesia, authoritarian rule maintained an uneasy unity and social order which disintegrated with the fall of the Suharto regime in 1998. The instability which has ensued has deterred foreign investors and added to the problems of economic recovery following the Asian financial crisis of 1997, which is explored in Case study 12.2.

SUMMARY POINTS

!!!

Models of multicultural societies

- **Assimilation** – Immigrants leave their home cultures behind and adopt the culture and language of their new society. Citizenship in the new country is easily available. (Examples: France, and the UK in the 1950s and 60s.)
- **Melting pot** – Society evolves its own identity and culture, based on a mixture of the different cultures of which it is composed. (Examples: 'settler' societies such as the US and Australia.)
- **Cultural pluralism** – Immigrants form social subcultures which remain distinct. (Examples: Germany and the US to some extent; however citizenship is more easily obtained in the US than in Germany.)

WEB ALERT!

Internet resources on race relations and refugees include:

The Commission for Racial Equality at http://www.cre.gov.uk

The Refugee Council at http://www.refugeecouncil.org.uk

The Institute of Race Relations at http://www.irr.org.uk/

The following is a site on ethnic studies: http://www.incore.ulst.ac.uk/. It provides a guide, plus links, to resources on conflict and ethnicity in regions across the world.

The UN Educational, Scientific and Cultural Organization (UNESCO) website is http://www.unesco.org. Here, 'culture' is one of the themes to click on

Cultural theories

Differences in national values and attitudes have been the subject of considerable research. Geert Hofstede (1994) has developed a theory of culture which holds that cultural and sociological differences between nations can be categorized and quantified, allowing us to compare national cultures. Hofstede's research was carried out in 50 countries, among IBM employees in each country. An obvious weakness of the research is its reliance solely on IBM employees, who are a special group in themselves and not necessarily representative of the countries in which they live. However, his research does yield interesting comparisons and contrasts between national cultures and has served as a benchmark for culture theories. Hofstede distinguishes four cultural dimensions – to which he later added a fifth – as variables. He uses these dimensions to compare value systems at various levels: in the family, at school, in the workplace, in the state and in ways of thinking generally. The cultural dimensions are:

1 *Power distance:* the extent to which members of a society accept a hierarchical or unequal power structure. In large power distance countries, people consider themselves to be inherently unequal and there is more dependence by subordinates on bosses. The boss is likely to be autocratic or paternalistic in these countries, in a type of management which subordinates may respond to positively or negatively. In small power distance countries, people tend to see themselves more as equals. When they occupy subordinate and superior roles in organizations, these situations are just that – roles, not reflecting inherent differences. Organizations in these countries tend to be flatter, with a more consultative style of management. Asian, Latin American and African countries tend to have large power distance, while Northern Europe has relatively small power distance.

2 *Uncertainty avoidance:* how members of a society cope with the uncertainties of everyday life. High levels of stress and anxiety denote high uncertainty avoidance countries. These cultures tend to be more expressive and emotional than those of low uncertainty avoidance countries. The latter have lower anxiety levels, but their easy-going exterior may simply indicate greater control of anxiety, not its non-existence. High uncertainty avoidance countries are in Latin American, Latin European and Mediterranean countries, along with Japan and South Korea. Ranking relatively low are other Asian countries and other European countries.

3 *Individualism:* the extent to which individuals perceive themselves as independent and autonomous beings. At the opposite pole is collectivism, in which people see themselves as integrated into 'ingroups'. High individualism scores occurred mainly in the English-speaking countries, while low individualism was prevalent in Latin American and Asian countries. Hofstede remarks that management techniques and training packages, which almost all originate in the individualist countries, are based on cultural assumptions which are out of tune with the more collectivist cultures (Hofstede, 1994).

4 *Masculinity:* the extent to which a society is inclined towards aggressive and materialistic behaviour. This dimension tends to present stereotyped gender roles. Hofstede associates masculinity with assertiveness, toughness and an emphasis on money and material things. At the opposite extreme is femininity, which denotes sensitivity, caring and an emphasis on quality of life. Conflict and competition predominate in more masculine environments, whereas negotiation and compromise predominate in more feminine environments. According to Hofstede's results, the most masculine countries are Japan and Austria, while the most feminine are Sweden, Norway, the Netherlands and Denmark.

5 *Long-term* vs. *short-term orientation:* people's time perspectives in their daily lives. Hofstede added this dimension as a result of work by another researcher, Michael Harris Bond, who found different time orientations between Western and Eastern ways of thinking. Short-term orientation stresses satisfying needs 'here and now', and is more characteristic of Western cultures, whereas long-term orientation stresses virtuous living through thrift and persistence, and is prevalent in Eastern cultures (Hofstede, 1996).

Hofstede was able to group countries together in clusters and make correlations between the different dimensions. Some of these are shown in the Table 6.4. For countries in group 1, high power distance combines with low individualism, suggesting that where people depend on ingroups, they also depend on power figures. Conversely, in cultures where people are less dependent on ingroups, shown in group 2, they are also less dependent on powerful leaders. There are some anomalies, however. France seems to have high individualism, but also medium power distance. Japan seems to be roughly in the middle in both power distance and individualism. Japanese companies are usually depicted as collectivist ingroups, akin to a family relationship. This apparent contradiction in the research could reflect the nature of his survey sample, which focused on employees of a large American multinational company.

More recent research by Fons Trompenaars also used the individualism/collectivism continuum as a key dimension. Trompenaars' research involved giving questionnaires to over 15,000 managers in 28 countries (Trompenaars, 1994). He identified five relationship orientations. These are:

1 *Universalism* vs. *particularism*: cultures with high universalism place more weight on formal rules, whereas more particularistic cultures value relationships more than formal rules or agreements. Western countries such as the UK, Australia and the USA, Trompenaars found, tend to rate highly in universalism, whereas China rated highly in particularism.

Table 6.4 Ranks of selected countries on four dimensions of national culture, based on research by Hofstede

	Power distance rank	Individualism rank	Masculinity rank	Uncertainty avoidance rank
Group 1 (high PD + low Individualism)				
Brazil	14	26–27	27	21–22
Indonesia	8–9	47–48	30–31	41–42
Malaysia	1	36	25–26	46
Mexico	5–6	32	6	18
Group 2 (low PD + high individualism)				
Finland	46	17	47	31–32
Germany	42–44	15	9–10	29
Netherlands	40	4–5	51	35
Sweden	47–48	10–11	53	49–50
UK	42–44	3	9–10	47–48
USA	38	1	15	43
Group 3 (varying patterns)				
France	15–16	10–11	35–36	10–15
Greece	27–28	30	18–19	1
Japan	33	22–23	1	7

Note: Rank: 1 = highest; 53 = lowest.
Source: Hofstede, G. (1994) *Cultures and Organizations* (London: HarperCollins), various tables.

2 *Individualism* vs. *collectivism*: this relationship mirrors one of Hofstede's four dimensions, but the findings were somewhat different. Trompenaars found Japan to be much further towards the collectivist extreme. On the other hand, Mexico and the Czech Republic, which Hofstede had found to be more collectivist, now tend to individualism. This finding could be explained by the later date of the research data, reflecting the progress of market economies in both regions: the impact of NAFTA in the case of Mexico, and the post-Communist transition to a market economy in the case of the Czech Republic.

3 *Neutral* vs. *emotional*: in a neutral culture, people are less inclined to show their feelings, whereas in an emotional culture, people are more open in showing emotion and expressing their views. In the findings, Japan has the most neutral culture and Mexico the most emotional.

4 *Specific* vs. *diffuse*: in a specific culture there is a clear separation between work and private life. In diffuse cultures, 'the whole person is involved in a business relationship', not merely the contracting role (Trompenaars, 1994, p. 9). Doing business in these cultures, therefore, involves building relationships, not simply focusing on the business deal in isolation. The US, Australia and the UK are examples of specific cultures, while China is an example of a diffuse culture.

5 *Achievement* vs. *ascription*: in an achievement culture people derive status from their accomplishments and record. In an ascription culture status is what matters, which could relate to birth, family, gender or age. The US and UK are achievement cultures, whereas China and other Asian cultures are ascription cultures.

The research of Hofstede and Trompenaars shed new light on the diversity among national cultures, dispelling the assumption that there is 'one best way' of managing and organizing people. International companies had assumed the universal application of management theories, but, in truth, many of their applications, such as pay-by-performance or management-by-objectives, were products of Anglo-Saxon culture, and unsuitable for other cultures with different values and norms. Just as standardized products do not suit all markets, organizations cannot be standardized, but must adapt to local social and cultural profiles.

SUMMARY POINTS

Cultural dimensions in Hofstede and Trompenaars

Hofstede's five cultural dimensions:

1 Power distance
2 Uncertainty avoidance
3 Individualism – collectivism
4 Masculinity – femininity
5 Long-term vs. short-term orientation.

Trompenaars' five relationship orientations:

1 Universalism vs. particularism
2 Individualism vs. collectivism
3 Neutral vs. emotional
4 Specific vs. diffuse
5 Achievement vs. ascription.

CRITICAL PERSPECTIVES

Cultural diversity

Research about the development of cultural values has shown repeatedly that there is very little evidence of international convergency over time, except an increase of individualism for countries that have become richer. Value differences between nations described by authors centuries ago are still present today, in spite of continued close contacts ... Not only will cultural diversity among countries remain with us: it even looks as though differences within countries are increasing. (Hofstede, 1994, p. 238)

▪ What evidence is there to support the two long-term trends highlighted by Hofstede: increasing individualism and cultural diversity within countries?

▪ What impact will they have on the ways in which international businesses operate?

Organizational culture

Organizational culture or 'corporate culture', like national culture, focuses on values, norms and behavioural patterns shared by the group, in this case, the organization. The elements of organizational culture can be found in the box below. The organization, however, unlike the nation, is an artificial creation, and a corporate culture is one that is deliberately fostered among employees, who may have come to the company from a variety of different cultural backgrounds. As we saw in Chapter 5, companies tend to reflect the national culture of their home country, despite globalization of their operations. Swiss multinationals, such as the food giant Nestlé, are among the most transnational, whereas American and Japanese companies are among the least transnational. Switzerland is highly multicultural, with a mixture of national cultures, including German, French and Italian. Its organizations are thus well attuned to appreciating cultural differences in overseas subsidiaries. American and Japanese companies, on the other hand, are from countries with a dominant national culture and a single language. Boardrooms of both American and Japanese companies are dominated by home nationals, in contrast to Nestlé, whose board resembles a miniature UN.

SUMMARY POINTS

!!!

Organizational or corporate culture

Characteristics of organizational culture include:

● Common language and shared terminology
● Norms of behaviour, such as relations between management and employees
● Preferences for formal or informal means of communication within the company and with associated companies
● Dominant values of the organization, such as high product quality and customer orientation
● Degree of empowerment of employees throughout the organization
● Systems of rules that specify dos and don'ts of employee behaviour.

Some multinational corporations see a strong corporate culture as a way of unifying the diverse national cultures represented by employees. Others evolve different organizational cultures in different locations, in effect incorporating multiculturalism within the company. The need to manage cultural diversity may arise through a number of routes: the acquisition of a foreign subsidiary, a merger with another company or a joint venture. In joint ventures, in particular, the need for cooperation and trust between partners is the key to long-term success.

The global merger – between countries of different national cultures – is an illustration of the difficulties that can arise when strong national cultures clash. The merger in 1998 of the two automotive giants, Daimler-Benz of Germany and Chrysler of the US, highlighted the difficulties of merging Chrysler's lean, flexible and open style with the more structured, bureaucratic and stiffer style of Daimler-

Benz (see Case study 6.4.). The two companies found huge differences in ways of working, decision-making, the conduct of meetings and the exchange of information. Blending the culture of different locations into a distinctive corporate culture – in which any of the company's employees feel at home in any of the company's locations – can strengthen the sense of corporate identity, but poses considerable challenges for international managers.

Case study 6.4 Can DaimlerChrysler turn an amalgam of corporate cultures to its advantage?

Mergers, it has been said, are about pride and control when two organizations with strong cultures join forces (Ibison, 24 January 2002). The merger of Chrysler Corp. of the US and Daimler-Benz AG of Germany in 1998 created DaimlerChrysler AG, the world's third largest manufacturer of motor vehicles. The aim expressed at the time was to blend their two very different corporate cultures into a new 'super culture' which drew from both sides: Chrysler had a reputation as a lean and flexible company, leading the way in cost-effectiveness, whereas Daimler was more structured and bureaucratic. In reality, the deal was a takeover of Chrysler by Daimler, rather than a merger of equals. The billionaire Kirk Kerkorian, who owned 13.7 per cent of Chrysler shares, later launched a lawsuit against DaimlerChrysler for $1.2 billion, claiming to have been misled into supporting the merger, and alleging that the German company bought Chrysler for a knockdown price by disguising the takeover as a merger. Evidence which emerged in the ensuing hearing suggested a merger of equals was not envisaged by Daimler-Benz, and that the intention was to turn Chrysler into a division of the larger company.

The differences of culture became apparent almost immediately, and turned out to be more difficult to overcome than had been anticipated:

- The official language became English, but the Americans found, not surprisingly, that their German colleagues were more comfortable in German and often used German in private conversations, which they found unsettling. They also

found that, without German, they could not integrate well at the social level.
- German managers were formal in their manner and dress, always wearing ties and addressing colleagues by title and surname, while Americans were accustomed to dressing more casually and addressing each other by first names.

The incompatibility of management styles was recognized, and German culture came to dominate. The key figures in the Chrysler management team had departed within 12 months, leaving Chrysler struggling to deal with a new management team (headed by a German former Mercedes executive, Dieter Zetsche) at a time when the competitive environment was particularly difficult. Under the chairmanship of Jurgen Schrempp, Daimler now views Chrysler as a stand-alone division, focusing wholly on the US market. In terms of corporate governance, the company retains the two-tier board structure as practised in Germany: the supervisory board, including 10 employee and trade union representatives, has ultimate authority, while the management board is responsible for day-to-day management. In 2001, the supervisory board approved the setting up of a 'chairman's council' of independent (non-executive) directors, reflecting American views of best practice. This move is seen as a hybrid between the German and Anglo-American models of corporate governance.

Chrysler, America's third largest car maker, struggled to compete in its home market and embarked on a recovery plan. In particular, it needed to replace some of its ageing models. Its new 300 and 300C saloons proved to be popular with customers and, by 2004, the company was returning to operating profit (see figure).

Meanwhile, it was concerned about losing out in its traditionally strong markets of light trucks and vans (a category which includes the popular sports utility vehicles). However, it is rebuilding market share in this segment (see second figure).

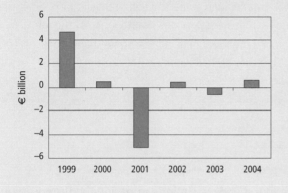

Chrysler operating profit/loss (to the first half of 2004)

Source: *Financial Times*, 18 August 2004.

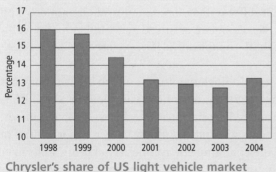

Chrysler's share of US light vehicle market

Source: *Financial Times*, 18 August 2004.

Insiders attribute many of Chrysler's troubles to the failure of the Germans to understand Chrysler culture. The group strategy of focusing on new models in the saloon market seems to be leading the revival of performance in the US. Of course, this segment is one in which Mercedes is able to bring expertise and a strong reputation for engineering excellence. Closer integration in developing models is therefore envisaged for the future. Chrysler will focus on 'centres of competence' within DaimlerChrysler globally. It is hoped this strategy will enhance Chrysler's position in the very competitive US market. The perception of quality, on which customer loyalty over the long term is based, is one of the strongest assets of the Daimler brand, which, it is hoped, will benefit Chrysler. The integration of manufacturing systems might finally be inching towards a point where 'Route 66 meets the Autobahn' (Grant, 9 August 2002). Zetsche now says of the company: 'Our processes have changed. We are a different company. Many things are now engrained in our culture: we are not satisfied with good any more' (Mackintosh, 1 November 2004).

Sources: 'DaimlerChrysler union challenges two cultures', *Detroit News*, 14 September 1998; 'Culture clash when car makers merge', *Detroit News*, 14 May 1998; 'Lessons from a casualty of the culture wars', *Business Week*, 29 November, 1999; Burt, T., 'Colliding with Chrysler', *Financial Times*, 10 October 2000; Burt, T., and Tait, N., 'Kerkorian versus Schrempp may add to Chrysler's woes', *Financial Times*, 28 November 2000; Ibison, D. 'Culture clashes prove biggest hurdle to international links', *Financial Times*, 24 January 2002; Grant, J. 'Chrysler seeks to gain from the Daimler brand', *Financial Times*, 9 August 2002; Burt, T. 'Daimler brings in council of non-execs', *Financial Times*, 28 September 2001; Grant, J., 'Chrysler hopeful it has turned the corner', *Financial Times*, 18 August 2004; Mackintosh, J., 'Why "good" is not enough for Chrysler', *Financial Times*, 1 November 2004.

Case questions

Describe the culture clash at DaimlerChrysler.

To what extent has it been resolved successfully?

CRITICAL PERSPECTIVES

Organizational culture

Organizational cultures are created in part by leaders, and one of the most decisive functions of leadership is the creation, management, and sometimes even the destruction of culture … If one wishes to distinguish leadership from management or administration, one can argue that leaders create and change cultures, while managers and administrators live within them. (Schein, 1992, p. 5)

 Why is leadership crucial in creating and managing corporate culture?

Looking back on case studies in this and previous chapters, assess the role of corporate leaders in forming organizational culture: some suggestions are Procter & Gamble (1.1), Disney (1.3), Ryanair (2.1), Coca-Cola (end of Part 1) and DaimlerChrysler (6.4).

Culture change

Hofstede and Trompenaars both found wide variations in national cultures among the nations studied. Studies such as these risk giving an impression that national cultures are static. However, individuals, organizations and even whole societies do change over time. Industrialization as a global phenomenon has impacted on the social and cultural environments of societies as they pursue economic development. Patterns of economic development differ and so too do cultural adaptations to the changes taking place. Capitalist development is linked with individualist values, which, while reflecting the growth of capitalism in Europe, are no longer seen as valid for all the world's peoples.

The growth of Asian capitalism in Confucian cultures, which are generally more collectivist than individualist, has demonstrated how cautious we should be in making assumptions about cultural predispositions. Nonetheless, growing material well-being and prosperity, the benefits of education, new career opportunities and urbanization are some aspects of the changing environment that bring shifts in cultural values in all countries, although their impact differs from society to society. For most societies, the impetus for cultural change comes about through external forces such as foreign investors who bring in new organizational forms and technological advances derived from more advanced Western economies. Global companies may take an ethnocentric approach, attempting to replicate their own national culture in each foreign location, but, increasingly, companies have found that managing cultural diversity through adaptation to local environments is more fruitful. In this way, change comes about gradually and impacts on both the local and the parent organizations.

Cultural globalization: myth or reality?

It has been argued by some notable commentators, such as Kenichi Ohmae, that economic globalization is leading to cultural globalization, which can be defined as movement towards a borderless world, in which cultural differences are fading in real significance (Ohmae, 1995). Ohmae points to the facts that some multinational corporations wield more power than governments, and that consumer markets are now globalized, rather than locally or nationally circumscribed. While Ohmae's views are persuasively argued, they risk oversimplifying a complex global picture. Cultural flows consist mainly of consumer products and entertainment. Both are now dominated by multinational companies from the developed world, but despite the globalization of their organizations and strategies, international tastes still show considerable diversity.

Role of the media in cultural globalization

The volume of information now available and the ease of instant access from any part of the globe are defining characteristics of the information age, distinguishing our world from that of all previous generations. International cultural flows have reached unprecedented levels and their reach potentially extends to all societies, from the richest to the poorest. Their reach is uneven, however, as is shown in Table 6.5. Whereas in developed societies, television, radio and telephone ownership have reached saturation levels, there are many parts of the world to which their reach still hardly extends.

Table 6.5 Growth in television ownership

	Number of television sets per 1000 inhabitants			
	1970	1980	1990	1997
World total	81	127	206	240
Africa	4.6	18	41	60
America (incl. whole of Americas)	209	328	404	429
Asia	20	40	153	190
Europe	205	324	385	446
Oceania	188	300	378	427
Latin America & Caribbean	57	98	162	205
Southern Asia	0.9	6.4	29	54
Developed countries	263	424	492	548
Developing countries	9.9	27	124	157
Least developed countries	0.5	3.5	13	23

Source: UNESCO, *1999 Statistical Yearbook* (Paris: Bernan Press), Table IV.S.3.

Broadcasts, films, commercial advertising, books, magazines and myriad internet resources offer larger amounts of cultural products than ever before available. They also familiarize consumers the world over with symbols and products which are increasingly seen as transnational, superseding the cultural bounds of nations. These cultural flows are dominated by large communications organizations, whose cultural reach and power are historically unparalleled. Media and telecommunications which were once under public ownership are now increasingly privatized and deregulated. Global media companies, such as Sony, Time-Warner, Disney or Bertelsmann, have dominated cultural output largely through capturing the latest technology. The takeover in 2000 of the media company Time-Warner by AOL, the internet company, is indicative of the perceived advantages of media mergers linking cultural content with the internet. Many see these developments, along with the predominance of English in the media, as signs of cultural globalization. On the other hand, despite Hollywood films and CNN, a remarkable diversity of cultural output persists, reflecting differing national tastes and languages.

In film, television and music, large media companies increasingly tailor entertainment output for local tastes and in local languages. In Asia and Latin America, where consumer markets are growing rapidly, audiences prefer local content over American popular culture (Rose, 1999). Media giants such as Sony have altered their strategies from the 1970s, when most of their output was American popular culture. Now, their growth area is international output of, for example, Hindi-language and Mandarin-language programming for satellite television, which reaches huge audiences (Rose, 1999). While imports, especially American films and television series, have global reach, local and regional broadcasters and producers find eager markets for local and 'alternative' broadcasting. Similarly, marketing research organizations who are monitoring the use of the internet now find that, as technology advances, websites are becoming more internationalized, offering multiple languages rather than English only (see minifile). Mass cultural consumption driven by global media does not seem to have swept away demand for local and national cultural products. This trend is particularly apparent in developing countries, as media penetration increases towards the levels of developed countries.

A further point which should be made in connection with cultural globalization is that cultural values and norms run deep and change only slowly. A person in Asia, for example, may listen to Western pop music, wear Levi jeans and drink Coca-Cola, but not subscribe to the value system they represent. Indeed, in many countries with strong cultural identities, high-profile American companies may attract hostility and accusations of cultural imperialism, prompting a kind of backlash consisting of positive moves towards reasserting local values and symbols.

Minifile

MULTILINGUAL WEBSITES

English dominates the internet. Estimates are that nearly 70 per cent of websites are in English, although only about 5.4 per cent of the world's population are native English speakers. But as international internet access grows, companies are increasingly making information available in multiple languages and conducting e-business in the consumer's own language. According to research, growth in Web usage and e-commerce in Europe and Asia will outstrip that of the US by between two and five times over the next few years. Global companies are now recognizing that cross-border commerce requires a new cross-cultural Web strategy. Language is an important element. Consumers are more likely to buy products and services online if they can use their own language. Sony sells its laptops to consumers through websites in 14 languages. The development of translation software, to respond quickly to queries in each language, was key to multilingual e-commerce. However, prices also need to be in local currency; dates must be expressed in the local format; and weights and measures should be in the local system. Website designers need to be sensitive to colour and style preferences in different countries. Bright colours may be considered cheerful in one country, but have negative connotations in another. As white signifies death in China, it should be avoided, unless your business is funeral services.

For a global company, Web strategy therefore goes well beyond simple translation into a local language. Even for French companies, because of different dialects, a generic French site will not succeed in Haiti or Mozambique (Woods, 2000). As the internet reaches more and more consumers, local companies, which have a full grasp of the cultural issues and local language, are well placed to exploit their inherent advantages in local markets.

Sources: Woods, L., 'Clique here', *Corporate Legal Times*, **10**(98), January 2000; Perkin, J. 'Multilingual websites widen the way to a new online world', *Financial Times*, 7 February 2001.

Global culture and national culture

Smith (1990, p. 180) contrasts national with global culture:

> Unlike national cultures, a global culture is essentially memoryless. Where a 'nation' can be constructed so as to draw upon and revive latent popular experiences and needs, a 'global culture' answers to no living needs, no identity-in-the-making. It has to be put together, artificially, out of the many existing folk and national identities into which humanity has been so long divided.

Smith argues that global culture is more transitory and ephemeral, in comparison with the depth of shared history of national cultures. Symbols of Western consumer culture are certainly widely accessible and highly visible, but it is a huge leap to conclude that they therefore represent universal values. Wherever these products are sold in the world, their significance is differently interpreted according to the national culture of that particular market. Marketing specialists are quick to point out that it is impossible to design a standard global marketing campaign guaranteeing success for a product in all markets. Although advanced media and communications technology bring people closer together in a spatial sense, this is a long way from the cultural shift which would be required to create a 'global village'.

Conclusions

1   Culture refers to a society's whole range of values and norms, which have developed through a shared history and experiences over a period of time. These cultural phenomena, which include language, religion and ethnicity, give a group of people a distinctive cultural identity.

2   The nation as a group of people is the dominant source of collective cultural identity. The growth in the number of nation-states since the Second World War reflects both the break-up of colonial empires and the pressures for national self-determination.

3   Most states are multicultural. While institutional design can accommodate minority identities, including religious and linguistic minorities, cultural conflict is a possibility, particularly in younger states whose institutions are not yet fully established.

4   Businesses are often ethnocentric in outlook, but in the international environment, a polycentric approach will make it easier for them to adapt to the different cultural environments of foreign operations.

5   The processes of industrialization and modernization have impacted on cultural values and social organization in all parts of the world, but their impact has varied from society to society. While Western individualistic values are traditionally linked to the development of capitalism, economic development in Asian countries has demonstrated the enterprise potential of Confucian value systems.

6   Research by Hofstede and Trompenaars, focusing on cultural dimensions as variables, while tending to present static pictures of national cultures, has provided useful tools for cross-cultural analysis, in terms of both organizational and societal cultural profiles.

7   Organizations, while they may develop their own specific values and behaviour, are also highly influenced by the national culture of their home country.

8   Cultures, both national and organizational, evolve over time, but changes are likely to take place only gradually, reflecting the deep-seated nature of cultural 'programming'.

9   The impetus behind cultural globalization has depended largely on the globalization of the media and the cultural symbols it represents. However, despite growing global economic integration, national cultural diversity shows little sign of fading into a uniform global culture.

Review questions

1   What are the main elements of culture?

2   What is meant by 'ethnocentrism'?

3   Explain the essential aspects of national culture. Why are strong national cultures often considered to be those of homogeneous societies?

4   What are the differences between a 'high-context' and 'low-context' language? Why do these differences matter in business negotiations?

5   In what ways are greater liberalization and Westernization taking place in some Muslim countries?

6   What has been the impact of Confucianism on firms in Asia, including their structures and ways of doing business?

7   Explain three approaches to multiculturalism in society. How do these different approaches affect business relations?

8   What are the essential cultural dimensions described by Hofstede in his research?

9   How do the rankings of national culture produced by Hofstede shed light on international management practices in different locations?

10 List the main elements of organizational culture. Why is 'culture clash' a common problem in mergers between large companies?

11 Describe the role of the media in cultural globalization. Why are media companies now expanding local production in local languages?

Assignments

1   It is sometimes said that local diversity will inevitably fade away under the tidal wave of cultural globalization. Examine the evidence which supports this view and also the evidence which contradicts it.

2   For a global company from a Western economy contemplating a joint venture with a foreign partner in China, what are the cultural difficulties likely to be encountered and what are your recommendations for how to enable the joint venture to succeed?

Further reading

Bartlett, C. and Ghoshal, S. (1998) *Managing Across Borders: A Transnational Solution*, 2nd edn (London: Random House).

Berger, P. and Huntington, S. (eds) (2002) *Many Globalizations: Cultural Diversity in the Contemporary World* (Oxford: Oxford University Press).

Harrison, L. and Huntington, S. (2000) *Culture Matters: How Values Shape Human Progress* (New York: Basic Books).

Held, D. (ed.) (2000) *A Globalizing World: Culture, Economics, Politics* (Andover: Routledge).

Hickson, D.J. and Pugh, D.S. (1995) *Management Worldwide* (London: Penguin Books).

Hofstede, G. (1994) *Cultures and Organizations: Software of the Mind* (London, HarperCollins).

Patten, C. (1998) *East and West* (Basingstoke: Macmillan – now Palgrave Macmillan).

Schein, E.J. (2004) *Organizational Culture and Leadership*, 3rd edn (London: John Wiley).

Schneider, S. and Barsoux, J.L. (2003) *Managing Across Cultures*, 2nd edn (Harlow: Pearson Education).

Smith, A.D. (1991) *National Identity* (London: Penguin).

Trompenaars, F. (1994) *Riding the Waves of Culture* (New York: Irwin).

Usunier, J.-C. (2000) *Marketing Across Cultures*, 3rd edn (London: Financial Times/Prentice Hall).

7

Society and business

Outline of chapter

- Introduction
- Types of society: the development of modern industrial societies
- Stratification in societies
  - Rigid social stratification
  - Social class
  - Changes in capitalist society
- Changing populations
  - Ageing societies and implications for business
  - International migration
  - Recent patterns of migration
- Urbanism
  - Urbanization in Western economies
  - Urbanization in the developing world
- Labour relations
- Gender and work
- Families
- Conclusions

Learning objectives

1 To identify the social groupings and interactions that make up societies.

2 To understand the social changes taking place in industrial, developing and transitional economies and their impact on business activities.

3 To appreciate how social stratification systems in diverse societies affect the international business environment.

4 To assess the importance of social change in a variety of contexts relating to business, including the changing nature of work in the IT age, gender and family issues.

Introduction

Social interaction and social relations are among the most basic of human activities. Every society has distinctive characteristics in terms of population and way of life, some of the greatest distinctions being between industrialized and developing societies. Within societies there may be numerous cross-cutting ties: religion, gender, age, race or ethnic grouping. At the personal level, family and workplace ties are also important strands in each person's web of social interactions. Social groupings vary greatly in their sense of identity, internal cohesion, cultures and structures. Virtually every social grouping, from the broadest level of a whole society down to a small organization such as the family, is stratified in one or more ways. Social and economic status, such as class divisions within societies, affect occupation, lifestyle and education, for virtually all the world's people. Differences in the social environment from country to country, therefore, have a direct effect on international business operations and, in particular, on business practices and consumer markets.

Globalization in the spheres of technology and communication has immensely broadened the possibilities for social interaction between people around the world. However, globalization, as we saw in the last chapter, has not as yet resulted in cultural homogenization. People are increasingly interconnected, but how do these changes affect societies and social relations? A main aim of this chapter is to delve into the nature of societies and other social groups, looking at the ways in which they interact in the international business environment. In a sense, this aim is focused on a 'moving target', as people and organizations proactively engage in changing and moulding the social environment, as well as responding to changes. An important second aim, therefore, is to understand the interactive dynamic between the individual and society, in the context of global economic forces.

SUMMARY POINTS

!!!

Social groupings

In any society, each person's attitudes and behaviour are formed in numerous social contexts. The first group of factors we have little control over, whereas those in the second group are mainly matters of choice.

1 **Social groupings derived from natural circumstances (primary groups):**
   - National society
   - Subnational grouping, such as immigrant community
   - Race
   - Religion
   - Gender
   - Class or other status system (such as caste)
   - Age
   - Family

2 **Social groupings based on individual choice (secondary groups):**
   - Occupation
   - Workplace organization
   - Trade union
   - Other voluntary associations, such as sport and leisure clubs, political parties, interest groups

Types of society: the development of modern industrial societies

A society may be defined broadly as 'a system of interrelationships which connects individuals together' (Giddens, 1997, p. 18). The word 'society' is used in many contexts. First, it is often used to refer to the national society of the modern nation-state. However, as we saw in Chapter , while shared culture is the lifeblood of nations, the modern state is seldom a homogeneous society reflecting a single national identity. Most are home to numerous subcultures representing ethnic and linguistic diversity. These subnational groups, both indigenous and immigrant, may have considerable cohesion, especially if they are clustered in geographical areas where they continue to speak their own language. Issues relating to the social integration of these groups will be examined later in this chapter.

A second use of the term 'society' is to designate types of society on the basis of their means of subsistence. We frequently use the terms, 'industrial society' and 'capitalist society', to refer to economies based on industrialized mass production – the type of society that most of us are familiar with. Industrialization refers to the shift from human and animal power to machine production, in which energy was derived from inanimate sources, such as water power, steam and the internal combustion engine. The Industrial Revolution, which started in the second half of the eighteenth century, brought about the dramatic social transformation of existing societies, beginning in Britain and spreading to other countries in Europe and America. Traditional societies, based primarily on agriculture, gradually evolved into industrial societies, whose economies were dominated by production and the exchange of mass-produced goods.

The transition to an industrial society can also be described as a shift from traditional to 'modern' society. Ties to the land loosened as people left the rural way of life for work in the new factories in cities. Major social changes brought about by industrialization, which are all discussed later in this chapter, included urbanization, changes in the nature of work and changes in family life. These changes can be observed today in transitional economies such as China, where large numbers of rural dwellers are moving to the cities, looking for opportunities in the fast-growing economy. Case study 7.1 reveals some of these changes in an increasingly affluent urbanized society. Developing countries are still predominantly agricultural, and the least developed, those in Africa, are only slowly becoming industrialized.

Case study 7.1   New era of the flexible friend in Asia

International banks and credit card companies are eyeing opportunities for new customers in the growing economies of Asia with growing enthusiasm. People in the Asia Pacific region held 448 million credit cards in 2002, broken down by country as shown in the figure. In the region as a whole, credit cards account for only 7 per cent of discretionary spending, while the figure in developed markets is about 40 per cent. A major factor is that credit card use is still in its infancy in China, the region's largest potential market. Consumers' new wealth has led to changing lifestyles, mainly in rapidly growing urban environments, reflected in a boom in consumer spending. Sales of televisions, motorcycles and air conditioners were among the first to experience rapid growth, followed by apartments and cars. Now, the growth in credit cards may be heralding a new 'plastic revolution'. Along with the opportunities, however, come a number of risks, for both the businesses and their new customers.

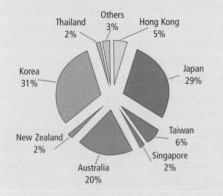

Density of credit card ownership in the Asia-Pacific region, by country (as of June, 2003)
Source: Mallet, 2 February 2004.

The rise of a credit card culture represents a radical cultural shift in Asian societies, where the virtues of saving and thrift are deeply rooted. In Japan, which has the largest number of affluent consumers, the use of credit cards is still limited. South Korea, with a long tradition of saving, experienced a credit card boom following the financial crisis of 1997–98. Here, credit cards were encouraged in order to increase consumer spending, which was a vital element in the country's economic recovery. The result was an explosion in the number of cards, with little check on creditworthiness – the average Korean accumulated four cards. The boom proved to be unsustainable, as debts mounted for customers who had little experience of managing household debt. The boom ended in disaster, leading to a mountain of unpaid debts, a sharp fall in domestic consumption and financial problems for the banks and credit card companies.

The lesson of Korea highlights the risks of lending too freely without a structure in place for credit checks. China presents the greatest potential market. Here, there are some 544 million bank debit cards, whereby money is directly debited from a bank account, and 25 million credit cards. According to Visa, the number of debit cards has risen quickly, 50 per cent in 2003, whereas the number of credit cards in the same period grew only 6 per cent. Consumers are only gradually shifting to the idea of using a card for credit rather than simply for payment. Visa's target market is people with a monthly salary equivalent to $300 or more, a category that already numbers about 60 million, but it could rise to 200 million by 2010. Expansion in credit card use will depend on putting in place systems which provide reliable credit information on individuals and on an increase in the number of outlets which accept cards. In addition, as in other Asian markets before they were opened, the Confucian cultural heritage of thrift has held back the spread of credit cards.

China's credit card companies have a fairly clear idea of their target market. The country manager for American Express says: 'Look at young, white-collar workers – there is clearly tremendous spending power in key cities. It's about balance. You don't want people to save too much, and you don't want people to spend too much' (McGregor, 2003). China Merchants, a bank based in Shenzhen, which launched its credit card in 2003, has few doubts about the market potential, sending salespeople into the commercial towers of Shanghai, cold calling on white-collar workers to sign them up as customers. This practice, by which salespeople receive bonuses for achieving targets, is associated with high-pressure tactics carrying negative connotations in markets where credit cards have long been established. The bank also operates incentive schemes for cardholders, giving gifts in return for a certain level of usage. The cautionary experience of South Korea, however, shows the risks in a credit card boom which got out of control.

Sources: Mallet, V. 'Asia's plastic revolution', *Financial Times*, 2 February 2004; McGregor, R. 'Credit comes cold calling in Shanghai', *Financial Times*, 29 December 2003; McGregor, R. 'Chinese set to make flexible friends', *Financial Times*, 19 October 2001.

Case questions

Describe the culture shift taking place in the growth of credit cards in Asia. What are the opportunities and risks?

Stratification in societies

Throughout history, all societies have exhibited social and economic inequalities to a greater or lesser degree. 'Social stratification' refers to this hierarchy of groups into which people in a society are classified. This classification may be rigidly institutionalized, as in caste systems, or it may allow for upward mobility, as in a capitalist class society. We look first at the more rigid systems of stratification and then at classes in industrial societies.

Rigid social stratification

Rigid social systems were once the norm in most societies. Under feudalism, a person's position in life was determined by birth, fitting into a hierarchical and inflexible social order. Under slavery, which existed in the Americas from the sixteenth century, human beings were owned and controlled by other people, effectively treated as chattels which were bought and sold. Colonial administrations also used forced labour in various parts of the world, in construction work and mining, for example. Slavery as an institution and slave trade were made illegal in most of the world in the nineteenth century. However, pockets of slavery have persisted, and new forms of forced labour are emerging in the modern global economy, aided by an alarming rise in the trafficking in human beings (ILO, 2001b). Forced labour in its modern incarnation can be broadly defined as work exacted by threats or coercion, restrictions on freedom of movement, with no or very little pay. It occurs in a variety of situations, including sweatshops, public works, domestic service, and commonly arises from bondage through indebtedness (often to traffickers). Vulnerable groups include women, children, migrants and ethnic minorities. While these new forms of exploitation are for shorter periods, rather than a lifetime, they share the essential characteristics of older forms of slavery – control over labour and lack of freedom. National authorities in almost all countries are now seeking to eliminate all forms of coercive labour, supported by a growing body of international law on human rights (ILO, 2001b).

A caste system is a rigid system of social stratification in which a person is born into a particular position which determines his or her place in society. India is perhaps the best-known example of a caste system based on religious beliefs. In Hinduism, a person is born into a caste and has no prospect of escape in his or her present lifetime. While the caste system was officially abolished in 1949, it is still very much a force in Indian society, especially rural society. The link between low caste and poverty in Indian society is thus perpetuated. Despite social inequalities based on caste, however, India's growing economy has provided educational and employment opportunities which cut across caste boundaries in growth areas such as computing and IT.

Stratification in societies

- **Slavery** – Extreme form of servitude, in which people are treated as forced labour and traded. While slavery and slave trade have been abolished, new forms of forced labour and trafficking in human beings have emerged in many countries.
- **Caste** – Status in society is determined by birth. The caste system is associated with the Indian subcontinent.
- **Class** – Status dependent on economic position. Class societies are associated with capitalist development, allowing for upward mobility from lower to higher status.

Social class

The dynamic of capitalist society is class-based divisions. Unlike systems of slavery and caste, a **class system** is not determined by birth, although the class of our parents does play a part in our educational and career prospects. A class may be defined as a grouping of individuals based on its economic strength in society, or, putting it in more theoretical terms, its position in relation to the means of production. Class differences rest essentially on economic inequalities, rather than any inherent characteristics of individuals. Social class is one of the key factors used by marketers in understanding consumer behaviour. There are a number of socioeconomic classification systems in use by government statistical offices and market research organizations. Table 7.1 sets out a typical scheme applied to the UK, with percentages of the population in each class. While this classification is based mainly on occupation, it should be remembered that a number of other factors help to determine social class, including income, education and wealth.

Table 7.1 UK socioeconomic classification scheme

Class name	Social status	Occupation of head of household	Percentage of population
A	Upper middle	Higher managerial, administrative or professional	3
B	Middle	Intermediate managerial, administrative or professional	14
C1	Lower middle	Supervisors or clerical, junior managerial, administrative or professional	27
C2	Skilled working	Skilled manual workers	25
D	Working	Semi-skilled and unskilled manual workers	19
E	Those at the lowest level of subsistence	State pensioners or widows, casual or lower grade workers	12

Source: Brassington, F., and Pettit, S., *Principles of Marketing*, 3rd edn, 2003 (Harlow: Pearson Education) p. 118.

In all class systems the upper class are the owners and controllers of economic resources. They may be self-made entrepreneurs who have accumulated wealth, or they may be senior managers in large corporations. The middle class comprises numerous professional and white-collar workers, in salaried posts. They may also be self-employed small businesspeople. A distinction is made between upper middle class, which includes managerial and professional people, and lower middle class, which includes people such as administrators and other office staff, nurses and teachers. The working class is made up of manual and blue-collar workers. Again, the upper working class, made up of skilled workers, is often distinguished from the lower working class of unskilled workers.

Class structures differ in different societies. The 'diamond' pattern of UK society (relatively few at the top and bottom, with a bulge in the middle – C1 and C2), as indicated in Table 7.1 is typical of many developed societies. But for many other societies, such as those in Latin America and Africa, the class structure is more of a pyramid, with a wealthy elite at the pinnacle and a large population of poor people at the base. Concentration of wealth in land ownership is one of the factors that perpetuates extreme inequalities in these countries. In the poorer countries whose economies are dominated by agriculture, the peasantry, who work on the land, form the largest class. Agriculture, including both farmers and labourers, is also economically and politically significant in many industrialized economies, as food is an important strategic resource.

Changes in capitalist society

All societies experience change, which may be gradual changes or radical transformations during particularly turbulent periods in their history. Some changes that have shaped modern capitalist societies are set out below.

The structure of corporate power

Today's large corporation differs from the nineteenth-century company in which ownership and control resided in the owner-entrepreneur. Ownership is now dispersed among a wide group of shareholders, many of them large financial institutions. Moreover, managers and corporate boards of directors must now be responsive to a variety of stakeholder interests, in addition to those of the company's shareholders. Corporate power has thus become more diffuse and complex than in the days of the owner-manager.

The changing nature of white-collar work

With the decline in manufacturing industries and the increase in the service sector, many more people now work in non-manual, white-collar jobs than in blue-collar jobs. However, many of these jobs are low-level clerical and administrative jobs, requiring little skill. The mechanization, or deskilling, of office work is largely responsible. Work which once involved individual responsibility has become routinized and repetitive, little individual initiative is involved and career prospects are few. This type of work may be hardly more skilled than manual labour used to be, but we probably still look on such jobs as middle class, rather than working class. Jobs that are subject to deskilling are likely to give way to automation, as workers are replaced by IT systems. These routine clerical jobs, such as work in call centres, are predominantly carried out by women (see Case study 7.3 on call centres). Job security and job satisfaction are low and career prospects are poor (Stanworth, 2000). Moreover, many of these jobs are shifting to low-cost locations such as the Caribbean, India and Malaysia.

Social
mobility and
the new
middle class

The growing middle class is associated with the growth of modern consumer society generally. Manual workers in industrial societies are now likely to be relatively far more affluent than their predecessors and enjoy the fruits of consumer society, such as home ownership. Many manual jobs have themselves changed with the introduction of computer technology, requiring a level of skill much higher than that needed for the manual jobs of old. In their lifestyles, these workers more closely resemble middle-class than working-class groups. They are likely to wear the same types of casual clothes in their leisure, enjoy the same types of entertainment and drive similar cars. The foreign package holiday has now become almost universally accessible, while the traditional seaside holiday camps, with their working-class image, have struggled to compete.

CRITICAL PERSPECTIVES

What happened to the working class?

The men and women who live in those starter homes in the great big housing estates around our cities may not work in huge factories any more but they remain just as at risk to capitalism, employer power and loss of work as their forbears were. The working class remains; it is working in the service sector, wears suits and is harder to organize into trade unions. It may not be so solidaristic, but because it's harder to recognize we shouldn't dismiss its existence. Its relations to work and power are critically very similar to those of the old working class. (Hutton, 2000, p. 25)

■ Think of types of work and lifestyle which fit the situation Hutton describes – these workers would probably think of themselves as middle class. Why is Hutton insistent that they are working class, and do you agree with him?

The tastes and purchasing decisions of this new middle class are being analysed by increasingly refined market research, providing information for marketing strategists in consumer goods and services. As seen in Chapter 2, marketing uses the concept of segmentation to break down consumer markets. Along with social class, segmentation can be based on geographic region, demographic factors (age, gender and family structure), education and lifestyle (Kotler et al., 2002). Geographic region may have a strong cultural bond linking residents, which cuts across class divisions. Similarly, lifestyle may be more indicative of consumer tastes than traditional socioeconomic indicators. Gender and age segmentation reflect prevalent social groupings and social interactions, also cutting across lines of social class. These groupings evolve over time, as Case studies 7.2 and 7.3 show. Marketing strategists seek to respond to these shifts by offering products and services designed for particular markets.

Changing populations

The world's population stands at 6.3 billion people. Asia is the most populous continent, with 3.8 billion people. The populations of the developing countries, encompassing Asia (excluding Japan and Russia), Latin America and Africa, account for five out of every six people, as Table 7.2 shows. It is notable that Europe stands out as an area where population has declined. World population is growing at 1.2 per cent per year, mostly accounted for by developing countries, as depicted in Figures 7.1 and 7.2. Populations of the least developed countries are growing the fastest, and are expected to jump from 11 per cent of total world population in 2003 to 19 per cent in 2050. This trend is a cause for concern, in that the bulk of the world's population growth will occur in the countries which are already struggling to provide sufficient food and improve the quality of life for their inhabitants.

Table 7.2 **Population in major areas of the world, 1950, 2000 and 2003 (millions)**

	1950	2000	2003
World	2,519	6,071	6,301
More developed regions	813	1,194	1,203
Less developed regions	1,706	4,877	5,098
Africa	221	796	851
Asia	1,398	3,680	3,823
Latin America and the Caribbean	167	520	543
Europe	547	728	726
North America	172	316	326
Oceania	13	31	32

Source: UN Population Division (2003) *World Population Prospects: The 2002 Revision*, at http://www.un.org/esa/population/unpop.

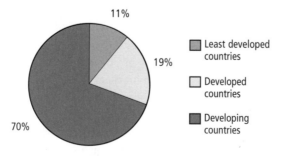

Figure 7.1 **World population in 2003**
Source: UN Population Division (2003) *World Population Prospects: The 2002 Revision*, at
http://un.org.esa/population/unpop.

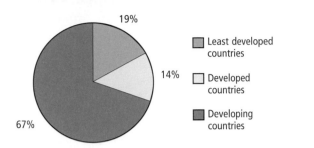

Figure 7.2 **World population estimates for 2050**
Source: UN Population Division (2003) *World Population Prospects: The 2002 Revision*, at
http://www.un.org/esa/population/unpop.

Populations are not static, but constantly changing. They change naturally over time and across space. **Demographic change** refers to these population changes. They include births, deaths and migration. The difference between births and deaths produces a natural increase (or decrease) in population. Natural increase – the excess of births over deaths – is the most common way in which populations grow, but migration is also an important factor. Migration may be within the same country, as in rural to urban migration or the international movement of people. These phenomena can have long-term effects on societies, both on the places people have left and those to which they migrate. (International immigration is discussed in detail in the next section.) Demographic changes can have profound long-term effects on societies, even though they happen gradually.

Ageing societies and Implications for business

In industrialized countries, low birth rates, coupled with a growing proportion of elderly people, are creating a looming **demographic crisis** in the twenty-first century. Figure 7.3(a) shows that, in the developed world, the proportion of children is projected to decline from 18 per cent in 1998 to 14 per cent in 2050, while the proportion of older people will rise from 20 per cent in 1998 to 35 per cent by 2050.

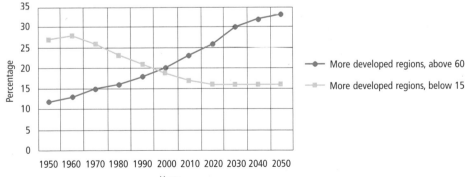

Figure 7.3a **Proportion of total population aged 0–14 and 60 and over, for more developed regions**
Source: UN Population Division (2003) *World Population Prospects: The 2002 Revision*.

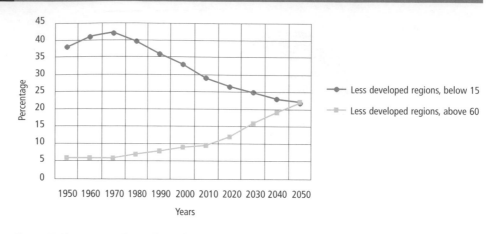

Figure 7.3b **Proportion of total population aged 0–14 and 60 and over, for less developed regions**
Source: UN Population Division (2003) *World Population Prospects: The 2002 Revision.*

Population ageing has been slower in less developed regions; the proportion of older people increased from 6 to 8 per cent between 1950 and 2000 (see Figure 7.3b). However, more rapid ageing seems to lie ahead, so that by mid-century, the less developed regions will probably have an age structure similar to today's more developed regions.

In developed countries, the percentage of older people (defined as those over 60) will rise from about one-fifth of the population at present to a third by 2050. Moreover, longevity is rising remarkably. Average life expectancy at the age of 65 rose by about 25 per cent between 1970 and 2000. A 65-year-old man in 1970 could expect to live another 12.6 years, while a man reaching 65 now can expect to live another 15.5 years. A women of 65 in 1970 could expect to live another 15.5 years, while now she would have another 19.5 years ahead of her. Paying for pensions and medical care for the elderly is a potential problem if pensions and health insurance schemes prove to be inadequately funded. France, Germany and Italy have had generous state pension arrangements, but are now seeking pension reforms to control spiralling public expenditure on pensions. It has been estimated that by 2050, pension payments could rise to as much as 17 per cent of GDP in Germany (Betts, 2003). In Britain, by contrast, where public provision is much less, the government pays only about 5 per cent of GDP in pensions, which is predicted to rise to 6 per cent by 2050 (HM Treasury, 2004a). Occupational and private pensions, which are commoner in the UK, face potential shortfalls as retirees live longer and falling stock markets have eroded the values of pension funds and other investments. Workers now and in the future must therefore come to terms with the need to pay a greater proportion of their earnings into pensions than their parents had to pay.

On the brighter side, older people are now likely to be healthier than those of earlier generations, given the advances in healthcare and the prevention of disabling illnesses, so that the length of ill health before death is shortening. Governments are now looking at raising the retirement age and encouraging older people to remain economically active. A UK government report (Cabinet Office, 2000) recommended the following:

- the introduction of age discrimination legislation (covered in the EU anti-discrimination directive, which must be implemented by 2006)
- raising from 50 to 55 the age at which early retirement schemes can be taken
- 'gradual' retirement arrangements with companies, to allow workers to continue working flexibly.

Advanced economies with ageing populations face skill shortages as a result of declining birth rates, and replacement migration to make up the shortfall is a possibility assessed in a UN report (UN Population Division, 2000). The report estimates that even a massive influx of immigrants would have only limited impact on the declining and ageing populations in Europe and Japan (UN Population Division, 2000). By 2025, it is estimated that nearly one-third of the population of Europe will be pensioners. In the case of Germany, for example, to maintain the current proportion between the working population and over-65s would require an average influx of 3.4 million migrants per year, more than ten times the number of immigrants entering Germany between 1993 and 1998. An alternative would be raising the retirement age to 77. The UN concludes that for the industrialized countries: 'Keeping retirement and healthcare systems for older persons solvent in the face of declining and ageing populations, for example, constitutes a new situation that poses serious challenges for Governments and civil society' (UN Population Division, 2000, p. 94).

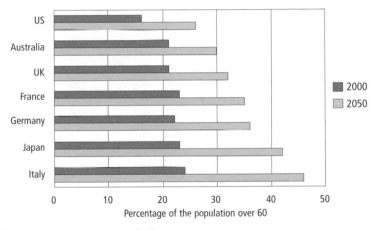

Figure 7.4 **Ageing populations**
Source: UN Population Division (2003) *World Population Prospects: The 2002 Revision*, Table 7.

There are long-term implications of these trends for business. Many businesses have seen opportunities for targeting older consumers, who have leisure time and money to spend. Saga Holidays specializes in holidays for over-50s, and has expanded into other services such as insurance (see Case study 7.2). Products and advertising targeted at these consumers present challenges for businesses which have traditionally focused on younger consumers, as the case study shows. With dwindling numbers of younger customers and a growing proportion of older ones, however, businesses are becoming aware of the needs and wants of older customers. Firms specializing in retirement flats, nursing homes, pharmaceuticals and healthcare products will experience market growth. Large food manufacturers in the US have found an eager market for products such as fruit juices and snacks which are fortified to give health benefits beyond their normal nutritional value. Called 'nutraceuticals', these products, with names like 'Wisdom', and 'Karma', are fortified with herbs such as gingko biloba and other supplements. This market nearly doubled from 1997, when it amounted to $2.68bn., to 2000, when it had grown to $4.7bn. (Barnes and Winter, 2001).

Case study 7.2   The growing power of the older consumer

A new Ferrari costing $660,000 and capable of a top speed of 217 mph would seem to be an unlikely product to be targeted at the older consumer, yet the company has felt the need to respond to the changing profile of its customers, whose average age is near 50 and getting older. Subtle design changes have involved enlarging the seat and altering the door height to make it easier for those with stiffer limbs to manage. These changes, engineered to give better accessibility and roominess, are not obvious to the eye and are designed to retain the sporty look desired by customers. By contrast, General Motors, catering for a mass market, has built a 'Sit-n-lift' motorized chairlift as an accessory for its minivan. Ford, too, has adapted door handles and dashboard lighting to cater for some of the problems common among older consumers, such as arthritis and poor eyesight. These examples point to contrasting strategies in the growing 'grey' market: should marketing explicitly address the ageing consumer, or should products be adapted in a way that does not remind people of their age? This strategy debate becomes increasingly important as the proportion of over-50s grows (see figure.)

The spending power of the grey consumer is seen by some businesses as a threat rather than an opportunity, particularly in advertising. Consumer goods companies have generally become accustomed to targeting the young adult consumer. A range of products, such as convenience foods and aerosol deodorants owe their success to the enthusiasm of young adults. These consumers, it is assumed, are more open to new products and brands and more likely to be influenced by advertising than their older counterparts. If advertisers shift their focus towards older consumers – as the changing demographics suggest they should – they fear an inbuilt resistance to their messages, as these customers are harder to persuade that they actually need the latest fashion accessory or high-tech gadget.

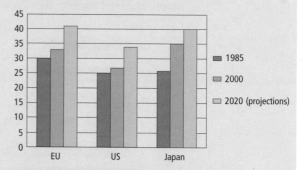

Population over 50 (percentages)
Source: Tomkins, 16 August 2002.

Older consumers, who are more experienced and more knowledgeable, are more discerning in making purchase decisions and less likely to buy what they perceive to be a mere fashion item. An implication for mobile phone companies, for example, is that the older customer is less likely to see the need of a video phone. On the other hand, there are pitfalls in making generalizations based on spending habits of previous generations of pensioners. Today's 'baby boomers' are people born between 1945 and 1965, who grew up in a changing social environment. Postwar industrialization was bringing better jobs and aspirations of a better lifestyle than their parents. They were also better educated and more liberal and free-thinking in their views. The fifty-plus consumers are now likely to have more free time, good health and a desire to spend their money in ways not dissimilar to more youthful consumers. And free from the financial burdens of thirty somethings, such as mortgage payments, they are finally able to indulge in products that make them feel good, such as sports cars and adventure holidays. Saga, a company which has catered for the over-50s, is indicative of changes taking place in this market. Started in 1951 as a family business, it began by offering off-peak holidays in British seaside resorts to retired people, who were likely to be the only people able to take holidays out of the peak summer period. The company diversified into a range of products, including insurance and publishing, as well as a hugely expanded holiday business, which now offers white-water rafting in Canada and jungle trekking in Borneo.

Internet use by older people confirms their influence. Market research indicates that those over 55 account for 16.7 per cent of users of online media and shopping sites, and they spend longer online, over 30 hours each quarter, than the average for the rest of the population, which is 28 hours. These well-informed and astute shoppers are posing challenges for marketers to think beyond the stereotypes of the 'old' market.

Sources: Tomkins, R. 'Grey power', *Financial Times*, 16 August 2002; Wendlandt, A., 'Champion of "grey pound" calls it a day', *Financial Times*, 27 November 2003; Roberts, D. 'The ageing business', *Financial Times*, 20 January 2004; Cohen, N., and Cookson, C., 'The planet is ever greyer', *Financial Times*, 19 January 2004.

Case questions

What are the challenges facing businesses in selling products and services to the older consumer?

International migration

The urge to move to 'greener pastures' is not a recent phenomenon. People have been on the move throughout history. Movements which result in a permanent change of residence are referred to as migration, and they are a normal aspect of most societies (de Haan, 1999). People move for a variety of reasons. Studies of the causes of migration divide these reasons into 'push' and 'pull' factors, and researchers find that often both sets of factors are relevant. Some push factors are escape from poverty, natural disasters or religious persecution. Often, when these factors are involved, people move en masse across borders. Pull factors include the prospect – real or imagined – of a better job and greater economic opportunities.

The most important historic examples of population outflow have been the movements of European settlers to the new worlds of the Americas and Australia. From about the sixteenth century, people emigrated in search of more space, economic riches, a better life and sometimes simply adventure. The exodus of Europeans, mainly to the Americas, in the nineteenth century created the world's largest international population flow, amounting to a million arrivals a year in the years leading up to the First World War. Push and pull factors both played a part. In the early phase, people left the densely populated areas of Northern Europe to seek more space and a better living in America, but later immigrants came from the poor areas of Southern and Eastern Europe.

Recent patterns of migration

In the postwar period, migration has involved economic migrants as well as refugees, who account for about 9 per cent of all migrants. Globalization has seen the rise of an international labour market and greater mobility of workers. About 175 million people, or 3 per cent of the world's population, reside in a country other than where they were born. A surge in migration has taken place since 1970, with a doubling in the number of migrants. International migration has been mainly from developing countries to developed ones, chiefly in North America and the industrial areas of Europe. This flow of labour reflects the gulf between richer and poorer economies, as well as the rapid rates of population increase in the developing countries. About 60 per cent of the world's migrants live in the more developed regions, amounting to one in every 10 people in developed countries. Recent trends are highlighted by the UN's *International Migration Report 2002*. The UN's forecasts for migration are shown in Figure 7.5. The largest growth in migrants is taking place in North America, Europe and Australia. However, given the pressures of growing populations in the developing world, forecasts of future migration appear modest. While the largest sending countries are forecast to be China, Mexico and India, it is also likely that migration from other Asian countries and Africa will be significant. A recent trend has been migration from countries in Africa and Asia to the oil-rich countries of the Gulf region, mainly Kuwait, the United Arab Emirates (UAE) and Saudi Arabia (UN Population Division, 2002).

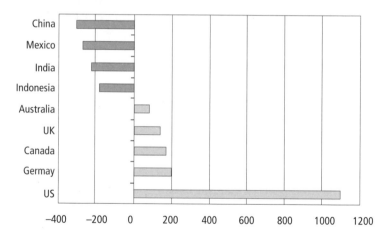

Figure 7.5 **Migration 2000–2050: major sending and receiving countries of migrants (thousands)**
Source: UN Population Division (2002) *International Migration Report 2002* (New York: UN).

Postwar economic development in France and Germany depended in large measure on immigrant labour. In Germany, many of these immigrants came as 'guest-workers', on short-term contracts. However, millions of these workers, a large proportion of whom were Turkish, stayed on and have become settled, although, as foreigners, they have not become assimilated into German society.

Migration impacts on both the sending and receiving countries. Highly skilled workers, such as scientists, doctors and engineers, come to industrialized regions

from developing countries, forming a 'brain drain', which deprives their home countries of their skills but provides broader individual opportunities for self-betterment.
These workers are welcomed by industrialized societies, to fill gaps in their own
workforces. On the other hand, poor, unskilled migrants, often without legal documentation, enter a country and find work in jobs that local people are reluctant to
take (for example, in agriculture). These people pose a number of issues for both government and society in the recipient countries. Employment, housing, healthcare
and education are some of the main areas where they have particular needs, often
because of language difficulties. Remittances contribute to household savings and
consumer spending in the home country and can be a major source of earnings for
countries sending migrants, as shown in Figure 7.6. Figure 7.7 gives an indication of
the importance of remittances in the economies of sending countries. In some, such
as El Salvador and Jordan, they amount to more than 10 per cent of GDP.

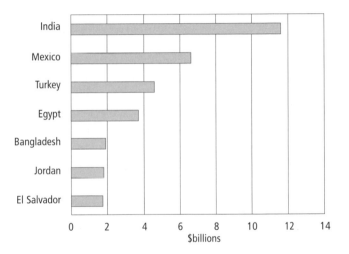

Figure 7.6 **Flows of remittances to home countries (2000)**
Source: *Financial Times*, 30 July 2003.

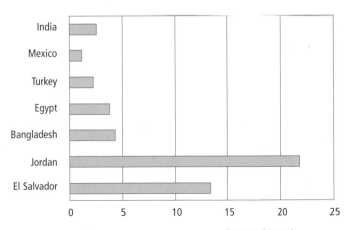

Figure 7.7 **Remittances as percentage of GDP (2000)**
Source: *Financial Times*, 30 July 2003.

In the postwar period, Western governments tightened immigration controls at borders, while recognizing an obligation under the UN Convention on Refugees (1951) to accept genuine refugees and asylum-seekers. However, the definition of refugee is interpreted differently in different states, some more broadly than others. There is an International Convention on the Protection of the Rights of all Migrant Workers and their Families (1990). The migrant who has little hope of entering as a refugee is tempted to use clandestine means, often relying on organized traffickers. Governments have consequently had to address the problems of controlling the growth of trafficking in humans, as well as the problems of individual asylum-seekers. In 2000, a Protocol on the Smuggling of Migrants was added to the UN Convention against Transnational Organized Crime, aiming to protect the most vulnerable migrants.

Within the EU, while non-citizens are subject to member states' separate immigration regimes, a long-standing principle is that EU citizens enjoy free movement. However, the recent enlargement of the EU, bringing in the poorer states of Central and Eastern Europe, has raised the issue of future immigration. The prospect of an influx of jobseekers from poorer countries into richer ones has pushed the immigration issue up the political agenda at both national and EU levels. Germany and Austria, in particular, would be likely destinations of new Eastern European migrants. Both have imposed two-year restrictions on the right of entry for people coming from the EU's 10 new member states, with a possible extension for five more years. In the 1990s, growing numbers of refugees from conflicts in Africa and the former Yugoslavia have entered EU countries, often illegally. In Britain, the official numbers leapt from 4000 to over 70,000 in 1999 (Home Office, 2000). Stricter laws on asylum-seekers came into force in 2000, in the Asylum and Immigration Act. The Act aims, above all, to streamline and speed up the processing of asylum-seekers and also impose penalties on traffickers. EU authorities now recognize that harmonization of the law is needed among its member states, in order to prevent a developing scenario of migrants 'shopping around' between countries.

SUMMARY POINTS

Changing patterns of international migration

- Historically, waves of immigrants from Europe to the new world have relieved population pressures in their homelands, and have been openly welcomed in their destinations.

- While the postwar modern state system presents considerable formal barriers to immigrants, most developed economies have benefited from immigrants' contribution to their economies.

- Migration of people between continents has grown with the globalization of labour markets, most of the movement being from developing to developed economies.

- Many of these newer migrants see themselves as following employment opportunities – part of a more mobile international labour pattern – in contrast to immigrants of earlier generations.

CRITICAL PERSPECTIVES

Illegal immigration

Since illegals will remain in our midst, and more will keep coming, the only meaningful, and indeed compelling, question for us becomes a moral one: How do we treat these illegal aliens with decency, assuring them and their families the civil rights that would rescue them from the afflictions of their illegal status? In my view, the answer has to take us in the direction of less internal enforcement, more protected and effective access by illegals to our welfare programs, and equal rights (for example, to education and health) for the children of illegals as for the children of legal aliens and citizens. (Bhagwati, 1999, pp. 330–1)

- Bhagwati is speaking in particular of Mexicans who cross into the US looking for work, but without legal documentation. Do you concur with Bhagwati's recommendation in principle?
- Most states at present do not operate such a liberal approach; what would be the effects if they were persuaded to do so in future?

Urbanism

Migration from rural areas to cities was commonplace long before industrialization. People were 'on the move' not just for economic motives, but for social and cultural reasons as well. The process by which a growing proportion of the population shifts to the cities is termed urbanization. At the start of the twenty-first century, approximately half the world's people live in urban areas. This proportion represents a rise from just over a third in 1975. By 2025, it is set to rise to two-thirds (World Bank, 2000a).

Urbanization is generally associated with economic development. Western countries, first to experience urbanization, are now 74.5 per cent urban, whereas developing countries, 42.1 per cent urban in 2003, are expected to become 57.1 per cent urban by 2030 (UN Population Division, 2004). Most of the global population increase expected during 2000–2030 will be concentrated in urban areas. The current rise in urbanization is now taking place mainly in developing countries, as indicated in the UN's forecast rise in urban populations, shown in Figure 7.8. The highest annual rate of urbanization forecast for the period 2000–2030 is in Africa (3.10 per cent), followed by Asia (2.22 per cent) (UN Population Division, 2004). Meanwhile, the world's rural population is decreasing slightly, a decrease which is almost all taking place in the more developed regions (see Table 7.3).

The pattern of urbanization and its social and economic effects have differed between the industrialized Western economies and the developing economies. We look first at urbanization in Western economies.

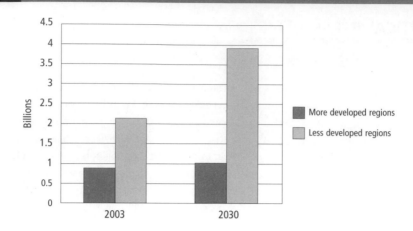

Figure 7.8 **Projected growth in urban populations, 2003–2030**
Source: United Nations Population Division (2004) *World Urbanization Prospects: The 2003 Revision.*

Table 7.3 **Distribution of the world's population in urban and rural areas**

	Population in 2003 (billions)	Population in 2030 (billions)	Annual average % growth 1950–2000	Annual average % growth 2000–2030
Urban population				
World	3.04	4.94	2.72	1.83
More developed regions	0.90	1.01	1.45	0.47
Less developed regions	2.15	3.93	3.73	2.29
Rural population				
World	3.26	3.19	1.17	−0.03
More developed regions	0.31	0.23	−0.43	−1.05
Less developed regions	2.95	2.96	1.46	0.06

Source: United Nations Population Division (2004) *World Urbanization Prospects: The 2003 Revision.*

Urbanization in Western economies

The technological developments of the Industrial Revolution provided the impetus to urbanization. These developments comprised three main elements:

1 The revolution in agriculture, which allowed farmers to produce more food with fewer workers
2 The transition to factory production systems, which attracted workers from the countryside
3 The transport revolution, which dramatically reduced the cost and increased the speed of transport of goods from one location to another, facilitating the distribution of food and other goods to an expanding urban population.

Urbanization accompanying economic development has followed a distinctive pattern, particularly observable in the US. With industrialization, firms were able to obtain scale economies by concentrating production in cities. The decision of a large firm to locate in a particular city can have a profound impact. For example, Detroit, the home of the motor industry in the US, attracted numerous firms connected with supplies to the major manufacturers. This phenomenon is known as the advantage of industrial agglomeration. Workers were attracted to the area, creating a healthy labour market. Detroit's heyday coincided with that of the mass production systems of Fordism, as we saw in Chapter 5. But with the shift to more flexible production in a global economy, firms looked carefully at advantages of a range of locations. High costs of labour, high costs of materials and scarcity of land were some of the factors that caused them to look to new locations. Factories closed down as companies looked for greenfield sites elsewhere, often abroad. The transition from the standardized Fordist economy to the flexible, information economy brought with it a more mobile workforce and changing industrial geography. A new urban economy based on financial and service activities has taken over from the older manufacturing businesses, and the major cities have become centres for international business and banking (Sassen, 1998).

The landscapes of many American cities reflect the shifting centres of economic activity. As the major cities of the industrial north grew, the more affluent moved to the surrounding area, the suburbs. This process of 'suburbanization' peaked in the 1950s and 60s. The congestion, pollution, lack of space and high crime rates in the cities were all factors. A continuing problem of the inner cities has been urban decay, marked by run-down property, poor living standards and high crime rates. Meanwhile, some smaller towns and cities are booming. Those that are booming are often in areas where the new businesses in the information economy have taken hold, again attracting those with capital, technological expertise and innovative talents.

WEB ALERT!

The World Bank has an urban development website, with links on all issues connected with urbanization, including the environment, transport and regional issues. It is at http://www.worldbank.org/urban

The Urban Institute's website concentrates on American issues. It is at http://www.urban.org

In the UK, too, suburbanization resulted in a decline in the inner cities, although not as extreme as in the US. The northern industrial cities declined as manufacturing industries either closed down or moved, leaving behind problems of unemployment and declining infrastructure. On the other hand, new industries have sprung up in smaller towns and cities. Cambridge, for example, has become a centre for technology companies. The regeneration of inner cities has been part of government policy, aimed to improve housing and amenities. An important aspect of this policy has been to tackle the problems of road congestion and pollution caused by long commuter journeys from the suburbs, by attracting people back to urban centres. Much urban development, however, such as the high-rise office blocks and luxury apartments of the Docklands development in London, risks alienating poor local residents and highlighting social divisions, rather than building a sense of community.

Table 7.4 The world's ten largest cities

	Population in 2003 (millions)	Population in 2015 (millions)	Annual average % growth 1975–2000	Annual average % growth 2000–2015
Tokyo, Japan	35.0	36.2	1.03	0.33
Mexico City, Mexico	18.7	20.6	2.10	0.89
New York, USA	18.3	19.7	0.47	0.66
São Paulo, Brazil	17.9	20.0	2.30	1.03
Mumbai (Bombay), India	17.4	22.7	3.13	2.28
Delhi, India	14.1	20.9	4.13	3.47
Calcutta, India	13.8	16.8	2.02	1.68
Buenos Aires, Argentina	13.0	14.6	1.28	0.97
Shanghai, China	12.8	12.7	0.48	−0.12
Jakarta, Indonesia	12.3	17.5	3.31	3.08

Source: United Nations Population Division (2004) *World Urbanization Prospects: 2003 Revision.*

Urbanization in the developing world

The developing countries are now experiencing the fastest rates of urbanization, but while urbanization has brought prosperity for the few, it has brought misery for masses of migrants to the cities. The growth is taking place with little planning and haphazard infrastructure (Linden, 1996). In 1950, only three cities in developing countries were among the top 10 in the world. As Table 7.4 shows, this position is now reversed – only two are in developed countries. Tokyo is the largest urban agglomeration, but its population is growing very slowly. Growth rates are highest in India's cities and Jakarta. Secondary cities in developing countries are also growing more rapidly, creating even greater pressures on limited infrastructure, although these cities do not receive the same international attention as the largest cities (Linden, 1996).

Cities in the developing world struggle to cope with the pressures of huge and growing populations. Traffic congestion, pollution, sanitation and inadequate housing are endemic problems. Slum areas, with their proliferation of shanty dwellings, are particularly vulnerable to disease and natural disasters. According to a World Bank report, the number of people in slum and squatter settlements will double in 25 years and the average age of slum dwellers is decreasing (World Bank, 1999). The urban landscape in the developing world, therefore, exhibits a stark juxtaposition between modern high-rise centres, symbolic of new economic wealth, and the slum areas inhabited by the poorest people.

CRITICAL PERSPECTIVES

The new urban economy

The new growth sectors – specialized services and finance – contain capabilities for profit-making vastly superior to those of more traditional economic sectors. Many of the latter are essential to the operation of the urban economy and the daily needs of residents, but their profitable survival is threatened in a situation where finance and specialized services can earn superprofits. We see sharp increases in socioeconomic and spatial inequalities within major cities. This can be interpreted as merely a quantitative increase in the degree of inequality. But it can also be interpreted as social and economic restructuring. (Sassen, 1998, p. 148)

■ Consider any changes that have taken place in an urban area that you are familiar with. What have been the social changes that have accompanied the changing economic activities?

Labour relations

Relations between management and workers vary considerably, depending on both the internal environment of the organization and the wider social and cultural environment. Workers traditionally organize themselves into **trade unions** in order to achieve higher wages, better working conditions and greater security of employment. Workers in almost every country have organizations of this type, although countries vary in their approaches to organized labour. In some countries, trade unions have limited recognition and limited rights of collective negotiation. The right to strike, which is the workers' concerted withdrawal of labour, is the most potent weapon possessed by unions. A prolonged or widespread strike can take a heavy toll, in both economic losses and relations between employers and employees. Virtually all countries legally control strikes in a number of ways: membership balloting requirements for the call of a strike; cooling-off periods; and the prohibition of strikes in key public sectors. While the strike is used as a bargaining tool to obtain better employment terms, the strike as a barometer of social tension can also have a much broader significance. The high-profile walkout can be directed not just against the employer, but against the political regime. Hence, the strike has been used to gain political voice in a number of countries. The Solidarity trade union in Poland, by orchestrating mass strikes in the shipyards, took the lead in the defeat of the Communist regime. The union's political party grouping has governed Poland through most of the 1990s. Ironically, perhaps, the birthplace of Solidarity, the Gdansk shipyards have now closed, victims of the harsh realities of global competition.

In industrialized countries, the growth in trade unionism took place in mass production factories such as those in the motor industry. As well as in manufacturing, trade unions in Britain have also been strong in coal mining and shipyards. The decline in these latter sectors, together with the general decline in manufacturing jobs, has brought a steady decrease in trade union membership from the 1970s onwards. Membership in UK trade unions has declined from 12.1 million workers in 1979 to 7.4 million in 2003. Figure 7.9 shows the rise and fall of trade union membership from 1950 to 2002. Trade unions now represent 26.5 per cent of the entire civilian workforce and 29 per cent of employees (ONS, 2004a). A factor in this decline has also been a tightening of the law on strikes, which meant, for example, that a union's funds could be sequestered or frozen, in the event of unofficial strikes. The unions have fought back with recruitment campaigns, aimed at a wider variety of workers.

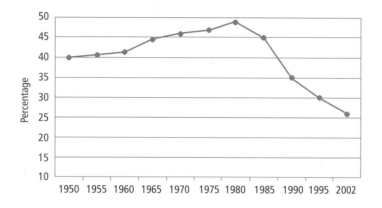

Figure 7.9 **Trade union density in the UK**
Source: ONS (2004) *Labour Market Trends March 2004* (London: ONS).

Only about 19 per cent of Britain's workers in the private sector are union members, while the percentage in the public sector is over 60 per cent. Union penetration is lower in the US, where less than 10 per cent of private sector workers are union members. Britain's largest union, UNISON, which represents professional, technical and administrative workers in the public sector, has 1.4 million members, 72 per cent of them women. By adapting to the new employment structures, UNISON has moved away from the traditional trade union model, built on the male-dominated, solidly working-class environment of manual work, to reflect the more diverse and flexible workforce in service and administrative employment. The president of the Trades Unions Congress (TUC) and joint general secretary of Amicus, the largest private sector union, has said: 'Members' concerns have changed dramatically since the 1960s. They used to be about pay and about terms and conditions in the specific workplace' (Turner, 2004). Now, he observes, they are about pensions, family life, discrimination, health and safety, long working hours and bullying. Research shows that this focus has had a positive effect, in that workplaces with recognized unions have more family-friendly policies, such as flexible working hours and job sharing, than those without (Turner, 2004). Still, in the private sector, two-thirds of workplaces have no union presence and one-third of workplaces have no formal structures for representing employee interests.

The EU Directive on worker consultation, requiring companies to consult workers over large-scale redundancies, corporate restructuring and other strategic issues, was initially opposed by the British government, and accepted only with provisos that it is phased in over seven years and does not apply to companies with fewer than 50 employees. Germany has had a longer history of this type of consultation, through 'workers' councils', which give employees a formal role in company decision-making, extending to operational measures, such as the hiring and firing of employees. The system of workers' councils has been criticized as inflexible, inhibiting the ability of companies to compete. However, attempts to reform the law on workers' councils have met resistance, as they are embedded in Germany's 'consensus' capitalism.

WEB ALERT!

Internet resources on trade unions offer insight into their activities and policy positions on a range of issues. Some are listed below:

For the UK perspective see the Trades Union Congress website at
http://www.tuc.org.uk

The International Confederation of Free Trade Unions has features on unions and the industrial environment throughout the world. It is at
http://www2.icftu.org/

UNISON's website is at http://www.unison.org.uk/home/index.htm

For the American perspective, the American trade union federation AFL-CLO has a site at http://www.aflcio/org/home.htm

Gender and work

Men enjoy greater status and wealth than women in virtually every society. Gender inequality has been accepted over many generations as somehow dictated by nature, reinforced by the stereotyped picture of the father as sole breadwinner and the mother as homemaker. This picture has persisted, even though in the developed world, women now make up on average over 60 per cent of the workforce outside the home, as the examples in Figure 7.10 show.

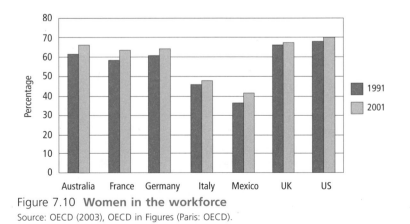

Figure 7.10 **Women in the workforce**
Source: OECD (2003), OECD in Figures (Paris: OECD).

Nonetheless, women still bear the major burden for bringing up children. Historically, women have lagged behind men in educational opportunities, career opportunities, pay and citizenship rights. Women achieved the right to vote and stand for public office in most Western societies in the last century, but only in the last 25 years of the twentieth century have they achieved legal rights to equal pay with men for equivalent work. In practice, however, while women's pay has improved in relation to that of men, they still fall behind in both pay and opportunities.

The gender pay gap is slowly narrowing, as shown in Figure 7.11. Average hourly pay for women in the UK in 2003 was 82 per cent of men's. Men's pay increased 2.2 per cent from 2002, whereas women's increased 3.4 per cent. It should be borne in mind that, as women work on average 3.5 fewer hours per week than men, there is a greater gap in weekly earnings. In 2003, a woman's weekly earnings were on average 75.4 per cent of those for men, up from 74.6 per cent in 2002 (ONS, 2003). The decreasing pay gap largely reflects the impact of legislation, including the UK Equal Pay and Sex Discrimination Acts, as well as European Community law. Under these laws, the employee is entitled to equal pay for work of equal value. Of EU countries, the UK has the highest percentage of women working part time. Here, approximately four out of every five part-time jobs (78.8 per cent) are filled by women (OECD, 2003a). Only in the 1990s, have part-time workers – as a result of EU initiatives – gained employment rights, such as pension rights and employment protection rights, on a par with full-time employees. The percentage of workers in part-time employment is rising in most OECD countries. In the UK, it accounts for 23 per cent of the labour force, well above the OECD average of 14.7 per cent. The rise in part-time work, along with other types of non-standard work, such as teleworking from home, are aspects of a growing flexibility in the definition of 'work' in response to global competitive pressures. 'Flexible working' includes the possibilities for any computer-based or telephone-based job, such as call centre work, to be located almost anywhere. Assuming a minimum level of infrastructure, services can be provided thousands of miles from the consumers. Case study 7.3 discusses the issues that arise when call centre jobs are moved to low-cost locations.

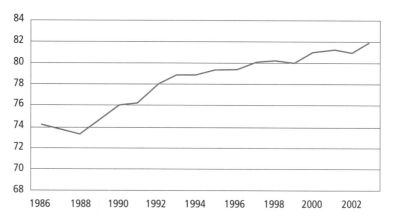

Figure 7.11 **Women's average hourly pay as a percentage of men's, for UK full-time employees**

Source: Office for National Statistics (2003) *Labour Market Statistics: Gender Pay Gap*, at http://statistics.gov.uk.

Work is now seen in the context of a 'learning society', where retraining and reskilling are needed to respond to changing technology. Even though women account for nearly half of all university enrolments, most women workers are in low-skilled jobs (Walby, 1999). In some sectors most affected by new technology, such as financial services, the information age has brought new divisions, between the professional 'knowledge' jobs, occupied mainly by men, and low-grade technical work, such as in call centres, in which women and ethnic minorities predominate (see Case study 7.3.). Women are scarce in company boardrooms. Research carried out by Singh and Vinnicombe, for the Cranfield School of Management, shows that, of Britain's largest 100 companies, the FTSE 100, women hold 101 seats, or 8.6 per cent of board seats. However, only 17, or 4 per cent, are in executive roles; 84 are non-executive directors (Singh and Vinnicombe, 2003). While nearly half of the FTSE 100 companies had no women at all on their boards in 1999, in 2003 there were still 32 with all-male boards. The research suggests a link between good corporate governance and the presence of women on the board. Companies with the highest scores on eight measures of best governance practice are more likely to have at least one female director (Singh and Vinnicombe, 2003).

Case study 7.3 Call centre jobs migrate to India

Call centres were once heralded as the providers of much-needed jobs in areas where the decline in manufacturing industry had left economic stagnation and high unemployment. Areas such as the northeast of England and Wales attracted call centres, largely in banking and financial services, where the need was for efficiency in handling large numbers of fairly routine queries from customers. An element of their attraction for businesses was the low-cost environment which they offered, and for employees, job and training opportunities. However, the reality turned out to be less rosy than expectations had suggested, and the quest for cost savings has led to a migration of these jobs to low-cost locations, particularly in India.

Call centre work acquired a reputation as a 'sweatshop' environment in the UK, which has been slow to shift. Low pay, poor working conditions and limited career prospects have led to high staff turnover and employees seeing this type of work as casual or temporary. A number of high-profile companies, including HSBC, Aviva (insurance) and BT, have shifted call centre jobs to India. HSBC, the world's second largest bank, cut 4000 UK jobs in 2003, relocating the work to India, Malaysia and China, in one of the largest transfers of British jobs to overseas locations. Its chief executive said: 'As one of the world's largest financial services companies, HSBC has a responsibility to all its stakeholders to remain efficient and competitive' (Croft, 17 October 2003). For HSBC's UK employees, the company's advertising slogan, 'the world's local bank', had a particularly hollow sound.

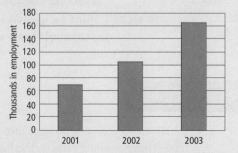

Growth in contact centres in India (includes computer and voice call centres)
Source: Roberts and Luce, 2003.

Announcing the shift of two call centres to India, BT's management highlighted the dilemma – the need to seek the low-cost locations, but also sensitivity to the employment implications for current UK employees (Singh, 10 March 2003). BT has outsourced jobs to service companies in the UK, reflecting a trend of 'outsourcing' which has developed in the industry. Under an outsourcing contract, a specialist call centre company agrees to provide call centre services for an organization such as BT. Garland Call Centres is one of these companies, employing 1300 people, making it the largest private sector employer in Hartlepool in the northeast of England. Customers phoning a helpline with a query regarding a gas provider, mobile phone provider or bank will probably have no idea they are speaking to a Garland employee rather than directly to the provider. For Garland, the attraction of Hartlepool was a pool of potential workers, many with a university education, with the added advantage that, because of high regional unemployment, they are willing to work for as little as £10,000–13,000 a year. A third of Garland's employees have university degrees.

By comparison, call centre jobs in India are mostly held by graduates, but the starting salary of the Indian graduate is £2000 per year. Here, specialist call centre companies are growing rapidly, fuelled by large numbers of graduates who speak English. These are considered desirable jobs, with relatively good conditions by local standards, but rates of staff retention are low, with annual turnover running at 40–50 per cent. Indian workers have found it difficult to adjust to the night shifts which are required of them, to deal with customers in time zones the other side of the globe. Then there are the pressures of the job, combined with the language and cultural adjustment needed to deal with customers in the US and Europe. They, like counterparts elsewhere, are unlikely to see their careers in call centres. The future of call centre workers, wherever they are, will depend largely on the extent to which automated technology is able to take over many routine tasks, through voice recognition, email and the internet. Deskilling leading to automation is a familiar occupational pattern which has affected manufacturing industries and is likely to be repeated in the call centre industry.

Sources: Croft, J., 'HSBC to cut 4,000 jobs in switch to Asia', *Financial Times*, 17 October 2003; Singh, S., 'The revolution revs up', *Financial Times*, 10 March 2003; Skapinker, M., Merchant, K. and London, S., 'A question of holding on to staff', *Financial Times*, 4 October 2002; Merchant, K., London, S. and Skapinker, M., 'Trying to keep the customer happy', *Financial Times*, 7 October 2002; Roberts, D. and Luce, E., 'Service industries go global: skilled white-collar jobs are starting to migrate to lower-cost centres overseas', *Financial Times*, 20 August 2003.

Case questions

In what ways can it be said that globalization is affecting the call centre industry?

HSBC's chief executive referred to the interests of stakeholders – what did he mean?

Families

Just as the roles of women are changing in modern societies, with the increase in paid employment outside the home, patterns of families are also changing. The unit of the 'nuclear family', consisting of mother, father and one or more children has been the basic family unit in European societies. The 'extended family', which also may include grandparents, brothers and sisters and their wives and husbands and children, has been the pattern in Asian and South Asian societies. In these societies, the extended family, or kinship group, is often an economic unit. The Asian family business built on kinship ties has been an important factor in economic development in Asia. Family relationships translated into business organizations have tended to be hierarchical and based on personal authority. They are also said to be at the core of Asian values, such as frugality and loyalty, discussed in Chapter 6.

Family patterns are changing in all modern societies. A major cause of change is the influence of Western values and culture, with its emphasis on the individual. There are a number of consequences for families. First, whereas in many societies, marriages are traditionally 'arranged' by families, the trend now is towards the free choice of a partner. Secondly, the extended family is less cohesive as a unit, partly as a result of urbanization, which brought greater scope for job opportunities further afield. And thirdly, there has been a growing recognition of women's rights to education and careers outside the home.

The result of these trends has been a greater diversity in the nature of families, and also a greater likelihood that the composition of families will change over a lifetime. In almost all Western societies, divorce is now accepted as a normal occurrence, and roughly one-third of marriages end in divorce. 'No-fault' divorces are now allowed by law in most Western countries, although countries which are predominantly Roman Catholic (such as Italy) are much less liberal in this respect. A rise in the number of lone-parent families has been brought about largely by divorce. But, in addition, there are growing numbers of people who deliberately opt for lone parenthood. In Britain in 1961, 38 per cent of households were of the traditional type, consisting of a couple and dependent children. By 1998–99, this proportion had decreased to 23 per cent (ONS, 2000a). In the US, the percentage of households consisting of married couple with children under 18 declined from 45 per cent in 1960 to 24 per cent in the 2000 census, further decreasing to 22.5 per cent in 2002 (Fields and Casper, 2001; US Census Bureau, 2002).

What are the long-term social implications of changes in family life for the business environment? There has been significant growth in the proportion of one-parent families. In Britain, the proportion has risen from 8 per cent of families in 1971 to 27 per cent in 2002 (ONS, 2004c). In most of these it is the mother who is the lone parent, whether from divorce (in which women usually obtain custody of children), widowhood or simply never having married. In nearly half of Britain's lone-parent families headed by mothers, the family is headed by a mother who has never married. As a growing segment of consumer markets, the lone parent has different needs for goods and services than larger families. Apartments rather than houses may be more suitable. While ready-meals for one are now quite common, package holidays are still typically based on two sharing and holiday operators charge a supplement for single people. For a lone parent, childcare facilities and flexible working hours may be crucial, but while some employers are accommodating, many, especially small organizations, lack the resources. State provision of childcare support has become an important issue as the numbers of lone parents have risen. Single mothers generally fare worse in terms of jobs and pay than other women workers, and a concern of governments is that lone-parent families can become caught in a 'poverty trap', dependent on state welfare.

CRITICAL PERSPECTIVES

Work and families

The imperatives of flexibility and mobility imposed by deregulated labour markets put particular strain on traditional modes of family life. How can families meet for meals when both parents work on shifts? What becomes of families when the jobs market pulls parents apart?

There has been a hollowing out of the business corporation as a social institution. The growth of contracting-out of labour tends to reduce the permanent workforce of late modern companies to a small cadre. (Gray, 1998, p. 72)

■ Would you agree that Gray's two points about labour flexibility are like two sides of the same coin: the negative side is the impact on families and the positive side is the efficiency gains for the organization? Are the two sides inevitably linked?

Conclusions

1 Modern societies are essentially industrial societies, based on capitalist economic principles. However, there is considerable diversity, including developing and transitional as well as developed industrial societies.

2 Social stratification is a feature of all societies. Classes in industrial society are evolving and becoming more flexibly interpreted, encompassing a new middle class based on consumption and lifestyle.

3 While populations in the industrialized world are growing only very slowly, and becoming greyer, populations in the developing world are growing more rapidly. Ageing populations have implications for governments and businesses, including skill shortages, pressure on healthcare provisions and pension systems.

4 The migration of people from the developing to industrialized regions of the world has become a trend, marked by increasing mobility of labour internationally.

5 Urbanization, while slowing in the developed world, is still a trend in the developing world, where seven out of the world's 10 largest cities are located.

6 The shift in industrial structure from manufacturing to services is reflected in reduced membership in trade unions, and also changes in labour relations in response to the changing work environment.

7 Women workers, while closing the gap in pay, in comparison with men, are predominant in low-skilled work and part-time work.

8 The nature of the family is changing in modern society, with a rise in numbers of lone-person and single-parent families.

Review questions

1   What are the characteristics of 'industrial society' and how are industrial societies changing?

2   It is often said that class no longer has any meaning in modern society. To what extent is this true?

3   What are the effects of the 'demographic timebomb' faced by industrialized societies and what steps can be taken to deal with them?

4   How does the international migration of labour affect businesses in industrialized countries?

5   What are the problems associated with urbanization and why have they become most acute in developing countries?

6   How has the role of trade unions changed in modern industrial societies?

7   What is meant by the deskilling of low-level, white-collar work?

8   The structure of families is changing in almost all societies. What are the changes and how do they affect the ways in which businesses operate?

Assignments

1   Assess the impact of demographic changes on the business environment in (a) advanced economies, and (b) developing economies.

2   The nature of work and its location are undergoing changes with the growth of the information economy. Examine the extent to which there are winners and losers emerging as a consequence of these changes, giving examples from different regions of the world.

Further reading

Brown, P. and Lander, H. (2001) *Capitalism and Social Progress* (Basingstoke: Palgrave Macmillan).

Castells, M. (2000) *The Rise of the Network Society*, 2nd edn (Oxford: Blackwells).

Cooper, C. (ed.) (2001) *The New World of Work* (Oxford: Blackwells).

Giddens, A. (2001) *Sociology*, 4th edn (Cambridge: Polity Press).

Grint, K. (2000) *Work and Society* (Cambridge: Polity Press).

Sassen, S. (1998) *Globalization and its Discontents* (New York: The New Press).

Savage, M., Warde, A. and Ward, K. (2002) *Urban Sociology, Capitalism and Modernity* (Basingstoke: Palgrave Macmillan).

8

The changing political environment: national, regional and international forces

Outline of chapter

- Introduction
- The political sphere and civil society: how political factors affect business
- Nation-states and political framework
  - Territoriality and the state
  - Sovereignty
  - Political risk and national security
- Sources of authority in the state
- Democracy and authoritarianism contrasted
- Democratic government: the criteria
- Unitary and federal systems
- Legislative assemblies
- Elections
- Political parties
- Systems of government: presidential, parliamentary and 'hybrid' systems
- Transitional democracies
  - Regional divergence in democratic transition
  - Transitional democracies and international business
- Global politics
  - The United Nations
  - The European Union
- Conclusions

Learning objectives

1 To appreciate the characteristics of nation-states and how these are evolving in the global environment.

2 To gain an understanding of political decision-making structures in different national systems and how they interact with business.

3 To assess the processes of building democracy and how democratic institutions affect the international business environment.

4 To appreciate the dimensions of political risk in business decision-making.

5 To understand the changing role of transnational and regional forces in political processes worldwide.

Introduction

Businesses, from global corporations down to family-run enterprises, desire a stable and reasonably predictable environment in which to carry on their activities. As interaction between government and business has grown, the importance of a stable political environment has become more apparent. In the political dynamics of every society, both internal and external factors come into play. First, internal governmental structures and processes form a political system, responsible for containing and channelling conflict and promoting the collective good of the society. Just as no two societies are identical, no two political systems are identical, and their differences can have a profound affect on their attractiveness as a business location and the likely success of any investment, for both home and foreign businesses. Secondly, regional and global forces outside its territory impact on a country's ability to control its affairs and these considerations also underpin a company's strategy to invest in a particular region. Two themes of this chapter are the diversity of political institutions and the extent to which political processes at all levels, from the local to the international, are becoming more connected in the wider global environment.

People everywhere wish to see public order maintained, public services function efficiently and government officers carry out their duties. But they want more besides. A police state can offer security, but it hardly offers a conducive environment for a happy life. People also wish to have a good education, a good job and the material prosperity it brings. A broad trend can be observed in the spread of democracy across the globe, most notably in the last 25 years. Yet these democratic systems diverge substantially from one to another, and by no means all deliver either the stability or prosperity hoped or expected of them. This chapter focuses first on national political systems and their public policy implications for business, looking in particular at democracy and democratization in its many permutations. Secondly, we look at the impact of globalization and the growth in transnational political institutions.

WEB ALERT!

The following site provides links to numerous web resources on political systems worldwide, international organizations (governmental and non-governmental) and other research resources:

http://www.politicalresources.net/

The political sphere and civil society: how political factors affect business

Politics has been defined in numerous different ways, but all highlight the function of conflict resolution in society. Broadly, politics refers to processes by which a social group allocates the exercise of power and authority for the group as a whole. Breaking down the definition into three elements, first there is the existence of a social group – the word 'politics' derives from the Greek word *polis*, meaning city-state, a political community. Conflict is inevitable within societies, and politics provides the means of resolving conflict in structured ways. Secondly, politics concerns power relations. The contesting of power in society arises from groups and individuals with a wide range of viewpoints – ideological, economic, religious, ethnic or simply self-interested opportunistic. In democratic societies, political parties are the most high-profile players on the political scene, but political authorities interact with a range of interests in society, including businesses and numerous interest groups, in arriving at policy decisions. Unilever's head of public affairs in the UK has said: 'The pervasive nature of government today means the need for dialogue between business and policy makers has never been greater ... It's absolutely vital that a business like ours keeps close to policy developments, and makes sure we have an input into the policy process' (*Financial Times*, 30 March 2001). The impact of policy is multidimensional, as shown in the summary box on political decision-making.

The third element is the terrain of politics – the social group as a whole. While politics occurs in every organization, we are here concerned with agenda-setting for a society as a whole. Its scope is thus public life, rather than particular organizations. For the citizen of ancient Athens, this distinction did not exist: participation in the city-state was both civic and moral in nature, the polis providing the means to the good life. Later developments, especially the growth of secular states in Europe and increasing emphasis on the worth of the individual, led to a separation between public and private spheres. The sphere of politics is public life, the institutions of the state, governmental structures and the process by which individuals come to occupy offices of state. The private sphere is often referred to as civil society, a term which covers the sphere in which citizens have space to pursue their own personal goals. Private individuals and businesses, trade unions, religious groups and the many subnational associations which exist in pluralist societies are all part of civil society (Linz and Stepan, 1997). The institutions of civil society may be limited, or even banned, in some states, but the trend in the postwar period has been towards greater pluralism, that is, a multiplicity of groups, a development which flows logically from liberalism (Sartori, 1997).

SUMMARY POINTS

Some areas of political decision-making which impact on business

- Extent of the welfare state and how it is financed (including health, education, housing, pensions, social security benefits).
- Regional development policies and funding.
- Fiscal and monetary policies, such as taxation and currency rules.
- Environmental policy and how to enforce it.
- 'Law and order' in society.
- The division of power between central, regional and local authorities.
- Agriculture and food.
- Defence, military establishment and decision to use armed forces in particular situations.
- Immigration.

Public and private spheres, however, are not as easily separated as the theoretical distinction suggests and their distinction has become blurred with the growth of the welfare state in the major industrialized societies since the Second World War, extending the reach of the state into the private sphere. The liberal's view of the public/private divide is that government interference in civil society should be kept to a minimum. However, the social and economic problems associated with growing inequalities in industrial societies, such as poverty and unemployment, have brought about a revision of this view, to encompass a more interventionist role for the state. The extent to which governments are justified in intervention to promote social welfare is one of the major issues giving rise to political divisions in all societies. It goes hand in hand with the issue of the extent that governments should intervene in markets. Most governments have undertaken wide-ranging privatization of public enterprises. In addition, we have seen the emergence of public/private partnerships in the provision of public services, such as education, transport, healthcare and prisons (Rhodes, 1996). The Labour Party, re-elected in the general election in 2001, reiterated its commitment to public/private partnerships, saying in its manifesto: 'Where private-sector providers can support public endeavour, we should use them. A "spirit of enterprise" should apply as much to public service as to business' (Labour Party, 2001). The simple dichotomy of public and private domains, therefore, is being replaced by a less polarized, more interlinking relationship between the state and civil society. Increasingly, businesses are becoming intertwined with government agencies and processes, in activities as diverse as air traffic control and hospitals.

Nation-states and political framework

The basic unit into which the world's peoples are divided is the nation-state The concept of the nation-state, introduced in Chapter 6, combines the principle of a people's right to self-determination with the achievement of a territorial state ruled by its own government and subordinate to no higher authority. New nation-states are often born of nationalist movements within existing states. The dismantling of colonial empires following the Second World War gave rise to a large number of new states, as the growing membership of the UN shows (Figure 8.1). Some 17 new states were born out of the break-up of the Soviet Union, falling mainly in the years 1991–2. Switzerland, with a long history of independence in the international sphere, became the 190th member in 2002, following a referendum.

The nation-state, or just 'state' for short, may be defined as:

> those specialized institutions that exercise a monopoly of law-making and adjudication over a given territory, and of the organized physical coercion necessary to enforce it.
> (Beetham, 1991, p. 121)

The definition highlights three defining principles of statehood: territoriality, sovereignty and the monopoly of coercive power. 'State' is a broader term than 'government'. While state encompasses people, territory and institutions, **government** refers to the particular institutions by which laws are made and implemented. It can also refer to the particular individuals in office at a given time, as in 'the government of the day'. The machinery of government may change from time to time while the state is a more enduring, and unifying, concept.

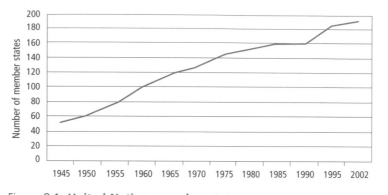

Figure 8.1 **United Nations member states**

Source: United Nations (2004) *Growth in United Nations Membership 1945–2002*, at www.un.org/Overview.

Territoriality and the state

The state occupies a geographically defined territory, within whose boundaries it has jurisdiction. Disputes over territory can be particularly bitter and have led to innumerable wars. Maintaining border controls, all would agree, has become more problematic, as territorial boundaries generally have become more permeable with the processes of globalization, such as improved communications, transport, the internet and the growth of e-commerce. Above all, these developments have facilitated the expansion of international business. Although the state is still the legal gatekeeper controlling what crosses its borders, this role has become more daunting with the growing international flows of goods, people, information and money. Importantly from a national economic standpoint, the state also controls access to the natural resources, such as mineral reserves and oil, in its territory. It is not surprising that countries such as Venezuela and Mexico, on gaining independence, nationalized their oil industries; but both are now taking steps towards liberalization and privatization. In 2001, the South African government and the mining industry reached a historic agreement: while mineral rights will belong exclusively to the state, the government will bring in a new system of objective criteria for granting licences to companies to exploit mineral rights, with a right of appeal against decisions. Through a stable regulatory regime, it is hoped to encourage overseas investors and also promote smaller mining companies.

The postcolonial states of Africa have generally followed inherited borders from the colonial period, which were artificially drawn and did not reflect ethnic groupings. Except for Rwanda and Burundi, none of the 34 modern African states corresponds to precolonial boundaries. Two consequences have followed: historic groupings are divided between states and a state's population may comprise groups which are historic enemies (Hawthorn, 1993). Ethnic conflict has been an inevitable result. In these situations, states struggle to maintain control and a sense of legitimacy over all their inhabitants (see Case study 8.1 on Nigeria). Internal tensions may lead to secession of national minorities within a state and the reforming of states. The pictures of flows of refugees from conflict into neighbouring countries have become a sad feature of modern politics, highlighting the vulnerability and interdependence of states.

Case study 8.1   Testing times for democracy in Nigeria

Nigeria, Africa's most populous state with a population of 120 million, is one of the world's largest producers of crude oil (see figure). Yet the 40 years since the country gained independence have seen a torrent of ethnic strife, military government, corruption and widespread poverty. Since 1999, Nigeria has had a democratically elected civilian government, headed by President Obasanjo, who is attempting to unite three traditionally hostile ethnic groups into a federal republic: the Muslim north, the Yoruba people of the southwest and the Ijaw people of the delta region, where the oilfields are situated. Mutual distrust has made it difficult for the federal government to establish the sense of legitimacy needed to bring about stability and economic reform. Regional political leaders in the country's 36 state governments and 774 local governments wield considerable political power in the own territories, bolstered by control over nearly half the national oil revenues. In a context of weak mechanisms for accountability and disclosure, corruption is able to flourish relatively unchecked. A leading human rights activist has said: 'Authoritarianism provides a kind of negative stability. Democracy creates space to do a lot of things, sometimes bad things, dangerous things. So democracy brings greater challenges to keep Nigeria together' (Vick, 2000).

Obasanjo's critics say that he has been weak in dealing with corruption and poor governance, noting the continued presence of officials from the military era. Conflict between ethnic groups has focused on political and social issues which go back to the military era, when local governments were set up. In Warri, in the oil-producing delta region, there have been violent conflicts between the Ijaw and Itsekiri ethnic groups. The Ijaw claim that they have too little representation in the regional government, proportionate to their population, and that the Itsekiri are overrepresented. This dispute highlights the problem that political boundaries cut across ethnic groups' traditional communities. The armed violence between the groups in 2003 had a direct impact on the oil industry, causing the multinationals to temporarily shut down more than a third of the country's oil production.

In the oil-producing delta region, some of the world's richest multinationals rub shoulders daily with its poorest inhabitants, but the local people see little of the wealth. Nigeria's people are among the world's poorest in terms of GNI (see figure), 70 per cent of the population live below the poverty line of less than $1 a day and nearly two-thirds of adults (over 15) are illiterate.

The world's crude oil reserves

Source: Energy Information Administration (2004) *World Proved Reserves of Oil*, at http://www.eia.doe.gov/emeu/international/reserves.

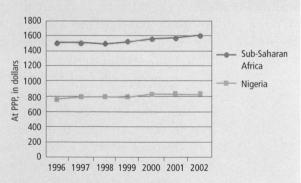

Nigeria's GNI per capita

Source: World Bank (2003) *Development Data for Nigeria*, at http://worldbank.org/cata/countrydata/aag/nga.
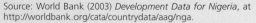

The major oil companies, including Nigeria's biggest producer, Royal Dutch Shell, operate as joint ventures with the state-owned Nigerian National Petroleum Corporation, providing more than 75 per cent of the federal government reserves. The efforts of the joint ventures have been hampered by a growing level of organized crime to steal oil from the delta's oilfields. Organized groups have been able to siphon off large amounts of oil, ship it out on barges and use the proceeds to buy arms. In 2003 it was estimated that the theft was the equivalent of a 95,000-tonne oil tanker being hijacked every week.

Building improved relations between the multi-nationals, the government and local people is a priority for restoring prosperity and security to the Niger Delta. People expected both the government and the multinationals to tackle pollution and crime and bring improvements in their economic situation and quality of life. The multinationals remain guardedly hopeful that relations are improving as their improved knowledge and sensitivity about community needs increases. Moreover, oil production is gaining momentum at more remote offshore sites, where the oil reserves are greater than on onshore sites. However, Nigeria's democratic transition, which was seen at its inception in 1999 as offering the best platform for dealing with the country's complex problems, has not as yet yielded the stability, accountability and transparency that it needs in order to make strides with its development agenda.

Sources: Vick, K., 'A delicate democracy', *Washington Post*, 29 January 2000; Holman, M., and Wallis, W., 'In office but out of power', *Financial Times*, 30 March 2000; Hawkins, T., 'Cornerstone of economic reform', *Financial Times*, 30 March 2000; Peel, M., 'Nigerian oil cutbacks continue as ethnic violence takes its toll', *Financial Times*, 30 September 2003; Goldman, A., Peel, M. and White, D., 'Nigeria suffers from slick operation to steal its crude', *Financial Times*, 29 May 2003; Peel, M., 'Deep well of troubles in Nigeria', *Financial Times*, 9 June 2004; Peel, M. and Mahtani, D., 'Nigeria wants a clean start from creditors, but is it doing enough to help itself?' *Financial Times*, 30 May 2005.

Case questions

What are the difficulties faced by Nigeria's young democracy?

What is the role of foreign multinational companies in the country's development?

Sovereignty

A second defining feature of statehood is sovereignty, which denotes the supreme legal authority of the state. Sovereignty has an internal and external aspect. A state has 'internal' sovereignty, in that it possesses ultimate authority to rule within its borders; all other associations within society are subordinate. The state's legal authority is supported by a monopoly of the use of coercive force, in the form of military and police forces. 'External' sovereignty refers to the position of states in the international context, in which all states recognize each other as supreme within their own borders. This principle of mutual recognition, known as the 'sovereign equality of states', has governed the conduct of international relations between states, although the growth of numerous other international actors is now questioning the dominance of state actors (as we examine in the section on global politics). Internal and external sovereignty are like reverse sides of a coin. Internal sovereignty declares the state master in its own house, whereas external sovereignty prohibits it from interfering in the affairs of another state.

Sovereignty must be distinguished from the actual exercise of power. In many societies, real power lies outside formal political structures. An example is the ascendancy of military over civilian rulers. Military regimes, arising through violent seizure of power (a coup d'état), are inherently unstable and there is a constant threat of social unrest and factionalism within the military leadership. In the 1970s and 80s, Latin America's military regimes gave way to democratically elected governments. Less extreme is rule by coordinated political and economic elites which effectively control a country. In such regimes, government and business leaders form links in networks often referred to as 'cronyism'. These personal ties are a major consideration for foreign investors. While some of these states, such as Indonesia, have impressive records of industrialization, they are prone to corruption and instability and are likely to have weak legal systems. They offer location advantages for investors, but may pose high political risk.

In the postwar period, sovereignty has become a live political issue, from national to international level. On the heels of an unprecedented surge in the numbers of sovereign states, anxiety has followed about whether a state can control its own destiny after all. Regional and global forces increasingly impact on states' governance processes, implying that, while sovereignty is intact in theory, in practice, all states are undergoing shifts in sovereignty. We return to this issue in greater detail in the global politics section.

SUMMARY POINTS

Attributes of the state

- Defined geographical territory.
- Internal sovereignty – supreme authority within the state.
- External sovereignty – mutual recognition by states of each other's authority.
- Monopoly of coercive power within its borders.

CRITICAL PERSPECTIVES

The persistence of nation-states

While nation-states, especially in Western Europe, have progressively lost the capacity to govern their economies and impose a political will on the free play of market forces on their territories, they have at the same time remained uniquely viable as political organizations and as foci of collective identification. The latter applies even where subnational communities try to break away from existing nation-states; what they aspire to is almost always to set up a nation-state of their own. (Streeck, 1996, pp. 302–3)

Why does the nation-state as a form of organization persist, despite the forces of economic globalization?

Political risk and national security

All states recognize their responsibility to maintain 'law and order' within their borders and defend their population against organized military aggression from outside. However, as notions of sovereignty are being revised, so too is the notion of national security. Spending on the armed forces and defence is a large element of public spending in many countries, used to purchase armaments and maintain forces. The priority that governments give to defence depends largely on perceptions of threats to national security. For this reason, many relatively poor countries spend proportionately more on defence than richer ones, as Table 8.1 shows. Ethiopia spends nearly twice as much on defence as on public health and education budgets combined. The US has the most widely dispersed defence establishment, including over 700 military bases outside the US. It also spends far more on defence than any other country (Figure 8.2). Indeed, its 2005 defence budget of $420bn. is just under that spent by all the other countries of the world put together. But, however much a government spends on arms, it cannot make its borders impregnable in the modern age. Threats to security are as likely to be from terrorists as from organized armed forces, since the diverse threats posed by terrorists to civilian populations are particularly difficult to deal with.

Table 8.1 Military commitment in selected states

Country	Total armed forces, 2002 (thousands)	Military expenditure as percentage of GDP
China	2,270	2.3
Ethiopia	253	5.2
France	260	2.5
Germany	296	1.2
Greece	178	4.3
India	1,298	2.3
Russian Federation	988	4.0
Saudi Arabia	200	9.8
Turkey	515	4.9
UK	210	2.4
US	1,414	3.4

Source: United Nations Development Programme (2004) *Human Development Report 2004* (New York: UNDP).

Most democratic states now recognize the need for international cooperation to reduce military and terrorist threats. Under the auspices of the UN, numerous international and regional conventions have aimed at reducing threats to security, including the prevention of nuclear proliferation and development of weapons of mass destruction, with recognized mechanisms for monitoring. States naturally turn to alliances for collective security. The North Atlantic Treaty Organization (NATO), formed in 1949, is perhaps the most influential. NATO became the first peacetime alliance the US had entered. Since 1949 NATO has expanded from 10 to 26 states, listed in the minifile.

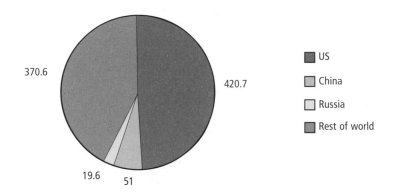

Figure 8.2 **US military spending compared to the rest of the world ($billions)**
Source: *The Economist* (2004) *The World in 2005* (London: *The Economist*).

Minifile

NATO

The North Atlantic Treaty is based on collective self-defence: an armed attack on any member is deemed to be an attack on all. There are now 26 members:

Belgium	Germany	Luxembourg	Spain
Canada	Greece	Netherlands	Turkey
Czech Republic	Hungary	Norway	UK
Denmark	Iceland	Poland	US
France	Italy	Portugal	Estonia
Latvia	Lithuania	Bulgaria	Romania
Slovakia	Slovenia		

Through a Partnership for Peace programme, additional countries, including neutral states (Austria, Finland, Ireland, Switzerland), former Communist satellite states, as well as former Soviet republics, have joined existing NATO members in the Euro-Atlantic Partnership Council. Russia became a new NATO partner in 2002. Partnership states are: Albania, Armenia, Austria, Azerbaijan, Belarus, Croatia, Finland, Georgia, Ireland, Kazakhstan, Kyrghyz Republic, Moldova, Russia, Sweden, Switzerland, Yugoslav Rep. Of Macedonia, Tadjikistan, Turkmenistan, Ukraine, and Uzbekistan.

WEB ALERT!

The NATO website contains links to the institutions of all these states, as well as background and news about NATO itself. It is at http://www.nato.int/

Terrorist threats may emanate from numerous sources, including disenchanted groups within society or from outside the state. **Terrorism** has been defined broadly as action meant:

to inflict dramatic and deadly injury on civilians and to create an atmosphere of fear, generally for a political or ideological (whether secular or religious) purpose. (UN Policy Working Group, 2002)

Terrorist acts are usually political in aim and criminal in nature. Dealing with crime is generally considered to be a matter for national security authorities. However, terrorist crimes pose particular challenges, particularly as much terrorism crosses national borders, eluding national authorities. Terrorists have become highly mobile, not just in terms of their activities, but also in regard to their funding networks and organization. Since the terrorist attacks on the World Trade Center in New York on 11 September 2001, which resulted in the deaths of 3000 people, the threat of terrorist attacks has risen to the top of the political agenda in virtually every country. In the wake of the 9/11 attacks, US President George Bush prioritized the 'war on terror', but the terrorist 'enemy' can be highly elusive. Historically, wars arise with attacks by a state or states against other states. For example, Iraq's invasion of Kuwait in 1991 prompted the first Gulf War. Terrorists may be organized in clandestine networks of small units and hard to track down. Notoriously, even when some members are arrested, others take up the cause. A response from governments has been anti-terrorism legislation, such as the Anti-terrorism Act 2001 in the UK and the USA Patriot Act 2001. These provisions, which include powers to arrest and detain people suspected of terrorism, are criticized as risking breaches of human rights law, to which most countries subscribe.

The war on terror took a dramatic turn with the US-led invasion of Iraq in 2003, in which American forces were joined by allies in a coalition, including the UK and Spain. The war aroused considerable controversy internationally, in contrast to the first Gulf War. A 'pre-emptive' strike against an enemy is usually considered justified in situations of imminent threat to national security (Walzer, 1992), while a 'preventive' strike is more problematic, based on dangers which it is felt are likely to materialize but which pose no immediate threat (Walzer, 2004). Opponents to the invasion of Iraq argued that it lacked UN authorization and there was little evidence that Iraq posed the serious threat to peace and security that had been cited as the justification for the invasion. President Bush urged the need for 'regime change' in Iraq, to replace the tyrannical government of Saddam Hussein. NATO allies, France and Germany, however, pointed out that this rationale was in breach of the UN Charter. There was vocal opposition in both the UK and Spain. While the regime was toppled within a few months, hardship and instability followed. Three days before Spain's general election in 2004, 192 people died in terrorist bombings in Madrid, which, evidence suggested, had been organized by Islamist extremists targeting Spain for its participation in Iraq. In the election which followed, the ruling centre-right party lost to the socialists, who immediately announced that Spanish troops would be pulled out of Iraq. The ruling party had had a strong law-and-order policy which had been credited with reducing the threat posed by Eta, the Basque separatist group in Spain. Following the Madrid bombings, however, Spanish voters seemed to see the greater threat from their alliance with the US in the Iraq invasion. The implications are considered in Case study 8.2 on Spain.

No government can provide national security on a scale to prevent terrorist attacks, if day-to-day life is to carry on as normal, because terrorists can easily find a host of 'soft' targets at which to strike. Recent research on transnational terrorism concludes that the formation by nations of governmental networks is needed (Sandler, 2003). Cooperation between states which includes sharing information and tracking funds to terrorist organizations is necessary. However, as the research indicates, 'modern-day terrorism taxes the ingenuity of governments worldwide' (Sandler, 2003, p. 26), and the partial cooperation that sovereign states engage in is often no match for terrorists' networks. At a deeper societal level, governments can look to dialogue and engagement with aggrieved groups within their societies, who are often minorities who feel alienated, so that would-be terrorists, it is hoped, will see that there is more to be gained from engaging in the political process than from seeking to destroy it.

SUMMARY POINTS

Political risk to international business

Businesses face political risk wherever they operate, but the risks are greater in locations with a history of political instability. Disruption can take the form of strikes and demonstrations, threats to people and property, and breaks in supplies.

Some of the contributing factors are:

● Disaffected groups in society, such as ethnic or religious groups, who feel alienated from the political processes and are likely to resort to violence to make their views heard

● External threats from terrorist groups who wish to destabilize the country, creating a climate of fear

● Armed groups, such as sections of the military, who have a political power base and pose a threat to the established government

● In federal or other decentralized countries, strong regional units can threaten the stability of central government and even assert independence from the centre

● Any government whose basis of control is military power rather than the ballot box – as they are liable to fall by the same means that they acquired power in the first place

● Factionalized political leadership based on personal ties ('cronyism'), where government assurances may last only as long as the faction holds the ascendancy

● Generally, countries without established democratic institutions to ensure transparency of processes and stable transition between governments.

Civil war refers to war by groups within the state's borders. A World Bank survey in 2000 found that in the period 1987–97, more than 85 per cent of conflicts were fought within national borders, and of 27 major armed conflicts in 1999, all but two were civil wars (Collier, 2000). Ninety per cent of the deaths were civilian, not military. These conflicts can cripple economic life and divert public money to military expenditure rather than productive activities. Civil wars and strife are heavily concentrated in the poorest countries, nearly 40 per cent in sub-Saharan Africa (Collier, 2000). Moreover, civil war may spill over into neighbouring countries. The capture and control of resources by those in government or other groups can fuel civil war.

Sources of authority in the state

In every viable state there is a source of legitimate authority. In a traditional monarchy, such as the Arab state of Saudi Arabia, heredity in the royal lineage is the legitimating principle. In a 'theocracy', religious prerogative is the guiding principle. Iran, which is a Muslim state, while it still has the religious leader (the ayatollah) as supreme leader, now has a dual, religious and secular, institutional hierarchy. Although tensions inevitably arise between secular and religious authorities, Iran's dual structure is widely seen as a step on the way to reform and liberalization. In 'patrimonial states', ruling families are recognized as having authority, but questions of succession and favouritism may cause instability if a power struggle ensues. Patrimonial states, therefore, are potentially unstable. The Suharto regime in Indonesia was overthrown in 1998 by popular uprising. North Korea is, in a sense, a patrimonial state, and its founder, adulated by the population, passed leadership to his son on his death in 1994. But North Korea is also a Communist state; hence, personal rule is reinforced by Communist ideology as a legitimating authority.

Ideology as a source of legitimacy is based a system of beliefs which permeate the whole of society, not just the system of government. Ideology is often used in a broad sense to refer to any set of political beliefs, such as liberalism or conservatism, but both these sets of beliefs embrace political pluralism, whereas the ideological state is monolithic, rejecting any competing belief systems. Fascism, an extreme nationalist ideology, reached its peak in the racist ideology of Fascist Germany and Italy. While these Fascist states were defeated in the Second World War, Fascist groups still form part of the political scene in many states. Historically, Communism has been one of the most important ideologies, originating in every case in Communist revolution. Since the collapse of the Soviet Union, China has been the leading Communist country, followed by a dwindling number of smaller states, such as Cuba and North Korea. Cuba and North Korea are still 'hardline' Communist states, but even these are taking tentative steps to opening their economies. Ideological regimes often rely on charismatic leaders, such as Fidel Castro in Cuba, to maintain ideological fervour. As in other non-democratic regimes, political succession can be a destabilizing event and constitutes an element of political risk for foreign investors.

In most modern states, legitimacy is founded on constitutionalism. **Constitutionalism** implies a set of rules, grounded in a society's shared beliefs, about the source of authority and its institutional forms. Constitutionalism stands for the 'rule of law', above both ruler and ruled. Its underlying principle is that the institutions of government, such as president, prime minister, elected assembly and bureaucracy derive their power from these pre-existing rules. Actual office holders will change from time to time – and, indeed, a vital function of a constitution is to provide for smooth change in the transfer of power – but the constitution, setting out the ground rules, provides continuity and legitimacy. Inherent in constitutionalism are the control by the civilian authority over the military and the existence of an independent judiciary (court system). Most of the world's constitutions are written. The major exception is the British constitution. However, while the UK has no separate constitutional document, much legislation, which is contained in Acts of Parliament, is constitutional in nature. This trend towards written constitutional law looks set to continue, with European integration, devolved powers for Scotland and Wales and the impact of the Human Rights Act 1998, which incorporates the European Convention on Human Rights into UK law (see Chapter 9). There are states, such as one-party states, where, despite a written constitution, there is only lip service to the rule of law. The mere existence of a constitution is thus no guarantee of accountable government.

SUMMARY POINTS

Sources of authority in nation-states

- **Traditional monarchy** – Absolute sovereignty is vested in a hereditary ruler. Most of these states have either been overthrown or gradually democraticized. A remaining example is Saudi Arabia. In Morocco and Jordan, traditional monarchies are making the transition to constitutional monarchy.

- **Constitutional monarchy** – The hereditary monarch in these states is little more than a head of state, and democratic institutions have taken over government. Examples: Belgium, Japan, Spain, the UK.

- **Theocracy** – In these states, the religious head is sovereign. The Muslim states come closest to theocratic rule, but all, to a greater or lesser extent, also have secular institutions of state.

- **Constitutional republic** – Here sovereignty rests with the constitution which guarantees civil and political rights. Examples: Canada, France, Poland (and other post-Communist states). In the UK, there is a body of republican opinion which supports abolition of the monarchy, in favour of a more modern head of state.

- **Communist state** – Although Communist states typically have written constitutions, in practice, sovereignty rests with the Communist Party, usually through a strong leader. Examples: China, Cuba, North Korea.

WEB ALERT!

A comprehensive guide to the constitutions of the world's nation-states can be found at http://www.uni-wuerzburg.de/law/index.html

Democracy and authoritarianism contrasted

Democracy broadly covers a range of political systems falling under the phrase, 'rule by the people', but popular sovereignty in theory can be found in a great diversity of institutional forms. Democracy is usually placed at one end of a continuum, with authoritarianism at the opposite end. **Democracy** is rule by the people, through elected governments, while **authoritarianism** is rule by a single leader or small group of individuals, with unlimited power, usually dependent on military support to maintain stability. Authoritarian regimes vary: the particularly repressive military regime in Myanmar is at one extreme, while other authoritarian states have limited elections among state-approved candidates. Opposition to the regime is seen as a threat and is typically suppressed by military force. In a number of countries, such as Indonesia and Egypt, authoritarian governments have led the drive for economic development, attracting extensive foreign investment. (Oil riches were an attraction in both Indonesia and Egypt.) For international companies which do business in authoritarian states, there is a high level of political risk, as security cannot be guaranteed and political dissent and social unrest may destabilize the system as a whole. In such situations, the company will find it difficult to remain 'neutral': its cooperation with the government may be seen as support for an oppressive military regime. An immediate concern is that its employees may be at risk if it becomes a target for those opposing the regime. A broader concern is the increasing pressure of international opinion against what is seen as complicity in human rights abuses. For this reason, a number of companies have pulled out of Myanmar. A further development is that major oil companies are now being pursued in the US courts for alleged human rights abuses in states such as Nigeria, Myanmar and Indonesia. While such lawsuits may take years to work their way through the legal system, their more immediate impact is the negative images of the companies' global operations.

Democratic government: the criteria

Most definitions of democracy focus on the formal institutional aspects of government, such as elections and suffrage, without which there is no democracy. However, as will be seen, even among institutional arrangements there are huge variations, and even with elections and universal suffrage, many states cannot really be considered democratic. Formal institutions are therefore necessary, but not sufficient, to construct a democracy. This minimal 'electoral democracy' can be distinguished from 'liberal democracy', which stipulates pluralism and political freedoms for individuals and groups (Diamond, 1996). Beyond liberal democracy lies 'social democracy', which focuses on the broader social and economic spheres in society. Social democracy is concerned with the underlying social and economic conditions in a society which contribute towards deeper participation than the simple exercise of the vote. A sharply divided or unequal society, in which power is concentrated in an entrenched ruling elite, is not a democracy in this substantive sense, even though it may have a constitution and regular elections. When attempting to measure democracy, the requirements of liberal democracy are generally accepted as the key criteria.

'Direct democracy' refers to direct participation in the governance of society. This model, workable only in a small community, is not transferable to a large society. The type of democracy which has evolved in the modern state is 'representative democracy', which can be defined as 'a system of governance in which rulers are held accountable for their actions in the public realm by citizens, acting indirectly through the competition and cooperation of their elected representatives' (Schmitter and Karl, 1993, p. 40). This definition, focusing on the institutional arrangements, is a commonly used measure of democracy. As its roots lie in liberalism and individualism, it is also equated with liberal democracy, although it is now seen as universally applicable, in countries with different, often authoritarian, histories. The following is a list of basic principles:

1 *The rule of law.* This is based on a constitution which establishes representative institutions, accountability of governments and an independent judiciary. Thus, executive power is kept in check.
2 *Free and fair elections.* These must be held at relatively frequent intervals. They must provide for a choice of candidates and the peaceful removal of representatives from office when they fail to secure enough votes, in accordance with the constitution. Reports of outside monitors are usually seen as a guarantee that the election has not been tainted by fraud.
3 *Universal right to vote for all adults.* This right extends to all citizens over a certain age, for example 18 in the UK. However, the increasing proportion of resident non-citizens in modern societies poses a problem for democratic participation. Moreover, voting alone is the most minimal form of participation.
4 *Freedoms of expression, speech and association.* These political rights are essential to ensure competitive elections, in which all interests and groups may put forward their candidates. There should be independent media, providing alternative sources of information, to which citizens have access.

These principles are general guidelines; they do not point to one specific type of political system. Democratic systems vary considerably from country to country. All must address constitutional questions such as the division of authority between central and regional or local government, the type of legislative assembly and its relationship with the executive and, importantly, the checks between different governmental authorities.

CRITICAL PERSPECTIVES

Democracy

Democracy is now seen, by those who want it and by those who have it (or are said to have it) and want more of it, as a kind of society – a whole complex of relations between individuals – rather than simply a system of government. So any theory which is to explicate, justify, or prescribe for the maintenance or improvement of, democracy in our time must take the basic criterion of democracy to be that equal effective right of individuals to live as fully as they may wish.
(Macpherson, 1973, p. 51)

- Which countries would you describe as democracies in this broad sense, and why?
- Which countries that call themselves democracies would Macpherson see as falling short of his basic criterion?

Unitary and federal states

In a **unitary system**, authority radiates out from the centre. There may well be local and regional governments but they are not autonomous actors, as their authority is delegated from the centre. Whether a state is unitary or federal has a direct impact on the business environment. Regulatory regimes, such as planning permissions, health and safety and the legal framework generally, may be regionally governed in a federal system, while they will be centralized in a unitary system. On the other hand, the UK is a unitary system, with devolved authority to local authorities and now also to Scotland and Wales. In a **federal system**, authority is shared between the centre and local or regional units, which retain autonomy in specific areas, such as education or regional development. Spain is an example of a state which, while not officially federalist in design, recognizes a high level of regional autonomy, accommodating strong historical regional identities. This arrangement is discussed in Case study 8.2.

Federalism is often seen as a solution for states with strong local identities which can be incorporated into the larger whole while retaining semi-autonomous status. Thus the separate 'states' of the US have separate legal systems and limited autonomy. However, the power granted by the US Constitution to the federal government 'to regulate interstate commerce' has opened the way for an increase in federal regulation. Separate authorities and inconsistencies in business regulations between states can pose headaches for businesses that operate in more than one state. Germany's constitution, too, provides for state governments, called *Länder*, which, historically, have had strong identities. For countries such as Canada and Belgium, federalism serves to accommodate separate founding nations, who wish to retain separate identities and languages within the federal structure: English and French in Canada, French and Flemish in Belgium. It is often said that a specifically democratic advantage of federalism is shifting decision-making closer to the people affected. The UK, although unitary in principle, in devolving limited authority to the Scottish Parliament and Welsh Assembly seems to be taking a step in this direction. Federalism is also seen by many as a solution to the governance of the EU, an issue which will be examined later in this chapter.

Case study 8.2 Challenging times for Spain's politicians

Spain has enjoyed remarkable economic and political development since the overthrow of the military dictatorship of General Franco in 1975 and its first democratic elections in 1977. Its new democratic institutions and programme of economic reform and liberalization led to an influx of foreign investors, attracted, it should be added, by its low costs of production. Its attraction was further enhanced by EU membership in 1986. Spanish companies have thrived in this new environment, particularly the large companies created from the former national industries, which have pursued impressive international expansion. The year 2004 brought a dramatic change of government, as well as EU enlargement. What impact will these changes have on Spain's business environment?

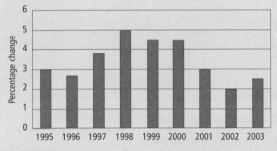

Growth in Spain's GDP during the Aznar years
Source: Crawford, 20 February 2004.

During its period of office from 1996 to 2004, the government of José Maria Aznar, the Popular Party prime minister, presided over unprece- dented economic prosperity. The Spanish economy enjoyed healthy growth during the eight years, an accomplishment unmatched by any other eurozone economy (see figure above). Also in contrast to eurozone partners, the government's budget balance was in surplus. Aznar's foreign policy was 'Atlanticist' – focusing on good relations with the US – a stance connected to the fact that American influence is a stabilizing force in Latin America, where many Spanish companies have invested heavily. Observers have argued, however, that Aznar paid a price for his special relationship with the US (to which he made 16 official trips), in that Spain's standing and influence in Europe suffered as a result (Crawford, 20 February 2004). This friendship undoubtedly played a role in his electoral defeat in 2004. Bomb attacks in Madrid

four days before the election were hastily attributed by the government to Eta, the Basque separatist group, before any proper investigation of the perpetrators had been made. When it emerged the following day that the chief suspects were Islamic terrorists, the public seemed to turn on Aznar's Popular Party, and voted in the Socialists under José Luis Rodríguez Zapatero, who became the new prime minister. Zapatero does not have an absolute majority in the Spanish Parliament, however, as the figure below shows, and must govern with the support of small parties. These include 11 Catalonian Moderate Nationalists, 8 Catalonian Radical Nationalists and 7 Basque Nationalists. Hence, working with regional interests will be needed in order to get his legislative agenda through parliament.

Spain's 17 regions (comunidades autónomas) have a high degree of self-government under the Spanish Constitution of 1978. They elect their own assemblies and run their own police forces, health and education systems. They also have some tax-raising powers. They account for 47 per cent of public spending. However, some of the regions, including the Basque region, Catalonia and Andalucia, are pressing for more autonomy and more control over tax affairs. The Basques seek separate citizenship, judiciary and social security systems. The new prime minister, like his predecessor, faces problems of appeasing regional leaders while holding the Spanish state together.

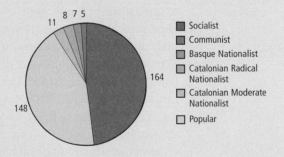

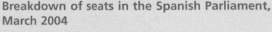

Breakdown of seats in the Spanish Parliament, March 2004
Source: Financial Times, 15 March 2004.

A further concern of the new prime minister is the loss of manufacturing jobs as companies move to lower cost locations in the enlarged EU. Among the companies that have shut manufacturing plants are Levi Strauss, Samsung, Alcatel, Ericsson, Bayer and Phillips. Some have relocated to Poland, the Czech Republic and Slovakia, where wages are a seventh of those in Spain. Of concern, too, is that Eastern Europeans generally spend more years in schooling than their Spanish counterparts (9.8 compared with 8 in Spain). While it is accepted that industries such as textiles and footwear will migrate, the motor industry poses particular risks for the Spanish economy. Car manufacturing accounts for one-tenth of Catalonia's GDP and employs 200,000 people. In 2003, Seat, Volkswagen's Spanish subsidiary, shifted 10 per cent of its production to a cheaper plant in Bratislava (Slovakia), citing labour inflexibility as the reason. Spanish companies, with their relatively low spending on R&D compared to European rivals, have struggled to move up the high-tech ladder. In looking for strategies to respond to the loss of low-wage manufacturing jobs, the new Socialist government is likely to look to investment in R&D and education.

Sources: Crawford, L., 'A jolt from Eta: the Basque separatists shake up Spain's election campaign as Aznar prepares to bow out of politics', *Financial Times*, 20 February 2004; Crawford, L., 'Spain's Socialists gain power', *Financial Times*, 15 March 2004; Peel, Q. and Dempsey, J., 'Triumph of terrorism or victory for democracy? Spain's stunning election result asks tough questions of Europe', *Financial Times*, 16 March 2004; Crawford, L, 'Socialists act fast on new policies', *Financial Times*, 15 June 2004; Levitt, J., 'In urgent need of new strategy', *Financial Times*, 15 June 2004; Crawford, L., 'Baptism of ire', *Financial Times*, 17 July 2004.

Case questions

What are the political challenges facing the Spanish government?

How has the business environment in Spain changed since the spring of 2004?

Legislative assemblies

At the centre of any democracy is the legislative assembly. It carries the main law-making function and, through the ballot box, it is the one tangible way that citizens express a say in the makeup of their government. Many countries have legislatures consisting of two houses (bicameral), where the lower house is the main law-making body. In the US both houses, the House of Representatives (the lower house) and the Senate (the upper house), are directly elected. In the UK only the House of Commons (the lower house) is elected. The House of Lords, upper house, has been the subject of much recent debate concerning its future composition and powers. Reforms have converted it from a hereditary chamber to a one composed of hereditary and appointed members. Its role has been gradually reduced to one of a revising chamber, and further reform plans have been put forward by the Labour government elected in 1997. The first stage of the reform took place in 1999, with the abolition of 600 hereditary peers, but, since then, there has been disagreement within the ruling party on the makeup of new House of Lords – whether members should be directly elected, indirectly elected, appointed or a possible combination of these categories. Other parliamentary systems have only a single chamber (a unicameral legislature). Sweden and New Zealand abolished the upper chamber.

Elections

Free and fair elections are a key element in political participation in a democracy. The electoral system may be the traditional first-past-the-post system or one of the more recent **proportional representation (PR)** systems, which allocate seats in proportion to the votes obtained. While the first-past-the-post system has predominated in the US and UK, most European countries (and also the European Parliament) have opted for PR. Outcomes in PR systems represent a broader political spectrum, giving small parties a greater prospect of winning seats than a first-past-the-post system, where they may win sizeable voter support but fail to win many seats. The Liberal Democrats in the UK have long campaigned for PR reforms: as a 'third' party in a two-party system, they attracted 23 per cent of the popular vote in the general election in 2005, but won only 10 per cent of the seats in the House of Commons. PR systems are also thought to be friendlier to women candidates. Women worldwide hold just 15.4 per cent of the seats in national legislatures (Inter-Parliamentary Union, 2004). The figures for EU states show that generally numbers of women representatives have risen, but there are wide disparities (see Table 8.2), from 45 per cent of the seats in Sweden to 9.8 per cent in Hungary. Women in the US hold just 14.3 per cent of seats in House of Representatives, which is below the world average.

Table 8.2 Women in national legislatures in selected EU countries (lower or single house)

Country	Percentage of women members, 2001	Percentage of women members, 2004
Sweden	42.7	45.3
Denmark	37.4	38.0
Finland	36.5	37.5
Netherlands	36.0	36.7
Germany	30.9	32.2
Spain	28.3	36.0
Austria	26.8	33.9
Belgium	23.3	35.3
Portugal	18.7	19.1
UK	17.9	19.3 (2005)
Luxembourg	16.7	20.0
Ireland	12.0	13.3
France	10.9	12.2
Italy	9.8	11.5
Greece	8.7	14.0
Hungary	8.3	9.8

Source: Inter-Parliamentary Union (2004) at http://www.ipu.org.

A drawback of PR is that in a multiparty system, if many parties secure seats, it may be difficult to form a government and political instability may result. A common requirement is that a party must obtain a minimum of 5 per cent of the total vote to gain any seats. Poland's first fully free election, in 1991, demonstrates the hazards of extreme PR: 111 parties or groups put up candidates, 29 parties or groups gained seats, including the Beer Lovers' Party, but none gained more than 13 per cent of the total. A series of unstable coalition governments followed, until a 5 per cent threshold was introduced in 1993. Since then, parties have settled into two main blocs.

Increasingly popular is the 'mixed' electoral system, combining first-past-the-post and PR systems. The leading example is Germany. The election of 1998 yielded a coalition between the Social Democrats (SPD) and the Greens, resulting in the gaining of a cabinet post for the Greens in the coalition government. Since then, they have used their voice in government effectively, securing, for example, assurance of the phasing out of nuclear power stations. Their position was strengthened in the elections of 2002, when they increased their share of the vote from 6.7 per cent to 8.6 per cent, as shown in Figure 8.3a. The two major parties each gained 38.5 per cent of the popular vote, but the SPD won 251 seats, 3 more than the CDU's 248, and, with the 55 Green members, formed the new coalition government, again led by Chancellor Schröder (see Figure 8.3b). Fischer, the foreign minister and a Green, enjoyed a stronger electoral mandate, which he used to press for economic reforms to tackle structural problems such as high labour costs, which have affected Germany's global competitiveness.

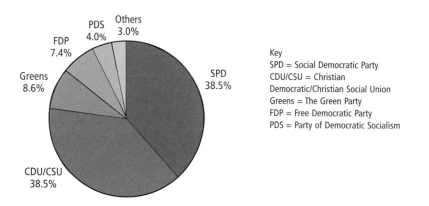

Figure 8.3a The German general election 2002: percentage of the vote
Source: Williamson, H., 'Schröder promises to "push forward with renewal"', *Financial Times*, 24 September 2002.

In 2000, Italy, which has had 54 different ruling coalitions in the past 53 years, attempted to change its voting system, from PR to first-past-the-post, to reduce the number of parties and bring about stable government. The proposal was required by the Constitution to be put to the voters in a **referendum**, but was rejected (see minifile on the use of the referendum). Since 2001, the centre-right government, headed by the billionaire businessman Silvio Berlusconi, has provided stability, although Italy's democracy still gives rise for concern, as the case study which closes Part 2 shows.

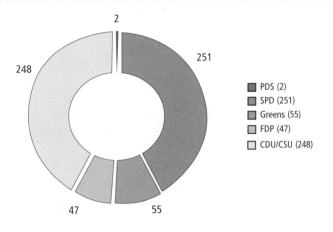

Figure 8.3b **The German general election 2002: composition of the Bundestag**
Source: Williamson, H., 'Schröder promises to "push forward with renewal"', *Financial Times*, 24 September 2002.

WEB ALERT!

The internet has provided political parties and other groups the means to reach a worldwide audience, even though they may have little or no media freedom in their own states, due to government controls

The following site contains links to political parties, interest groups and other social movements worldwide – international first and then country by country: http://www.politicalresources.net/

For elections, parties and parliaments, the following are useful: International Foundation for Election Systems: http://www.ifes.org/ http://www.electionresources.org/

Minifile

THE REFERENDUM IN DEMOCRATIC SYSTEMS

The referendum is an example of direct democracy and has become increasingly popular for governments seeking a mandate for a particularly important issue. In some states (for example Italy) it is a constitutional requirement in others (for example the UK) it is optional.

Examples of the varied uses of the referendum are:

● Devolution in Scotland and Wales, 1997

● Decision to join the UN by the Swiss in 2002, following earlier rejection in 1986

● The end of apartheid in South Africa, 1992

● The decision not to join the eurozone by Denmark (2000) and Sweden (2002).

The advantages of the referendum are that it acts as a check on elected governments, giving citizens an opportunity to express a view on an issue of the day. A drawback, however, is that citizens are typically asked to make a yes/no decision although the issues may be complex. Moreover, ordinary citizens are not as well informed as elected representatives about the ramifications of proposed changes.

Political parties

Political parties form the link between voters and legislative assemblies. In democratic states, parties perform several functions:

1 They provide candidates for public office, who rely on their organizational machinery and funding to get elected. The independent candidate faces an uphill battle and needs to be very rich.
2 They provide a policy platform, on which voters can decide who to support. Many voters are traditional party loyalists, not caring who the individual candidate is.
3 When in office, they provide an agenda for government, against which performance can be judged.

Parties vary in their political agendas and their views of society. Some embrace strong ideological positions, such as communist parties. Others are religious in origin, such as Muslim parties and numerous Christian parties. Many countries have rural-based, or peasant, parties which exist mainly to foster rural interests. Parties may also emerge from interest groups, such as the Green Party, which concentrates on ecological issues. Most of the narrowly based parties have little hope of gaining a majority of legislative seats and forming a government; instead, they seek publicity and political influence for their views. They are more likely to win seats in multiparty systems with PR. In two-party systems, such as the US and the UK, the trend has been towards the 'catch-all' party, with weaker ideological underpinning and greater direct appeal to voters via the media, in which personalities are as important as policies. Political parties depend on funding largely from supporters, and, although most states attempt to regulate funding, this is fertile ground for corruption scandals, in which politicians and corporate donors can become enmeshed.

SUMMARY POINTS

Party systems

- **Two major parties** (for example the US and UK). The two major parties are catch-all parties aiming to capture the middle ground on the main issues. Both examples have first-past-the-post electoral systems. Third parties, while they obtain electoral support (for example the Liberal Democrats in Britain) are unlikely to gain seats in proportion to their overall support, unless there is a shift to a PR system.
- **Multiparty system** (for example Italy, Poland and other Central and Eastern European countries). In these states, which have PR systems, parties cover a greater range of ideological positions, from left to right. Centre-left or centre-right coalitions are a typical outcome of elections.
- **Single dominant party** (for example Japan and Mexico up to 2000). In these states, while there are numerous smaller parties, the single dominant party has such a reservoir of loyalty that it is extremely difficult to shift from office.

● **One-party state** (for example China, Cuba, North Korea). These Communist states differ from the preceding category in that pluralist elections are not tolerated and there is no institutional means of change of government. Clearly, these regimes are not democratic (they are classed as 'not free' in Figure 8.7).

Case study 8.3   The voices of Indian democracy

India's political landscape changed dramatically following elections in May 2004, when the country's voters emphatically swept the ruling Bharatiya Janata (BJP) coalition government out of power and voted in the Congress Party, led by the unlikely figure of the Italian widow of former Prime Minister Rajiv Gandhi. This was a political upset unpredicted by the polling experts, which highlighted the vibrancy of India's democracy. India is the world's largest democracy, with a population of over one billion, and 900 political parties, many regional, religious and caste-based. The BJP Hindu nationalist coalition under Prime Minister Vajpayee had guided the country to impressive levels of economic growth and prosperity (see figure below). Its economic reforms had brought privatization of the country's large and bureaucratic public sector, attracted foreign investment, particularly in the new high-tech industries. Why, then, had the voters turned on it?

The answer lies in the vast countryside where a rural population of some 600 million people live in 650,000 villages. For the vast majority of Indians, reality is not the IT industry or modern call centres, but a subsistence livelihood in areas where water and electricity are scarce and only one in 10 villages is connected to a road. Spending on rural development fell during the rule of the BJP coalition government (see figure below). The Congress Party addressed the vast rural population, promising investment in rural infrastructure, including roads, wells and irrigation. In marked contrast, the BJP spoke mainly to the prosperous urban dwellers who have been the chief beneficiaries of the country's economic growth. Realizing the need to attract a wide audience, it used the campaign slogan, 'India shining' as a unifying message. The BJP coalition rests on 19 Hindu nationalist parties, some elements of which have a history of intolerance and even violence against other religious groups, mainly Muslims and Christians. In retrospect, it seemed that the campaign failed to convince the public of the new tolerant image of the BJP. Muslim Indians, in particular, who comprise 14 per cent of the electorate, were solidly against the Hindu nationalists. This failure to convince voters of its legitimacy in a multicultural India, coupled with the weakness of its record in dealing with impoverished villages and urban slum dwellers, proved its downfall. India's long tradition as a multifaith society with a secular government seemed to be reasserted.

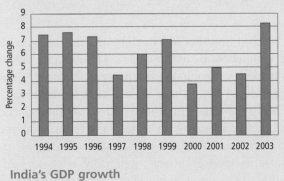

India's GDP growth
Source: Luce, 18 May 2004.

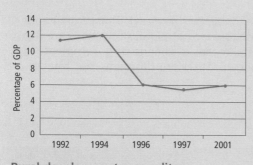

Rural development expenditure
Source: Luce, 18 May 2004.

The new Prime Minister Manmohan Singh himself governs with a coalition of 12 parties, some of which are Communist. He promised that economic reform is still on the agenda, but it is 'economic reform with a human face' (Luce, 28 May 2004). Progress on promised reforms has been slow during his first year in office. Privatization plans have met with resistance from Communist coalition members. His social programme aims to double spending on education and health, but progress has been slow. Increasing inflows of FDI is a priority: FDI inflows are one-tenth of the level China receives and would be valuable in building much-needed infrastructure. In order to attract FDI for manufacturing industries, the government is planning to introduce special economic zones,

modelled on those in China, offering benefits such as tax and labour incentives to match those enjoyed in the country's IT sector. Perhaps ironically, the former BJP Finance Minister Jaswant Singh, in an interview four months before the 2004 election, said that while India's growth model seems to be built on IT and outsourcing, agriculture is in fact the key to its economic success. Agriculture still represents 25 per cent of its GDP, while business process outsourcing represents 2 per cent. He went on to muse on the 'natural checks and balances of a democratic culture' (Luce et al., 5 December 2003). India's voters, especially the rural and urban poor, held high expectations after the unexpected Congress Party victory in the elections of 2004, but the new coalition government has had to please both 'markets and Marxists' in shaping its reform policies.

Sources: Luce, E., Ridding, J. and Mallet, V., 'India's farms seen as its seedcorn', *Financial Times*, 5 December 2003; Luce, E., 'Vajpayee trampled by bullock cart economy', *Financial Times*, 14 May 2004; Luce, E., 'India's new leaders vow reform with "human face"', *Financial Times*, 28 May 2004; Tully, M., 'Indians have little relish for hardline Hinduism', *Financial Times*, 20 April, 2004; 'India is shining: through its voters', editorial *Financial Times*, 14 May 2004; Luce, E., 'From India's forgotten fields, a call for economic reform to lift the poor', *Financial Times*, 18 May 2004; Johnson, J., 'Coalition politics damps zeal of 'Holy Trinity' reformers', *Financial Times*, 6 May 2005.

Case question

Assess how India's political culture is likely to impact on current and future foreign investors.

Political parties are usually described in terms of left, right and centre, with the modern catch-all parties falling somewhere near the centre. The modern Labour Party in Britain has shifted from being a left-wing socialist party to a broader-based centre-left party. However, pinning down what these labels stand for in terms of policy can be bewildering, especially as their meanings have shifted over time. Parties to the 'left' generally support high public spending on social services, protection of workers and trade union rights; they tend to oppose privatization. Parties on the 'right', known almost universally as 'conservatives', generally wish to see a minimum of government intervention in business, reduced public spending and low taxes. They favour more privatization of the economy, reducing the size of government bureaucracy. However, all modern parties, the British Conservatives included, support the welfare state. Nationalist tendencies are associated with the right, but most parties of the right (except extremist right-wing parties) support multiculturalism. With its election in 1997, New Labour in Britain expressly moved closer to business-friendly policies and distanced itself from its working-class ideological roots. The new Social Democratic parties across Europe are said to represent the 'third way', between Socialism and market liberalism.

Defence and foreign policy have become more important issues for voters, as fears over security have grown. In a poll of voters' opinions in the UK in August 2004, 38 per cent felt defence and foreign affairs to be the major issues, while the more familiar electoral issues of unemployment and education were less important (Figure 8.4). Foreign affairs also took centre stage in the US elections of 2004.

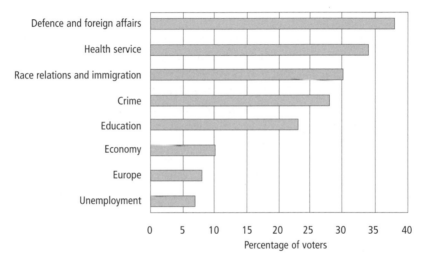

Figure 8.4 **Shifting priorities of voters**
Source: MORI (2004) *MORI Political Monitor*, August 2004, at www.mori.com.

Systems of government: presidential, parliamentary and 'hybrid' systems

It is customary to think of government as comprising three functions or branches: legislative, executive and judicial. The division of functions between the three is known as the **separation of powers**. In practice, most systems have considerable overlap between these functions, and the main safeguard that no one branch comes to dominate the others is a system of checks and balances between them. The legislative power, located in an elected assembly, exercises the main law-making function. The executive, although it drafts much legislation and must normally give its assent to legislation, is mainly an administrative authority. The judicial function, located in the court system, interprets the law and thereby keeps a check on the other two branches. Law and policy therefore emanate mainly from legislative and executive branches and, more specifically, from the political interplay between the two, depending on the balance of power within the system.

A **presidential system** is thought of as producing a stronger chief executive, as presidents are normally directly elected by the people and thus have a personal mandate. The US is the leading example of a presidential system. Checks on executive power are provided by the Constitution and a vigorous two-party system. The other main proponents of the presidential system have been Latin American countries, for whom a strong presidency is more grounded in political culture, in which nationalism has been a prominent feature. The inherent drawbacks of the 'winner-takes-all' nature of presidential elections are that supporters of the losing candidate may feel alienated, while the winner may overestimate the popular mandate, 'conflating his supporters with the people as a whole' (Linz, 1993, p. 118).

The US presidential election in 2000 was the closest result in the country's history. After five weeks of recounting and several court cases, culminating in a decision of the US Supreme Court, George W. Bush emerged the winner. Despite his wish to bring a sense of national unity after such a protracted and bitter episode, his Cabinet and legislative agenda, including major tax cuts, were distinctly rightist, reflecting traditional conservative Republicanism. However, in the 100-seat Senate, which was divided 50/50 between Republicans and Democrats when Bush took office, one Republican senator abruptly left the party in May 2001, causing a dramatic shift in power in the Senate to the Democrats, who gained chairmanship of all 20 committees. Suddenly, healthcare reforms, labour rights and the environment came back onto the agenda. Given the system of checks and balances in the US, law-making can be hampered by wrangles, or even 'gridlock', between the president and Congress when parties are closely balanced in Congress. Since then, the Republicans have gained firm control and, coupled with the re-election of Bush in 2004, they are in a strong position to push their legislative programme through Congress.

Businesses, including those abroad which do business in the US and those who are indirectly affected by US economic and trade policies, look for a clear and coherent legislative agenda on issues such as trade liberalization and regional trade agreements. However, the system seldom delivers the political mandate which elections promise and policies emerge piecemeal through negotiation and compromise among numerous competing interests, even when the voters deliver a decisive majority to the president.

In a **parliamentary system**, the voters elect members of parliament, from whom a prime minister and Cabinet are selected, usually from the political party with the majority of seats. This is often called the 'Westminster model', as the leading example is the UK. The efficient running of a parliamentary system depends greatly on the nature and number of a country's political parties. It is usually felt that it works best in a stable two-party system of 'government' and 'opposition' parties, in which the opposition is in effect an alternative government. However, the UK general election in 2005 revealed a more fragmented pattern, as shown in Figure 8.5. The Labour share of the overall vote was 36 per cent, while the Conservative share was 33 per cent, and Liberal Democrat share was 23 per cent. However, of the 646 seats in the House of Commons, Labour won 355 to the Conservatives' 197, securing a comfortable majority of 66. Although down from its nearly two-thirds majority in 2001, the Labour Party still holds 55 per cent of the seats, as shown in Figure 8.6. Despite capturing 23 per cent of the popular vote, the Liberal Democrats hold only 62 seats. Labour won its majority in 2005 with the lowest ever share of the vote by a winning party, having been positively supported by just 21.8 per cent of the electorate, or just over one in five of eligible voters. While it has a comfortable 66-seat parliamentary majority, it hardly achieved a ringing endorsement from the electorate.

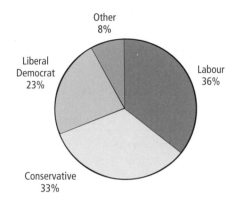

Figure 8.5 **Parties' share of votes in UK general election, 2005**
Source: *Financial Times*, 7 May 2005.

Low turnout in democratic elections is a concern, as it indicates apathy or lack of engagement in the democratic process. Turnout in UK general elections was in the 70–80 per cent region throughout the postwar period, and dived to a low of 59.6 per cent only in 2001. The 2005 election was a slight improvement, at 61.3 per cent of eligible voters. Also worrying is that the turnout among younger voters was particularly low: less than 40 per cent of people under 25 voted. Apart from the obvious conclusion that people are disillusioned with politics, it is also arguable that they are turned off by the mainstream political parties which seem remote. A trend has been the rising profile of various lobby groups and single-interest groups which seek to influence policy on particular issues, rather than play a direct role in politics. Consultation by government with lobby groups of all descriptions – from animal rights groups to railway users – have become routine, arguably sidelining established political parties.

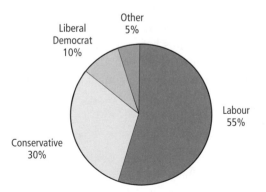

Figure 8.6 **Parties' share of seats in House of Commons after UK general election, 2005**
Source: *Financial Times*, 7 May 2005.

In multiparty systems, a **coalition government**, made up of two or more parties, is the likely outcome. Aware of its power to bring down the government, a minor party in a coalition may demand a 'price' for its cooperation, in terms of key policies, to keep it on board. Small right-wing religious parties in Israel are an example of this phenomenon, wielding more political power than their number of seats alone would justify. It could be argued that coalition government is more representative of electoral support, and hence more democratic, but a major disadvantage is its potential instability.

Table 8.3 Summary of systems of government

	Presidential	Parliamentary	Hybrid system
Advantages	Strong executive based on popular mandate; fixed term of office	Executive reflects electoral support in Parliament	Strong executive imparts unity; prime minister coordinates parliamentary programme
Disadvantages	Possible disaffection among electorate	Thin majority may lead to breakdown of government	Conflict between president and prime minister
Stability	Stable executive, but legislature may be dominated by the opposing party, stifling law-making agenda	Stable if prime minister has a large majority; coalition and minority governments can be unstable	Fixed-term president imparts stability; but successive coalition governments can be unstable in multiparty systems

The so-called 'hybrid system' (summarized in the final column of Table 8.3) aims to achieve both a stable executive and maximum representation, with an independently elected president and a prime minister selected by Parliament to head the Cabinet. The model for this system, also known as the dual executive, is the Fifth French Republic. Apart from Hungary, which has a parliamentary system, the post-Communist states of Central and Eastern Europe have adopted this model. The theory is that the nationally elected president can foster national unity, playing the role of head of state, while the prime minister plays more of a party political role, maintaining support for the government in Parliament. In practice, these systems may not run as smoothly as envisaged if the two executives are of different parties (called 'co-habitation' in France) or, as is almost inevitable, each sees the other as a rival and political rivalry develops between the two. In new democracies such as Poland and the Czech Republic, where politics tends to focus on personalities, the role of president can be seen as a strong political platform.

Transitional democracies

Where democratic institutions have become settled, democracy is said to be 'consolidated', meaning that democratic processes have become so routine and internalized in people's attitudes and behaviour that democracy is the 'only game in town' (Linz and Stepan, 1997). Consolidated democracies will still change and evolve, of course, but the overwhelming likelihood is that change will come about in peaceful ways within well-oiled institutions, with minimum risk of system instability. Where states are still putting in place the basic representative institutions, they are referred to as **transitional democracies**, and the process of building democracy, democratization. The earliest democracies were established in the nineteenth century, in the 'first wave' (Huntington, 1991). A second wave occurred after the Second World War, and a third wave gathered pace in the 1970s, as Figure 8.7 shows. However, some of these democracies may be described as 'shallow', consisting of electoral systems but limited political rights and civil liberties (Diamond, 1996). In Figure 8.7, free states are those with a high degree of political and economic freedom and respect of basic liberties. In 2003, 88 of the world's 192 sovereign states fell into this category, covering 44 per cent of the world's population. Partly free states offer more limited civil rights, in a context which often includes corruption, weak rule of law, dominance by a single party and ethnic or religious strife. In 2003, there were 55 countries in this category, home to 21 per cent of the world's population. Countries designated not free deny basic civil and political rights. There were 49 countries in this category, covering 35 per cent of the world's population.

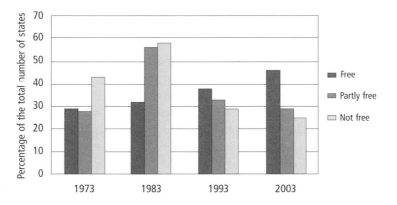

Figure 8.7 **Freedom survey among the world's independent states**
Source: Freedom House (2004) *Annual Global Survey of Political Rights and Civil Liberties*, at www.freedomhouse.org.

Regional divergence in democratic transition

Democratic institutions in the Western industrialized states grew in a piecemeal way, out of the social conflicts which emerged with capitalist development, as existing systems came under pressure for greater political participation. The post-Communist states in Eastern Europe, by contrast, are making a dual transition – putting in place democratic institutions and a market economy at the same time. In these changing social and economic environments, the success of democracy depends in large part on the new institutions bringing economic prosperity to the people. Those left behind by the new economy are more likely to support anti-reform parties (Kullberg and Zimmerman, 1999). The transition from a collectivist society to one based on individual civil and political rights has been easier for the Central European satellite states than for the former Soviet republics, which had a much longer history of authoritarian rule and have struggled to establish workable democratic institutions.

WEB ALERT!

Background information and up-to-date reports on transitional democracies and the general issues related to sustainable democracy can be found at the website of the International Institute for Democracy and Electoral Assistance, http://www.idea.int/

The states of East Asia and Latin America present a somewhat different picture, generally having a history of authoritarian rule. An exception has been Costa Rica, which has combined a strong democracy with economic development, as Case study 8.4 shows. In East Asia, state-led economic development has preceded democratic reforms. Japan was the earliest to democratize, but its parliamentary system was the product of the American occupation, rather than its own (weak) representative institutions. Since the war, it has been governed almost continuously by a single dominant party, albeit one with much factional in-fighting. In contrast, changes of political power in South Korea and Taiwan indicate the growth of more pluralist electoral contests.

Single-party dominant systems have also been a feature in Latin America, but here the strong state has not produced economic success on the scale of the Asian economies. Ruling elites have done little to heal deep social divisions, deal with land reform or ameliorate extreme poverty. The defeat of Mexico's ruling party in July 2000, after 71 years in power, could mark the beginnings of genuine democratic contests in Mexico, as well as economic liberalization. Mexico's new president sees NAFTA as the way to obtain a better deal for Mexicans. An early success was a NAFTA ruling allowing Mexican trucks to carry export goods to US destinations, rather than to reload cargo onto US trucks at the border.

Case study 8.4 Costa Rican democracy reaps FDI rewards

Costa Rica was once thought of simply as a 'banana republic', but in the past decade it has attracted impressive flows of foreign investment which have transformed its economy. Costa Rica now attracts about $517bn., or 53 per cent of the total foreign investment in Latin America. Schuler and Brown (1999) argue that a major factor in attracting multinational corporations has been the country's political and institutional stability. Costa Rica has established a strong democracy with transparent institutions, competitive elections and a solid social welfare state. *The Citizens' Audit on the Quality of Democracy 1998–2001* has produced evidence on the experience of democracy by citizens from all walks of life within the country (O'Donnell et al., 2004). The audit revealed high spots such as the electoral system, but also weaknesses, such as poor treatment of citizens by bureaucrats. In general, it brought to light that democracy is deeper than simply electing governments, but is about human rights, accountability of those in power and the rule of law. It highlighted the importance of social and economic inequalities in assessing the quality of political participation.

Costa Rica's biggest FDI success story has been Intel, whose chip factory now accounts for 37 per cent of the country's exports. Costa Rica was competing against Mexico for the factory, and both governments offered incentives. The Costa

Rican government offered Intel tax-free status for eight years, followed by a 50 per cent discount for another four; a commitment to invest more in infrastructure and education; and a favourable regime on energy prices. Mexico offered enhanced incentives and had the advantage of lower wages than those in Costa Rica. Notwithstanding, Intel opted for Costa Rica. This evidence suggests the decisive role played by a strong democracy, along with membership in a number of international accords (such as GATT and WTO).

Schuler and Brown (1999) also argue that democracy seems to influence the way multinationals behave once they have settled in the host country. Lively democratic institutions and interest groups which represent and channel citizens' views can provide valuable feedback to the company and aid it in developing beneficial relationships with the community. For example, Ston Forestal, a US company which invested in a reforestation project in Costa Rica, changed the location of its planned chipping factory after environmental groups, mainly Greenpeace, had lobbied the government. The company then set up a multiparty watchdog group to monitor its operations. This development is indicative of Costa Rica's approach to conservation of its biodiversity through decentralized decision-making and localized management of protected areas.

How does Intel benefit Costa Rica? The company enjoys a tax holiday for eight years, and it brings 90 per cent of its supplies from abroad, as there is no local electronics industry. Still, the enthusiastic workforce at the new factory see the benefits of a constant education in the new economy. The agreement between the government and Intel provided for cooperation in developing new programmes for worker training. One twenty-something employee says chips are far more challenging than bananas, the country's other major export: 'Bananas will be bananas today and bananas tomorrow. When you're making chips ... you always learn something new.'

The Intel experience in Costa Rica indicates that the existence of robust democratic political institutions gave Costa Rica significant advantages in attracting investment. While the multinational company possesses significant bargaining power in its relations with governments, in that it has geographical mobility and ownership of the technology, states are in a position to build 'institutional comparative advantage', as Costa Rica has successfully shown.

Sources: Schuler, D. and Brown, D. (1999) 'Democracy, regional market integration and foreign direct investment', *Business & Society*, **38**(4), pp. 450–74; 'A silicon republic', *Newsweek*, 28 August 2000, **136**(9), pp. 42–5; United Nations Development Programme (UNDP) (2002) *Human Development Report 2002*; UNDP (2002) *Human Development Report 2003*; O'Donnell, G., Cullell, J. and Iazzetta, O. (eds) (2004) *The Quality of Democracy* (Notre Dame, IN: University of Notre Dame Press).

Case questions

Why does democracy reduce political risk for foreign investors in Costa Rica?

What specific lessons can multinational organizations learn from Intel's experience in Costa Rica which can be applied in assessing locations globally?

The postcolonial states of Africa have had limited success so far in making the transition to democracy. Social inequalities and ethnic conflict have inhibited the building of viable states. Politics has been largely based on ethnic, religious and tribal loyalties and ruling elites have been reluctant to accept the notion of competition for power through genuine elections, in which they may face the real possibility of losing power to a rival group. The aid that has gone into these weak economies, both bilateral and multilateral, from the World Bank and the IMF, is necessarily channelled through government offices, a process which has enhanced the power of political elites over scarce resources. There are some hopeful signs of democracy gaining ground. Following military dictatorship, Nigeria now has a fragile democracy, but is struggling to control disenchanted groups (see Case study 8.1). In 2000, the authoritarian regime of President Mugabe in Zimbabwe received an electoral shock, despite intimidatory tactics aimed at opposition politicians and their supporters.

Transitional democracies and international business

Transitional democracies are now in the international spotlight, as they represent emerging markets seeking to attract international business. Most of these states are developing economies in which popular governments have replaced colonial rule, which also includes the former Soviet satellite states. In some of these states in Central and Eastern Europe, multipartyism has produced fragile democracies. Because they seem to be on the path to consolidation, they present relative stability for investors. On the other hand, privatization has been subject to political influence from vested interests (EBRD, 2000). At the other extreme are the 'partial democracies', with elected assemblies, but within single-party states where civil and political rights are limited. While these regimes see unity in the single party, their intolerance of opposition makes them closer to authoritarianism. Transitional democracies look to outside sources to provide economic development, through investment and financial aid, and, increasingly their political systems are brought into the economic equation. For foreign investors, they represent new markets, but carry considerable political risk, as businesses cannot be insulated from local political life. Indeed, successful operations often hinge on trust and cooperation with host political authorities. However, if the political risk becomes too high, investors will flee. As the example of Costa Rica has shown, stable and transparent political institutions seem the best long-term guarantee of economic development, a more attractive business environment and a better quality of life for citizens.

Global politics

It is increasingly recognized by governments that states no longer have the means to deliver national security and material well-being on their own. Interdependence and cooperation have generated numerous alliances and international organizations, the most influential being the UN. Organizations, both governmental and non-governmental, regional and international, have emerged in the postwar period. **Non-governmental organizations** (NGOs) have gained in political influence and become part of the international institutional process in some areas of global concern, such as human rights (for example Amnesty International) and the environment (for example Greenpeace).

Political leaders of the major industrial democracies, known as the **G7** countries, have been meeting annually since 1975, to discuss important economic and political issues facing their societies and the international community generally. The members are Canada, France, Germany, Japan, Italy, the US and the UK. With the addition of Russia at the more recent meetings, they have in practice become the 'G8'. Their discussions provide a forum for setting priorities and highlighting new issues on the international agenda. They cover a wide range of subjects, including macroeconomic policies, international trade, security matters and human rights. While their formal meetings are at ministerial level, they have set up a number of task forces and working groups on specific issues such as money laundering and nuclear safety. The G7 provides a forum for arriving at consensus positions on important global issues. They have also attracted numerous NGOs seeking to influence policies, as well as the more negative and disorderly anti-globalization protesters.

The United Nations

Founded in 1945, the UN has grown from 50 to nearly 200 states. The UN's institutions and processes have evolved considerably in 50 years, and so too has the body of international treaties and conventions (discussed in Chapter 9), which are increasingly recognized in international law. The UN does not constitute a world government, however, as it operates on the basis of intergovernmental cooperation between member states. Its secretary-general, while not having the executive powers that state leaders possess, commands considerable confidence in the international community and exemplifies the UN's aim of achieving peaceful negotiated settlement of conflicts between states. The General Assembly, in which all member states have one vote, can be contrasted with the Security Council, in which the major postwar powers – the US, UK, France, China and Russia (formerly the Soviet Union) – were made permanent members and given the right of veto. Although the Security Council was therefore less effective than anticipated during the cold war period, the UN was able to provide a forum for international debate and expand its social and economic activities through its many agencies and affiliated bodies. The International Labour Organization (ILO), which actually predates the UN, has set standards for health and safety, workers' rights and child labour; its conventions have been ratified by dozens of states, who, by so doing, show a commitment to be bound by them. Similarly, the human rights covenants have been ratified by over 140 states (see Chapter 9).

Minifile

CHARTER OF THE UNITED NATIONS

Article 1

The purposes of the United Nations are:

1 To maintain international peace and security, and to that end:

• To take effective collective measures for the prevention and removal of threats to the peace, and for the suppression of acts of aggression or other breaches of the peace, and

• To bring about by peaceful means, and in conformity with the principles of justice and international law, adjustment or settlement of international disputes or situations which might lead to a breach of the peace

2 To develop friendly relations among nations based on respect for the principle of equal rights and self-determination of peoples, and to take other appropriate measures to strengthen universal peace

3 To achieve international cooperation in solving international problems of an economic, social, cultural or humanitarian character, and in promoting and encouraging respect for human rights and for fundamental freedoms for all without distinction as to race, sex, language, or religion

4 To be a centre for harmonizing the actions of nations in the attainment of these common ends.

WEB ALERT!

A full text of the UN Charter may be found on the UN's website at
http://www.un.org

While state practice sometimes falls far short of these commitments, they do
represent an acknowledgement of commitment to the principles they contain: the
Covenant on Civil and Political Rights (in Article 25) lays down minimum standards
for democratic government, including free and fair elections, universal suffrage and
secret ballots. The acceptance by states of the principle that these conventions
impose on them a 'higher' duty to comply is an indication of a shift away from the
pure theory of state sovereignty. The UN itself has taken the lead by giving humanitarian intervention priority over state sovereignty by intervening in states' domestic
affairs, in cases of human rights violations in Iraq, Somalia and Bosnia. Under its
Charter, the UN can take measures to enforce or maintain international peace,
including peacekeeping operations and sanctions against particular countries. Sanctions include a range of measures: they may be economic and trade sanctions, arms
embargoes, travel bans or financial restrictions. Countries affected have included
Libya, Somalia, Sudan, Sierra Leone and Iraq. Sanctions, however, may have negative effects, in that ordinary people suffer while regimes find ways of getting round
the sanctions, as happened in Iraq under Saddam Hussein. A framework of 'smart'
sanctions approved by the Security Council in 2002 against Iraq was designed to
target arms exports while allowing goods needed by civilians to enter the country.
The UN is currently examining how sanctions may be targeted more effectively (UN
Security Council, 2004).

Looking back over its first 50 years, two parallel trends have emerged: the UN has
grown in authoritative stature in relation to states, while state sovereignty has weakened its grip as the sole source of legitimate authority. While there are some who
would like to take this process further and make the UN a world government, there
are also those who warn that controversial interventions can undermine confidence
in its position generally. Any reform of its structure will therefore probably focus on
enhancing confidence in its institutions and processes, while retaining the principle
of state sovereignty.

CRITICAL PERSPECTIVES

Global politics

The idea of 'global politics' challenges the traditional distinctions between domes-
tic/international, inside/outside, territorial/non-territorial politics … It also highlights the richness and complexity of the interconnections which transcend states
and societies in the global order. Although governments and states remain, of

course, powerful actors, they now share the global arena with an array of other agencies and organizations. (Held et al., 1999, p. 50)

■ Assess the way states and governments are evolving in relation to the international organizations, both governmental and non-governmental. To what extent do these changes impact on 'domestic' politics?

The European Union

Regional groupings of states have also grown in numbers in the postwar period. Most of these are trading alliances, but the European Union (EU), the most advanced, represents much deeper economic, social and political integration. Originally comprising a group of six states (Germany, France, Belgium, Luxembourg, the Netherlands, and Italy) under the Treaty of Rome in 1957, the European Community, as it was then, envisaged a 'pooling' of national sovereignty. When Britain joined in 1973, the possibility of the erosion of parliamentary sovereignty was a major issue and it has remained so, particularly among 'Euro-sceptics'. Despite misgivings about national sovereignty, perceived economic benefits have made the EU more popular than ever. It has expanded to 25 members, and accession negotiations are taking place with Bulgaria, Romania, Turkey and Croatia. Other Eastern European countries such as Ukraine, with its new democratic government, are also aspiring to membership. The enlargement debate has raised questions about the effectiveness and democratic credentials of EU structures, perceived as unwieldy, overbureaucratic and lacking in democratic accountability. Protracted discussions on a proposed new Constitution for the enlarged EU resulted in agreement in 2004 on several key issues, summarized in the box below. While negotiators were mindful of the need to achieve a workable union, there was much concern from the smaller states in particular, that the new enlarged EU would be dominated by the larger states. Supporters of federalism argued that the EU Constitution should take the federalist route, but the federalist principle has proved controversial among other member states, fearful of the weakening of national institutions and greater centralization. The new Constitution agreed in 2004 is, strictly speaking, a Constitutional Treaty, rather than a Constitution in the sense of state constitutions discussed earlier in this chapter. The reason is that the legal status of the document, like previous constitutional documents such as the Nice Treaty, remains a treaty between sovereign states. However, echoing the Bill of Rights which became part of the US Constitution, the Constitutional Treaty contains a Charter of Fundamental Rights. To take effect, the new treaty must be ratified by all EU member states, either by a parliamentary vote or referendum, the deadline for which was set at November 2006. Following the German Parliament's approval and overwhelming support by Spain's voters in a referendum, the voters of France and the Netherlands rejected it decisively in their respective referenda in 2005, leaving considerable doubt over the treaty's future. There follows a discussion of the main EU institutions and how they would be reformed under the new Constitution.

The European Union Constitutional Treaty of 2004

- Enhances powers of the European Parliament over legislation and EU budget.
- Abolishes the national veto in the Council of Ministers, in immigration and asylum policy.
- Introduces a new system of weighted voting in the Council of Ministers: a yes vote requires at least 55 per cent of member states representing at least 65 per cent of the EU population.
- Reduces the size of the European Commission from 2014: members to be sent from only two-thirds of member states on a rotation basis.
- Creates new offices of president of the Council (serving a term of up to five years) and foreign minister.
- Incorporates an EU Charter of Fundamental Rights.

The highest law-making authority in the EU is the Council of Ministers, renamed the Council of the European Union in 1993. Members are ministers in their own states. The new Constitution provides for a new president of the European Council, to replace the previous arrangement of a six-month rotation presidency among member states. Originally, unanimity among its members was required for a proposal to proceed, but this requirement has been relaxed in some key areas (for example agriculture, the environment and transport) by 'qualified majority voting' (QMV), whereby votes are carried in the Council with 232 votes out of a total of 321, representing 62 per cent of the total population. This system, extended by the Nice Treaty in 2000, applies to 80 per cent of its decisions. The Nice Treaty established a system of weighted voting, shown in Table 8.4, which only partially reflects size of population. As can be seen, there is voting parity between Germany, France, the UK and Italy, although the German population is much larger than the others. Under the new Constitution, voting is more in proportion to the size of population: Germany would enjoy 18 per cent, while France, Italy and the UK would have roughly 13 per cent each. However, further enlargement would require adjustments to be made. In particular, Turkey, with its large population of 70 million, would gain a significant voice in the council, and it is possible that these enlargement issues boosted the 'no' vote among the French and Dutch electorates. A safeguard for small countries is the provision that a vote is carried if it is supported by at least 55 per cent of member states, representing 65 per cent of the overall population of the EU. Importantly, the new Constitution provides that the issues of immigration and asylum policy, formerly outside the QMV voting system, now fall within it. National veto is still retained on issues of tax, defence, foreign policy and financing the EU budget. There would be a new office of foreign minister, however, and a diplomatic service, to raise the foreign affairs profile of the EU.

Table 8.4 The Council and Parliament of the European Union

EU15 Members	Population, millions	Vote in Council	Allocation of seats in Parliament	Accession 10 members, 2004	Population, millions	Vote in Council	Allocation of seats in Parliament
Germany	82	29	99	Poland	38.5	27	54
UK	60	29	78	Czech Rep.	10.2	12	24
France	61	29	78	Hungary	10	12	24
Italy	58	29	78	Slovakia	5.4	7	14
Spain	40.2	27	54	Lithuania	3.6	7	13
Netherlands	16.2	13	27	Latvia	2.3	4	9
Greece	10.7	12	24	Slovenia	1.9	4	7
Belgium	10.3	12	24	Estonia	1.4	4	6
Portugal	10.1	12	24	Cyprus	.7	4	6
Sweden	8.9	10	19	Malta	.4	3	5
Austria	8.2	10	18				
Denmark	5.4	7	14				
Finland	5.2	7	14				
Ireland	3.9	7	13				
Luxembourg	0.45	4	6				

Source: The European Commission, in *Financial Times*, 15 June 2004; European Council, at http://ue.eu.int/cms.

The European Commission is at present composed of 25 appointed commissioners headed by a president. The 24 directorates-general of the commission are the heart of the EU's civil service, responsible for its day-to-day running. Importantly, in addition, the Commission takes the lead in proposing legislation and thus enjoys considerable political power from its 'agenda-setting' initiatives, such as the Single Market and Monetary Union. The Constitutional Treaty provides for a reduction in the number of commissioners to 18 from 2014.

The European Parliament is composed of members from each state in proportion to the state's population. The EU Parliament has grown in size from 78 to 732 members. Although Members of the European Parliament (MEPs) have been directly elected by EU citizens since 1979, Parliament does not play the pivotal role which is customary in national systems. The Treaty of Rome gave the EU Parliament little direct say in legislation, but, with later treaties, it gained greater influence, with an increase from 15 to 38 areas in which it has 'co-decision-making' powers with the Council (amounting to two-thirds of all EU legislation). These reforms have come in response to criticism that EU institutions lack sufficient democratic accountability and are bureaucratic and inefficient. The new Constitutional Treaty also provides for increased scrutiny of proposed legislation by national parliaments.

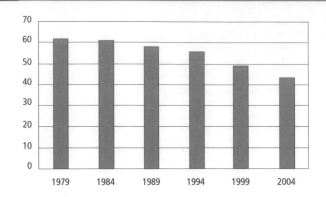

Figure 8.8 **Voter turnout in European Parliament elections**
Source: European Parliament (2004) *Turnout trends at European elections,* at http://www.elections2004.eu.int/ ep-election/sites/en/results1306/turnout.

The European Parliament has not as yet resonated with voters to the same extent that national parliaments do, as voter turnout in elections to date have been disappointing. As Figure 8.8 shows, voter turnout has declined with each successive election, reaching a low of 45.3 per cent in 2004. It had been hoped that the prospect of a greater role for the Parliament in the new European Constitution would persuade voters to take greater interest. However, the popularity of Euro-sceptic parties and politicians in many countries suggests that national issues loom larger with the electorate than pan-European issues. It is perhaps ironic that 93 seats out of the total 732 are filled by non-aligned MEPs of a Euro-sceptic or nationalist leaning. By contrast, the 25 European green parties mounted a unified campaign, deciding to focus on Europe-wide issues, and pronounced their strategy a success as they increased their share of the vote in five countries and achieved a 6.8 per cent share of the overall vote, up from 5.5 per cent in the previous election. The fact that candidates representing ruling parties in a number of countries, including the UK, Germany and France, faired poorly suggested that voters were using the European elections to register disenchantment with ruling national parties. While institutional designers of the new Europe forge ahead, it would seem that the political challenges for European institution-building at grassroots level remain formidable. These challenges have surfaced in the constitutional debates held in the countries which have held a referendum on the constitutional treaty in 2005. In both France and the Netherlands, the 'no' vote reflected anti-government sentiment as well as disquiet over the new Constitution. For the referendum, the turnout in France was 70 per cent, in marked contrast to the usual turnout in EU parliamentary elections.

WEB ALERT!

EU internet resources can be found at http://www.europarl.eu.int/. This site contains links to national parliaments and political groups

The EU's main website is http://europa.eu.int/

The EU institutions website is http://www.europarl.eu.int/institutions/en/ default.htm

CRITICAL PERSPECTIVES

The future of the EU

Either the European Community will take firm action soon, and will introduce supranational structures, or it will remain a loose league of nations, in which Europe will revert to the former rivalry of hostile nation-states. (Glotz, 1995, p. 221)

■   The EU is attempting to bring member states into a structure somewhere between these two extremes. Critically assess how successful it is likely to be.

Conclusions

1   The political sphere concerns decision-making processes for resolving conflict in society as a whole. Interactions between state and private actors are blurring the traditional distinctions between state and civil society.

2   The nation-state is the basic unit into which all the world's people are divided. Sovereignty and territoriality, however, are being eroded, with the growing interdependence of states.

3   States vary in their sources of legitimacy. Traditional sources of legitimate authority have given way to constitutionality and democratic forms.

4   Democratic government may take a number of forms: these include presidential, parliamentary and hybrid systems. A stronger executive is associated with presidential systems, while the legislative is predominant in parliamentary systems. The favoured design of new constitutions is the dual executive, or hybrid system.

5   Political parties and pluralistic political debate are characteristic of democratic systems. Two-party systems are associated with the first-past-the-post type of electoral system, while multiparty systems, often leading to coalition government, are characteristic of PR systems.

6   While democracies are increasing in number globally, many of these are transitional democracies, in the process of building institutions of participation and accountability, as well as introducing economic liberalization. The states of Central and Eastern Europe and Latin America are examples.

7   The growth of global political forces has led to a questioning of traditional notions of sovereignty in an interdependent world. In particular, the changing structure of the EU towards a supranational body is sparking a reappraisal of the role of nation-states.

Review questions

1   What are the defining characteristics of the nation-state? How is globalization threatening state sovereignty?

2   What are political risks to international business?

3   What is federalism and what are its alleged advantages? Would it be workable in the EU?

4   List the main defining features of democracy.

5   What are the sources of possible instability in transitional democracies?

6   How do presidential systems compare with parliamentary systems of government? The hybrid system is said to combine the best of both worlds, but does it?

7   Looking at the main institutions of the EU, how democratic are they?

8   What are the proposals for reforming the EU?

Assignments

1   Assume that a company is considering moving production to a location in a developing country (for example Mexico), but is concerned about political instability. What particular aspects of the country's political structure and processes should it take into account when assessing political risk?

2   What are the links between democratization and economic development? Give two examples and assess how successful they have been.

Further reading

Baylis, J. and Smith, S. (eds) (2004) *The Globalization of World Politics* (Oxford: Oxford University Press).

Heywood, A. (1997) *Politics* (Basingstoke: Macmillan – now Palgrave Macmillan).

Hague, R. and Harrop, M. (2001) *Comparative Government and Politics: An Introduction* (5th edn) (Basingstoke: Palgrave – now Palgrave Macmillan).

Held, D. (ed.) (1993) *Prospects for Democracy* (Cambridge: Polity Press).

Held, D. and McGrew, A. (2002) *Governing Globalization: Power, Authority and Global Governance* (Cambridge: Polity Press).

McGrew, A. and Lewis, P. (1992) *Globalization and the Nation-State* (Cambridge: Polity Press).

9

The international legal environment of business: moving towards harmonization

Outline of chapter

- Introduction
- How legal systems affect business
- National legal systems
  - Civil law tradition
  - Common law tradition
  - Non-Western legal systems
- Legal framework of the European Union
- International business transactions
  - International codification
  - Cultural factors in international contracts
- Resolution of disputes in international business
  - Contractual disputes
  - Negligence and product liability
- Crime, corruption and the law
- The growing impact of international law on business
  - Treaties and convention
  - Settlement of disputes in international law
- Human rights
- Conclusions

Learning objectives

1 To understand the interrelationships between national, regional and international legal frameworks in their impact on the international business environment.

2 To appreciate the divergence in structures, processes and content between national legal systems.

3 To assess the impact of evolving regional, in particular EU, law-making on enterprises, workers and consumers.

4 To apply principles of international law, in particular human rights, to organizations and their workforces.

Introduction

The legal dimension of international business has grown as business relations across national borders have deepened and become more complex. Historically, the legal environment has been determined by national legal systems stemming from state sovereignty. All commercial transactions across national borders, from the simplest export contracts to complex joint ventures, exist within the framework of national legal systems. The globalization of markets and production has provided the impetus for harmonization in the legal systems between states. We now see the dual effects of a weakening of state sovereignty and a burgeoning body of international law. Modern international managers, therefore, require an understanding of the workings of international law, as well as a familiarity with different national legal systems.

The speed of some developments such as e-commerce has far outpaced the development of the law to cover them. While governments have slowly woken up to the legal implications of technology advances, they have also realized their own limitations in regulating international transactions. Law-makers are now cooperating in international legal reform and the reform of national systems to take account of new ways of doing business. All countries appreciate the need for an efficient, modern, impartial legal system, to attract enterprises (both local and overseas investors) and retain their confidence in its processes. They also see the benefits of harmonization of laws to facilitate international transactions. The legal environment can be divided into three interacting spheres, as shown in Figure 9.1: national legal systems; regional law-making authorities, of which the EU is the major example; and international law emanating from recognized international bodies such as the UN and its agencies. This chapter sets out the 'boundaries' of each and explores the ways in which these overlapping spheres of law impact on international business.

Figure 9.1 **The three interlocking spheres of the international legal environment**

How legal systems affect business

Law refers to the rules which a society defines as binding on all its members. Whereas groups within a society, such as sports bodies, create rules for their own members, the distinguishing feature of law is that it creates obligations for society as a whole, encompassing individual citizens, businesses and government agents. In modern societies, law has expanded into almost all aspects of business. While businesspeople are inclined to see legal rules in a negative light, constraining their activities (for example an application for planning permission), in fact, much law is of an enabling nature (for example eligibility to apply for public funding). Market-driven economies aim to strike a balance between freedom of enterprise and sufficient regulation to guard the public interest. In the postwar era, with an upsurge in welfare state provisions, the law has extended to areas such as employment protection, consumer protection and health and safety in the workplace. More recently, with advances in telecommunications, data protection for personal details has come into the ambit of legal protection. As can be seen in Table 9.1, legal obligations now cover a wide range of business activities.

Table 9.1 Summary of major areas of law affecting business and relevant authorities

Area of law	Legal authorities
Contract	National; international conventions
Property and planning	National
Employment	National; EU; international conventions
Company	Mainly national; EU
Competition	National; EU
Health and Safety	National; EU; international conventions
Environment	National; EU; international conventions
Intellectual property	National; EU; international conventions
Negligence and product liability	National; EU
Human rights	National; EU; international conventions

Law may be broadly classified into two categories: **public law**, which concerns relations between citizens and the state, and **civil** (or private) **law**, which concerns relations between individuals (including companies). Tax and social security fall within public law, whereas contract law and employment law are areas of civil law. The state plays a significant, although less direct, role in civil law. Legislatures enact law regulating employment relations, for example, and the state's courts may be called on to settle disputes between the parties. In a dispute over a contract or an accident at work, the person who has suffered loss or injury (the 'plaintiff') may bring a claim for monetary compensation ('damages') or a range of other remedies against the 'defendant' in the state's courts. Monetary claims are by far the most common remedy sought: they accounted for 86 per cent of claims in the civil courts of England and Wales in 2003 (ONS, 2004b).

A major body of public law is the **criminal law**, under which certain types of wrong-doing are designated by society as criminal offences. In these cases, state authorities initiate proceedings, known as a 'prosecution', in the criminal courts, which, on conviction for a crime, will lead to a fine or the imprisonment of the offender. While we tend to think of crime in terms of individual crimes, such as assault and theft, companies, as well as their directors, can be guilty of criminal offences. Breaches of health and safety law are a common type of corporate crime. In Britain, corporate liability has been extended by new offences of corporate killing, following unsuccessful prosecutions for manslaughter in relation to ferry and train disasters, including a crash at Paddington Station, London, in 1999, in which 31 people died. Directors cannot hide behind the façade of the company: they may be personally liable for its crimes. On the other hand, enforcement of the criminal law, which is mainly rooted in national systems, poses major challenges, as criminal activities have become increasingly globalized and also highly organized. Table 9.2 provides a breakdown of the distinctions between civil and criminal law. Note that the 'burden of proof' is higher in a criminal case, which means that a greater degree of certainty is required for criminal guilt than for the judgment as to which party succeeds in a civil case.

Table 9.2 Outline of civil law and criminal law

	Criminal law	Civil law
What is it about?	Offences against society	Disputes between private individuals or companies
What is the purpose of the action?	To preserve order in the community by punishing offenders and deterring others	To seek a remedy for the wrong which has been suffered, usually financial compensation
Who are the parties?	A prosecutor, usually representing the state, prosecutes a defendant, the accused	A plaintiff sues a defendant
Where is the action heard?	State, regional or local criminal courts	Civil courts, at local, regional or state level
Who has to prove what?	The prosecutor must prove a case against the defendant beyond all reasonable doubt	The plaintiff must establish a case on the balance of probabilities
What form does the decision take?	A defendant may be convicted if found guilty, or acquitted if found not guilty	A defendant may be found liable or not liable
What remedies are handed down by the court?	Imprisonment, fine, probation, community service	Damages (financial compensation) to the successful plaintiff is the commonest
What are some common types of legal action?	Offences include theft, assault, drunken driving, criminal damage	Actions for breach of contract; actions in negligence for breach of a duty of care owed to the plaintiff

For a business, the bulk of the relevant law stems from national law-making authorities, as each of the world's sovereign states has its own legal system, which has both the law-making capacity within its territory ('jurisdiction') and the capacity to apply its law to legal disputes within its jurisdiction. Before looking at legal institutions, it is important to note that legal systems do not exist in a vacuum, but are influenced by the society's social, political and cultural environment. The legal environment, including the content of law and legal processes, is an indication of the attitudes to law in general, as well as the wider values of a society. As is often remarked on, there are over seventeen times as many lawyers per head of population in the US as in Japan (one for every 400 in the US, compared to one for every 7000 in Japan). People in individualistic societies such as the US make far greater use of the courts to settle disputes (known as **litigation**) than those in the more group-oriented societies. As values change, the law – and people's readiness to use it – are changing in harmony. In China's expanding market economy, for example, individuals are now seeking redress in the courts over defective consumer products and workers' rights. China's legal system is becoming more transparent, partly as a result of the influence of foreign investors (McGregor, 2001). Table 9.3 provides an outline of how Chinese law has evolved in its treatment of foreign enterprises. The law in 1986 to open the door to wholly foreign-owned enterprises was significant, in that it created an environment in which businesses could seek to strengthen property rights (Story, 2003).

Table 9.3 Legal protection of foreign investors in China

1979	Law on joint ventures between Chinese and foreign enterprises
1982	Constitutional amendment to authorize FDI in China
1983	Law to protect trademarks
1984	Law to protect patents
1985	Law on contracts with foreign enterprises
1986	Law allowing FDI by enterprises wholly foreign-owned in special economic zones
1990	Revision of law on joint ventures to allow non-Chinese chairperson; protection from nationalization
1994	Revision of tax law to gradually bring in equal treatment of domestic and foreign enterprises
2000	Regulation to allow individuals to make franchise agreements with foreign corporations
2001	WTO commitments towards non-discriminatory treatment of foreign and domestic enterprises

Source: Story, J. (2003) *China: The Race to Market* (Harlow: FT/Prentice Hall), p. 206.

However, reflecting cultural differences as well as the extent of economic development, some areas of legal protection (for example health and safety legislation), while commonplace in industrialized societies, are much less prevalent in the developing world. Although formal legal systems may look much alike between countries, the ways in which they work in practice may be very different. The extent to which a legal system has the capacity to adapt and respond to changes in the environment is a recurring issue in comparisons between national legal systems. Court systems, too, vary enormously in their user-friendliness. The 'wheels of justice' may turn so slowly that a would-be plaintiff, faced with a judicial process lasting years, may decide against litigation. In 2000 India, for example, had some 25 million cases pending. Even if no new actions were filed, the backlog would take an estimated 324 years to clear (Bearak, 2000).

Many disputes involving legal issues are settled by the parties 'out of court', saving costs and achieving an agreement more quickly than judicial proceedings. There are now many mechanisms available which help to facilitate settlements – such as mediation and negotiation – and which fall short of full court proceedings. In business disputes, **arbitration**, whereby the parties agree to allow a third party to step in to settle disputes, is much more efficient than litigation. Partly because of the trends towards alternative means of settling disputes, the number of claims in the civil courts in England and Wales has dropped, following a peak in the late 1980s and early 1990s, as shown in Figure 9.2. (Alternative means of settling disputes in international contracts are discussed later in the chapter.)

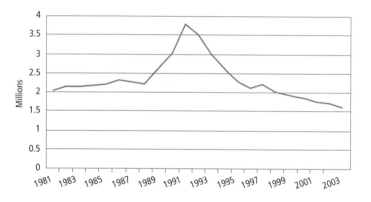

Figure 9.2 **County Court claims in England and Wales**
Source: ONS (2004) *UK 2005: The Official Yearbook* (London: ONS).

National legal systems

The pre-eminence of national legal systems derives from the theory of the sovereign state (see Chapter 8). Every legal system may be divided into two main sets of functional institutions. These are legislation (law-making) and adjudication (the settlement of disputes). Legislation, or statute law, is 'law made by a person or institution with the power to make law' (Miers and Page, 1990, p. 3). In democracies, elected legislative bodies link directly with the political system. Much law-making follows the social and political agendas of elected governments. Legislators can get it wrong, of course. The prohibition law in the US in the 1930s, banning alcoholic beverages, met widespread opposition and had to be repealed.

The system of courts, or **judicial system**, interprets and applies the law in particular cases. The extent to which judges thereby shape legal development, overlapping with the law-making function, differs between systems, and, even within systems, is a matter of differing opinions. As will be seen below, 'case law' (judge-made law) is more important in some countries than in others. A general rule is that legal systems attempt to draw a line between law-making and judicial functions. Court systems are designed to prevent the intrusion of political and personal considerations, and judges should be seen to be fair and impartial. Figure 9.3 presents the findings of the World Bank in its survey of the investment climate in developing countries. Senior managers were asked to agree or disagree with the statement: 'I am confident that the judicial system will enforce my contractual and property rights in business disputes' (World Bank, 2004). Figure 9.3 shows the percentage of managers in each country who disagreed with this statement. Foreign businesses, in particular, are often wary of evolving court systems in developing economies, as they feel that they are at a disadvantage compared to local people. This is due in part to a lack of familiarity with the system and language, but they may also perceive that there is a bias against them as outsiders. The notion of equality before the law is an aspect of the **rule of law**. For transitional democracies, establishing the rule of law and an independent judiciary are as important as instituting a free and fair electoral system. Case study 9.1 on legal reform in Turkey provides an example of the links between democratization and embedding the rule of law.

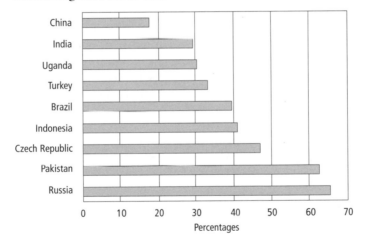

Figure 9.3 **Businesses' lack of confidence in courts**
Source: World Bank (2004) *World Development Report 2005* (Washington, DC: World Bank)

The world's legal systems can be classified in terms of legal traditions or legal families. The two major Western historical traditions are the civil law tradition and the common law tradition. The **civil law system**, prevalent in Continental Europe, is founded on a comprehensive legal code, whereas the **common law** tradition, which is English in origin, emphasizes case law. Both have been adopted in a variety of non-Western contexts, as part of modernization processes. Newly independent states have tended to adopt the legal tradition of their former colonial power. For this reason, a lawyer from Ghana will find it much easier to understand a lawyer from Kenya or England, than one from the Ivory Coast just next door, which falls within French colonial influence (Zweigert and Kötz, 1998).

Civil law tradition

The civil law tradition is by far the older of the two, and has its origin in the ancient Roman *ius civile*, which was codified in the sixth century in the Justinian Code. Civil law relies on a legal code for the basic groundwork of the system, on which further law-making is built. The legal code is a comprehensive, systematic setting out of the basic law for a country. The modern models of codified law are the French Civil Code of 1804, known as the Napoleonic Code and the German Civil Code of 1896. Codified law is in fact divided into a number of different codes, depending on the subject matter. The civil code, which contains the body of private law (that is, between citizens), is complemented, for example, by a commercial code and a criminal code. These codes have demonstrated their adaptability by providing models for numerous other countries in Europe, Latin America, Africa, Asia and the Middle East (see Table 9.4). They are adaptable in federal systems, as in Germany itself, or in unitary systems, as in France. In the UK, Scotland falls into the civil law tradition. Japan's choice of the civil code model coincided with the country's initial industrialization and modernization policies in the late nineteenth century. The attraction of the civil law model lies in the supremacy of the single authoritative source of the law. The principles and concepts contained in the codes form the basis of legal reasoning. Although the accumulated decisions of judges are useful as guidelines, they are not in themselves a source of law. This is the major distinction between the civil law and common law systems. The distinction has been described as one between different legal styles. The urge to regulate and systematize has dominated Continental legal thinking, whereas English lawyers have tended to improvise, not making a decision until they have to, on the view that 'we'll cross that bridge when we come to it' (Zweigert and Kötz, 1998, p. 70).

Table 9.4 Selected civil law and common law countries

Civil law	Common law
Argentina	Australia
Brazil	Bangladesh
Chile	Canada
China	Ghana
Egypt	India
France	Israel
Germany	Jamaica
Greece	Kenya
Indonesia	Malaysia
Iran	Nigeria
Italy	Singapore
Japan	England
Mexico	United States
Sweden	Zambia

Case study 9.1   Legal reforms win business in Turkey

With the prospect of EU membership, Turkey is undergoing a transformation of its economic, political and social environment. Legal reforms are an important element of this process, providing an underpinning for the changes taking place, which the government hopes will assure citizens, EU authorities and prospective investors of an efficient, impartial legal system. The country, however, has had a long way to go to achieve this goal. Turkey's legal system is firmly in the civil law family, dating from the foundation of the republic in 1923. Its commercial code was borrowed from Germany, and its system of administrative law from France. However, four decades of military rule, weak procedural safeguards and poor human rights records have taken their toll, and many reforms have been necessary to meet EU requirements.

The democratically elected government of Recep Tayyip Erdogan, who heads the Justice and Development Party (AKP), elected in 2002, has wasted no time in bringing about reforms. While its background is Islamist, the AKP is firm that it supports secular government and the principle of inclusion for the multiple ethnic groups that make up the population. In particular, it has brought in legislation to establish the rights of the Kurdish minority, including Kurdish language broadcasting. A Turkish commentator has said of the threat of Kurdish separatism: 'The best way to fight these threats is in a democratic state based on the rule of law' (Bolton and Gardner, 6 June 2003). It has abolished the death penalty and is reforming its criminal procedures to rule out the gaining of evidence by torture. The major challenge, however, is establishing a culture based on the rule of law.

The military has been a dominant force in Turkish society, often seen as a bulwark of secular authority counterpoised to Islamist forces. There have been four military coups in as many decades, and the sense of the residual authority of the military is a deeply rooted tradition which is difficult to change. But change it must, if Turkey is to achieve the goal of persuading the EU that it is a functioning democracy. Legislation has now established civilian control over the military, providing that the National Security Council, the military stronghold, is advisory only.

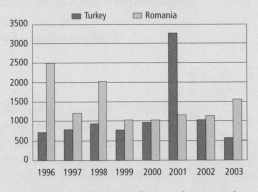

Comparison of inward flows of FDI: Turkey and Romania

Source: United Nations, *World Investment Reports 1999 and 2004* (Geneva: UN).

Turkey's increasing stability and modernization should help to attract foreign investors. It boasts a low-cost environment, a strategic location at the crossroads of Europe and Asia and a huge potential market of 70 million consumers. Judging by its inflows of FDI, however, one commentator likened Turkey to 'the frog that never gets kissed' (Munir, 2003). As the figure shows, inward flows of FDI fell in 2002 and 2003, whereas flows to Romania, with which it is competing for foreign investment, increased. Political instability in the region was a factor, as was the failure of its political leaders to prioritize an improvement of the investment climate. Its weak legal climate has been an impediment, as Cargill, the US agricultural company found in 2000. The company was optimistic when it invested in a $90m. sugar-substitute plant. Having secured the necessary government permissions to build the plant on agricultural land, it built the plant and started producing, only to be told that the plant violated the Constitution. Judicial proceedings were commenced against Cargill. It is hoped that the new investment law will prevent this type of confusion in future. Turkey's leaders need to attract foreign investors, and, of course, the prospect of EU membership enhances its allure.

Sources: Boulton, L., 'Greenfield factory highlights the perils', *Financial Times*, 25 June 2002; Boulton, L. and Gardner, D., 'Ankara stand-off', *Financial Times*, 6 June 2003; Çakmak, M., 'It's the way it's implemented', *Financial Times*, 10 December 2002; Munir, M., 'The frog that never gets kissed', *Financial Times*, 1 April 2003.

Case questions

What reforms have taken place in Turkey's legal environment?

How are they contributing to a more attractive business climate for potential investors?

WEB ALERT!

For information on FDI in Turkey, look at the factfile on Turkey in the FDI magazine at http://www.fdimagazine.com/

Also interesting is the Turkish government's 'Investment in Turkey' website, designed to provide information (and encouragement) to would-be investors, at http://www.investinginturkey.gov.tr

Common law tradition

The common law tradition originated in England some 900 years ago – long before Parliament had become the supreme law-making authority. Common law is essentially judge-made law, known as case law. In deciding a particular dispute, the judge creates a precedent to be followed in similar cases in the future. The body of law builds up through the accumulation of precedents in decided cases. The system has both flexibility and rigidities in practice. Precedents may be applied more loosely or more strictly in later cases, lending flexibility. However, as the court system is hierarchical, the decisions of higher courts form precedents which must be followed by lower courts. Faced with what seems to be a bad precedent, the judge in a lower court has little choice but to follow it. The growth in statute law, in the form of Acts of Parliament, mainly in the past 100 years, has come about largely in response to the complexities of economic and social changes. Modern judges spend a great deal of their time interpreting and applying statute law, including, it should be added, European law. The growing importance of statute law (also referred to as enacted law) suggests a convergence with the civil law tradition, although, when it comes down to interpreting the law in particular factual situations – which is what matters to litigants – the judge still holds a good deal of power.

Common law systems have been transplanted to countries as diverse as the US and India. Like all legal systems, the tradition has been adapted to the local environment. The US, with its division between federal and 50 state jurisdictions, has evolved a particularly complex system, with overlapping jurisdictions that can be confusing to outsiders (and even insiders). Each state constitutes a system within a system – Louisiana even has remnants of French codified law from its own colonial past. The individual states have made efforts to achieve consistency in the law in key areas that affect business, notably through the Uniform Commercial Code, which has been adopted by all the states (although only partially in Louisiana). The American Law Institute has spearheaded the efforts to bring about consistency by producing its Restatements of the law in areas such as contract and product liability (see Case Study 9.4 on Firestone). These restatements resemble codified law in all but name, but they do not have the status of a statute as they are not passed by Congress. Their aim is to clarify the law and act as guidance to lawyers and judges.

Table 9.5 Summary of civil law and common law traditions

	Civil law tradition	Common law tradition
Sources of the law	Comprehensive legal codes	Judge-made law and statutes
Role of case law	Guidance, but not binding	System of binding precedent
Legal style	Systematic application of principles	Pragmatic and piecemeal

Non-Western legal systems

The growth in commercial law has reached almost all countries, aware that economic development depends on a sound legal framework and an efficient and accessible court system. As has been seen, the groundwork for modern legal systems in much of the world was the legacy of colonial regimes. Legal traditions in many countries, which are based on customary law, predate Western systems and continue to form an important part of the overall legal environment. In many countries, therefore, we now find a mixture of pre-modern customs, colonial forms and newer codes designed to keep up to date with business needs. The study of evolving legal systems in developing countries reveals much about the relationship between law and social change.

Non-Western legal traditions include Islamic, Chinese and Hindu law. Of these, Islamic law, called Shari'a law (or God's rules), is perhaps the most highly developed. Islamic law can have a direct impact on the way business is conducted in Muslim countries such as Saudi Arabia and Sudan. Because the Shari'a prohibits 'unearned profits', the charging of interest is forbidden. Financing through banks can still be arranged, by devising alternative legal forms to cover transactions, such as profit-sharing and loss-sharing by a lending bank. Islamic countries have introduced codes for the secular regulation of activities such as the formation and enforcement of contracts, foreign investment and the employment of foreign workers. Accordingly, most now have secular tribunals for these areas.

Both Western and non-Western legal traditions have evolved and adapted to different cultural contexts, in response to two related forces. First, there has been a perceived need to modernize national legal structures as societies have become more complex and legal relations, such as consumer and employment contracts, have become more common. Most of this development has come through legislation, such the Consumer Protection Act 1987 and Employment Rights Act 1996 in the UK. Secondly, the growth of global markets has led to increasing international efforts to achieve uniformity and standardization of laws across national borders. Much of this latter effort has come through multilateral international conventions signed by a number of sovereign states, which, when ratified by national authorities, become incorporated into the domestic law of the state. In particular, international conventions have played an important role in bringing common legal frameworks for international trade in goods (as will be discussed below). Within the EU, harmonization has gone further, putting in place supranational legal structures for both law-making and adjudication (Denza, 1999).

WEB ALERT!

A good source for the legal environment generally, including both national and international materials, is http://www.law.cornel.edu/world/

A site for international trade and commercial law is http://www.jus.uio.no/lm/index.html. This site has been expanded to include e-commerce, environmental law, human rights, Islamic law and much more

CRITICAL PERSPECTIVES

The rule of law

In an individualistic and pluralistic society, where there are few common standards, where strong binding collectivities have declined and been replaced by communities of choice, and where informal social sanctions have weakened, then the rule of law is more rather than less necessary. This does not mean that states will be able to cope fully with the multiple problems and conflicts that arise from the growing pluralism of modern societies; rather we are claiming that without a public power that mediates between these plural groups through the rule of law, such conflicts will become intolerable. (Hirst and Thompson 1999, p. 179)

■ Why is the rule of law essential in societies? Think of societies in which the rule of law is weak or non-existent: what are the drawbacks from the business perspective?

Legal framework of the European Union

For each member state, the EU provides a growing source of law, which has become intertwined with their own national law. The foundation Treaty of Rome 1957, referred to as the EC Treaty, has been greatly expanded, with articles renumbered as a result of the Treaty of Amsterdam 1997. The law of the EU is still technically referred to as EC law. The current constitutional structure is the product of the Treaty of European Union 1992 (TEU), also known as the Maastricht Treaty. EU law-making touches a wide range of areas, including:

- Elimination of trade barriers between member states
- A common agricultural policy
- A common commercial policy
- A common transport policy
- Harmonization of competition law
- Harmonization of social policy
- Economic and monetary union (EMU).

The UK recognizes the supremacy of European Community (EC) law in the European Communities Act 1972 (as amended in 1986, 1993 and 1998). The European Court of Justice (ECJ) is the sole interpreter of European law and can override national legislation in cases of conflict. Although national supreme courts (such as the House of Lords in the UK) have ultimate authority in domestic matters, in issues involving EU institutions and EC law, the ECJ is the ultimate authority. Case study 8.1 highlights the importance of European law for business.

SUMMARY POINTS

!!!

EC law and institutions

- **Treaties** creating the EU, which must be ratified by member states.
- **Law-making** by the Commission and Council (plus co-decision procedure with European Parliament):
  - *Regulations* – directly applicable throughout the EU; incorporated automatically into the law of each member state; create individual rights and obligations
  - *Directives* – require member states to implement their provisions, usually within a given period of time, for example two years; may have direct effect, allowing individuals to enforce rights directly, if the member state does not implement the directive in the required time limit.
- **European Court of Justice** (situated in Luxembourg): interprets the treaties and other legislation; modelled on courts in the civil law tradition, in that it is not bound by its previous decisions, but its case law has in fact shown consistency.

Case study 9.2   **Legal battle between Tesco and Levi Strauss**

In legal battles that have gone to the High Court in England and the European Court of Justice, Tesco attempted to establish a right to sell Levi jeans in its supermarkets at prices undercutting high-street shops. The case had wide implications for stores which sell popular designer brands at discount prices. The issue is whether the brands, which are registered trademarks, should be allowed to control which retailers sell their products. In a practice known as 'parallel imports', Tesco and other retailers had been able to buy branded goods cheaply in, say, Southeast Asia, bypassing the brand owners' official distribution channels in Europe. The law is clear that, within Europe, manufacturers cannot prevent a retailer from buying goods in one country and selling them in another. In a 1998 decision seen as a victory for brand owners, the ECJ held that retailers could not import goods from outside Europe without the manufacturer's consent. Levi were therefore tempted to sue parallel importers such as Tesco. Tesco then sued Levi for 'groundless threats', with a claim for damages.

From the consumer's point of view, it has been argued that parallel imports put pressure on prices and give the consumer more choice. Levi jeans bought at Tesco cost considerably less than those bought at Levi's stores. Levi argued that the issue was not essentially about price, but that super-markets could not provide the expert sales staff needed: 'Customers need advice on what's on offer and the difference between loose and baggy, straight and slim ... We're not saying you need a university degree to sell jeans, but if a person is cutting bacon and filling shelves one minute, it's not possible for them to sell jeans as well.' Levi said that Tesco has never met the standard to become a licensed outlet and lack of training was one of the main reasons. Tesco replied, 'It's not rocket science to sell jeans ... we don't think giving five minutes extra training than our staff get justifies an extra £20 on the price and neither do our customers.'

The ECJ ruled in Levi's favour, but winning the legal battle was something of a shallow victory. The ruling confirmed that sourcing from cheaper locations within the EU is still permissible. Tesco had succeeded in portraying the supermarkets as the consumer's champion in the battle against greedy brand-owners. The case highlighted the broad trend in mass-market retailing, in which the supermarkets are targeting a wider range of non-food products, including branded goods, which they are selling at much lower prices than traditional retail outlets such as department stores. Targeted areas have included perfumes, sunglasses, watches and jewellery. Brand-owners are having to adjust to the shifting retail landscape. In a shift in strategy in 2003, Levi launched a bargain jeans brand, to be sold in mass-market channels, namely super-markets, beginning with Wal-Mart. A retailing specialist at Asda (the UK supermarket chain owned by Wal-Mart) was sceptical. He said of Asda customers: 'They do not want a value version. They want the right version at the right price' (Voyle, 1 May 2003).

Sources: Hargreaves, D., 'Showdown in the supermarket', *Financial Times*, 22 January 2001; Hargreaves, D., 'Levi puts case for "special" sales skills', *Financial Times*, 16 January 2001; Eaglesham, J., Voyle, S. and Hargreaves, D., 'European Court leans to Levi over cheap imports', *Financial Times*, 6 April 2001; Voyle, S., 'Levi's leaps into mass mar-ket', *Financial Times*, 1 May 2003.

Case questions

What is the essential issue of the Tesco/Levi case?

What are the wider implications for retailers of branded goods?

WEB ALERT!

Tesco's website is http://www.tesco.com

Levi Strauss's website is http://www.levistrauss.com

The website of the International Trademark Association is http://www.inta.org. It offers various relevant topics, including 'parallel imports', to click on

International business transactions

Laws covering trade between businesses in different countries have existed since the medieval period, when the *law merchant* came into being – the customary rules used by the merchants of the period. These rules, relating to the sale of goods and the settlement of disputes, were gradually incorporated into national bodies of law, codified in the case of civil law countries, and part of common law in common law countries. In England, the law became enacted in the Sale of Goods Act 1894, and in the US the Uniform Commercial Code (1951) harmonized the law between the 50 states. Impetus to achieve international harmonization has come from a number of initiatives.

International codification

Set up in 1966, the UN Commission on International Trade Law (UNCITRAL) attempted to devise a framework to satisfy the needs of businesses from trading nations of all continents. The result was the Convention on Contracts for the International Sale of Goods (CISG) of 1980 (the Vienna Convention), which came into force in 1988. The CISG does not apply automatically to international sales. The convention must be ratified by individual states, becoming incorporated in their domestic law. The number of countries which have ratified the convention (65 by August 2005) continues to rise, and they now account for two-thirds of the world's trade. Among major trading nations, the US, Germany, France and China have ratified, but neither the UK nor Japan has done so. The convention applies to contracts falling within its scope which are concluded by firms in countries which have ratified, or to contracts whose performance is carried out in a country which has ratified. For transactions between firms in non-ratifying countries, the rules of private international law apply (these are discussed below).

The CISG makes a major contribution in harmonizing the rules concerning the formation of contracts for the sale of goods, the obligations of the parties and remedies. It attempts to bridge the gap between civil and common law jurisdictions on questions such as the 'meeting of minds' between the parties over the existence of an agreement and its particular terms. These are the key areas in which disputes arise, and the CISG attempts to compromise between countries which require certainty and those which allow greater flexibility. For example, the requirement that a contract must be in writing is traditional in common law countries (although of diminishing importance), whereas civil law countries tend to have no writing requirement. The CISG allows ratifying countries the option, in keeping with their own national law. China, for example, has preserved its writing requirement.

WEB ALERT!

The UN's main international law website is http://www.un.org/law/

The UNCITRAL home page is http://www.uncitral.org

Texts of the conventions can be found at
http://www.uncitral.org/english/texts/sales/index.htm

The UNIDROIT principles are available in full at
http://www.cisg.law.pace.edu/cisg/principles.html

The International Institute for the Unification of Private International Law (UNIDROIT) has complemented the CISG, and approached the need for unification from a different perspective. The UNIDROIT *Principles of International Commercial Contracts*, published in 1994, offer general rules for international contracts, and are broadly similar to the CISG, but of wider application. The Principles are not confined to the sale of goods. Moreover, as they are not embodied in any binding international convention, they can be incorporated into contracts by firms from any country, not just those that have ratified the CISG. It has been suggested that they come closest to 'the emerging international consensus' on the rules of international trade (Moens and Gillies, 1998, p. 81). Because the Principles do not themselves have any force of law, they can be adopted and modified as needed, and have even provided models for legislators as diverse as Mexico, Quebec and the Netherlands. In particular, they have facilitated the growing trade between Australia and its Asian neighbours.

Cultural factors in international contracts

The negotiation of international contracts usually involves the use of a foreign language for at least one of the parties. Apart from problems of translating technical terms, the cultural context of negotiations varies considerably. High-context and low-context languages will have different styles of negotiation. Attention to detailed terms and confrontational bargaining are far more significant in the Anglo-American context than in Asian contexts, for example. The formally agreed contract may be in one language, with an unofficial translation in another, which clarifies the terms. Alternatively, the contract may have two official versions in two different languages. An inescapable difficulty is possible misunderstandings in the translation process. The CISG exists in six languages (Arabic, Chinese, English, French, Russian and Spanish), and unofficial translations into other languages must be made for negotiators who need them. The interpretation of terms, even between speakers of the same language, can differ from country to country. For example, the French word *droit* can mean either 'law' or 'right' in English, giving considerable scope for misunderstanding. Hence, it should be remembered that while the contract creates legal obligations, these are not necessarily interpreted in exactly the same way by all parties, and, in cases of dispute, an arbitrator or judge faces the unenviable task of finding out what the parties intended in a particular situation.

The role of the contract itself is viewed differently in different cultures. In individualistic cultures, the detailed formal contract governs business relationships, whereas in the more group-oriented societies, such as Japan and Southeast Asia, business relies more on informal, personalized relationships. **Relational contracting**, as the latter is known, is rooted in societies where personal ties built on trust, often over a number of years, matter more than formal written documents. In these societies, the preferred method of settling disputes is out of court, rather than through litigation. In more individualist societies, **arm's length contracting** (in which the agreement is paramount) is more the norm. With the growing numbers of joint ventures and expanding markets across cultural boundaries, an understanding of cultural sensitivities is essential in cross-border contracts. While written contracts are now part of the modern legal systems that have been adopted in non-Western societies, the underlying cultural environment is still influential in their negotiation and interpretation. It goes without saying that a 'meeting of minds' over both the terms and the working relationship that flows from the agreement is good insurance against a breakdown which could lead to the courts.

Resolution of disputes in international business

Sooner or later, every international business becomes involved in a dispute with a foreign element. The exposure to legal risk is greater for international businesses than domestic ones, mainly because of multiple jurisdictions (see summary box on international business and legal risk). Disputes are likely to arise over contractual terms, licence agreements and in the area of tort, in which the firm either alleges wrongdoing or is the defendant in a negligence or product liability claim. The area of the law concerned is **private international law**, defined as the law applying to the private law between individuals and firms in more than one country. Also referred to as 'conflict of laws', private international law seeks to establish rules for deciding which national law to apply to a particular situation. The rules of private international law give guidance on three broad issues:

1 the choice of law governing transactions
2 the choice of forum, that is, the country in which a case should be heard
3 the enforcement of court judgments.

The harmonizing of private international law has been an important aim of international conventions. The Rome Convention on the Law Applicable to Contracts 1980 and the Brussels Convention on Jurisdiction and Enforcement of Judgments in Civil and Commercial Matters 1968 have both been incorporated into English law.

Both arbitration and litigation involve choice-of-law rules, depending on the type of dispute. We look at two types of dispute: contractual disputes and those involving negligence or product liability claims.

Contractual disputes

In the basic transaction of buying or selling goods, at least one of the contracting firms is likely to find its rights governed by foreign law, thereby adding to the legal risk in a number of ways. First there is the question of what contract law in the foreign jurisdiction actually stipulates. Then there is the possibility of having to go through the courts in that country to obtain redress. Finally, the firm may face problems of getting a judgment of the foreign court enforced in its own country.

Litigation is costly, time-consuming and may bring unwanted publicity if the case is a high-profile one. Added risks in international disputes are the distance, unfamiliarity of the law and unfamiliar legal cultural environment. While US business have become accustomed to a culture of litigation, the costs in damages can be astronomical, and the high cost of liability insurance is a consequence. In contract disputes, the incentives to find other means of dispute resolution are therefore strong. Practising lawyers, far from suggesting litigation in all cases, emphasize the benefits of 'alternative dispute resolution'. Alternatives to litigation are:

● *Settlement* by the parties 'out of court'
● *Mediation*, in which the parties agree to bring in a third party, who attempts to settle their differences

● *Arbitration*, the submission of the dispute to a named person or organization in accordance with the agreement. Arbitration is not a cheap alternative and can be lengthy, but is, nevertheless, usually thought to be preferable to litigation. It has become popular in licensing disputes and international construction contracts.

Contracts between firms based in different countries may specify a 'choice of law' to govern their contract. This choice will also normally govern the forum in which any disputes will be heard. Most countries recognize choice-of-law clauses. For EU member states, the Rome Convention provides that if the parties have not made a clear choice of law, then the contract is governed by the law of the country with which it is most closely connected. In practice, this is likely to be the law of the party who is to carry out performance of the contract. The Brussels Convention provides that jurisdiction depends on whether the defendant is 'domiciled' in the EU (which, for a firm, means that it must have a 'seat' of business there). In employment contracts, the employee can sue where he/she carries out his/her duties. In consumer contracts, the Brussels Convention (now an EU regulation) gives the consumer the right to sue in local courts. This regulation will have profound implications for online traders, who may be liable to be sued in the national courts of any EU member state where their business activities are directed. For enforcement of judgments, most states will recognize the judgment of a foreign court if the foreign law and procedure are broadly compatible with their own. Within the EU, this recognition is automatic, as it is between states within the CISG.

Whereas the Brussels and Rome Conventions envisaged international contracts to be almost all business-to-business, the growth in e-commerce has greatly expanded the numbers of consumer deals across national borders. An online trader, even an SME, may sell goods to consumers in many states from one website. A survey in 2000 found that over 50 per cent of European online traders are accessed in ten or more countries (Landwell, 2000). The online trader thus needs to be familiar with the relevant national law, such as the consumer's right to cancel. Moreover, the online trader may be liable to be sued in the courts of all the states in which its website is accessed. In 2000, an EU directive on electronic commerce recognized the need for a uniform legal framework across Europe, balancing the desire to encourage e-commerce with the need for protection of consumers. Part of the solution is to provide alternative ways of solving disputes. In the US, Dell Computers has been selling its products online since 1996, and now sells to consumers in 85 different countries. The company has devised a system whereby, in cases of complaint, the consumer has redress from a local office.

International business and legal risk

International businesses may be exposed to legal risk in a number of ways:

● Contractual risks in overseas markets: for example in France and Portugal consumer contracts must be in local language to be legally binding

● Protection of intellectual property: trademarks require registration both at home and in other countries where customers are located; copyright materials, such as software, also require protection; lax enforcement is a problem in many countries

● Risk of liability for injuries or defective products and subsequent litigation in foreign jurisdiction

● Risk of infringement of data protection requirements, designed for protection and security of personal data

● Risk of dealings with local officials, especially where local regulations are complex and the possibility of corruption arises; a firm could incur criminal liability under home-country laws (for example, the US Foreign Corrupt Practices Act).

CRITICAL PERSPECTIVES

What are investing firms looking for in the legal environment of a host country?

Firms do not make decisions based on the formal content of laws, regulations, or policy statements alone. Because investment decisions are forward looking, firms need to assess the likelihood of those policies actually being implemented and sustained over the life of their proposed investment. Addressing firms' concerns about uncertainty, and building policy credibility, are fundamental to creating a better investment climate. (World Bank, 2004, p. 45)

■ This passage addresses improvements in the investment climate in developing countries. What specific aspects of the legal environment, in addition to the content of the laws, will influence firms' decision-making?

Negligence and product liability

While obligations under contracts are defined by the particular agreement, obligations in tort arise from a range of broadly defined obligations owed by those in society to fellow citizens generally. The plaintiff may suffer personal injury or damage to property in an accident caused by the activities of the defendant. If the plaintiff's reputation has been damaged by something the defendant has said publicly, the claim is in libel. There are many different areas of tort law, but the areas which are of greatest relevance to business are negligence and product liability. In a negligence claim, the defendant is alleged to have failed to take reasonable care and so caused the plaintiff's injuries or loss. Product liability claims impose a duty which is much nearer to 'strict' liability, in which the defendant (usually the producer) is made liable for defective products that cause harm to consumers. The development of tort law in these areas parallels the growth of modern consumer society. Factory-produced goods, mass transport, advanced pharmaceutical products and medical procedures and industrialized food production have all carried risks of accidents and injury, sometimes on a wide scale. All industrialized countries have in place laws protecting consumers and other victims in these cases. In the EU, product liability laws have been harmonized by a directive in 1985, which has been incorporated into national law (in the UK, by the Consumer Protection Act 1987). The directive, which includes a 'development risks defence', providing an escape route for producers who have achieved an industry standard level of product testing, is perceived to be less consumer-friendly than US law.

In the US, tort litigation, particularly product liability, has developed into a booming industry. While product liability laws vary from state to state, the legal climate has facilitated litigation in three key ways: (1) the use of the **class action**, whereby a group of plaintiffs may come together to bring legal proceedings; (2) the award by courts of 'punitive' damages (intended to punish the defendant for the wrongdoing) to plaintiffs, in addition to compensatory damages. Huge sums have been awarded by American juries as punitive damages (although often reduced on appeal, it should be added; punitive damages are also capped in some states); and (3) the 'contingency' fee system for lawyers' fees, also known as the 'no-win-no-fee' system, whereby the legal fees are an agreed percentage of the damages. With this prior arrangement, the potential plaintiff without huge resources can still bring a claim. In a Florida case, three sick smokers brought a class action on behalf of 500,000 Florida smokers. At the end of the two-year trial in 2000, they were awarded $12.7m. in compensatory damages and $144.8bn. in punitive damages against the five major tobacco companies.

Total tort costs in any jurisdiction include compensation, insurance, lawyers' fees and administrative costs. The cost of the US tort system is nearly twice as high as a percentage of GDP as the average of other industrialized countries (see Figure 9.4).

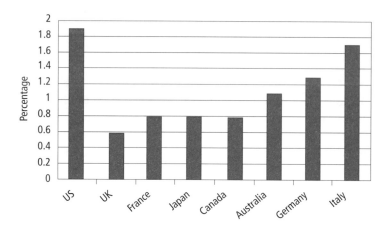

Figure 9.4 **Cost of the tort system as percentage of GDP**
Source: Institute of Actuaries (2002) 'The cost of compensation culture: Working Party Report', at http://www.actuaries.org.uk.

Clearly, the successful plaintiff in a negligence or product liability claim in the US stands to gain greater damages than his or her equivalent in most other countries. One of the largest groups of claimants has been workers who have suffered from asbestos. These workers are located all over the world, as the case study below shows. Plaintiffs, like all consumers of services, shop around, and 'forum shopping' is a continuing issue in the international legal environment. The rules of private international law provide guidelines on where claims in tort should be brought (choice of forum), which hinge on where the damage suffered by the plaintiff took place. In Bhopal, India, in 1984, a chemical disaster resulted in the deaths of 2000–4000 people, and injuries to several hundred thousand others. The victims attempted to sue Union Carbide, the parent company, in New York, arguing that negligence in the design of the plant caused the accident, in which a massive escape of poisonous gases occurred. Their claim failed, as much of the design and engineering that went into the plant was carried out by local engineers in India. The plaintiffs then sought damages in India. Undeterred, foreign plaintiffs from poorer countries have continued to press claims against defendant corporations in richer countries. The Bhopal case is highlighted in the minifile, along with other examples of TNCs which have been criticized. (The overlap between legal and ethical responsibilities is considered further in Chapter 14.)

In the US courts, a recent development has been an upsurge in claims from plaintiffs abroad who allege that their injuries from pollution accidents and sweatshop conditions fall within international human rights law, allowing them to establish jurisdiction in the US. Indians in Ecuador have sued Texaco in a federal court in New York, for the alleged dumping of crude oil in the Ecuadorian jungle. In a decision in 2004, the US Supreme Court narrowed the categories of case that can be heard in the US from these non-US plaintiffs to specific laws with definite content rather than to broad human rights claims.

Minifile

GLOBAL COMPANIES UNDER FIRE

1984: Union Carbide
Escape of poisonous gases from pesticide plant in Bhopal, India killed 2000–4000 people

1989: Exxon
The *Exxon Valdez*, supertanker, spilt 10 million gallons of crude oil into William Sound, Alaska

1995: Shell
Campaigners criticized Shell for failing to influence the Nigerian government over the execution of dissidents

1997: McDonald's
The company won a long libel case against two UK anti-globalization campaigners, who accused it of destroying rainforests, but McDonald's attracted considerable adverse publicity in the process

1997: Nike
Protests against Nike in 50 US cities and 11 countries for sweatshop conditions in factories in Asia

WEB ALERT!

Background and later developments following the Bhopal tragedy can be accessed on the internet. Two dedicated websites are:
http://www.bhopal.net
http://www.bhopal.org

Case study 9.3   Asbestos: liability goes global

Asbestos was the name given to a fire-retardant mineral widely used in industry and construction for much of the twentieth century. Over the years, however, it was gradually discovered that the tiny fibres of asbestos cause long-term illness, mainly lung diseases, including cancer. Illnesses can be very slow in developing, as long as 40 years. Workers who have been exposed to asbestos have been seeking compensation from employers and former employers for many years, in what has become a torrent of claims. The possible extent of asbestos litigation is staggering. It was estimated in 2001, that in the US alone, as many as 100 million people were exposed to asbestos in the twentieth century. Claims for compensation could amount to $200bn. Moreover, because of the large numbers of potential plaintiffs, effects have been felt by an increasingly wide range of corporations, some of which were only indirectly involved in asbestos.

Johns-Mandeville, the largest US asbestos producer, went bankrupt under the weight of claims in 1982, after which a trust fund was set up for future claimants. The trust is still deluged with claims, 101,000 in 2003, and is able to pay as little as 5 cents for every dollar of compensation awarded by the courts. The number of bankruptcies has risen – there were nine in 2001 and eight in 2002. Encouraged by entrepreneurial lawyers, claimants have turned to other possible defendants who are solvent, even though they were not producers. These include car manufacturers, who used asbestos in brake linings. Ford had 41,500 cases filed against it in 2003, up from 25,000 in 2002. Defending these cases is expensive and potentially the company's finances could be affected, whether or not plaintiffs are successful. In fact, most of the claims now being filed are from plaintiffs who are not actually sick, but who fear that exposure to asbestos in the past will cause future illness.

For non-US asbestos-related claims, the situation has been bleak. Turner & Newell (T&N), the largest UK asbestos manufacturer, was taken over by Federal Mogul, a US company, shortly before hundreds of British sufferers from asbestos-related cancer were awarded compensation. Sums awarded in the English courts were small compared to those awarded in the US. However, weighed down by the weight of US claims, Federal Mogul filed for bankruptcy. The plaintiffs then turned on T&N's insurers, who claimed that the particular insurance policy had not covered asbestos-related liabilities.

Companies have tried to settle these large class action cases once and for all, taking in future liabilities. However, this has required advertising widely to alert potential claimants in the class that the move was being undertaken. The effect of the publicity has been to attract even more claimants. Despite the fact that many of these people are not sick, the long latency period, of perhaps up to 40 years from first exposure, means that many more people will become ill and die from asbestos-related diseases. Experts believe that since the use of the mineral peaked in 1973, perhaps half a million people will die from such exposure over the next 35 years. One has said: 'The bankruptcies and lost jobs from asbestos far outweigh the effects of Enron or WorldCom, but it's happening very slowly and it's difficult to get people's attention.'

Sources: Mackintosh, J., 'Asbestos suits against Ford rise by 16,500', *Financial Times*, 25 March 2004; Bowe, C. and Roberts, D., 'Asbestos lawsuits "affect 85% of the US economy"', *Financial Times*, 10 September 2002; Roberts, D., 'The toxic time-bomb exploding throughout the corporate world', *Financial Times*, 9 September 2002.

Case questions

What are the advantages of class action lawsuits from the point of view of plaintiffs and defendants?

In what ways have claims for asbestos-related diseases caused strains in both the legal and corporate worlds?

When a consumer suffers harm as a result of a product defect, a manufacturing company can find itself on the end of product liability claims, where the damage may be multiplied in relation to the number of consumers. The large corporation which manufactures for global markets may face claims from millions of consumers worldwide, as Case study 9.4 shows. The product recall is a means of limiting the damage and is effective in some cases, such as the Tylenol case, in which contamination of painkilling tablets resulted in the deaths of eight people and the removal of the product from retailers' shelves. The recall in the Firestone case has been on a much larger scale.

Case study 9.4 Firestone recalls 6.5 million tyres

Firestone, the US tyre company taken over by Bridgestone of Japan in 1997, announced to US consumers in August, 2000, that it would replace free of charge about 6.5 million tyres, most of them fitted on Ford Explorers, a sports utility vehicle (SUV). The product recall announcement was the culmination of investigations that are continuing into injuries and an estimated 148 deaths that have been linked with the tyres since the late 1990s. At least 100 lawsuits were filed against Firestone, and two national class action lawsuits, in Texas and Florida, were filed. One of the class actions claimed $50bn. in damages. In one individual case, a child was killed in Florida when the tyre on her mother's Ford Explorer blew out and the vehicle flipped over two and a half times. (SUVs require more reliable tyres than cars, because they are more likely to roll over when they lose a tyre.) It appears that the tyres were inclined to split in hot weather, and the majority of the lawsuits were in southern states. Bridgestone recalled the same tyre in a number of overseas markets in 1999, including the Middle East, Thailand, Malaysia, Venezuela and Columbia, apparently confirming the tyre's weakness in hot climates.

If Firestone and Ford knew of the problems and did nothing, they could face criminal as well as civil legal action. In Venezuela, where there is very little legal scope for consumers to launch civil actions for compensation, government authorities threatened prosecution in 2000, insisting that Bridgestone and Ford shared responsibility. Ford maintained that it did not know of safety problems with the tyres until they managed to extract the information from Firestone. For Firestone, these problems were not new. It had been forced into a large recall in 1978, having denied for over a year that there was a problem. When it was finally compelled to hand over documents, they showed that the company had known about the problems of the Firestone 500 tyre for years and covered them up.

The recent tyre crisis has been more damaging for Firestone than for Ford. In addition to the massive tyre replacement programme, it has faced growing litigation expenses and had to restructure the company, closing its factory in Decatur, Illinois. Civil suits against both Firestone and Ford have come from plaintiffs who made personal injury claims and also many others who claimed economic damage only, for example alleging that the failure risks have lessened the resale value of their cars. This latter group of plaintiffs were granted class action status, but this decision was overturned by a federal appeal court. While this decision seemed to be a victory for the defendant companies, they might have little cause for relief, as they will now face large numbers of individual lawsuits, which could go on for years.

Sources: Bradsher, K., 'Documents portray tire debacle as a story of lost opportunities, *New York Times*, 11 September 2000; Rohter, L., 'Bridgestone agrees to recall 62 000 tires in Venezuela', *New York Times*, 5 September 2000; Grimaldi, J., 'Tiremaker moves to settle suits', *Washington Post*, 10 August 2000; Valkin, V., 'Court overturns Ford/Firestone class-action', *Financial Times*, 3 May 2002.

Case questions

What are the lessons which should be learnt from the case?

Should the companies involved have handled the situation differently, once the faults emerged?

Crime, corruption and the law

A body of criminal law forms an important part of every national legal system. However, societies differ markedly on which activities are designated as crimes and crime prevention and enforcement vary from society to society. Moreover, attitudes towards corruption also differ among countries. What is seen as criminal dealing in one society may be accepted as normal in another. For international businesses, the robustness of criminal law enforcement and the society's attitudes towards corruption are aspects of the location which form part of its legal risk. Corruption can adversely affect the investment climate in a country and, when it involves high-ranking government officials, it can undermine the government's overall credibility (World Bank, 2004). Foreign direct investors seeking a stake in the privatization projects of transition economies may find themselves in a grey area, required to make payments to officials which seem to be of doubtful legality, but in cultures where a certain level of corruption is tolerated. The World Bank's investment climate survey has found that the majority of firms in developing countries expect to pay bribes, but there are variations between regions and between sectors. Regional variations are shown in Figure 9.5.

Figure 9.5 **Firms reporting bribes: regional variations**
Source: World Bank (2004) *World Development Report 2005* (Washington, DC: World Bank).

Criminal activities, such as smuggling, trafficking in goods and people and 'money laundering' of illicit gains, are all areas of considerable business involvement, which generate huge sums of money. Globalization, while it has opened up enormous opportunities for good, has also provided unprecedented scope for transnational crime, which national authorities struggle to contain and prosecute. The illegal drug trade is estimated to be worth $400bn. per year, amounting to 8 per cent in value of world trade – greater than that in motor vehicles. The UN agency for crime prevention estimates that well-organized criminal organizations with trafficking infrastructure in place can shift any product line at will – from human beings or body parts to cultural artefacts to nuclear products (UN Office for Drug Control and Crime Prevention, 1999). Criminal justice systems, by contrast, are national in scope, and, although they coordinate their crime detection efforts, the differing systems and differing laws make it difficult to control transnational crime.

Also lucrative is the **grey market** of business activity, which handles a variety of goods and services through informal channels, outside national regulatory systems. The 'black' economy is the market in goods which are being bought and sold illegally. An example is the trade in products that are much in demand, such as alcohol and cigarettes, which, when traded illegally, avoid payments of customs duties. Other products traded include pirated goods such as software, CDs and DVDs, counterfeit designer goods and counterfeit pharmaceutical products, all of which find buyers eager to avoid the higher prices charged through legitimate markets. A breakdown of counterfeit goods seized in the EU in 2003 appears in Figure 9.6. The two largest categories are cigarettes and CDs and DVDs, which includes other audio products such as games and software. Among 'other goods' are food, alcoholic and other drinks, and computer equipment. While most would agree that illegitimate trade harms legitimate businesses as well as consumers, efforts to control such trade have encountered difficulties in an environment where there seems to be considerable consumer demand, coupled with cross-border supply networks.

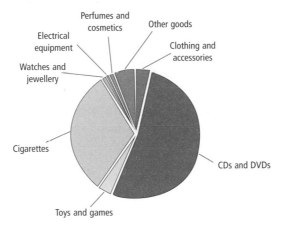

Figure 9.6 **Breakdown of counterfeit goods seized in the EU, 2003 (total seized = 50,314,886 articles)**

Source: European Taxation and Customs Union (2003) 'Counterfeiting and piracy: Statistics recorded at the external borders of the EU', at http://europa.eu.int/comm./taxation_customs.

The growing impact of international law on business

International law covers the body of rules recognized by the international community as governing relations between sovereign states. It is also referred to as public international law, to distinguish it from the rules of private international law discussed above. The world's sovereign states, while recognizing international law, have not (as yet) created a supranational legal system with enforcement mechanisms mirroring those at national level. The functions of law-making and dispute settlement, therefore, rely on the cooperation of states and the willingness of state authorities to submit to international law as a matter of obligation. Since the Second World War there has been an accelerated growth in international law, which has coincided with the processes of globalization described in Chapter 5. While states are still inclined to see national interest as paramount, they increasingly recognize that, in the long run, state interests are interdependent. The growth in international law has been largely due to a growing awareness of the following:

● The need to protect the global environment (see Chapter 13)
● Global security and the need to control nuclear and other weapons
● Human rights as transcending national law.

Treaties and conventions

Most international law comes about through treaties and conventions, and most are the result of initiatives by UN-affiliated bodies. Treaties may be multilateral, involving many countries, or bilateral, between two countries. An extradition treaty is an example of a bilateral treaty, requiring states to cooperate on the handing over of persons accused of crimes. Major multilateral treaties may take years in the drafting stages and do not become law until ratified by a given number of individual states specified in the treaty itself (see Chapter 13 for a detailed discussion of this process in relation to the Kyoto Protocol on climate change). There is no cutoff date – additional states may ratify indefinitely. However, even when a state does ratify, there is no guarantee that it will abide by treaty obligations, especially if national interest seems to conflict. It is in these circumstances that the effectiveness of international law is tested. International public opinion, encouraged by the many NGOs, plays an important role in putting pressure on governments. The UN can impose sanctions on individual states which are in serious breach of international law. Sanctions against Iraq for its failure to cooperate with UN weapons inspectors are an example. Alleged breaches of international law can also be subject to judicial proceedings in a variety of legal settings, considered in the next section.

Settlement of disputes in international law

Despite the fact that there is no overarching international legal system equivalent to a national one, judicial means are available for settling disputes in international law. First, national courts interpret and apply international law, thereby acknowledging its binding force. In Belgium in 2001, four Rwandans were found guilty and given lengthy prison sentences for war crimes in Rwanda. This landmark trial was the first ordinary jury trial for crimes committed in another country. Other countries could follow suit, including France, Germany and Switzerland, which all allow ordinary courts to try war crimes. Secondly, the International Court of Justice (ICJ), which sits in The Hague, in the Netherlands, hears a limited range of international cases. The ICJ is a UN body, whose authority derives from its governing Statute, attached to the UN Charter. While the ICJ's prestige is acknowledged, its effectiveness is limited by the restrictions to its jurisdiction. The major one is that it hears only disputes between sovereign states. A non-state organization cannot apply to it, although cases can involve activities of individuals and companies. Examples are the cases involving the handing over for trial of two Libyans accused of planting the bomb which caused the explosion over Lockerbie, Scotland of a Pan American jet in 1988, in which 270 people lost their lives. An agreement was reached under the auspices of the UN for the accused to be tried in a Scottish court sitting in the Netherlands in 2000, at which one was acquitted and the other found guilty of the bombing.

WEB ALERT!

The home page of the International Court of Justice is http://www.icj-cit.org/
Informative documents about the ICJ can be found at
http://www.icj-cij.org/icjwww/ibasicdocuments.htm

Thirdly, other international tribunals have been set up in the area of criminal law. Beginning with the Nuremberg trials after the Second World War, those who are alleged to have committed war crimes and genocide have been subject to international criminal proceedings. In the 1990s the ICJ set up an International Criminal Tribunals for Rwanda and Yugoslavia. Beyond these special tribunals, considerable international effort has gone into establishing a permanent international criminal court to hear cases of crimes against humanity, from any country. A UN Conference meeting in Rome in 1998, in which 120 nations participated, agreed a convention, the Rome Statute of the International Criminal Court. The treaty has now been signed by 139 countries and ratified by 97. The treaty came into force in 2002, on the ratification of the 60th country, and the court itself is now set up in The Hague in the Netherlands. The International Criminal Court (ICC) is complementary to national courts, which have the first opportunity to investigate and prosecute crimes such as genocide, crimes against humanity and war crimes. Although the treaty was signed by the US under former President Clinton in 2000, President Bush renounced the treaty, and the US has taken steps to secure guarantees from governments that would exempt US citizens. Governments which are party to the ICC and do not reach such immunity agreements risk losing US aid funding (*Washington Post*, 26 November 2004).

Fourthly, there is the dispute settlement procedure established by the WTO for member states, in its capacity to oversee world trade. This process will be examined in Chapter 10.

Human rights

Human rights may be defined as basic, universal rights of life which transcend social and cultural differences. The first general enunciation of human rights came in the Universal Declaration of Human Rights, adopted by the UN General Assembly in 1948. It did not have the legal authority of a convention or treaty, but it did give expression to a consensus on fundamental freedoms, including social, cultural, political and economic rights. These took more concrete form with the adoption of two conventions in the 1960s: the International Covenant on Civil and Political Rights and the International Covenant on Economic, Social and Cultural Rights. These conventions take a broad view of the content of human rights, stretching the concept from principles such as freedom from slavery and torture to the right to vote for governments and bargain collectively in the workplace. A majority of the world's states have ratified both covenants, committing themselves to implementation. However, subscribing to these goals in principle does not readily translate into practice, especially for developing countries, where economic development has often taken precedence over human rights issues. For example, child labour is tolerated in many developing countries and large TNCs which have affiliated manufacturers in these countries have been criticized for failing to take a stronger stand against the practice.

Other conventions cover specific areas of human rights. These include:

- Convention on the Elimination of All Forms of Racial Discrimination, 1966
- Convention on the Rights of the Child, 1989
- Convention on the Elimination of Discrimination against Women, 1979
- Convention against Torture and Other Cruel, Inhuman or Degrading Treatment or Punishment, 1984
- Convention Relating to the Status of Refugees, 1951.

SUMMARY POINTS

The International Covenant on Civil and Political Rights

- Right to life.
- Right not to be held in slavery.
- Right against arbitrary arrest or detention.
- Freedom of movement and freedom to choose place of residence.
- Freedom of thought, conscience and religion.
- Right of peaceful assembly.

(Can be accessed in full at http://www.unhcr.ch/html/menu3/b/a_cpr.htm)

The International Covenant on Economic, Social and Cultural Rights

- Right to just and favourable conditions of work.
- Right to fair wages and a decent living.
- Right to join trade unions.
- Right to medical attention in the event of sickness.
- Right to free primary education.
- Right to take part in cultural life.

(Can be accessed in full at http://www.unhcr.ch/html/menu3/b/a_cescr.htm)

WEB ALERT!

The Universal Declaration of Human Rights is at
http://www.un.org/Overview/rights.html

The Convention on the Rights of the Child is at
http://www.unicef.org/crc/convention.htm

The website of the UN High Commissioner for Human Rights is at
http://www.unhchr.ch/

The Charter of Fundamental Rights of the European Union is at
http://www.europarl.eu.int/charter/en/default.htm

In the increasing global awareness of human rights issues, one trend has been to place responsibility on companies to answer for their practices and policies, irrespective of the national laws in host countries (see minifile). What standards should the company apply? While it was once thought that local standards suffice, this view is no longer considered to be tenable. Companies are now expected to maintain consistent standards and policies across their operations, whatever the location. Both legal and ethical issues are involved. As we have seen, companies can be sued in their home countries for alleged wrongdoings in foreign operations. Importantly, too, companies are now perceived as having a duty of social responsibility to the local communities in which they are located. The strategy implications for companies are examined further in Chapter 14.

The European Convention on Human Rights (ECHR) was produced by the Council of Europe in 1950. Its permanent legacy was the establishment of the European Court of Human Rights (in Strasbourg), which hears cases of alleged breaches of its provisions brought by individuals in member states. The rights defined in it are similar to those in the Covenant of Civil and Political Rights. The UK government, while not a party to the convention, has recognized decisions of the Strasbourg court brought by UK citizens and has now incorporated the convention into UK legislation, in the Human Rights Act 1998, which took effect in October, 2000. The new statute has far-reaching implications, giving the right to sue public bodies for breaches and stating that courts and tribunals are obliged to interpret all legislation, past and future alike, in light of the convention. In addition, the EU has stepped into the human rights arena with the Charter of Fundamental Rights of the European Union enshrining 50 basic rights. This document would seem to overlap with the ECHR, and confusion could arise over whether grievances should go to national courts, the European Court of Human Rights, or the EU's European Court of Justice. The new charter has become incorporated into the EU Constitutional Treaty.

WEB ALERT!

The website of the Charter of Fundamental Rights of the EU is
http://europarl.eu.int/charter/default/en.htm

SUMMARY POINTS

The European Convention on Human Rights, now enacted in the Human Rights Act 1998

- Right to life.
- Prohibition of torture, slavery, and forced labour.
- Right to liberty and security.
- Right to a fair trial.
- No punishment without lawful authority.
- Right to respect for private and family life, home and correspondence.
- Freedom of thought, conscience and religion.
- Freedom of expression.
- Freedom of assembly and association.
- Right to marry.
- Right to an effective remedy.
- Prohibition of discrimination on any ground.

(The Act can be found at http://www.homeoffice.gov.uk/hract)

Minifile

IMPLICATIONS FOR BUSINESS OF THE HUMAN RIGHTS ACT 1998

- All public bodies, including any company or organization performing a public role, can be sued for breach of the convention. Hence privatized utilities could be sued for breach of the Act, for example by objectors claiming that proposed electricity pylons or airports interfered with home and family life.

- Tribunals such as employment tribunals must take account of the Act, so that in deciding whether a firm had acted fairly and reasonably with respect to an employee it had dismissed, the new right to privacy must be taken into account. Companies therefore need to review their policies on monitoring internet usage and surveillance of employee emails.

- Businesses, as well as humans, have rights under the Act. When they appear before numerous regulatory bodies such as the Financial Services Authority and the Takeover Panel, new, more stringent standards of a fair and impartial hearing and respect for property must be observed. This far-reaching provision would affect, for example, decisions to withdraw or refuse licences in many different contexts, from pharmaceutical products to bus routes.

CRITICAL PERSPECTIVES

Interlocking human rights

History shows that even without the full set of civil and political rights, rapid progress is possible in economic, social and cultural rights. But withholding civil and political rights in no way helps to achieve these rapid advances. Quite the reverse, for civil and political rights empower poor people to claim their economic and social rights – to food, to housing, to education, to decent work and to social security. (UN, 2000, pp. 85–6)

■   Which countries can be cited as having made economic progress while withholding civil and political rights? To what extent do you agree with the authors in seeing these rights as integral to economic development?

Conclusions

1   The legal environment of international business may be depicted as interacting spheres, consisting of national legal systems, regional authorities and international structures.

2   Most of the law affecting business transactions emanates from national legal authorities, but an increasing amount is international in scope, and, for EU member states, the product of EU law-making.

3   Civil law and common law legal traditions have been established all over the globe, in many cases existing alongside non-Western legal systems, such as Islamic and Chinese.

4   EU law-making increasingly penetrates the national legal systems of EU member states, taking precedence when there is a conflict between EU and national laws.

5   While commercial transactions across national borders are governed by national law, the harmonization of national laws through international convention and codification is moving forward apace, in recognition of the global interconnectedness of modern business.

6   Resolution of disputes in contract and tort can lead to lengthy (and costly) litigation. Out of court settlements, mediation and arbitration are alternatives to litigation.

7   Law-making and enforcement in the area of criminal law has increasingly encountered the globalization of criminal activity. Levels of corruption, which are higher in some countries than in others, can deter investors and create an uncertain legal environment.

8   International law focuses on relations between sovereign states, enshrined in treaties and conventions. Nonetheless, increasingly, individuals and organizations are being brought within their scope, in human rights and environmental law.

Review questions

1   What is meant by the interlocking spheres of national, regional and international law? Which is the most important in the business environment and why?

2   What are the differences between civil and criminal law?

3   What are the main functions of a national legal system?

4   How do codified legal systems differ from common law systems? What are the difficulties for a federal system such as the US?

5   What international conventions exist for the harmonization of national trade law?

6   Distinguish between arm's length contracting and relational contracting. What are the consequences for joint ventures across the two traditions?

7   What factors account for the global growth in negligence and product liability claims?

8   List the factors involved in 'legal risk' for an international business.

9   What is the impact of treaty activity in environmental law on business operations?

10 Name at least three examples of human rights law. How does the law on human rights impact on business?

Assignments

1   Looking at the specific areas of contract law and tort law, assess the ways in which the national legal system provides a workable framework for the regulation of business activities in two different national environments.

2   Human rights law is now enshrined in international, regional and national law. To what extent is it having an impact on the ways in which businesses operate in diverse national environments?

Further reading

Adams, A. (1999) *Law for Business Students*, 2nd edn (London: Longman).

Akdeniz, Y., Walker, C. and Wall, D. (eds) (2000) *The Internet, Law and Society* (London: Longman).

Harris, D. (2004) *Cases and Materials on International Law* (London: Sweet & Maxwell).

Keenan, D. and Riches, S. (1998) *Business Law*, 5th edn (London: Pitman).

Sands, P. (ed.) (2003) *From Nuremberg to The Hague: The Future of International Justice* (Cambridge: Cambridge University Press).

Schaffer, R., Earle, B. and Augusti, F. (1999) *International Business Law and its Environment*, 4th edn (Cincinnati: West Educational Publishing).

Steiner, H. and Alston, P. (eds) (2000) *International Human Rights in Context: Law, Politics, Morals*, 2nd edn (Oxford: Oxford University Press).

Wallace, R. (1997) *International Law*, 3rd edn (London: Sweet & Maxwell).

END OF PART 2 CASE STUDY

Fiat: Italian champion struggles to compete globally

In the eyes of the world, Fiat is seen as a national champion of Italy, its legendary patriarchal founder, Gianni Agnelli, a more well-known leader than most of Italy's postwar prime ministers. While Fiat as a brand represents above all Fiat Auto, the motor manufacturers, in its 100-year history, the company grew into a vast conglomerate covering a multitude of businesses. At its height, the motor industry businesses include the Iveco truck manufacturer, the CNH farm and construction machinery company, Magnetti Marelli car component manufacturer, FiatAvio aero-engine company and Ferrari sports cars. More expansionist forays were into insurance, energy and publishing. It is Fiat Auto, however, that defines the company's image. Its mounting difficulties from the late 1990s onwards caused anguish, not just among those associated with Fiat, but within the Italian government and general public. The very thought that this Italian icon might collapse under a pile of debt, to be taken over by a foreign owner, was turning painfully into a probability. How did it get into this perilous position and how could it claw its way back? Key to finding answers to these questions is the cultural and political environment of Italy, coupled with the external pressures of the EU and the globalization facing the car industry worldwide.

Fallen Icon

Like most Italian businesses, Fiat has been dominated by a family. The Agnelli family controls about 34 per cent of the ordinary shares, through two holding companies, Ifi and Ifil. Maintaining family control has been a priority, making it difficult for Fiat to enter alliances and joint ventures, common among its competitors. Fiat Auto has enjoyed a dominant share in the Italian market, helped in large measure by successive governments, which have protected its position. This is not to say that the company had been entirely cushioned from external pressures. It went through a difficult period in the 1970s, when its factories and managers became targets of extreme left-wing, Red Brigade terrorists, who caused widespread disruption, including the assassination of Aldo Moro, president of the Christian Democrat party, in 1978. The company was forced to restructure following the oil shocks of the 1970s. However, it was helped by government policies which held back the introduction of anti-pollution requirements, such as catalytic converters, which competitors elsewhere were compelled to install, giving the company a price advantage in the 1980s and early 1990s. The government also barred the import of Japanese cars into Italy until the mid-1990s, keeping at bay, in particular, the threat posed by Japanese small cars to Fiat's market share. Fiat had been slow to invest in quality improvements and other innovations, leaving it in a weak position in terms of quality guarantees when the market was finally opened to competition. A further aid for Fiat was the succession of currency devaluations which helped it to remain price-competitive. With the adoption of the euro in 1999, Italy could no longer devalue its currency, and by then global competitors were making inroads into the Italian market. Fiat's debts were rapidly accumulating. A deal was done with General Motors (GM) in 2000, by which GM would buy 20 per cent of the shares in the Auto division. In addition, Fiat had an option to sell the other 80 per cent of Fiat Auto to GM between 2004 and 2009.

Fiat's market share in Italy dropped from over half in 1990 to 28 per cent in 2002 (see Figure 1). With debts in the order of €6bn. and sales falling, Fiat was staring into the abyss, with operating losses of €1348m. in 2002 (see Figure 2). In the restructuring which followed, some 6000 jobs were lost and production was cut back at 18 plants. Some of the businesses were sold, including the insurance and aero-engines operations. In 2002, Fiat's car operations still employed 36,000 in Italy and a further 100,000 indirectly, and were estimated to account for about 1.5 per cent of the country's GDP. When Prime Minister Silvio Berlusconi was elected in 2001, he promised as much support as he could give to Fiat, while keeping within the EU's strict rules on state aid to industry. He described the crisis at Fiat as a 'national problem' (Betts, 2002).

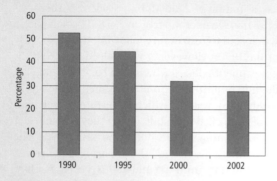

Figure 1 Fiat's market share in Italy
Source: Kapner, F., 'Trouble with Fiat', *Financial Times*, 4 March 2003.

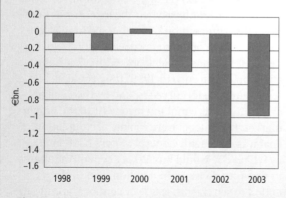

Figure 2 Fiat Auto's operating profit/losses
Source: Fiat S.p.A., Annual Report at 31 December 2003.

Mounting problems for the Italian government

Mr Berlusconi has been in office longer than any postwar Italian prime minister, navigating his centre-right coalition through a series of problems. He had promised a reinvigorated

economy, tax cuts and structural reforms, but has had troubles keeping his four-party coalition together and met public resistance to unpalatable reforms. He introduced some reform of Italy's rigid labour laws, providing for greater flexibility in labour markets. Unemployment remains high, at 9 per cent, and rising inflation, persistently above the EU average, is a worry. Tax cuts are not universally applauded, causing disagreement within the coalition and objections from the EU Commission. The EU Commission has advised him to raise taxes, mindful that the national debt stands at 106 per cent of GDP, the highest in the EU. Italy has one of the highest rates of early retirement in Europe and about 14 per cent of GDP is spent on pensions. The government aims to reduce the pension bill by 0.7 per cent by requiring many workers to work until they are 60, rather than 57, to qualify for a full state pension (those who have paid 40 years of contributions into the system could still retire at 57 with the full pension). This would take effect from 2008 onwards. Many observers, particularly within the EU, see this measure as too weak, but the government faced stiff resistance, including surviving a vote of confidence, in getting even this modest reform passed into law in 2004.

Berlusconi himself has been the subject of much criticism – criticisms which go to the heart of Italy's democracy. These criticisms focus, first, on his alleged criminal activities, which are still going through the courts. Judicial proceedings are pending against him for alleged crimes involving multiple business interests. Secondly, criticism focuses on his media empire, which constitutes a conflict of interest with his public office. As Italy's richest man, Berlusconi owns a media empire which includes the country's three main television channels, its largest publishing house and largest advertising agency. He is also accused of exerting pressure on RAI, the state-owned network. He has acknowledged that there is a possible conflict of interest between his media businesses and his public role and has proposed legislation on conflict of interests. However, critics argue that this measure is too weak, and, importantly, would not require him to divest any companies, but simply refrain from exploiting his privileged position. Why Italians would vote for a man who had been the target of a number of serious criminal investigations, and whose media domination would be considered intolerable in many democracies, is a question which exercises many inside and outside Italy (Lane, 2004). Lane argues that the concentration of media power makes it difficult for Italian voters to form informed judgments. The country has a history of power politics overlaying political institutions and close ties between business and politics which breed corruption. The collapse of the dairy empire, Parmalat, another family business, which hinged on large-scale false accounting, is indicative of weak corporate governance, facilitated by opaque ties between political and business players.

Fiat's recovery prospects

Parmalat's collapse sent a shiver through Italian businesses. They are facing the realities of global competition at a time when favours from the government are drying up. Generational changes have taken place at Fiat, with the deaths of both Gianni and Umberto Agnelli (in 2003 and 2004 respectively). The new chairman is Luca Cordero di Montezemolo, the chairman of Ferrari. Product development has been pushed up the agenda, along with quality improvements. Two new models have been introduced, and the management is focused on improving the brand image. Development of the new models of course added to the borrowings. The operations in developing markets are improving and good profits are being generated in Brazil. But restructuring and debt reduction are priorities. Improvement in shareholder value in 2004 indicated that the restructuring was producing results (see table).

Nonetheless, the prospect of takeover by GM still loomed on the horizon. For its part, GM was regretting its agreement to take over Fiat, as its market share at home was on the slide, and the takeover of the loss-making Italian car maker would constitute a further headache. By 2005,

both companies were looking for a way out of the deal, and the parties agreed that GM would pay Fiat €1.55bn. to terminate the takeover agreement and other aspects of the relationship. Some of their successful joint ventures would continue, but Fiat is now free to devise more deals with other car companies. The much-needed cash can be used by Fiat for restructuring and, as part of the deal, it retains the benefits of being part of GM's worldwide purchasing operations. What of the future role of the family? Following the deaths of its two elder members, new appointments to the board were soon made. They included grandsons of Gianni and Umberto Agnelli, both 28 – an indication that the family intends to keep its grip on the tiller.

Total shareholder return: comparisons of leading automakers, 2003–4

Company	Percentage change in total shareholder return, 2003–4
Fiat	23.4
DaimlerChrysler	41.0
Ford	46.8
Renault	49.4
Toyota	58.4
General Motors	35.6
Volkswagen	3.2

Source: Armstrong, J. (2004), 'Automakers' 2nd quarter is sound', *Automotive News*, 78(6103), p. 40.

Sources: Betts, P., 'Fiat's fate', *Financial Times*, 30 May 2002; Barber, T., 'Italy passes bill on pensions reform', *Financial Times*, 29 July 2004; Kapner, F. 'Champion that can't turn round', *Financial Times*, 22 July 2002; Kapner, F., 'Trouble with Fiat', *Financial Times*, 4 March 2003; Kapner, F., 'Leaning towards change: why Italy's companies must reform to prosper', *Financial Times*, 2 June 2004; Barber, T., 'Berlusconi's burden: Italy's economy languishes and reforms have stalled,' *Financial Times*, 25 May 2004; Armstrong, J., 'Automakers' 2nd quarter is sound', *Automotive News*, 78(6103); 'Whither Fiat after Umberto Agnelli?', *The Economist*, 5 June 2004; Fiat S.p.A., *Annual Report at December 31*, 2003; Lane, D. (2004) *Berlusconi's Shadow: Crime, Justice and the Pursuit of Power* (Harmonsworth: Penguin); Michaels, A. and Simon, B., 'GM pays Fiat €1.55bn to end legal disputes', *Financial Times*, 14 February 2005; Michaels, A. and Simon, B., 'Fiat and GM still face problems after deal', *Financial Times*, 14 February 2005.

End of Part 2 case questions

1 What factors caused Fiat's difficulties from the 1990s onwards?

2 In what ways have links with the Italian government helped or hindered Fiat?

3 Describe the tensions which exist in the Italian political environment.

4 What are the global pressures facing Fiat? How is it responding?

Part 3

Global Forces

10 World trade and the international competitive
    environment 313

11 Technology and innovation 349

12 International financial markets 386

End of Part 3 case study 416

In this part, attention turns to international forces which shape the competitive environment of businesses, whether they operate only in their domestic or regional markets or global markets. Chapter 10 takes an overview of the international competitive environment, focusing on trade. Recall the liberalization of national economies discussed in the context of national economic systems and foreign direct investment (Chapters 3, 4 and 5). Running parallel with these developments has been the evolution of the world trading system over the last half-century. While much of the focus has been on trade liberalization, national interests, and perceptions thereof, still play a crucial role in patterns of global and regional trade. Developments in specific regions will be highlighted, along with the perspectives of developing countries in world trade.

Two dimensions of the international environment which have been at the forefront of global change have been technology and financial markets. Innovation and the technological environment are the subject of Chapter 11. As will be seen, national innovation systems are closely linked with other dimensions of the national environment such as cultural values, political forces and legal frameworks. How companies can nurture innovation as a platform for competitive advantage in different sectors, and through coordination of activities globally, is a major challenge for international businesses. One of the sources of uncertainty is the international financial environment, which is the subject of Chapter 12. The chapter looks first at developments in national and global financial markets and the institutions which are in place to maintain stability and regulatory oversight. As will be seen in the case of major financial crises, there can be widespread ripple effects, and international institutions such as the IMF and World Bank have come under strain. The chapter focuses on the effects of financial uncertainty on business decision-making, looking at merger and acquisition (M&A) strategies. Takeovers and mergers are some of the most important strategic moves a company can make, as the case examples will show. The closing case study in Part 3, on General Electric (GE), provides a synthesis of the issues discussed in the three chapters. A large conglomerate, GE has continued to pursue a strategy of acquisitions across the globe, but it has strained to achieve innovative synergies in its diverse businesses. It has also been adversely affected by volatility in global financial markets.

10 World trade and the international competitive environment

Outline of chapter

- Introduction
- International trade theories
  - The theory of comparative advantage
  - Newer trade theories
  - Porter's theory of competitive advantage
  - Product life cycle theory
- Trade policy and national priorities
  - Promoting industrialization
  - Protecting employment
  - Protecting consumers
  - Promoting national interests
- Tools of governmental trade policy
- International regulation of trade
  - GATT principles
  - World Trade Organization (WTO) and the regulation of world trade
- Trade liberalization: the Doha Round
  - Labour standards and environmental protection
  - International competition policy
- Regionalism
  - The European Union (EU)
  - NAFTA
  - Regionalism in Asia
- Developing countries and world trade
- Globalization and the world trading system
- Conclusions

Learning objectives

1 To appreciate the contributions of international trade theories to an understanding of the ways in which companies, industries and nations compete in the global environment.

2 To understand the rationale and mechanisms of national trade policies.

3 To understand the evolution of the multilateral trading system, in terms of its structures, processes and issues to be resolved.

4 To assess the impact of regional integration on the business environment.

Introduction

Across the ages, businesses seeking markets have looked to trade beyond their home country. Growth in international trade has been a major contributor to the rise of the major industrialized countries, stretching back to the Industrial Revolution. Indeed, when we look at the flourishing trade between Asia and Europe as far back as the medieval era, we are tempted to think that globalization has been happening a long time. However, both the volume of trade and the patterns of trade between nations have changed greatly over the years. The postwar era has seen trade grow at a remarkable rate: between 1950 and 1998, the volume of world exports multiplied 18 times, while production went up 6.5 times. In the 1990s, trade grew on average 6.5 per cent annually, while output grew at 2.5 per cent annually. Three major trading regions, Europe, North America and Asia, account for over 80 per cent of global trade. From Figure 10.1, it can be seen that, from the late 1990s, Asia's share in global merchandise exports has gradually increased, whereas the North American share has slightly decreased and the Western European share has recovered from a dip in 2001, but not to the level of 1990.

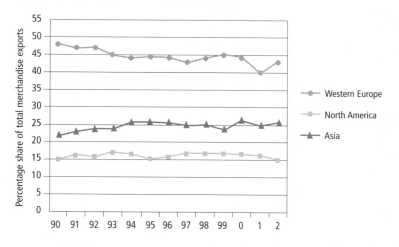

Figure 10.1 **Shares of merchandise exports of the major exporting regions (1990–2002)**
Source: WTO (2004) International Trade Statistics 2003, at www.wto.org.

China's expansion has been the outstanding feature from 2000 to 2002, as Figures 10.2(a) and (b) show. Between 2000 and 2002, both its exports and imports rose by 30 per cent and it is now the world's fourth largest trader if the EU is counted as a single trader. The combination of declining exports and rising imports by the US led to a record trade deficit. Expansion and deepening of trading relations, along with increased regional integration, have become important globalizing trends in the world economy.

This chapter looks first at why trade takes place, examining some of the theories which help to explain patterns of world trade. Second, it analyses the divergent views on the issues of free trade and protectionism. Finally, the chapter looks at the recent developments in the patterns of world trade, with the growth of regionalism and the changing role of the WTO. It should be borne in mind that world trade involves a number of different perspectives. There is the perspective of the individual business wishing to expand beyond its home market. Then, there are national governments focusing on national interests. Thirdly, there are the consumers, looking for a variety of goods and services, both domestic and imported. And consumers are themselves workers in industries which, in today's world, are more likely than ever to be engaged in exporting. In an ideal world, all would benefit and none would lose out in the trading environment. In reality, however, the issues have become complex and even contentious, drawing political, social and ethical issues into the global competitive environment.

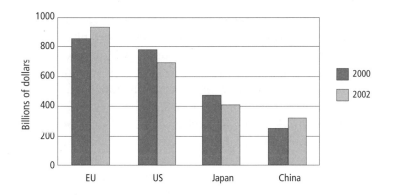

Figure 10.2a **World merchandise trade: leading exporters (excluding intra-EU trade)**

Source: WTO (2004) *World Trade Developments 2002* at http://www.wto.org.

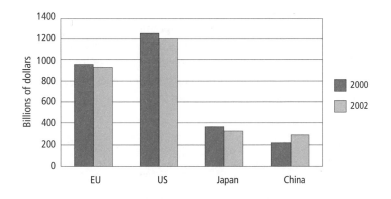

Figure 10.2b **World merchandise trade: leading importers (excluding intra-EU trade)**

Source: WTO (2004) *World Trade Developments 2002* at http://www.wto.org.

International trade theories

The first major theorist of international trade was Adam Smith, who believed that all countries benefit from unrestricted trade. Free trade is said to exist where citizens can sell abroad (export) and buy from abroad (import) without restrictions, or barriers, by governments of either the exporting or importing country. In his book, *The Wealth of Nations* (published in 1776), Smith argued in favour of the 'the invisible hand' of market forces, as opposed to government intervention. When countries produce the products in which they are the most efficient producers, they are said to have an 'absolute advantage' in these products. A country may then sell these goods overseas, and purchase from overseas goods which are produced more efficiently elsewhere. Thus, both countries benefit from trade.

The theory of comparative advantage

Starting from the principle of absolute advantage, David Ricardo ([1817]1973), writing some 40 years after Adam Smith, developed his theory of comparative advantage. His theory contends that, if Country A is an efficient producer of wheat and Country B an efficient producer of clocks, it pays A to purchase clocks from B, even if it could itself produce clocks more efficiently than B. According to Ricardo, if countries specialize in the industries in which they have comparative advantage, all will benefit from trade with each other, consumers in both countries enjoying more wheat and more clocks than they would without trade. According to Ricardo's theory, therefore, trade is not a 'zero-sum' game, that is, where one side's gain is the other's loss, but a 'positive-sum' game, that is, one in which all parties benefit.

In reality, most countries do not specialize in ways envisaged by Ricardo's theory. Further, the model does not allow for dynamic changes that trade brings about. Economists base the benefits of free trade on 'dynamic gains' that lead to economic growth. Free trade leads to an increase in a country's stock of resources, in terms of both increased capital from abroad and greater supplies of labour. In addition, efficiency may improve with large-scale production and improved technology. Opening up markets and creating more competition can provide an impetus for domestic companies to become more efficient. Trading patterns are also influenced by historical accident, government policies and the importance of TNCs in the global economy – all of which have been incorporated into newer trade theories. The impact of government policy can be seen in Case study 10.1.

Case study 10.1 The impact of oil in world trade

The two oil crises of the 1970s, which saw the price of oil increase tenfold, left an enduring impact on patterns of world trade. In 1973, the Organization of Petroleum Exporting Countries (OPEC), the oil producers' cartel whose members controlled 85 per cent of the world's oil, decided to raise the price of oil fourfold and limit the amount of oil produced. OPEC member countries are Saudi Arabia, Iran, Venezuela, Iraq, United Arab Emirates, Kuwait, Nigeria, Libya, Indonesia,

Algeria and Qatar. The seemingly endless supply of cheap oil, which had fuelled industrial growth, mainly in the US, in the previous decades, came to an abrupt halt. Further price rises were to follow, culminating in the 1979 crisis brought about by the Islamic revolution in Iran and the Iran–Iraq war, which disrupted supply. For a time, OPEC countries grew rich from oil revenues, but their market dominance (and their oil wealth) was to decline in the 1980s, as demand fell. The crisis led to world recession, the search for alternative energy supplies, reduced demand for OPEC oil and increased output by non-OPEC countries, notably Norway, Mexico and Russia.

In the period 1997–8, both OPEC and non-OPEC oil-producing countries saw prices fall as a result of the Asian financial crisis, down to $10 a barrel in 1998. Some, including Saudi Arabia and Iran, then decided to cut production drastically. By then, the Asian recovery was under way, demand surged and the result was a trebling of oil prices, bringing fears of another oil crisis. Could there be a repeat of the 1970s' crises?

Oil prices rose to over $40 a barrel in 2004, amid fears of terrorist disruption to supplies and political instability in the Middle East. Economic growth in industrializing economies has sent demand surging. While oil-producing countries have increased output, fears remain that oil supplies are vulnerable. Oilfields, pipelines, refineries and ports could all be vulnerable to terrorist attack. Should prices continue to rise, faltering economic growth in the rapidly developing countries would impact on the world economy. Net exporters would gain from higher earnings, but this gain would be more than offset by the depressing effect on net importers. Countries dependent on oil imports would suffer, but effects would vary. Eurozone countries dependent on oil imports would see rising inflation and slowing in GDP growth. Oil-importing developing countries would be more seriously affected, as they use on average twice as much oil to produce a unit of output as advanced economies, which have become much more energy efficient (see figure).

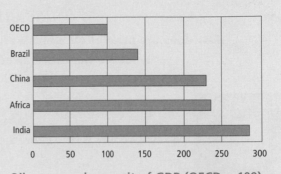

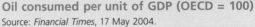

Oil consumed per unit of GDP (OECD = 100)
Source: *Financial Times*, 17 May 2004.

Demand is increasing most rapidly in China, which has overtaken Japan to become the world's second biggest consumer of oil after the US. China's energy demand accounted for nearly half of the annual global growth in demand in 2004. Its energy infrastructure is struggling to cope with demand and it has become the world's most rapidly growing vehicle market. The Chinese government has been active in pursuit of deals with oil-producing countries to provide it with energy security. Much attention is turning to Russia and the Caspian, where oil reserves are estimated to be greater than previously thought. Developing these sources would help to reduce reliance on imports from the Middle East. Building infrastructure, including pipelines, to exploit these resources has attracted the large oil companies to Russia. The lesson remains from previous oil crises, however, that spreading the risk should focus on developing alternative energy supplies, promoting efficient technology and conserving energy.

Sources: Gause III, G.F. (2000) 'Saudi Arabia over a barrel', *Foreign Affairs*, **79**(3), pp. 80–95; Crooks, E., 'A barrel of woes', *Financial Times*, 26 January 2000; 'The end of opaque?', *The Economist*, 22 April 2000; 'Lifting the veil', *The Economist*, 8 July 2000; 'Oil's taxing times', *The Economist*, 16 September 2000; Mallet, V., 'Power hungry: Asia's surging energy demand reverberates around the world', *Financial Times*, 12 May 2004; Morrison, K., Hoyos, C. and Khalaf, R., 'Terror attacks, capacity shortages and a herd of speculators: how can Opec bring calm to the world oil market?', *Financial Times*, 3 June 2004; Crooks, E. and Morrison, K., 'A new surge in prices raises fears for the world economy. But this is not the next great oil shock – at least, not yet', *Financial Times*, 17 May 2004.

Case questions

How does the price of oil affect world trade and economic development?
What are the concerns of oil-importing countries?

WEB ALERT!

OPEC's website is http://www.opec.org. The site has links to member countries

Newer trade theories

More recently, theorists have turned their attention to the growing importance of TNCs in international trade, taking into account the globalization of production and trade between affiliated companies (see Chapter 5). In his book *Rethinking International Trade* (1994), Krugman emphasized features of the international economy such as increasing returns and imperfect competition. More precisely, he went on: 'conventional trade theory views world trade as taking place entirely in goods like wheat; new trade theory sees it as being largely in goods like aircraft' (Krugman, 1994, p. 1). For companies, innovation and economies of scale give what are called **first-mover advantages** to early entrants in a market. This lead cumulates over time, making it impossible for others to catch up. For firms able to benefit in this way, an increased share of global markets has led to oligopolistic behaviour in some industries, such as the aircraft industry. For countries, there are advantages to be gained from encouraging national firms which enjoy first-mover advantages. There are clear implications here that government intervention can play a role in promoting innovation and entrepreneurship, thereby boosting the competitive advantage of nations.

Porter's theory of competitive advantage

In his book *The Competitive Advantage of Nations*, published originally in 1990, Michael Porter developed a theory of national **competitive advantage**. His considerable research, which is set out in the book, attempts to find out why some countries are more successful than others. Each nation, he says, has four broad attributes that shape its national competitive environment (Porter, 1998b, p. 71). They are:

- *Factor conditions.* The nation's position in factors of production, such as skilled labour or infrastructure and natural resources necessary to compete in a given industry
- *Demand conditions.* The nature and depth of home demand for the industry's product or service
- *Related and supporting industries.* The presence or absence in the nation of supplier industries and related industries that are internationally competitive
- *Firm strategy, structure and rivalry.* The conditions in the nation governing how companies are created, organized and managed, and the nature of domestic rivalry.

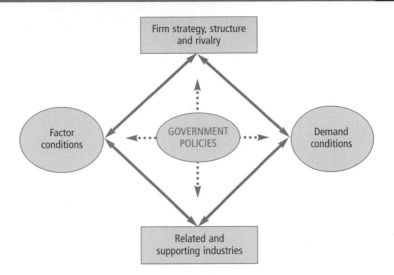

Figure 10.3 **Porter's diamond: the determinants of national advantage**
Source: adapted from Porter, M., *The Competitive Advantage of Nations* (Basingstoke: Macmillan – now Palgrave Macmillan, 1998), p. 72.

The four attributes, or determinants, form a diamond shape, as shown in Figure 10.3. The first two determinants, factor conditions and demand conditions, relate to the national environment, which, for Porter, includes social and cultural environment as well as natural resources and labour market attributes. The third and fourth determinants relate to the nation's firms and industries. Porter stresses that the four determinants are interdependent. Favourable demand conditions, for example, will contribute to competitive advantage only in an environment in which firms are able and willing to respond. Advantage based on only one or two determinants may suffice in natural resource-dependent industries, or those with lower technological input, but to sustain advantage in the modern knowledge-intensive industries, advantages throughout the diamond are necessary.

Porter adds that there are two additional variables in his theory. They are chance and government. Chance can open up unexpected opportunities in a variety of ways: new inventions, external political developments and shifts in foreign market demand. (The fall of Communism and the opening up of Central and Eastern Europe is an example.) Government policies can be highly influential and are therefore shown in the centre of Figure 10.3. Government policies highlighted by Porter include a strong antitrust policy, which encourages domestic rivalry, and investment in education, which generates knowledge resources. Government policies can play a crucial role in building national competitive advantage. Porter (1998c, pp. 184–6) stresses that this role, however, is indirect rather than direct. Although government remains an 'influence' rather than a 'determinant' in his model, it is arguable that government policy has been a key to international success in some countries, most notably Japan (see Chapter 4). In the more recent case of Chinese economic development, which has relied heavily on FDI, business-friendly taxation regimes and the setting up of special economic zones are two aspects of government policy that have been influential (see Chapter 9). In addition, government policies are instrumental in the development of infrastructure. China and India provide contrasting examples: transport and other infrastructure has developed rapidly in China, but has progressed slowly in India, largely because of lack of government impetus. On the other hand, the Indian government has prioritized investment in high-tech education, in order to attract computing and IT services industries, which have driven the country's economic growth.

CRITICAL PERSPECTIVES

Competitive advantage of nations

Competitive advantage is created and sustained through a highly localized process. Differences in national economic structures, values, cultures, institutions, and histories contribute profoundly to competitive success. The role of the home nation seems to be as strong or stronger than ever. While globalization of competition might appear to make the nation less important, it seems to make them more so. (Porter, 1998b, p. 19)

- What is the apparent paradox in Porter's theory in relation to globalization and the competitive advantage of nations?
- Assess the ways in which Porter's theory can impact on firms' global corporate strategy.

Case study 10.2   Two cheers for Australia's wine exporters

Traditional wine production for centuries been dominated by Old World producers of Europe, whose labels were steeped in history and exclusivity. The past 20 years have seen a rapid rise in New World producers from Australia, South Africa and the US, whose ethos, production methods and marketing strategies have shaken the industry. Wine producers in Australia have been particularly successful in building competitive advantage, through innovative technology and vineyard mechanization which reduced costs. As wine-drinking comes well behind beer in the domestic market, they have focused on increasing exports, rising from the bottom of the world's exporters 20 years ago to become the world's fourth largest wine exporter, behind European producers, France, Italy and Spain.

Australia's largest producer is Southcorp, which owns the upmarket Lindemans and Penfolds brands among its portfolio of 23 brands. Southcorp merged with rival producer Rosemount in 2001, adding the valued brand, Rosemount, to its portfolio. However, this apparent strengthening of Southcorp seemed to be short-lived. A glut of red-grape varieties led to overcapacity. The company responded with a robust discounting strategy, but this turned out to be ill conceived and led to losses. The powerful retailers had a major say in the discounting. In the UK, which is its biggest export market (see figure), supermarkets in particular were keen to offer discounts and promotions, but the value of UK sales remained stagnant. The effects of the discounting strategy were a disaster for the company. The company was forced to issue six profits warnings in two years and the CEO was forced out.

The new GEO had to re-examine the company's overall strategy, looking at costs, improvements in efficiency, global promotional strategy and relationships with large retailers. The company needed to focus on the positioning of its valued brands. A bright note was its increasing market share in the US, caused in part by a backlash among American consumers against French producers, following France's antagonism to the US position in Iraq. Brand names can be deceptive, of course. The Australian brand Jacob's Creek enjoyed a boom in sales in the US, bringing delight to its French owners, Pernod Ricard.

Like other brand owners who are keen to preserve the premium image of their brands, Southcorp is faced with the pricing pressure exerted by the supermarkets. This situation is exacerbated by the supermarkets' introduction of their own-brand wines. Another worry for Southcorp has been the increasing presence in the market of Foster's, the brewing company. Foster's, a recent entrant in the wine market, has adopted a strategy of outsourcing supplies, requiring lower working capital, which has enabled it to produce cheaper wines.

Having taken over Rosemount, Southcorp found itself vulnerable to a takeover. Diageo, the UK drinks giant, and Robert Mondavi of the US were possible bidders, but the strongest bidder turned out to be Foster's, which was encouraged by the steps Southcorp had taken to restructure. The prospect of continued strong growth in the US for Australian brands enhances Southcorp's value. Following the takeover, Foster's chief executive said: 'We will be the owners of "brand Australia" both in beer and wine as we grow this business globally' (*Business Asia*, 22 April 2005).

Sources: Jones, A., 'Rivalries bubble over in the world of wine', *Financial Times*, 19 August 2003; Marsh, V., 'Southcorp pins hope on shake-up', *Financial Times*, 3 September 2003; Fifield, A., 'Australian wine exports drown margins', *Financial Times*, 3 September 2003; Sinclair, L., 'Southcorp rises to the occasion', *The Australian*, 8 July 2004; 'Foster's increased takeover bid wins over majority of Southcorp Board', *Business Asia News*, 22 April 2005, at http://business.asia.news.

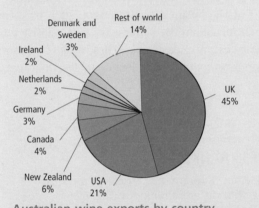

Australian wine exports by country

Source: Australian Bureau of Statistics (2002) *Australian wine exports*, at http://www.export61.com.au/Australian-wine-exports.asp.

Case question

Analyse the competitive advantage of the Australian wine industry, using Porter's model.

Porter emphasizes that the diamond is a tool not just for explaining past competitive advantage, but also for predicting how industries will evolve in the future. The theory is useful in demonstrating the interaction between different determinants of national competitive advantage, but it probably underemphasizes world economic integration. For example, both capital and managers are now likely to be mobile.

Similarly, related and supporting industries are increasingly internationalized, thanks largely to cheaper transport, reductions in import duties and the advances in communications technology. By the 1990s, an estimated one-third of all manufactures trade involved parts and components (World Bank, 2000a). Intra-firm trade between TNCs and affiliates account for about one-third of world exports (ILO, 2004, p. 32). Business-to-business (B2B) e-commerce has further opened up opportunities for sourcing components and materials globally. Growth in the export of commercial services is similarly linked to e-commerce developments.

Hirst and Thompson (1999) remind us of the essential difference between comparative advantage, which pertains to the national economy; and competitive advantage, which pertains to the companies that make it up. Competitive advantage in areas such as manufacturing and services can be deliberately created and maintained (through government policy and corporate strategy), whereas comparative advantage obtains where natural factor endowments are paramount, as in agricultural and extractive industries (Hirst and Thompson, 1999; Gilpin, 2000). Hirst and Thompson go on to suggest that, on the whole, it makes more sense to speak of companies, rather than countries, competing with each other. Countries do compete in, for example, attracting FDI, but here, as was seen in Chapter 5, location advantages often focus on particular regions and cities, rather than on whole countries. And the competition is based on many aspects of the business environment, such as social and cultural values, which are not measurable in the same ways that relative cost structure, productivity and exchange rates are measurable (Hirst and Thompson, 1999, p. 122). Nonetheless, international competitiveness 'league tables' do attempt to rank countries (see minifile).

Minifile

GLOBAL COMPETITIVENESS RANKINGS

Two league tables of competitiveness are compiled annually. They are the *Global Competitiveness Report*, published by the World Economic Forum (WEF) in Geneva, and the *World Competitiveness Yearbook*, published by the International Institute for Management Development (IMD) in Lausanne. They use somewhat different indicators and arrive at somewhat different rankings. The WEF is weighted towards economic indicators, including economic creativity, while the IMD criteria are broader, including quality of life and cultural values. Rankings for 2004 are below:

Global Competitiveness Index (WEF)

1	Finland	9	Norway
2	USA	10	Australia
3	Denmark	11	Japan
4	Sweden	12	Netherlands
5	Taiwan	13	Germany
6	Singapore	14	New Zealand
7	Switzerland	15	UK
8	Iceland		

World Competitveness Scoreboard (IMD)

1	USA	9	Luxembourg
2	Singapore	10	Ireland
3	Canada	11	Sweden
4	Australia	12	Taiwan
5	Iceland	13	Austria
6	Hong Kong	14	Switzerland
7	Denmark	15	Netherlands
8	Finland		

Perhaps surprisingly, the US, ranked first in 2002, slipped to second in the Global Competitiveness Index in 2004, behind Finland, home of Nokia, the world's largest mobile phone manufacturer. In the WEF's other indexes, Growth Competitivessness and Economic Creativity, Finland also came top. One notable discrepancy between the two league tables is that the UK is ranked 15 by WEF and 22 by IMD, just behind Germany.

Sources: World Economic Forum (2004) *Global Competitiveness Report 2003–2004* (Geneva: WEF); International Institute for Management Development (2004) *World Competitiveness Yearbook 2004* (Lausanne: IMD).

WEB ALERT!

Highlights of global competitiveness league tables may be found on the following websites: http://www.imd.ch/wcy/wcy/cfm and http://www.weforum.org/

Product life cycle theory

Raymond Vernon's theory of the international product life cycle explains trade from the perspective of the firm (Wells, 1972). It traces the product's life from its launch in the home market, through to export to other markets and, finally, its manufacture in cheaper locations for import into its original home market (see Figure 10.4). Vernon's theory dates from the 1960s, a period when, owing to the size and prosperity of the American consumer market, any new consumer product was likely to begin life in the US. In the first phase, the firm produces only for the American market. Products which began life in this way include televisions, fridges and washing machines. In this early phase, demand at home leads to expansion, and demand overseas, which is limited to high-income groups, is satisfied by exports. As the market matures in the second phase and overseas demand grows, foreign producers begin to produce for their own markets, limiting the appeal of US imports. At the same time, cost considerations take on greater importance and the product becomes more standardized. US producers are likely to shift production overseas, first to the higher income markets (such as Europe). In the third phase, producers in these countries, where labour costs are lower than in the US, will begin exporting to other countries and even to the US. Finally, in the last phase, production shifts to low-cost environments, such as Asian industrializing economies. Over the cycle, production has moved from the US to other advanced countries and finally to developing countries.

The product life cycle model as conceived by Vernon assumed that most innovations would originate in the US, a view which reflected US manufacturing dominance in consumer durables up to the 1970s. While many products did follow the pattern described by Vernon, the model has become less valid as globalization has evolved. The scenario presented in Figure 10.4 uses Vernon's concept of the product life cycle as it would play out in the global economy in which industrializing economies provide a low-cost environment. Global companies with dispersed production (as discussed in Chapter 5) may use components from various locations and choose yet another for assembling the final product. Because of the rapid pace of technological innovation and short product life cycles, a company in an industry such as consumer electronics may well introduce a new product simultaneously in a number of markets, wiping out the leads and lags between markets. (This point will explored further in the next chapter.) The model is useful in explaining production patterns for some types of products, such as standardized consumer goods, but is less useful in predicting future patterns, especially in industries dominated by a few global players.

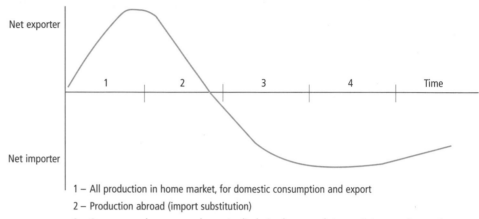

1 – All production in home market, for domestic consumption and export

2 – Production abroad (import substitution)

3 – Overseas producers expand exports, displacing home market exports to emerging markets

4 – Production in low-cost locations for export to global markets

Figure 10.4 **International product life cycle**

Source: Adapted from Wells, L.T. (ed.) (1972) *The Product Life Cycle and International Trade* (Boston, MA: Harvard Business School Publishing).

WEB ALERT!

The Institute of International Economics website is http://www.iie.org. It contains numerous resources and links for all trade issues

A comprehensive website on US trade issues is http://www.mac.doc.gov/. This is the US Department of Commerce Market Access and Compliance site

The International Trade Administration of the US Department of Commerce also has an extensive website at http://www.ita.doc.gov/

Trade policy and national priorities

National economic prosperity for almost all countries is tied in more than ever with international trade. However, benefits are not spread evenly, either between countries or between groups within individual countries. Governments face innumerable political, social and economic pressures to intervene in trade. Government policy which seeks explicitly to benefit domestic producers is known as protectionism. In this section we look at the reasoning behind government policy. The four major policy areas are briefly discussed below.

Promoting industrial-ization

Industrialization may be promoted by restricting the flow of imported products, thereby encouraging domestic manufacturing. We have seen in Chapter 4 that industrialization in many countries, such as Japan and the newly industrialized economies (NIEs) of Southeast Asia, has been guided by government, through industrial policy. These countries have made rapid transitions from mainly agricultural to industrial economies. The 'infant industries' argument holds that developing countries should protect infant industries in which they have potential comparative advantage until they are strong enough to survive when protections are removed. Japan is an example of both successful infant industry support and industrial policy (Gilpin, 2000). In the cases of Japan and South Korea, domestic producers benefited, while for Singapore and other tiger economies, foreign direct investors provided the impetus of development. Industrialization may focus on import substitution, that is, producing goods for domestic consumption which would otherwise have been imported. Domestic industries nurtured through protective measures in this way do not always become competitive in world markets. Export-led development, by contrast, focuses on growth in export-oriented goods. Industrialization in Taiwan and South Korea has taken this route.

SUMMARY POINTS

!!!

Free trade and protectionism: the pros and cons

'Free trade' as a term is misleading. There has never been 'free' trade in the sense of no barriers at all. 'Trade liberalization' is therefore more accurate, to indicate measures *towards* free trade.

Those in favour argue:

● Free trade benefits all countries
● Capitalism is driven by competition. A country risks falling behind if it cuts itself off from competition
● Costs of protecting industries can be high. Protecting *infant* industries can be justified, but too often protection is for *senile* industries.

Opponents of free trade argue:

● Protection of national industries promotes independence and security
● Levels of domestic employment can only be maintained through protectionist measures
● National industries, if aided by government, can compete globally, increasing national wealth. After all, other countries will aid *their* industries.

Protecting employment

By restricting imports, governments aim to safeguard domestic jobs. However, the situation is seldom as simple as it seems. A common fear of US workers in manufacturing jobs is that their jobs have gone to lower paid overseas workers. Work in lower skilled jobs, as in the textile industry, is particularly vulnerable to being lost to low-cost imports. However, proponents of trade liberalization would argue that protectionist measures are damaging to the economy in the long term. They argue that restricting imports may lead to retaliation, so that a country's exporters in profitable sectors may suffer, causing job losses in those sectors. Import restrictions may also have a dampening effect on foreign workers' incomes, which translates into a decrease in jobs in domestic export industries. Workers in industrialized countries who are displaced by global competitive forces are usually those without the skills to benefit from the newer job opportunities. Payment of unemployment and other benefits for displaced workers fall on the public purse and whole regions can suffer decline as a result. It could be argued that in the long term, governments need to look at the education and training needs of the economy to enhance competitive advantage. Nonetheless, protectionist pressures are very strong: special interests' regional strongholds are often effective in mobilizing political support.

Protecting consumers

Conventional wisdom holds that consumers benefit from free trade, in that competition in markets brings down prices and increases choice. More recently, consumer interest has shifted somewhat, to focus on issues of health and safety. The industrialization and globalization of the food chain have resulted in agricultural produce and livestock being transported hundreds – even thousands – of miles to markets. Contamination such as BSE in beef can thus have global ramifications. Governments have at their disposal a variety of regulatory measures on consumer products such as food and medicines, whether produced at home or abroad. Often they target imported products through an outright ban or labelling and packaging requirements. Restrictions raise controversy if they are perceived as simply a device for controlling imports under the guise of safety. However, the issue is often not straightforward. In the area of new developments in food production, scientific evidence may be incomplete or apparently conflicting, and consumer perceptions may understandably be cautious, or even negative. Hormone-treated beef from the US was banned in the EU, but found not to be in breach of WTO rules. The use of genetically modified (GM) foods, also originating in the US, while not totally banned, is under consideration and is resisted by many European consumers. For governments, it is therefore difficult to distinguish genuine safety concerns from protectionist pressures. As will be seen later in this chapter, WTO rules focus on the product, not on its production methods, but this stance is one of the current controversial issues facing the WTO.

Promoting national interests

National interest covers a number of considerations. First, it is thought that the strategic sensitivity of defence industries dictates that domestic suppliers are preferable to foreign ones and thus should be protected. The *strategic necessity* argument can be extended to a great number of products. It was used to provide federal funding for the semiconductor industry in the US in the 1990s, as semiconductors are crucial to defence systems. Food production is one of the most heavily protected industries, because of the strategic importance of safeguarding food supply and also agricultural employment. On this reasoning, subsidies and import restrictions have long benefited Japanese farmers, while Japanese consumers have paid well above world prices for their food. These barriers are only slowly coming down.

Second, national governments have evolved strategic trade policies, by which they target industries in which national competitive advantage can be gained. *Strategic trade policy* holds that governments can assist their own firms in particular industries to gain competitive advantage. This theory mainly applies to oligopolistic industries such as the aerospace industry, in which the US helped Boeing by providing it with lucrative defence contracts, while European governments helped Airbus through subsidies.

Third, trade policies may be linked to *foreign policy objectives*, as was clearly demonstrated during the cold war, when trade followed political and military alliances. Government overseas aid packages to developing countries may be tied to trade. Trade policies are often based on historical relationships between countries, such as those between the former colonial powers of Europe and their former colonies. The long-running dispute between the EU and US over the banana trade had its roots in the preferential treatment that former colonies in the Caribbean have continued to receive, which, the US has argued, contravened WTO rules. The US has used trade sanctions against Iran and Libya, both considered dangerous to US national interests. Although sanctions are generally thought to be ineffective, it is estimated that the US has imposed sanctions 61 times on 35 countries (Gilpin, 2000). A controversial piece of US trade legislation has been the Helms-Burton Act, under which US firms can sue (in US courts) foreign firms that deal with Cuba, which has been subject to a US trade embargo since the Communist revolution of 1959. There has been much hostility among the US trading partners to this statute. A thaw in US-Cuba trade relations has been evident from 2000, with a relaxation of the embargo on shipments of food and medicines to Cuba.

Fourth, national interest concerns *maintaining the national culture and identity*, for which cultural products such as literature, film and music are particularly important. The growth of the internet and global media has led to fears of cultural globalization, prompting some national authorities to limit foreign content and foreign ownership in these sectors.

SUMMARY POINTS

Why governments intervene in trade

- To nurture infant industries and promote industrialization.
- To protect domestic employment, especially in low-skill jobs, from low-cost imports.
- To protect consumers from unsafe products.
- To safeguard national interests:
  - through government purchasing in strategic industries
  - through strategic trade policy for globally competitive industries
  - as instruments of foreign policy
  - as means of maintaining national culture and identity.

Tools of governmental trade policy

Government policies affect trade in numerous ways, both directly and indirectly. Direct impact comes from the manipulation of exchange rates. Devaluing a country's currency will have the immediate effect of making exports cheaper and imports more expensive (see Chapter 12). However, governments now have less scope for manipulating exchange rates in increasingly interlinked currency markets. Similarly, most governments are now party to multilateral and regional trading arrangements which curtail their ability to control trade. We will therefore look at government policy options in the context of changing global and regional contexts. The traditional tools for controlling trade are tariffs and **non-tariff barriers** such as quotas, subsidies and VER.

The classic tool of trade policy is the **tariff**, or duty payable on imported goods. When we think of protectionism, that is, the deliberate policy to favour home producers, we think of tariff barriers. The tariff raises the price of an imported product, thereby benefiting domestic producers of the same product. Japanese whisky producers have been protected in this way, by huge import duties levied on foreign whisky. The sums collected also swell government coffers. The main losers are the consumers, who pay higher prices for the imported product. While tariffs on manufactured goods have diminished dramatically, thanks to the multilateral GATT (to be discussed later), tariffs on agricultural products are still common.

The **import quota** limits the quantity of an imported product that can legally enter a country. Licences may be issued annually to a limited number of firms, each of which must stay within the amounts specified in its import licence. Limits are set so as to allow only a portion of the market to foreign goods, thus protecting the market share of domestic producers. Restricting supply in this way is likely to result in higher prices for consumers. Import quotas are sometimes evaded by companies shipping goods via other countries with quota to spare when their home country's quota is used up. An exporting firm may ultimately set up production in a country to avoid the imposition of quotas. This is the situation which has evolved in the global garment industry (highlighted in Case study 14.1), where production has migrated to many developing countries, in order to circumvent import quotas.

An alternative to the import quota is the **voluntary export restraint (VER)**, which shifts the onus onto the exporting country to limit its exports, or possibly risk the imposition of quotas or tariffs. A leading example of the VER has been Japanese car exports to the US. In the 1980s, when the Japanese motor industry was growing apace and making rapid inroads into the American market, the US government persuaded Japan to agree to a VER. A way round these restrictions is to set up local production, which Japanese manufacturers have done in the US and other markets. The protectionist urge is still strong, however, as governments have imposed **local content requirements**, to ensure that local component suppliers gain. Japanese motor manufacturers have responded by locating associated Japanese component manufacturers near to assembly plants in the overseas location, thus facilitating just-in-time operations and maintaining high local content.

Government **subsidies** are payments from public funds to domestic producers. For advocates of strategic trade policy, the line of reasoning is that the extra funds will boost the local company's competitive position in the global market. Funds in the form of R&D grants are intended to give competitive advantage to the local producer over foreign competitors. Export subsidies are a means of ensuring that domestic producers can sell abroad at competitive prices. In general, subsidies benefit domestic producers by enabling them to compete with low-cost imports in the home market, and in export markets.

Besides direct funding, there are other types of subsidies, including loans at preferential rates and tax concessions. Countries in the 'strong-state' tradition, such as France, Germany, and other continental states, have tended towards higher state subsidies, whereas those in the more laissez-faire, 'weak-state' tradition, such as the US and UK, have tended towards lower subsidies. However, in the US, individual state governments have provided lavish incentives to German and Japanese car assembly and component plants (Dicken, 2003, p. 306). The state of Alabama has provided $372m. in incentives to the Mercedes automotive plant in Tuscaloosa, amounting to nearly 40 per cent of the total investment in the plant, which celebrated the opening of a $600m. expansion in 2005 (Simon, 2005).

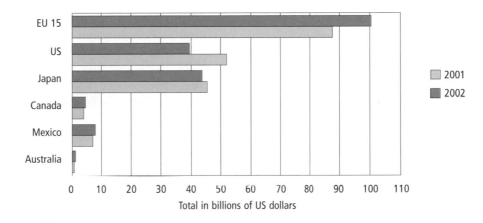

Figure 10.5 **Agricultural subsidies in selected economies**
Source: OECD (2003) *OECD in Figures* (Paris: OECD), p. 26.

Advocates of trade liberalization criticize subsidies on several grounds. Subsidies work against a level playing field for trade, as unsubsidized foreign firms argue that they face unfair competition. And, although they aim to increase the competitiveness of domestic firms, they do not encourage local firms to be more efficient. Often, they protect inefficient producers (and jobs), creating a culture of dependence on subsidies. Agriculture is a traditionally heavily subsidized sector (see Figure 10.5). The EU, through the CAP, has provided substantial subsidies for farmers since 1962, creating considerable trade friction with other nations. The extent of EU support has diminished in the 1990s, but agriculture continues to be a highly politically sensitive sector. In the EU in 2001, 35 per cent of total farm income still came from subsidies, while in the US the share was 21 per cent. As Figure 10.5 shows, the total amount paid out in subsidies was reduced in the US in 2002, whereas it rose in the EU 15.

As trade in the postwar period has expanded, tariff barriers have generally come down, largely as a result of multilateral initiatives (discussed below). On the other hand, many non-tariff barriers have proliferated, in both developed and developing countries. Trade disputes between countries have led to a good deal of tension in international relations. This trend reflects the fact that trade issues, as the discussion above has shown, have become enmeshed in numerous other areas of policy, including industry, investment and employment. At the same time, national trade policy, once seen as a defining attribute of the nation-state, is becoming embedded in an international regulatory framework We look next at the changing institutional environment of trade at international level.

Tools of government trade policy

- Manipulating the exchange rate of the country's currency.
- Tariffs: duties imposed by government on imported goods, which protect home producers; used heavily in agriculture sector.
- Non-tariff barriers:
  - **Import quotas:** limit the quantity of an imported product that can enter a country, protecting home producers, but resulting in higher prices to consumers; common in textiles
  - **Voluntary export restraint (VER):** an alternative to the import quota, which obliges the exporting country to 'voluntarily' limit exports, or risk the imposition of a quota; Japanese car exports to the US are an example
  - **Subsidies:** government payments to local producers, including loans at preferential rates, tax concessions and state 'bailouts'; examples: price support for farmers, export subsidies for domestic industries.

CRITICAL PERSPECTIVES

Government trade policy

I recommend that the nation's trade laws be used to deter or compensate for foreign practices that are not adequately regulated by existing multilateral rules. Unlike most traditional and even many moderate free traders, I am convinced that such practices can inflict substantial long-term injury on American producers ... US policymakers should be guided by the principle of selective reciprocity and motivated by the goal of opening foreign markets. Wherever possible, they should favor approaches that encourage trade and competition over those that discourage them. (Tyson, 1992, p. 13)

Laura Tyson is writing particularly about American high-tech industries and has been described as a 'cautious activist' in terms of government trade policy. What types of policies would fall into this category, and would they amount to protectionism?

International regulation of trade

Institutional arrangements put in place in the immediate aftermath of the Second World War have played an major role in establishing a global trading order. The preceding era, scarred by the Great Depression of 1929–30, had seen protectionism and a decline in world trade. Under the **Bretton Woods agreement** reached at a conference of the allied nations in 1944, exchange rate stability would be achieved by pegging every currency to gold or the US dollar (see Chapter 12). It also envisaged the **multilateral agreement** as a means of dismantling barriers to trade. Negotiators laid plans for an international trade organization (ITO) to bring down tariff barriers, but the charter eventually drawn up in 1948 met with little enthusiasm from nations, still reluctant to endorse free trade. Instead, a more modest set of proposals for a weaker institutional framework was formulated in the **GATT (General Agreement on Tariffs and Trade)**. Under GATT, successive rounds of negotiations have brought about global trade liberalization, leading to the establishment in 1994 of the WTO, reminiscent of the stronger body envisaged in early days after the war. The WTO now has 147 member states. Two other institutions set up as a result of postwar initiatives were the International Monetary Fund (IMF) and the International Bank for Reconstruction and Development (IBRD – the World Bank), which are discussed in Chapter 12. The Bretton Woods system disintegrated in the early 1970s, bringing about a resurgence of protectionism. The period 1945–70 has been called the 'golden age of capitalism' (Michie and Kitson, 1995).

WEB ALERT!

The WTO website is http://www.wto.org

The IMF website is http://www.imf.org

The World Bank's website is http://www.worldbank.org

GATT principles

The GATT provided the principles and foundation for the development of a global trading system which were carried forward into the WTO. Perhaps the most important of these is non-discrimination, or the **most-favoured-nation** principle (MFN). There are two aspects to this principle:

1 Favourable tariff treatment negotiated with one country will be extended to similar goods from all countries
2 Under the principle of 'national treatment', imported goods are treated for all purposes in the same way as domestic goods of the same type.

MFN status is negotiated between countries and, while it is the norm among trading partners, there are exceptions. US legislation has linked MFN treatment with a country's human rights record. Because of its poor human rights record, China was granted only temporary MFN status from 1980 onwards, which was renewed annually. Unconditional MFN status came in 2000, paving the way for WTO membership.

Other GATT principles include reciprocity, requiring tariff reductions by one country to be matched by its trading partners, and transparency, ensuring that the underlying aims of all trade measures are clear. The principle of fairness allows a country which has suffered from unfair trading practices by a trading partner to take protectionist measures against that country. Defining fair practice is at the heart of many trade disputes, as countries naturally have differing perspectives on what is and is not fair. One example is dumping, or the sale of goods abroad at below the price charged for comparable goods in the producing country. The GATT anti-dumping agreement of 1994 allows anti-dumping duties to be imposed on the exporting country by the importing country, in order to protect local producers from unfair competition.

The Uruguay Round, culminating in the 1994 GATT, laid the groundwork for future trade liberalization, while allowing countries to take limited steps to safeguard national industries. It resulted in worldwide tariff reductions of about 40 per cent on manufactured goods. Less spectacularly, it made strides in the more difficult areas of reducing trade barriers in agricultural products and textiles. It also initiated agreements on intellectual property rights and services, both crucial areas in growing world trade. Finally, the 1994 GATT created the WTO as its successor institution.

WTO and the regulation of world trade

Whereas in 1947 the GATT created only a weak institutional framework, the World Trade Organization (WTO), which came into being in 1995, was designed on firmer legal footing, with a stronger rule-governed orientation. This approach is reflected in its organizational structure. A Ministerial Conference, consisting of trade ministers of all member states, now numbering 147, is the main policy-making body, which meets every two years. A Dispute Settlement Body oversees the dispute settlement procedure for specific trade disputes between countries. This new legal procedure for resolving disputes marks a sharp departure from the GATT procedure, which had no power of enforcement.

The WTO's dispute settlement procedure aims to resolve trade disputes through impartial panels before they escalate into damaging trade wars in which countries take unilateral action against each other. A country which feels it has suffered because of another's breach of trading rules may apply to the WTO, which appoints an impartial panel for hearing the case within a specified timetable. A country found to be in breach of trade rules by a panel may appeal to the Appellate Body. If it is again found to be in the wrong, the WTO may authorize the country whose trade has suffered as a result to impose retaliatory trade sanctions. An example is given in Case study 10.3 on the US government's imposition of tariffs on steel, which grew into a damaging trade dispute with many of its trading partners.

Case study 10.3 Trade war averted over steel tariffs

At the outset of 2002, the US steel industry was suffering from a number of woes. Costs of pensions and healthcare for some 600,000 retired workers had spiralled. Thirty-one steel companies were bankrupt and the list was growing. Many remaining companies were uncompetitive, but stronger companies were deterred from taking over weaker ones because of the potential bills for pensions and healthcare they would incur.

Meanwhile, steel production in China has grown rapidly in response to domestic demand, gaining China an 18 per cent share of global steel production (see figure). Moreover, China's new plants produce steel of good quality and low price, giving the industry an edge in global markets.

US steel makers asked for a government bailout of $21bn., along with other support for the industry, including the imposition of tariffs of up to 40 per cent on imported steel. Steel makers in other parts of the world were alarmed by this prospect, which looked like outright protectionism, prohibited under WTO rules. The US authorities pointed to the rule which would allow protectionist measures in the case of dumping, but there was no evidence of dumping – indeed, US steel imports had fallen by a third in the previous two years. Nonetheless, the US president announced tariffs of between 8 and 30 per cent on steel imported from a number of countries, including the EU, Japan, China, and South Korea, but not Canada and Mexico (which are NAFTA members) or some 80 developing countries.

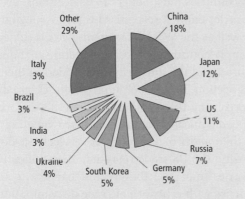

Share of world steel production by country
Source: *Financial Times*, 9 April 2003.

The reaction of the EU was to launch a complaint to the WTO. It also announced emergency tariffs of between 14.9 and 26 per cent on imported steel, to prevent a flood of imports diverted from other markets. In the EU, the prevailing view was that US protectionism was masking problems in its steel industry which had evolved over the years: while European companies had gone through painful restructuring in the 1970s and 80s, to make them more competitive, the American steel industry had remained essentially the same structure for 25 years. Most of the companies, which are heavily unionized, suffered from high costs and overstaffing. Smaller, non-unionized 'mini-mills' were in fact much more competitive. The government, they argued, was seeking to protect the older inefficient plants.

A WTO dispute settlement panel was set up, following complaints by the EU and several other trading partners, including Japan, China and South Korea. The WTO ruled that the tariffs were in breach of trade rules, paving the way for retaliatory action against the US by the trading partners who brought the complaints. An increasing worry among European governments was the rise in imports diverted from Asia and South America, which had been destined for the US.

The EU announced sweeping trade sanctions on all manner of products, including citrus fruits from Florida and steel from Pennsylvania, designed to have maximum impact. Late in 2003, the US government backed down and rescinded the tariffs, which had been in place for nearly two years, following a final ruling by the WTO's Appellate Body that the tariffs violated WTO rules. Complaints by American steel-using manufacturers was a factor, which the government had to weigh against its wish to support the steel makers. The move was welcomed in Europe and Japan, as an indication of the robustness of the WTO when confronted with protectionism on the part of the world's most powerful trading nation. On the other hand, it was felt that the dispute had weakened the American position in calling for international trade liberalization. At the height of the dispute, the heads of the world's three main multilateral organizations, the IMF, the World Bank and the WTO, had issued a statement, condemning US protectionism, saying that it sent 'the wrong signal, threatening the ability of governments everywhere to build support for market-oriented reforms', and asking: 'How can leaders in developing countries or in any capital argue for more open economies if leadership in this area is not forthcoming from wealthy nations?' (de Jonquières, 17 May 2002).

Sources: Alden, E., 'Washington puts high price on steel industry bail-out', *Financial Times*, 14 February 2002; Smith, D., 'Steeling away', *Sunday Times*, 10 March 2002; de Jonquières, G., 'US attacked over trade curbs', *Financial Times*, 17 May 2002; Alden, E., de Jonquières, G. and Sanchanta, M., 'Bush bows to WTO and ends tariffs on steel', *Financial Times*, 5 December 2003; Kynge, J., 'Poised to undercut the world', *Financial Times*, 9 April 2003.

Case questions

What were the main factors which caused the steel dispute?
How would you assess its resolution in terms of strengthening worldwide adherence to the WTO's fair trade rules?

WEB ALERT!

A website on the steel industry is at http://www.steelnews.com

The EU Commission's Enterprise and Industry home page has a specialist page on steel and other metals at http://europa.eu.int/comm./enterprise/steel

For the WTO's procedure to succeed, countries must adhere to its decisions, even when they disagree with them. All countries enjoy a recognized right to safeguard national interests, but this principle, as well as the WTO rules themselves, is subject to considerable latitude in interpretation. If countries impose unilateral sanctions, bypassing the WTO, then WTO procedures, and the authority that underlies them, could be eroded. The US law known as Section 301 is such a provision. Originally enacted in the Trade Act 1974, it authorizes the US to retaliate unilaterally against other countries (as opposed to specific companies) which it judges are violating a GATT provision or unfairly restricting the import of US goods or services. Section 301 was strengthened in 1988, authorizing the US trade representative to identify 'priority trade practices' of other countries that pose the greatest barriers to US trade, and to single out particular countries with a history of trade discrimination. Under this legislation, a country could lose access to the entire US market, not merely that of the offending product. The legislation has been criticized for its aggressive unilateral approach which, some argue, is in breach of WTO rules (Sell, 2000). In February 2000, in what was seen by a number of developing countries as an unsatisfactory decision, a WTO panel ruled that Section 301 is not incompatible with WTO rules, so long as the US refrained from taking unilateral action.

Trade liberalization: the Doha Round

Although only ten years old, the WTO has made a dramatic impact in focusing international attention on issues of world trade and also sparked considerable controversy. The WTO's planned ministerial meeting in Seattle, Washington (USA) in December 1999 had to be abandoned in the midst of heated divisions among the delegates within the meeting and violent demonstrations by anti-globalization protesters on the streets of Seattle. The meeting was intended to initiate a new trade liberalization round. Areas to be targeted were services and agriculture, which had been brought onto the agenda in the Uruguay Round, but on which progress had been limited. Divisions emerged between the triad powers – the US, EU and Japan – and the many developing countries who are the majority of the WTO's members.

While industrialized countries urged that core labour standards and environmental policy should be linked with trade policy, developing countries argued that these links are a pretext for legitimizing protectionist measures against their exports. Demonstrations in the streets reminded all that global economic integration, while it was previously seen as an issue mainly between governments, is now seen as one mobilizing ordinary consumers, worried about issues such as food safety. NGOs have been instrumental in vocalizing environmental and human rights issues, and the 1999 meeting provided a high-profile occasion for intensive lobbying. The disintegration of multilateral negotiations tarnished public perception of the WTO.

A new round of multilateral trade negotiations commenced in Doha, Qatar in 2001, known as the Doha Round. Negotiation continued at the Ministerial Conference in Cancún, Mexico in 2003, but the major policy areas which had been carried forward from the Uruguay Round again generated a sharp divergence of perspectives, mainly between developed and developing countries. Areas in which agreement was sought included agriculture, the opening of markets and access to patented drugs. Other issues were labour standards, environmental protection and competition policy. Doha was described as a 'development' round, focusing on issues central to developing countries. These countries have been firm in their view that progress must be made by rich countries in reducing farm subsidies and tariffs. A loose grouping of poorer nations, the 'Group of 20', formed to put the developing countries' case more forcefully. Among the proposals for farm reform they advanced were reducing tariffs, phasing out export subsidies and domestic support. The US, the EU and Japan have been reluctant to go as far as the G20 countries proposed, and a 2003 deadline passed without agreement. A framework agreement on the principle of reducing farm subsidies was reached in 2004, but it lacked detailed provisions. A draft accord on measures to ease access to cheap medicines for poor countries was also agreed in 2004. Welcomed by developing countries, it caused alarm in the pharmaceutical industry, as explored in the Case study on GlaxoSmithKline at the end of Part 4.

Labour standards and environmental protection

The Doha Round placed issues of labour standards and the environment on the agenda for future consideration. Awareness of humanitarian and environmental goals has impacted on both companies and governments. But whether trade policy should take these areas into account has become a controversial issue. Those in favour of trade liberalization argue that these issues, important as they are, should be kept separate from trade, and that bringing them into trade negotiations will increase protectionism. Myanmar, which is a WTO member, has drawn condemnation from the ILO and other bodies for its persistent use of forced labour. In 1997, the US banned investment in Myanmar, but the US remains the biggest market for its exports, particularly clothing exports – up 400 per cent between 1997 and 1999. The US could not impose restrictions on Myanmar's clothing exports without violating WTO rules as they now stand. Human rights groups have pressed for a 'social clause' in WTO trade agreements to allow a ban on both trade with and investment in Myanmar.

Environmentalists argue that if issues such as global warming and the protection of the rain forests are not brought into the equation, commercial goals will win out and the environment will suffer. Trade unionists in industrialized economies, fearful of job losses, argue for the inclusion of labour standards in trade policy. Moreover, labour standards, including practices such as child labour, have come to be included in human rights principles generally. These issues crystallized over China's application for WTO membership: its poor human rights record and weak environmental protection regulation were major hurdles to its eventual gaining of WTO membership.

WEB ALERT!

Background information and agreements arrived at during the Doha Round can be accessed via the WTO website at http://www.wto.org, by clicking on Doha

Numerous groups and campaigns critical of the global trading system present their arguments and supporting materials on the internet. A range of these may be accessed via the website of the Fairtrade Foundation at http://www.fairtrade.org.uk

The EU Commission offers a website dedicated to trade and social issues at http://europa.eu.int/comm./trade/issues/global/social/fairtrade/

International competition policy

Competition policy which, as has been seen in Chapter 4, is subject to varying national frameworks, has become a thorny issue at WTO panels. In 1997 the EU threatened to impose trade sanctions on Boeing, objecting to its merger with McDonnell Douglas on the grounds that it adversely affected the competitive position of Airbus, the European aerospace manufacturer. In another case, the US claimed, on behalf of Kodak, that Fuji of Japan benefited from restrictive practices in the Japanese market, which discriminated against Kodak products. To the dismay of the US, the panel decided that Japan had not violated WTO rules, as there had been no connection between government action and Japan's market structure. Clearly, however, countries differ enormously on competition policy, including merger regulation and scope for restrictive practices (see Chapter 4). National competition regimes can amount to institutional barriers to trade and foreign investment.

There are two proposals under consideration for regulating competition policy. One is to devise an international code, aimed at harmonizing competition policy, to be overseen by the WTO. This approach is favoured by the EU, but has so far been resisted by the US, as it entails giving the WTO powers to override national competition authorities. The US Justice Department's Antitrust Division would seem to favour bilateral cooperative agreements as an alternative, while stressing the need for controlling international cartels. Between the US and the EU competition authorities, cooperation in pursuing international cartels has progressed and could lead to some form of multilateral antitrust organization in the future.

SUMMARY POINTS

The Doha agenda

- Agriculture – expand market access; reduce farm subsidies.
- Review dispute settlement procedure.
- Review food safety rules.

● Continue negotiations on services liberalization.

● Reach agreement on international patent protection for drugs and access to medicines by poor countries.

● Attempt to resolve tensions between world trade rules and environmental agreements (multilateral environmental agreements, or MEAs).

● Explore possible role for WTO in competition policy.

● Revitalize efforts to negotiate an agreement on FDI policy.

● Review possible insertion of core labour standards clause in trade agreements.

● Review policy on regional trade agreements.

● Labour standards – note taken on social dimensions of globalization by the ILO.

Regionalism

Countries in all regions of the world look naturally to trade with their neighbours. Not only does regional trade make sense in terms of cost, it is likely that familiarity with local markets and regional ties will foster regional trade. Intra-regional merchandise export flows are presented in Figure 10.6. Looking at the major regions, intra-regional trade flows in 2002 accounted for 67 per cent of merchandise exports in Europe, 40 per cent in North America, and 49 per cent in Asia.

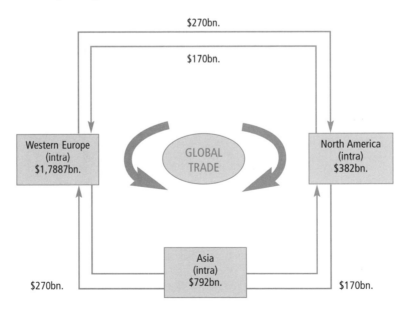

Figure 10.6 **Export flows within and between major regions (merchandise flows)**
Source: WTO(2004) *International Trade Statistics 2003*, at www.wto.org.

While the WTO represents a multilateral approach to trade liberalization, regional trade agreements have been growing in importance in the postwar period. **Regional trade agreements (RTAs)** are formed between countries in a broad geographic area, such as the continents of Europe and North America. They are designed to bring down trade barriers among their member states, thus opening up regional markets for national producers. However, their impact can be much broader, as strong regional markets can have a considerable impact on world trade patterns. Political considerations also play a key role, as economic integration is inseparable from the political power balance within any region and regional trading blocks are influential in global politics. We begin by looking at the categories of regional groupings, expanded from the one originally devised by Balassa (1962) in *The Theory of Economic Integration*. They can be categorized accordingly:

- **Free trade area.** Member states agree to remove trade barriers among themselves, but keep their separate national barriers against trade with non-member states
- *Customs union.* Member states remove all trade barriers among themselves and adopt a common set of external barriers
- **Common market.** Member states enjoy free movement of goods, labour and capital
- *Economic union.* Member states unify all their economic policies, including monetary, fiscal and welfare policies
- *Political union.* Member states transfer sovereignty to the regional political and law-making institutions, creating a new superstate.

There are now nearly 250 regional trade groupings. RTAs must be notified to the WTO, and GATT provides that they are allowable, provided they do not harm non-members or the global trading system as a whole. Although there does seem to be built-in discrimination against non-members, the review of these agreements to date has been lenient (Gilpin, 2000). Their numbers have grown dramatically from the 1990s onwards, as shown in Figure 10.7.

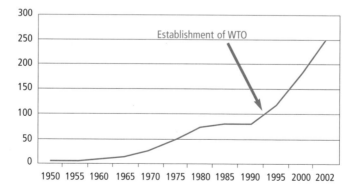

Figure 10.7 **Increase in numbers of regional trade agreements notified to GATT/WTO, 1950–2002**
Source: WTO (2004) *Facts and Figures*, at wto.org.

This upsurge can be explained by their appeal as a collective counterbalance against globalization. They provide an enlarged domestic market and offer a platform for global competitiveness. Most of the world's nations belong to at least one regional grouping, the vast majority of which fall into the first two categories – free trade area and customs union (see Table 10.1). The categories can be seen as successive steps towards deepening economic integration. Only the EU has reached the stage of economic union; political union is in the formative stages, but many issues are outstanding, including the relationship between member nations and EU institutions. In the Americas, NAFTA has been followed by the South American common market, but no hemispheric economic integration as yet. Negotiations to create a Free Trade Area of the Americas (FTAA) continue. Asian nations in ASEAN have increased their cooperation, while APEC countries, embracing all the Pacific region, have set their sights on a free trade regime by 2020. We look at differing examples of regionalism in Europe, North America and Asia.

Table 10.1 Regional trade groupings

Region	Group	Member countries	Date of formation	Type of agreement
South America	ANCOM (Andean Common Market)	Bolivia, Colombia,Ecuador, Peru, Venezuela	1969	Customs union
Asia Pacific	APEC (Asia Pacific Economic Cooperation)	21 countries: Australia, Brunei, Canada, Indonesia, Japan, South Korea, Malaysia, New Zealand, Philippines, Singapore, Thailand, US, People's Rep. of China, Hong Kong (China), Taiwan, Mexico, Papua New Guinea, Chile, Peru, Russia, Vietnam	1989	Free trade area (to be in place by 2020)
Southeast Asia	ASEAN (Association of South East Asian Nations)	Indonesia, Malaysia, Philippines, Singapore, Thailand, Brunei, Cambodia, Laos, Myanmar, Vietnam	1967	Cooperation agreement, free trade by early 2010
Caribbean	CARICOM (Caribbean Community)	15 Caribbean nations: Antigua, Bahamas, Barbados, Belize, Dominica, Grenada, Guyana, Haiti, Jamaica, Montserrat, St. Lucia, St. Kitts and Nevis, St. Vincent, Surinam, Trinidad and Tobago	1973	Common market
Europe	EU (European Union)	Austria, Belgium, Denmark, France, Finland, Germany, Greece, Ireland, Italy, Luxembourg, Netherlands, Portugal, Spain, Sweden, the UK, Czech Republic, Poland, Hungary, Slovenia, Slovakia, Estonia, Lithuania, Latvia, Cyprus, Malta	1957	Economic union, moving towards political union
South America	MERCOSUR (Southern Common Market)	Argentina, Brazil, Paraguay, Uruguay	1991	Common market
North and Central America	NAFTA (North America Free Trade Agreement)	Canada, Mexico, US	1994	Free trade area

The European Union

As early as the Treaty of Rome in 1957 the founding six members of the European Economic Community envisaged both economic and political integration. The institutions set up, dominated by the Commission and Council, have remained the structural foundations, and the European Court of Justice has established its legal supremacy (see Chapters 8 and 9). No other regional grouping begins to approach this level of structural autonomy. The European Monetary Union (EMU), discussed in Chapter 4, to which 12 of the 25 current member states have subscribed, will encourage further cross-border trade. However, the goal of the Single European Market, which was the cornerstone of European economic integration, has come about only gradually, amid a good deal of political and bureaucratic stalemate. The Single European Act of 1987 aimed to dismantle internal barriers and establish a single market by 1992. Businesses would be able to move seamlessly from one member country to another, without bureaucratic frontier procedures. Product standards would be recognized between member states. Financial services would be liberalized, so that firms such as banks and insurance companies could compete across national borders.

SUMMARY POINTS

!!!

European Union enlargement

1957 – Belgium, France, Western Germany, Italy, Luxembourg and the Netherlands

1973 – Denmark, Ireland and the UK

1981 – Greece

1986 – Portugal and Spain

1995 – Austria, Finland and Sweden

Total = 15

1998 – Applications received from 13 countries

2004 – 10 new members: Cyprus, Estonia, Poland, Czech Republic, Slovenia, Hungary, Slovakia, Latvia, Lithuania, Malta

Total = 25

Other applicants – Bulgaria, Romania, Turkey, Croatia

Possible total = 29

In reality, progress in internal liberalization has been neither as swift nor easy as many predicted back in 1987. Liberalization of financial services began in the mid-1990s. Banks and investors urge speeding up the necessary legislation, which has taken years. The deregulation of telecommunications and utilities, such as water, gas and electricity, has been uneven. Histories of protected industries and varying degrees of state ownership have slowed progress. Deeply rooted national cultural differences were underestimated and domestic political considerations have loomed large. The latter have sparked continuing debate on principles of sovereignty and national identity, and also the economic interests of groups of workers affected by liberalization. For agriculture, the effect of the GATT agreement of

1994 was to reduce the CAP budget, but it still amounts to half the EU's annual budget. Liberalization has taken on renewed urgency in negotiations on EU enlargement, as the countries waiting in the wings are concerned to protect farming interests, creating more strain on the CAP in propping up relatively inefficient agriculture.

WEB ALERT!

The NAFTA website is http://www.nafta-sec-alena.org/english/home.htm

APEC's home page is http://www.apecsec.org.sg/

MERCOSUR is at http://www.mercosur.org

The ASEAN Secretariat is at http://www.aseansec.org/

The EU Commission's main website is http://europa.eu.int

The FTAA's website is http://www.ftaa-alca.org/

NAFTA

The **North American Free Trade Agreement (NAFTA)**, which came into effect in 1994, comprises the US, Canada and Mexico. While NAFTA does not envisage the degree of economic integration of the EU, its provisions and future developments raise similar issues, including political concerns and the question of sovereignty. In contrast to the EU, NAFTA is centred on one dominant power, the US, whose GDP is 10 times that of Mexico, a much bigger gap than that between the rich and poor EU members. Fear of economic dependence on the US has bred nationalism in both Canada and Mexico, although rather more virulent in nature in its Mexican form. In the postwar period, their economies became increasingly integrated into that of the US, as US companies set up branch plants and subsidiaries to export to US markets. A free trade agreement, securing free access to markets, offered advantages to all three countries. The US looked for advantages of low-cost labour in Mexico, the opening of Canada and Mexico to US financial services and improved access to oil in Canada and Mexico. For the two smaller states, advantage consisted of negotiated rules to put their access to US markets on more secure footing, replacing the informal relationships of the past.

Market access provisions are the main substance of NAFTA, by which the parties agreed to eliminate tariffs on most manufactured goods over a 10-year period. NAFTA's investment rules allow investors from any of the three countries to be treated in the same way as domestic investors. These rules apply to both FDI and portfolio investment. For matters other than investment, NAFTA introduced a dispute settlement procedure. While it aimed to satisfy the worries of smaller partners that the stronger partner always has the upper hand, there is the problem for smaller countries that US pressure may be backed up by retaliatory measures such as anti-dumping measures to restrict imports into the US. Two 'side accords' of NAFTA concern labour standards and environmental standards, stemming from concern in the US over firms moving production to Mexico in order to avoid the higher US standards. Commissions were set up in both areas to monitor and enforce national standards (rather than international ILO standards), but enforcement procedures are weak.

Unlike the EU, NAFTA operates no common external trade policy. Also in contrast to the EU, it has no institutions for dealing with exchange rates. The Mexican peso crisis of the mid-1990s was left to individual governments to resolve. NAFTA aimed to increase exports between partners, who already traded heavily with each other, and create jobs in all three countries. By 1996, the US president reported to Congress that trade between the US and its NAFTA partners had grown 44 per cent since the agreement was signed (Schaffer et al., 1999, p. 457). US and Canadian citizens had feared that their jobs would be lost to Mexico, a fear articulated by American trade unions in particular. Presidential candidate Ross Perot, in the 1992 campaign, warned Americans of 'a giant sucking sound going south' if the border with Mexico was opened. However, there seems to be a rough balance between employment gains in the US and Canada due to NAFTA, and job losses due to imports from Mexico (Schaffer et al., 1999). On the other hand, despite the benefits of NAFTA investment, living conditions in Mexico have remained poor.

Plans to create a Free Trade Area of the Americas (FTAA), which would encompass all the states of North and South America except Cuba, are being actively pursued, driven mainly by impetus from the US. The first FTAA talks took place in 1994, amid much optimism. But more recently, negotiations between the US and the 33 other countries have run into difficulties, particularly over opening of markets for agricultural products, mirroring somewhat the difficulties which caused the breakdown of the WTO's Cancún talks. Brazil, a leader in the G20 group in Cancún and joint chair of the FTAA talks, has become a highly competitive regional exporter, as Case study 10.4 shows, and has strongly put forward its own position, leading to confrontation with the hemisphere's superpower, the US. The US position on free trade across the hemisphere is complicated by divergent interests within the country. Many farmers and manufacturers are concerned about the possible influx of commodities and other products from South America, while trade unionists are arguing for tougher provisions on labour standards than NAFTA contains. As the case study shows, Brazil is keen to access the large American market, but on terms that it views as fair; meanwhile it is building trading relations farther afield.

Case study 10.4 Brazil's trading relations: signalling shifts in global trade

With a domestic market of 177 million consumers, Brazilian industries have tended not to be as interested in exporting as those in other developing economies. However, in recent years, their focus has been turning more to exports, aided by successive devaluations of their currency. After two good years of export performance (see figure), the country now enjoys a trade surplus, allowing it to accumulate foreign reserves, which will help it to withstand volatility in foreign exchange markets. Foreign trade in 2004 was just 27 per cent of GDP, which is still relatively low, but it is increasing, thanks to new initiatives and the continuing relative weakness of the currency. China has become Brazil's largest export market, its booming industries looking to imports to provide a range of essential products. Exports of iron ore and agricultural commodities such as soya beans have been particularly strong areas of export growth for Brazil's cultivation of Chinese markets. Other countries in Latin America, too, have enjoyed a boost due Chinese demand, including Argentina, Peru and Chile.

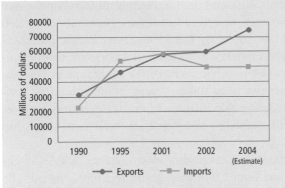

Brazil's merchandise exports and imports

Sources: WTO (2003) *International Trade Statistics 2003*, at http://www.wto.org; *Brazilian government statistics*, at http://www.tesouro.fazenda.gov.br.

Brazilian farmers have become highly competitive, often as productive as their counterparts in developed countries. Critics have warned that as China develops its own capacity to supply domestic demand, it will rely less on imports. Brazilian exporters, however, maintain that trading relations with China are leading to other opportunities to do business which have sustainable long-term prospects. One Brazilian banker says: 'The Chinese are looking for long-term suppliers of food and technology and we have both. They are coming to us to set up joint ventures' (Colitt, 11 November 2003). To satisfy China's growing thirst for instant coffee, currently supplied by two multinationals, Kraft and Nestlé, a Brazilian company has launched Café Pelé in the Chinese market. Beyond commodities, Chinese/Brazilian joint ventures in steel, textiles and computers are investing in Brazil for re-export to China.

Luiz Inacia Lula da Silva, Brazil's president, came to power in 2003, on the crest of a popularity wave, promising economic growth to bring financial stability and improvements in social and economic conditions, especially for the country's estimated 35 million people living in poverty. He has promoted trade diversification, saying: 'We need to be where the opportunities are ... We need to broaden our portfolio of trading partners' (Colitt, 3 December 2003). The left-wing Lula da Silva, undeterred by US disapproval, has made trips to Cuba, Libya, Syria and Egypt, among other countries, to promote Brazil's exports, especially farm products. Closer to home, his Workers' Party has been distinctly unenthusiastic about the FTAA, fearing an extension of US hegemony. Among Brazil's businesses, farmers and industries such as textiles, footwear and vehicles, FTAA progress is encouraged, as a means of expanding exports. Of course, the prospect of access to the American market is the source of greatest concern to US farmers, who produce highly protected crops such as citrus fruits, sugar and soya beans. Brazil continues to look beyond regional horizons. The growing ties between Latin America and China, cutting across regional relations, are indicative of shifts in global trading patterns.

Sources: de Jonquières, G., 'The divided Americas', *Financial Times*, 17 November 2003; Wheatley, J., 'A year of impressive performance', *Financial Times*, 5 May 2004; Colitt, R., 'Lula takes political risk to widen Brazil's trade horizon', *Financial Times*, 3 December 2003; Colitt, R., 'China fever drives Brazil's exporters to frenzied activity', *Financial Times*, 11 November 2003.

Case questions

Explain the reasons behind Brazil's export drive into China. How do the new trading relations indicate a shift in global trading patterns?

Regionalism in Asia

Regionalism has proceeded more slowly in the Asia Pacific region than in either Europe or the Americas. One explanation is the extreme sociocultural, political and economic diversity that has inhibited the development of a shared regional identity or sense of shared 'destiny'. ASEAN comprises the NIEs of Southeast Asia, while APEC encompasses the entire Pacific region (see Table 10.1). While economic integration has grown, impetus towards a free trade area has been weak among the major powers of the region – Japan, China and the US. Japan's multinationals have pursued a strategy of Asian expansion, investing heavily in 'regional production alliances' and increasing their Asian trade. By the 1990s, Asia Pacific had over-taken the US as Japan's largest export market. Production networks in Asian coun-tries have enabled Japanese companies to retain competitive advantage in Western markets, by exploiting the comparative advantages offered by neighbouring low-cost economies. Japan's economic leadership in the region, however, has been set back by its own economic woes (discussed in Chapter 4), as well as by the Asian financial crisis.

Meanwhile, China's star has risen rapidly, causing alarm among ASEAN coun-tries, which see FDI which they had hoped to attract going to China instead. The issue of China's membership of the WTO has caused divisions in APEC. One group, consisting of the US, Canada, Australia and Singapore, wishes to bring down trade barriers, while the less developed countries, notably Malaysia and China, have been reluctant to endorse free trade. Japan, meanwhile, has established bilateral talks on free trade with South Korea and Singapore. While Japan had tried to reassert its posi-tion as the economic centre of the region, the power in the region is shifting to China, which is trying to create a free trade area with the ASEAN countries by 2010. Shifting power balances in Asia are therefore affecting regional economic integra-tion and the prospects for future trade liberalizaition.

Developing countries and world trade

Trade has grown faster than GDP since 1986. However, trade itself does not guarantee development. While some developing countries have seen economic expansion linked with trade, the vast majority of developing countries have not seen significant trade expansion. The least developed countries (LDCs), which include most of the countries in sub-Saharan Africa, have not increased their share in global exports, as can be seen in Figure 10.8. These countries, which export mainly low-value primary commodities, remain poor. While developing countries' share in world trade in manufactures increased from 6 per cent in 1965 to 20 per cent in 1995, developed economies still pre-dominate. And the dominance is particularly strong in the high-value, high-tech prod-ucts (Castells, 2000a). The benefits of technical knowledge to be gained by low-cost producers has largely been confined to the newly industrialized economies (NIEs) of Southeast Asia. In the increasingly important trade in services, all countries, developed and developing alike, stand to gain. Services now account for about 70 per cent of GDP in industrialized countries and about 50 per cent in developing countries. In the 1990s growth rates in exports of commercial services were highest in East Asia and Asia Pacific, growing at about 18 per cent annually (World Bank, 2000a, p. 34). Poorer developing countries have been keen to attract foreign investors to improve infrastruc-ture services, such as telecommunications and banking, which underpin modern eco-nomic activities. However, the investment climate, including legal and financial infrastructure, remains weak (World Bank, 2004). Indeed, the mineral wealth that a number of developing countries rely on to promote growth has often been associated with a unstable investment climate, deterring investors (World Bank, 2004, p. 36).

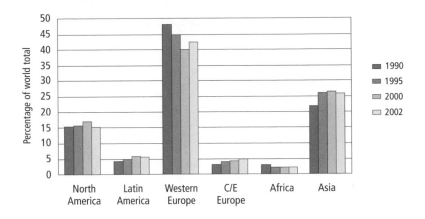

Figure 10.8 **Shares of world merchandise exports by region**
Source of data: WTO (2003) *International Trade Statistics 2003*, at www.wto.org.

While developing economies have huge potential for trade expansion, they often complain that the world trade system is stacked against them. They make up more than three-quarters of the membership of the WTO, but the organization, like GATT before it, does not operate on democratic principles, but on the rule of consensus. This means that no decision can be approved without the consent of the main trading nations. Developing countries point to the fact that GATT barely touched barriers to developed countries' markets in products such as textiles and agricultural products. On the other hand, developing countries have slowly gained expertise in trade matters, enhancing negotiating skills. The dispute resolution procedure has been used extensively by developing countries, for example by India against the US on textiles. The WTO estimates that the Uruguay Round resulted in tariff reductions of 37 per cent on industrial products relevant to developing countries, which is slightly less than the average. Developing countries have won a number of concessions over longer transition times to comply with WTO rules, but even so, the administrative resources and technical expertise entailed by compliance procedures are beyond the means of the poorest developing countries. Broadening the WTO agenda to include labour standards and environmental measures is resisted by many developing countries, as disguised protectionism. However, the fact that, on the contentious issues, developing countries are now taking an active part is indicative of the impact of globalization.

CRITICAL PERSPECTIVES

Trade liberalization and developing countries

The fact that trade liberalization all too often fails to live up to its promise – but instead simply leads to more unemployment – is why it provokes strong opposition … The Western countries pushed trade liberalization for the products that they exported, but at the same time continued to protect those sectors in which competition from developing countries might have threatened their economies. This was one of the bases of the opposition to the new round of trade negotiations that was supposed to be launched in Seattle; previous rounds of trade negotiations had protected the interests of the advanced industrial countries – or more accurately, special interests within those countries – without concomitant benefit to lesser developed countries. (Stiglitz, 2002, pp. 60–1)

- How can developing countries achieve a more equitable position in world trade?
- How likely is it that the imbalance in world trade will be resolved?

Globalization and the world trading system

Trade involves both political and economic considerations. Nation-states have traditionally relied on tariffs, quota restrictions and other policies which rested on the assumption that protection and economic development naturally went together. In modern economies, the level of productivity, technological innovation and investment are dependent more than ever on participation in the global economy. Participation no longer simply means increasing trade, although expansion of trade has been one of the major trends of the postwar era. Increasingly, through the global strategies of TNCs, foreign investment has been the driver of trade. The processes of globalization in integrating national economies can largely be attributed to TNCs' global production networks. Global competition has led to growing interdependence of states and a strengthening of multilateral institutions. Protectionist voices still abound, but governments are now constrained by numerous multilateral agreements designed to liberalize trade.

The 1980s and 90s, however, saw a tension between two apparently contradictory trends: trade liberalization, sponsored by the WTO, on the one hand, and growing regional trading blocs on the other. In this context, regionalism has served two purposes. First, regional trade agreements have permitted firms to build a better competitive base in the internal market. Secondly, it has allowed groups of states in regional trade blocs to enhance their political and economic power. Economists have argued that regional agreements put up barriers to free trade with outsiders, but predictions of a regionalized economy have not yet come to fruition (Castells, 2000a). As we have seen, few of these groupings are homogeneous or cohesive. Apart from the EU, institutional structures are limited. And even in the EU, which is the most economically integrated, nation-states have not yet been superseded as defining units for a population's economic interests. But those interests are now played out in regional, as well as multilateral, institutions. Moreover, **bilateral trade agreements** are a continuing trend. Under such agreements, two countries, sometimes separated by thousands of miles, draw up a trading accord between themselves. The US has concluded many, with countries all over the world, in a trend that has accelerated. This bilateralism, like regionalism, by discriminating against third parties, is a concern to the WTO, which sees both as a threat to multilateralism.

Conclusions

1   The postwar period has seen a growth of international trade and a trend towards liberalization of the world trading system. Although trade, both exports and imports, is predominantly between the three main trading powers – the US, the EU and Japan – other countries, notably the industrialized nations of Southeast Asia, are now important players.

2   International trade theories offer explanations of why countries, as well as companies, compete and how comparative and competitive advantages can be exploited.

3   Government policy, highly influential in international trade, rests on concerns of national producer and consumer interests.

4   Tools of government trade policy include exchange rate manipulation, tariffs and non-tariff barriers to trade. However, the growth of the multilateral trading system, initiated by GATT, has limited the scope of governments to act unilaterally in managing trade.

5   The WTO, successor to GATT, has strengthened the rule-governed system of international trade regulation, particularly in regard to dispute settlement. Tensions nonetheless remain over the decision-making and implementation of WTO decisions in trade disputes.

6   The Doha Round of negotiations has made progress in some respects, such as a framework for reductions of agricultural subsidies, but differences between developed and developing countries have slowed negotiations. Outstanding issues facing the WTO remain whether to link issues such as core labour standards and environmental protection to trade policies.

7   The postwar trend towards regional trade agreements represents growing regional economic integration. However, regional groupings differ considerably in their internal cohesiveness and structures, the EU being the most integrated.

8   World trade can best be viewed in the context of globalization, in which the large TNCs with globalized production capacities have been major players.

Review questions

1   How relevant is the theory of comparative advantage to modern trade patterns?

2   What are the main contributions of Porter's theory of competitive advantage?

3   What is meant by strategic trade policy?

4   Outline the motivations underlying government trade policy.

5   Summarize the arguments for and against free trade.

6   What are the main tools of government trade policy?

7   Define the GATT principles of most-favoured nation and national treatment.

8   In what ways does the WTO represent a step on from GATT?

9   What progress has been made in the Doha Round of trade negotiations?

10 What are the outstanding issues facing the WTO and why has it struggled to arrive at a consensus?

11 Why have regional trade groupings become popular and in what ways, if any, do they undermine multilateral trade liberalization efforts?

12 Contrast the EU and NAFTA in terms of regional integration. What are the prospects for the FTAA?

13 Why do developing countries have ambivalent feelings about trade liberalization?

Assignments

1   Assess the contrasting perspectives and interests of developed, industrializing and developing countries with respect to global trade liberalization.

2   Is regionalism a 'stepping stone' or 'stumbling block' to free trade? Compare the progress of regional integration in three regions: Europe, North America and Asia.

Further reading

Berry, B., Conkling, E. and Ray, D. (1997) *The Global Economy in Transition*, 2nd edn (New Jersey: Prentice Hall).

Frieden, J. and Lake, D. (1999) *International Political Economy: Perspectives on Global Power and Wealth* (Oxford: Routledge).

Gilpin, R. (2000) *The Challenge of Global Capitalism* (Princeton: Princeton University Press).

Gilpin, R. (2001) *Global Political Economy: Understanding the International Economic Order* (Princeton: Princeton University Press).

Hirst, P. and Thompson, G. (1999) *Globalization in Question*, 2nd edn (Cambridge: Polity Press).

Mattli, W. (1999) *The Logic of Regional Integration: Europe and Beyond* (Cambridge: Cambridge University Press)

Michie, J. and Kitson, M. (eds) (1995) *Managing the Global Economy* (Oxford: Oxford University Press).

11 Technology and innovation

Outline of chapter

- Introduction
- Concepts and processes
- Technological innovation theories
  - Schumpeter's industrial waves theory
  - Product life cycle theory reconsidered
- National innovation systems
  - Education and training
  - Science and technology capabilities
  - Industrial structure
  - Science and technology strengths and weaknesses
  - Interactions within the innovation system
  - Some conclusions on national innovation systems
- Patents and innovation
  - What is a patentable invention?
  - Patent rights
  - The Trade-related Aspects of Intellectual Property (TRIPS) agreement
- Technology transfer
  - Channels for international technology transfer
  - Technology diffusion and innovation
- Information and communications technology (ICT)
  - The technology revolution
  - The internet and e-commerce
- Biotechnology
- Globalization and technological innovation
- Conclusions

Learning objectives

1. To appreciate the role of technological change in economic progress.
2. To gain an insight into the ways in which innovation is generated and diffused in different societies.
3. To understand the interactions between national innovation systems and processes of globalization and technology transfer.
4. To gain an overview of the impact of the rapidly changing technological environment on business processes and structures.

Introduction

Technology is a key driving force in the world economy. Technological innovation and the capacity to sustain a technological lead are crucial to success in the competitive environment, for both companies and countries. No longer the preserve of engineering and design departments, technology now penetrates every aspect of business, linking R&D, design, production and distribution in global networks. In particular, advances in computing, telecommunications and transport have had widespread implications in all sectors, from manufacturing to media. Moreover, technology changes have impacted on the ways in which organizations operate, both internally and, increasingly, in interdependent global networks. The declining costs of transport and communications, shown in Table 11.1, give an indication of the changes that have taken place. The result has been a host of wide-ranging changes in the ways in which we live and work, taking in all manner of developments, from convenience food to the internet.

Table 11.1 Declining costs of transport and communications (1990, US$)

Year	Sea freight (average ocean freight and port charges per ton)	Air transport (average revenue per passenger mile)	Telephone call (3 minutes, NY/London)	Computers (index, 1990=100)
1920	95	–	–	–
1930	60	0.68	245	–
1940	63	0.46	189	–
1950	34	0.30	53	–
1960	27	0.24	46	12,500
1970	27	0.16	32	1,947
1980	24	0.10	5	362
1990	29	0.11	3	100

Source: IMF, World Economic Outlook 1997, in UN (1999) *Human Development Report 1999* (Oxford: Oxford University Press), p. 30.

Cutting-edge technology can be an important source of competitive advantage. However, the relationships between knowledge, technological innovation and markets are now recognized to be more complex than was once thought. The growth of international markets has focused attention on differences between national systems of innovation and differences in organizational structures that can promote or inhibit innovation. Social, cultural and political factors in national environments can influence the creation and adoption of technological know-how. Globalization processes have raised these questions particularly in relation to technology and knowledge transfer. Thus, while organizations see the need for a strong focus on technological innovation, they are becoming increasingly aware that technology must be viewed in the context of the wider business environment. This chapter first explains the broad processes of technological innovation and diffusion, in the context of national and organizational environments. Then key developments in IT and biotechnology are examined, highlighting trends of technological globalization. Finally, some conclusions on the future impact of technology on the competitive environment are put forward.

Concepts and processes

Technology can be defined as the methodical application of scientific knowledge to practical purposes. It is a concept at the intersection of learning and doing. Throughout history, there have been talented, imaginative individuals, able to assimilate scientific knowledge and transform its principles into practical inventions. An **invention** is a product or process which can be described as 'new', in that it makes a significant qualitative leap forward from the state of existing knowledge. The term **innovation** is broader in its scope, in that it covers not just inventions, but a range of technical improvements to products and processes that are commercially exploitable. While many inventions, including patented ones, are never commercially produced, innovations, by definition, are economically valuable. Technical innovation has thus been described as the matching of new technology to a market, or 'the first commercial application or production of a new process or product' (Freeman and Soete, 1997, p. 201). Inventions can be legally protected by a patent, which gives the inventor (or more often, a company) 'ownership' of its rights of exploitation. An innovation may be a less dramatic step forward, for example an improvement that speeds up an industrial process. While not patentable, it is nonetheless significant, in that it can lead to economies of scale.

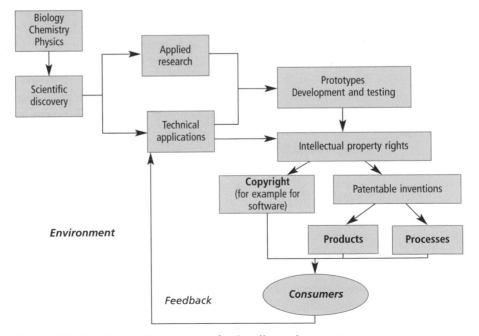

Figure 11.1 **The innovation process for intellectual property**

Scientific knowledge plays a crucial role in technical innovation. As Figure 11.1 depicts, however, there are many steps along the way from turning a scientific discovery into a workable invention which can be commercially exploited. Figure 11.1, although highly simplified, shows the flow of ideas from science to applied research, and then to development for commercial application. Note that consumer feedback is integrated into the process, helping to generate improved products and further innovation. It is important to remember that this process takes place within distinctive national and corporate environments, which may greatly facilitate the bringing of innovative ideas to commercial fruition.

Historians puzzle over two key questions in relation to technology. First, why science and invention flourish in particular societies during certain eras, but not in others. And secondly, why some societies, with high levels of learning, scientific knowledge and creative inventors, still seem unable to convert learning into invention, or invention into technological advancement at the level of society. David Landes points to two examples. Islam, in its golden age, 750–1100, 'produced the world's greatest scientists, yet a flourishing science contributed nothing to the slow advance of technology in Islam' (Landes, 1998). More remarkable were the Chinese, with a long list of inventions, including the wheelbarrow, compass, paper, printing, gunpowder and porcelain. In the twelfth century, the Chinese were using a water-driven machine for spinning hemp, anticipating English spinning machines by some 500 years. Yet technical progress made little impact on the Chinese economy. The Chinese, it seems, had the scientific knowledge to produce the steam engine, but for some reason that still baffles historians, failed to do it. Summarizing the debate, Landes points to China's lack of 'a free market and institutionalized property rights' as key factors that discouraged initiative (Landes, 1998, p. 56).

We generally assume that in societies where learning is valued, a high level of science education will lay the foundations for people with technological talent to flourish and that these skills will feed into the country's industries, fostering economic prosperity. However, the relative importance of 'demand-pull' and 'science-push' is debated. Both forces play a role in technological innovation. Emphasis on demand-pull factors, as in product life cycle theory, have been criticized as one-sided. How, it might be asked, can consumers judge a revolutionary new product of which they have no knowledge? (Freeman and Soete, 1997, p. 200). Many of the early inventors, with their scientific backgrounds, had little idea of the economic potential of their innovations or the many possible applications of their technology. Science-push was clearly important among the early inventors and entrepreneurs, who formed new companies in order to exploit their inventions. However, there were instances where demand predominated, and these certainly became more prevalent when innovation became 'routinized' within large firms. It is arguable that even today, although large firms with vast R&D expenditure account for the bulk of innovations, radical innovations often come from small firms. As smaller firms tend to lack the resources to exploit their own inventions, they may license the technology to large companies, or they may be bought out entirely by large companies which are able to reach global markets.

SUMMARY POINTS

Concepts and processes

- **Technology** is the methodical application of scientific knowledge to practical purposes.
- **Innovation** is the creation or improvement of products or processes, including incremental improvements, which bring commercial benefits.
- An **invention** is a new product or process which is industrially applicable (many inventions fall by the wayside for lack of commercial exploitation).
- **Research and development (R&D)** is the systematic search for new knowledge in specific academic disciplines (basic research), and also new knowledge for specific applications (applied research).

WEB ALERT!

The innovation website of the UK Department of Trade and Industry is at http://www.innovation.gov.uk/

The OECD's Directorate on Science and Technology has a website featuring many relevant specialist topics. Click on the directorate from the OECD's main home page at http://www.oecd.org

Technological innovation theories

Technological innovation theories start from the assumption that innovation is a key to economic progress. In terms of competitive advantage, technological innovation, as Porter has pointed out, can create first-mover advantages, which governments can promote (see Chapter 10). The importance of 'improvements in machines' was recognized by Adam Smith at the outset of his *Wealth of Nations* ([1776]1950). However, for a long period, economic theorists tended to see technological change as an 'exogenous variable', that is, outside the traditional inputs of labour and capital. Against this background, Schumpeter stands out for his analysis of technological innovation as central to economic development.

Schumpeter's industrial waves theory

Schumpeter's work spanned a long period, 1912–42. As industrial economies developed during that time, his analysis of the role of technological innovation evolved. From the outset in 1912, he stressed the importance of the individual entrepreneur in the innovative process. Schumpeter saw that innovation can encompass not just technical, but also marketing and organizational innovations. The key actors in the Industrial Revolution were both talented inventors and entrepreneurs, who often went into production, making (and improving) their own inventions. The cotton-spinning industry, for example, was transformed by the inventions of Arkwright, Hargreaves and Crompton in the late eighteenth century. Richard Arkwright, for one, embodied important qualities as inventor and entrepreneur, protecting and exploiting his patents, with a partner, Jedediah Strutt, providing the necessary capital for further investment. Large-scale machine production dramatically increased output and brought down prices.

Schumpeter saw the shift in technical innovation from the individual inventor to R&D specialist professionals within firms. Two developments were particularly important. The first was the increasing importance of scientific research as the basis of innovation, and the second was the growing bureaucracy of large organizations, with their specialist R&D departments. He viewed the changes that take place within capitalism as involving 'creative destruction'. New products, new methods of production and new forms of organization emerge, 'revolutionizing economic structure, *from within*' (Schumpeter, 1942, p. 83).

He used the notion of business cycles, devised by the Russian economist Kondratieff, to describe successive 'waves' of economic development, in which technological innovation played a crucial role. The first long wave is the Industrial Revolution and the development of factory production (1780s–1840s). The second wave is that of steam power and the growth of the railways, lasting until the 1890s. The third wave, which lasted until the Second World War, was dominated by electricity and steel. Following Schumpeter's death shortly after the war, theorists have added a fourth wave, that of Fordist mass production (1940s–1990s) (see Chapter 5), and a fifth, that of microelectronics and computing, from the 1990s (see Table 11.2). Each Kondratieff wave is based on technological changes and their widespread diffusion in the economy, creating changes in investment opportunities and employment. While Schumpeter could not have foreseen the pace of technological change of recent decades, an enduring contribution of his analysis, which is echoed in more recent theorists, is the interdependence between technological innovation, economic progress and the social environment.

Table 11.2 Summary of long waves of technical change

Approx. timing	Kondratieff waves	Science, technology, education and training
First 1780s–1840s	Industrial Revolution: factory production, for example in textiles	Apprenticeship; learning by doing; scientific societies
Second 1840s–1890s	Age of steam power and railways	Professional mechanical and civil engineers; institutes of technology; mass primary education
Third 1890s–1940s	Age of electricity and steel	Industrial R&D labs, national laboratories
Fourth 1940s–1990s	Age of mass production ('Fordism') of automobiles and synthetic materials	Large-scale industrial and government R&D; mass higher education
Fifth 1990s–	Age of microelectronics and computer networks; the internet	Data networks; R&D global networks; lifetime education and training

Source: Adapted from Freeman, C. and Soete, L. (1997) *The Economics of Industrial Innovation*, 3rd edn (London: Cassell), p. 19.

CRITICAL PERSPECTIVES

Where do innovators come from?

Technological progress is increasingly becoming the business of teams of trained specialists who turn out what is required and make it work in predictable ways. The romance of earlier commercial adventure is rapidly wearing away, because so many more things can be strictly calculated that had of old to be visualized in a flash of genius. (Schumpeter, 1942, p. 132)

■ Is there still a role for the creative genius?
■ In what type of organization is the intuitive innovator likely to be found?

Product life cycle theory reconsidered

According to product life cycle theory (outlined in Chapter 10), the introduction of a new product by a firm depends on a large market in the firm's home country, which will bear the costs and risks of R&D. Demand from high-income consumers in the US in the 1950s and 60s thus resulted in a lead in consumer durables. The theory holds that this monopoly advantage is gradually whittled away as the product becomes standardized and production moves to less advanced countries. Maintaining competitive advantage requires continually introducing new products. The theory can be criticized for its static view of technology. More recent consideration of the product life cycle model points out that it overemphasizes consumer demand and misses the dynamic implications of technology development (Cantwell, 1989). As technology accumulates, innovation becomes diffused and the 'technology gap' closes. A further shortcoming of the product life cycle model is its focus on products independently of each other, with each new product seen as a radical innovation (Freeman and Soete, 1997). In reality, product innovations are interrelated and technological changes evolve across ranges of products. Hence, the narrow focus of product life cycles does not capture the dynamic quality of innovation processes.

Theories of how innovation is generated now take into account the diffusion of technology across the globe. The competitive positions of countries and firms may shift over relatively short time spans, as technological changes play out in markets (see case study below). The technological lead of European countries before 1900 was eroded, as the US (and later, Japan), caught up and eventually surpassed European countries. European countries were then in the position of catching up. TNCs' geographical expansion has led postwar technological change, reshaping the competitive environment between firms and between countries. It is clear that industrial 'latecomers' have benefited from technology transfer, although the evidence is that the diffusion of technology differs between different national environments.

Foreign direct investment has brought about the globalization of production, but whether this has led to the globalization of technological innovation is open to debate. Large companies have tended to concentrate their R&D activities in their home countries, but there are now indications that specialized R&D is being decentralized to overseas locations, to benefit from different areas of excellence in different localities (Patel and Pavitt, 1991; Archibugi and Michie, 1997b). Automotive R&D, once dominated by the major car makers, is now being undertaken more by specialist suppliers, who, it is now estimated, are responsible for nearly 60 per cent of the industry's R&D. Part of the reason is that the electronics content of the average car, which was less than 10 per cent in the 1970s, is expected to be over 40 per cent by 2010 (Grant, 2004). Much current debate on the generation and diffusion of technological innovation, and its relation to economic growth, highlights the importance of national innovation systems on the one hand and the forces of globalization on the other.

Case study 11.1   Sony aims to keep a step ahead

Sony is famous for creating the Walkman and the Playstation, but how does the company, which has become an electronics giant, see itself in the future? Through expansion in the 1980s, it acquired CBS Records, which was to become Sony Music, and Columbia Pictures. Both acquisitions were in the field of content provision, but the company's focus continued to be on consumer electronics. Consumer electronics, however, is rapidly changing, mainly due to the spread of networks. Senior executives feel that, whereas electronics manufacturing remains their core business (see figure), the challenge will be to adapt to the networked world, where wireless devices become more versatile and there will be a convergence between different platforms.

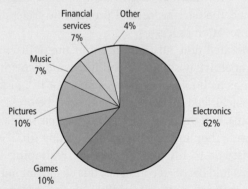

Breakdown of Sony's businesses by share of sales

Source: Nakamoto, 2004.

Sony executives now think that integrating an array of devices, rather than producing stand-alone products, is the way forward. Thus, TVs, PCs, camcorders and mobile phones will be access points to the internet. This may seem like a radical departure for the company, but it is perhaps well placed to gain innovative leads on its rivals as it straddles the electronics, software and media sectors. Its president says: 'I think Sony's mission is to make our own products obsolete. Otherwise, somebody else will do it' (Burt, 10 February 2003).

One of the factors that have influenced Sony in its new direction has been the competitive environment in its core business, consumer electronics. Competition has come from lower priced manufacturers in South Korea and China. Thanks to digital technology, companies can outsource semiconductors cheaply, enabling them to build consumer electronics products relatively quickly, rapidly eating into the market share of the early leaders. This commoditization has left Sony needing to reposition itself in the new era. The president of Sony's Network Solutions Company says: 'With DVDs, we invested a huge amount in development and competitors walked off with the profits' (Burt, 10 February 2003).

There are organizational changes implied by the more integrated strategy. The different arms of the business, which had become separate divisions, will need to be more integrated. In particular, audiovisual and IT operations will need to work more closely with the hardware and software businesses. The games business is being integrated with its consumer electronics, giving it a more central role. Games account for about 35 per cent of Sony's operating profits. Interestingly, in an organizational departure, regional management structures are being introduced, to develop shared services across the group. Meanwhile, in the interactive research laboratory in Tokyo, new and far-fetched ideas for touch screens are being created. One of the inventors says: 'We like to look five to 10 years ahead an ask ourselves the big "what if?" question, without constraining ourselves with the current state of technology. That will allow us to stay ahead of the current trends and push Sony's vision into the future' (Fitzpatrick, 25 June 2003).

Sources: Nakamoto, M., 'Sony promotes games innovator Kutaragi', *Financial Times*, 1 April 2003; Nakamoto, M. and Burt, T., 'Sony's mission is to make our own products obsolete', *Financial Times*, 10 February 2003; Fitzpatrick, M., 'Sony's flexible approach pays dividends in lab', *Financial Times*, 25 June 2003; Nakamoto, M., 'Sony struggles to get back in the race', *Financial Times*, 28 October 2004.

Case questions

What are Sony's innovative strengths?

How can it continue to turn these to competitive advantage?

WEB ALERT!

Sony's website is http://www.sony.com. Its global headquarters is http://www.sony.net

National innovation systems

First Britain, then the US and later Japan and Germany have all been able to achieve high levels of technological innovation coupled with economic growth. It has long been recognized that the national environment is important in stimulating or inhibiting innovation. Writing in 1841, Friedrich List, in his *National System of Political Economy*, addressed ways in which Germany could catch up with England. Significantly, he emphasized the importance of both social and cultural factors and also government policy in, for example, the protection of infant industries and setting up technical training institutes (Archibugi and Michie, 1997a). Indeed, List anticipated many of the aspects of the national environment which were later to be grouped together under the term 'national innovation system'. There is now a considerable body of literature on national systems, their different approaches to innovation and how they interact (Lundvall, 1992).

A national innovation system is broadly defined as the structures and institutions by which a country's innovation activities are encouraged and facilitated, both directly and indirectly. The term 'system' might imply that these institutions and policies are coordinated, when in fact levels of coordination vary between countries. The word 'network' has been used to describe the relevant linkages between companies, disciplines and institutions (Patel and Pavitt, 2000). Summing up these threads, Mowery and Oxley define a national innovation system as 'the network of public and private institutions within an economy that fund and perform R&D,

translate the results of R&D into commercial innovations and effect the diffusion of new technologies' (Mowery and Oxley, 1997, p. 154). The key aspects, outlined by Archibugi and Michie (1997a), are education and training; science and technology capabilities; industrial structure; science and technology strengths and weaknesses; and interactions within the innovation system. Each is now discussed in turn.

Education and training

Learning covers a number of processes in addition to formal education. It includes learning by doing and interactive learning, which are influenced by social and cultural factors. Moreover, learning is increasingly perceived as a lifelong process of acquiring new skills and knowledge. Technological innovation relies on both institutionalized scientific research and interaction between people with different kinds of knowledge (Lundvall, 1992).

In general, governments are responsible for the formal provision of education. Achieving high rates of participation at all levels, from primary through to higher education, is a key to national economic growth. Clearly, too, qualitative issues are important and governments are keenly aware of the need to maintain high-quality graduates in the new technologies, such as IT and biotechnology. In countries with federal systems, such as the US and Germany, it is usual for the separate states to take responsibility for education. A consequence is that priorities and resources differ between states, richer states able to afford better educational systems than poorer ones. Looking at Figure 11.2 on performance by students aged 14–16 in science, Asian countries have the highest scores among OECD countries. Scores of students in Germany are significantly lower, causing concern for the German federal government and highlighting the need for cooperation between federal and state authorities to improve standards. Note the position of the Czech Republic. Here, the supply of high-quality workers in a relatively low-cost environment provides location-specific advantages for investors – a fact which causes further concern to the German government. To make up a skills shortage in the short term, Germany, like the US and UK, has offered work permits to foreign IT specialists.

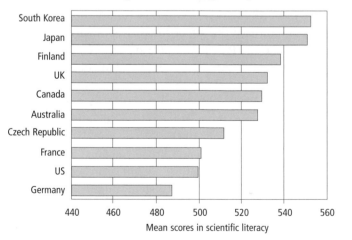

Figure 11.2 **Student performance in science in selected OECD countries**
Source: OECD (2002) *Education at a Glance – OECD Indicators 2002* (Paris: OECD).

The flow of university graduates with science and engineering degrees is another indicator of innovative capacity. In this respect, as Figure 11.3 shows, European countries have relative strength in comparison to the US and Japan, but, again South Korea's achievement stands out. South Korean students' educational achievement, however, owes more to private evening tuition than the excellence of its state schools. An estimated 80 per cent of South Korean pupils attend evening schools (an $11bn. a year industry), even though parents have to pay fees which many struggle to afford. The schools, which specialize in preparing pupils to pass exams, are considered questionable in terms of general education and creative thinking, but status in South Korea is so closely linked to educational achievement that parents' financial sacrifice and pupils' long hours in the classroom are considered justified (Ward, 2004).

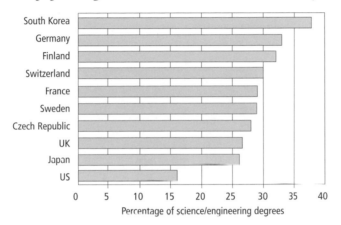

Figure 11.3 **University graduates with science and engineering degrees**
Source: OECD (2003) *Science, Technology and Industry Scoreboard 2003* (Paris: OECD).

Science and technology capabilities

Countries differ considerably in the resources devoted to R&D activities. Priorities differ on what to fund and how to meet the expenditure. Figure 11.4 shows the gross amount per capita devoted to R&D, indicating the proportion spent on business enterprise R&D. The richer countries devote about 3 per cent of GDP to R&D activities as shown in Figure 11.5, while for most countries the percentage is much lower. However, some developing countries, including China, India and Brazil, have rapidly increased their R&D expenditure, to levels on a par with those of the world's richer countries (OECD, 2003b). The bulk of funding for R&D is provided by businesses rather than governments. Much direct funding of R&D by governments is targeted on defence. The US comes top in this respect, devoting 54 per cent of government R&D funding to defence R&D. Among the other big spenders on defence R&D are the UK, where 34 per cent of government R&D spending goes on defence, and Spain, where the figure is 37 per cent (OECD, 2003b). Other countries, including Denmark, Canada and New Zealand, target government support on biotechnology R&D. As was pointed out in Chapter 10, supporters of the 'new trade theory' in the US generally favour greater government spending to enhance competitive advantage (Tyson, 1992). The UK government has introduced a scheme of R&D tax credits to encourage businesses to invest more in R&D.

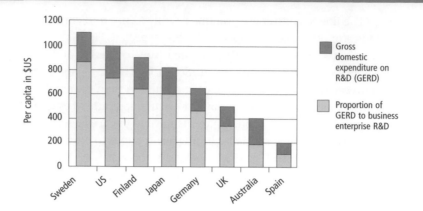

Figure 11.4 **Expenditure on R&D in selected OECD countries**
Source: OECD (2003) *Science, Industry and Technology Scoreboard 2003* (Paris: OECD).

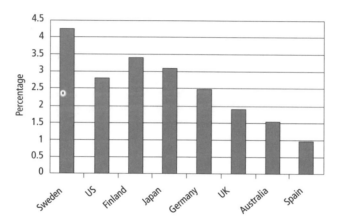

Figure 11.5 **R&D expenditure as a percentage of GDP**
Source: OECD (2003) *Science, Industry and Technology Scoreboard 2003* (Paris: OECD).

Industrial structure

Large-scale investment in R&D is borne mainly by a country's large firms, as only they are able to undertake the long-term R&D programmes and accompanying risks. Research has shown that the share of large firms is on average about 49 per cent, but it varies considerably between sectors (Patel and Pavitt, 1994). Of course, simply spending a lot of money on R&D does not ensure successful innovation. Interfirm rivalry and competition in home markets can lead to 'imitative' increases in R&D in particular product fields (Patel and Pavitt, 1994). Small firms can play a role, as has been the case in high-tech areas. The small start-up is flexible and less bureaucratic than the large established firm, and may be a rich source of ideas. Microsoft, and many other high-tech companies, began life as a start-up. In the US, venture capital for start-up firms has been more developed than in either Europe or Japan. The rapid growth of biotechnology start-ups in the US in the 1980s owed much to funding by venture capital. By 1999, the attraction had worn off, and almost half of all venture capital investment in the US in 1999 was in internet-related companies (OECD, 2000c).

Science and technology strengths and weaknesses

Countries differ in their areas of specialization and the intensity of R&D activities. Where a country pursues a particular technological strength in an area of growing global importance, it stands to gain competitive advantage. Japan's intense investment in R&D in the fast-growing consumer electronics industry in the 1970s and 80s is an example. Japanese electronics firms overtook both European and US firms in taking out patents, both at home and in the US (Freeman, 1997). India's growth in software development is a more recent example of building competitive advantage.

Interactions within the innovation system

Interactions, whether formal coordination or informal networking, contribute to innovation activities within a country and their diffusion. Government guidance differs considerably from country to country. The coordinating role of Japan's Ministry of International Trade and Industry is often cited for its crucial role in the country's economic development. Strong state guidance in the Soviet Union, by contrast, was much less successful. There, separate research institutes for each industry sector had only weak links with each other. The Soviet system's concentration of R&D expenditure on military and space projects (3 per cent of GNP), coupled with the rigid command economy, left little scope for civilian innovation links to develop (Freeman, 1997). A more recent trend globally has been the growing interaction between academic researchers and firms, as scientific research plays a more important role in the development of many new technologies, such as life sciences.

SUMMARY POINTS

National innovation systems

Definition of a national system of innovation: 'the network of public and private institutions within an economy that fund and perform R&D, translate the results of R&D into commercial innovations, and effect the diffusion of new technologies' (Mowery and Oxley, 1997, p. 154).

Elements of a national system of innovation:

● Education and training, including learning by doing and interactive learning
● Science and technology capabilities, involving public and business sectors
● Science and technology strengths and weaknesses, whereby countries' national specialisms differ
● Interactions within the innovation system, including government/business links and inter-firm collaborations.

WEB ALERT!

The OECD features research on national innovation systems which can be reached via its home page at http://www.oecd.org

The UN Industrial Development Organization (UNIDO) also offers research on innovation systems and related topics at http://www.unido.org

CRITICAL PERSPECTIVES

Societies' technological capacities

The ability or inability of societies to master technology, and particularly technologies that are strategically decisive in each historical period, largely shapes their destiny, to the point where we could say that while technology per se does not determine historical evolution and social change, technology (or the lack of it) embodies the capacity of societies to transform themselves, as well as the uses to which societies, always in a conflictive process, decide to put their technological potential. (Castells, 2000a, p. 7)

■ Castells steps back from a deterministic view of technology, but recognizes its transformative nature. Think of examples of transformations in society brought about by technological change. What individuals, groups or institutions (such as government) took the transformative lead and what changes resulted in the society?

Some conclusions on national innovation systems

There is no one model of innovation system that can be said to be superior in generating and diffusing technological innovation. While it is clear from the example of the industrialized countries that innovation is linked to economic growth, countries show a good deal of diversity in their national innovation systems. Simple quantitative comparisons of R&D expenditure tell only a partial story. Social, cultural and historical differences influence the ways in which learning, scientific curiosity and entrepreneurial flair are allowed to flourish in national environments (Lundvall, 1992). Government initiatives are more influential in some countries than in others. Huge investment in industrial R&D in Germany and Japan in the postwar period was crucial in their efforts to catch up economically. The ability to assimilate and imitate innovations from elsewhere as the basis of further local innovative developments has been a particular feature of Asian economic development. This process of technology transfer holds out to all nations the possibility of benefiting from innovation. However, technical change has proceeded unevenly among countries. The adaptation of technology and use in local environments is still dependent on diverse national systems. Diffusion of technology is in part governed by ownership structures of intellectual property, which have tended to be heavily concentrated in the producing countries. Hence, control of the ownership of technology can limit the extent of the benefits of technology transfer enjoyed by firms in industrializing countries.

Case study 11.2   New start for South Korea's GM Daewoo

GM Daewoo was formed in 2002, when General Motors (GM) of the US bought the assets of the bankrupt Daewoo Motor Co. of South Korea. Elements of the collapsed South Korean conglomerates, or chaebol, were picked up by several large Western companies, in the hope that, with new investment and new management, they could become success stories. These included Renault, which acquired a share in Samsung, and DaimlerChrysler, which acquired a share in Hyundai. GM purchased 44.6 per cent of Daewoo's stock, joined by Suzuki, which purchased 14.9 per cent, and Shanghai Automotive Industries, which bought 10 per cent (the remaining stock is in the hands of Daewoo's creditors). It emerged later that the Korean government had granted the new company exemption from all corporation taxes for seven years after it returns to profitability, to be followed by a 50 per cent discount in taxes due the next three years. The newly formed GM Daewoo, it was hoped, would rebuild its reputation in the South Korean market, where consumers overwhelmingly buy home-produced cars. Looking into the future, the new company could export into China, which is the world's most rapidly growing car market.

Sceptics questioned GM's strategy, pointing out that an uphill competitive battle was waiting in the Korean market. Import restrictions combined with consumer loyalty to national manufacturers have given South Korea a reputation as a 'hermit kingdom' for car sales, with foreign manufacturers taking only 3 per cent of the market. Daewoo had enjoyed a 20 per cent share of the South Korean car market, but its share had slumped to 10 per cent following the bankruptcy (see figure) and its reputation had suffered. Korean consumers might not show the same loyalty to their own brands once foreign management had taken them over. Hyundai, which with its affiliate Kia Motors, enjoys 70 per cent of the domestic car market (see figure), has been highly successful at transforming itself from a volume producer of small cars to a producer of higher quality vehicles and, in particular, SUVs, which are preferred by 65 per cent of Korean purchasers. To compete, GM Daewoo would need to develop an SUV itself. GM was also aware that South Korea has a history of turbulent labour relations, which could de-rail its plans.

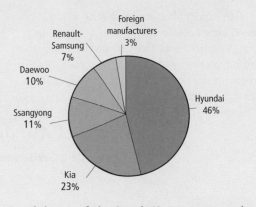

Breakdown of the South Korean car market
Source: Ward, 30 April 2002.

The new chief executive of GM Daewoo remained upbeat about the prospects. He argues that the advantages offered by Korea's highly skilled workforce more than outweigh the disadvantages of poor labour relations, pointing out that Korea produces more engineers each year than any Western country. The takeover of the company was approved by the major trade unions, which had the power to veto the deal. Union expectations are high: wage negotiations, which take place annually, yielded a 15 per cent rise in 2003, on the heels of which they demanded further double-digit rises in 2004. The company is hoping to go over to a system of multiyear agreements to avoid the near-continuous rounds of pay talks. Importantly, the management is hoping that restructuring will produce efficiencies which will give the company a competitive edge. The CEO sees the depth of its engineering expertise as key to developing new vehicle platforms at low cost. He says: 'GM Daewoo can produce a platform for $300m., half the cost of one developed in Germany. Reasons for this advantage include the lower cost of the engineering talent and an inexpensive supplier base' (McCormick, 2004).

GM Daewoo plans to increase its engineering and R&D in Korea, giving the company the capability to develop its own product portfolio. The aim is to make GM Daewoo the third largest engineering centre in the GM empire, behind Warren, Michigan and Russdsheim, Germany. The new management is confident that GM Daewoo will succeed in export markets, producing models designed for specific markets, such as the Matiz, which it sells in China. The CEO says: 'Initially there was much concern that GM Daewoo would be just an assembly operation for GM worldwide, but we are a lot more than that' (McCormick, 2004).

Sources: McCormick, J. (2004), 'GM's big bets in Asia pay off', *Automotive Industries*, **184**(1), pp. 27–30; Chang, P. (2003), 'GM Daewoo gets Korea tax holiday', *Automotive News*, **78**(6086), p. 61; Ward, A., 'Workers clear Daewoo sale to General Motors', *Financial Times*, 17 April 2002; Ward, A., 'GM's bid to conquer the "hermit kingdom"', *Financial Times*, 30 April 2002; Ward, A., 'Korean employees work for GM', *Financial Times*, 22 July 2004.

Case question

Carry out a SWOT analysis of GM Daewoo.

WEB ALERT!

GM Daewoo's website is at http://www.gmdaewoo.co.kr/kor/main.jsp

Patents and innovation

Patents are often referred to as a type of 'industrial' property, and patent activity is an indicator of levels of innovation. We should be cautious, though, not to read too much into patent statistics, as many innovations, such as informal and incremental improvements, fall outside patent activity. That said, patent statistics are an often-cited barometer of innovative activities.

Protection of property which exists in inventions and other products of human intellect have been the subject of heated policy debates from the days of the Industrial Revolution through to the present. Many would argue that technology should be freely available for anyone anywhere to use. Governments of industrialized countries, on the other hand, have long established policies for protecting intellectual property (IP), in the belief that only by doing so will the incentive be provided for people to devote time and resources to innovation. From research and design through to testing, a new product can take many years before it reaches consumers. Companies, it is felt, would be unwilling to commit resources in the absence of a system for granting exclusive rights over the product for a reasonable period of time. It is acknowledged that limited monopolies are created, restricting competition, but it is argued that this is a price that must be paid to ensure technical progress (Bainbridge, 1996). Many in developing countries, on the other hand, argue that they are effectively frozen out by these policies because of the concentration of IP ownership in the industrialized countries. This is a recurring issue in relation to innovation policies, to which we will return when we look at technology transfer. In this section, we look at the nature of IP rights and how they come into being.

WHERE WOULD WE BE WITHOUT...?

- Self-adhesive tape, invented in 1929, by a lab worker in 3M.
- Paper tissues, invented in 1924 by Kimberley Clark, and launched in 1930 as Kleenex.
- The power drill, invented in 1895 by Wilhelm Fein of Stuttgart, Germany. Black & Decker's first portable drill was produced in 1910.
- Contact lenses, originally made of glass, were fitted to six patients by Dr Rudolf Frick in 1888. The first plastic contact lens was made by I.G. Farben in Germany in 1936.
- The ring-pull, first used on canned beer by the Iron City Brewery of Pittsburgh in 1962.
- The paper cup, created by Hugh Moore in 1909, for his watercooler with disposable cups.
- The Post-it note, invented by Art Fry at 3M in 1975, now sold in over 200 countries.

Source: *Financial Times Business*, 18 December 1999 and 2 December 2000.

What is a patentable invention?

The patentable invention is a new product or process which can be applied industrially. These basic requirements are similar across most countries, with some variations. In Europe, the main source of law is the European Patent Convention 1973 (EPC), which member states have incorporated into national law (these are EU states plus Switzerland, Monaco and Liechtenstein). The European Patent Office (EPO) was set up under the convention. In the UK, the relevant law is the Patents Act 1977. US patent law requires that the invention be 'useful', rather than 'industrially applicable', as required by the EPC. The requirement that the invention must be an industrial product or process rules out discoveries, scientific theories and mathematical methods, as they relate to knowledge and have no technical effect. Mere ideas or suggestions are also excluded, as a complete description of the invention must be submitted as part of the patent application. Moreover, the invention must not have been disclosed prior to the patent application, as once disclosed, it becomes 'prior art' and can no longer be said to be new. Most inventions are not totally new products, but improvements on existing products. For a pharmaceutical drug, for example, a new patent can be obtained for a new one-a-week dosage, rather than one a day. This can be a means of extending the life of a patent. While we tend to think of only the most formal inventions as patentable, in fact the scope of potentially patentable inventions is expanding all the time, extending to software, microorganisms and business methods.

Computer software and business methods are both patentable in the US, but only to a limited extent in Europe. In Europe a software-based invention is patentable if it has a 'technical effect'. This means that a new program which affects how the computer operates is patentable, whereas a computer game is not. The game, like most software, is protected by copyright, but the expansion of software patents has been a trend in the US since they were recognized as patentable by the Supreme Court in 1981. In the US a 'way of doing business' is patentable, whereas it would not be in Europe, although there are ways of getting round this restriction. The US has seen growing numbers of business methods patent applications, especially for e-commerce patents, such as Amazon.com's 'one-click' shopping method in 1999. The European Commission is considering widening European law, but many believe that the US has gone too far in granting monopoly protection where there is little justifiable case. They argue that it is difficult to see how a miracle cure for AIDS and an online retailer's system for repeat orders are at all comparable. On the other hand, US companies are seeking to extend their coverage to Europe, where they accounted for 52 per cent of business methods applications to the EPO in 1999 (Amazon.com was among them) (*Financial Times*, 26 October 2000).

WEB ALERT!

The website of the UK Patent Office is http://www.patent.gov.uk

The US Patent and Trademark Office is at http://www.uspto.gov

The European Union's site for intellectual and industrial property is http://europa.eu.int/ISPO/ecommerce/. Latest proposals, directives and reports are all available here. There are also links to research institutes and sites on e-commerce in other regions of the world

Patent rights

The patent gives its owner an exclusive right for a limited period to exploit the invention, license others to use it and stop all unauthorized exploitation of the invention. Eighty per cent of patent holders are companies, not the actual inventors. The duration of a patent in the UK is four years, renewable up to 20 years. Renewal fees become steeper over time, and most inventions have been superseded by new technology long before the 20 years have expired. In the US, the normal duration is 20 years at the outset, with 'maintenance' fees payable at intervals. Being able to license the technology to other manufacturers entitles the patent holder to collect royalty fees agreed with the licensee. Much FDI relies on the licensing of technology. A patent may also be sold outright ('assigned') to someone else, who is then is entitled to exploit it commercially. In common with other IP rights, 'exhaustion of rights' applies to patents. Under this principle, once the patent holder has consented to the marketing of the product in specific countries, he or she cannot prevent 'parallel imports', that is, importation of the product from another country, usually a lower cost one. A consequence is that the owner of a patent for a product which is sold in a number of countries might find it difficult to maintain price differentials between them.

SUMMARY POINTS

Legal requirements for a patentable invention

The four legal requirements for a UK patent are that the invention must:

● be new, that is, not part of the 'state of the art'

● involve an 'inventive step', that is, not obvious to a person skilled in the art

● have an industrial application, either a product which can be made industrially, or a process which is a means of achieving a concrete result

- not be excluded from patentability. Excluded categories are scientific discoveries; literary works (for which copyright is available); transgenic animals.

Categories which *may* be patentable if the invention has a 'technical effect':

- computer software
- business method.

For an inventor, the process of applying for a patent can be complicated, long and expensive. The process of patent office 'examination' of a patent application typically takes from two to four years. The help of expert professionals is almost always needed, stacking the odds against the individual inventor-entrepreneur. The simplest route for the inventor is to apply for a patent in his or her home country, but in that case, the patent granted will only cover that country, which most nowadays would find inadequate. There is no such thing as a global patent! For the multinational company with global markets, there are means available to alleviate the need to make separate applications in every country. The EPO in Munich (established by the EPC) provides one route. Application to the EPO allows the applicant to designate particular countries, typically eight, in which the patent will be valid. However, the grant will be a bundle of individual national patents, each of which must be translated into the national language and enforced in national courts. The expense of translation into several languages adds considerably to the overall expense, making European patents several times more expensive than US or Japanese patents. For many years, businesses have pressed the European Commission for a simplified system which would allow a single application submitted in one language, making the process more efficient and cheaper. Protracted negotiations have now made significant progress towards this goal. Disputes would be settled under the European Court of Justice, rather than in the many national legal systems.

An alternative route is offered by the Patent Co-operation Treaty (PCT) procedure, which covers over 100 countries. Under the PCT, the applicant makes one application, to a regional office, and the process is divided into an 'international' phase and a 'national' phase. For the applicant with a global market in mind, there are considerable savings to be made in comparison with multiple individual country applications. The process is overseen by the World Intellectual Property Organization (WIPO) in Geneva. There were 2625 PCT applications in 1979, each designating on average 6.66 countries. In 2003, PCT applications numbered 114,944 (WIPO, 2004). It is possible to use multiple routes to gain competitive advantage. For example, an initial application may be filed through the national route, obtaining a filing date, or 'priority date', and then application is made to the EPO, which takes the same priority date if done within 12 months of the original application. This apparent 'backdating' can be a crucial advantage to an application, as the priority date is used for determining the prior art relevant to the application.

Table 11.3 Patent applications to the European Patent Office

Country of applicant	Total number	Number in ICT	Number in biotechnology
US	28,109	10,761	2,625
Germany	20,397	4,775	637
Japan	10,230	7,461	585
France	7,050	2,015	297
UK	5,492	1,887	428
Italy	3,638	528	60
The Netherlands	2,873	1,248	137
Switzerland	2,424	506	93
Finland	1,367	814	37
Korea	972	442	54
Australia	885	350	75

Source: OECD (2003) *Main Science and Technology Indicators* (Paris: OECD).

The US Patent Office receives the largest number of applications – over 300,000 in 2003 (US Patent Office, 2003). It issued 173,072 patents in 2003. Every patent system receives a significant number of applications from abroad every year. As can be seen from Table 11.3, the US, Germany and Japan account for the bulk of applications to the EPO. These three countries are also the leaders in PCT international applications, depicted in Figure 11.6(a). Nearly 36 per cent of all PCT applications in 2003 were US in origin, followed by 15 per cent from Japan and 13 per cent from Germany. However, of the three, only applications from Japan show sustained growth from 2000 to 2003, and US applications decreased slightly. Looking at the patenting numbers in other countries, shown in Figure 11.6(b), France, South Korea and India saw steady growth, whereas China's progress has been more uneven. India's progress has been remarkable. Starting from an admittedly small base, PCT patent applications grew 302 per cent between 2000 and 2003.

The extent to which patent activity indicates innovative capacity is much debated. It has been suggested by specialist researchers in patent statistics that weighting should be given to ground-breaking technological discoveries, to give a better indication of where the greatest innovative capacity lies (CHI/MIT, 2004). On this basis, the US and Japan have by far the greatest innovative capacity. Despite its economic woes, Japan's technological strengths have been sustained in areas such as office equipment, consumer electronics and cameras. However, Germany, which has high levels of patent activity, is less highly rated by this research, as its strengths, mainly in manufacturing and automotive engineering, are rated as less valuable. As Table 11.3 shows, Japanese companies filed over 10,000 patent applications to the EPO, 7461 of them in the ICT area, whereas German applications numbered just over 20,000, but only 4775 were in ICT.

(a) PCT applications from the three top-ranking countries

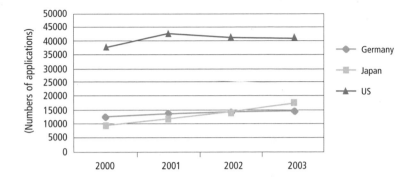

(b) PCT applications from other key countries

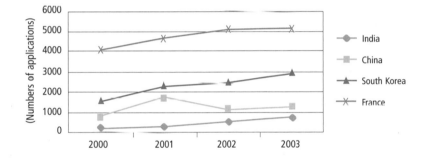

Figures 11.6a and b **PCT international applications**
Source: WIPO (2004) *PCT Statistical Indicators Report* (Geneva: WIPO).

Patent activity, however measured, should be placed in perspective when looking at overall innovative behaviour. Patented inventions, however excellent, must be commercially viable and meet consumer needs. The capacity to build brands and reputation are as critical as winning products in achieving competitive advantage. Moreover, many innovations, such as new working practices, lie outside the category of patentable inventions.

The Trade-related Aspects of Intellectual Property agreement

There have been significant efforts to harmonize national laws on intellectual property rights through multilateral agreements. Following the Uruguay Round of GATT, the agreement on **Trade-related Aspects of Intellectual Property (TRIPS)** attempted to bring national legal regimes into harmony. Obligations of national treatment (equal treatment for foreign and domestic individuals and companies) and most-favoured-nation treatment (non-discrimination between foreign individuals and companies) apply. These provisions took effect from 1996 for most countries, with transitional periods allowed for developing countries to comply. Most developing countries had a further five years, but the least developed countries have ten years to comply (that is, until 2006). TRIPS does not aim to make all countries conform to a single system, but to set certain 'minimum standards', with latitude for national variations. In the controversial area of plants and animals, TRIPS provides that plant varieties must be patentable, but members may exclude certain types of plants and animal inventions. The TRIPS Council of the WTO monitors national laws for conformity. Disputes under TRIPS are settled through the WTO dispute settlement procedure.

TRIPS has come in for a great deal of criticism from developing countries. Industrial countries hold 97 per cent of all patents worldwide and global corporations hold 90 per cent of all technology and product patents (United Nations, 2000). Critical areas for developing countries are new drugs to fight diseases such as AIDS and new seeds for crops. Both areas rely on research in biotechnology, or life science technology. In industrial countries, the trend away from publicly funded research to private funding has brought the increasing domination of a few large multinationals in these areas. Many developing countries have either a weak patent system, or none at all. In pharmaceutical drugs, India allows patenting of processes, not products. The result has been a booming local industry producing generic drugs for sale to many poor countries, where the inhabitants cannot afford the prices charged by the multinational drug companies. The TRIPS agreement will therefore require much tighter regulation of IP rights, as it provides 20-year protection of both process and products. More than 80 per cent of the patents granted in developing countries go to residents of the industrial countries (United Nations, 1999b). The TRIPS agreement therefore seems to consolidate the hold of the multinationals from industrial countries over IP rights.

WEB ALERT!

Text and discussion of TRIPS may be found at http://www.wto.org/english/tratop
The website for the World Intellectual Property Organization (WIPO) is http://www.wipo.int/. Information on the Patent Co-operation Treaty may be found here

Technology transfer

Acquiring technology from other countries is known as **technology transfer**. While the term usually refers to transfers from the advanced economies to industrializing economies, it also covers transfers between industrialized countries. Technology transfer has been crucial to the processes of industrial growth and global integration. It is now recognized that technology transfer is not a simple one-way process, but more interactive and complex. Research has reopened basic issues of how knowledge and skills are acquired and how imitation and innovation are interlinked.

Channels for international technology transfer

The postwar period has seen the emergence of four main channels of technology transfer. These are foreign direct investment, joint ventures and strategic alliances, licensing and trade in capital goods (Mowery and Oxley, 1997). We look at each in turn.

FDI

FDI investment by TNCs is a major source of technology for developing countries. For the host country, the benefits derive from observing, imitating and applying the technologies, including the management methods. Spillover effects can include linkages developed with domestic suppliers, but to exploit spillover effects requires incentives for local firms to adopt the new technologies. A recent trend among TNCs has been to relocate R&D activities from the home country to overseas locations, enhancing the parent company's overall innovative capacity (United Nations, 1999a). The late industrializing countries of Asia and Latin America have benefited from FDI flows, mainly from the US and Japan. From the 1980s, outflows from newly industrialized countries, mainly South Korea, Taiwan and China, have also increased, reflecting a successful build-up of technological capabilities.

Joint ventures and strategic alliances

Collaborative innovation is a growing trend among firms in industrialized countries, and also between firms in industrializing and advanced economies. As costs of innovation have increased and companies have become more specialized in R&D activities, companies see the benefits of marrying expertise and sharing costs. OECD research shows that numbers of new strategic alliances grew over the 1990s, from just over 1000 in 1989 to over 7000 in 1999 (OECD, 2000c).

Technology licensing

The owner of a patent may license a foreign manufacturer to produce the product under licence, in return for royalties. Many late industrializing countries have relied significantly on licences for technology, particularly from the US and Japan. South Korea's spending on licences increased tenfold in the period 1982–91 (Mowery and Oxley, 1997). The age of technology transferred through licensing, however, is significantly older than that transferred through FDI.

Capital goods trade

Sometimes called 'embodied' technology transfer, the importation of machinery and equipment provides a means to assimilate the technology. By 'reverse engineering', discovering how a product has been made, it is possible to develop and refine the technology further. Japan's postwar industrial development is a good example of the benefits of imported technology, which were assimilated and complemented by local R&D and engineering capabilities. Japanese firms similarly benefited from licensed technology, building on substantial investments in R&D and engineering (Bell and Pavitt, 1997). Importing foreign technology is not limited to imitation, but part of a larger process of technological accumulation.

SUMMARY POINTS

Channels for international technology transfer

- FDI, whereby opportunities to apply and adapt advanced technology can provide a foundation for local technological innovation.
- Joint ventures and strategic alliances between firms in different countries, bringing together expertise in different disciplines.
- Technology licensing, which allows a manufacturer to produce another's patented product, in return for royalties.

● Capital goods transfer provides a means, by 'reverse engineering', of learning how a product is made, and then to adapt and refine the technology further.

Technology diffusion and innovation

Technological diffusion was once thought to be the simple acquisition and adoption by developing countries of the technologies of developed countries, akin to adopting a set of 'blueprints', without any further creative contribution. It is now recognized that this view is oversimplified, in that the processes of diffusing technology are more dynamic, involving technical changes and adaptations to specific local conditions. Technological learning, or 'absorptive capacity', is at the heart of these processes. Formal education and training clearly play a part, but much learning is also acquired by doing, as in 'on the job' training. To benefit from technological accumulation, firms need to develop skills and know-how to improve the technology acquired from abroad. Japan and Germany are examples of countries that have combined imported technology with the development of local technological capabilities. On the other hand, late industrializing countries, while they have been able to increase productive capacity, have varied in their capacities for technological innovation.

Some economies seem to have become locked into sectors where competitiveness depends on low-wage production and are unable to break into the more knowledge-based sectors. Examples are the Latin American economies. A scale-intensive motor industry grew up in Argentina in the 1950s and 60s, along with the beginnings of specialist supplier industries, but these seemed not to have progressed further in the 1990s (Bell and Pavitt, 1997). To the extent that this is the case, economies are said to be 'path-dependent'. By contrast, some of the Asian late industrializing economies have moved from labour-intensive sectors (which are supplier dominated) to sectors such as cars and consumer durables and then to specialized equipment. Singapore is an example of this trajectory. Certainly, while technological innovation would seem to have become more difficult for late industrializing countries, there are even greater gaps between these and other developing countries, despite increasing access to international higher education and training. It has been suggested by Bell and Pavitt that for today's developed countries, productive capacity and technological capacity developed in parallel. Doing and learning went hand in hand. By contrast, in the current, fast-moving world of technical change, 'the skills needed to use and operate technologies, and those required to create and change technology' have become separated (Bell and Pavitt, 1997, p. 123).

The activities of global companies in expanding their global reach through FDI and licensing have been major forces behind the diffusion of technology. The processes of technology transfer can thus be viewed from different perspectives. While they can be seen as part of a larger picture of globalization, they can also be seen as nation-specific, that is, dependent on national systems of innovation, rather than superseding them. It follows that national action, including government policies, can give much-needed impetus, as has happened in India in the software industry. LDCs, where well-trained workforces earn much lower salaries than in developed countries, may exploit opportunities in an area such as IT, for which geographic location is not a key issue.

CRITICAL PERSPECTIVES

Global strategy for competitive advantage in technology

The technological imperative would seem to point to a shift in the particular competitive advantages of the MNE, from those based on the intangible assets which it possesses and utilizes in different countries, to those which stem from its ability to identify, source and utilize a group of inter-dependent and internationally located technological inputs, which may then be used to produce a range of products. The extent of its product range will depend both on the efficiency of the MNE as an innovator and producer, and on how far it is able to exploit cross-border economies of scope and arbitrage, not only in R&D and production, but also in sales and marketing activities. (Dunning, 1993b, p. 299)

■ How does this shift towards globalized technological and R&D inputs of multinational enterprises (MNEs) impact on national technological environments? (See the case study on General Electric Corporation at the end of Part 3 for an example of the shift described by Dunning.)

Information and communications technology (ICT)

The IT revolution has been compared to the Industrial Revolution in its pervasiveness, amounting to a further long wave, to use Schumpeter's terms. It began just after the Second World War, when, with army sponsorship, a team at the University of Pennsylvania produced the first electronic computer, a monster weighing 30 tons and using so much electricity that it caused Philadelphia's lights to flicker. The 1950s saw the commercial development of mainframe computers, spearheaded by IBM.

The technology revolution

In the early postwar period, many in the industry did not see the huge potential of computing. Those who did felt that it would be a long time before computer-based automation would bring about the 'automatic factory', and many feared it would bring mass unemployment. Diffusion of computer technology in the 30 years after the war rested on clusters of both radical and incremental innovations, such as computer-aided design (CAD) and software engineering. Economic factors also played a crucial role in diffusion, in that technical advantages were combined with falling prices. The arrival of microelectronics in the 1960s and the microprocessor in the early 1970s enabled SMEs, as well as large firms to computerize and ensured diffusion of computer technology across industries. The spread of the microcomputer started with Apple Computer in 1976, followed by IBM's 'personal computer' (PC) in 1981, whose name has become the generic name for microcomputers. IBM's PC relied not on its own software, as Apple's machine had done, but on Microsoft's MS-DOS operating system. The number of PCs leapt from 2 million in 1981 to 5.5 million in 1982, due in large part to cloning, which served to diffuse the technology all over the world and create a common standard.

Microprocessors have been described as the 'fundamental building block of the new technology', making it possible to produce better products more cheaply and efficiently (Baily, 2000). A single memory chip now holds 250,000 times as much data as one from the early 1970s. In 1970 a state-of-the-art computer cost about $4.7m., which was equivalent to 15 times the lifetime wages of the average American worker. Now, a PC with more than ten times as much computing power can be purchased for less than two weeks' wages for an average worker. The average cost of processing information fell from about $75 per million operations in 1960 to one-hundredth of a cent in 1990. As Table 11.4 shows, however, PCs are much more prevalent in richer countries than in poorer ones. The implications of this gap in the diffusion of technology will be discussed in Chapter 14.

Table 11.4 PCs and internet users across the world (2003)

Country/region	PCs per 100 inhabitants	Internet users per 10,000 inhabitants
Africa	1.38	147.93
Nigeria	0.71	60.82
South Africa	7.26	682.01
Asia	4.45	674.25
China	2.76	632.48
India	0.72	174.86
Japan	38.22	4,488.56
South Korea	55.14	6,034.20
Europe	21.44	2,373.19
France	34.71	3,656.08
Germany	43.13	4,726.70
Italy	23.07	3,366.60
Poland	10.56	2,324.50
Sweden	62.13	5,730.74
UK	40.57	4,230.98
Americas	28.95	2,592.71
US	65.89	5,513.77
Brazil	7.48	822.41
Oceania	42.40	3,763.99
Australia	56.45	4,817.41
New Zealand	41.35	5,262.37

Source: *International Telecommunication Union* (2004), *ICT indicators*, at www.itu.int/ITU/ict/statistics.

The internet and e-commerce

Further networking capacities were opened up with the creation and rapid development of the internet. Like computing technology, the internet was a product of military research, the first network dating from 1969. Initially, the US Defense Department and university research centres, including the National Science Foundation, were able to communicate via the network, but commercial exploitation and corporate use were not far behind, and in 1979, the network was able to link up computers through ordinary phone lines. From military-inspired innovation, the internet became available to anyone anywhere with a PC, decreasing in price all the time. In 2003, half the population of the EU 15 states between 16 and 74 used the internet, while the percentage of enterprises using the internet was 87 per cent (see Figure 11.7). It is noteworthy that internet use varies significantly with educational level, as shown in Figure 11.8.

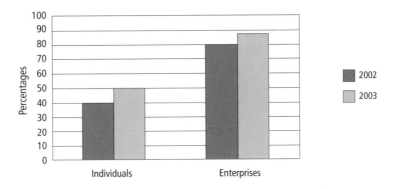

Figure 11.7 **Growth in EU internet use by individuals and enterprises**
Source: Eurostat (2004) *Statistics in Focus: Industry, Trade and Services* (Luxembourg: Eurostat).

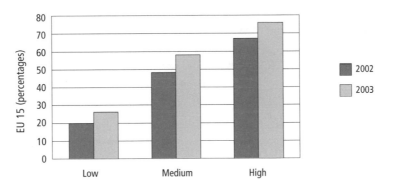

Figure 11.8 **Internet usage by individuals, compared according to educational level**

Note on educational level:
Low – primary education and lower secondary education; this normally constitutes compulsory education.
Medium – upper secondary education and post-secondary, non-tertiary education, for example vocational training.
High – tertiary education, including completion of first degrees and higher degrees which lead to an advanced research qualification.

Source: Eurostat (2004) *Statistics in focus: Industry, Trade and Services* (Luxembourg: Eurostat).

While three-quarters of Europeans with higher education use the internet, the proportion of those with high school education using the internet remains low, at only one-quarter. This discrepancy highlights the importance of education in taking the opportunities provided by the new technology. Internet penetration is highest in the US, where 69 per cent of inhabitants are online, but they account for only about 25 per cent of the global online population. Internet users in China, who make up only 6.8 per cent of the Chinese population, number 87 million, and account for nearly 11 per cent of the global online population. A breakdown of global internet users is given in Figure 11.9.

The diffusion of computer technology led to the reorganization of factories and increases in productive capacity. Changes in the workplace required both new skills and new management structures. The pervasive effects on social and economic organization brought about by technical changes have been termed a new 'technological paradigm'. These changes are the basis of the 'new economy', or the 'knowledge economy', whose fundamental features are that it is 'informational, global and networked' (Castells, 2000a, p. 77). In the process referred to as 'technological convergence', telecommunications technology is now integrated with information processing technology. Innovations in ICT can thus be major drivers of globalization, making possible a networked, interdependent global economy traversing nation-states.

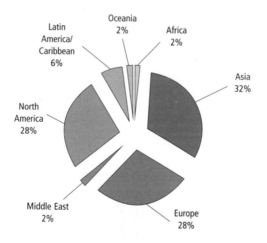

Figure 11.9 **Breakdown of global internet use by region**
Source: *Internet World Statistics 2004*, at www.internetworldstats.com.

WEB ALERT!

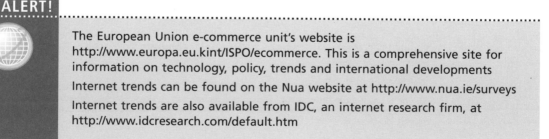

The European Union e-commerce unit's website is http://www.europa.eu.kint/ISPO/ecommerce. This is a comprehensive site for information on technology, policy, trends and international developments

Internet trends can be found on the Nua website at http://www.nua.ie/surveys

Internet trends are also available from IDC, an internet research firm, at http://www.idcresearch.com/default.htm

E-commerce, the use of the internet to replace traditional paper transactions for buying and selling, has been one of the major recent developments in the rapidly growing world of communications technology. While the major centres are still the industrialized countries, with the highest density of internet users, e-commerce is expanding in other parts of the world as well, particularly in Asia. E-commerce has opened up enormous opportunities for both business-to-consumer (B2C) and business-to-business (B2B) commerce. E-retailing has grown as PC density has increased, mainly in the industrialized countries, as shown in Table 11.4. As with internet use generally, however, the growth of e-commerce varies greatly between countries. The marked preference among those who use e-commerce, both individuals and enterprises, is to use the internet predominantly for purchasing rather than selling. Within the EU, 19 per cent of individuals used e-commerce to purchase goods and services in 2003. Among enterprises, 12 per cent use e-commerce to make purchases and 7 per cent use it to sell (Eurostat, 2004). The British, Danish or German consumer is much more likely to buy on the internet that other European consumers: over 20 per cent of consumers in these countries bought goods or services online in 2003 (Eurostat, 2004).

Some internet businesses, such as Amazon and eBay, were conceived as e-retailing models. The dot-com boom of the 1990s saw numerous e-commerce start-ups which attracted huge investment, but the crash in 1999–2000 was a warning that only sound business models will succeed in the long term, whether based on 'virtual' or bricks-and-mortar enterprises. Amazon and eBay have survived and expanded their 'e-tailing' models, developing new technologies to add value. Amazon now offers 'search inside the book', using search technology to allow customers to search inside a book. eBay, the online auction site, claims to handle 22 per cent of online retailing in goods.

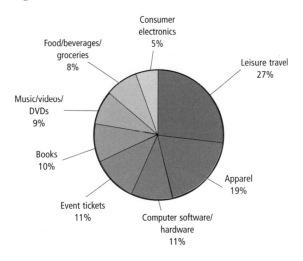

Figure 11.10 **Online retail sales in Europe, 2004**
Source: *Financial Times*, 10 June 2004.

Online services too, including travel, banking and other financial services, have expanded rapidly. Online booking of flights, hotels and entertainment accounts for

38 per cent of all online trading in Europe, as shown in Figure 11.10. Much e-tailing is substitution, shifting business from high-street retailers and banks to online equivalents. E-tailing has dramatically increased the potential not just for sales, but also for marketing, advertising and customer relations. The rise of internet search engines, such as Yahoo! and Google, are linked to the growth in e-commerce. As case study 11.3 illustrates, the consumer now tends to reach first for a search engine when looking to shop online. There are still drawbacks to online purchases of goods and services, a major one being security. Although the technology of security systems is improving, security breaches are a serious threat in e-commerce.

Case study 11.3   Feeling lucky with Google

The meteoric rise of Google, the internet search engine company, has lifted the gloom which followed the dot.com crash of 1999–2000. Since its launch in 1998 by Stanford University students, Larry Page and Sergey Brin, it has become the most visited site on the web, and, like its biggest rival, Yahoo!, Google has become a global brand. Google's rapid increase in revenues is shown in the figure opposite. Has it learnt the lessons of the earlier dot.com failures? One factor is the apparent soundness of its business model. It was conceived purely as an internet search engine. It has prided itself on its impartiality, allowing internet users to find the sites which would be of greatest value to them, rather than directing them to companies that had paid for promotion. Advertising, which generates 96 per cent of its revenue, is kept separate from the search results. The 'sponsored search' allows the consumer to click on sites related to the particular search – advertisers pay for each 'click' that the consumer makes on their website. The price is determined by advertisers bidding against each other in a real-time online auction for the privilege of having their messages displayed when certain key words are entered in the search engine. A second factor is the fact that, as a private company, Google was insulated from the investment fever that surrounded the dot.com bubble. However, with its huge popularity, the owners decided to turn Google into a public company with an initial public offering (IPO) in 2004. The prospects looked good, especially as the search engine has increasingly become a driver of e-commerce.

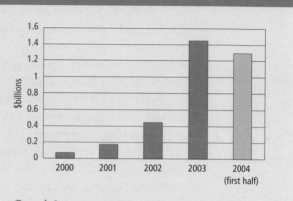

Google's revenues
Source: *Financial Times*, 19 August 2004.

One in every five consumers who is looking for a specific product turns first to a search engine, rather than a specialist e-tailer. Google has been particularly successful in capturing this market (see second figure). However, challengers have also been active in expanding into e-commerce. Yahoo!, in particular, has made a number of acquisitions of companies, combining search technology with other services to the consumer. For example, when the consumer turns first to a search engine to find specific products, often what is sought is comparisons of different prices and products. Yahoo! has acquired a company to provide this service, while Google's equivalent, Froogle, is still in the formative stages. Although Google is the most popular search engine, it has no unique content and no long-term customer relationship with those who use its search engine. It has been remarked that Google 'is only as good as its last search' (Gapper, 28 October

2003). This is in marked contrast with Yahoo!, which has is own databases and customer networks. Google's engineers have developed email technology and are confident that their new free email service, Gmail, will compete with rivals, Yahoo! and Microsoft.

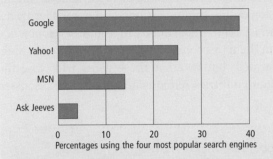

US consumers using search engines to reach e-commerce sites, Christmas 2003
Source: Waters, 23 February 2004.

A concern for Google is that, however successful the model, the history of the internet demonstrates that competitors are soon at work copying and improving it. Biggest among these is Microsoft, which is developing a new search engine. Because of Microsoft's ability to integrate it with other services and content, bundling search with the Windows operating system, Microsoft will be guaranteed a large market, constituting a serious challenge to Google's supremacy.

A second concern is that the growing internationalization of the internet makes it more difficult for the one-size-fits-all search engine to satisfy consumers. Google's international advertising revenues are a growing proportion of its total revenues, having grown from 14 per cent in 2001 to 30 per cent in 2004. This reflects the fact that more than half its user traffic is outside the US. The number of internet users outside the US is estimated to grow at 13 per cent per annum, twice the rate of growth within the US. While Google's service is provided in 97 languages

worldwide, the growth in international usage offers opportunities for internet start-ups to provide services in local markets which the 'one-size-fits-all' approach cannot satisfy. One backer of a European internet venture has said: 'You can't use overwhelming firepower with a limited number of troops on the ground and no understanding of the locals or the culture and then expect you're going to win and be the market leader' (Waters and Nuttall,10 June 2004).

In launching itself as a public company in 2004, Google chose the novel method of inviting the public to bid for its shares in an auction. The founders hoped for a sound send-off, underlining the company's value while avoiding speculation which led to the boom and bust that afflicted earlier internet companies. In the event, when shares began trading, they rose 20 per cent on the first day, in a solid, but undramatic, start. In a letter to potential investors, Google has said that it 'has a responsibility to the world', not just to shareholders who invest in the company (London, 30 April 2004.) Its apparently idealistic stance is rather tempered by the dual share structure, by which the two founders will retain control of the company. Its letter also advises investors that, as the company matures, growth will be expected to slow. This amounts to a note of timely realism in view of the multiple challenges it faces from competitors in both technology and marketing.

Sources: Waters, R., 'Google's buried treasure', *Financial Times*, 23 July 2003; Gapper, J., 'Why Google's technology may have reached its peak', *Financial Times*, 28 October 2003; Waters, R., 'A tussle for power in online shopping: the sites may have the goods, but search engines have the eyeballs', *Financial Times*, 23 February 2004; London, S., 'Method of sale puts onus on each investor', *Financial Times*, 30 April 2004; Waters, R. and Nuttall, C., 'Going global: from shopping to search, America's online giants have their sights set on international expansion', *Financial Times*, 10 June, 2004; Waters, R., 'Google's rivals in search for supremacy', *Financial Times*, 30 April 2004; Schurr, S., 'Google's offering heralds an end to boom and bust', *Financial Times*, 21 August 2004; London, S., 'Google search finds concern with structure', *Financial Times*, 23 August 2004.

Case questions

What has been Google's recipe for success?
How is its search engine supremacy being challenged?

B2B e-commerce provides opportunities for worldwide sourcing for all sectors, including raw materials, components and services. The internet can save costs by streamlining purchasing, distribution and marketing. While the benefits have been apparent to multinationals, SMEs have also benefited. SMEs are able to form networks linked to multinational companies, opening up new avenues for the cooperative development of technology as well as markets. The transnational 'web' of global production networks is transforming supply chains. In 1999, General Motors and Ford announced plans to develop online trading exchanges for supplier transactions. Again, there are social and labour implications of these developments. Developing countries may gain from the new economy, as software centres in India and the Philippines have demonstrated, but whether these gains will close the 'digital divide' between rich and poor countries remains an issue (to be discussed further in Chapter 14).

WEB ALERT!

The UK Government sponsors a global information network for SMEs at http://www.businesslink.gov.uk

Biotechnology

Biotechnology is 'the application of scientific and engineering principles to the processing of materials by biological agents to provide goods and services' (OECD, 1999). Because biotechnology is concerned with the manipulation of living organisms, it is often called 'life science' technology. Practical applications extend from primary sectors (such as agriculture and forestry) to secondary industries (such as food, chemicals and drugs). The growth in biotechnology is a further aspect of technological convergence, made possible by the advances in computing. Research on the genetic makeup of living organisms has led to 'genetic engineering' or genetic modification. The research is relatively young, having begun only in the 1980s. Genetically modified (GM) bacteria producing human insulin for the treatment of diabetes was approved in 1986, as was the first vaccine using DNA. The use of vaccines to prevent disease is one of the greatest potential benefits from the new science of microbiology. Whereas treatment for many diseases is expensive and inaccessible, vaccines offer an affordable alternative. In developing countries in particular, the death toll from preventable diseases, especially the childhood killer diseases, could be dramatically reduced (Freeman and Robbins, 1995).

Biotechnology research has not been without controversy. Scientists have inserted foreign genes into animals in their efforts to study human diseases and possible cures. PPL Therapeutics, a company based in Scotland, created Dolly the sheep and was successful in obtaining a patent from the EPO. Researchers in the US have created a cloned monkey, the first GM primate. Under the EU Biotechnology Patents Directive, neither DNA nor the human genome can be patented, as they are discoveries of realities which already exist. However, an invention based on gene sequences, requiring the isolation and manufacture of genes, can be patented, as human intervention is involved, assuming the process is capable of industrial application.

WEB ALERT!

Many biotechnology resources may be found at
http://www.cals.Arizona.edu/biotechnology

The OECD provides links to biotechnology resources at http://oecd.org. From here, go to 'topics' and click on 'biotechnology'

Sources on biotechnology in food and agriculture are available through the website of the UN Food and Agriculture Organization at
http://www.fao.org/biotech/news

Research has made possible the breeding of high-yield, disease-resistant plants, with a reduced reliance on pesticides and herbicides. However, it has given rise to ethical questions which have generated heated debate, centred on food safety and the environmental impact. One of these concerns is doubts over the research underpinning GM foods, including food safety and environmental effects. North American consumers have so far been relatively unperturbed about GM foods, whereas European consumers have been much more sceptical, as discussed in Case study 11.4. Some experts argue that scientific advances hold out genuine prospects of revolutionizing food production, to feed the growing populations of developing countries. This raises a second ethical concern, which is the powerful position of the few global companies, all based in industrialized countries, that now dominate the world's agribusiness sector. The expansion of the use of patents to cover seed varieties has helped to consolidate their economic power, but also raised questions of public policy and accountability. Farming communities in developing countries fear the risk to local ecosystems from GM crops, while reducing their scope to produce alternative crops.

Case study 11.4 Food for thought in the debate on genetically modified organisms

The production of genetically engineered plants to endow them with various qualities, such as the corn that produces its own pesticide, is altering farming and food systems, but there are doubts about the long-term effects in both developed and developing countries. In 1996, genetically modified (GM) crops were planted on 1.7 million hectares worldwide. In 2002, altered soya, corn, cotton and other crops were grown on 58.7 million hectares, most of it in the US, Argentina, Canada and China. In 1996, just six countries grew GM crops, while the number had grown to 16 by 2002, and nine of these are developing countries, where the growth in GM crops has been the strongest (see figure). In 2002, India, Colombia, Honduras and the Philippines approved biotech crops. However, the US is far ahead of other countries. It is estimated that as much as 70 per cent of the foods on the shelves of US supermarkets contain GM ingredients, although it is difficult to tell, as there is no mandatory labelling in the US. US biotechnology companies have invested heavily in developing GM strains, which now account for 75 per cent of the soya bean crop, 71 per cent of the cotton crop and 34 per cent of the maize crop in the US.

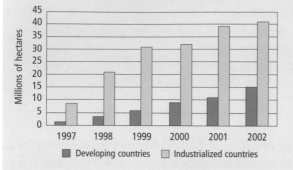

Global area of genetically modified crops
Source: Mason, 16 January 2003.

European consumers have been sceptical about GM foods. Eurobarometer, the European market research group, has found that European consumers question the safety of GM foods: 44 per cent felt GM foods to be less safe than other foods; 28 per cent said they have confidence in GM foods; and 27 per cent said they do not know (Mason, 14 May 2003). The EU has imposed a moratorium on the import of GM products, which the US has maintained is in contravention of WTO rules. However, the case is not clear-cut: WTO rules do allow for trade restrictions where there is a risk to health. The US has argued that there are no risks posed to health, and that the European ban is unjustified. The EU response has been a cautious one, reflecting disagreement among scientists on the possible long-term effects of GM foods and also highlighting a wide range of concerns of European consumers, whose confidence has been dented by a succession of food scares, including foot-and-mouth disease. The EU is legislating to require the labelling and traceability of GM foods, and setting a threshold above which the presence of GM products in food (for humans and animal feed) must be indicated on the packaging. Trials of GM crops in the UK, one of the world's largest such experiments, found that the crops were damaging for birds, insects and plantlife, causing concerns for biodi-

versity. Increasingly in Europe, farming exists alongside tourist and leisure industries. The report of the trials highlights the balance that needs to be made between agricultural production and opportunities for biodiversity. There is also concern over the 'co-existence' of GM and non-GM farming, as cross-pollination inevitably occurs.

For developing countries, research has made possible a high-protein maize and 'golden rice' enriched with Vitamin A, which can aid the estimated two million children vulnerable to diseases related to Vitamin A deficiency in poor countries. Both were invented by Western scientists, funded by research institutes, but IP rights have been acquired by global life science corporations, Monsanto (now part of Pharmacia & Upjohn) and AstraZeneca. In a friendly gesture, they are giving developing countries' farmers free access to the grain. Sceptics question the use of golden rice as a 'quick-fix' remedy, pointing to more low-tech, cost-effective alternatives, such as the reintroduction of the diverse food plants which farmers used to grow before the 'green revolution' of the 1960s brought high-yield hybrid plants, also produced by Western laboratories. In 2002, despite widespread food shortages in Africa, a number of African countries rejected GM emergency relief food from the US, for fear that if it finds its way into their agricultural systems, it could affect their ecosystems. It could also affect their prospects of exports to the EU. In addition to the issue of food safety, the wider issue of environmental impact has risen up the agenda in the debate over GM crops. Meanwhile, scientific research proceeds on future generations of more complex organisms.

Sources: Mason, J., 'Scientists disagree, but farmers' harvests grow', *Financial Times*, 14 May 2003; Mason, J., 'World production of biotech crops keeps growing, *Financial Times*, 16 January, 2003; de Jonquières, G., Alden, E. and Buck, T., 'Sowing discord', *Financial Times*, 14 May 2004; Marquis, C., 'Monsanto plans to offer rights to its altered-rice technology', *New York Times*, 4 August 2000; Pollack, A., 'On the trail of genetically altered corn flour from Azteca', *New York Times*, 30 September 2000; Pollack, A., 'Kraft recalls taco shells with bioengineered corn', *New York Times*, 23 September 2000.

Case questions

What are the concerns highlighted in the case study over GM food?
In your view, how would it be possible to derive the benefits offered by
GM crops without risk to health and biodiversity?

Globalization and technological innovation

Howells and Wood (1993, p. 7) pose the question: 'How is the global shaping of production (in terms of overall corporate structures) influencing the distribution and character of R&D and technical competence?' According to them: 'Corporate, and consequently, national, performance [is at] the interface between research/technical know-how and production'. We have seen in this chapter that the globalization of production has led to a diffusion of technology, but also that technological capacities still depend to a large extent on national innovation systems. It is also true that technological innovation increasingly depends on links between scientific research and industrial R&D, both of which differ between national technological environments. The R&D strategies of global companies aim to draw on sectoral specializations offered by specific countries. Archibugi and Michie (1997b, p. 191) observe: 'Nations are becoming *increasingly* different and the international operations of large firms are exploiting and developing this diversity.'

In generating innovation and exploiting its fruits, globalization processes highlight the continued role of national government policies. By providing incentives to companies for innovative activities and supportive infrastructure such as industry/university partnerships, governments can attract the innovative activities that generate competitive advantage. It is for this reason that Michael Porter and others stress the importance of government in fostering innovation (Porter, 1998b). Technological innovation thus has a national as well as global dimension. Countries which have concentrated on low-cost, labour-intensive manufacturing industries have been less successful in developing the more technologically advanced production systems. It is arguable that businesses in these countries may find opportunities in the knowledge-intensive industries of the new economy, where geographic location is less important. On the other hand, poor developing countries risk falling further behind, opening up a 'digital divide' between rich and poor countries. We return to this issue in Chapter 14, with a discussion of the challenges facing international businesses.

Conclusions

1   Technology is central to economic development and prosperity. Technological innovation can lead to competitive advantages in the world economy.

2   Innovation is a broad term, ranging from seemingly modest improvements in operations to radical new inventions that transform the way we live.

3   Technological development can be seen in terms of 'long waves' or cycles, each wave denoted by its dominant new technology, which transforms both the methods of production and organizational structures. The current wave is that of microelectronics and computer networks.

4   The national system of innovation is defined as the institutions by which a country's innovation activities are encouraged and facilitated. Education and training, as well as industrial structures, are important components. Interactions, both formal and informal, are increasingly seen as contributing to innovation networks.

5   Patents are an indication of the amount of formal innovation in a society, and also the sources of innovation. Both products and processes, if new and industrially applicable, can be patented. Patent law regimes are still essentially national.

6   For developing countries, technology transfer represents a variety of means for acquiring technology from other countries. They include FDI, joint ventures, licensing and trade in capital goods. The diffusion of technology is increasingly seen as an interactive process, in which host countries can develop independent innovative capacities over time.

7   Information and communication technology (ICT) has led to transformational change in all aspects of business life. The growth in B2B e-commerce, in particular, is bringing about greater efficiencies in design, production and distribution.

8   The impact of the globalization of production on the generation of global technological innovation is much debated. The R&D activities of TNCs are becoming more dispersed, benefiting from nation-specific specialisms.

Review questions

1   Explain science-push and demand-pull in the development of new technology.

2   What is Schumpeter's view of technological innovation and waves of economic development?

3   Outline the elements of a national system of innovation. How relevant is the educational and training environment of the country?

4   Which countries have evolved particularly successful national innovation systems and why?

5   Why are patents crucial to a technological lead?

6   What are the conditions which must be satisfied before a patent may be obtained for a process or product?

7 Why is the TRIPS agreement said to be disadvantageous to developing countries?

8 Describe briefly the four ways in which technology transfer takes place, pointing to the advantages and disadvantages of each.

9 In what ways has the revolution in IT transformed business?

10 Assess the possible benefits and the ethical issues of biotechnology research.

Assignments

1 Assume that you are advising the government of an industrializing economy on (a) policies designed to bolster national innovative capacities; and (b) policies to gain maximum benefit from technology transfer afforded by its inward investors in manufacturing. What would these policies be?

2 To what extent is R&D becoming 'globalized', and in what ways may developing countries reap R&D advantages which could spill over into their domestic companies?

Further reading

Afuah, A. (2003) *Innovation Management* (Oxford: Oxford University Press).

Archibugi, D. and Michie, J. (1997) *Technology, Globalisation and Economic Performance* (Cambridge: Cambridge University Press).

Castells, M. (2000) *The Rise of the Network Society*, 2nd edn (Oxford: Blackwells).

Freeman, C. and Soete, L. (1997) *The Economics of Industrial Innovation*, 3rd edn (London: Cassell).

Landes, D. (1998) *The Wealth and Poverty of Nations* (London: Abacus).

Pearce, R. (1997) *Global Competition and Technology* (Basingstoke: Palgrave – now Palgrave Macmillan).

Tidd, J., Bessant, J. and Pavitt, K. (2005) *Managing Innovation* (London: John Wiley).

12 International financial markets

Outline of chapter

- Introduction
- International capital markets
  - Stock exchanges
  - Bond markets
- Development of the international monetary system
  - The gold standard
  - The Bretton Woods agreement
- Foreign exchange in the contemporary environment
  - Exchange rate systems
  - Money markets
- The International Monetary Fund (IMF) and the World Bank
- The Asian financial crisis
  - Genesis of the crisis
  - Aftermath of the crisis
- Global markets for corporate control
  - Mergers and acquisitions
  - Trends in cross-border mergers
- Regulation and TNCs
- The global financial environment and developing countries
- Conclusions

Learning objectives

1 To gain an overview of the evolving structures and processes that make up the international financial system, including the extent and implications of financial globalization for international business.

2 To analyse the ways in which shifting patterns of global finance have impacted in diverse economic environments, including developed, industrializing and developing countries.

3 To gain an insight into the role of transnational corporations in driving globalization through strategies of acquisition and control.

Introduction

Smoothness and efficiency in financial transactions are valued by all businesses, whether local, national or international. For business dealings which are entirely within national boundaries, these aims are more easily achieved than cross-border dealings. With globalization, many more firms, including SMEs, are internationally active. There is therefore a growing need for businesspeople to grasp the essential aspects of the international financial environment. Growing trade networks lead to a demand for cross-border financial services. These include currency exchanges, stock exchanges, banks and other financial intermediaries by which money transfers take place and credit is arranged. Like international trade in goods, cross-border financial flows have existed for centuries. However, the twentieth century saw major changes in international finance. Growing overseas investment, as well as trade, led to the growth of global capital markets and global financial institutions. Facilitated by improvements in communications technology, cross-border capital flows have become more extensive, and national financial systems have become more deeply enmeshed than ever before in global financial networks.

Global financial markets are now 24-hour-a-day, fast-moving and complex processes, whose operations are on a scale which dwarf many national governments: world foreign exchanges deal with an average $1490bn. every day. This chapter attempts to demystify these processes as they impact on businesses. It explains in relatively simple terms how international financial institutions interact with businesses, investors and national financial systems. As will be seen, sharply differing perspectives have emerged between enterprises, consumers and governments. The growth of international financial institutions, raising broad questions of stability and control in financial markets, has drawn both praise and criticism. From the business point of view, there are huge benefits from integrated markets, which have been particularly evident in emerging markets, but there are also risks of instability and vulnerability to financial shocks. TNCs have been major drivers of financial globalization and this chapter explores their role in global financial markets. Shifting patterns of corporate control, now evident on a global scale, have revealed the differing perspectives of corporate management, shareholders, lenders, consumers and governments. With globalization has come greater awareness of the interactions between market, national and international forces that increasingly impact on international business.

International capital markets

Access to capital is essential for every company. Firms may turn to banks and other institutions for loans, raising capital by debt financing, or they may raise capital through share offerings, known as equity financing. In practice, companies rely on both equity and debt financing. When share prices have been buoyant, investors have flocked to purchase shares. With high-tech shares in particular, investors became accustomed to dramatic increases in share prices in the 1990s, but these giddy heights could not be sustained and prices tumbled in 2000. When a company is publicly 'floated', it is listed on a stock exchange, and its shares are offered through an initial public offering (IPO). In the 1990s, European countries saw a steep rise in the number of IPOs, largely because of privatizations in major industries such as telecommunications (see Figure 12.1). The largest in 2000 was the flotation of Deutsche Post, Europe's biggest postal service operator, in a market capitalization of €23.4bn. IPOs lost momentum towards the end of 2000, as investor sentiment cooled. Since then, companies have cautiously resumed flotations. Most notably, Google's successful flotation, discussed in Case Study 11.4, is an indication of renewed confidence. On the other hand, Deutsche Post, which came back to the market in 2004 with the flotation of Postbank, had been overconfident in anticipating what German investors would be willing to pay and scaled back the initial price just before the launch.

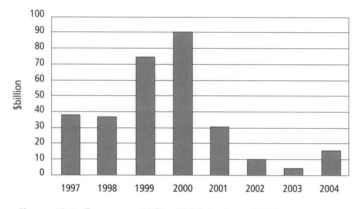

Figure 12.1 **European IPOs, 1997 to June 2004**
Source: *Financial Times*, 24 June 2004.

Stock exchanges

By 2000, the total capitalization of the world's publicly traded equity was over $20 trillion (New York Stock Exchange, 2000). Capital markets refer to capital flows, including equity investments (portfolio investment) and also government securities. They are handled through stock exchanges, which facilitate the buying and selling of shares and other securities, in an increasingly integrated global economy. Companies may apply for a 'listing' on a stock exchange, allowing their shares to be traded publicly in equity markets. Stock exchanges are located in financial centres around the world. Along with traditional exchanges, such as the New York Stock Exchange (NYSE) and London Stock Exchange, there are rapidly growing newer exchanges, such as the NASDAQ (National Association of Securities Dealers Automated Quotations) in New York. Founded in 1971, the NASDAQ focuses on technology and other 'new economy' stocks. These stocks suffered generally in the crash of dot-com stocks in 2000, but have been regaining value since 2003. The successful launch of Google on the NASDAQ in 2004 helped to rebuild confidence. In Europe, the Frankfurt Neuer Markt was founded in 1997, amid great optimism over technology stocks, but fell victim to their downfall in 2000 and was closed down in January

2003. As can be seen in Figure 12.2, share prices fell generally in the early years of the new millennium, starting to rise again in 2003.

There are many indices following the movement of share prices, including the Dow Jones Industrial Average and NASDAQ Composite in New York and a number of FTSE indices, including the FTSE 100 index in London. These indices, which represent baskets of shares, only give a performance benchmark and have been criticized as not reflecting true market performance (Coggan, 2000). The typical picture of frantic trading on the floor of stock exchanges is now becoming outdated, with the rise in electronic trading systems, which facilitate global trading. The New York Stock Exchange now handles 40 per cent of its volume through SuperDOT, its computerized trading system (New York Stock Exchange, 2000).

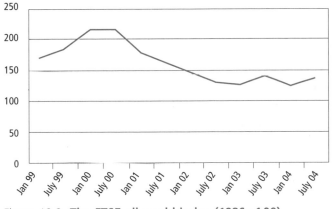

Figure 12.2 **The FTSE all-world index (1986=100)**
Source: The Economist Group (2004) *The World in 2004*; FTSE Group.

While stock markets historically served the needs of investors within their national borders, global companies now often seek listings outside their home countries in order to attract more international investors. The NYSE, NASDAQ and the London Stock Exchange all have significant numbers of foreign companies listed (see Figure 12.3). An important trend in capital markets has been the growth of institutional investors, such as pension funds and other investment funds. On the other hand, some foreign companies have recently delisted from the New York exchanges, following the implementation of the Sarbanes-Oxley Act in the US, which increased criminal liabilities of directors for financial reporting requirements of their companies. Investment institutions have broadened their horizons from their national markets to international markets. The largest are the US institutional investors, who have assets six times the size of their European counterparts. The US-based index fund managers lead the world in international investment, accounting for about 70 per cent of the entire market for internationally traded equities (Conference Board, 1999). Some of these institutional shareholders, such as the California Public Employees (CalPERS), with $24.3bn. in foreign equities, are noted for their shareholder activism. Their greater participation in international markets is likely, as the Conference Board points out, to lead to greater pressures on company boards to maintain a focus on shareholder value.

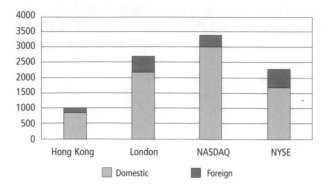

Figure 12.3 **Number of shares listed on major stock exchanges (2003)**
Source: *Financial Times*, 19 September 2003.

Stock exchanges are subject to national regulation. Regulatory systems aim to establish transparency and 'market integrity, that is, ensuring that the market is fair and efficient and warrants public confidence' (OECD, 2000a). Cross-border markets present new challenges to national systems of regulation. Integration in capital markets has not been matched by integrated regulatory frameworks. The advent of e-commerce, which facilitates almost instantaneous securities transactions around the globe, benefits investors but is vulnerable to market abuse. Protection of the investing public is a major concern of stock market regulators. In the US, the Securities and Exchange Commission (SEC) provides oversight, but there has been a tradition of self-regulation for stock markets. Recent scandals have shaken confidence in the NYSE, which acts as both a marketplace and regulator, raising the possibility of reforms which would separate the roles of running the stock market and regulating the companies which trade in it. Such a reform would bring the NYSE more into line with other exchanges, such as the British and German, where the regulator is an independent body. The NASDAQ provides an example of this separation of powers, whereby the regulator, the National Association of Securities Dealers, is under separate ownership from NASDAQ.

In the UK, the regulation of financial services was reformed by the Financial Services and Markets Act 2000. Under the new framework, the Financial Services

Authority (FSA) took over from nine former regulatory authorities, acquiring wide powers of regulation in insurance, investment business and banking. These are summarized in the box below.

Minifile

THE UK FINANCIAL SERVICES AUTHORITY

The expanded role of the FSA under the Financial Services and Markets Act 2000 includes:

- Authorization and supervision of stockbrokers and financial advisors
- Oversight of the new offence of 'market abuse', aimed to protect the investing community

- Banking supervision
- Regulation of building societies
- Protection of investors, taking over from the Investment Management Regulatory Organization and Personal Investment Authority
- Supervision of insurance services, taking over from the Insurance Directorate.

Most stock exchanges have gone through a period of liberalizing, 'big bang' reforms, dismantling restrictions on trading and opening up markets. Although much of the EU has adopted a single currency, it has been much slower to integrate financial markets. The persistence of home country supervision has allowed fragmentation in financial markets to persist, with the result that investors have not as yet been able to take advantage of the full benefits of the single currency. One stumbling block has been the contentious issue of harmonizing tax rules, which has been politically highly sensitive. Businesses within the EU have urged government finance ministers to speed up the integration of financial regulatory systems, in order to enhance the efficiency (and investor appeal) of its capital markets. A single regulatory regime for the EU would facilitate investment across borders and protect consumers who purchase financial products anywhere in the EU. Framework EU legislation was put in place in 2004, to bring a single regulatory regime closer to reality, but much detail remained to be filled in.

WEB ALERT!

The UK Financial Services Authority is at http://www.fsa.gov.uk. This site provides a summary of the Financial Services and Markets Act 2000

The US Securities and Exchange Commission is at http://www.sec.gov/

Bond markets

Debt financing has given rise to an international bond market which facilitates trade in a variety of loan instruments. A **bond** is a loan document promising to pay a specific sum of money on a fixed date and to pay interest at stated intervals (Held et al., 1999, p. 205). Bonds are marketable securities which can be issued in different currencies. An 'external bond' is one issued by a borrower in a capital market outside the borrower's own country. The external bond may be a foreign bond, which is denominated in the currency of the country in which it is issued. **Eurobonds**, by contrast, are denominated in currencies other than those of the countries in which they are issued. Dollar-denominated bonds issued outside the US are examples of eurobonds. Their attraction has been that they escape official regulation. Global bonds are the most flexible of bonds, as they may be sold inside as well as outside the country in whose currency they are denominated. Dollar global bonds are regulated by the US SEC. The World Bank is the leading issuer of global bonds. Governments have also raised money in this way, with the recent addition of developing countries. However, as Case Study 12.1 shows, such investments can be risky, even though they are government, or 'sovereign', debt. In the international bond market, eurobonds account for about 70 per cent, while foreign and global bonds amount to 30 per cent (Kim and Kim, 1999, p. 276). Banks are the largest borrowers, followed by corporations and governments.

Companies must listen to bondholders as well as shareholders when taking strategic decisions. As can be seen in Figure 12.4, corporate bonds grew in popularity from 2000 onwards, largely because of weak share performance, but, as equities recovered, the attraction of bonds diminished. Telecommunications companies have relied heavily on the issue of bonds, in particular, to pay government authorities for 3G mobile phone licences. In 1998, telecoms companies issued $65bn. of debt globally, whereas the figure for 2000 was $155bn. As of December 2000, the biggest ever multicurrency corporate bond issue was that of Deutsche Telekom in June 2000, amounting to $14.6bn. of debt.

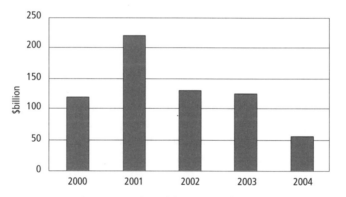

Figure 12.4 **Corporate bond issues in the US, 2000 to June 2004**
Source: *Financial Times*, 6 September 2004.

Development of the international monetary system

Besides equity investment and debt financing, global finance also includes the important element of cross-border flows of money, via money markets. Currencies are generally controlled by national central banks, although the European Central Bank is more akin to a 'supranational' institution. Currencies, however, are linked in global financial networks, which have become more integrated as trade and FDI have grown. The growth in global financial flows has outpaced both trade and output (Held et al., 1999, p. 203). For businesses, consumers and governments, stability in international finance is a priority. However, achieving an effective international system has relied on cooperation between sovereign states, which has encountered numerous hurdles. In order to understand the challenges currently confronting international financial institutions, we need to look briefly at how they have evolved.

The gold standard

The rise in trade and financial flows from the late nineteenth century led to the growing internationalization of finance. To facilitate these movements, the world's major trading nations adopted a global gold standard system, which lasted from the 1870s to 1914, a period in which Britain was the strongest trading nation. Under the gold standard, all currencies were 'pegged' to gold, which removed the uncertainty of transactions involving different currencies. For each currency, a conversion rate into gold ensured stability. The system required countries to convert their currency into gold on demand, and did not restrict international gold flows. Governments willingly endorsed the system, even though, in theory, it reduced their control over their own economic policy. In practice, governments did not always play by the 'rules of the game', and there was more national monetary autonomy than supposed (Eichengreen, 1996, p. 28). Significantly, national interest rates, while they showed some convergence, were largely influenced by domestic conditions. Nonetheless, the gold standard period represented the emergence of a global financial order.

The maintenance of the gold standard depended on central banks' continuing commitment to external convertibility. Eichengreen (1996, p. 46) comments:

> The essence of the pre-war system was a commitment by governments to convert domestic currency into fixed quantities of gold and freedom for individuals to export and import gold obtained from official and other sources.

This system broke down with the First World War, when governments used precious metal to purchase military supplies and restricted movements in the gold market, thus causing currencies to float. The system collapsed, despite efforts to resurrect it in the interwar period, during which government priorities had shifted from exchange rate stability to domestic economic concerns. Moreover, the domination, or hegemony, that Britain had exerted over capital markets had declined and the rise of American commercial and financial power did not lead to its taking on a similar role in the international system (Eichengreen, 1996, p. 92).

The Bretton Woods agreement

The Bretton Woods agreement at the close of the Second World War was meant to usher in a new international financial order and a restoration of stable foreign exchange. It was not, however, simply a revamped gold standard system. It differed from the gold standard system in three ways:

1 Currencies were pegged to the dollar, with the dollar fixed in terms of gold at $35 an ounce. This was an 'adjustable peg'. A country could alter its currency only if it was in 'fundamental disequilibrium', which was not fully defined.
2 Controls were permitted, to limit private financial flows.
3 A new institution, the International Monetary Fund (IMF) was created to monitor national economic policies. The IMF could also help out countries with balance of payments difficulties.

The Bretton Woods system has been described as 'a compromise between the free traders, who desired open global markets, and the social democrats, who desired national prosperity and full employment' (Held et al., 1999, p. 201). It aimed to liberalize world trade, but also took into account governments' wishes to maintain systems of social protection and other domestic objectives. This meant that governments had considerable autonomy to pursue domestic economic policies.

During the 1950s and into the 60s, international capital flows were low, largely because of national capital controls and also the limited infrastructure for private international capital flows. This situation was about to change dramatically. Events in the 1960s and 70s led to the collapse of the Bretton Woods system. Three factors can be highlighted. First, the US in the 1960s was gripped by inflation and a mounting trade deficit, fuelled by increasing imports, largely from the growing economies of Europe. Secondly, there rose the 'euromarkets', which were systems for taking foreign currency deposits, such as dollar deposits, in European banks (Kapstein, 1994, p. 32). The source of the dollars could be individual investors, central banks or firms. From the 1950s, the eurocurrency market grew, as funds flowed into European banks and European economies were growing. European banks were able to expand their eurocurrency business, unrestrained by national regulations and capital controls. Thirdly, OPEC's quadrupling of the price of oil (see Case study 10.1) had the effect of transferring huge sums from the oil-importing countries to the oil-exporting countries. The oil exporters, with their mounting surpluses, invested in international money markets, swelling the funds of international banks. Much of this OPEC surplus was recycled to developing countries, thus contributing to the expansion of global financial flows. The effects of a booming eurocurrency market, combined with US inflation and a growing trade deficit, led to speculative activities against the US dollar, the linchpin currency of Bretton Woods. In 1971, President Nixon announced that the dollar would no longer be convertible to gold, heralding the collapse of the Bretton Woods system, with its system of fixed exchange rates. This brought about extreme volatility in exchange rates.

SUMMARY POINTS

Stages in the development of an international monetary system

The gold standard (1870s to 1914):
- Exchange rates fixed to the value of gold
- Freedom to export and import gold.

The Bretton Woods system (1944–71):
- Currencies pegged to the dollar, in turn fixed to the value of gold
- Controls on private financial flows permitted
- Establishment of the IMF, to oversee stable foreign exchange.

Post-Bretton Woods:
- Countries determine exchange rates, under oversight of the IMF
- By the Jamaica Agreement of 1976, the IMF allows greater exchange rate flexibility.

Foreign exchange in the contemporary environment

When firms carry out transactions across national borders, the need to convert from one currency to another arises leading to cross-border **currency flows**. The mechanisms for paying in other currencies are referred to as **foreign exchange**. The 'exchange rate' is the number of units of one currency that are needed to purchase one unit of another currency. The US dollar is the basis of much international business although its value fluctuates (see Figure 12.5). The US dollar is said to be 'fully convertible', or a 'hard' currency. This means that it can be exchanged by both residents and non-residents, without exchange controls, that is, with no limits on the amount. Many currencies, by contrast, are 'weak' and not fully convertible.

Exchange rate systems

Exchange rate systems vary from fixed exchange rates at one extreme to floating exchange rates at the other. A **fixed exchange rate** may be set by government, whereas a **floating exchange rate** allows the value of the currency to be determined by day-to-day trading in the foreign exchange markets. An alternative is the **pegged exchange rate**, by which a country's currency is tied to another currency, such as the US dollar, and moves up or down in accordance with the other currency. With the collapse of the Bretton Woods fixed exchange rate system, the IMF altered its rules to allow greater exchange rate flexibility. Accordingly, countries can maintain their own exchange rate policy. Exchange rates pegged to the dollar, which allow only limited flexibility, are often cited as one of the causes of the Asian financial crisis (which is discussed below), as governments struggled to maintain the peg.

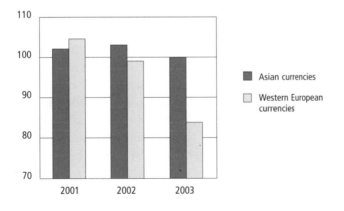

Notes:
Indices, January 2001=100.
Western European currencies are those of the eurozone, the UK, Switzerland, Sweden and Norway.
Asian currencies are those of Japan, China, Republic of Korea, Taiwan, Singapore and Hong Kong.

Figure 12.5 **Dollar fluctuation against Western European and Asian currencies**
Source: WTO (2003) *International Trade Statistics 2003*, at www.wto.org.

Floating exchange rates can allow rapid movements in value, which may hamper governments' wishes to maintain low inflation. In practice, most systems allow for 'managed' exchange rates allowing fluctuation within specified bands. In 1979, the

European Community set up the Exchange Rate Mechanism (ERM), which limited fluctuations within a target zone of 2.25 per cent either side of an agreed value. The British pound and Italian lira were both forced out of the system in 1992, largely, it is thought, because of the activities of well-known hedge fund managers (see next section). After these events, the bands were widened to 15 per cent. The ERM has been superseded by the European Monetary Union, from 1999. This is a fixed exchange rate system, using a common currency (see Chapter 3 for a fuller description of EMU).

SUMMARY POINTS

!!!

Determination of exchange rates

- **Fixed exchange rates** – determined by government or other agreement, for example the member states' national currencies within the eurozone.
- **Pegged exchange rates** – value of the currency is linked to the value of another currency, or basket of currencies, for example the US dollar.
- **More flexible arrangements** – allow the currency to float according to supply and demand, with limited government intervention. The major industrial countries fall into this category, including the US and Japan. The euro also falls into this category.

Money markets

Companies which do business internationally are directly affected by foreign exchange rates. Their transactions thus expose them to financial risk. To protect them from adverse currency fluctuations, they may turn to trading in currency markets. The 'currency futures contract' allows a business to buy or sell a specific amount of foreign currency at a designated price in the future. They are therefore said to have a hedge against future fluctuations which can adversely affect their business. For TNCs, importers, exporters and others, dealings on the currency markets are incidental to their main business. If a firm's main business is to buy and sell currencies with a view to profit, it engages in 'arbitrage'. This is a type of speculation, in which the buying and selling of a commodity, such as currency, contains considerable risk, but also a chance to make handsome profits. A wide range of financial instruments, known as 'derivatives', have been devised, so named because they are derived from primary dealings in equities, commodities and currencies. Derivative contracts allow companies to transfer financial risk between parties, although not to eliminate it (Brown, 2000).

Trade in derivatives grew enormously in the 1990s. Hedge funds are associated with fund managers such as George Soros, who acquired a 'troublemaker' image from the point of view of governments, fearful of speculation against their currencies. The downfall of the fund, Long Term Capital Management (LTCM), is often highlighted as the most spectacular example of the risks of hedge funds. LTCM was based on what was thought to be a low-risk arbitrage strategy built on an efficient market model. Founded in 1994, it seemed like a 'money machine' at the time, so masterful were its managers (Stulz, 2000). But a collapse in bond markets, triggered by Russia's debt default in 1998, brought LTCM to the brink of bankruptcy, threatening to destabilize world financial markets. It was rescued by a consortium of 14 financial institutions, which provided a $3.63bn. bailout at short notice. The failure of LTCM was a graphic lesson that risk management is not an exact science. Since then, hedge funds have become more cautious and closer to mainstream investments. Moreover, the global economy has changed and developing countries in particular have seen the risks in adopting currency pegs. This point is illustrated in Case study 12.1 on Argentina.

The International Monetary Fund (IMF) and the World Bank

Although the Bretton Woods system of fixed exchange rates disintegrated in the 1970s, the IMF and the World Bank, which were created in the 1940s by the Bretton Woods agreement, have continued to grow and become important actors in international finance. Both organizations have grown from the original 44 member states to over 180 today, most of these developing countries. The changes that have taken place in the world economic environment over their more than 50 years in existence have led to different roles for both organizations from those intended by their founding agreement. Moreover, both have come in for a good deal of criticism in recent years. We concentrate here on how their roles have changed.

The IMF was originally designed to promote exchange rate stability. It had a pool of money contributed by member countries, and could provide short-term loans to members suffering from balance of payments deficits. The aim was to allow a country to maintain imports, avoid the imposition of controls and thus reduce pressure on its currency and restore equilibrium. The IMF would consider a devaluation of more than 10 per cent if a country's currency was in 'fundamental disequilibrium', according to its Articles of Agreement. Changes in the IMF's functions have come about as developing countries have increased participation in global financial flows. The IMF's role has shifted to providing assistance to developing countries, aimed at achieving long-term development objectives. It has also been called on for assistance in financial crises, in three countries in Asia in 1997, followed by Brazil, Turkey and Argentina. Loans to these latter three countries totalled $67.5bn. in 2003, amounting to 72 per cent of the IMF's overall lending (Wolf, 2004). In giving assistance, it imposes strict monetary and fiscal conditions on recipient countries, which have given rise to criticisms of its role as contributing to the problems (Mikesell, 2000). The IMF has shifted 'from being an overseer of the Bretton Woods system to being a key player in poor countries' development' (Harris, 1999, p. 200). The IMF's monitoring role has also changed. While traditional monitoring has focused on countries' macroeconomic policies, a broadened 'surveillance' role takes in the country's entire financial structure, including the soundness of its banks, in keeping with the role of lender of last resort (Harris, 1999, p. 207).

WEB ALERT!

The IMF website is at http://www.imf.org
The World Bank's website is at http://www.worldbank.org

The **World Bank**, which comprises the International Bank for Reconstruction and Development (IBRD) and the International Development Association (IDA), has also undergone changes in its role. From the outset, the World Bank was envisaged as assisting in development, beginning with postwar reconstruction. The money would be channelled through governments towards specific development projects. As the organization has evolved, however, it has gone in more for financing broad programmes, rather than specific projects, bringing it closer to the IMF's changed role of making general purpose loans. It has funded programmes in Africa, Asia and the transition economies of Central and Eastern Europe – all areas in which the IMF is also active. It provides low-interest loans and grants to developing countries. In 2002, the IDA provided $8.1bn. to help finance 133 projects in 62 low-income countries. Like the IMF, the World Bank now imposes a range of conditions attached to loans, including institutional changes, such as the privatization of banks, legal reforms, including property rights, and conditions regarding foreign investment (Mikesell, 2000). There is thus overlap between the IMF and the World Bank, not envisaged by the Bretton Woods agreement, as both organizations have become involved in general economic and social development.

SUMMARY POINTS

The IMF and the World Bank

International Monetary Fund (IMF): organization founded in 1947, under the Bretton Woods agreement. Its members now number 182, and the fund, contributed by member states, is administered by a Board of Executive Directors. Its defined purposes are:

● to help members suffering from balance of payments difficulties

● to maintain stable exchange rates.

The World Bank: also founded by the Bretton Woods agreement, the World Bank began operations in 1946. It is funded by member states and the issue of bonds. Its purposes are:

● to help fund development projects, for example power generation projects

● to help fund broad development programmes.

Case study 12.1   Argentina tests international financial institutions

In the 1990s, Argentina was heralded as a model for emerging markets, but by 2001, the country was in financial chaos, causing it to default on IMF loans and devalue its currency, which had been pegged to the US dollar. Financial collapse was accompanied by political crisis and social instability, as ordinary Argentines saw their savings wiped out. Two presidents were forced out of office within the space of two weeks by protests and demonstrations. How did Argentina, a country rich in natural resources, manage to plunge into financial crisis?

Argentina enjoyed strong economic growth in the 1990s. Privatization schemes, most notably in electricity, gas and telecommunications, attracted foreign investors and contributed to the impressive modernization of the country's infrastructure. The economy grew on average 4.4 per cent a year from 1993 to 1998. However, high levels of public spending led to growing public deficits. The country became dependent on foreign capital, but it did not put in place a strong internal financial system or a system of internal borrowing. Nor did it develop an effective regulatory system for overseeing the newly privatized industries. The Asian and Brazilian financial crises, combined with the failure of the hedge fund, LTCM, led to a dramatic fall in capital flows in 1998, which had a devastating effect on Argentina. It looked to international financial institutions for loans, most notably the IMF. An IMF condition was the preparation of a coherent economic plan, but Argentina was unable to meet repayments and defaulted on a total of $141bn. debt in December 2001. Its liability to the IMF amounts to $15bn., while it owes $7.5bn. to the World Bank and $8.4bn. to the Inter-American Development Bank. As urged by the IMF, the currency was devalued in 2002, decoupling it from the dollar.

During the heady days of the 1990s, Argentina issued a huge array of debt instruments, to both institutions and private investors, taking full advantage of global capital markets. In all, there were 152 types of bonds issued in eight jurisdictions and seven currencies. Moreover, many small investors across the globe bought Argentine bonds, which held out the hope of higher returns than their own governments could offer. They included, in particular, Italian and Japanese investors, who are now nursing losses. In all, there was more than $100bn. in defaulted sovereign debt. Some of these investors have mounted lawsuits against the Argentine government, including an American investor who won a $700m. lawsuit in 2003. They are encouraged by the recent economic recovery which has taken place in Argentina.

The depth of Argentina's recovery, however,

is open to question. Its economy grew at a rate of 8 per cent in 2003 (see figure), hardly imaginable two years earlier, and second only to China. The devaluation of the currency gave an impetus to local industries and also helped agriculture. The record highs of international commodity prices also aided recovery. Surging demand from China for products such as copper, soya and iron is helping to swell current accounts. However, structural problems, such as the weak banking system, remain. While unemployment had been reduced to 14.5 per cent by the end of 2003, the new prosperity is very unevenly spread and 50 per cent of the population live below the poverty line.

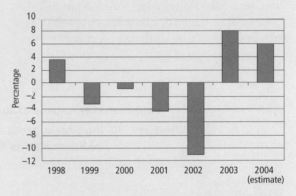

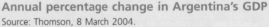

Annual percentage change in Argentina's GDP
Source: Thomson, 8 March 2004.

The government of Néstor Kirchner now enjoys fiscal surpluses, but was slow to engage in restructuring the country's debt. It devised a scheme to settle with private bondholders by paying them only about 30 cents in each dollar they hold. When questioned about the debt restructuring plan, President Kirchner said: 'We will not pay if that means an increasing number of Argentines having to go without education, healthcare, housing, a decent job' (Thomson, 8 March 2004). By March, 2005, the deal was accepted by 76 per cent of the private creditors, a level deemed to be sufficient to satisfy the IMF that the country had acted in good faith. However, many questions remain for both Argentina's prospects and the IMF's approach to the default crisis.

The case of Argentina highlights the weaknesses of current arrangements for dealing with sovereign default in bond markets. A group representing the private investors maintain that Argentina did not act in good faith and that the 30 cents in the dollar offered to them was far below the country's present ability to repay. Sensitive to the global issues, the former economics minister has said: 'I agree that you must not use the money of American plumbers and carpenters or German dentists to bail out Argentina' (Thomson, 8 March 2004). Argentina had damaged its credibility in the world's capital markets and alienated potential investors in the country's future growth. Its behaviour could undermine the IMF system in the long term, as the countries which advance money to the IMF for borrowing by countries in distress might be reluctant to do so in future. The sustainability of

Argentina's recovery is a cause for concern, resting, as it has done, on a favourable international environment and the country's failure since 2001 to service the debt to its private creditors. The country again seems to be at loggerheads with the IMF, which continues to press for structural reforms which the government is resisting.

Sources: Catán, T., 'Bad luck is mixed with some bad management', *Financial Times*, 8 March 2002; Thomson, A., 'Rising fast from the lower depths of crisis', *Financial Times*, 29 March 2004; Thomson, A., 'Argentina on the edge: what are the consequences of another default?', *Financial Times*, 8 March 2004; 'Argentina again', *Financial Times*, 28 September 2004; Balls, A. and Thomson, A., 'Argentina goes head to head over debt restructuring offer', *Financial Times*, 2 February 2005; Wolf, M., 'Argentina's debt deal leaves it holding a weak hand', *Financial Times*, 9 March 2005; Thomson, A., 'All to play for on investment as left-wing leadership revisits a decade of disposal', *Financial Times*, 9 May 2005.

Case questions

What were the causes of financial crisis in Argentina?

What are the long-term prospects of restoring international confidence in its financial system?

WEB ALERT!

For further information on Argentina's debt restructuring process, see the website of the Ministry of Economy and Production at http://www.mecon.gov.ar/finance

CRITICAL PERSPECTIVES

Financial globalization

Beyond the degree of autonomy states may still possess in macroeconomic policy or exchange rate management, there is a perception that financial globalization is transforming the form and functions of the modern state in the global political economy. Global financial markets are conceived as central to inducing a convergence of political and social agendas among governments of varied ideological persuasions to 'market-friendly' policies: a general commitment to price stability; low public deficits and indeed expenditure, especially on social goods; low direct taxation; privatization and labour market deregulation. These developments are argued to be particularly unfavourable to organized labour; public sector employees, welfare state beneficiaries, and other traditional interest groups of the left. (Held et al., 1999, p. 232)

 The authors are quite specific on the groups that are perceived to be disadvantaged by the effects of global financial markets. Who are the beneficiaries and how are societies changing as a consequence of financial globalization?

The Asian financial crisis

The financial crisis that struck three Southeast Asian countries and South Korea in 1997 was to generate a general rethinking of international finance, the relationships between national and international institutions and the role of the IMF. The crisis that spread from Thailand to Korea, Malaysia and Indonesia startled the world, largely because it occurred in high-growth economies, against a backdrop of seemingly stable economic conditions, with neither the large budget deficits nor the inflation commonly associated with financial crisis, as had occurred in the peso crisis in Mexico. Interpretations of why it occurred differ widely, but it is generally agreed that there was no single cause, but a mixture of both national domestic conditions and global financial movements.

Genesis of the crisis

The roots of the crisis lie partly with the nature of economic development within what has been called the 'Asian model' of capitalism (see Chapter 4), which was based on 'guided capitalist development' rather than on market forces (Singh, 1999, p. 11). In all the Asian economies, government links with banks and investors had led to 'cosy' relationships, in which banking regulation was weak.

The policies of liberalization and deregulation in the 1990s led to inflows of capital, as investors were attracted to high rates of interest and trusted that governments would not allow their banks to fail. Net capital inflows more than doubled between 1994 and 1996 in the four countries (Singh, 1999). The investment boom was largely financed by borrowed money, much of the borrowing in US dollars. As in other developing countries struck by financial crisis, banks and businesses across Southeast Asia borrowed in dollars and then either loaned in local currency or invested in local assets. Asian currencies were pegged to the dollar and interest rates on dollar loans were generally lower than on local currency loans. The collapse of the Bangkok Bank of Commerce in 1996 started a bank run which led to a banking crisis in Thailand. Thai financial institutions had engaged in imprudent lending on local property development and found themselves at risk of defaulting on dollar-denominated debt to international financial institutions. The Thai government attempted to defend its currency, the baht, by increasing interest rates and buying baht with its own foreign currency reserves, but this effort exhausted the reserves of the central bank. Under increasing pressure, the baht was floated in 1997 and immediately dropped 20 per cent in value (see Figure 12.6). In summary, overinvestment had been followed by a swift deterioration in confidence. Declining confidence caused investors to flee. Banks and businesses found the burden of dollar debts increasingly crippling. The banking crisis was thus directly related to the currency crisis, the combined effect of which was to send the economy into meltdown (Krugman, 1999).

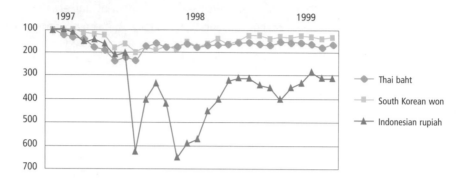

Figure 12.6 **Exchange rates of Asian currencies against the US dollar (6th June 1997=100)**
Source: *The Economist*, 9 October 1999, p. 106.

Authorities were surprised by the rapid spread of the crisis to neighbouring countries, in a process that has been described as 'contagion' (Krugman, 1999, p. 96). Before long, the currencies of the Philippines, Malaysia, Indonesia and South Korea were also under pressure, as the flight of capital continued. For the Southeast Asian region, an inflow of capital on the order of US$93bn. in 1996 turned into an estimated outflow of US$12bn. in 1997 (Bhagwati, 1998; Griffith-Jones, 1999). A major factor was the interconnectedness of their economies, as much of the money that flowed into the region was through 'emerging market funds', which grouped all of them together. The enthusiasm of investors for the region as a whole had been based on a perception of the Asian 'miracle'. When one stumbled, investors lost faith in all of them (Krugman, 1999, p. 97).

Aftermath of the crisis

Thailand, Indonesia and South Korea applied for IMF bailouts. Large sums by way of credits were made available by the IMF to South Korea and Indonesia, to support the currency and meet external debts. IMF conditions to strengthen fiscal and monetary stability were imposed, in the hope that confidence in capital and foreign exchange markets would be restored. As can be seen from Figure 12.6, with the exception of Indonesia, the affected currencies gradually recovered. Foreign bank lending, which had nose-dived, did not recover so well, as Figure 12.7 shows. FDI flows into the affected countries, with the exception of Indonesia, held their ground. According to the *World Investment Report 1999*, the reasons lie in the integrated production networks of TNCs which were established in the region – in some cases, they increased their stakes by buying out weakened joint venture partners (United Nations, 1999a, p. 56). Moreover, the more attractive FDI regimes that have been instituted seem to have encouraged investors. In 2000, businesses of the insolvent South Korean conglomerate, Daewoo, were slowly being sold off. The Korean government's proposal in

2000, for forming a state-run holding company to take over its troubled banks, met with scepticism from the IMF, as its three-year, $58bn. rescue plan for the country was coming to an end. Indonesia's plight, highlighted in Figure 12.7, was compounded by social and political instability, as is shown in Case study 12.2.

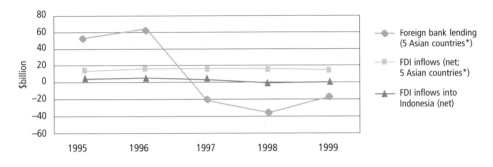

Note: *Indonesia, South Korea, Malaysia, Philippines, Thailand

Figure 12.7 **Foreign bank lending and FDI flows for Indonesia and five Asian economies**
Sources: United Nations (1999) *World Investment Report 1999* (Geneva: United Nations), pp. 56 and 479 (Table B.1); *Financial Times*, 10 April 2000.

Case study 12.2 The lessons of financial crisis in Indonesia

Indonesia was particularly severely affected by the Asian financial crisis, which was compounded by social and political turbulence. With a population of 212 million people, Indonesia is the world's fourth most populous country. It is also one of the most geographically dispersed and ethnically diverse. While nearly 90 per cent of its people consider themselves Muslims, there are some 300 ethnic groups clustered on about half the 3000-mile stretch of 13,000 islands that make up the country. Indonesia's colonial legacy was a mixture of Dutch, Portuguese and British, leaving a fragmented structure which is still evident. The 32-year military regime of President Suharto brought national unification and economic growth, but the regime was dominated by patronage and corruption. This legacy has been difficult to overcome. Following the currency and banking crisis of 1997, the IMF launched a $43bn. assistance programme conditional on austerity measures, but the economy deteriorated alarmingly, violent unrest erupted and Suharto

was forced out of office. The IMF suspended its assistance until a new interim government could be established in 1998. Critics of the IMF approach argue that, while austerity measures were appropriate in the high-spending countries of Latin America, they were ill conceived in East Asian countries such as Indonesia where they triggered a recession, exacerbating poverty and unemployment (Stiglitz, 2000). Recession in Indonesia was particularly devastating, due to the ethnic divisions which led to social and political turmoil. Indonesia's GDP plummeted in 1998 (see figure), making it the worst hit of the countries affected by the Asian crisis (Donnan, 2003).

The transitional government paved the way for elections in 1999, which saw the first democratically elected president take office. However, economic and political stability still seemed a long way off. The young democracy has faced extreme problems of tackling entrenched interests in pushing through reforms of the banking system, the legal system and corporate governance – all of which have been slower than hoped. Because of the slowness of reform, the IMF briefly suspended lending in 2000, but then altered its policy to one of greater flexibility, recognizing that developed world systems of governance were not realizable instantly and efforts to bring about reforms too quickly could actually deter investors. Among the government's worries are the threats to stability posed by numerous separatist movements, unleashed following the overthrow of the Suharto regime. Formerly Portuguese East Timor has broken away and is now administered by the UN. Gas-rich Aceh province threatens separatism, as do the 'Spice Islands', the Moluccas, half of whose population is Christian.

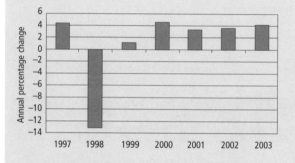

Indonesia's GDP: effects of the financial crisis
Sources: Donnan, 19 December 2003; *The Economist* (2004)
Indonesia: Economic data, at http://www.economist.com.

The government has taken steps to avert a financial crisis in future by building up foreign exchange reserves to $33.7bn. However, the slowness of economic reforms, combined with the weak judicial system and continuing corruption, are still holding back potential

foreign direct investors. Indonesia is ranked among the top ten of the world's most corrupt countries by Transparency International (2004). An anti-corruption commission, long recommended by the IMF, was set up in 2003 by the Indonesian Parliament as part of the programme of reforms, but sceptics questioned the credibility of its chairman, a former member of the powerful military faction, which is accused of being embroiled in the country's corruption. Indonesia's prospects of attracting FDI were set back by two terrorist attacks – one in Bali in 2002, in which 202 people died, and one in the centre of Jakarta in 2003, in which 16 people died and 150 were injured. Indonesia's new president, elected in 2004, is aware of potential investors' doubts about Indonesia's investment climate. He has promised firm policies to combat terrorism and corruption, aiming to increase the flows of FDI needed to stimulate economic growth, particularly needed for rebuilding following the devastation of the December 2004 tsunami.

Sources: Mydans, S., 'Indonesia's many faces reflect one nation, divisible', *New York Times*, 5 September 1999; Montagnon, P. and Thoenes, S., 'Indonesia in a hole', *Financial Times*, 8 June 1998; Montagnon, P. and McCawley, T., 'Boxed in', *Financial Times*, 16 May 2000; Burton, J., 'Jakarta blast may deter new investors', *Financial Times*, 7 August 2003; Donnan, S., 'Relief and resentment as Indonesia prepares to graduate from IMF-dictated reform programme', *Financial Times*, 19 December 2003; Donnan, S., 'Yudhoyono keen to make reformist mark', *Financial Times*, 22 September 2004; Stiglitz, J. (2000) 'The insider', *New Republic*, **22**(16/17) (17 April), pp. 56–60; Transparency International (2004) *Transparency International Corruption Perceptions Index 2004* (Berlin: Transparency International).

Case questions

In the aftermath of the financial crisis, what reforms have taken place in Indonesia?

What are now the advantages and disadvantages of Indonesia as a business location and investment?

WEB ALERT!

Further information on Indonesia's reforms can be found on the website of the Indonesian Ministry of Finance, which is at http://www.depkeu.go.id/Eng

In its Asian rescue packages, the IMF has been criticized for exacerbating the problems, rather than curing them. In particular, its one-size-fits-all, market-oriented solutions, administered as shock therapy, have been criticized as not taking into account national conditions which vary from country to country. This view is expressed by Joseph Stiglitz, former chief economist at the World Bank, who has pointed in particular to the fact that recession in ethnically divided Indonesia contributed to social and political strife (Stiglitz, 2000) (see Case study 12.2 on Indonesia). An important lesson from the Asian experience is that financial crisis may have multiple causes, some of which stem from specific aspects of the national environment. Solutions therefore need to address the realities of particular national conditions.

SUMMARY POINTS

The Asian financial crisis, 1997–8

Causes:

● Rapid liberalization of national financial systems, bringing in greater trade and investment, but with the risks of volatility

● Weak banking systems, characterized by imprudent lending for development

● Flight of capital caused by departure of large inward investors.

Lessons to be learnt:

● Financial crises may arise from a mixture of causes, some rooted in the specific national environment. Solutions should therefore be tailored to national conditions

● Liberalization of the national financial system requires a sound, independent banking system, to maintain confidence

● Vulnerability of pegged exchange rates when waning confidence leads to pressure on the currency

● Risks in short-term capital flows, which are more volatile than long-term investment.

CRITICAL PERSPECTIVES

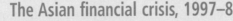

Why did financial 'contagion' spread in Asia?

In Malaysia, in Indonesia, in Korea, as in Thailand, the market's loss of confidence started a vicious circle of financial and economic collapse. It did not matter that these economies were only modestly linked in terms of physical flows of goods. They were linked in the minds of investors, who regarded the troubles of one Asian economy as bad news about the others; and when an economy is vulnerable to self-validating panic, believing makes it so. (Krugman, 1999, p. 98)

■ What vulnerabilities to loss of investor confidence did these countries share?

■ Can contagion on this scale be prevented in future?

Global markets for corporate control

The opening of markets to flows of private capital has been a trend of the postwar period, and one which has accelerated with the fall of the Communist states of Central and Eastern Europe. Through FDI, TNCs have been the major players in this process. As has been seen in earlier chapters, FDI is associated with a number of processes: globalization of production (Chapter 5); increases in world trade (Chapter 10); and the diffusion of technology (Chapter 11). An often-cited characteristic of TNCs is their ability to 'shop around' between countries, taking advantage of different investment regimes in different countries (Tolentino, 1999, p. 171). The main vehicle for FDI has become merger and acquisition activity (M&A) (OECD, 2000b). The *World Investment Report 1999* commented: 'the increased competition brought about by liberalization and globalization and the special needs and conditions of particular industries leading to a consolidation on a global scale, especially in developed countries, are driving cross-border M&As' (United Nations, 1999a).

Mergers and acquisitions

A **merger** occurs where two or more companies agree to come together to form a new company. One example of a merger is that of Grand Metropolitan and Guinness to form Diageo. In the case of an acquisition, or **takeover**, a stronger company takes over a weaker one. The company may simply buy the weaker one if the smaller company is a private company. If the smaller company is a public one, however, the shareholders become involved and a majority of their shares must be acquired by the bidding company. Their board of directors may recommend selling out to the bidder, but in the case of a hostile takeover, the bidder bypasses the board and makes an offer directly to the shareholders of the target company. A further type of acquisition is the **leveraged buyout (LBO)**, by which a group, usually managers of the company, make an arrangement, through a loan or venture capital finance, to buy out the company's equity. The LBO is thus a means for achieving corporate restructuring, often financed by venture capitalists. According to the Centre for Management Buy-Out Research (reported in Rivlin, 2000), buyouts rose 62 per cent from 1998 to 1999 in Europe, from €20.1bn. in 1998 to €30.4bn. in 1999, with much of the focus on restructuring. The bulk of these deals were in the UK, one of the biggest being the sale of United Biscuits to a group of trade and finance bidders.

Mergers and acquisitions are key to companies' growth strategies. This point is highlighted in the case study on General Electric at the end of Part 3. A major driving force has been the enhancement of shareholder value, bringing cost savings and efficiencies. M&A activities may be **horizontal integration**, that is, between companies in the same industry, often referred to as 'consolidation'. There have been waves of consolidation in the pharmaceuticals and chemicals sector, for example, in the late 1990s, the main rationale being the increasing returns in R&D from economies of scale. **Vertical integration**, that is, between firms in successive stages of production or distribution, can also be strategically valuable, bringing benefits of internalization (see Chapter 5). An example is the $182bn. takeover of Time Warner by AOL in 2000. In this mega-deal, an internet provider (AOL) took over a media and entertainment company (Time Warner), exemplifying a new economy predator taking over an old economy conglomerate. The deal required approval of the US antitrust authority, the Federal Trade Commission, which imposed stringent conditions.

Some large companies have grown by diversification, acquiring subsidiaries in businesses only loosely related to each other. Diageo, formed from a merger of Grand Metropolitan and Guinness, is an example. Although mainly a drinks company, Diageo acquired a packaged food business and the Burger King chain of restaurants. A recent trend has been for highly diversified companies to slim down to what is conceived to be their core business, and 'demerge', or spin off, the non-core businesses. In the case of Diageo, wine and spirits were seen to be the core business, and it sold off the packaged food and Burger King businesses.

SUMMARY POINTS

!!!

Mergers and acquisitions

- **Merger** – the coming together of two or more companies to form a new company.
- **Acquisition** – the takeover of a company by another company. Acquisitions also include the takeover of a state-owned enterprise by a private sector company (privatization).
- **'Hostile' takeover** – a company targets a prospective acquisition, but the board of directors of the target company reject the acquisition proposal. The would-be acquiring company therefore makes an offer directly to the shareholders of the target company.
- **Demerger** – the spinning off of a part of a company's business, such as a division, which is viable on its own. Demerger is usually part of a corporate strategy to refocus on the core business.
- **Leveraged buy-out (LBO)** – a group, often managers of a company, obtain finance to buy out part or all of the company's equity.

Trends in cross-border mergers

Historically, there have been periods of heightened merger activity generally, resulting in the rise of large conglomerates, as happened in the 1960s in the US and Europe. From the 1980s onwards, waves of privatizations in former state-owned industries, such as telecommunications and utilities, have accounted for much acquisition activity, attracting foreign investors, usually global companies keen to expand into new markets. The telecommunications industry accounted for 20 per cent of the world's total M&A activity in 1999, with the chemical industry second and petroleum and gas exploitation third (OECD, 2000b). The oil industry saw a radical transformation of the competitive environment, with the $57bn. merger between BP and Amoco, which was followed three months later by a deal between Exxon and Mobil worth $80bn. Ironically, the Exxon–Mobil merger reunited two offshoots of Standard Oil, forced to be dismantled under antitrust law by the US Supreme Court in 1911. In today's global economy, these major players in the oil and gas industry are aiming to secure partnerships with national oil companies in the world's major oil-producing countries. The year 2000 marked a peak in cross-border M&As, reaching a global total of $1,143bn.; the major acquisitions and sectors are shown in Table 12.1. The value of sales fell to $297bn. by 2003, as shown in Figure 12.8. In 2003, there were only 56 deals of $1bn. or more, one-third the number achieved in 2000 (United Nations, 2004). One factor in the fall in M&A activity has been the slowdown in privatizations. The sale of state-owned assets fell in value from a global total of $50bn. in 2000 to less than $20bn. in 2003 (United Nations, 2004).

Table 12.1 Global acquisitions, 1999–2000

Target	Acquirer	Value ($billion)	Sector
Mannesmann (Germany)	Vodafone (UK)	198.9	Telecoms
Time Warner (US)	AOL (US)	181.9	Internet/media
Sprint (US)	MCI Worldcom (US)	127.3	Telecoms
Warner-Lambert (US)	Pfizer (US)	87.9	Pharmaceuticals
Mobil (US)	Exxon (US)	86.4	Oil
SmithKline Beecham (UK)	Glaxo Wellcome (UK)	78.4	Pharmaceuticals
Citicorp (US)	Travelers (US)	72.6	Banking/financial services

Source: *Financial Times*, 5/6 February and 30 June 2000.

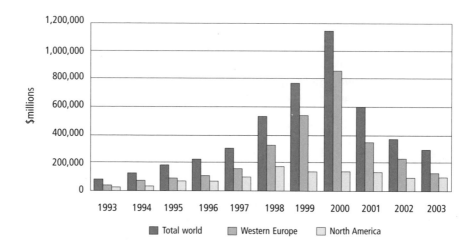

Figure 12.8 Cross-border mergers and acquisitions by economy of purchaser
Source: United Nations (2004) *World Investment Report 2004*, Annex table B.8.

While M&A activity has a long history within national economies, in 1999, cross-border mergers had grown in number, to half of all reported mergers in the US, EU and Asia (Paul, 2000). In the 1990s, cross-border M&A activity increased fivefold in OECD countries. What is even more striking, though, is the increase in the average deal value, which rose from $29m. in 1990 to $157m. in 1999 (OECD, 2000b). Of UK TNCs, research suggests that 95 per cent of those that expanded abroad during the late 1980s did so via acquisition (Hubbard, 1999). The UK overtook the US in 1999 as the most active source of M&A investment and remained in that position in 2000. The 1999 figures were swelled by Vodafone's acquisition of AirTouch in the US (for £41.25bn.), and the 2000 figures are boosted by Vodafone's takeover of Mannesman (for £101.2bn.) (National Statistics, 2000). Like banking and public utilities, telecommunications have been dominated in many countries by state-controlled companies, but are experiencing rapid changes in the competitive climate, as Case study 12.3 indicates.

Case study 12.3   **Vodafone's takeover of Mannesmann: a turning point for European takeovers?**

Vodafone, the UK mobile phone operator, has pursued a strategy of expansion by acquisition. Its 1999 acquisition of US mobile phone operator, AirTouch, was a notable success. But its hardest battle has been takeover of Mannesmann, the German engineering and mobile phone group, in 2000. The takeover, valued at just over €178bn. (£100bn.), came at a time when the mobile phone market was booming. For most of its 110-year history, Mannesmann had been essentially an engineering group. It entered the mobile phone business only ten years previously, greatly boosting its position by its acquisition of Orange, a major rival to Vodafone. The deal had to clear the EU competition authorities, which required Orange to be sold off (it was acquired by France Telecom). The new, enlarged Vodafone became Europe's largest publicly traded company and the world's largest telecommunications group.

Vodafone became the first foreign company to have succeeded in a hostile bid for a large German company. Pirelli, the Italian tyre maker, had failed in a bid for German tyre maker Continental in 1990. Germany is well known as a fortress against foreign takeovers. This may be attributed partly to the ways in which postwar German capitalism developed. Extensive cross-shareholdings between companies, often linking in banks, provided a bulwark against outsiders, as only a relatively small proportion of shares were 'free-floating'. Trade unions, who are represented on supervisory boards, ensure that any takeover proposal will be

scrutinized for any potential loss of jobs. Vodafone's success came from winning over Mannesmann's shareholders. Unusually for a German company, 70 per cent of Mannesmann's shareholders were foreign, including some large US institutional investors, who were persuaded that the deal would be in shareholders' interests. To their voices were added Jurgen Schrempp, chairman of DaimlerChrysler, and Josef Ackermann, chief executive of Deutsche Bank. Opposed to the deal were the head of IG Metall, the powerful union, and Klaus Esser, Manessmann's chief executive. The German government was also opposed, arguing that the deal risked upsetting Germany's stakeholder culture, which valued employees before shareholders. However, the overwhelming pressure from investors resulted in approval of the deal by the supervisory board on 3 February 2000.

Vodafone's victory was seen as a turning point in the cross-border takeover market in Europe, as shareholder value and market considerations had triumphed over Germany's entrenched corporate structures. However, within Germany there remains ambivalence towards the Anglo-American style of capitalism. Reforms initiated by Schröder's government have encouraged market liberalization. First, the 58 per cent capital gains tax on corporate stakes held by banks and insurance companies has been abolished. Secondly, the reform of the state pension system has encouraged more active investors looking for better returns than the rather low levels typical of many German companies. Thirdly, Germany has a new code of corporate governance, which discourages the multiple directorships of corporate leaders on Germany's supervisory boards, and encourages greater transparency on the pay of executive and supervisory board members. A new takeover code, adopted in 2002, however, allows defence mechanisms, known as 'poison pills', to be invoked in the case of a hostile takeover, which are designed to discourage predators. They include, for example, a process whereby the supervisory board can impose conditions on acquirers which could prevent redundancies for up to five years.

In a bizarre final act of the Vodafone takeover, criminal proceedings were launched against six former directors of Mannesmann in 2004, including Klaus Esser and Josef Ackermann, alleging receipt of illegal bonuses, which were approved on 4 February 2000, the day following the takeover approval. Esser himself pocketed €15m. as an 'appreciation award', in a total of €60m. of executive bonuses, as well as pension enhancements for 18 former executives. If convicted, they could have faced 10-year jail sentences. Although the high-profile criminal trial, which lasted six months, ended in acquittals on the criminal charges of breach of fiduciary duty, the judge expressed concern that the bonuses were inadmissibly high in corporate law terms (Jenkins, 23 July 2004). The case highlighted continuing unease over Germany's transition towards Anglo-American style markets for corporate control.

Vodafones's investors are now looking to see the benefits in terms of cost and operational synergies that the global company has gained from its aggressive acquisition strategy. However, despite its unrivalled economies of scale, its success in global markets has been uneven (see figure). In Japan, where 3G is well advanced, it has lost market share to Japanese rivals. When the takeover boom subsided, Vodafone faced the long-term challenges of operating in highly competitive markets.

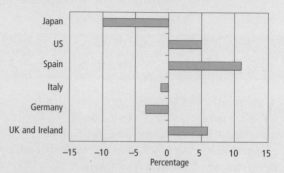

Vodafone's average revenue per user (April–September 2004)
Source: Budden, 17 November 2004.

Sources: Plender, J., 'Whirlwinds of change', *Financial Times*, 4 February, 2000; Atkins, R. and Lewis, W., 'Triumph for Vodafone as Mannesmann gives in', *Financial Times*, 4 February 2000; Lorenz, A., 'Mobile mania', *Sunday Times*, 9 January 2000; Lorenz, A., 'V for victory', *Sunday Times*, 6 February 2000; Barber, T., 'Shareholder democracy gets a bigger say', *Financial Times*, 15 May 2002; Swann, C., 'The weak will become prey', *Financial Times*, 30 June 2000; Betts, P., 'Buyers beware', *Financial Times*, 20 December 2001; Benoit, B., 'Effects of hostile takeover still being felt in Germany', *Financial Times*, 6 November 2002; Jenkins, P. 'Germany on trial', *Financial Times*, 15 January 2004; Jenkins, P., 'Court clears bosses over bonuses', *Financial Times*, 23 July 2004; Budden, R., 'Healthy returns mask Vodafone's global challenges', *Financial Times*, 17 November 2004.

Case questions

What does the case study reveal about the market for corporate control in Germany, and has it changed as a result of the Vodafone takeover of Mannesman?

How has the acquisition strategy benefited Vodafone?

WEB ALERT!

The EU Commission's competition website offers a variety of links related to M&A activity at http://europa.eu.int/comm./competition/index

Regulation and TNCs

The sheer size of many newly merged TNCs has renewed the debate on the concentration of economic power in corporate hands and the domination of some global industries by only a few powerful companies. The Vodafone–Mannesmann deal, as the *Financial Times* noted in an editorial, 'is on a par with the gross domestic product of Denmark' (*Financial Times*, 5 February 2000). But whereas countries are enmeshed in international regulatory regimes, such as those for international trade (WTO) and international monetary issues (the IMF and the World Bank), there is no regulatroy framework for TNCs at the international level. Industrialized countries have all enacted competition (or antitrust) legislation, designed to curb monopolists (see a fuller discussion in Chapter 4). Within the EU, there are both EU and national regulatory frameworks to comply with, which, it is intended, will be harmonized across the EU. However, in the wake of the Vodafone–Mannesmann deal, the EU Parliament added amendments (opposed by Britain and Ireland) to the proposed EU takeover directive, to give workers a greater say in takeover situations.

Mergers must be notified to national authorities, as well as to the EU Commission, for clearance, and can be blocked under competition law if they constitute an abuse of a dominant market position, or allowed through with conditions attached. Indeed, national rules have become more complex and the list of countries with merger regulations is growing. Merger notification regimes are in place in 57 jurisdictions and, between 1994 and 2000, 35 of these have enacted new or substantially revised rules, creating a 'daunting landscape' for companies contemplating cross-border mergers (Paul, 2000).

Competition policy, like company regulation generally, is subject to wide variations of interpretation and also changing public perceptions about big business in general. A 'national champion' is seen as enhancing competitive advantage for the home nation, and some governments welcome the consolidation of companies within some sectors, in order to create a single entity stronger than its former constituent parts, fit to compete globally. A shift of attitudes towards a greater acceptance of takeovers, especially hostile ones, has taken place in a number of countries, such as France and Germany, opening up the market for corporate control and with a greater focus on shareholder value. This shift stems from the growing equity culture and a move away from the stakeholder model. In Germany, the number of shareholders grew from 5 million in 1992 to 8 million in 1999, while trade union membership fell from 12 million to 10 million (*The Economist*, 20 November 1999). Notwithstanding Germany's legislation on corporate governance, which is stacked against the hostile takeover, Mannesman shareholders, in supporting the Vodafone deal, went 'in favour of shareholder value and against national champions' (*The Economist*, 20 November 1999).

As globalization processes have encompassed more countries, developing and transitional economies have run the risk of becoming dependent on foreign capital, as well as technology. Thus, while TNC investments have brought benefits to societies, they have also created concentrations of economic power which in many ways are perceived as escaping the control of governments. Foreign-owned companies in

Hungary accounted for 80 per cent of manufacturing investment in 1996, providing a third of the country's employment (United Nations, 1999b). National authorities typically offer incentives to attract foreign investors. Regulatory frameworks for FDI serve two purposes: to control the activities of TNCs in the interests of host countries; and to protect TNCs in overseas locations from, for example, arbitrary seizure of assets (Tolentino, 1999). From 1995, a Multilateral Agreement on Investment (MAI) has been under consideration, under the auspices of the OECD. Such a treaty would aim to regulate FDI at the international level, balancing the interests of host countries and foreign investors. However, the negotiation process has been dominated by the developed countries and thus is perceived by developing countries as flawed in the area of control of TNCs (Tolentino, 1999). While MAI negotiations seemed to stall, countries have proceeded with bilateral agreements, tailoring agreements to fit particular needs on a country-by-country basis. A shortcoming of this piecemeal approach, however, is that it does not cover as many countries as a multilateral agreement would cover, bypassing especially the poorest developing countries.

The global financial environment and developing countries

The globalization of production and FDI have led to increases in capital flows from advanced countries to many developing countries, but their benefits have been unevenly distributed. Only a relatively small group of developing countries attract the lion's share of private capital flows. Asian and Latin American countries have been successful in attracting investment, whereas African and Middle Eastern countries have been much less so. Where FDI has contributed significantly to economic growth, fluctuations in these flows and changes in exchange rates have brought financial instability, and even crisis, in Asian industrializing countries, Mexico, Brazil and Russia. Thus, globalization has brought problems of overinvestment in some countries and underinvestment in others.

For the first group of countries, *The World Development Report 1999/2000* (World Bank, 2000a) examined ways to capture the gains from financial globalization without running the risks of volatility in capital markets. Liberalizing the domestic financial environment, it recommends, needs to be complemented by strengthening bank regulation and stabilizing the macroeconomic environment. These aims have been echoed in IMF rescue packages in the crisis-struck Asian economies. The second group of countries, those yet to see sustained economic development, present greater long-term problems. In 1997, Africa received only 2 per cent of the world total of FDI. For this reason, many countries have had to rely on assistance from the IMF and the World Bank. Loans and grants from rich nations now account for 10 per cent of all economic activity in Africa. Despite this help, these countries remain poor, amassing a huge debt burden that, many argue, has made matters worse. These broad issues are discussed in greater detail in Chapter 14. A general problem seems to be that countries become dependent on the IMF, making it even more difficult for them to attract private capital. The situation has been likened to that of individuals who become dependent on welfare aid. A study found that of 89 less developed countries that received IMF aid between 1965 and 1995, by 1998, 48 were no better off than they were before receiving the loans, and 32 were actually worse off (Longman and Ahmad, 1998).

Debate on changing the role of the IMF has thus focused on the different functions it fulfils in different types of developing country. While Asian programmes are seen as rescue packages in countries which have dynamic economies, aid to sub-Saharan African countries has taken on the quality of permanence. It has been argued that the IMF and the World Bank should coordinate their roles in countries which have yet to develop the basic systems for growth, including legal structures, public administration and social services. Alternatively, there are those who say that the IMF should revert to short-term loans and dealing with financial crises, allowing the World Bank to concentrate on development programmes in poor countries. Attention has also focused on easing the debt problems of the poorest countries and opening up more export opportunities for crops and textiles produced in these countries. Granting debt relief would at least ease the burden of interest payments. Among the 41 countries eligible for debt relief in 2000, the average debt load was 125 per cent of their GDP (*New York Times*, 1 October 2000). Debt relief, like trade reforms, relies on the will of authorities in wealthy countries. The IMF's former managing director, Horst Köhler, has said: 'We have to tackle the selfishness of wealthy countries. This is a question of morals' (*New York Times*, 1 October 2000).

CRITICAL PERSPECTIVES

Development and the role of international financial institutions

Overall, the successful countries have pursued a comprehensive approach to development. Thirty years ago, economists of the left and the right often seemed to agree that the improvement in the efficiency of resource allocation and the increase in the supply of capital were at the heart of development. They differed only as to whether those changes should be obtained through government-led planning or unfettered markets. In the end, neither worked. Development encompasses not just resources and capital but a transformation of society. Clearly, the international financial institutions cannot be held responsible for this transformation, but they can play an important role. And at the very least, they should not become impediments to a successful transformation. (Stiglitz, 2002, p. 242)

To what extent do you agree with Stiglitz's analysis? Reassess the role of international financial institutions in light of the examples of their activities discussed in this chapter.

Conclusions

1 All business requires access to capital. A firm may borrow funds or raise capital by issuing shares, known as an initial public offering (IPO).

2 Stock exchanges handle flows of publicly traded shares in systems which are becoming increasingly globalized. Moreover, investors, especially institutional investors such as pension funds, are seeking advantageous investments abroad.

3 Foreign exchange refers to currency dealings across national borders. Exchange rates can be determined in a number of different ways, including fixed exchange rates, pegged exchange rates and more flexible arrangements.

4 With the collapse of the Bretton Woods fixed exchange rate system in the early 1970s, volatility in exchange markets set in. The IMF, founded under the Bretton Woods agreement, has responsibility for maintaining stability in the international monetary system.

5 The IMF and the World Bank have evolved considerably since they were established in the 1940s, particularly to address problems of financial crisis, as in the Asian crisis of 1997–8, and the many problems of developing countries.

6 The Asian crisis highlighted the risks of volatile capital flows and posed challenges for the Asian economies in restructuring, to attract foreign investors in a more stable financial environment.

7 TNCs have become drivers of financial globalization, largely through merger and acquisition (M&A) activities. The benefits of global integration, however, must be weighed against the concentration of economic power enjoyed by merged global companies, especially in relation to host economies.

8 The problems of heavily indebted poor countries have come to be recognized as major challenges for the developed world, sparking a debate among all players, including corporate leaders, the IMF and government authorities.

Review questions

1   How have capital markets become globalized and what are the implications for listed companies?

2   How can a company benefit from the issuing of bonds and how do bondholders differ from shareholders?

3   Explain the benefits that were enjoyed under the gold standard system.

4   What were the aims of the Bretton Woods agreement? What were the reasons behind its collapse in the 1970s?

5 Explain the differences between fixed, floating and pegged exchanged rates.

6 Summarize the initial aims of the Bretton Woods institutions – the IMF and the World Bank. How have their roles evolved since their formation?

7 What were the causes of the Asian financial crisis of 1997–98?

8 How have the Asian economies been restructured and reformed since the crisis and what has been the role of the IMF? To what extent have their combined efforts been a success?

9 Mergers and acquisitions have become increasingly important in the markets for corporate control. What is the driving force behind them?

10 In what ways are developing countries' economies vulnerable to global financial movements?

Assignments

1 Globalizing capital markets have provided investment opportunities for outside investors, but have also posed risks for both investors and national authorities. Assess the lessons have been learned from the Asian financial crisis for companies wishing to invest in the region in future.

2 Growing through M&A is one of the main ways in which companies seek to expand internationally. Often, however, expectations outrun reality and the difficulties of merging two companies are underestimated. Examine a cross-border takeover or merger of your choice, discussing the balance between the benefits it has generated and the difficulties that had to be overcome.

Further reading

Eichengreen, B. (1996) *Globalizing Capital: A History of the International Monetary System* (Princeton: Princeton University Press).

Eichengreen, B. (2002) *Financial Crises and What to Do About Them* (Oxford: Oxford University Press).

Grosse, R. (2004) *The Future of Global Financial Services* (Oxford: Blackwells).

Harwood, A. (ed.) (1999) *Financial Markets and Development: The Crisis in Emerging Markets* (Washington: Brookings Institution Press).

Kapstein, E.B. (1994) *Governing the Global Economy: International Finance and the State* (Cambridge, MA: Harvard University Press).

Kohn, M. (2003) *Financial Institutions and Markets*, 2nd edn (Oxford: Oxford University Press).

Krugman, P. (1999) *The Return of Depression Economics* (Harmondsworth: The Penguin Press).

Kuttner, R. (1991) *The End of Laissez-Faire: National Purpose and the Global Economy after the Cold War* (New York: Alfred A. Knopf).

Michie, J. and Grieve Smith, J. (eds) (1999) *Global Instability: The Political Economy of World Economic Governance* (Andover: Routledge).

END OF PART 3 CASE STUDY

GE seeks growth in a globalized environment

General Electric (GE) is the world's largest industrial company and an icon of American capitalism. A descendant of the Edison Electric Light Company, founded by Thomas Edison in 1878, GE was formed in 1892. It is the only company listed on the NYSE today that was listed on its original index in 1896. It has grown into a conglomerate, spanning many different types of business and employing 300,000 people worldwide. Nearly half these employees are now located outside the US, while in 1999, US employees outnumbered those in overseas locations by over 20,000. GE retains its lighting and consumer appliances businesses, which are traditionally associated with the company in consumers' minds but its driving forces have become, first, its financial and insurance arm, and second, its higher margin technology businesses. This latter category includes aerospace engines, power systems (including gas turbines for power stations) and medical systems (including X-ray equipment). In addition, it has ventured into media interests, acquiring NBC, the major US television network, and Universal Studios, purchasing the latter from the crisis-struck French conglomerate, Vivendi International. In principle, the strength of the conglomerate is that diversified streams of income allow it to offset a downturn in one business with growth in another. GE prospered during the 1990s, but in the new millennium, its businesses encountered a more difficult environment. Economic downturn and the effects of the terrorist attacks of 11 September 2001, impacting on many fronts, causing it to rethink its global strategy.

A hard act to follow

Legendary Chairman and CEO Jack Welch presided over 25 years of uninterrupted growth at GE. His strong leadership style had propelled the company to high levels of performance, reflected in high share prices and glowing credit ratings by analysts. GE Capital, the financial and insurance arm, was a major driving force, accounting for 40 per cent of revenues in the booming 1990s. He left the company on 10 September 2001 and was succeeded by Jeffrey Immelt on the day of the attacks on the World Trade Center in New York.

The world in late 2001 presented an uncertain and insecure environment. In the wake of the Enron collapse, questions were raised across America about the transparency of corporate finances and corporate governance. Following the terrorist attacks, demand for aerospace products weakened and customers for GE power systems either cancelled their orders for new gas turbines or decided against putting in new orders. GE's insurance subsidiary, Employers Reinsurance Corporation, was one of the insurers of the World Trade Center which had to pay out on liability claims. Immelt was compelled to look at the elements of GE Capital. It had grown rapidly, but was exposed to risks, such as potential bad loans should customers of the consumer and commercial financing

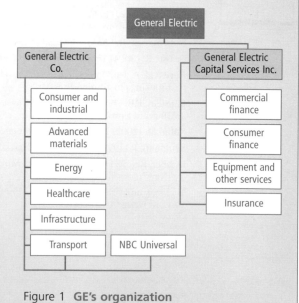

Figure 1 **GE's organization**

businesses default. For example, if customers for aircraft and power plants defaulted, there were assets to back up loans, but the value of these assets was falling. GE also operates a large aircraft leasing business, many of which were returned to it, as airlines no longer had use for them. Despite the growth in earnings of financial businesses, profit margins were low, at 9.6 per cent, compared to other parts of the GE empire, such as the 20 per cent produced by medical systems and transport.

The uncertain business climate and the exposure of the financial businesses took their toll on GE's share price, which halved from 2000 to 2002. GE strategists concluded that a refocus on industrial strengths, with a concentration on technology and services, would be the more prudent long-term strategy. The many businesses that make up GE were reorganized into 11 business units. The industrial segments were grouped under General Electric, and the financial businesses were grouped under General Electric Capital Services, as shown in Figure 1.

Brighter prospects for future growth

GE has faced concerns over the proportion of earnings coming from the financial businesses (see Figure 2). Consumer and industrial suffered from higher costs, lower prices and the weakness of the US dollar. The energy segment was affected by the fall in the number of gas turbines sold, from 362 in 2002, down to 208 in 2003. Overall, GE reported a healthy rise in profits of 45 per cent in 2003. Sales grew 1 per cent, to $134bn., just over half coming from the industrial and consumer products divisions. These are the areas in which Immelt sees growth through technology and services. Aircraft engines and gas turbines, for example, will benefit from new research and more service-based contracts, both of which should lead to higher margins. As Figure 3 shows, profits from services are gradually rising in relation to goods.

Traditionally, acquisitions have greatly contributed to growth of GE. An example is the energy business, which has expanded largely by acquisitions: between 2000 and 2002, it bought

more than 30 companies, with an eye to buying in new technology. It has about 60 per cent of the world market for gas turbines. It sees future growth coming mainly from sales of power generation equipment outside the US, which are about 60 per cent of the unit's sales. Building up the services side of the business will also strengthen its position in the group, with an operating margin of 24 per cent. GE acquired the wind energy operations of the collapsed Enron, making it now among the largest producers of wind turbines, which is seen as a growth area. Purchasing Amersham International, the British medical research and bioscience company, was part of the strategy to strengthen research and innovation.

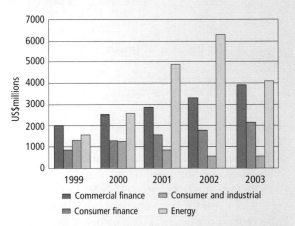

Figure 2 **GE's profits in contrasting segments**
Source of data: *GE Annual Report 2003.*

The head of GE Europe says: 'Our size means it is not very easy to achieve our growth targets intrinsically because you bump your head against the market share, so we have to grow into new areas by acquisition' (21 June 2002). For a company the size of GE, achieving growth by acquisitions is not as simple as it might seem in the current regulatory environment. The European Commission blocked GE's proposed acquisition of Honeywell, a rival aero engine company, in 2001, holding that it would make GE too powerful. Immelt commented: 'In America you can say, "I am GE, I am big and I make a lot of money". That generally works. In Europe you have to be more subtle' (Hamilton, 3 February 2002). The company has therefore focused on a series of smaller acquisitions which, while not individually transformational, have added up to a substantial spending spree. Acquisitions in 2004 amounted to $42bn., which is equivalent to its unsuccessful bid for Honeywell.

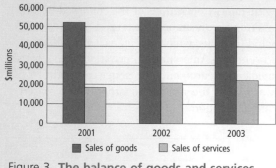

Figure 3 **The balance of goods and services at GE**
Source of data: *GE Annual Report 2003.*

Internationalizing R&D

Until 2000, almost all GE's research was based in the US. It now has a new research centre in Munich, as well as new research units in Bangalore and Shanghai. These steps to globalize its research aim to tap into a broader range of scientific expertise than is available in the US, and also reflects the international nature of the businesses. GE has been slower to internationalize its R&D than global competitors, such as Siemens of Germany and Philips of the Netherlands. GE's R&D budget has risen from $2.2bn. in 2000 to $2.7bn. in 2003. It aims to focus research on new technology in the many businesses. The research centres will focus on 'core' technologies in areas such as metallurgy, organic chemistry, solid state physics, biosciences, electronics and imaging technology. Projects include controlling emissions from power stations, making quieter, less pollutant jet engines and improving medical scanning systems. Coordination is needed between the different research centres and between the researchers and the technology specialists in each division. Ultimately, the

research needs to yield product developments and success in the marketplace. Does the quest for innovation on multiple fronts, and in geographically dispersed locations, risk spreading its efforts too thinly?

GE's global challenges

Overcomplexity and slowness have long been associated with conglomerates, which largely explains why there are so few remaining. The cumbersome structure of the conglomerate made it ill suited to achieve agility in innovation and respond quickly to new market opportunities. GE executives face huge management challenges in coordinating the disparate parts of the business. There are cultural differences to accommodate, ranging from engineers and research scientists to the creative people in the entertainment industries. Immelt recognizes that they must be managed differently, but feels that all will fit into GE's well-established processes. Thanks in large part to Welch, the company has built a strong corporate culture. Having acquired NBC in 1985 under Welch's leadership, GE now has 20 years' experience in managing a media company.

Immelt sees expansion in growing markets as essential to future success, in production, sourcing of parts and in markets. GE has been selling its jet engines in China since the early 1990s. But China is now far more significant in the global economy due to its recent rapid growth, in terms of both production and potential market. The new research unit in Shanghai is an indication of its growing importance in innovation as well. For GE, globalization presents cultural challenges, as well as management challenges. Immelt admits that in 1981, when Welch became chairman, most of GE's executives did not even have passports. Now, he says, 'we have to look at the world as our market' (Roberts, 27 December 2003).

Sources: Hill, A., and Roberts, D., 'GE must hone predatory instincts to ensure survival', *Financial Times*, 21 June 2002; Hamilton, K., 'Too good to be true?', *Sunday Times*, 3 February 2002; Hill, A., 'A different direction for the GE way', *Financial Times*, 3 January 2003; Gapper, J. and

Roberts, D., 'The friendly face of American capitalism in a cynical and dangerous era', *Financial Times*, 27 December 2003; Marsh, P., 'GE taps a world of local skills', *Financial Times*, 18 February 2004; Roberts, D., 'Plugging in to the global deal machine', *Financial Times*, 2 December 2004; Roberts, D., 'GE keeps to takeover trail with $16bn outlay', *Financial Times*, 2 December 2004; *GE Annual Report 2003*, at www.GE.com/en/company.

End of Part 3 case questions

1 **What problems did GE face in the new millennium?**

2 **What are the elements of its new strategy under the new chairman and CEO? In particular, what is the role of acquisitions?**

3 **How has R&D been internationalized at GE? To what extent will these moves give GE competitive advantage in international markets?**

4 **What are the challenges facing GE in the future?**

Part 4

Issues and Challenges

13 Environmental challenges: global and local perspectives 423

14 Global challenges and the responsible business 447

End of Part 4 case study 474

This part looks into the future, taking a critical perspective on the ways in which businesses are impacting on the natural and social environments globally. Chapter 13, discusses the challenges facing businesses in the ecological environment. For centuries, the processes of industrialization and urbanization have wreaked damage in the form of environmental degradation, depletion of natural resources and pollution. Through scientific research, the effects of these processes are now becoming widely known, creating pressure for governments and businesses to address ways of pursuing more sustainable development, while striving to maintain the consumer lifestyles that people in advanced economies enjoy and those in developing economies aspire to. Environmental management has become a priority for businesses, as regulatory regimes impact to a greater extent on operations and, importantly, consumers look to businesses to raise standards of environmental protection.

A related challenge is the impact of businesses on the societies in which they operate, which is the focus of Chapter 14. It begins with a review of the dimensions of the international environment which have occupied earlier chapters, noting the different levels of interaction, in local, national, regional and international spheres. Discussion then turns to the problems confronting the very poorest countries, where economic and human development remain more aspirational than real. These pressing global issues, once considered matters for governments and international governmental organizations, are now recognized as a concern of businesses as well. While businesses have traditionally seen themselves as playing an exclusively economic role, their multidimensional effects in the societies in which they operate are now the focus of critical examination. We look at theories of corporate social responsibility (CSR) and stakeholder management as pointing towards new strategic perspectives on companies' changing role in societies. Finally, there is a case study on GlaxoSmithKline (GSK) which concludes Part 4. Through the perspective of this global pharmaceutical company, the case confronts the various global challenges discussed in this final part of the book. While GSK seeks to maintain profitability and market share, mainly in the advanced economies whose inhabitants are its predominant consumers, it is also enmeshed in the problems of very poor developing countries where drugs are desperately needed but where neither people nor their governments can afford them. GSK's experience in balancing these stakeholder interests is illustrative of changing corporate strategies to respond to the social issues arising in the global environment.

13 Environmental challenges: global and local perspectives

Outline of chapter

- Introduction
- Environmental degradation
- Climate change
- Transboundary pollution and implications for energy policies
- International legal frameworks
- Challenges of environmental protection for business
  - Sustainable development in the business context
  - Environmental management
- EU initiatives on the environment
- Green consumerism
- Environmental protection and changing values
- Conclusions

Learning objectives

1 To understand the nature and causes of the major environmental challenges, such as climate change and transboundary pollution.

2 To appreciate interconnections between local, regional and global concerns.

3 To gain insight into the role of governments and international cooperation in tackling environmental challenges.

4 To identify at a practical level the initiatives that businesses can take in environmental management and sustainable development strategy.

Introduction

Challenges posed by the environment are increasingly impacting on societies, governments and businesses. They include global warming, the depletion of natural resources and pollution. These and other processes are detrimental to human well-being and also harm plants and animals, both on the land and in the seas. While it may not be possible to bring back species which have become extinct or replace resources which have become exhausted, it is possible to slow down and control harmful processes and, with the aid of research, find ways of combating the harmful effects. Whereas environmental issues were once seen as mainly local, they are increasingly perceived in the wider context of regional and global implications. Similarly, because it is about the public interest, the environment was once seen mainly as a matter of government concern, whereas the role of businesses – whether for bad or good – is now attracting more attention. Governments and businesses now cooperate in environmental protection, at national, regional and international level. Often, this cooperation includes international organizations, both governmental and non-governmental (NGOs). The role of specialist environmental NGOs has been important in raising awareness of 'green' issues and also in promoting green alternatives to environmentally damaging activities. Greater weight has been given to these efforts by advances in scientific research, which have shed light on trends affecting the planet as a whole and also provided details on the effects of different types of pollution in specific locations.

Much past and present environmental damage stems from the effects of economic development. These processes include industrialization, changes in farming methods and the depletion of natural resources. As has been seen in Chapter 8, industrialization leads to urbanization, as rural dwellers flock to urban areas in search of work in new industries. While these twin processes began two centuries ago in the advanced economies, the centres of today's industrialization are in the developing world, and the processes are taking place more quickly than in the first wave of industrialization. Moreover, current environmental changes are occurring in a context of unprecedented population pressures, mainly in the developing world. Protecting the environment, therefore, is now seen as part of a broad view of development, known as 'sustainable development', which takes into account not just the well-being of today's generation, but also the needs of future generations. Sustainable development is increasingly incorporated into the strategic thinking of international managers.

This chapter first highlights the major environmental challenges, their causes and effects, both long and short term. It then looks at responses to challenges at the level of business enterprises. Environmental management strategies adapted to sustainable development goals are evolving in a context of changing institutional and legal frameworks. Recent years have seen an increasing involvement of business players in both responses and initiatives in the area of environmental protection.

Environmental degradation

While environmental changes can occur naturally through changes in climate and weather, environmental degradation refers specifically to environmental change caused mainly by human activity (Held et al., 1999, p. 382). The development of agriculture in Europe and North America in the seventeenth and eighteenth centuries is an example, which saw a huge expansion in the area of cultivated land, technological innovations and the emergence of capitalist market relationships in agriculture (Maddison, 2001). Forests were cut down, heathland was cleared and numerous species of wildlife declined as their habitats were destroyed. With the Industrial Revolution, the capacity for environmental degradation started to grow dramatically, in both intensity and geographic scope. Factory production relying on power sources such as coal were joined by newer industries, such as synthetic chemicals, which generated a mixture of old and new pollutants. As urban areas grew up around these industries, environmental problems also grew, posing threats to health associated with air pollution and poor access to clean water and sanitation. As Maddison points out, although city dwellers in the early period of industrialization enjoyed higher incomes than those in rural areas, their mortality rates were significantly higher, mainly due to the spread of infectious diseases, which took their greatest toll among infants and recent migrants (Maddison, 2001).

It is estimated to have taken 10,000 years for the earth's population to reach its current level of 5 billion. Two billion of these have been added in the last 30 years, mostly in developing countries (World Bank, 2002). This represents a huge leap in terms of demands on the environment. As Chapter 7 highlighted, almost all the current population growth is now taking place in the developing world, where another billion people will be added over the next 20 years. In general, these countries' economies are heavily reliant on agriculture, but agriculture can be precarious and is unlikely to promote sustained economic growth in today's world. Wealth is more likely to come from natural resources such as oil and minerals, or industrialization. In both these scenarios, foreign direct investors, usually large TNCs able to fund inward investment, have been the catalysts. China and India are examples of developing economies that have attracted FDI, mainly through their abundant low-cost labour, and where industrial production is now fuelling economic growth (see Chapters 3 and 4).

Although industrial development has brought much-needed employment and income, it has also led to environmental degradation, including resource depletion and pollution (Miller, 1995). Industrial production requires land for factories and also for housing and other services, such as roads and infrastructure. It is estimated that nearly 23 per cent of all the world's cropland, pasture, forest and woodland have been degraded since the 1950s (World Bank, 2002). Similarly, in this period, nearly one-fifth of all tropical forests have been cleared, most of them in the developing world (World Bank, 2002). One result has been the severe threat to biodiversity: many plants and animals are unique to particular areas and become extinct when the ecosystem is disrupted. Urbanization often encroaches into land which had been agricultural, while growing urban populations place greater pressure on supplies of food, water and energy. Burning fossil fuels such as coal is highly pollutant and resources are finite. The result can be the stifling smogs which envelop cities in the developing world, causing health problems and increased burdens on health infrastructure. Moreover, interconnections between local, regional and global phenomena are increasingly being revealed. For example, air pollution or waste dumped into a river from a single factory may travel long distances, heedless of national boundaries. In the wider picture, we now know that air pollution generated by industrial agglomeration depletes the ozone layer of our atmosphere.

The large TNCs from the developed world, who are at the forefront of FDI, have found themselves enmeshed in the societies in which they operate, facing conflicting agendas. Shareholders, mostly in the developed world, see foreign expansion swelling profits. Governments in host societies welcome the investment and people appreciate new job opportunities. Potential environmental damage may not seem to be a big issue, or, if it is assessed at the decision-making stage, it seems a price worth paying. Only later do the effects become apparent, and some, like health problems, may not emerge for years. Environmental degradation in a host society may take many forms: a forest may be cleared to build a factory; waterways may be polluted by waste from the factory; and the air may be polluted by emissions from its operations. In addition, emissions from factory production pose dangers not merely to local populations, but the build-up of certain gases in the atmosphere contributes to the global phenomenon of climate change. The notion of 'global commons' in the atmosphere and the seas has led environmental researchers to view the entire planet as made up of interrelated ecosystems, where actions in a specific locale can have wide-ranging effects across the globe, some very unpredictable (Held et al., 1999, p. 378).

CRITICAL PERSPECTIVES

Environmentalism and economic growth

The fear is widespread among environmentalists that free trade increases economic growth and that growth harms the environment. That fear is misplaced. Growth enables governments to tax and to raise resources for a variety of objectives, including the abatement of pollution and the general protection of the environment. Without such revenues, little can be achieved, no matter how pure one's motives may be. How do societies actually spend these additional revenues? It depends on how getting rich affects the desire for a better environment. Rich countries have more groups worrying about environmental causes than do poor countries. Efficient policies, such as freer trade, should generally help environmentalism, not harm it. (Bhagwati, 1999, p. 233)

▪ Do you broadly agree with the argument put forward?
▪ What points could be raised which question its validity?

Climate change

Climate experts generally believe that a slow process of global warming is occurring, caused by the build-up of heat-trapping gases, or 'greenhouse gases', in the earth's atmosphere. In particular, carbon dioxide is to blame. Carbon dioxide emissions quadrupled over the second half of the twentieth century, a period of rapid economic growth in Europe, the US and Japan. The burning of fossil fuels is a major cause. Other contributing factors are associated with industrialization and modern consumer societies: they include factories, power stations and the rise of the car. As can be seen from Figure 13.1, which presents comparisons between countries, poorer developing countries tend to have lower levels of emissions per capita than industrialized and advanced economies.

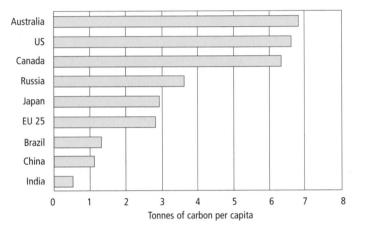

Figure 13.1 Greenhouse gas emissions per capita
Source: *Financial Times*, 31 December 2004.

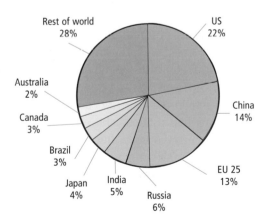

Figure 13.2 Percentage share of world greenhouse gas emissions
Source: *Financial Times*, 31 December, 2004.

The effects of climate change are complex, as climate is more than just temperature, but includes interactions of temperatures with winds and rainfalls in different locations. It is estimated that all continents can expect shifts in their climate and thus their ecology as a result of global warming. Severe flooding is occurring in some places and desertification in others. Arid and semi-arid areas in Africa and Asia will have higher temperatures, causing loss of vegetation and depletion of water sources. Because the polar icecaps are melting, sea levels may rise. Island nations and low-lying regions, such as Bangladesh, risk submerging beneath the sea, while the Sahara Desert in Africa is expanding. Subterranean aquifers are becoming depleted and rivers are drying up. Extremes of drought and flood, as well as extreme events such as storms, pose risks to agriculture and lead to insecurity of supplies of food and clean water. They also contribute to the spread of airborne and waterborne diseases. In arid regions of the world, securing a sustainable supply of water is posing increasing problems, as shown in Case study 13.1, which examines the implications of water scarcity.

The evidence for global warming emanates from a panel of hundreds of scientists, the Intergovernmental Panel on Climate Change, which has published reports in 1990, 1995 and 2000. This theory has been around over a hundred years, but only in the last two decades have scientists been able to monitor the changes with precision in a variety of locations. Most conclude that the process threatens ecology and human well-being. While experts point to the need to curtail emissions to slow down the warming process, arriving at an international consensus on how to achieve this aim has proved difficult. It is argued that the damaging rise in carbon dioxide might be offset by the absorptive capacity of the sea, which acts as a sink. However, recent research indicates that the sea's absorptive capacity might be more limited than experts had thought, implying a quicker rate of global warming (Wright, 2004). Deforestation, for example, in the rainforests of South America, also diminishes the capacity of the environment to absorb carbon dioxide, accelerating global warming.

The Kyoto Protocol, initiated in 1997, contains a framework for international cooperation to deal with the effects of climate change. This treaty set targets for the reduction in carbon dioxide emissions, mainly by the industrialized countries. It also introduces a system of emissions trading to achieve this objective. The overall target is that by 2008–12, industrial countries would reduce their combined greenhouse gas emissions to 5 per cent below 1990 levels. The treaty was signed by over 150 countries, but would not come into force until countries accounting for 55 per cent of greenhouse gas emissions had ratified. The US produces more greenhouse gas emissions than any other country, accounting for about 22 per cent of the global total (see Figure 13.2). As can be seen in Figure 13.3, the US would have needed to reduce emissions by nearly 300 million tonnes from 2000 levels, representing a 19.3 per cent reduction by 2008–12. The US rejection of the treaty in 2001 cast doubt on the treaty ever coming into effect. Australia, which would need to reduce emissions by 15.4 per cent of 2000 levels, also declined to ratify it. However, in 2004, with the ratification by Russia, which accounts for 17 per cent of global emissions, the 55 per cent threshold was met and the treaty was set to come into force in international law in 2005.

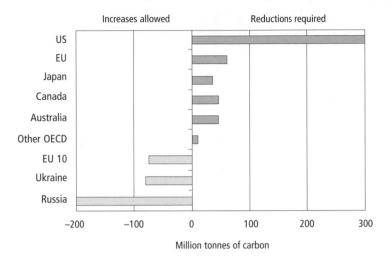

Figure 13.3 **Gap between emissions in 2000 and Kyoto targets**
Source: *Financial Times*, 20 May 2004.

Despite its having achieved the necessary ratifications to take effect, environmentalists have doubts about the effectiveness of the Kyoto Protocol. For a start, its emission reduction targets are very modest and only extend to 2008–12. Without US participation, the targets will achieve a reduction of only 2 per cent in the amount of carbon dioxide in the world. A 60 per cent reduction in emissions would be needed to halt climate change, and achieving international consensus on a tougher agreement to succeed the Kyoto Protocol looks remote. Moreover, the Kyoto targets for reducing emissions exclude the major developing countries, such as China and India. Finally, environmentalists doubt the effectiveness of the principle of 'emissions trading', pointing to the fact that it allows polluting industries simply to buy emission 'credits' from other countries in order to meet their targets, without actually cutting emissions in their domestic economy. The EU, Japan and Canada can simply buy surplus credits from the countries in the former Soviet Union. In particular, as Figure 13.3 indicates, Russia is potentially a major seller of credits in global carbon markets. On the other hand, the market-based scheme can be readily assimilated by businesses, providing them with incentives and flexibility that a purely regulatory regime would not accommodate.

WEB ALERT! Websites with specific content on climate change:

The Intergovernmental Panel on Climate Change is at http://www.ipcc.ch/

The UN Framework Convention on Climate Change, which includes the Kyoto Protocol, is at http://unfccc.int

Materials on climate change can be accessed via the World Wildlife Fund's website at http://www.panda.org; click on 'climate change'

Case study 13.1   Global water resources become precarious

The world is becoming drier. Many vital rivers and lakes, once offering abundant water, have shrunk, mainly due to climate change, irrigation and demands of growing populations. Moreover, rivers and lakes in some parts of the world have become so polluted that their water is unusable – a situation that is made worse by the effects of climate change. It is estimated by the UN that nearly a third of the world's population, at least 2 billion people, will be affected by water scarcity by 2025 (see figure). Resources in groundwater, the water stored in underground aquifers, is increasingly being drawn on, and in some areas, such as northern China, serious depletion is occurring.

Farmers are the biggest consumers of water, irrigation accounting for 75 per cent of all water drawn from rivers, reservoirs and aquifers. Growing the food for a person to eat requires a thousand times as much water as that person needs for drinking purposes. Growing populations demand more food, and agricultural scientists estimate that farm water use will need to be increased by 15–20 per cent in the coming 25 years to maintain food supplies. On the other hand, environmental scientists say that water use is severely threatening ecosystems and needs to be reduced by 10 per cent to maintain rivers and lakes. According to the *World Development Report 2003*, much of the world's land surface is 'fragile', that is, 'vulnerable to degradation, erosion, floods and landslides' (World Bank, 2002, p. 60). These areas are mainly in East and South Asia, sub-Saharan Africa, the Middle East and North Africa. Between 1950 and 2000, the rural populations tripled and even quadrupled in some of the countries where people living on fragile lands make up half the total population. To make matters worse, a high proportion of the countries which have significant populations living on fragile lands have suffered from civil conflicts in the last decade. Nineteen countries in sub-Saharan Africa fall into this category (World Bank, 2002).

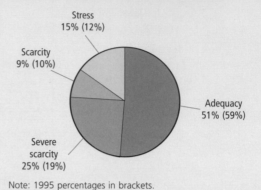

Note: 1995 percentages in brackets.

The world's water availability (as estimated percentage of population in 2025)
Source: Houlder, 14 August 2001.

Improving water management and seeking innovative ways to improve efficiency are recommended by water experts. More than half the water that is used in irrigation systems never reaches crops, due to leakages, evaporation and poor management. Drip irrigation systems and precision sprinklers can alleviate this wastage. Scientists have made progress in developing crop strains which are drought-resistant. New water-saving techniques are being designed to reduce the water needed to grow rice. For some countries, importing food alleviates the problems of water scarcity, but this solution is only feasible for wealthier countries, such as Jordan. It would not be workable in the poorest countries. For China and India, the world market would not be able to meet the needs of their large populations. Both are engaged in major hydrological schemes to transfer water long distances. However, the experience in India has been that the promises of political leaders and bureaucrats that reliable water infrastructure would reach rural villages remain unfulfilled. Self-help has stepped in, with extensive rainwater harvesting systems, relying on man-made ponds, tanks, channels and a variety of other structures, some medieval in origin.

While the World Bank recommends that new infrastructure projects are needed, environmentalists argue that some of these have caused ecological destruction and are very costly. They urge that large projects on their own are not the solution: conservation and better water management are the keys to combating water shortages and protecting the environment. In addition, building desalination plants to use water from the world's oceans, while expensive, is an alternative. New desalination technology is reducing the costs, bringing the process within the reach of poorer countries. The solar-powered desalination plant represents the kind of innovative approach that offers hope of future sustainable water supply.

Sources: Houlder, V., 'Low water', *Financial Times*, 14 August 2001; Houlder, V., 'World in drier straits', *Financial Times*, 11 August 2003; World Bank (2002) *World Development Report 2003*; Houlder, V., 'Parched cities turn to the sea to quench their thirst', *Financial Times*, 23 June 2004; Luce, E., 'Supply and demands: what has water to do with politics', *Financial Times*, 24 July 2004.

Case questions

How does water supply highlight the tension between economic growth and environmental protection?

What solutions does the case study highlight for combating water shortages?

Transboundary pollution and implications for energy policies

Transboundary pollution refers to the transmission of pollutants through the water, soil and air from one national jurisdiction to another. The transmission may be intentional, as in the transport of hazardous waste, or it may be unintentional, as in an accident at a nuclear power plant. Industrial enterprises have long been releasing waste into rivers and emissions such as sulphur dioxide into the atmosphere. However, only in the twentieth century was there a dramatic increase in the capacity for pollution on a large scale, with the potential for devastating environmental effects. In addition, industries such as nuclear power generation raised the possibility of catastrophic accidents. The cataclysmic event which is usually cited as causing a shift in the environmental paradigm was the meltdown of the nuclear power station at Chernobyl in the former Soviet Union in 1986 (Landes, 1998). The fire, which burned for five days, released more than 50 tonnes of radioactive poison into the atmosphere, affecting Belarus, the Baltic states and the Scandinavian countries. The disaster and the inept handling of the aftermath are factors which contributed to the eventual collapse of the Soviet command economy (Landes, 1998).

Less dramatic has been the quiet destruction that acid rain has caused in the environment, becoming visible only when rivers and forests appear to be dying. 'Acid rain' is the term used to describe acid which falls out of the atmosphere. It may be wet, in the form of rain, fog and snow, affecting the soil on which plants and animals depend. Or it may be dry, in the form of acidic gases and particles, which may blow onto buildings and trees and into homes. Its main components are sulphur dioxide and nitrogen oxides. It causes trees to gradually wither, buildings to decay and aquatic life to die. Aquatic ecosystems are particularly endangered. The burning of fossil fuel, such as coal, for electricity is particularly blamed for acid rain. International cooperation for lowering acid rain emissions in Europe and North America has helped to reduce levels, but industrialization in the developing world has spread these problems to more countries.

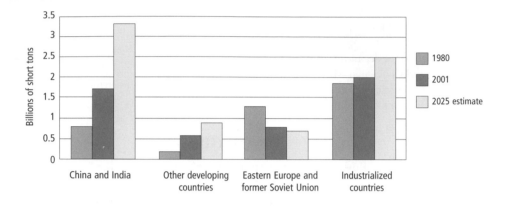

Figure 13.4 **World coal consumption by region**
Source: *Financial Times*, 4 October 2004.

China still relies on coal-burning power stations for nearly 70 per cent of its power. It aims to reduce its reliance on coal as an energy source to 60 per cent by 2020, as it builds gas and nuclear-fired power stations. However, China's rapid economic growth has relied on increasing its output of coal for both power generation and steel production. As a result, China's coal mining industry is booming, output climbing from 1.67 billion tonnes in 2003 to 1.9 billion in 2004. This trend is likely to continue, as Figure 13.4 shows, whereas reliance on coal is decreasing in Eastern Europe and Russia. Apart from the indirect damage wreaked by environmental pollution, China's mining industry has also attracted attention, it should be added, for its direct cost in human life. Over 5000 miners lost their lives in China's unsafe mines in 2004, a statistic which, incredibly, represents an improvement on 2003 and is cited by Chinese authorities as an indication that their campaign, 'Putting people first', to encourage safety in mine management is succeeding (Dickie, 2004).

China's embrace of the private car as a centrepiece of its thriving economy is also contributing to the pollution problems. Pollution from the Pearl River delta in Guangdong province is travelling across the delta to neighbouring Hong Kong, causing smog and water pollution. A World Bank report in 2004 found that the Guangdong region had the capacity to treat only 28 per cent of the waste water that it generates every day (Harney, 2004).

The case for nuclear power generation rests on its low level of emissions, combined with concerns over the depletion of non-renewable energy sources such as coal and oil. France and Japan, both poor in these natural energy sources, have gone over to nuclear power for electricity, as Figure 13.5 shows. However, the expansion of nuclear power has brought risks. An accident at a nuclear power station in Japan, in which four workers died in 2004, shook the confidence of the Japanese people in their nuclear industry. Further risks have emerged with the growth in the nuclear reprocessing and recycling industries, combined with the need for safe treatment and storage of nuclear waste. Further, the safe transport of nuclear waste across land and sea, to reach reprocessing sites, has created new concerns, not only because of the risk of accidents, but also from the fear of terrorist attack. The risks associated with nuclear-related industries have become dispersed geographically as these industries have grown. The Ukrainian president opened a new nuclear reactor in 2004, the first since the Chernobyl meltdown. Significantly, he emphasized the country's need for the export income it would generate (Taylor and McNulty, 2004). Sweden voted in a referendum in 1980 to phase out its nuclear industry by 2010, but an opinion poll in 2004 indicated that nearly half of respondents wished to keep existing reactors (Taylor and McNulty, 2004).

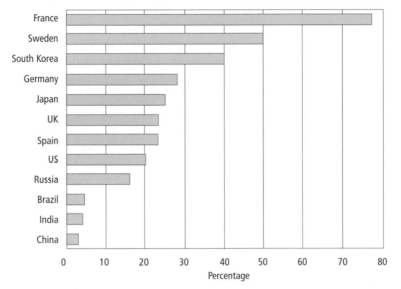

Figure 13.5 **Share of nuclear power in electricity generation (2003)**
Source: *Financial Times*, 10 August 2004.

Damage caused by transboundary pollution, whether intentional or unintentional, may be long-lasting and, in some cases, the full extent of the damage is not apparent for many years. How to apportion responsibility and compel polluters to compensate (insofar as possible) for the harm they cause is complicated by the fact that different legal jurisdictions are involved. Often, the victims are in developing countries, with little in the way of resources to seek legal redress, especially if they must resort to litigation in another country, as was seen in the example of the Bhopal explosion, discussed in Chapter 9. Cooperation between governments has led to numerous international regulatory regimes designed to monitor pollution and reduce the risk of accidents.

International legal frameworks

Environmental disasters, such as the *Exxon Valdez* oil spill off the Alaskan coast in 1989 and the Chernobyl nuclear plant disaster in 1986, have dramatically raised public consciousness of the need for cooperation between states. The United Nations Environment Programme (UNEP) dates from 1972. The UN Conference on Environment and Development (UNCED), at the Rio Summit in 1992, adopted the concept of **sustainable development**, which refers to 'meeting the needs of present generations without compromising the ability of future generations to do the same' (Wallace, 1997, p. 197). The conference produced the Declaration on Environment and Development (the Rio Declaration), which includes principles which apply to a variety of activities and incidents, whether involving state agencies or commercial enterprises (see minifile). Note that, although the principle of state sovereignty over resources is acknowledged, it is qualified by the principle of sustainable development. The 'polluter-pays' principle is acknowledged, although, when it comes to dispute resolution (discussed in Chapter 9), the polluting state will seldom consent to international adjudication or arbitration. Finally, the link is made between sustainable development and poverty reduction in Principle 5. Critics have argued that this principle seems to indicate an underlying assumption of the Rio Declaration that reducing poverty requires economic development, although the historical evidence suggests a more complex relationship than simple cause and effect (Castro, 2004). What is meant by 'poverty' is discussed in Chapter 14, but it is relevant to note here that the definition includes dimensions other than purely economic ones, especially in the context of sustainable development. Moreover, as the benefits of market-based economic development are not spread evenly in societies, policy-making in relation to resource allocation and social priorities are factors in reducing poverty (Castro, 2004).

Minifile

THE RIO DECLARATION ON ENVIRONMENT AND DEVELOPMENT, 1992

Working towards international agreements which respect the interests of all and protect the integrity of the global environmental and developmental system.

● Principle 2: States have, in accordance with the UN Charter and the principles of international law, the sovereign right to exploit their own resources pursuant to their own environmental and developmental policies, and the responsibility to ensure that activities within their jurisdiction or control do not cause damage to the environment of other States or of areas beyond the limits of national jurisdiction.

● Principle 3: The right to development must be fulfilled so as to equitably meet developmental and environmental needs of present and future generations.

● Principle 5: All States and all people shall cooperate in the essential task of eradicating

poverty as an indispensable requirement of sustainable development.

● Principle 8: To achieve sustainable development and a higher quality of life for all people, States should reduce and eliminate unsustainable patterns of production and consumption and promote appropriate demographic policies.

● Principle 13: States shall develop national law regarding liability and compensation for the victims of pollution and other environmental damage ...

● Principle 16: ... the polluter should, in principle, bear the cost of pollution ...

● Principle 25: Peace, development and environmental protection are interdependent and indivisible.

The full statement of principles is available in Evans, M.D. (1999) *Blackstone's International Law Documents* (4th edn), London: Blackstone Press.

The Rio conference also adopted the Convention on Biological Diversity and the Convention on Climate Change. The Biodiversity Convention aimed to protect and sustain biodiversity by a number of measures, including national monitoring of biodiversity, environmental impact assessments and national progress reports from individual countries. It reinforced the principle of sustainable development. In 1992, the UN also adopted a Convention on the Transboundary Effects of Industrial Accidents, placing an onus on states to take preventive steps and also to respond responsibly when accidents occur. A Convention on Nuclear Safety followed in 1994. While these international instruments focus on state responsibility for implementation of their provisions within their own jurisdictions, it should be noted that states vary in their commitment to prevent and control harmful activities. Developing countries, above all, may lack the resources to regulate environmental protection. Awareness of environmental implications by business enterprises is therefore a crucial factor in the environmental protection landscape. In particular, the responsibility of the large TNCs as important global players is increasingly recognized in environmental issues.

WEB ALERT!

A website on environmental resources is the Socioeconomic and Applications Centre at http://sedac.ciesin.Columbia.edu

The Biodiversity Conservation Information System's website is http://www.biodiversity.org

The UN's Food and Agriculture Organization (FAO) offers resources on many topics related to land and water themes, including biodiversity. These include a soil biodiversity portal at http://www.fao.org/ag/agl/agll/soilbiod

The Forest Conservation portal is at http://forests.org

Challenges of environmental protection for business

Land, water and air are the components of the physical environment which have been affected by industrial processes associated with economic development. Managers have become accustomed to dealing with local pollution problems arising from their operations, entailing interaction with local community authorities. However, wider issues such as climate change and biodiversity, while nonetheless real, seem remote, complex and insusceptible to the usual means of resolution. What is more, scientific evidence is not always clear cut, and regulatory regimes are still in doubt, partly over difficulties of measurement and enforcement. It is largely down to the lobbying and, more recently, active involvement of 'green groups' that environmental issues and climate change are now seen as urgent issues on the global agenda, engaging governments, corporations and consumers alike.

Sustainable development in the business context

Businesses are becoming more conscious of the need for new, cleaner technologies, partly because of growing social and ethical considerations, and also because international instruments signed up to by governments, such as the Kyoto Protocol, are growing in number. But how does a broad principle like sustainable development translate into a business strategy? The following provides some indication:

For the business enterprise, sustainable development means adopting business strategies and activities that meet the needs of the enterprise and its stakeholders today while protecting, sustaining and enhancing the human and natural resources that will be needed in the future. (International Institute for Sustainable Development, 1992)

In terms of strategy, the statement is still rather general, but it does highlight the duty to stakeholders, and also the duty to both human and environmental resources. Companies now take a broader view of their 'environmental footprint', looking at all phases of their operations, from production processes to the nature of the products they sell, to assess whether they can be made more environmentally friendly. Consumers have been a source of pressure, creating new demand, for example for recyclable products. Environmental protection and economic efficiency, once seen as posing a dilemma of choice, are now therefore seen as merging together, in that protecting the environment is now regarded as a primary objective of a business, rather than a constraint, as was felt in the past.

WEB ALERT!

In the UK, the Department for Environment, Food and Rural Affairs (DEFRA) is at http://www.defra.gov.uk

There are many websites run by NGOs, including:

The National Environmental Trust at http://www.net.org
Friends of the Earth at http://www.foe.org.uk
Greenpeace at http://www.greenpeace.org
Worldwide Fund for Nature at http://www.panda.org

CRITICAL PERSPECTIVES

Competitiveness and the environment

Although pollution prevention is an important step in the right direction, ultimately companies must learn to frame environmental improvement in terms of resource productivity. Today managers and regulators focus on the actual costs of eliminating or treating pollution. They must shift their attention to include the opportunity costs of pollution – wasted resources, wasted effort, and diminished product value to the customer. At the level of resource productivity, environmental improvement and competitiveness come together. (Porter and van der Linde, 1995, p. 355)

The authors suggest that innovation in terms of resource productivity should be substituted for the old dichotomy that posited environmental improvement as diminishing competitiveness. To what extent is this argument borne out in the global economy of the present day?

**Environ-
mental
management**

Environmental management, assessing environmental impact and devising suitable strategies, is now seen as central to companies' operations, especially in the industries which are by nature more pollutant. These include chemicals, mining, pulp and paper, iron and steel, and refineries. For the large TNCs which use subcontracting and licensing arrangements, there is a question of how much control can be exerted on subcontractors in terms of environmental management. This question is often posed for TNCs operating in developing countries with weaker environmental protection regimes. Although it is difficult to assess the impact of industries in different locations, research suggests that the ratio of pollution-intensive industries in FDI stock is higher than in domestic investment (United Nations, 1999a). Historically, state-owned production was highly pollutant, partly because of obsolete technology, whereas the flow of new investment has brought cleaner technology and greater environmental protection, as has happened in Central and Eastern Europe. FDI to many countries that have relied on mineral exports has increased as a result of liberalization and privatization. However, the riches from oil and mineral wealth may prove difficult to harness towards goals which improve the well-being of society generally, as has been the case in resource-rich regions of Africa (World Bank, 2004). Equatorial Guinea's new oil wealth has seen FDI inflow increase from $323m. in 2002 to nearly $1.5bn. in 2003 (World Bank, 2004). Of the world's five top-ranking countries in inward FDI performance, three owe their attraction mainly to oil (United Nations, 2004). They are Azerbaijan, Brunei and Angola, all of whose economies are dependent on income from natural resources. The large TNCs which characterize the extraction industries, such as global oil companies, may therefore dominate the economies of host developing countries, causing tension between corporate goals and local environmental protection. Weak or unstable host governments, eager for the revenues from resource wealth, have been poorly placed to exert pressures on foreign investors to pursue sustainable development goals. Ecuador is an example, where serious environmental degradation was caused by Texaco's operations in the 1970s and 80s. Because environmental restoration requirements agreed by the company with the Ecuadorian government were so minimal, there was little the inhabitants could do to make the company clean up and restore sites when they left the country in 1992 (Olsen, 2001).

Developing countries with weak environmental policies and weak enforcement are also host to manufacturing industries, which enjoy the traditional comparative advantages due to low-cost labour. Where these plants are export-oriented, consumers in developed countries' markets can be a source of pressure for environmental protection. The International Organization for Standardization, which produces ISO standards, has developed a certification for standards of environmental management (ISO 14000). Although research suggests that foreign affiliates in manufacturing industries might have higher environmental standards, the adoption rate of ISO 14000 certification does not show any noticeable differences between foreign and domestic firms (United Nations, 1999a, p. 302). Recall the differences in energy efficiency between developed and developing countries highlighted in Case study 10.1. TNCs are finding that, in the new context of social responsibility, it is advantageous to integrate systems of environmental management across all their corporate activities globally, wherever the location.

Aspects of environmental management

Processes

Air
- Emissions of gases, particle matter, metals, organic chemicals and odours.
- Risks of fires and explosions.

Water
- Use of process water and emission of process water.
- Emissions of water contaminated, for example, by metals or oil.
- Contamination of surface water or underground water.

Land
- Waste disposal, including hazardous waste.
- Extraction of raw materials.
- Soil contamination by metals.
- Surface disturbance, such as erosion or subsidence.

Products
- Contaminating components, such as metals, chemicals, pesticides.
- Recyclability, including recyclable packaging.

Research and increased awareness of the damaging effects of climate change have impressed on businesses the need to look at the green implications of their operations, especially their levels of emissions. One consideration is that reductions are likely to be required under future treaties and it is preferable to get a head start. Another is that companies are in a position to take the lead in positive action to alleviate potentially harmful global warming, especially in industries that have high levels of emissions. Cutting pollution, while it can be seen as a cost, is also a business opportunity. Case study 13.2 on Ecover highlights how a company has made environmental protection the centrepiece of its strategy. Large car makers, such as General Motors, Toyota and Ford, have committed considerable research to less polluting cars, run on fuel cells. They thus have an advantage over less sophisticated rivals. General Motors reported in 2004 that it had reduced its greenhouse gas emissions 72 per cent in 13 years (Harvey, 2004). Low-emission technologies have opened opportunities in the energy industry and also in a range of manufacturing industries. DuPont has already cut greenhouse emissions 69 per cent below 1990 levels (Harvey, 2004). It has found ways to end emissions of nitrous oxide, a greenhouse gas that was emitted in the production of nylon. Clean technology can also be exported to countries in the developing world. Environmental reporting, detailing the ways in which a company's operations impact on the environment, has become an element in 'triple-bottom-line' reporting. In addition to financial reporting, companies may report on social and environmental aspects of their operations, making up the three elements of triple-bottom-line reporting. While the latter two impact reports are voluntary, they are increasingly viewed by shareholders and other stakeholders as indicative of good governance. These issues will be revisited in Chapter 14 in the context of the socially responsible enterprise.

Case study 13.2   Ecover cleans up with green consumers

Ecover is a company which manufactures environmentally friendly cleaning products. It was founded in Belgium in 1979 and since then has had success in its 'niche' market. The company's aim is to produce cleaning products that cause as little harm to the environment as possible. Its products are plant-based and biodegrade rapidly, causing a minimum of harm to the aquatic environment. Detergents and other cleaning products made by the large multinationals, by contrast, contain chemicals such as phosphates, which cause a proliferation of bacteria in waterways. While governments have banned some chemicals, eroding some of the differentiation between Ecover and its rivals, Ecover's managers point out that there are many common ingredients which are potentially harmful, such as optical brighteners and scent.

As Ecover is scrupulous about using only rapidly biodegradable ingredients, its raw materials are more expensive than those of larger rivals, who also benefit from economies of scale. Ecover's commitment to environmentally safe ingredients won it many consumers in the 1980s and 90s, despite the fact that its products are about 10 per cent more expensive than those of its rivals. Taken up by the major supermarkets in the UK in 1990, it had 3 per cent of the British detergent market. In 1992, it built an ecological factory which featured recycled bricks and a grass roof, which kept the building cool in summer and warm in winter, as well as blending in with the environment. The company's fortunes soon took a downturn, however. In the late 1990s, consumers became reluctant to spend premium prices for its products. It was forced to retreat back to the health food shops.

The boom in organic products in the new millennium brought renewed interest in the environment, which presented an opportunity for Ecover to win consumers back to its products. Its marketing stressed a broader appeal, on health as well as environmental grounds, extending beyond the 'pure' green consumer to the more health-conscious consumer. Adjusting to the changing consumer profile, the company stresses that its products must work well. One analyst has said of green products generally: 'To succeed in the marketplace products have to be more than just green. They have to be better products' (Murray, 2001). The EU's strong environmental policies on testing chemicals and recycling packaging reflect renewed concern over the environment. Ecover will hope that changing consumer preferences towards more environmentally and socially responsible products are here to stay and will not evaporate in future economic downturns.

Sources: Murray, S., 'Green products: consumers count cost over ecology', *Financial Times*, 5 November 2001; Houlder, V., 'Greener brand of cleaner finds organic growth', *Financial Times*, 16 July, 2004; Wendlandt, A., 'A crushing burden on industry', *Financial Times*, 24 September 2002; Ecover's website at http://www.ecover.com.

Case questions

What problems are faced by a company such as Ecover in consumer markets?

What are its prospects for growth?

EU initiatives on the environment

Governments in European countries and the EU itself have taken a lead in environmental protection measures, including 'economic instruments' such as fuel taxes, and market approaches such as emissions trading. The UK and Germany are roughly on target to meet Kyoto targets. UK emissions of the basket of greenhouse gases are expected to be about 13.5 per cent below 1990 levels in 2010, and emissions of carbon dioxide (which comprises about 80 per cent of the total greenhouse gas emissions) about 7 per cent below (DEFRA, 2001). The distribution in reductions across the UK economy are shown in Figure 13.6.

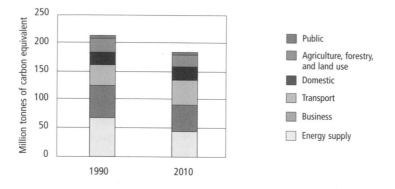

Figure 13.6 **UK greenhouse gas emissions in 1990 and projections for 2010**
Source: UK Department of Environment, Food & Rural Affairs (2000) *Climate Change: Draft UK Programme*, at http://www.defra.gov.uk/environment.

In the UK, the March 2000 budget introduced a number of environmental tax reforms, including a climate change levy on business to encourage energy efficiency (see minifile), which has met with criticism from businesses that jobs and production will suffer. Although discounts will be available for heavy energy users, a report for the Engineering Employers' Federation showed that more than 3000 UK companies have annual energy bills of over £100,000, but will be ineligible for the discount. Particularly hard hit when the climate levy starts to bite will be SMEs, some of whom, according to one British managing director of a US-owned company, may consider shifting production to the US if productivity suffers (*Financial Times*, 21 November 2000).

The EU agreed a greenhouse gas emissions trading scheme in 2003, as part of its strategy to meet its target of an 8 per cent reduction between 1990 and 2010. Since then, national governments have drawn up plans for how to implement it. In particular, the plans will affect the most pollutant sectors: power generation, steelmaking, glass and cement manufacture together account for 46 per cent of Europe's carbon dioxide emissions. Permits will be given to individual plants, linked to emissions allocations. If a plant exceeds its target, it will have to buy permits from businesses which have not used all their allocations. Companies which are able to reduce their emissions by greater energy efficiency and cleaner technology stand to gain, as they are able to sell surplus permits to companies which have exceeded allocations. The latter companies, which include those who find it too expensive to convert to cleaner technology, face the added cost of permits. They may thus be encouraged to invest in cleaner technology. Issues of international competitiveness and pricing will be critical. Much depends on the whether extra costs can be passed on to customers. Recall that the US, China, India and Australia are outside the Kyoto Protocol. The extent to

PROTECTING THE ENVIRONMENT: THE UK BUDGET 2000

The following is a summary of key provisions in the green budget of 2000:

Tackling climate change

- Extension of reduced Vehicle Excise Duty (VED) rate to existing cars with engines up to 1,200cc.
- Introduction of graduated VED system for new cars based primarily on their carbon dioxide emissions.
- An additional £280 million allocated to tackling congestion hot-spots and modernizing public transport.
- Further encouragement for emissions trading.
- Implementing the climate change levy to encourage energy efficiency in the business sector.

Improving air quality

- A fiscal incentive to encourage the take up of cleaner ultra-low sulphur petrol.

- Lower rates of tax for vehicles which use less polluting fuels.

Regenerating our cities and protecting our countryside

- Introduction of an aggregates levy to tackle the environmental costs of quarrying and encourage recycling.
- Preannounced increases in landfill tax to encourage waste minimization and recycling.
- Consultation on possible stamp duty relief for new developments on brownfield land to encourage an urban renaissance.
- Further discussions on a voluntary package to reduce the environmental impacts of pesticides use.

Source: HM Treasury (2000) *Budget: March 2000*, at http://www.hm-treasury.gov.uk/budget2000.

which their businesses will voluntarily set targets for emission reduction will affect global progress in emission reduction. Moreover, the burden in the EU, as business leaders in Britain have noted, falls on business, rather than motorists and households, which, as Figure 13.6 showed, are two of the biggest polluters. For Britain, the reliance on coal-fired power stations for 35 per cent of its electricity is likely to lead to rises in the price of electricity.

The EU has also embarked on a series of far-reaching measures in environmental legislation. Concerned about the effects of excessive packaging on the environment, it is raising minimum targets for recycling packaging waste. The new targets require 55 per cent of packaging to be recycled by 2008. Critics argue, however, that packaging is only a small part of the overall problem of increasing environmental awareness. Research in 2004 indicated that changing a four-wheel-drive SUV for a more fuel-efficient car would, in one year, save the same amount of energy as recycling a family's bottles for 400 years (Houlder, 2004). A new landfill directive aims to reduce the risk of polluting water and soil from landfill sites. From 2004, hazardous and non-hazardous waste cannot be disposed of jointly in landfill sites and the categories of hazardous waste have expanded – tyres, for example, cannot be disposed of in landfill sites. With fewer sites able to deal with hazardous waste, the costs of disposal are likely to rise. A growing problem is how to dispose of the mountain of old white goods, televisions, computers and other household electrical equipment – these are sources of heavy metals and organic pollutants. From 2005, the EU requires manufacturers and importers to take back and recycle these appliances, from mobile phones to washing machines. These requirements, which place the responsibility on the manufacturers, will add to costs but should create incentives to design products that are easier to recycle.

The polluter-pays principle was established in a directive on environmental liability agreed in 2003. Under the directive, a company would be liable for a variety of harms which might arise from its operations, including water or soil pollution, damage to bio-diversity and harm to human health. The company would be responsible for repairing the damage insofar as possible. Of course, damage may be irreversible and effects may take some time to emerge. The aims, as with the use of other mandatory legislation, is to encourage companies to take into account the environment at the planning stage, and develop cleaner, less invasive ways of operating. But how effective is this top-down approach to changing the way we think about the environment?

CRITICAL PERSPECTIVES

Environmental regulation and corporate strategy

If innovation in response to environmental regulation can be profitable – if a company can actually offset the cost of compliance through improving resource productivity – why is regulation necessary at all? If such opportunities exist, wouldn't companies pursue them naturally and wouldn't regulation be unnecessary? That is like saying there will rarely be ten-dollar bills to be found on the ground because someone already will have picked them up. Certainly, some companies do pursue such innovations without, or in advance of, regulation ... But the belief that com-panies will pick up on profitable opportunities without a regulatory push makes a false assumption about competitive reality – namely, that all profitable opportunit-ies for innovation have already been discovered, that all managers have perfect information about them, and that organizational incentives are aligned with inno-vating. (Porter and van der Linde, 1995, p. 362).

What is the authors' approach to environmental regulation? What are the implications for corporate strategists?

Green consumerism

When we think of green consumerism, we tend to think mainly of recycling waste and buying organic produce. However, green consumerism covers a wide range of lifestyle decisions. Besides shopping for environmentally friendly products and recy-cling, it covers using less pollutant transport, using complementary medicine, exploring ecotourism for our holidays and investing our money in socially respon-sible funds. In addressing the role of consumers in environmental issues, the UNEP focuses on a broad notion of 'sustainable consumption', which covers the many lifestyle decisions made by consumers which impact on the environment, directly or indirectly. The UK National Consumer Council has found that consumers want to 'do their bit', but they point to the hurly-burly of daily life and pressures which take precedence. There is an element of feeling guilty about purchasing habits, which, the UNEP notes, does not help to encourage changes in behaviour (Houlder, 2003). Rather than making people feel guilty, it would be more fruitful to try to rid green consumerism of its dreary image and emphasize the benefits to be enjoyed from living in ways that are more in harmony with nature.

Sceptics about green consumerism argue that, even if consumers in rich countries change their buying habits to more environmentally friendly products, the effects will be limited unless people are persuaded to consume less. They point out that improvements in products to make them less detrimental to the environment are often offset by growing demand. In transport, for example, although new cars are fuel-efficient, the growing number of vehicles on the roads cancels out the benefits of greater fuel efficiency. For businesses, especially manufacturing firms, the notion of defining sustainable consumption as reduced consumption meets with little appeal. Similarly, for governments, reduced consumption is not likely to find favour. Reduced consumer spending tends to pose headaches, as highlighted in Chapter 3: reduced output is linked to decreases in employment, falling tax revenues and weak economic growth. Governments, however, are in a position to promote changes in consumer behaviour and changes in manufacturers' approaches which fall within the notion of sustainable consumption. The head of policy research at the UK National Consumer Council has said of consumers' environmental awareness: 'People are getting more interested in the processes behind the product, that's a growing trend. But from the point of view of trying to transform markets it will never be enough. You'll still need the regulators' (Murray, 2001).

Environmental protection and changing values

Much of the thrust of EU regulation has fallen on businesses, rather than directly on consumers. It is recognized that the lifestyle decisions of consumers are important in society's adoption of more eco-friendly behaviour, but these involve culture change in the developed world, where, in terms of the attributes that consumers seek in products and services, the environment comes well down the list, behind price, brand and quality (Murray 2001). In parts of China at present, people are now buying cars and other consumer products in their millions, thanks to their new prosperity, which has come with modern, FDI-driven industrialization. Is this sustainable development or just plain development?

CRITICAL PERSPECTIVES

Sustainable consumption

Recent history suggests that those living in wealthier countries do not intend to consume and waste less. Given that the other 80 per cent of the planet's people seek to emulate those consumption habits, the only hope for sustainability is to change *forms* of consumption. To do so, we must innovate. We must produce more energy, but with lower carbon intensity; more wood and paper, but from planted forests rather than virgin forests; more food, but not in ways that spread deserts and waste water. Sustainable consumption is not necessarily about consuming less, but consuming differently; consuming efficiently. (World Business Council for Sustainable Development, 2002)

■   Is this approach sufficient to achieve sustainable consumption, without consuming less?

In developing countries, where infrastructure is struggling to catch up, urbanization is causing problems for provision of clean air, access to clean water and sanitation. These sprawling cities are also prone to suffer from food and energy shortages. Whereas these locations were once seen as matters of local concern, we now see them as global issues, involving sustainable development. Similarly, in areas of the world where population pressures and the depletion of natural resources are causing hardship to humans, animals and wildlife, as well as adversely affecting ecosystems, the issues are of global concern. As a result of the globalization of the environment, there has been a proliferation of regimes for international monitoring, cooperation among states to reach international environmental agreements and the growth of many NGOs, whose activities have raised the public's awareness of environmental issues.

Development has tended to be equated with Western consumer lifestyles, dependent on cars, cheap air travel and throwaway appliances, all of which are becoming problematical in today's ecologically stressed environment. Can it, or should it, be held up as a model for other developing countries, or even for the vast swathes of China as yet untouched by modernity? As has been seen in this chapter, development, both past and present, tends to mean economic growth, with little heed for environmental consequences. What is added by the notion of sustainability may, at its most minimal interpretation, simply mean sustained economic growth, rather than sustaining the environment (Castro, 2004). However, a question mark hangs over sustained economic growth, as non-renewable energy resources such as oil become depleted. Given the observable effects of environmental degradation in today's world, failure to heed the ecological messages will jeopardize the prospects of long-term economic growth.

Conclusions

1   Environmental issues, including climate change, the depletion of natural resources and pollution, are now seen as global issues, to be addressed by governments, businesses and consumers alike.

2
Human activity, particularly the processes of industrialization and urbanization, result in environmental degradation such as pollution from emissions. While promoting economic development in host societies, TNCs are enmeshed in the environmental consequences of their operations on societies.

3
Climate change, a process of global warming, is caused by a build-up of heat-trapping gases. Carbon dioxide emissions associated with industrialization are highlighted as a major factor.

4
International efforts to reduce global greenhouse gases took a step forward with the Kyoto Protocol, which aimed to reduce levels of these emissions to 1990 levels by 2008–12. However, even if these reductions are achieved, much further reduction is needed to have an impact on global warming.

5
Transboundary pollution, such as acid rain, can have wide-ranging effects, calling for cooperation between countries to reduce the levels.

6
While there is a strong case for nuclear power, resting on its low level of emissions, and concern over the depletion of non-renewable energy sources, there remain concerns over its safety, including the nuclear reprocessing and recycling industries.

7
International legal frameworks now cover a variety of environmental concerns. Most notably, the principles enunciated by the Rio Declaration in 1992 formed the basis of sustainable development policies.

8
Businesses face specific environmental challenges depending on their particular industry. In response, they now look at their 'environmental footprint' in a strategic light.

9
Environmental management addresses the specific environmental aspects of a firm's operations, including those of subcontractors. In some industries, such as extraction, companies operating in host countries face challenges to operate according to international standards, rather than local standards, which are likely to be lower and weakly enforced.

10
The EU has taken a lead in environmental protection, particularly with new legislation on recycling and emissions trading. These initiatives are helping to bring emissions down to Kyoto targets.

11
Green consumerism, often considered to focus on buying environmentally friendly products, can be seen in the wider context of 'sustainable consumption', which impacts on a range of lifestyle decisions, such as transport and recreation.

12
The challenges of sustainable development are particularly acute for the developing world, where development has been equated with the stereotypical Western consumer lifestyle.

Review questions

1   In what ways do industrialization and urbanization impact on the environment?

2   What does environmental degradation refer to and what are its effects?

3   What are the causes of climate change and what are the effects of global warming?

4   What are the aims of the Kyoto Protocol and what is the likelihood of their being achieved?

5   Why has transboundary pollution become a global concern? Give some examples of transboundary pollution and examine ways of dealing with it through collaboration between countries.

6   Define 'sustainable development'. How does it differ from plain economic development?

7   What are the implications of sustainable development for business strategists?

8   What is meant by environmental management?

9   What initiatives are being taken by the EU in environmental protection?

10   How does a system of emissions trading work? What are the advantages and disadvantages of this type of system over a mandatory regulatory system in achieving targets for reducing emissions?

11   What is meant by 'sustainable consumption'? Are consumer attitudes in rich countries changing as a result of green campaigns and the greater availability of information on environmental issues?

12   What are the challenges posed by a sustainable development agenda in the developing world?

Assignments

1   Devise an outline environmental management strategy for a company in the international construction industry specializing in building factory production units.

2   To what extent is sustainable development a realistic proposition for the developing world?

Further reading

Barrow, C.J. (1999) *Environmental Management: Principles and Practice* (Oxford: Routledge).

Daly, H.E. (1996) *Beyond Growth: The Economics of Sustainable Development* (Boston: Beacon).

Dresner, S. (2002) *The Principles of Sustainability* (London: Earthscan).

Goldblatt, D. (1996) *Social Theory and the Environment* (Cambridge: Polity Press).

Hecht, A.D. (1999) 'The triad of sustainable development: Promoting sustainable development in developing countries', *Journal of Environment and Development*, **8**: 111–32.

Landes, D. (1998) *The Wealth and Poverty of Nations* (London: Little, Brown).

Miller, M.A.L. (1995) *The Third World in Global Environmental Politics* (Boulder, CO: Lynne Reinner).

Young, O. (1994) *International Governance: Protecting the Environment in a Stateless Society* (Ithaca: Cornell University Press).

14 Global challenges and the responsible business

Outline of chapter

- ■ Introduction
- ■ Global and national environments: an overview
- ■ Change in the business environment
- ■ Left behind? The least developed nations
  - • Poverty: its many dimensions
  - • Development prospects for Africa
- ■ Social responsibility of the firm
  - • Theories of corporate social responsibility
  - • Raising corporate standards
  - • Reaching for international standards
- ■ Challenges of the new information age
- ■ Globalization and national diversity: the way ahead
- ■ Conclusions

Learning objectives

1 To gain an overview of how each dimension of the international business environment fits into a dynamic overall picture.

2 To focus on some of the primary challenges facing all societies, such as poverty and quality of life, particularly in the context of developing societies.

3 To examine how businesses are placed to respond positively and, in particular, in socially responsible ways, within strategies characterized by corporate social responsibility.

4 To grasp the pros and cons of how globalization impacts in differing national environments, offering broadening opportunities for international businesses, as well as benefits for host societies.

Introduction

Preceding chapters have each presented a key aspect of the international environment which impacts on businesses. While each of these aspects is identifiable as possessing its own characteristics, they do not function independently, but as facets of an overall picture of the environment, rather like pieces in a jigsaw. For a business, therefore, an understanding of how the 'pieces', such as economic, cultural, social, and other inputs, are put together is essential to long-term success. This chapter shifts the focus, firstly, to an overview of the how the parts interact in the changing environment and, secondly, to the challenges and opportunities that are emerging for businesses in the future.

The themes of globalization and local diversity have run throughout the preceding chapters and they are taken up here in the context of the challenges that lie ahead. Attention is given to the wider issues in the world economy: global inequalities, development prospects, social responsibility and the new frontiers of the information age. Questions about the impact that economic activities have on societies and the environment for present and future generations are generating debate, not just in the business community, but in the international community generally. The opportunities are immense, but so are the threats. Businesses, from the small firm to the global company, are uniquely placed to take proactive approaches in a rapidly changing environment, and an understanding of the multifaceted nature of the issues will enhance their ability to meet the challenges ahead.

Global and national environments: an overview

Two themes have recurred throughout this book. First, globalization, defined as the expansion and deepening of ties across national borders, has gained ground in all aspects of the business environment. Secondly, national differences, rather than melting away, seem to have persisted and adapted in the changing environment. These themes are presented in Table 14.1, which summarizes how organizations (such as the WTO) and processes (such as economic integration) fit into the larger picture. The headings, global and national environments, are used here not to represent separate 'containers', but as aids to help visualize relationships. In reality, these categories are increasingly shading into each other, in dynamic interactive processes that are redefining their contours. In all these categories, global changes have brought improvements which are valued by people in their immediate national and local situations. Change, of course, can have numerous effects, both benefits and detriments, as its consequences are played out in societies and as businesses, governments and consumers assess their impact. From a firm's point of view, one of the major advantages of understanding the forces that go to make up the environment is to be able to assess more accurately the ways in which change will affect its activities and thus, by managing change, reduce the risks.

Table 14.1 Global and national environments

Dimension	Global environment	National environment
Economic	Global and regional economic integration; globalization of production	National economic systems
Cultural	Media and internet penetration; consumer society and global markets	National and subnational cultural, including linguistic and religious, groupings
Social	International division of labour; international migration	National and subnational social groupings, for example family and ethnic groups
Political	International and regional political interdependence and integration	National political systems; political parties in pluralist states
Legal	International law and practice (in, for example, human rights and environment); international tribunals	National legal systems, including national legislative processes and national judicial systems
Trade and competitive	Multilateral trade agreements (for example GATT); multilateral organizations (for example WTO); regional trade groupings	National strategic trade policy; bilateral trade agreements
Technological	Global R&D by transnational corporations and international bodies	National innovation systems
Financial	Global capital markets; international institutions (for example IMF and World Bank)	National financial systems, including banks and other financial institutions
Ecological	Climate change; international regulation	Resource depletion; environmental degradation; national regulation; national energy policies

Change in the business environment

The preceding chapters have each focused on a selected aspect of the business environment. Each has emphasized the changes that are currently taking place and the ways in which businesses are both responding to them and bringing about further changes themselves. The pace of change clearly varies from place to place and not all change is for the better. Change is almost universally perceived as involving winners and losers. Technological innovation has brought untold benefits in quality of life, healthcare and working environment, but has also resulted in the displacement of low-skilled workers in advanced economies, as their jobs migrated abroad to low-cost locations. The industrialization of production has also produced harmful side effects, such as pollution, and it has depleted the world's non-renewable energy resources. Much depends on the viewpoint of the speaker. In the case of foreign direct investment (FDI), for example, host country perspectives may differ markedly from those of the foreign investor's home country.

Changes in the business environment can largely be attributed to the processes of globalization and liberalization. Globalization encompasses the processes of techno-logical innovation, deepening FDI, and expanding trade and financial networks. Indeed, improvements in technology, including transport and communications, have been instrumental in bringing about the other developments just listed. They make up the flows of money, goods, and information that characterize modern society. The countries whose populations have benefited to the greatest extent are the advanced economies of the world which have been at the forefront of both tech-nological innovation and its commercial exploitation. These developments have owed much to liberalization, that is, opening economies to market forces, and have had a broad impact across the whole spectrum of the business environment, including cultural and social environments and legal and political systems. For many countries, mainly the advanced Western economies, individualist cultures fostered capitalist enterprises, along with legal systems to protect property and democratic national political systems responsive to citizens. The defining character-istics of the market economy, stemming from the early industrializing Western economies, have come to be identified with liberal market reforms in the context of nation-states.

By contrast, the histories and cultures of the countries of Asia, Latin America and Africa represent an array of differing environments, commonly featuring the pre-eminence of community and family values over individual values. Changes, includ-ing more open markets and social mobility, have come less from indigenous forces and more from external forces, specifically growing FDI, reflecting the globalization of production. While liberalization in these countries offers manifold opportunities for business enterprises, it has also had a downside of market volatility and inequali-ties, which have posed challenges for good governance. The experiences of these countries demonstrate the importance of understanding how changes in one sphere have repercussions in others.

Globalization and liberalization have brought opportunities for economic develop-ment and technological diffusion, but also instability, as changes occur in established ways of doing things and established structures in society. Asian countries, in partic-ular, have welcomed the opportunities opened up by technological innovation and have set out to adapt them to existing social and cultural values. In this way, nations have aspired to grasp the best of both worlds: stability from established systems and economic growth from FDI and imported technology. Foreign investors that have succeeded in establishing themselves, often with local partners, have demonstrated the value of cooperation through cross-cultural management approaches, which work within the local environment, rather than trying to recreate the home country structures in the foreign location. Even during the financial crisis of 1997–8, these long-term investors provided an element of stability amidst the volatility of short-term capital movements.

China is an example of a transitional economy, in which market reforms are taking place in a rapidly changing business environment. Daily it is becoming easier for Western businesses to enter China, as barriers come down, but changes in other aspects of the business environment are moving more slowly. An independent legal system, private property rights and intellectual property (IP) rights are still underdeveloped by Western standards. And political decision-making is still closer to authoritarianism than democracy. Whether the marketization of the economy will lead to social and cultural change, and ultimately a peaceful transition to democracy, has become a tantalizing question for observers of China. There are the beginnings of democratic forms in China. Many point to the fact that at the height of the cold war, few would have predicted the relatively peaceful overthrow of Soviet Communist regimes in Central and Eastern Europe. On the other hand, the post-Communist transitions have varied considerably, from the relatively smooth progress of Poland and Hungary to the erratic progress of Russia. In general, countries with deep legacies of authoritarianism, as in the former Soviet republics, have found the path to economic reforms more difficult than countries with a stronger civil society, such as those in Central and Eastern Europe. Economic reforms, it seems clear, do not take place in isolation from other dimensions of the national environment. They can stimulate change in social and cultural spheres and also come about as a result of pressures within societies.

Left behind? The least developed nations

It was once thought, optimistically, that globalization would spread economic growth and prosperity from the advanced countries to the developing countries, eventually bringing the benefits of a better quality of life to all. Since 1980, not only has the gap between rich and poor within countries widened, the gap between rich and poor countries has grown, as shown in Figure.14.1. The average income in the 20 richest countries is 37 times that in the 20 poorest countries. Increased trade and internationalized production have delivered benefits to some nations, but left others marginalized, with little prospect of catching up. There has been an improvement in economic growth in China and India, two countries which account for over a third of the world's population. In the last decade, their economies have grown at rates of 9 per cent and 7 per cent, respectively. By contrast, 55 developing countries grew at less than 2 per cent per annum between 1985 and 2000, and of these, 23 saw their economies slide backwards (ILO, 2004). These variations owe much to the fact that the economies of China and India have forged ahead in manufacturing for export markets, while poorer developing countries are reliant on exports of primary commodities. In general, the countries with manufacturing industries have enjoyed growth, whereas those which export mainly primary commodities (other than oil) have seen only slight growth (UNDP, 2003). A combination of broad factors have been responsible. They include tariffs and other trade barriers set up to protect markets in the developed countries from imports from the developing world, and subsidies paid by governments in the developed world to their own farmers. For most of the 1990s, commodity prices fell in global markets; only in 2001 did they start to rise again, largely due to rising demand in China (UNCTAD, 2004). For the last two decades, export volumes of developing countries have risen, largely because of improvements in agricultural production, but the purchasing power of these exports has not risen in parallel. Although this phenomenon is traditionally associated with exporters of primary commodities, research indicates that it has also affected developing countries which export low-tech manufactured goods (UNCTAD 2004). The implication is that these goods have to some extent become commoditized, and that the poorer developing countries are losing out to those which embody a higher level of technology in their manufactured goods.

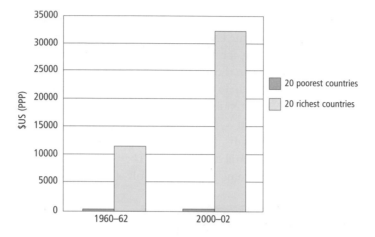

Figure 14.1 **GDP per capita in the poorest and richest countries**
Source: ILO (2004) *A Fair Globalization* (Geneva: ILO) p. 37.

Poverty: its many dimensions

Poverty in a narrow sense is simply inadequate income to sustain life, or 'income poverty'. However, it can also be viewed in broader terms, recognizing that human life is more than the economic dimension alone. The UN has coined the term, 'human poverty', to cover this broader spectrum of deprivation (United Nations, 2000, p. 73). It includes lack of capabilities to enjoy a long, healthy life, to be educated and have a decent standard of living. These more qualitative dimensions are captured in the UN's human development measures, which take into account life expectancy, healthcare and access to education. This broader view of deprivation's dimensions mirrors the distinction between economic development and sustainable development, discussed in Chapter 13. Sustainable development takes into account not just economic benefit, but the impact of environmental degradation, damage to ecosystems and loss of cultural goods. Similarly, environmental and cultural detriments are dimensions of human poverty beyond the measures of income poverty.

Among the UN's Millennium Goals for 2015 is halving income poverty in the world and halving the numbers of people without access to clean water (United Nations, 2000). It is now looking unlikely that these goals can be achieved. For 59 poor countries, the 1980s and 90s saw declining GNI per capita. The number of people living in absolute poverty (defined as living on less than $1 a day) declined from 1,237 million in 1990 to 1,100 million in 2000. However, as Figure 14.2 shows, most of this improvement came in China and, to a lesser extent India, but there are still large numbers of very poor people in these two most populous countries, amounting to 17 per cent of the population of China and 35 per cent of the population of India (UNDP, 2004). Economic growth, it should be borne in mind, does not automatically lead to poverty reduction: a country may do well on average, but overall figures may conceal growing inequalities or poverty-stricken areas (UNDP,

2003). In sub-Saharan Africa, Europe, Central Asia and Latin America, poverty has increased, as Figure 14.2 shows. According to the World Bank, about half of Africa's 600 million people live on $0.65 a day (World Bank, 2000b).

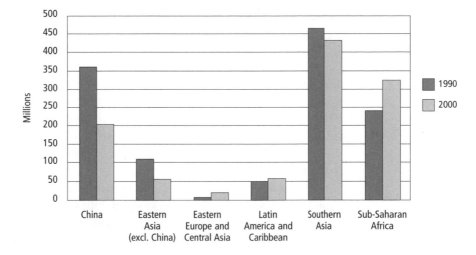

Figure 14.2 **People living on less than US$1 per day**
Source: ILO (2004) *A Fair Globalization* (Geneva: ILO), p. 45.

The poor are likely to be undernourished and lack access to clean water and sanitation. More than one billion people in poor countries lack access to sanitation and two billion lack access to safe water (World Bank, 2002). The UN's Food and Agriculture Organization (2003) estimates that about 842 million people were undernourished in the period 1999–2001, and of these, 10 million were in industrialized countries, 34 million in transitional countries and 798 million in developing countries. Asian countries have made greater progress in reducing undernourishment, due to their economic expansion and slowing population growth, while the poorest countries in Africa, which have experienced the greatest depth of hunger, are not progressing so well. The ILO's report on globalization concludes that:

> the least-developed countries are trapped in a vicious circle of interlocking handicaps including poverty and illiteracy, civil strife, geographical disadvantages, poor governance and inflexible economies largely dependent on a single commodity. (ILO, 2004, p. 38)

For the poor countries of the world, therefore, poverty is linked to social, environmental and political issues. Growing populations, fragile ecosystems and fragile lands prone to disasters of drought and flood cause insecurity in food and water supplies. Poor countries, particularly in sub-Saharan Africa, have suffered most from the AIDS epidemic, which has severely impacted on economic activity. Conflicts have also taken a heavy toll. Of the 46 countries that suffered conflicts in the 1990s, 17 were poor countries, half of the 33 poorest countries in the world (World Bank, 2002). The effects have been setbacks for economic development and also setbacks in human development, including life expectancy, healthcare and education.

WEB ALERT!

The UK government has published a comprehensive White Paper on globalization and economic development, *Eliminating World Poverty: Making Globalisation Work for the Poor*, at http://www.globalisation.gov.uk
The UN's Food and Agriculture Organization is at http://www.fao.org

Hunger and lack of clean water make the poor particularly vulnerable to natural disasters and disease. The HIV/Aids epidemic that struck sub-Saharan Africa has had devastating effects, more difficult to cope with in poor countries lacking the money for medicines, which are supplied by global pharmaceutical companies. The WHO estimated that by the end of 2000, the rate of new infections in the region was stabilizing. From 4 million newly infected people in 1999, the figure for 2000 was an estimated 3.8 million newly infected people. For a region that is home to 10 per cent of the world's population, Africa still accounts for 70 per cent of the global total of people living with HIV/Aids, and 80 per cent of deaths from Aids. The World Bank has made loan funds available to fight the disease, for which ten countries applied in 2000. When the $1bn. allocated is used up, the World Bank promised more would be forthcoming, as another 13 countries are applying. A spokesperson said: 'It is more than a health issue. It is now a development issue, and in many countries it is a matter of peace and security' (*Washington Post*, 1 December 2000).

In 2000, five multinational drug companies agreed to cut their prices of Aids drugs for African countries, and Pfizer offered a $50m. donation to the South African government, for the purchase of a key Aids drug. However, even at a discount of 90 per cent, 'a cocktail of Aids-suppressing drugs for an single African patient might cost $2000 per year, which is more than four times the average per capita income in many of the worst-afflicted countries' (Kahn, 2000). The broader issue is that of drugs patents generally. As has been seen in Chapter 10, the WTO reached agreement in the Doha Round of negotiations to bypass the rights of patent-holders in cases of national emergency.

As Case study 14.1 highlights, international competitive pressures have led to the globalization of production systems. However, the quality of employment and working conditions in labour-intensive industries in developing countries are often overlooked by local authorities, keen to attract manufacturing industries. The poor, illiterate and unskilled are particularly vulnerable. New industrial areas provide economic opportunities for salaried work, but at a price: often workers are housed in cramped, dormitory accommodation, away from their families, often leading to the breakdown of social and family life. Similarly, indigenous peoples are vulnerable in the face of the economic might of multinational companies which can transform whole communities. Traditional livelihoods, social ties, ecosystems and culture may undergo changes which are detrimental to the quality of life in the long term.

Case study 14.1   The worldwide garment industry: winners and losers

The clothing industry employs some 40 million people worldwide, most of them in developing countries. It accounts for trade worth about $350bn. a year. Asian countries are the largest exporters, and their largest markets are consumers in the US and EU. From the 1950s onwards, trade barriers have been in place, to protect the clothing and textile industries in Western economies, fearful of being undermined by cheaper Asian imports. In particular, import quotas restricted access to Western markets. However, an agreement stemming from the Uruguay Round of trade negotiations spelled the end of import quotas at the end of 2004. This global industry is therefore undergoing massive restructuring, but who will be the winners and losers?

China and India are set to be the biggest winners in the industry's reshaping. China, already accounting for a quarter of global exports, is in an especially strong position, with its large-scale, low-cost production, which it is able to expand to meet new demand. India, too, is expected to gain, but its firms are less advantageously placed. Indian factories are smaller, as those which employ over 100 people are subject to inflexible labour laws which make it almost impossible to shed workers. Electricity and raw materials are both considerably more expensive in India than in China: electricity costs about 30 per cent more, and India's cotton farmers achieve yields two-thirds smaller than their Chinese counterparts. To compete with China, India's garment industry needs restructuring and the infrastructure needs to be improved.

Garment and cotton workers in over 40 other countries, mostly poor developing countries, have benefited from the import quota system, known as the Multifibre Arrangement. As major exporting countries hit their quota ceiling, production would migrate to smaller producing countries which had quota to spare, in a system of 'quota-hopping'. Globalized production has therefore

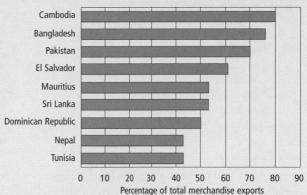

Dependency on clothing and textile exports
Source: de Jonquières, 19 July 2004.

reached many poor countries such as Mauritius and Bangladesh (see figure above), whose industries would not have been able to compete in open markets. Now, in a seemingly ironic twist, both have lobbied the WTO to preserve the barriers. These small producers cannot match China's manufacturing capabilities. Survival for the garment industry in these instances will depend on finding niche markets, diversifying or moving upmarket. Honduras is fearful for the future of its garment industry, as about 80 per cent of its production is simple products like T-shirts. It is aiming for vertical integration, producing materials, using computer-aided-design to cut the cloth and stitching shirts in a quick turnaround time. In Columbia, the local textile industry is confident that shorter transport times to US markets will compensate for the fact that wages in Columbia are 50 per cent higher than in China. New production methods in the Columbian textile industry are enabling it to deliver quality products for brands such as Tommy Hilfiger and Pierre Cardin.

For the poorest developing countries, mainly in Africa, the outlook is bleaker, as readjustment is harder, diversification possibilities are minimal and creating new jobs for displaced workers is too costly. However, the phasing out of subsidies to cotton farmers in the US in particular, should

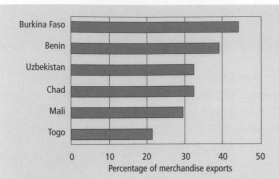

Dependency on cotton exports of developing countries

Source: Boffes (2004).

benefit West and Central Africa's 10 million cotton farmers. Cotton is the main export product in some of the world's poorest countries, including Benin, Burkina Faso, Chad, Mali and Togo (see figure above). Farmers have seen cotton prices halve between 1997 and 2002, resulting in the loss of an estimated $1bn. annually in foreign earnings, while the US has paid $3.3bn. annually to its 25,000 cotton farmers (de Jonquières, 11 September 2003).

Sources: Boffes, J. (2004) 'Cotton: Market Setting Trade Policies, and Issues', World Bank Policy Research Working Paper No. 3218, February 2004 (Washington, DC: World Bank); Williams, F. and de Jonquières, G., 'US fights plea by Africans over cotton', *Financial Times*, 11 September 2003; Morrison, K., 'Low-cost cotton producers to pick up business as era of subsidies unwinds', *Financial Times*, 6 August 2004; Lapper, R., 'Garment companies fight back for share of market', *Financial Times*, 27 July 2004; de Jonquières, G., 'Clothes on the line: the garment industry faces a global shake-up as quotas end', *Financial Times*, 19 July 2004; Marcelo, R., 'India's garment industry needs to be retailored', *Financial Times*, 22 July 2004; UNDP (2003), *Human Development Report 2003* (New York: Oxford University Press).

Case questions

Which countries stand to benefit from the end of import quotas and which will lose out?

What are the effects of opening markets for the poorest developing countries?

WEB ALERT!

Globalization in the apparel industry is one of the topics to be found at http://www.sweatshopwatch.org

---

SUMMARY POINTS

Poverty in all its dimensions

- **Income poverty** – economic measure of poverty. There are still over a billion people, mostly in the poorest developing countries, living in absolute poverty, defined as less than $1 per day.

- **Human poverty** – broader measure of deprivation, looking at quality of life, healthcare and education, as well as sustainable environmental practices.

CRITICAL PERSPECTIVES

What is prosperity?

Prosperity is the ability of an individual, group, or nation to provide shelter, nutrition, and other material goods that enable people to live a good life, according to their own definition. Prosperity helps create space in people's hearts and minds so that they may develop a healthy emotional and spiritual life, according to their preferences, unfettered by the everyday concern of the material goods they require to survive. (Fairbanks, 2000, p. 270)

■ Do you agree with this definition of prosperity?

■ Think of some countries which in your view are prosperous and then think of some that are struggling to build prosperity. What are the key differences?

Development prospects for Africa

Some African countries have reaped new wealth from natural resources. Equatorial Guinea is an oil-rich West African state which has attracted the interest of oil companies from the US, concerned about possible insecurities of supplies from the Middle East. However, despite oil wealth, the ordinary people remain poor. Corruption and the mismanagement of billions of dollars of oil revenues by the country's leaders are responsible for poverty and a lack of civic services. The country ranks sixth in the world in income per person, but in the UN's human development rankings, Equatorial Guinea ranks 109th: life expectancy at birth is just 49; school enrolment is just 58 per cent of the population; and public expenditure on education is only 0.5 per cent of GDP (UNDP, 2004). This is in a country where GDP per capita is nearly US$30,000.

For the poorest countries of Africa, whose economies are mainly agricultural, trade has not delivered the hoped-for gains. Although Africa only accounts for just over 2 per cent of world trade, its countries are deeply integrated in the world economy, as Case Study 14.1 highlights. A problem for African countries is that their exports are primary commodities, which are vulnerable to swings in the commodity markets. Reliance on natural resources as a strategy can be characterized as a comparative advantage strategy (see Chapter 10). Such strategies are common in the developing world, and become embedded in a country's institutions and habits of thinking, making change difficult (Lindsay, 2000). It has been argued that greater prosperity requires a shift to strategies based on competitive advantage, which entail a broader view of how wealth is created in a society, beyond exploiting factor endowments. Strategic change often faces resistance from the very business and political leaders whose policy changes are needed, but who tend to be locked into traditional ways of thinking. Further, shifting to competitive strategies requires change on many fronts. A better educated workforce, higher levels of innovation and the nurturing of an ability to produce more complex goods and services are all needed, as well as investment in infrastructure.

Economic diversification would help to reduce the dependency on comparative advantage. The World Bank has called on the developed world to open markets to African agricultural produce. OECD subsidies for agriculture total $311bn. a year, about the equivalent of Africa's GDP. This figure dwarfs the amount given in official development assistance (ODA) by OECD countries (see Figure 14.3). With the OECD, the US and EU account for the greatest expenditure in both subsidies and development support. Comparative data appear in Figure 14.4: aid from both rose slightly in the 2000–2002 period. However, while EU agricultural subsidies have reduced, subsidies to US farmers have grown.

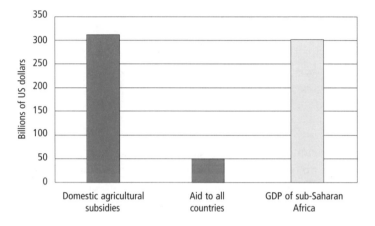

Figure 14.3 **OECD agricultural subsidies in perspective**
Source: UNDP (2003) *Human Development Report 2003* (New York: Oxford University Press), p. 156.

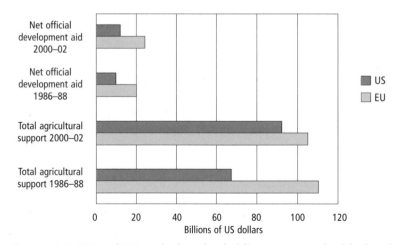

Figure 14.4 **US and EU agricultural subsidies contrasted with development aid**
Source: World Bank (2004) *2004 World Development Indicators*, at http://www.wto.org.

The IMF and World Bank initiated a programme of debt relief for heavily-indebted poor countries (HIPCs) in 1996. Its aims were to relieve low-income countries of debt which had reached unsustainable proportions and promote reforms aimed at promoting human development and reducing poverty. There are two stages to the debt relief: at the first stage, the country may receive debt service relief, and, at the second stage, debt stock relief. Countries must provide detailed programmes for how the freed-up money will be used. By 2003, 16 HIPCs had reached the first stage, and 8 had completed the second stage (Benin, Bolivia, Burkina Faso, Mali, Mauritania, Mozambique, Tanzania and Uganda) (UNDP, 2003).

Official development assistance by rich countries fell in the 1990s from 0.33 per cent to 0.22 per cent of GNI. Aid started to rise again at the end of the 1990s, but 31 of the 49 least developed countries (LDCs) received less aid in 2003 than they had in 1990. Problems of corruption and the inefficient use of the funds have deterred donor countries. A number of OECD countries have pledged more aid by 2006, along with debt relief. However, there has been less action in opening markets and transferring technology. Table 14.2 gives a picture of what rich countries are doing for the LDCs. Note that Norway is relatively generous with aid, but imposes high trade barriers. The US, by contrast, has lower trade barriers, but gives relatively little in aid. France remains the leading country in the cancellation of debt of HIPCs. The OECD Development Assistance Committee recommends that rich countries look at their actions as part of an overall strategy for aid, trade and debt relief.

Table 14.2 Rich countries' policies towards the least developed countries

Country	Aid (ODA) US$millions 2001 (% of GNP in brackets)	Cancellation of bilateral debt 1990–2002 US$millions	Average tariff barriers 2000 (%)	Goods imports from LDCs 2001 (% of total imports in brackets)
Australia	873 (0.25)	72	13.4	11 (0.2)
Denmark	1,634 (1.03)	359	21.6	12 (0.3)
France	4,198 (0.32)	13,043	21.4	236 (0.8)
Germany	4,990 (0.27)	4,996	21.4	218 (0.4)
Japan	9,847 (0.23)	3,908	34.8	110 (0.3)
Norway	1,346 (0.83)	237	61.1	12 (0.4)
UK	4,579 (0.32)	1,886	20.9	132 (0.4)
US	11,429 (0.11)	8,062	9.7	982 (0.8)

Source: UNDP (2003) *Human Development Report 2003* (New York: UNDP).

Political instability and corruption have inhibited development, and, as international institutions now stress, the restructuring of political and social institutions is an essential part of the process, if sustainable improvements are to be made. The World Bank's report, *Can Africa Claim the 21st Century?*, stresses that African countries have a 'window of opportunity', requiring action in four main areas: 'conflict resolution and improved governance; more investment in people; increasing competitiveness and diversifying economies; and better support from the international community' (World Bank, 2000b). These are broadly defined areas and the emphasis seems to be on the internal restructuring that is needed, rather than on help from outside. It is generally true that in low-income countries, growth in per capita income has a noticeable effect on the speed of poverty reduction (Dollar, 1999). A more stable environment will encourage business, economic growth and diversification. Foreign investors, as in Asia and Latin America, can provide much-needed impetus, provided that necessary infrastructure can be built and maintained in relative peace and security.

SUMMARY POINTS

Bridging the gap between rich and poor countries

What rich countries can do:

- Open markets to commodities and manufactured goods from LDCs
- Participate in debt reduction programmes for HIPCs
- Increase development aid to LDCs
- Promote technology transfer to LDCs.

What poor countries can do:

- Promote transparent institutions
- Channel aid effectively to social programmes such as health and education
- Foster programmes for improvements in agriculture and water conservation
- Promote diversification in national economies.

WEB ALERT!

A general site on Africa is http://www.africa-business.com

For news, policy, economic information and business links, see http://www.allafrica.com

The site for the Common Market for Eastern and Southern Africa (COMESA) is http://www.comesa.int/home

Social responsibility of the firm

Transnational companies have been the drivers of globalization and the beneficiaries of the liberalization policies of national governments. Should expanding freedoms to pursue corporate goals be balanced by greater social responsibility for corporate players? Social responsibility refers to a group of related issues, including human rights, human development and environmental protection issues (discussed in the last chapter). In the past, they have been seen as public policy matters falling within the ambit of governments, which formulate laws and policies. So long as businesses adhered to existing legal obligations, they were free to focus on 'the bottom line', that is, profits and shareholder value. This simplistic view, which separates social responsibility concerns from business has now become outdated, giving way to the view that the power companies enjoy entails duties of social responsibility in the community. As was seen in Chapter 9 on the legal environment, there is a growing body of law in areas of human rights, workers' rights and environmental protection, both national laws and international treaties. The company, as employer and producer of goods and services for global markets, is directly involved in employment conditions and operating processes. It is thus in the 'driving seat' in relation to upholding human rights, improving working conditions and protecting the environment. Therefore, it is argued, corporate leaders should take a more proactive role in moving ahead of the minimal standards required by law.

Two factors can be highlighted in bringing about this change in the approach to social responsibility. Firstly, while markets have delivered economic results, they have left out of the equation considerations of human and environmental values. The insertion of these concerns in social market economies is a recognition of market limitations. The human rights and environmental questions posed daily for large corporations, such as oil companies in developing states, also show the inadequacy of viewing business in isolation from the community. No longer can a TNC doing business in a developing country remain disengaged from the live community issues in its places of operation. Secondly, the sheer size of the world's global corporations now dwarfs many national economies. Questions of how they are using this power in socially responsible ways are now being addressed to companies, as well as governments. Moreover, as Case study 14.2 shows, consumers are important in driving the social responsibility agenda. Critical natural resources, such as water, are now privatized and the trend is continuing. Two large transnational water companies, Générale des Eaux and Lyonnaise des Eaux, now operate in 120 countries, some of which, such as those in the Middle East, have chronic problems of water scarcity (discussed in Case study 13.1). As water is now seen as a big business opportunity, questions of social responsibility inevitably arise, as the public interest may conflict with that of the shareholders of water companies. It has been said that, once a company passes a certain size, it ceases to be seen as entrepreneurial (a good thing) and starts to be seen as too powerful (a bad thing).

Case study 14.2 Vibrant coffee culture contrasts with woes for producers

While affluent consumers sip their cappuccinos in Starbucks and other coffee bars, the behind-the-scenes story is one of a world coffee crisis which has impoverished field workers and devastated rural economies, particularly in Central America, which depend on coffee production. More than 2 billion consumers around the world drink coffee regularly, and about 20–25 million families depend on coffee for their income. These producers are mostly smallholder farmers in developing countries, in many of which coffee accounts for a high proportion of export earnings. Surging demand and high prices encouraged farmers to switch to coffee from other crops from the 1980s onwards, but the result was eventually oversupply and falling prices. Production increased particularly in Vietnam and Brazil (see figure below) sending the prices of green, unroasted coffee beans tumbling. The world price has fallen from $3.30 a pound in the 1980s to 60 cents, which is below the estimated 80 cents a pound it costs farmers to produce them. In the mid-1990s, farmers' share of the final price to the consumer was only 10 per cent, but this has fallen to 7 per cent. The lion's share of the price goes to middlemen. These are roasters, retailers and global buyers, or brokers. Each of these sectors is characterized by a few dominant firms, creating a market in which buyers are concentrated and powerful, while producers are mainly small farmers in a weak bargaining position.

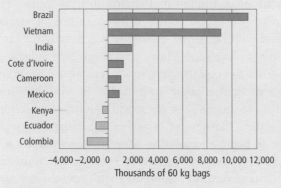

Changes in coffee production of the main producers, from 1994 to 2004
Source: Lewin et al. (2004).

Responses to this deteriorating position can be grouped together under the heading 'sustainable coffee' initiatives. These include organic, ecofriendly and fair trade coffee. Demand for sustainable coffee has come mainly in the more developed consumer markets (see figure below). The fair trade movement, exemplified by Cafédirect, was set up in 1991 by the charity, Oxfam. The principle behind fair trade coffee is to pay the producer a price above market price, for a premium product, and cutting out the middlemen. It also works with farmers to improve expertise in production. Fair trade coffee has grown to a 15 per cent share of the coffee market in the UK, and now operates on a commercial basis. In 2004, Cafédirect was floated as a public company, appropriately, on a small ethically based stock exchange. Despite the unconventional IPO, the issue was oversubscribed, as investors snapped up the shares, making the £5m. issue a success.

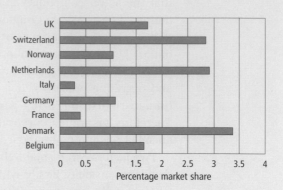

Share of sustainable coffees consumed in key European markets, 2001
Source: Lewin et al. (2004).

A second response to the coffee crisis has come from the large companies in the industry. The world's two largest coffee brokers, Neumann and Volcafe, entered an agreement with the Rainforest Alliance to promote the production of ecofriendly coffee, based on environmental and social standards. A spokesman for the companies says: 'the image of coffee is endangered ... It is becoming a product where farmers are dying and birds are being denied habitats' (Silver, 14 May 2003). If farmers convert their farms to sustainable practices, they will raise the quality of the coffee, curb environmental damage and improve the prospects of a better livelihood than they have at present. Ecofriendly coffee will require an industry-wide set of standards and their implementation. Meanwhile, four of the world's largest coffee companies – Nestlé, Sara Lee, Kraft Foods and Tchibo – have made an agreement with producers to improve working conditions and environmental standards. Called the Common Code for the Coffee Community, it will apply to coffee producers in Brazil, Central America and Africa, and it has been signed by Oxfam, Greenpeace and trade unions representing coffee workers. This code, to be monitored by independent auditors, is targeted at the mainstream market, rather than the fair trade segment. It represents a response to pressures from consumers, retailers and NGOs. At the same time, there is a 'business case' for these moves, in that, as Cafédirect has shown, consumers are willing to pay a premium price for quality coffee, which benefits all in the coffee industry.

Sources: Lewin, B., Giovannucci, D. and Varangis, P., 'Coffee markets: new paradigms in global supply and demand', *World Bank Agriculture and Rural Development Discussion Paper 3* (Washington, DC: World Bank); 'Growers left tasting dregs of coffee culture', editorial in *Financial Times*, 23 May 2002; Silver, S., 'Coffee's crisis stirs traders to take action', *Financial Times*, 14 May 2003; Harford, T., 'Fair trade coffee has a commercial blend', *Financial Times*, 12 September 2003; John, P., 'Cafédirect floats with its ethical principles', *Financial Times*, 12 February 2004; Williamson, H., 'Coffee trade pact on better standards', *Financial Times*, 10 September 2004.

Case questions

How did the coffee industry come to be in such a perilous state?

How do the fair trade initiatives and sustainable coffee initiatives differ from each other?

WEB ALERT!

The website of the Fair Trade Foundation is http://www.fairtrade.org.uk

Cafédirect is at http://www.cafedirect.co.uk

Starbucks is at http://www.starbucks.com

Theories of corporate social responsibility

For a number of years, management theorists and corporate strategists have been addressing the question of what the role of the company in society should be. While most now agree that its role extends beyond the purely economic dimension, there is much debate on the extent of this expanded social role and how social performance can be measured. Adding complexity to the discussion is the reality of global companies which operate in a number of different societies. Theories which attempt to define the company's responsibility to society are generally grouped together as theories of **corporate social responsibility (CSR)**. These theories typically make reference to stakeholder groups (discussed in Chapter 1), as well as to society in general, and therefore it is useful to look at theories of CSR in conjunction with stakeholder theories, which have also been the subject of academic focus in recent years (Mitchell et al., 1997).

A 'weak' theory of CSR focuses on philanthropic or charitable contributions and activities, which the firm engages in as an adjunct to its business activities: any costs are weighed against the benefit to be gained in terms of the firm's enhanced reputation as a good corporate citizen. On this view, CSR 'is fine, if you can afford it' (Freeman, 1984, p. 40). Critics of this approach argue that it is 'skin deep', entailing no rethinking of the firm's strategy and operations in terms of social issues – in theory, a company might be a socially responsible in this limited sense while exploiting its workforce and polluting the environment.

A stronger strategic approach to CSR is found in the work of Carroll (1991), who has devised a four-dimensional model of CSR, which takes into account economic, legal, ethical and philanthropic dimensions (see Figure 14.5). This model, which can be envisaged as a pyramid, places the economic obligations of the company at the base, recognizing that the business must be economically profitable in order to survive. Above economic activities are legal responsibilities. Legal obligations cover many areas, including employment law, environmental law and health and safety regulations. Of course, the law sets minimum standards, which may differ from country to country. The firm with a strong CSR policy will aim to go beyond minimum legal standards. Carroll's model sees this exceeding of minimal legal requirements as an aspect of ethical responsibility, along with respect for ethical norms in the society in which the firm operates. The last element is philanthropy, such as charitable giving, which, while desirable, is less important than the other three – the icing on the cake. Carroll stresses that the model does not posit an inherent conflict between making profits and being socially responsible: for the manager, all four dimensions of the firm's responsibility should be central to corporate strategy.

Figure 14.5 **Carroll's pyramid of corporate social responsibility**
Source: Adapted from Carroll, A.B. (1991) 'The Pyramid of Corporate Social Responsibility: Toward the Moral Management of Organizational Stakeholders', *Business Horizons*, **34**, p. 42.

While Carroll's model provides an overall framework, analysis of the 'social' component of CSR is provided by stakeholder theory (see Figure 1.8 for a diagram of stakeholder groups). First developed by Edward Freeman, stakeholder theory points to the many different groups and interests that affect the company. Freeman (1984, p. 46) defines them broadly as 'any group or individual which affects or is affected by the achievement of the organization's objectives'. Stakeholders may be classified according to the strength of their influence on the company, and how critical they are to the company's operational success at any given time. Some of these, such as shareholders and employees, are internal to the company, while suppliers, customers and the community in general are outside the organization itself, although these relationships may come to be seen as integral to the company's strategy. Situations in which stakeholder interests conflict with each other pose particular challenges for managers. For example, the decision to outsource a particular operation to a low-cost location will save money, but cause loss of employment in the company's home country, where most of its shareholders are likely to be located. Corporate boards, as was highlighted in Chapter 1, have a primary obligation to serve shareholders' interests, but those interests may be complex and not susceptible to simple either/or decision-making. Moreover, shareholders increasingly look beyond short-term financial criteria to long-term value creation, in which CSR and stakeholder perspectives come more into play.

Demand for CSR as integral to corporate strategy is likely to be driven by a number of stakeholder groups, including investors, consumers, employees and the community (McWilliams, 2001). Research on the link between CSR and firm performance has been inconsistent (McWilliams and Siegel, 2000). McWilliams argues that, analysed in terms of costs and benefits, a 'business case' for CSR can be based on a differentiation strategy and become a source of competitive advantage. Examples of CSR approaches in this context are:

- Products made from CSR resources, such as recycled materials
- Products made through CSR-related processes, such as organic foods
- Advertising which provides information about CSR attributes, such as dolphin-free tuna labels
- Building brand reputation on CSR attributes.

This approach supports a view of CSR based on market considerations, treating the choice of CSR attributes as analogous to the other strategic choices a firm makes, in terms of the demand for the attribute and the costs of providing it. This 'instrumental' view of CSR is akin to the weak version of the theory, but it does highlight the fact that demand exists and is coming from numerous stakeholder groups – an indication that social responsibility is one of the criteria guiding consumers and investors in their evaluation of corporate performance.

SUMMARY POINTS

Social responsibility

- Social responsibility comprises a group of issues, including:
  - **Human rights**, including rights such as freedom from torture and right to privacy (see Chapter 9)
  - **Workers' rights**, such as the right not to be discriminated against on grounds of race, sex, religion or nationality; and also working conditions (for example health and safety measures) (see Chapter 7)
  - **Environmental protection**, including reducing pollutants, protecting ecosystems and reducing demands on non-renewable natural resources (see Chapter 13).
- While there are national and EU laws, as well as international treaties, laying down minimum standards in all these spheres, the socially responsible company will go beyond the minimum required by law.
- TNCs are often criticized, especially by numerous watchdog groups, when their operations in developing countries do not come up to international standards and they are perceived as exploiting cheap labour, rather than behaving as good 'corporate citizens'.

CRITICAL PERSPECTIVES

Corporate social responsibility

Corporations are social institutions. If they don't serve society, they have no business existing. The argument that they serve society by making money and creating jobs is coming apart. (Mintzberg, quoted in Skapinker, 2003)

■ What factors have caused this undermining of the purely economic view of the company's role?

■ To what extent does the view of the corporation as a social institution suggest a radical transformation in its role, or, alternatively, a reformulation of what corporations have always been doing?

Raising corporate standards

Large TNCs operate in a huge range of national cultural environments. While it was once thought that local standards sufficed, companies are now expected to maintain consistent standards and policies across their operations, whatever the location. In many countries, however, practices such as child labour are commonplace. Accurate data on the extent of child labour are difficult to obtain, but it is estimated by the ILO (2002) that there were about 211 million children aged 5–14 at work in economic activities in 2000. The equivalent number for 1995 was 250 million, but the ILO cautions that this apparent reduction should not be interpreted as a trend, as different ways of collecting statistics have been used (ILO, 2002). The number of child workers is greatest in the Asia Pacific region, as Table 14.3 shows, but the highest proportion of child workers is in sub-Saharan Africa, where almost one child in three is economically active (29 per cent). Moreover, about one in every four children in this region is working by the age of 10. Nearly 171 million children aged 5–17 were involved in hazardous work, which includes mining, construction, work with dangerous machinery and work involving exposure to dangerous substances. In addition, there are an estimated 8.4 million children involved in the worst forms of child labour, which include forced labour, trafficking, armed conflict and prostitution (ILO 2002, p. 25).

Table 14.3 **Economic activity of children in different regions, 2000**

Region	Number of children (in millions)	Work ratio (%)
Developed economies	2.5	2
Transition economies	2.4	4
Asia and the Pacific	127.3	19
Latin America & Caribbean	17.4	16
Sub-Saharan Africa	48.0	29
Middle East & North Africa	13.4	15
Total	211	18

Source: ILO (2002) *Every Child Counts: New Global Estimates on Child Labour* (Geneva: ILO).

Many companies have introduced voluntary codes of conduct, outlining their principles on legal and ethical standards. Levi Strauss, which relies on more than 400 subcontractors overseas, discovered that 25 per cent of the local subcontractors were abusing the workforce. As part of its programme to stop such practices, it devised new sourcing guidelines for the future, which address legal, ethical, environmental and employment standards (Schaffer, et al., 1999). Such codes have now become accepted practice. While they are doubtless part of a public relations exercise to deflect criticism, they underline the sense in which the modern corporation is aware of its responsibility as a good corporate citizen. These codes tend to be worded in general terms, and most lack mechanisms for external monitoring and audit. Nike has 700 contract factories in 53 countries, with varying legal, social and economic environments. Having been a target of protesters, Nike has issued a code of conduct which is complemented by internal and external monitoring and has begun to involve NGOs in its monitoring processes.

Reaching for international standards

On an international level, there are three initiatives which have addressed ethical issues. The first is from the Organization for Economic Co-operation and Development (OECD). Its *Guidelines for Multinational Enterprises*, first issued in 1976, were strengthened in 2000 (OECD, 2000d). The 2000 version includes standards for corporate governance, workplace conditions, environmental safeguards, bribery and protection for whistleblowers. While they are not binding, these guidelines are supported by the OECD's considerable ability to publicize abuses and bring pressure to bear on governments and corporations. The OECD's 1976 version prompted changes in national law in its member states.

Secondly, the International Labour Organization (ILO), which dates from 1919, sets standards and provides monitoring of working conditions. Now a UN agency, its organization includes representatives of government, labour and employers from each member state. It aims to set up national mechanisms for employment protection and monitoring and, in addition, it aims to promote the recognition of basic rights, including freedom of association.

Thirdly, the UN has initiated a Global Compact between governments, corporations and NGOs. The Compact lists nine key principles from the Universal Declaration of Human Rights, the core standards of the ILO, and the Rio Declaration. They include support of human rights, the elimination of child labour, free trade unions and the elimination of environmental pollution. These are 'aspirational' rather than binding in their effects. The significance of the initiative is the bringing together of the major players in a single forum for debate about the issues. Nike, Daimler-Chrysler, Unilever and Royal Dutch Shell were among the corporations that signed the accord, as were Amnesty International and the World Wildlife Fund. The UN secretary-general said: 'Companies should not wait for governments to pass laws before they pay a decent wage or agree not to pollute the environment ... If companies lead by example, the governments may wake up and make laws to formalize these practices' (*New York Times*, 27 July 2000).

The launch of the Global Compact illustrates three points that are indicative of the current global legal and ethical environment:

- The line between what is ethical and what is legal has become blurred. What is legal in a particular country may not pass muster by international ethical – and often legal – standards.
- Global corporations, with a presence in all continents, are often in a stronger position than governments to take a lead in implementing higher ethical standards.
- The bringing together of corporate, governmental and NGO representatives in an, as yet, embryonic framework under the auspices of the UN emphasizes that the changing environment encompasses both state and non-state players.

WEB ALERT!

The ILO's website is http://www.ilo.org

There is a website dedicated to the UN Global Compact at http://www.globalcompact.org. There are many relevant topics to click on for further details, including corruption and human rights

Challenges of the new information age

The last two decades of the twentieth century saw the explosion of IT and the spread of networked information systems to virtually all types of industry. The internet has been described as 'globalization on steroids' (World Bank, 2000c). Advances in IT, and especially telecommunications and internet technology, have been crucial to the emergence of what is called the 'new economy', based on electronic networks (see Chapter 11). Combined with the deregulation of financial markets, globalization has brought enormous opportunities for investment and hastening market integration, but it has also exposed serious risks, which threaten to undermine the undoubted benefits. There is no doubt that near-instantaneous electronic trading in capital markets has facilitated the radical movements in capital flows that have contributed to various financial crises – Mexico in 1994, Asian countries in 1997, Russia in 1998 and Brazil in 1999 (Castells, 2000b, p. 52). While investors flocked to join the rush to emerging markets, financial collapses brought hardship and suffering to millions of innocent victims in stricken economies (see Chapter 12).

The new economy has tapped wellsprings of entrepreneurial energy all over the globe, as internet start-up companies leapt onto the bandwagon. Here too, investors were not lacking. Some of the dot-com companies saw amazing growth, on a scale of 400–500 per cent rise in share prices almost overnight, following glittering initial public offerings. In the US in 1997, a higher proportion of households' assets were in securities than in property (Castells, 2000b, p. 54). These inflated values were bound to come down to earth, however, on the realization that the business foundations of many of the dot-com enterprises were unsound and that 'virtual' retailers face all the familiar problems of the old economy, such as product quality and prudent accounting. The surviving dot-coms and the more recent arrivals have been more realistic in their expectations.

Has the globalized world of the internet left behind the national borders of the old economy? In *The Invisible Continent*, Kenichi Ohmae (2000) argues that there is a new borderless world of the emerging internet-based economy, which he calls the 'invisible continent' of cyberspace, or 'Cyberia'. While he speaks of leaving behind the national borders of the 'old-world' environment, he does envisage nations, companies, individuals and regions moving at different paces towards the new continent. He offers a score card of national readiness to move into the invisible continent (Ohmae, 2000, p. 238). Unsurprisingly, the US is at the forefront.

In the new economy, as in the old, there are inequalities and exclusions, as well as opportunities. Developing and transition economies, for example in Eastern Europe and Asia, have benefited from the trend towards outsourcing by TNCs. India is an example: while at one end of the value spectrum, it has become a host to call centre operations, its engineers and scientists are building computing, software and pharmaceutical businesses (see Case study 8.3 on India and the Case study on Glaxo-SmithKline at the end of this chapter). Countries in the developing world, however, risk losing their highly skilled workers to the greater allure of opportunities in the more advanced economies. For the lives of the bulk of the population in poor countries, there is little change. While nearly half the population of the US has internet access, the figure is about 0.6 per cent in developing countries, which risk being marginalized by poor access to information. A 'digital divide' may thus be opening up between rich and poor countries (World Bank, 2000c).

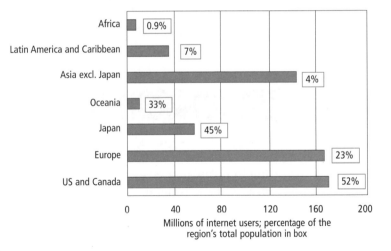

Figure 14.6 **Prevalence of internet use in different regions (2002)**
Sources: UN (2003) *World Population Prospects, The 2002 Revision*; ILO (2004) *A Fair Globalization* (Geneva: ILO).

There are huge potential benefits from new technologies, but the problems of the global economy seem to persist, and are even becoming more threatening. Castells argues that:

> the global economy is at the same time extraordinarily inclusive of what is valued in the networks of business interaction, and highly exclusive of what has little or no interest in a given time and space. (Castells, 2000b, p. 53)

He cites examples of the AIDS epidemic, the global trade in people, the destruction of the world's forests and the expansion of global criminal activity. The technology itself is not to blame, but where are the safeguards that will be used to serve the values of human well-being for present and future generations?

CRITICAL PERSPECTIVES

Development revisited

Development is not about helping a few people to get rich or creating a handful of pointless protected industries that only benefit the country's elite: it is not about bringing in Prada and Benetton, Ralph Lauren or Louis Vuitton, for the urban rich and leaving the rural poor in their misery. Being able to buy Gucci handbags in Moscow department stores did not mean that country had become a market economy. Development is about transforming societies, improving the lives of the poor, enabling everyone to have a chance at success and access to health care and education. (Stiglitz, 2002, p. 252)

■ In what ways does this passage evoke the notion of sustainable development?

■ This chapter has highlighted that development poses challenges for both businesses and policy-makers. What recommendations would you make to each group in respect of a sustainable development agenda?

Globalization and national diversity: the way ahead

Neither the extreme views of the hyperglobalizers, who predicted a withering away of national differences, nor those who deny globalization altogether have yet come to pass. The increasing integration of economic and financial systems has not as yet brought about convergence. Globalization has enhanced the powers of TNCs and weakened the abilities of nation-states to set national agendas. At the same time, the Fordist organization has given way to the flexible organization, global in strategic outlook, but adapting to the diversity of different locations, in terms of social and cultural environment, economic systems and systems of innovation. An understanding of the relationship between the forces of globalization and local distinctiveness is increasingly seen as essential for companies in international markets.

There are some who argue that, with the demise of nation-states' ability to set moral, legal and economic rules, there needs to be a strengthening of supranational organizations, to take on the mantle of governance in the global economy (Drucker, 1997; Giddens and Hutton, 2000). Giddens and Hutton (2000, p. 223) point to the growing role of the EU in taking over the authority formerly allotted to national governments, as the beginnings of 'cosmopolitan governance with mechanisms for proper democratic accountability and continental citizenship'. Drucker (1997,

p. 170) says, that 'a central challenge ... is the development of international law and supranational organizations that can make and enforce rules for the global economy'. On the other hand, the experience of the Bretton Woods institutions, the IMF and the World Bank, has been one of finding that a one-size-fits-all approach has proved unsuitable in the divergent economic, social and political settings that exist from country to country. The experience of the EU, the most highly developed supranational organization to date, has been primarily one of struggling both to reconcile divergent national interests and establish structures of legitimacy and accountability, essential for the institutional foundation on which enlargement rests.

For the developing world, the benefits of globalization have been unevenly distributed. Some have enjoyed wealth from the exploitation of natural resources and others have attracted manufacturing industries, but often the benefits of development have neglected broader societal needs. For international business, the way ahead opens opportunities to grasp the dynamic interaction between the forces of globalization, on the one hand, and the needs and expectations of people in diverse national environments, on the other.

Conclusions

1   The themes of globalization and persisting national diversity have emerged in each of the spheres of the business environment discussed in earlier chapters. These themes represent interactions rather than countervailing forces in the environment.

2   Change in the international environment, through the processes of globalization and liberalization, has brought opportunities for economic development, but also exposure to instabilities, as in financial markets.

3   Attention is increasingly focused on the widening gap between rich and poor countries and the possible solutions. Heightened awareness of the problems of poverty, disease and hunger has led to initiatives from governments in developed countries, as well as initiatives to encourage foreign investment.

4   Economic development can be framed in a broader picture of human development, which takes in improvements in education, health and cultural well-being.

5   Social responsibility, including human rights, human development and environmental protection, is now engaging the managers of TNCs, responding to growing awareness of ethical and environmental issues by shareholders and consumers.

6   Theories of corporate social responsibility (CSR) stress that companies' impact on society should become central to their strategy formation. Assessing social interactions is often envisaged in terms of stakeholder groups, including investors, consumers, employees and society in general.

7   Globalization has perhaps been most pervasive in the information revolution and the rapid spread of the internet. Like the old economy, however, the new economy presents risks as well as opportunities, and divergent national environments for its successful exploitation.

8   While some would argue that the weakening of nation-states implies that newer global forms of governance are needed, international institutions at present seem not to fulfil that role.

9   For international business, therefore, globalization implies local adaptation and sensitivity to local business environments. Global challenges are particularly acute in developing countries, where TNCs in conjunction with governments may wield considerable economic power. Building socially responsible strategies and societal relations represents both opportunities and challenges.

Review questions

1   In which dimensions of the international business environment has globalization penetrated more deeply and in which is national diversity still the norm?

2   What has been the impact of liberalization in national economies on the business environment globally?

3   What factors account for the gaps between rich and poor countries? In what ways is economic development reducing poverty?

4   How is economic development contrasted with the broader concept of human development? What is the role of companies in the latter?

5   What is meant by 'social responsibility' in relation to the modern company? How do CSR theories contribute to strategy formation?

6   Identify the main stakeholder groups which impact on a TNC and their potential power in influencing corporate behaviour.

7   In what ways has the new information age created a digital divide? In what ways does the knowledge economy represent both globalization and national diversity?

Assignments

1   Discuss (a) the possibilities for economic development in the poorest countries, in particular those of sub-Saharan Africa; and (b) the current problems which present obstacles to development.

2   Compare the traditional view of the role of the firm, in relation to its shareholders and society, to the new view envisaged by the broader emphasis on social responsibility.

Further reading

Agittey, G. (2000) *Africa in Chaos* (Basingstoke: Palgrave Macmillan).

Allen, T. and Thomas, A. (2000) *Poverty and Development*, 2nd edn (Oxford: Oxford University Press).

Crane, A. and Matten, D. (2003) *Business Ethics* (Oxford: Oxford University Press).

Hutton, W. and Giddens, A. (2000) *On the Edge: Living with Global Capitalism* (London: Jonathan Cape).

Kotler, P. (2004) *Corporate Social Responsibility* (London: John Wiley & Sons).

Meyer, A. (2000) *Contraction and Convergence: A Global Framework to Cope with Climate Change* (Newton Abbot: Green Books).

Lomborg, B. (ed.) (2004) *Global Crises, Global Solutions: Priorities for a World of Scarcity* (Cambridge: Cambridge University Press).

Ohmae, K. (2000) *The Invisible Continent: Four Strategic Imperatives of the New Economy* (London: Nicholas Brealey).

Stiglitz, J. (2002) *Globalization and its Discontents* (London: Allen Lane).

END OF PART 4 CASE STUDY

GlaxoSmithKline and what the world expects from a big pharmaceutical company

GlaxoSmithKline (GSK), the world's second largest pharmaceutical company, was formed in 2000, combining Glaxo Wellcome, which had research expertise in chemistry, with SmithKline Beecham, which specialized in biology and genomics (research on the human genome). Hopes were high that the complementary strengths of the two companies would lead to reductions in costs and improved performance in global markets. The prevailing view in the pharmaceutical industry favoured consolidation to achieve economies of scale. In common with all drug companies, GSK needs to maintain a steady flow of new drugs to take the place of those which become superseded by newer ones or to replace those whose patents expire. The long lead time for drugs requires a resource commitment over several years, to see the drug through lengthy trial phases, before it is finally released. A drug company seeks to have numerous drugs in the pipeline, to compensate for those that fall by the wayside. For example, the patent application could founder or the trials could reveal harmful side effects. Importantly, every drug must be navigated through the regulatory authorities in each market, before it can be prescribed or sold over the counter. It is little wonder that big is thought to be better in the pharmaceutical industry. The research figures of GSK were impressive: it had a $4bn.-a-year budget and employed 15,000 scientists. Still, it had to find the winning drugs and get them successfully to market.

Decentralized research units: the recipe for innovation?

At the time of the merger, there was the risk that research would be smothered by bureaucracy. GSK decided to devolve research into six separate units, each with its own budget, called 'centres of excellence for drug discovery'. Each focuses on a particular area of research, such as cancer treatment. These drug discovery units were intended to foster the entrepreneurship and creativity that is found in smaller biotech companies. However, realizing this ideal in practice turned out to be difficult. The creation of the units came on the heels of the upheaval caused by the merger, creating uncertainty among the scientists, some of whom left. Older researchers had endured a long period of uncertainty, dating back to the SmithKline Beecham merger in 1989 and the Glaxo Wellcome merger in 1995. The remaining scientists have found that bureaucracy was reduced in the new research units, making it easier to get new drugs into the trial phase. To provide incentives, 20 per cent of scientists' remuneration in the new centres is performance-linked.

What was in the pipeline in the aftermath of the merger? The research cupboard looked rather bare. Glaxo and SmithKline had each suffered setbacks in the run-up to the merger, as three potential money-spinners had had to be pulled in the late stages of tests. Its top-selling drug, the anti-depressant, Paxil, is reaching the end of its patent life, and the threat of generic producers is looming. Augmentin, an antibiotic, generated $1.4bn. for GSK in 2001, but in 2002, an American court ruled that three of its patents were invalid. As a consequence, cheaper generic copies gained sales and Augmentin's sales fell 42 per cent in the following year. By 2004, 70 per cent of GSK's turnover came from products whose sales were declining. Looking to the future, the company's investment in genomics is expected to bring long-term benefits which will yield advantages over its competitors. Biotechnology has become the basis of most new drugs and vaccines.

Buying in winners: a winning strategy?

When there seem to be too few 'blockbuster' drugs in the pipeline, the large drug companies look to buy in drugs from the smaller biotech companies. Researchers in these smaller companies create drugs which often stall in the experimental stages, as their companies lack the resources to take the development through to the later phases and clinical trials. They also lack the marketing expertise to promote the drug globally. The large company steps in, agreeing to produce the drug under licence, for which it may have to pay. Known as 'in-licensing', these deals can be risky, as the drug may turn out not to be the money-spinner that had been hoped. Marketing these licensed drugs created by others now contributes about 24 per cent of total revenues of the major pharmaceutical companies. GSK has become the leader in in-licensing agreements. Between 2001 and 2003, GSK bought rights to almost twice as many drugs as its rivals (see Figure 1). It is perhaps a sign of the trend that Bayer, the German group which created aspirin, has turned to GSK to market one of its drugs.

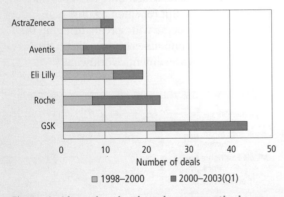

Figure 1 **Licensing in the pharmaceutical industry**

Source: Firn, D., 'GSK "tops drug purchase league"', *Financial Times*, 19 May 2003.

While licensing deals are beneficial to the small biotech companies, they raise questions over the innovative capacity of the large companies' in-house researchers. GSK has developed the marketing side of the business, aided by its 17,000 salesmen across the world, but doubts remain about its R&D productivity. Investors fear that there are too few drugs of its own in the pipeline, despite the assurances of the Chief Executive Jean-Pierre Garnier that licensing is merely a short-term strategy until its own drugs come to market. The use of licensing may be a sign of changes in the structure of the pharmaceutical industry, with smaller, specialized companies discovering drugs and the large companies marketing them. Yamada, the GSK research director, seemed further to cast doubt on GSK's research when he said: 'I am not sure that we are any better than a biotech company, a small pharmaceuticals company or a university department' (Durman, 17 March 2002).

Dilemmas in global markets

GSK is the world's largest producer of HIV/Aids drugs. The company has found itself at loggerheads with the governments of developing countries, where the disease has been most widespread and where sufferers are least able to afford the drugs. Of the world's 38 million people living with HIV/Aids, 25 million (66 per cent) live in sub-Saharan Africa, where only 12 per cent receive treatment (see Figure 2) (UNAIDS, 2004). Generic drug makers have been producing HIV drugs in breach of patents held by GSK, Merck, Pfizer and other drug companies, which launched legal action against the South African government. The negative image of these companies which this action created eventually persuaded them to drop the cases. GSK, having led the action, then licensed three HIV medicines to a South African generics company free of charge in 2002. The inability of poor people in developing countries to afford life-saving drugs led to pressures from GSK's institutional investors to reduce prices. In response, it halved the prices of its biggest Aids drug, bringing it more into line with prices charged by Ranbaxy, the Indian generics company (which manufactures without patent infringement under the much laxer Indian law). The new prices, which it said allowed for no profit, applied to 63 developing countries, including sub-Saharan Africa. However, even the reduced prices were more than their generic rivals.

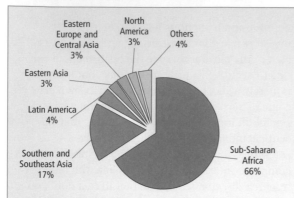

Figure 2 HIV/Aids in the world: percentages of sufferers in the most affected regions (total number of adults and children estimated to be living with HIV/AIDS: 38 million)

Source: United Nations (2004) *2004 Report on the Global AIDS Epidemic* (Geneva: UN).

Forging links with its erstwhile enemy, GSK announced in 2003 a link-up for drug research with Ranbaxy. Ranbaxy's scientists would be able to do early-stage research into new drugs, helping it to diversify away from generics. The alliance resembled an outsourcing arrangement, in that Indian scientists in Indian laboratories are paid much less than those in Western economies. The company denies the outsourcing allegation, saying that: 'the idea is to combine their skill sets, which include excellent chemistry, with our technology infrastructure' (Dyer, 23 October 2003). There are risks, however, lurking in the weak intellectual property protection that is afforded in India. GSK is actually suing Ranbaxy in the US for its manufacture of a generic version of Augmentin.

Corporate social responsibility rises up the agenda

The price of Aids drugs in poor developing countries highlights the problems faced by the pharmaceutical industry generally. Suffering negative publicity over their pricing, companies reduced prices for poor countries. However, the generic producers, who have borne none of the development costs, are still undercutting them in these countries. The WTO's Doha Round of negotiations reached an agreement which would allow 'compulsory licensing' of life-saving drugs where public health is at risk. On the face of it, this agreement was a blow to the pharmaceutical industry, as it would allow governments to override patents in the interest of public health. In practice, however, patent protection had already become eroded by generic copies.

Further price-cutting pressures are coming from governments generally, as they increasingly question the prices of medicines that public health systems are being asked to pay. Health authorities, because of their huge buying power, are in a position to exert pressures on the pharmaceutical companies to cut prices. It is notable that healthcare expenses are much higher in the US than in other countries, as Figure 3 shows. Canada, having successfully managed to negotiate lower prices for its citizens, is finding that US citizens are increasingly 'reimporting' cheaper Canadian drugs in preference to those with higher US price tags. Canada's internet pharmacies are particularly benefiting from increased sales. Future drug innovations, companies argue, depend on maintaining revenues, the bulk of which have been provided by US consumers. But rebellion against high prices has now become widespread, bringing the pharmaceutical companies into conflict with consumers and governments worldwide.

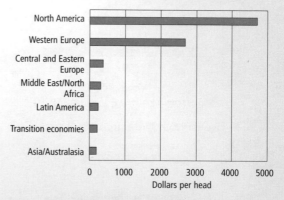

Figure 3 Healthcare and pharmaceutical sales (estimates for 2004)

Source: The Economist (2003) *The World in 2004* (London: *The Economist*) p. 106.

Investors, too, have been raising their voices. In 2002, at a time when shareholders were having doubts about the long-term health of the large pharmaceutical companies, GSK announced plans to double the remuneration of its CEO. This proposed leap in remuneration was contained in a complex package estimated at $18m., including bonuses, share options, pension provisions and other benefits. Besides concern over the proposed increase itself, there were concerns that the remuneration package was so complex as to make it difficult to discern the total remuneration and that links to performance were unclear. The plan was rejected by shareholders. The rejection was considered a landmark in UK shareholder activism by UK institutional investors. The CEO, nonetheless, received a 26 per cent increase in remuneration in 2003, making him one of the UK's highest paid executives. The executive remuneration issue highlighted a further dimension of corporate responsibility, again focusing on the values underlying GSK.

Sources: Durman, P., 'Week of stress leaves Glaxo looking sick', *Sunday Times*, 17 March 2002; Dyer, G., 'GSK in Indian drugs link-up', *Financial Times*, 23 October 2003; Dyer, G., 'Sagging morale, departing scientists, a dwindling pipeline: when will GSK's research overhaul produce results', *Financial Times*, 24 October 2002; Jenkins, P., 'GSK drops Garnier pay plan', *Financial Times*, 27 November 2002; Dyer, G., 'GSK cuts price of top Aids treatment', *Financial Times*, 28 April 2003; Michaels, A., 'Symptoms grow worse for world's drug companies', *Financial Times*, 15 January 2002; Firn, D., 'GSK "tops drug purchase league"', *Financial Times*, 19 May 2003; Dyer, G., 'As the pandemic spreads, developed nations must respond to a new challenge from the White House', *Financial Times*, 2 June 2003; 'Health-care', *The World in 2004* (London: *The Economist*); Jack, A. 'Glaxo's catalyst for creativity', *Financial Times*, 18 March 2005; Urry, M., 'New leader rings change at GSK', *Financial Times*, 30 March 2005.

End of Part 4 case questions

1 **What were the benefits of the merger of SmithKline Beecham and Glaxo Wellcome to form GSK?**

2 **What are the specific difficulties that arise for R&D in the pharmaceutical industry? Assess the success of GSK's decentralization of R&D.**

3 **How has licensing of other companies' drugs represented a change of strategy for GSK?**

4 **What issues of corporate social responsibility are highlighted in the case study? How successfully has GSK handled them?**

Glossary

antitrust laws	laws designed to control monopolies and anti-competitive practices such as price-fixing agreements.
arbitration	means of resolving disputes between parties to a contract, through an independent body agreed by the parties, thereby averting the need for court proceedings.
arm's-length contracting	business dealings between people who interact only for the purpose of doing business; contrasted with relational contracting. Arm's length contracting is more prevalent in individualist societies.
assimilation of cultures	process by which minority cultures of, for example, immigrants, become integrated into the mainstream culture of a nation.
auditor	independent professional accountant or firm of accountants appointed by a company to prepare its annual financial report.
authoritarianism	rule by a single leader or group of individuals, with unlimited power; contrasted with constitutionalism.
balance of payments	credit and debit transactions between a country's residents (including countries) and those of other countries.
balance sheet	detailed statement giving a picture of a company's financial position in terms of assets and liabilities; specific requirements set by regulatory authorities.
bilateral trade agreements	agreements with the status of treaties between two countries, designed to regulate trading relations between them.
biotechnology	the application of scientific and engineering principles to the processing of materials by biological agents to provide goods and services.
bond	a loan document promising to pay a specific sum on a due date.
brand	visual identity of a product or company, such as a name or logo, known as a trademark.

Bretton Woods agreement	the 1944 agreement between Allied nations in the aftermath of the Second World War, which was intended to bring about exchange rate stability and regulate international finance. It established the IMF and the World Bank.
Buddhism	Asian religion with over 300 million followers worldwide. Emphasizing spiritual attainment rather than worldly gain, it has subdivided into a number of sects.
bureaucracy	organizational form based on hierarchy of status and a multiplicity of formal rules governing operations.
business	economic activity in which goods and services are supplied in exchange for payment, usually money.
business cycle	regular pattern of fluctuations in business activity, divided into phases of prosperity, recession, depression and recovery.
capital account	account on the balance of payments statement which shows the transactions involving the sale and purchase of assets, including investments in shares.
capital flows	the flow of private funds between countries.
capitalism	economic systems based on the ownership of the means of production, including the individual's ability to sell his or her own labour.
cartel	grouping of producers of a product who, through a continuing cooperative agreement exert control on prices and output. Members of the cartel may be companies or nations.
caste system	social stratification system based on birth; associated with Hinduism.
central bank	bank which is responsible for monetary policy for an economy and the issuance of notes and coins. It is the banker to the government and the lender of last resort.
centralization	the concentration of power and control among relatively few decision-makers in an organization.
chaebol	industrial conglomerates characteristic of business organizations in South Korea.
chief executive officer (CEO)	chief officer at the head of a company's organizational structure.
civil law	in any legal system, the law pertaining to relations between private individuals and companies.
civil law system	legal system based on comprehensive legal codes which form the basic law; contrasted with common law systems.
civil society	sphere of activities in society in which citizens are free to pursue personal goals and form associations as they wish; characteristic of pluralist societies.
civil war	armed conflict which takes place between different groups within a state's borders.
class action	legal action in courts brought by a number of injured parties acting as a group. Class actions are often brought against manufacturers of defective products which have been widely distributed, or against companies that are

alleged to have caused widespread harm to the public, as in pollution accidents.

class system	system of social stratification based on economic status in society.
coalition government	government formed by two or more parties following elections in which no single party wins a majority of votes; likely to occur in multiparty systems and those which have proportional representation.
co-determination	a system of relations and corporate governance structures between business management, trade unions and government, based on cooperation rather than confrontation in labour relations (associated mainly with Germany).
common law	legal system based chiefly on the accumulation of case law in decided judgments through a system of binding precedent; contrasted with civil law (codified) systems.
common market	grouping of countries which agree to remove trade barriers such as tariffs among members and operate a common trade policy towards non-member countries.
company	organization recognized as a legal entity with a separate corporate identity from its members and employees.
comparative advantage	the theory (devised by Ricardo) that a country should specialize in producing the products which it can produce more cheaply and efficiently than other countries.
competitive advantage	the theory (devised by Porter) that a country's international competitive position is based on four factors: demand conditions; factor conditions; firm strategy and structure; and related and supporting industries.
Confucianism	Asian moral philosophy which emphasizes family relationships and duties of loyalty. While not a formal religion, it has had a huge impact on the social and cultural environment in most Asian countries.
constitutionalism	source of state legitimacy based on accepted institutional rules, applying to both rulers and ruled; contrasted with, for example, personal or military rule.
convertibility	the characteristic of a currency which can be exchanged for other currencies without government restrictions and controls.
corporate governance	structures and processes by which a company is controlled at the highest level, in particular the mechanisms for accountability of the board of directors to the shareholders. Corporate governance has come to take on a broader definition, encompassing the interests of stakeholders as well as shareholders.
corporate social responsibility (CSR)	approach to the company's role in society which encompasses economic, legal, ethical and philanthropic obligations, often in terms of stakeholders.
corruption	practices such as payments and favours between businesses, individuals and officials (usually for personal gain), which are outside formal legal channels, and can significantly permeate the business environment.
criminal law	laws which designate offences and set out legal procedure for prosecution by state authorities against those charged with criminal offences. There is now

also a body of international criminal law, overseen by the International Criminal Court in The Hague, the Netherlands.

cultural globalization
process of gradual fading of national cultures in the face of global values and symbols, such as global brands, fast food and Western-dominated media.

cultural pluralism
the recognition of numerous subcultures within a society; contrasted with the policy of assimilation of immigrants and minority groups into a dominant national culture.

currency flows
movements of currency between countries, which influence exchange rates and are an important element of risk for international business.

current account
the account on the balance of payments statement that shows the level of trade in merchandise and services.

decentralization
in large organizations or countries, processes for transferring decision-making authority to lower levels; associated with empowerment.

demand
the aggregate amount of a product that consumers are willing to purchase at a particular price.

democracy
system of elected government, based on fair and free elections and universal suffrage.

demographic change
changes in whole populations brought about by rises and falls in the birth rate and death rate, as well as migration of people.

demographic crisis
problems experienced generally in ageing societies, where there is a growing proportion of elderly people.

deregulation
process by which government restrictions and controls are lifted.

developing country
a country which is less industrialized and poorer than the advanced industrial economies; also referred to as less developed countries.

direct taxation
the imposition of taxes directly on income, as in income and corporation tax.

director (of a company)
person in whom ultimate responsibility for a company's actions rests; may be an active manager ('executive') director or an independent ('non-executive') director who takes little part in management.

division of labour
organizational principle by which each phase in production is conceived as a specialized task assigned to a particular person. The international division of labour, similarly, assigns particular phases to particular locations.

dumping
the sale of goods abroad at below the price charged for comparable goods in the producing country. Under GATT, importing countries are allowed to impose anti-dumping duties on the exporting country.

e-commerce
business transactions, both business-to-business and business-to-consumers, which are negotiated and agreed on the internet.

economic growth
a country's increase in national income over time, associated with industrialization, increasing investment and technological improvement.

economies of scale
lower costs of production arising from increases in the volume of products produced.

elasticity	the proportionate change in a dependent variable, as in the price elasticity of demand, whereby demand responds to price changes.
embargo	the prohibition imposed by a government on trade with another country by its nationals (as in the embargo imposed by the US on trade with Cuba).
empowerment	management approach which allows employees decision-making authority and responsibility for their own actions.
entrepreneur	person who sets up in business, often referred to as the 'start-up' enterprise, and commits his or her own funds, as well as energy, to the enterprise.
environmental degradation	environmental change caused mainly by human activity which has detrimental effects on ecological systems.
environmental management	assessment of environmental impact and formulation of environmental strategies from the perspective of a company's total operations.
equity	A company's shares (known as 'stock' in the US).
ethnocentrism	view of the world which centres on one's own culture only.
euro	the single currency adopted by the EU under EMU.
eurobond	a bond denominated in a currency other than that of the country in which it is issued.
eurodollars	US dollars held on deposit in banks outside the US. They need not be European banks.
European Monetary Union (EMU)	The EU programme centred on a single European currency (the euro) and an independent central bank which sets monetary policy. Launched in 1999, there are now 12 states in the eurozone.
eurozone	member states in the EU which have satisfied the Maastricht criteria and joined the EMU. Their number rose to 12 with the admission of Greece in 2000.
European Union (EU)	the regional grouping of European countries which evolved from a common market to the deeper integrative framework of economic union, changing its name from European Community to European Union in 1994. Its membership rose to 25 countries in 2004.
exchange controls	restrictions and controls imposed by governments on the movement of currency.
expatriate	in international business, an employee, usually a manager, from the home country of an organization who takes up a post in the company's foreign operations.
export	the sale of goods or services to a buyer in another country.
externalization strategy	the severing of ties with linked suppliers in a supply chain, in favour of more competitive terms from other suppliers in global markets.
factors of production	inputs into the production process, including land, labour, capital and technology.

federal system — system of government in which authority is divided between the centre and regional units (examples are the US and Germany).

financial reporting — business function which provides information on the company's financial performance, including profit and loss account and balance sheet.

first-mover advantages — precept that countries or firms which are first to produce a new product gain an advantage in markets which makes it virtually impossible for others to catch up.

fiscal policy — a government's policy concerning budgetary matters, including taxation and public expenditure.

fixed exchange rate — government policy of fixing the value of a country's currency, by specifying the number of units which can be exchanged for a specific number of units of a foreign currency.

flexible mass production — production model, chiefly associated with Japanese manufacturing companies, which allows for flexibility in production and organization within a hierarchical structure.

floating exchange rate — government policy of allowing the country's currency to be determined by market forces, rather than government control; in contrast to a fixed exchange rate.

Fordism — industrial organization based on large factories producing standardized products for mass consumption, named after the automobile magnate, Henry Ford.

foreign direct investment (FDI) — the establishment by a company of a productive base in another country, usually involving substantial shareholding in the foreign operation.

foreign exchange — any financial instrument for making payment in another country's currency.

franchise — form of business organization whereby a trader agrees with a company to carry on business under licence to use the company's brand in a particular area, in exchange for a share of the profits (McDonald's is an example).

free trade area — trade grouping of countries, by which member states agree to eliminate trade barriers such as tariffs on trade among themselves, but operate no uniform trade policy in respect of non-members (NAFTA is an example).

function (within a business) — type of activity that forms part of the overall process of providing a product for the consumer, from the design stage to the delivery to the customer.

functional approach — organizational structure based on business functions, such as finance, HRM and marketing.

GATT (General Agreement on Tariffs and Trade) — succession of multilateral agreements on reducing trade barriers, begun in 1947. The most recent 'round', the Uruguay Round, or GATT 1994, has now been subsumed in the World Trade Organization (WTO), from 1995.

globalization — multidimensional processes which are leading to broader and deeper integration between countries and peoples.

global warming — process of climate change by which temperatures are gradually rising and sea levels are rising; generally thought to be caused by the build-up of heat-trapping gases, or 'greenhouse gases'.

gold standard	the setting of exchange rates in terms of the value of gold (in operation from the late nineteenth century to the Second World War).
government	structures and processes of the state by which laws are made and administered; also refers to the particular office holders at any given time.
grey market	'unofficial' trade in goods, usually designed to circumvent customs duty and other government restrictions.
Gross domestic product (GDP)	the total flow of goods and services produced by an economy over a particular period.
Gross national income (GNI)	GDP plus the income accruing to residents from investments abroad, less income in the domestic economy which accrues to foreigners abroad (formerly gross national product).
Group of Seven (G7)	Canada, France, Germany, Japan, Italy, the US and the UK. The G7 was formed in 1975, and joined by the European Community in 1977. From 1998, they have been joined by Russia, creating the G8.
hedge	in international business transactions, to buy or sell currency in international currency markets for future delivery, as a means of reducing the risk of fluctuations in exchange rates.
hierarchy	vertical differentiation of people in an organization or society generally.
high-context culture	culture in which communication relies heavily on the behavioural dimension, such as 'body language'; contrasted with low-context culture.
Hinduism	Asian religion centred on the Indian subcontinent, polytheistic in nature and associated closely with a caste system of social stratification.
holding company	company whose main purpose is ownership of other companies, known as subsidiaries.
horizontal integration	mergers or acquisitions between two or more companies in the same industry.
human resource management (HRM)	business function which focuses on relations, both formal and informal, between employees and managers within an organization.
human rights	basic, universal rights enjoyed by all individuals, which are recognized in national and international law.
ideology	all-encompassing system of beliefs and values, or 'world view'.
import	the purchase of goods or services by a buyer in another country.
import quota	a non-tariff barrier to trade which consists of limiting the quantity of an imported product, often requiring a licence specifying the quantity authorized.
import substitution	a policy adopted by many industrializing economies, under which industries are encouraged in areas which produce goods formerly imported.
indirect taxation	taxes which are charged other than on income, such as VAT, tariffs and customs duties.

industrial agglomeration	the concentration, or clustering, of several producers in a particular industry in a single location.
industrial society	society based on industrial production and employment, characterized by stratification on the basis of class. Industrial societies are thought of as 'modern', to distinguish them from traditional agricultural societies.
industrialization	process of transition from a mainly agricultural economy to one based on machine production.
inflation	increase in the general level of prices in an economy.
initial public offering (IPO)	offering shares in a public company to the public, which are then traded on a stock exchange.
innovation	creation or improvement of products or processes, including incremental improvements, which bring commercial benefits.
innovation system	structures and institutions which shape a country's innovative capacity, including educational system, level of science and technology and industrial structure.
intellectual property (IP)	products of the human mind protected by law, including patents for inventions, copyright for original written, musical or artistic works and trademarks.
internalization strategy	company strategy which aims to acquire control of raw materials or components, as an alternative to reliance on markets.
international business	business activities, including the buying, selling and production of goods, as well as the provision of services between two or more countries.
international law	body of rules recognized by the international community as governing relations between sovereign states; mainly contained in treaties and international conventions.
International Monetary Fund (IMF)	agency of the UN dating back to the Bretton Woods agreement, which oversees the international financial system.
intra-firm trade	the sale of goods or services between units of the same parent company operating in different countries.
invention	a new product or process which can be applied industrially. Intellectual property law provides a patent system for recognition and protection of patents.
Islam	major world religion with over a billion followers (known as Muslims). In countries where it is the dominant religion, Islamic law is an important element of the business environment.
joint venture	an agreement between companies to produce or sell a product or service. Joint ventures may take many forms, often involving equity holdings, and are typically between a foreign investor and a local partner.
judicial system	system of courts, usually divided between civil courts and criminal courts.
just-in-time	production system which relies on delivery of materials just before they are needed in the production process, thereby reducing the need to hold large stocks of inventory.

kaizen	management philosophy of continuous improvement, involving an entire workforce; developed by the Japanese.
keiretsu	grouping of Japanese companies, usually around a main bank, and characterized by cross-shareholdings.
legislative assembly	elected body of representatives which holds the central law-making function in democratic systems of government.
leveraged buy-out (LBO)	acquisition of a company's equity by a group of persons (often managers of the company), through a loan.
liberalization	policies of deregulation of government controls of the economy, and allowing market forces to determine prices.
licensing agreement	usually in relation to intellectual property rights, a firm which owns a patent or trademark may license another firm to produce the product under licence, in return for a royalty fee.
litigation	the practice of using the courts to resolve disputes and settle other claims for compensation, as in negligence and product liability cases.
local content requirements	government rules requiring foreign investors to maintain minimum levels of material and components supplied by local suppliers.
location advantage	aspects of a country's business environment which constitute an attraction for investors, including natural resources and low-cost labour.
low-context culture	culture in which communication is clear and direct, rather than relying on patterns of behaviour; contrasted with high-context culture.
macroeconomics	the study of whole economic systems, in particular, national economies.
management	process of planning, organizing, leading and controlling the work of organization members.
management accounting	business function which provides information on costs (such as labour and materials) required by the firm as part of the planning and control processes.
market economy	economy in which ownership of production is in private hands and allocation of resources is determined by supply and demand.
marketing concept	the philosophy that an organization should try to provide products that satisfy customers' needs through a coordinated set of activities that also allows the organization to achieve its goals.
marketing mix	combination of the 4 Ps (product, price, promotion and place) which creates an integrated offering to potential customers that satisfies their needs and wants.
matrix structure	organizational structure incorporating both functional and divisional structures.
melting pot	in relation to societies with large numbers of immigrants, the blend of people from many different cultures to form a single nation. The most notable example is the US.

merger	agreement of two companies to unite to form a new company. An example is the merger of Grand Metropolitan and Guinness to form Diageo.
microeconomics	the study of economic activity at the level of individuals and firms.
migration	movements of people which result in a permanent change of residence.
monetary policy	policies for determining the amount of money in supply, rates of interest and exchange rates.
monopoly	market situation in which a single firm is the sole supplier.
most-favoured nation (MFN)	GATT principle negotiated between countries, by which the most favourable tariff treatment negotiated with one country is extended to similar goods from all countries.
multiculturalism	in societies, the recognition of minority cultures, ethnic groups and languages, with institutional and legal safeguards to prevent discrimination.
multidivisional structure	organizational structure with decentralized divisions based on product lines or geographical areas.
multilateral agreement	international agreement between a number of countries, such as the GATT in the area of free trade.
nation	social grouping based on cultural bonds such as language, shared history, shared sense of collective identity and usually a territorial homeland.
nation-state	social, administrative and territorial unit into which the world's peoples are divided.
national culture	distinctive values and patterns of behaviour which distinguish one nation from another and influence organizational culture and economic and political structures.
national debt	the total debt accumulated by a central government's borrowings over the years.
national security	principle of sovereign states whereby a government protects its inhabitants and territory from armed aggression such as terrorism and invasion.
negligence	in law, the breach of the duty to take reasonable care which causes injury or other harm to another, for which legal redress may be sought in the civil courts. In extreme cases, cases of criminal negligence may give rise to criminal prosecution.
network organization	organization characterized by flexible lines of communication and informal links between different teams and functional groups.
networking	informal ties and communication which cut across formal structures in organizations.
non-governmental organizations (NGOs)	organizations formed by private individuals for particular causes, which aim to influence public policy-makers and also offer assistance in specialist fields alongside official agencies. An example is the Worldwide Fund for Nature.
non-tariff barrier	tool of government trade policy which acts indirectly to form barriers to trade; include import quotas, subsidies and voluntary export restraint (VER).

North American Free Trade Agreement (NAFTA)	free trade grouping consisting of Canada, Mexico and the US.
OLI paradigm	also known as the 'eclectic' paradigm, devised by Dunning, to explain the rationale behind foreign direct investment. It highlights ownership, location, and internalization advantages.
oligopoly	market situation in which a few large producers dominate the market.
operations	the creation and provision of goods or services to be offered to the consumer.
organization	two or more people who work together in a structured way to achieve a specific goal or set of goals.
Organization for Economic Co-operation and Development (OECD)	international organization comprising the major industrialized and industrializing countries. The OECD monitors economic performance and policies among member states.
organizational culture	an organization's values, behavioural norms and management style; also known as 'corporate culture'.
parliamentary system	system of government in which the voters elect members of parliament, from whom the prime minister and cabinet (the executive) are chosen, usually from the political party with the majority of seats.
partnership	two or more people carrying on a business in common, with a view to profit.
patent	type of intellectual property which gives the owner of a new invention or new process exclusive rights for a limited period to exploit the invention commercially, to license others to use it and stop all unauthorized exploitation.
pegged exchange rate	linking the value of a currency to the value of another currency.
PEST analysis	analytical tool for scanning the business environment, representing political, economic, social and technological environment.
planned economy	economic system based on total state ownership of the means of production, in which the state controls prices and output; contrasted with the market economy.
pluralism	type of society characterized by freedom of association, under which multiple groups and interests, including multiple political parties, can flourish.
politics	processes by which a social group allocates the exercise of power and authority for the group as a whole.
polycentrism	view of the world which takes in other cultures besides one's own.
portfolio investment	investment in a company's shares as an investment only, with a relatively short-term perspective; usually involving a holding of under 10 per cent. Portfolio investment is contrasted with foreign direct investment, in which the aim is to play a more active role.
post-Fordism	industrial organization in which diversity, flexibility and specialization have replaced the mass production ethos of Fordism.

presidential system system of government in which the head of the executive branch, the president, is elected directly by the voters.

private international law the law determining decisions on the question of which national law prevails in legal issues between individuals or companies in different countries.

privatization process of transferring assets from state ownership to the private sector; extensively used in the transition economies of post-Communist European countries.

product in marketing, defined broadly to include anything that can be offered to consumers which fulfils a consumer need; includes both goods and services.

product liability liability of a producer of a defective product to consumers harmed by the product.

product life cycle theory of the evolution of a product in four stages: introduction, growth, maturity and decline.

profit and loss account statement giving details of an organization's income and expenditure over a set period of time; specific requirements set by regulatory bodies.

proportional representation (PR) system of electoral representation in which seats are allocated in proportion to the votes obtained by each party; seen as more favourable to smaller parties.

protectionism trade policy stance of governments which seeks to promote domestic producers and to curtail competing imports.

public law body of law covering relations between citizens and the state.

public sector borrowing requirement (PSBR) with respect to national economies, the extent to which public spending exceeds receipts.

purchasing power parity (PPP) an exchange rate which takes account of the differing purchasing power of different currencies; in particular, a means of measuring the number of units of a foreign currency which would be needed to buy goods or services equivalent to those which the US dollar would buy in the US.

referendum example of direct democracy, in which electors cast a vote on a particular issue, such as joining the EU; may be incorporated in a country's constitution.

regional trade agreement (RTA) agreement between countries in the same broad geographical region to bring down trade barriers among themselves.

regionalism the growth of economic integration within geographic regions through, for example, free trade agreements, common markets and, in the more advanced phases, economic and political union. The EU represents deeper regional integration than exists in either Asia or the Americas.

relational contracting business dealings in which personal relations between the parties are more important than formal written agreements; contrasted with arm's-length contracting.

research and development (R&D) the systematic search for new knowledge in specific academic disciplines (basic research); and also new knowledge for specific applications (applied research).

royalty	payment by an individual or company to the owner of intellectual property (such as a patent or trademark) for the right to manufacture or sell the product under licence.
rule of law	principle of supremacy of the law over both governments and citizens, entailing equality before the law and an independent judiciary.
sanctions	actions by governments or UN authorization, which disrupt free trade to a particular country, in order to attain some purpose, such as condemnation of that country's political or humanitarian policies; may also be authorized by the WTO against countries in breach of WTO rules.
segmentation	division of a market into distinct groups of buyers with different characteristics and needs, requiring separate products or marketing strategies.
separation of powers	in systems of government, the separation of legislative, executive and judicial powers in separate authorities, with checks and balances incorporated to assure that no one branch becomes too powerful. The foremost example is the US.
share (in a company)	type of personal property denoting ownership of a company, with accompanying legal rights, such as voting rights in the company's annual general meeting; also known as 'stock'.
shareholders	owners of a company's shares; also known as 'stockholders'.
small-to-medium-size enterprise (SME)	classification of businesses which have fewer than 50 employees (small) or 50–249 (medium), although sizes vary from industry to industry and country to country. Flexible specialization and the use of subcontracting have fostered an increase in numbers of SMEs.
social market model of capitalism	capitalist market economy with a strong social justice dimension, including substantial welfare state provisions.
social responsibility	emphasis on issues of human rights, human development and environmental protections, especially in relation to management of transnational companies.
society	a system of interrelationships which connects individuals together.
sole trader	business under the ownership and control of an individual, often extending to family members.
sovereignty	supreme legal authority in the state; also the principle of autonomy and mutual recognition of states in international relations.
stakeholder	anyone who has an interest in a company, even indirectly; includes shareholders, employees, creditors, suppliers and also the investing public generally; usually in the context of stakeholder theory of corporate governance.
state-owned enterprise (SOE)	an entity owned and controlled by government, such as a nationalized industry; known as a public sector enterprise.
stock exchange	market in which shares in large public companies and other securities are traded. Share prices are an indicator of confidence in companies'

	performance, and in economic activity generally. Major stock exchanges are New York, London and Tokyo.
strategic thinking	bringing together all the information available from those within the organization and converting that knowledge into a vision of the aims that the business should pursue.
strategy	the determination of the basic long-term goals and objectives of an organization and the adoption of courses of action and the allocation of resources necessary for carrying out these goals.
structure	the design of an organization through which the enterprise is administered.
subcontractor	a legally independent firm which supplies goods or services to another on the basis of market exchange.
subculture	minority culture in a society, often associated with immigrant communities and reinforced by separate language and religion.
subsidiary	a firm which is owned by a parent company.
subsidies	payments by governments from public funds to domestic producers, as part of a strategic trade policy aimed at strengthening local firms' competitive positions.
supply	total availability of a good from all producers in the market in a particular period.
sustainable development	approach to economic development which stresses long-term environmental impact.
SWOT analysis	strategic tool used by businesses to assess the organization's strengths, weaknesses, opportunities and threats; combines analysis of both internal and external environments of the business.
takeover	the acquisition of one company by another; usually agreed between the directors of the two companies, but in a 'hostile' takeover the predator company makes an offer directly to the shareholders of the target company to buy them out.
tariffs	taxes imposed by governments on imported goods and services, which act as a barrier to trade.
technology	methodical application of scientific knowledge to practical purposes.
technology transfer	processes of acquiring technology from another country, especially in manufacturing industries. The transfer is commonly through licensing or foreign direct investment.
terrorism	action intended to inflict dramatic and deadly injury on civilians and create an atmosphere of fear, generally for a political or ideological purpose.
tort	branch of the law which concerns obligations owed by all organizations and individuals to others within the society.
trademark	type of intellectual property, which consists of a firm's distinctive logo or symbol, which distinguishes it from other firms. The trademark may be

registered, thus giving the proprietor exclusive use of it, and a right to sue in the courts those using it without authority. There is, however, a good deal of illicit use of trademarks, known as 'counterfeiting', particularly in the area of luxury brands.

Trade-Related Aspects of Intellectual Property Rights (TRIPS) — multilateral international agreement on the protection of intellectual property rights.

trade union — organization of workers which aims to achieve higher wages, better working conditions and greater security of employment; usually based on occupations or industries.

transformation process — system by which inputs such as resources are processed or transformed to produce outputs which are delivered to customers. The transformation process model is central to operations management.

transition economy — an economy making the transition from state planning to a market-driven orientation; usually involving privatization of state-owned industries, as in the economies of Central and Eastern Europe.

transitional democracy — state in which democratic institutions such as free elections are in the early stages, often following a period of authoritarian or military rule. These states are prone to political instability; an example is Nigeria.

transnational corporation (TNC) — firm which has the power to coordinate and control operations in more than one country.

treaties — chief instruments of international law.

Triad blocs — the US, EU and Japan, each of which is seen as a trade bloc.

unemployment — percentage of the labour force who are willing to work but are without jobs.

unitary system — system of authority within a state, in which all authority radiates out from the centre; contrasted with federalism.

urbanization — population movement from rural areas to cities.

vertical integration — mergers or acquisitions between firms in successive stages of production or distribution; often referred to as internalization.

voluntary export restraint (VER) — tool of government trade policy by which companies wishing to export into the country are encouraged to limit their exports, or else risk the imposition of quotas or tariffs; used by the US government against Japanese companies wishing to export to the US market.

welfare state — the provision of social benefits, such as health service and social security payments, from public funds.

World Bank — Bretton Woods organization set up to fund development projects and broader development programmes; funded by member states.

World Trade Organization (WTO) — founded in 1995 as a successor organization to GATT, for the purpose of regulating world trade, including multilateral trade agreements and the settlement of trade disputes between member states.

References

Aaker, D. (2004) *Brand Portfolio Strategy* (New York: Free Press).

Amin, A. and Thrift, N. (1994) 'Living in the global', in Amin, A. and Thrift, N. (eds) *Globalization, Institutions, and Regional Development in Europe* (Oxford: Oxford University Press), pp. 2–5.

Archibugi, D. and Michie, J. (1997a) 'Technological globalisation and national systems of innovation: an introduction', in Archibugi, D. and Michie, J. (eds) *Technology, Globalisation and Economic Performance* (Cambridge: Cambridge University Press), pp. 1–23.

Archibugi, D. and Michie, J. (1997b) 'Globalisation of technology: a new taxonomy', in Archibugi, D. and Michie, J. (eds) *Technology, Globalisation and Economic Performance* (Cambridge: Cambridge University Press), pp. 173–240.

Baily, M. (2000) 'Innovation in the new economy', *OECD Observer*, 11 October 2000.

Bainbridge, D. (1996) *Intellectual Property*, 3rd edn (London: Pitman Publishing).

Balassa, B. (1962) *The Theory of Economic Integration* (London: Allen & Unwin).

Barnes, J.E. and Winter, G. (2001) 'Stressed out? Bad knee? Try a sip of these juices', *New York Times*, 27 May.

Barrett, D. (1997) 'Annual statistical table on global mission: 1997', *International Bulletin of Missionary Research*, **1**(1): 24–5.

Bartlett, C.A. and Ghoshal, S. (1990) 'Matrix management: not a structure, a frame of mind', *Harvard Business Review*, **90**(4): 138–45.

Bartlett, A. and Ghoshal, S. (1998) *Managing Across Borders: A Transnational Solution*, 2nd edn (London: Random House).

Bearak, B. (2000) 'In India, the wheels of justice hardly move', *New York Times*, 1 June.

Becht, M., Betts, P. and Morck, R. (2003) 'The complex evolution of family affairs', *Financial Times*, 3 February.

Beeson, M. (2000) 'The political economy of East Asia at a time of crisis', in Stubbs, R. and Underhill, G. (eds) *Political Economy and the Changing Global Order*, 2nd edn (Oxford: Oxford University Press), pp. 352–61.

Beetham, D. (1991) *The Legitimation of Power* (Basingstoke: Palgrave Macmillan).

Bell, M. and Pavitt, K. (1997) 'Technological accumulation and industrial growth: constrasts between developed and developing countries', in Archibugi, D. and Michie, J. (eds) *Technology, Globalisation and Economic Performance* (Cambridge: Cambridge University Press), pp. 83–137.

Berle, A. and Means, G. (1932) *The Modern Corporation and Private Property* (New York: Macmillan).

Betts, P. (2003) 'Ageing Europe faces the need for pension reform', *Financial Times*, 28 August.

Bhagwati, J. (1998) 'The capital myth', *Foreign Affairs*, **77**(3): 7–13.

Bhagwati, J. (1999) *A Stream of Windows* (Cambridge, MA: MIT Press).

Birkinshaw, J. (2000) 'The structures behind global companies', in *Mastering Management*, Part 10, *Financial Times*, 4 December.

Bourke, A. (2000) 'Overseas pharmaceutical firms in Ireland – insiders or outsiders?', in *Conference Proceedings of the Third Global Change Conference* (Manchester: The Manchester Metropolitan University), pp. 35–48.

Boyer, R., (1996) 'State and market: a new engagement for the twenty-first century?' in Boyer, R. and Drache, D. (eds) *States against Markets: The Limits of Globalization* (London: Routledge), pp. 84–114.

Bradshaw, M.J. (1996) 'The prospects for the post-socialist economies', in Daniels, P.W. and Lever, W.F. (eds) *The Global Economy in Transition* (Harlow: Addison Wesley), pp. 263–88.

Brassington, F. and Pettitt, S. (2003) *Principles of Marketing*, 3rd edn (Harlow: Pearson Education).

Bratton, J. and Gold, J. (2003) *Human Resource Management*, 3rd edn (Basingstoke: Palgrave Macmillan).

Brown, G.W. (2000) 'Seeking security in a volatile world' in *Mastering Risk*, Part Four, *Financial Times*, 16 May.

Buckley, P. (1999) 'Foreign direct investment by small- and medium-sized enterprises: the theoretical background', in Buckley, P. and Ghauri, P. (eds) *The Internationalization of the Firm*, 2nd edn (London: International Thomson), pp. 99–113.

Cabinet Office (UK) (2000) *Winning the Generation Game* (London: Cabinet Office).

Cantwell, J. (1989) *Technological Innovation and Multinational Corporations* (Oxford: Basil Blackwell).

Carroll, A.B. (1991) 'The pyramid of corporate social responsibility: toward the moral management of organizational stakeholders', *Business Horizons*, **34**: 39–48.

Castells, M. (2000a) *The Rise of the Network Society*, 2nd edn (Oxford: Blackwells).

Castells, M. (2000b) 'Information technology and global capitalism', in Giddens, A. and Hutton, W. (eds) *On the Edge: Living with Global Capitalism* (London: Jonathan Cape), pp. 52–74.

Castro, C. (2004) 'Sustainable development: mainstream and critical perspectives', *Organization & Environment*, **17**(2): 195–225.

Chandler, A. (1990) *Strategy and Structure: Chapters in the History of the Industrial Enterprise* (Cambridge, MA: The MIT Press).

Charkham, J. (1994) *Keeping Good Company: A Study of Corporate Governance in Five Countries* (Oxford: Oxford University Press).

CHI/MIT (2004) Technology Review Patent Scorecard 2004, at http://www.technologyreview.com.

Coates, D. (1999) 'Why growth rates differ', *New Political Economy*, **4**(1): 77–95.

Coggan, P. (2000) 'The weighting game', *Financial Times*, 8 June.

Coggan, P. (2004) 'The unravelling mystery: how will a sudden change in investor sentiment affect global markets in the long run?' *Financial Times*, 11 May.

Collier, P. (2000) *Economic Causes of Civil Conflict and their Implications for Policy* (World Bank).

Conference Board (1999) *International Patterns of Institutional Investment* (New York: The Conference Board) cited in *Financial Times*, 6 May 1999.

DEFRA (Department for Environment, Food & Rural Affairs) (2001) *Climate Change: Draft UK Programme*, at http://www.defra.gov.uk/environment.

De Haan, A. (1999) 'Livelihoods and poverty: the role of migration – a critical review of the migration literature', *The Journal of Development Studies*, **36**(2): 1–47.

Denza, E. (1999) 'Two legal orders: divergent or convergent?' *International and Comparative Law Quarterly* (48): 257–84.

Diamond, L. (1996) 'Is the third wave over?', *Journal of Democracy*, **7**(3): 21–39.

Dibb, S., Simkin, L., Pride, W. and Ferrell, O.C. (1997) *Marketing*, 3rd European edn (New York: Houghton Mifflin).

Dicken, P. (2003) *Global Shift*, 4th edn (London: Sage Publications).

Dicken, P. and Lloyd, P.E. (1990) *Location in Space: Theoretical Perspectives in Economic Grography*, 3rd edn (New York: Harper & Row).

Dickie, M. (2004) 'Chinese miners learn to live with danger', *Financial Times*, 21 December.

Dollar, D. (1999) *Aid and Poverty Reduction: What We know and What Else We Need to Know*, Paper for World Development Report on Poverty and Development 2000/01 (Washington, DC: Stiglitz Summer Research Workshop on Poverty).

Dreher, G. (2003) 'Aligning HR with business goals', in Pickford (ed), *Mastering People Management* (Harlow: FT/Prentice Hall), pp. 25–9.

Drucker, P. (1997) 'The global economy and the nation-state' *Foreign Affairs*, **76**(5): 159–72.

DTI (Department of Trade and Industry) (2000) *Small and Medium Enterprise (SME) Statistics for the UK, 1999* (London: Office of National Statistics).

Dunning, J.H. (1993a) *Multinational Enterprises and the Global Economy* (Wokingham: Addison Wesley).

Dunning, J.H. (1993b) *The Globalization of Business* (London: Routledge).

EBRD (European Bank for Reconstruction and Development) (2000) *Transition Report 2000* (London: EBRD).

Eichengreen, B. (1996) *Globalizing Capital: A History of the International Monetary System* (Princeton: Princeton University Press).

Eurobarometer (1998) *Eurobarometer 48*, at http:europa.eu.int/comm./dg10.

Eurostat (2004) *Statistics in Focus: Industry, Trade and Services* (Luxemburg: Eurostat).

Fairbanks, M. (2000) 'Changing the mind of a nation: elements in a process of creating prosperity', in Harrison, L. and Huntington, S. (eds) *Culture Matters: How Values Shape Human Progress* (New York: Basic Books), pp. 268–81.

Fields, J. and Casper, L. (2001) *America's Families and Living Arrangements: March 2000*, Current Population Reports, No. P20–537 (Washington, DC: US Census Bureau).

Freeman, C. (1997) 'The "national system of innovation" in historical perspective', in Archibugi, D. and Michie, J. (eds) *Technology, Globalisation and Economic Performance* (Cambridge: Cambridge University Press), pp. 24–49.

Freeman, C. and Soete, L. (1997) *The Economics of Industrial Innovation*, 3rd edn (London: Cassell).

Freeman, P. and Robbins, A. (1995) 'The promise of biotechnology for vaccines', in Fransman, M., Junne, G. and Roobeek, A. (eds) *The Biotechnology Revolution* (Oxford: Blackwells), pp. 174–83.

Freeman, R.E. (1984) *Strategic Management: A Stakeholder Approach* (Boston, MA: Pitman).

Fukuyama, F. (1999) *The Great Disruption: Human Nature and the Reconstitution of Social Order* (London: Profile Books).

Gallup Europe (2002) 'Entrepreneurship', Eurobarometer 134, at http://eosgallupeurope.com.

Gankema, H., Snuif, H. and Zwart, P. (2000) 'The internationalization process of small and medium-sized enterprises: an evaluation of stage theory', *Journal of Small Business Management*, **38**(4): 15–28.

Gerlach, M. (1991) *Alliance Capitalism: The Social Organization of Japanese Business* (Berkeley: University of California Press).

Giddens, A. (1997) *Sociology*, 3rd edn (Cambridge: Polity Press).

Giddens, A. and Hutton, W. (2000) 'Fighting back', in Giddens, A. and Hutton, W. (eds) *On the Edge: Living with Global Capitalism* (London: Jonathan Cape), pp. 213–23.

Gilpin, R. (2000) *The Challenge of Global Capitalism: The World Economy in the 21st Century* (Princeton: Princeton University Press).

Global Reach (2004) 'Global Internet Statistics (b Language)' at http://glreach.com/globstats/.

Glotz, P. (1995) 'East European reform and West European integration' in Walzer, M. (ed), *Toward a Global Civil Society* (Providence, RI: Berghahn Books), pp. 211–22.

Glynn, J., Perrin, J. and Murphy, M. (1998) *Accounting for Managers*, 2nd edn (London: International Thomson Press).

Graham, R. (2001) 'Corsica hope of autonomy rises with historic law', *Financial Times*, 23 May.

Grant, J. (2004) 'Vehicle suppliers "to extend R&D role"', *Financial Times*, 22 July.

Grant, J. and Mackintosh, J. (2004) '"Year of the car": how the Big Three are battling to regain the lead in one of their most crucial markets', *Financial Times*, 5 January.

Gray, J. (1998) *False Dawn: The Delusions of Global Capitalism* (London: Granta Books).

Griffith-Jones, S. (1999) 'Stabilizing capital flows to developing countries', in Michie, J. and Grieve Smith, J. (eds), *Global Instability: The Political Economy of World Economic Governance* (London: Routledge), pp. 68–96.

Grimes, C. (2004) 'Big shift forecast in US ethnic make-up', *Financial Times*, 18 March.

Hall, M.R. and Hall, E.T. (1960) 'The silent language of overseas business', *Harvard Business Review*, **38**(3): 87–95.

Hamel, G. and Prahalad, C.K. (1994) *Competing for the Future* (Boston, MA: Harvard Business School Press).

Hamel, G. and Skarzynski, P. (2001) 'Innovation: the new route to new wealth', *Leader to Leader*, **19**(Winter 2001): 16–21.

Harney, A. (2004) 'Politics complicates neighbours' battle against pollution', *Financial Times*, 13 August.

Harris, L. (1999) 'Will the real IMF please stand up: What does the Fund do and what should it do?', in Michie, J. and Grieve Smith, J. (eds), *Global Instability: The Political Economy of World Economic Governance* (London: Routledge), pp. 198–211.

Harvey, F. (2004) 'Cashing in on climate change: trade in carbon credits takes off', *Financial Times*, 22 October.

Hawthorn, J. (1993) 'Sub-Saharan Africa' in Held, D. (ed.) *Prospects for Democracy* (Cambridge: Polity Press), pp. 330–54.

Held, D., McGrew, A., Goldblatt, D. and Perraton, J. (1999) *Global Transformations: Politics, Economics and Culture* (Cambridge: Polity Press).

Hirst, P. and Thompson, G. (1999) *Globalization in Question*, 2nd edn (Cambridge: Polity Press).

HM Treasury (2000) *Budget: March 2000* (London: HM Treasury) at http://www.hm-treasury.gov.uk/budget2000.

HM Treasury (2004a) *Budget 2004* (London: The Stationery Office).

HM Treasury (2004b) 'Public Sector Finances, April 2004' at http://www.statistics.gov.uk.

Hofstede, G., (1994) *Cultures and Organizations: Software of the Mind* (London: HarperCollins).

Hofstede, G. (1996) 'Images of Europe: past, present and future' in Joynt, P. and Warner, M. (eds), *Managing Across Cultures: Issues and Perspectives* (London: International Thomson Business Press), pp. 147–65.

Home Office (1999) *A Consultation Paper on the Integration of Recognised Refugees in the UK* (London: The Home Office).

Home Office (2000) *Control of Immigration: Statistics, United Kingdom, First Half 2000* (Croydon: Immigration Research and Statistics Service).

Hoon-Halbauer, S.K. (1999) 'Managing relationships within Sino-foreign joint ventures', *Journal of World Business*, **34**(4): 344–72.

Howells, J. and Wood, M. (1993) *The Globalisation of Production and Technology* (London: Belhaven Press).

Houlder, V. (2003) 'Guilt is no solution', *Financial Times*, 16 October.

Houlder, V. (2004) 'Industry says the environmental case overlooks consumer responsibilities', *Financial Times*, 28 February.

Hubbard, N. (1999) *Acquisition: Strategy and Implementation* (Basingstoke: Macmillan – now Palgrave Macmillan).

Huntington, S. (1991) *The Third Wave: Democratization in the Late Twentieth Century* (Norman: University of Oklahoma Press).

Huntington, S. (1996) *The Clash of Civilizations and the Remaking of World Order* (New York: Touchstone).

Hutton, W. (2000) 'Anthony Giddens and Will Hutton in conversation' in Hutton, W. and Giddens, A. (eds) *On the Edge: Living with Global Capitalism* (London: Jonathan Cape), pp. 1–51.

Ibison, D. (2003) 'Japan spurns small business despite Tokyo's best efforts', *Financial Times*, 21 November.

ILO (International Labour Organization) (2001a) *World Employment Report 2000*, (Geneva: ILO)

ILO (International Labour Organization) (2001b) *The Elimination of all Forms of Forced or Compulsory Labour* (Geneva: ILO).

ILO (International Labour Organization) (2002) *Every Child Counts: New Global Estimates on Child Labour* (Geneva: ILO).

ILO (International Labour Organization) (2004) *A Fair Globalization: Creating Opportunities for All* (Geneva: ILO).

International Institute for Sustainable Development (1992) 'Business strategies for sustainable development', at http://www.bdsglobal.com.

Inter-Parliamentary Union (2004) 'Women in National Parliaments', at http://www.ipu.org.

Jackson, S. and Schuler, R. (2000) 'Turning knowledge into business', *Mastering Management*, Part 14, *Financial Times*, 15 January 2001.

Johnson, C. (1982) *MITI and the Japanese Miracle* (Stanford: Stanford University Press).

Juergensmeyer, M. (2003) *Terror in the Mind of God: The Global Rise of Religious Violence*, 3rd edn (Berkeley: University of California Press).

Kahn, J. (2000) 'U.S. offers Africa billions to fight AIDS', *New York Times*, 19 July.

Kapstein, E.B. (1994) *Governing the Global Economy: International Finance and the State* (Cambridge, MA: Harvard University Press).

Keynes, J.M. (1936) *The General Theory of Employment, Interest and Money* (London: Macmillan – now Palgrave Macmillan).

Kim, S.K. and Kim, S.H. (1999) *Global Corporate Finance: Text and Cases*, 4th edn (Oxford: Blackwells).

Knight, G. and Cavusgil, S. (2004) 'Innovation, organizational capabilities and the born-global firm', *Journal of International Business Studies*, **35**(2): 124–41.

Kotler, P., Armstrong, G., Saunders, J. and Wong, V. (2002) *Principles of Marketing*, 3rd European edn (London: Prentice Hall Europe).

Kovacic, W. and Shapiro, C. (2000) 'Antitrust policy: a century of economic and legal thinking', *Journal of Economic Perspectives*, **14**(1): 43–60.

Krugman, P. (1994) *Rethinking International Trade* (Cambridge, MA: MIT Press).

Krugman, P. (1999) *The Return of Depression Economics* (Harmondsworth: The Penguin Press).

Krugman, P. (2004) *The Great Unravelling* (Harmondsworth: The Penguin Press).

Kullberg, J. and Zimmerman, W. (1999) 'Liberal elites, socialist masses and problems of Russian democracy', *World Politics*, **51**: 323–58.

Kynge, J. and McGregor, R. (2002) 'China sees role for private sector in need to create jobs for millions', *Financial Times*, 11 November.

Labour Party (2001) *Ambitions for Britain: Labour's manifesto 2001* (London: The Labour Party).

Landes, D. (1998) *The Wealth and Poverty of Nations* (London: Little, Brown and Company).

Landwell (2000) *Time for law and order*, at http://www.Landwellglobal.com.

Leys, S., translator and editor (1997) *Analects of Confucius* (New York: W.W. Norton & Co.).

Linden, E., (1996) 'The exploding cities of the developing world', *Foreign Affairs*, **75**(1): 52–66.

Lindsay, S. (2000) 'Culture, mental models and national prosperity', in Harrison, L. and Huntington, S., (eds) *Culture Matters: How Values Shape Human Progress* (New York: Basic Books), pp. 282–95.

Linz, J. (1993) 'Perils of presidentialism', in Diamond, L. and Plattner, M.F. (eds), *The Global Resurgence of Democracy* (Baltimore: The Johns Hopkins University Press), pp. 108–26.

Linz, J. and Stepan, A. (1997) 'Toward consolidated democracies', *Journal of Democracy*, **7**(2): 14–33.

Liu, B. (2004) 'Krispy Kreme looks to its global roll-out', *Financial Times*, 25 March.

London School of Economics (1998) *Social Welfare Systems in East Asia: A Comparative Analysis* (London: LSE Centre for Analysis of Social Exclusion).

Longman, P. and Ahmad, S. (1998) 'The bailout backlash' *U.S. News & World Report*, **124**(4), 2 February 1998.

Lundvall, B.-A. (ed.) (1992) *National Systems of Innovation*, (London: Pinter).

Macpherson, C.B. (1973) *Democratic Theory* (Oxford: Clarendon Press).

Maddison, A. (1991) *Dynamic Forces in Capitalist Development* (Oxford: Oxford University Press).

Maddison, A. (2001) *The World Economy: A Millennial Perspective* (Paris: OECD).

Marchington, M. (1995) 'Involvement and participation', in Storey, J. (ed.) *Human Resource Management: A Critical Text* (London: Routledge), pp. 280–305.

McGregor, R. (2001) 'Legal evolution with strings attached', *Financial Times*, 2 May.

McWilliams, A. (2001) 'Corporate social responsibility: a theory of the firm perspective', *Academy of Management Review*, **26**(1): 117–28.

McWilliams, A. and Siegel, D. (2000) 'Corporate social responsibility and financial performance: correlation or misspecification?, *Strategic Management Journal*, **21**: 603–9.

Michie, J. and Kitson (eds) (1995) *Managing the Global Economy* (Oxford: Oxford University Press).

Miers, D.R. and Page, A.C. (1990) *Legislation*, 2nd edn (London: Sweet & Maxwell).

Mikesell, R.F. (2000) 'Bretton Woods – original intentions and current problems', *Contemporary Economic Policy*, **18**(4): 404–15.

Miller, M.A.L. (1995) *The Third World in Global Environmental Politics* (Boulder, Colorado: Lynne Reinner).

Mintzberg, H. (2000) *The Rise and Fall of Strategic Planning*, (London: Pearson Education).

Mitchell, R.K., Agle, B.R. and Wood, D.J. (1997) 'Toward a theory of stakeholder identification and salience: defining the principle of who and what really counts', *Academy of Management Review*, **22**(4): 853–86.

Moens, G. and Gillies, P. (1998) *International Trade and Business: Law, Policy and Ethics* (Sydney: Cavendish Publishing).

Monks, R. and Minow, N. (1996) *Watching the Watchers: Corporate Governance for the 21st Century* (Cambridge, MA: Blackwells).

Morse, G., (1991) *Partnership Law*, 2nd edn (London: Blackstone Press).

Morse, G. (1995) *Charlesworth & Morse Company Law*, 15th edn (London: Sweet & Maxwell).

Mowery, D.C. and Oxley, J. (1997) 'Inward technology transfer and competitiveness' in Archibugi, D. and Michie, J. (eds) *Technology, Globalisation and Economic Performance* (Cambridge: Cambridge University Press), pp. 138–71.

Murray, S. (2001) 'Green products: count cost over ecology', *Financial Times*, 5 November.

National Statistics (UK) (2000) *Acquisitions and Mergers Involving UK Companies*, 3rd quarter 2000, 7 November 2000 (London: National Statistics).

New York Stock Exchange (2000) *An International Marketplace* (New York Stock Exchange).

OECD (Organization for Economic Co-operation and Development) (1999) 'The core of the matter', *OECD Observer*, 2 October 1999.

OECD (Organization for Economic Co-operation and Development) (2000a) 'Cross-border trade in financial services: economics and regulation', *Financial Market Trends*, **75**, March.

OECD (Organization for Economic Co-operation and Development) (2000b) 'Recent trends in foreign direct investment', *Financial Market Trends*, **76**, June.

OECD (Organization for Economic Co-operation and Development) (2000c) 'Science, technology and innovation in the new economy', *OECD Observer*, September.

OECD (Organization for Economic Co-operation and Development) (2000d) *Guidelines for Multinational Enterprises* (Paris: OECD).

OECD (Organization for Economic Co-operation and Development) (2002) *OECD Small and Medium Enterprise Outlook* (Paris: OECD).

OECD (Organization for Economic Co-operation and Development) (2003a) *OECD in Figures* (Paris: OECD).

OECD (Organization for Economic Co-operation and Development) (2003b) *Science, Industry and Technology Scoreboard 2003* (Paris: OECD).

OECD (Organization for Economic Co-operation and Development) (2004) *OECD Principles of Corporate Governance* (Paris: OECD).

Ohmae, K. (1995) *The End of the Nation State* (London: HarperCollins).

Ohmae, K. (2000) *The Invisible Continent: Four Strategic Imperatives of the New Economy* (London: Nicholas Brealey Publishing).

Olsen, J.E. (2001) 'Environmental problems and ethical jurisdiction: The case concerning Texaco in Ecuador', *Business Ethics: A European Review*, **10**(1): 71–7.

ONS (Office for National Statistics) (2000a) *Social Trends 30* (London: Stationery Office).

ONS (Office for National Statistics) (2000b) *Labour Force Survey: Labour Market Trends* (London: Stationery Office).

ONS (Office for National Statistics) (2003) *Labour Market Statistics*, at http://www.statistics.gov.uk

ONS (Office for National Statistics) (2004a) *Labour Market Trends* (London: ONS).

ONS (Office for National Statistics) (2004b) *UK 2005: The Official Yearbook* (London: ONS).

ONS (Office for National Statistics) (2004c) *Living in Britain: The 2002 General Household Survey* (London: ONS).

Parkin, M., Powell, M. and Matthews, K. (1997) *Economics*, 3rd edn (Essex: Addison Wesley).

Patel, P. and Pavitt, K. (1991) 'Large firms in the production of the world's technology: an important case of "non-globalisation"', *Journal of International Business Studies*, **22**: 1–21.

Patel, P. and Pavitt, K. (1994) 'National innovation systems: why they are important and how they might be measured and compared', *Economics of Innovation and New Technology*, **3**: 77–95.

Patel, P. and Pavitt, K. (2000) 'National systems of innovation under strain: the internationalisation of corporate R&D', in Barrell, R., Mason, G. and O'Mahony, M. (eds) *Productivity, innovation and economic performance* (Cambridge: Cambridge University Press), pp. 217–35.

Patten, C. (1998) *East and West* (Basingstoke: Macmillan – now Palgrave Macmillan).

Paul, R. (2000) 'The Increasing Maze of International Pre-Acquisition Notification', *International Company and Commercial Law Review*, April 2000, at http://www.whitecase.com/

Pauly, L.W. and Reich, S. (1997) 'National structures and multinational corporate behavior: enduring differences in the age of globalization', *International Organization*, **51**(1): 1–30.

Peiperi, M. (1997) 'Does empowerment deliver the goods?', in *Mastering Management*, (London: Financial Times/Pitman), pp. 283–7.

Piercy, N. and Giles, W. (1989) 'Making SWOT analysis work', *Marketing Intelligence and Planning*, **7**(5): 5–7.

Pettigrew, A.M. (1997) 'Context and action in the transformation of the firm', in Pugh, D.S. (ed.) *Organization Theory: Selected Readings*, 4th edn (Harmondsworth: Penguin), pp. 460–85.

Pontusson, J. (1997) 'Between neo-liberalisim and the German model: Swedish capitalism in transition', in Crouch, C. and Streeck, W. (eds) *Political Economy of Modern Capitalism* (London: Sage), pp. 55–70.

Porter, M. (1998a) *Competitive strategy: techniques for analyzing industries and competitors* (with new introduction) (New York: Free Press).

Porter, M. (1998b) *The Competitive Advantage of Nations* (Basingstoke: Macmillan – now Palgrave Macmillan).

Porter, M. (1998c) *On Competition* (Boston: Harvard Business Review Publishing).

Porter, M. and van der Linde, C. (1995) 'Green and competitive: ending the stalemate' in Porter, M. (1998) *On Competition* (Boston: Harvard Business Review Publishing), pp. 351–75.

Pugh, D.S. (1997) 'Introduction to the fourth edition', in Pugh, D.S. (ed.) *Organization Theory: Selected Readings* (Harmondsworth: Penguin Books), pp. xi–xiii.

Ramirez, R. and de la Cruz, G. P. (2002) 'The Hispanic Population in the United States: March 2002' *Current Population Reports*, No. P20–545 (Washington, DC: US Census Bureau).

Reich, R. (1991) *The Work of Nations: Preparing Ourselves for 21st Century Capitalism* (London: Simon & Schuster).

Reynolds, A. (1999) 'Women in the legislatures and executives of the world: knocking at the highest glass ceiling', *World Politics*, **51**: 547–72.

Rex, J. (1996) *Ethnic Minorities in the Modern Nation State* (Basingstoke: Macmillan – now Palgrave Macmillan).

Rhodes, R.A.W. (1996) 'The new governance: governing without government', *Political Studies*, **XLIV**: 654–67.

Ricardo, D. ([1817] 1973) *Principles of Political Economy and Taxation* (London: Dent).

Rivlin, R. (2000) 'Old economy, new private optimism', *Financial Times*, 9 June 2000.

Rose, F. (1999) 'Think globally, script locally', *Fortune*, **140**(9): 156–60.

Rozman, G. (1991) 'Comparisons of modern Confucian values in China and Japan' in Rozman, G. (ed.), *The East Asian Region: Confucian Heritage and Its Modern Adaptation* (Princeton, N.J.: Princeton University Press), pp. 157–203.

Sabel, C.F. (1994) 'Flexible specialisation and the re-emergence of regional economics', in Amin, A. (ed.) *Post-Fordism: A Reader* (Oxford: Basil Blackwell), pp. 101–56.

Sandler, T. (2003) 'Collective Action and Transnational Terrorism', Leverhulme Centre for Research On Globalisation and Economic Policy, Research Paper Series, No. 2003/13 at http://www.nottingham.ac.uk/economics/leverhulme/.

Sartori, G. (1997) 'Understanding pluralism', *Journal of Democracy*, **8**(4): 58–69.

Sassen, S. (1998) *Globalization and its Discontents* (New York: The New Press).

Schaffer, R., Earle, B. and Agusti, F. (1999) *International Business Law and its Environment*, 4th edn (Cincinnati: West).

Schein, E.J. (1992) *Organizational Culture and Leadership*, 2nd edn (San Francisco: Jossey-Bass).

Schmitter, P.C. and Karl, T.L. 'What democracy is ... and is not', in Diamond, L. and Platnerr, M.F. (eds) *The Global Resurgence of Democracy* (Baltimore: The Johns Hopkins University Press, 1993), pp. 39–52.

Schumpeter, J.A. (1942) *Capitalism, Socialism and Democracy* (New York: Harper & Row, 1975 edn), originally published in 1942.

Sell, S. (2000) 'Big business and the new trade agreements' in Stubbs, R. and Underhill, G., *Political Economy and the Changing Global Order*, 2nd edn (Oxford: Oxford University Press), pp. 174–183.

Simon, B. (2005) 'A tale of two states: how Alabama is motoring as Michigan slows down', *Financial Times*, 6 May.

Singh, A. (1999) '"Asian capitalism" and the financial crisis', in Michie, J. and Grieve Smith, J. (eds) *Global Instability: The political economy of world economic governance* (London: Routledge).

Singh, V. and Vinnicombe, S. (2003) *The Female FTSE Report 2003* (Bedford: Cranfield School of Management).

Skapinker, M. (2003) 'In search of a balanced society', *Financial Times*, 16 September.

Slack, N., Chambers, S. and Johnson, R. (2004) *Operations Management*, 4th edn (Harlow: FT/Prentice Hall).

Smith, A. ([1776]1950) *An Inquiry into the Nature and Causes of the Wealth of Nations* (London; Methuen).

Smith, A.D. (1990) 'Towards a global culture' in Featherstone, M. (ed.) *Global Culture: Nationalism, Globalization, and Modernity* (London: Sage Publications), pp. 171–91.

Smith, A.D. (1991) *National Identity* (London: Penguin Books).

Stanworth, C. (2000) 'Women and work in the information age', *Gender, Work and Organization*, **7**(1): 20–31.

Statham, P. (1999) 'Political mobilisation by minorities in Britain: negative feedback of "race relations"', *Journal of Ethnic and Migration Studies*, **25**(4): 597–626.

Stiglitz, J. (2000) 'The insider', *New Republic*, **222**(16/17) 17 April 2000: 56–60.

Stiglitz, J. (2002) *Globalization and Its Discontents* (London: Allen Lane).

Stoner, J. and Freeman, R. (1992) *Management*, 5th edn (New Jersey: Prentice-Hall).

Storey, J. (ed.) (1995) *Human Resource Management: A Critical Text* (London: Routledge).

Story, J. (2003) *China: The Race to Market* (Harlow: FT/Prentice Hall).

Streeck, W. (1996) 'Public power beyond the nation-state' in Boyer, R. and Drache, D. (eds) *States against Markets: The Limits of Globalization* (London: Routledge), pp. 299–315.

Streeck, W. (1997) 'German capitalism: does it exist? Can it survive?' *New Political Economy*, **2**(2): 237–56.

Stulz, R. (2000) 'Why risk management is not rocket science', *Mastering Risk*, Part 10, p. 6, *Financial Times*, 27 June, 2000.

Stutz, F.P. and deSouza, A.R. (1998) *The World Economy: Resources, Location, Trade and Development*, 3rd edn (Upper Saddle, NJ: Prentice Hall).

Taylor, A. and McNulty, S. (2004) 'The nuclear option: why atomic power is creeping back into political favour', *Financial Times*, 10 August.

Terpstra, V. and David, K. (1991) *The Cultural Environment of International Business* (Cincinnati: South-Western Publishing Co.).

Therrien, M. and Ramirez, R. (2000) *The Hispanic Population in the United States: March, 2000*, Current Population Reports, P20–535 (Washington, DC: US Census Bureau).

Thomas, J.B., Clark, S.M. and Gioia, D.A. (1993) 'Strategic sensemaking and organizational performance: Linkages among scanning, interpretation, action, and outcomes,' *Academy of Management Journal* (April, 1993): 239–70.

Tolentino, P.E. (1999) 'Transnational rules for transnational corporations: What next?', in Michie, J. and Grieve Smith, J. (eds) *Global Instability: The Political Economy of World Economic Governance* (London: Routledge), pp. 171–97.

Trompenaars, F. (1994) *Riding the Waves of Culture* (New York: Irwin).

Turner, D. (2004) 'Awkward times for trades unions struggling to win members and regain influence', *Financial Times*, 17/18 April.

Tyson, L.D. (1992) *Who's Bashing Whom? Trade Conflict in High-Technology Industries* (Washington, DC: Institute for International Economics).

UNCTAD (United Nations Conference on Trade and Development) (2004) *Trade and Development Report 2004* (New York: UNCTAD).

UNDP (United Nations Development Programme) (2003) *Human Development Report 2003* (New York: UNDP).

UNDP (United Nations Development Programme) (2004) *Human Development Report 2004* (New York: UNDP).

United Nations (1999a) *World Investment Report 1999* (Geneva: United Nations).

United Nations (1999b) *Human Development Report 1999* (Oxford: Oxford University Press).

United Nations (2000) *Human Development Report 2000* (Oxford: Oxford University Press).

United Nations (2003) *World Investment Report 2003* (Geneva: United Nations).

United Nations (2004) *World Investment Report 2004* (Geneva: United Nations).

United Nations Food and Agriculture Organization (2003) *The State of Food Insecurity in the World*, at http://www.fao.org.

United Nations Industrial Development Organization (UNIDO) (2000) *Enhancing Competitiveness of SMEs in the Global Economy: Strategies and Policies*, at http://www.unido.org/doc/ee1214.htmls.

United Nations Office for Drug Control and Crime Prevention (1999) *Global Report on Crime and Justice* (Oxford: Oxford University Press).

United Nations Policy Working Group (2002) *Report of the Policy Working Group on the United Nations and Terrorism*, Ref. A/57/273, at http://www.un.org/terrorism/a57273.htm.

United Nations Population Division (2000) *Replacement Migration: Is it a Solution to Declining and Ageing Populations?*, http://www.un.org/esa/population/migration/htm.

United Nations Population Division (2002) *International Migration Report 2002* (New York: UN).

United Nations Population Division (2003) *World Population Prospects: The 2002 Revision* (New York: UN).

United Nations Population Division (2004) *World Urbanization Prospects: The 2003 Revision* (New York: UN).

United Nations Security Council (2004) *Security Council Sanctions Committee: An Overview*, at http://www.un.org/Docs/sc/committees.

US Census Bureau (2002) *American Community Survey Profile 2002*, at http://www.census.gov/acs.

US Patent Office (2003) *2003 US Patent and Trademark Office Performance and Accountability Report*, at http://www.uspto.gov.

Vitols, S. (2000) 'Globalization: a fundamental change to the German model:' in Stubbs, R. and Underhill, G. (eds) *Political Economy and the Changing Global Order*, 2nd edn (Oxford: Oxford University Press), pp. 373–81.

Walby, S. (1999) 'Transformations of the gendered political economy: changes in women's employment in the United Kingdom', *New Political Economy*, 4(2): 195–213.

Walzer, M. (1992) *Just and Unjust Wars*, 2nd edn (HarperCollins).

Walzer, M. (2004) *Arguing about War* (New Haven: Yale University Press)

Ward, A. (2004) 'Lessons leave no time to play in Seoul', *Financial Times*, 18 February.

Waters, M. (2001) *Globalization*, 2nd edn (London: Routledge).

Weber, M. (1930) *The Protestant Ethic and the Spirit of Capitalism* (New York: Scribner's).

Weir, G. (2003) 'Self-employment in the UK labour market', *Labour Market Trends* 111(9): 441–51.

Wells, L.T. (ed.) (1972) *The Product Life Cycle and International Trade* (Boston, MA: Harvard Business School Press).

Whitley, R.D. (1999) *Divergent Capitalisms* (Oxford: Oxford University Press).

WIPO (World Intellectual Property Organization) (2004) *PCT Statistical Indicators* (Geneva: WIPO).

Wolf, M. (2004) 'The Fund is ill equipped for the job it was meant to do', *Financial Times*, 10 March.

Wolin, S. (1993) 'Democracy, difference, and re-cognition', *Political Theory*, 21(3): 464–83.

World Bank (1999) *Cities Alliance for Cities without Slums* (World Bank).

World Bank (2000a) *Entering the 21st Century: World Development Report 1999–2000* (Oxford: Oxford University Press).

World Bank (2000b) *Can Africa Claim the 21st Century*, at http://www.worldbank.org/afr.

World Bank (2000c) *Global Economic Prospects and the Developing Countries, 2001*, at http://www.worldbank.org/prospects/gep2001.

World Bank (2002) *World Development Report 2003* (Washington, DC: The World Bank).

World Bank (2004) *World Development Report 2005* (Washington, DC: The World Bank).

World Business Council for Sustainable Development (2002) *The Business Case for Sustainable Development* (Geneva: World Business Council for Sustainable Development).

Wright, L. (2004) 'Acid test for the marine web of life', *Financial Times*, 24 September.

Zimmerer, T. and Scarborough, N. (1998) *Essentials of Entrepreneurship and Small Business Management*, 2nd edn (New Jersey: Prentice Hall).

Zweigert, K. and Kötz, H. (1998) *Introduction to Comparative Law*, 3rd edn (Oxford: Clarendon Press).

Index

A

ABB, 17, 162
AB Electronics (Cardiff), 157–8
accounting and finance, 37, 56–9, 63
   international, 58
Aceh, 404
Acid rain, 431–2, 445
Ackermann, Josef, 409–10
acquisitions, 406–8, 416–18
   global (1999–2000), 408
Adidas, 143
adjudication, 280–1
advertising, 47–50, 104–5, 130–2, 177, 215–17
   and ethics, 50
aerospace industry, 326–7, 416–18
Africa, xviii, 206, 238, 246, 265–6, 176, 382, 428, 437, 450, 462
   and AIDS, 454, 475–6
   child labour, 466–7
   colonial boundaries, 238
   and cotton, 456
   debt, 412
   development prospects, 457–60
   and FDI, 412
   political elites, 265–6
   population, 221
   poverty, 453–7
   vulnerability of ecosystems, 430
age discrimination, 214–15
ageing, 213–16
Agnelli, Gianni, 307, 309
agriculture, 70–1, 122, 125–6, 210, 222, 236, 328–9, 332, 335–6, 340, 381–2, 425–6, 457–8
   subsidies, 458
   and water, 430–1
Ahold, 160
AIDS, 453–4, 470, 475–6
airlines, 104, 109
Air Touch, 409
air travel, 39–40
   and global warming, 40
AKP (Justice and Development Party, Turkey), 283
Albania, 183
Algeria, 183, 316
alliance capitalism, 113
al-Qaeda, 184
Amazon.com, 6, 7, 366, 377

America, see US
American Express, 207
Amicus, 226
Amnesty International, 266, 467
Amoco, 407
ANCOM (Andean Common Market), 339
Angola, 437
anti-terrorism legislation, 244
anti-trust law (US), 106–7, 127, 131–2, 336, 407, 411
AOL, 200, 406–8
APEC (Asia Pacific Economic Cooperation), 339, 341, 343
Apple Computers, 24, 60–1, 374
arbitrage, 396
arbitration, 280, 291–2, 305
Argentina, 69, 224, 381, 372
   financial crisis, 397–400
   and the IMF, 398–400
   motor industry, 372
   recovery, 399–400
Arkwright, Richard, 353–4
Arthur Andersen, 57
asbestos, 294–6
   class action, 294–6
Asda, 160
ASEAN (Association of South East Asian Nations), 127, 339, 341, 343
Asia, xix, 428, 450, 455
   and child labour, 466–7
   and credit cards, 206–7
   and families, 230–1
   and FDI, 412
Asian
   culture, 187
   family business, 231
Asian financial crisis (1997), 113–15, 138, 190, 317, 395, 397, 401–5, 450, 468
   causes, 401–2, 405
   and the IMF, 402–5, 412–14
Asian
   model of capitalism, 401
   religions, 180, 186–7
   'tiger' economies, 112–16, 325
   values, 169, 173, 186–8, 231
assimilation, 189–90
AstraZeneca, 382, 475
Atrica, 344
Australia, 69, 96, 162, 176, 183, 190, 192, 218, 320–2, 368, 459

ageing population, 215
   greenhouse gas emissions, 427, 429
   and Kyoto Protocol, 428
   wine exports, 320–1
Austria, 123, 192, 220, 271, 322, 358
authoritarianism, 239, 247–9, 263, 451
authority, 235, 240, 246–50, 259
automobile industry, see motor industry
Aventis, 475
Aviva, 229
Avon Automotive, 158
Ayatollah Khomeini, 183
Azerbaijan, 437
Azriar, José Maria (Spain), 251

B

baby boomers, 216–17
balance of payments, 75–6, 91, 393, 397
Balassa, *Theory of Economic Integration*, 338
Bangkok Bank of Commerce, 401
Bangladesh, 219, 428, 455
Bank of England, 82, 85
banks, 80–2, 85–6, 90, 91, 109, 114, 147, 177, 206–7, 229, 340, 387, 391, 401–2, 405
   Muslim, 183
   role in the economy, 81–2
Bayer, 475
behaviour and norms, 168–9, 172–3, 201
Belgium, 123, 162, 247, 250, 269, 271, 439
Benin, 456, 459
Berlusconi, Silvio (Italy), 254, 308–9
Bertelsmann, 200
Bezos, Jeff, 6, 7 see also Amazon.com
Bhopal, India, 295, 433
biodiversity, 382, 435,
   industrial threat to, 425–6
biotechnology, 359–60, 370, 380–2, 474–5
   and cloning, 380
   and patent applications, 368
   and vaccines, 380

BJP (Bharatiya Janata Party), 186, 257
Boeing, 327, 336
Bolivia, 459
bond markets, 391–2, 396–400
   global bonds, 392, 399
Bond, Michael Harris, 192
boom and bust, 80, 155
borderless world, 469
Bosnia, 119, 174, 268
BP, 145, 407
brain drain, 219
branding, 45–9, 105, 120, 130–2, 160, 170, 287–8, 320–1
   and cultural differences, 176–7
   brand recognition, 105, 120
brands, global, 130–2, 143, 144, 169–72
Brazil, 69, 100, 159, 176, 183, 193, 224, 342, 359, 461–2, 468
   and China, 342
   and coffee, 461–2
   and exports, 342–3
   and FDI, 412
   financial crisis, 397, 399
   greenhouse gas emissions, 427, 433
Bretton Woods international monetary system (1944–1971), 155, 331, 393–5, 397–8, 414, 471
bribery, 298, 467
Bridgestone tyres, 297
Brin, Sergey, 378–9
British Airways, 39–40
Brunei, 437
Brussels Convention, 292
BT (British Telecom), 11, 15, 108, 229–30
Buddhism, 180, 185–6
building societies, 391
Bulgaria, 119, 125–6
bureaucracy, 21
   Fordist, 156
bureaucratic structures
   reform of, 21–2
Burger King, 9, 407
Burkina Faso, 456, 459
Burma, 186
Bush, George W., 260
business
   born-globals, 6

classification of, 7–12: by size, 11–12
cycles, 79–80, 91, 354
definition of, 5
as an economic activity, 2, 4–5
and the environment, xxvi, 37, 43, 424–6, 435–43
environment/s, xxiii–iv, 2–6, 30–3, 95–7, 114, 156, 449–50
and family, 25, 26, 113–14, 230–1
see also chaebol; Confucian ethic; Disney; Fiat
functions, 6, 30–3, 36–63
global, and competition, 106
global nature of, xxiii–iv, 4–6
hierarchies, 14–16, 21–2, 23, 34
and innovation, 17
internal/external environment, 4, 30–33, 43
international, see international business
internationalization of, 43, 54–6
and legal systems, 136, 146, 276–84
networks, 21–2
operations, see operations
organization, 5–6, 13–17
ownership, 5, 7–10 see also family business; partnership; private ownership; state-ownership
and politics, 136, 146, 235–41, 245–6, 250–2, 260, 264–6
and pollution, 437–42
and social change, 204–32
and society, 136
state ownership, 94–5, 105, 108–10, 117, 122, 128
and sustainable development, 424, 434–6, 443–4
business strategy, 18–21, 30, 33, 34, 37, 39, 57, 59, 61–3
analysis: PEST, 30–1, 34: SWOT, 31–4
and change, 21
and developing countries, 457
emergent strategy approach, 20
planning approach, 20
tools, 30–33
top-down, 19
see also operations
business structure, 23, 33 see also companies; corporations; organizations
B2B e-commerce, 380, 384

C
Cafédirect, 462–3
call centres, 71, 210, 228–30
abroad, 229–30

Cambodia, 143, 455
cameras, digital, 39, 59
Cameroon, 462
Canada, 162, 175, 218, 247, 250, 266, 322, 341–2, 358–9, 381
greenhouse gas emissions, 427, 429
internet pharmacies, 476
CAP (Common Agriculture Policy), 125, 329, 341
capital, 56, 387, 414
flows, 388, 394, 401–2, 405–6, 412, 468
goods transfer, 370–2
markets, 388–91
share, 10, 56
capitalism, 93–109, 126–7, 263, 325, 450
alliance, 113
Asian model, 112–16, 127–8
crony, 114
free-market, 94–109, 126–7
German, 409; and takeovers, 409
and globalization, 155
golden age of, 331
laissez-faire model, 95, 109–10, 127
new European, 126–7
and social class, 209–10
and social justice, 109–10
social market model, 109–12, 127–8
and social welfare, 94, 101, 109–12
Cargill, 10, 283–4
CARICOM (Caribbean Community), 339
car industry, 42, 44–6, 60
in China, 48
in Japan, 46
in the US, 45, 46
see also motor industry
Carrefour, 160–1
Carroll's pyramid of CSR, 464
cartel/s, 105–6, 127, 316, 336
caste system, 186, 208
Castro, Fidel, 246
Catholic Church, 181–3, 188, 231
central banks, 81–2, 85–6, 89–91, 392–3
Chad, 456
Chandler, Alfred, 15, 18–19
change, 21 see also organizational change
chaebol (South Korea), 114, 362
Chanel, 160
Chernobyl, 431
child labour, 336, 466–7
Chile, 69
China, 17, 48, 69, 71, 73, 76–7, 94–7, 100, 112–13, 116–19, 132, 142–4, 153, 159, 186–7, 192, 206, 218, 224, 239, 242–3, 246–7, 257, 319–20, 331, 336, 344,

359, 363, 368, 381, 430, 433, 450–3
China
and Brazil, joint ventures, 342
and call centres, 229
and change, 450–1
and coal, 432
Confucianism, 186–8
consumers, 443
and credit cards, 206–7
and democracy, 451
economic reform, 117–19
economy, 117–19
entrepreneurs in, 96–7
expansion 2000–2002, 314
and FDI, 142–4, 148, 425
and greenhouse gas emissions, 427, 429
and instant coffee, 343
and internet use, 376
joint ventures, 117–18, 143, 153, 279
legal systems and international business, 279
low cost labour, 142–3
manufacturing, 142–3
and McDonald's, 170
and oil, 317
and pollution, 432
and poverty, 452–3
religion, 186–7
socialism, 117–18
steel, 332, 432
Christianity, 180–2, 185
and business, 181–2
and the megachurch, 182
Chrysler, 46, 195–7
CISG (UN Convention on Contracts for the International Sale of Goods, 1980), 289–92
Citicorp, 408
cities, 224
and inequality, 225
inner, 223–4
world's ten largest, 224
Citroen, 147
civil law, 277–85, 305
countries using, 282
civil rights, 302–5
civil war, 245–6
Clairol, 17
class
action, 294–7
middle, 209–11
system, 209–10
working, changes to, 209–11
cleaning products, environmentally friendly, 439
clerical work, 210
climate change, 300, 427–30, 435, 438–40, 444–5, 449
levy, 440
coal, 425–7, 431–2
Coca-Cola, 45, 50, 130–3, 170, 172, 200
coffee
fair trade, 462–3
world crisis, 461–3

cold war, 146
collectivism, 94, 113, 116–17, 157, 169, 192–4
collectivism/individualism, 116–17, 192–4, 263
colonialism, 208
Colombia, 381
Columbia, 455, 462
commercial liability, 285
common law, 281–2, 284–5, 305
countries using, 282
common market, 338–9
communism, 114–15, 117, 121–5, 128, 142, 146, 173–4, 187, 225, 246–7, 257
companies, 7–11, 29
as capitalist enterprise, 163
consolidation, 406
customer-led, 44–6, 55
demerger, 407
diversification, 407
as family, 128
global, 198
Japanese view of, 112–13, 116
limited, 7–8, 9–11
ownership, 154
private, 10, 11
public, 10, 11, 23–4
and strategy, 406
structure, 23
see also business; corporation; directors; firm; management; TNCs
comparative advantage, 457–8
competition, 97–100, 102, 105–8, 127, 192, 318–20, 322, 325
business, 102–5, 122
first-mover advantage, 353
and global business, 106
and government policy, 105–7
law, 277
policy, international, 336–7, 411
and price, 104–5
Treaty of Amsterdam (1999), 106
Competition Commission (UK), 105–6
competitive advantage, 318–21, 326, 355, 359, 361, 373, 457
national, 318–21, 326
computer/s, 60, 70, 106–7, 350, 354
first, 373
and international business, 373–4
and patent laws, 365–7
revolution, 60
see also internet; Microsoft
Confucian ethic, 188, 202, 207
Confucianism, 186–8
Confucian values, xxviii, 113–14, 116, 128, 202

conglomerates, 416–18
Congress Party (India), 257–8
constitutionalism, 246–7, 260
Consumer Price Index (CPI), 72
consumer protection, 277, 326–7
  Act (1987), 285
consumers, 44–51, 59, 63, 68–9, 97–100, 105, 118, 120, 130–3, 142, 155–6, 159, 206–7, 231, 288, 355
  ageing, 215–17, 232
  black economy, 299
  Chinese, 117–18
  and class, 209–11
  and credit cards, 206–7
  demand and supply, 97–100, 102
  and the environment, 422, 436, 439
  green, 442–3, 445
  health-conscious, 50–1, 130–1, 170–1
  Hispanic, 176–7
  Japanese, 160
  Russian, 120
  and social responsibility, 461
  sustainable consumption, 443–5
  in transitional economies, 120, 122
  and the US, 355
  see also products; product liability
contagion, financial, 402, 405
Continental tyres, 409
contract
  law, 277, 291–2
  liability, 285
contracting
  arm's length, 290
  relational, 290
contracts, 277, 290–3, 305
contracts, international, 289–93
  and cultural factors, 290
  and disputes, 291–3
  see also CISG; joint ventures
conventions, 277, 300–5
copyright, 101, 365, 367
corporate
  bond issues US (2000–2004), 392
  culture, 60–1, 195–8
  entrepreneurship, 60–1
  legal liability, 278
  social responsibility (CSR), 463–6, 471, 476
  strategy, 57, 406–7, 464–5; global, 159, 161
corporate governance, 23–9, 34, 108–9, 112, 127, 132, 196, 229, 410, 467
  OECD Principles, 24, 25
  and women, 229
corporation/s 9–10, 466
  modern, 210, 232
  structure, 23
  transnational (TNCs), 105
  see also MNCs; TNCs

corruption, 298–9, 305, 308–9, 403–4, 457, 459
Corsica, 178
Costa Rica, 264–6
Côte d'Ivoire, 462
cotton, 456
credit, 387
credit cards, use and spread, 206–7
CRH Plc, 162
criminal law, 278
Croatia, 119, 125–6, 174
crony capitalism, 114
cronyism, 241
CSR (corporate social responsibility), 463–6, 471, 476
C Two (Japan), 160–1
Cuba, 94, 246–7, 257, 327
cultural differences, 168–72, 177, 189–90, 195
  and business, 168–72, 177, 290
  and global brands, 170–2
cultural
  diversity, 190, 194–5, 198
  flows, international, 199
  globalization, 327; myth, 194, 199, 202; and the media, 199–200, 202
  homogenization, 205–6
  identity, 172–3, 177, 189–90, 201–2; and Hispanic Americans, 176–7, 190
  pluralism, 190
  rights, 302
cultural values, 94, 112–14, 116, 121, 127, 157–9, 161, 167–9, 172–4, 177, 183, 189, 191–202
  and democracy, 169
  and language, 168–9, 172–9, 190, 201
  and religion, 168–9, 172–4, 179–88, 201
  see also collectivism; individualism
culture, 52, 54–6, 151, 167–202
  Asian, 173–5, 187
  and business, 167–70, 187–8, 191–8
  change, 198
  definition of, 168–9
  global, 168, 194, 199; and national, 201
  global flows, 151
  high/low context, 174–5
  and markets, 172, 177
  national, 168–9, 172–4, 191–8
  native, 175–6
  organizational, 18, 21
  theories of, 191–4
currency
  devaluation, 397–9
  flows, 395, 397
  futures contract, 396

  hard, 395
customs union, 338–9
Cyberia, 469
Cyprus, 123, 125–6, 271,
CzechInvest, 147
Czechoslovakia, 119, 122
Czech Republic, 74, 119–20, 122–3, 125–6, 146–8, 153, 174, 193, 252, 262, 271, 358–9

D
Dae-jung, Kim, 115
Daewoo, 114, 363–4, 402
  and China, 363–4
  and R&D, 363
Daft, Douglas, 131–2
Daimler-Benz, 195–6
DaimlerChrysler AG, 196–7, 309, 363, 409, 467
Danone, 50–1
data protection, 50
DBK Technitherm Ltd., 73
debt
  financing, 387, 391–2
  national 84
  relief, 458–9, 458–9
deflation, 71
  and Japan, 71
Dell Computers, 143, 292
Delphi Automotive Systems, 159
demand management, 81
democracy, 235–6, 239–40, 247–9, 252–64, 268, 273, 451
  vs. authoritarianism, 247–9
  direct, 248
  liberal, 248–9, 253
  and MNCs, 264–5
  representative, 248–9
  social, 248, 254, 259
  transitional, 262–6, 273
Democrats, 260
demographic change, 213–16
denationalization, 161
Denmark, 87, 123, 183, 192, 271, 322, 359, 459
  and the EU, 87
depression, economic, 80–1
deskilling, 210, 230
Detroit, 223
Deutsche Bank, 409
Deutsche Post, 388
Deutsche Telekom, 10, 108, 392
developing countries, 451–3, 466–71
  and aid, 459
  business and strategic change, 457
  and capital flows, 412
  challenges, 470
  clothing industry, 455
  debt relief, 413, 458–9
  and financial globalization, 412
  gap between rich and poor, 451–60, 470–1

  and growth, 451
  and the IMF, 411–13
  and trade, 344–5
Diageo, 406–7
di Montezemolo, Luca Cordero, 309
directors, company, 23–9 see also management
Disney Corporation, 24, 25, 26–7, 28, 200
Disney, Roy, 27
Disney, Walt, 26
dispute resolution, 291–2, 300, 305
diversity, xxiv, 159
  and globalization, 167–202
  linguistic, 175–8
divorce, 231
Doha Round, 334–6, 347, 454
Dominican Republic, 455
Donato's Pizzerias, 171
dot.com
  boom (1990s), 377–8, 387–8
  business, 6, 33, 468
Dow Jones Industrial Average, 389
drinks, carbonated, 130–3 see also Coca-Cola
Dr Martens, and China, 143
dumping, 332–3
Dunning, John, 152–4
duopoly, 105
Du Pont, 15, 438

E
East Timor, 404
easyjet, 39–41
eBay, 377
e-business, 200–1
  and language, 179
EC (European Community) law, 286–7
ECB (European Central Bank), 86, 89–91
ECJ (European Court of Justice), 287–8, 340
e-commerce, 159, 217, 322, 377–80, 384, 390
  and international law, 292–3
  and law, 276
  and security, 378
economic activity, 70–6, 79–80, 91
  sectors, 70–1, 91
economic concentration, 102, 105
  and globalization, 102
  and government regulation, 102
  mergers, 102
  and monopolies, 102, 105–7
economic development, waves theory, 354
economic fragmentation, 139
economic growth, 76–8, 81
  and environmentalism, 426
  and poverty reduction, 452–3
economic integration, 80,

86–90, 112, 127–8, 139–41, 147, 335, 338, 449
common market, 338–9
customs union, 338–9
economic union, 338–9
free trade area, 338–9
political union, 338–9
theory of, 338–9
economic policy, 78–89
and banks, 81–2, 85–6
fiscal, 81–4, 86, 89, 91
and globalization, 82, 85, 90
monetary, 81–2, 85–6, 91
social market, 88
see also EMU; Friedman; Keynes
economic reform, 450–1
economics, 81
Keynesian school, 81
economic systems, 93–128 see also capitalism; socialism
economic union, 338–9
economy/ies,
Asian 'tiger', 112–16, 138
command, 117
internet-based, 469
market, 95–100, 126–7, 146
mixed, 109
national, 66–89
planned, 117, 121–3, 127, 128, 146
role of government, 71–6, 78–86, 109–11, 121–2, 126–7
of scale, 155, 157, 223, 351, 406, 410
transitional, 128, 206
urban, 223–5
e-consumers, 201
Ecover, 438–9
Ecuador, 295, 437, 462
Edison, Thomas, 416
education, 209, 211, 217
and internet use, 375–6
and social class, 209, 211
and training, 358–61, 372, 384; on the job, 372
and women, 231
Egypt, 183, 219, 248
Eisner, Michael (CEO Disney), 26–7
elasticity
income, 99
price, 98–9
elections, 248–9, 251–61, 268, 272
UK 2005, 260–1
US 2000, 260
electronic networks, 468 see also internet
El Salvador, 219, 455
e-mail, 379
emissions, greenhouse gas, 427–9, 438, 440 see also Kyoto Protocol
emissions trading, 429, 443
employee relations, 52–5
international, 54–5

employment, 51–5, 74, 76, 79–80, 325–6
law, 277, 464
and protectionism, 327
reward systems, 52–5
standards, 467
training, 53
see also labour; unemployment
empowerment, 21–3
EMU (European Monetary Union 1999), 82, 84, 86–7, 89–91, 340, 396
energy efficiency, 440–2
English language, 175–8, 200–1, 250
and call centres, India, 230
as global language, 178, 200–1
Enron, 25–6, 57–8, 416
enterprise/s,
free, 95–7
small-to-medium size (SMEs) 11, 26
state-owned (SOEs), 10
entertainment industry, global, 200
entrepreneur/s, 5–9, 12, 209, 352–3, 468
entrepreneurship, 37, 60–1, 95–7, 474
environment, 163
business, 95–7; and government regulation, 95–7, 114; post-industrial, 156
cultural, 167–202, 449
economic, 138–9, 142, 151–2, 449
ethical, 460–8
global and national, interrelated, 448–9
global business, changing, 449–50
international business, post-war, 145–6
international legal, 276–80, 289–300, 305, 460–8
and the law, 277
legal, 276–86, 449
macroeconomic, 66–72, 91
national cultural, 173–4
natural, 97
political, 138–9, 142, 151–2, 234–73, 449
social, 138–9, 142, 151–2, 157, 205–32, 449
environmental
challenges, global, 422–45
degradation, 425–6, 430–1, 445, 452
footprint, 436, 445
management, 422, 436–8, 445
pollution, 467
protection, 435–42, 465, 471
scanning (PEST), 30–1, 34
environmental protection, 435–6, 443, 460–1

and changing values, 443–4
and consumers, 422
international legal frameworks, 433–4, 445, 461
EPC (European Patent Convention 1973), 365, 367
EPO (European Patent Office), 365, 367
and patent applications (2003), 367–8
Equal Pay and Sex Discrimination Acts, 228
equal rights, 228, 231
Equatorial Guinea and oil, 437, 457
equity
financing, 387
investment, 388, 392
Ericsson, 15
ERM (Exchange Rate Mechanism 1979), 395–6
Esser, Klauss, 409–10
Estonia, 119, 123, 125–6, 271
Eta, 244, 251
ethical issues, global, 467
Ethiopia, 242
ethnic minorities, 189, 206
ethnocentrism, 168
EU (European Union), 74, 80, 86–90, 123–8, 146–7, 149, 151, 247, 250, 269–70, 272–3, 286, 339–42, 346, 470–1
and agriculture, 125–6
Constitutional Treaty, 269–72
and cultural differences, 340
emissions trading, 440, 445
and the environment, 439–43, 445
financial regulation, 391
formation and development of, 269, 340–1
and gender, 228
greenhouse gas emissions, 427, 429, 440–1, 445
harmonization of law, 285–7, 294
human rights, 303–4
labour relations, 227
legal framework, 286–7, 305
legislation, 270–1
and liberalization, 340–1
member states, 123–6, 269–71, 340
and migration, 218
patent law, 365–6
sanctions, 334, 336
subsidies, 458
EU 15, 123–4
euro, 86–90, 396
Eurobonds, 391–2
euro currency market, 394
euromarkets, 394
Europe, xxii
and GM crops, 381–2
Europe, Central and Eastern, 118–25, 128, 146, 148–9, 398, 406, 451

and culture, 173–4
national identity, 173–4
European
Central Bank, 392
Commission, 270–1
identity, 174
Parliament, 271–2
Eurozone, 101, 86–91, 251
members, 86–7
exchange rates, 76, 85–7, 89–91, 155, 330–1, 342, 394–7, 412, 414
fixed, 395–7
floating, 395–6
pegged, 395–6, 405
externalization, 159, 163
Exxon, 407
merger, 408
Exxon Mobil, 145, 295
Exxon Valdez, 433

F
factory, growth of the, 154–5
fair trade, 336
movement, 462
family
and business, 25–6, 113–14, 128, 192, 230–1
changing patterns of, 230–1
extended, 230–1
firm, 110, 231
nuclear, 230
one-parent, 231, 233
values, 169, 172–3, 177, 186–7, 450
see also chaebol; Confucian values; Disney; Fiat
farm subsidies, 335
Fascism, 246
FDI (foreign direct investment), 140, 142–4, 146–52, 163–4, 257–8, 264, 283–4, 298, 319, 325, 337, 346, 355, 370–2, 392, 402, 406, 412, 449–50
and Asia, 149, 371
and China, 142–4, 159
and the Czech Republic, 146–8
and developing countries, 425
flows, 148–9, 151, 159, 163
and international business, 140, 142, 371–2
Federal Mogul, 296
federal system, 250
Ferrari, 216, 307–9
Fiat, 15, 26, 307–9
and Italian government policy, 307–8
national icon, 307
film and TV, global, 199–200
finance
and accounting, 6, 13
industry, 206–7, 225
financial
contagion, 402, 405
globalization, 400

institutions, international, 387–91
management, 56–8, 63
markets, 387–400
reporting, 57–8, 63
services, 229
transactions and globalization, 387–91
Finland, 123, 183, 193, 271, 322–3, 358–9, 368
Firestone tyres, 297
and class action, 297
firm, 9
economic theory of, 152
internationalization of, 152–4
and international trade, 323
social responsibility, 460
first-mover advantage, 353
Flextronics, 143
food production, globalization of, 326
footwear, 46, 48–9
marketing, 48–9
Ford, Henry, 154
Fordism, 154–9, 164, 223, 354, 470
Ford Motor Co, 25, 45, 144–5, 154–6, 159, 216, 296, 309, 380, 438
Explorers, tyres, 297
foreign exchange, 387, 393–6, 414
Foster's brewing, 321
France, 8, 69, 74, 109–11, 123, 162–3, 178, 183, 189–90, 192–3, 214, 218, 242, 244, 247, 262, 266, 269–71, 329, 358–9, 368, 411, 432–3
and aid, 459
and capitalism, 109–10, 128
economy and government, 109–11
and privatization, 110–11
France Telecom, 109, 145, 409
franchises, 5, 9, 171
freedom, 263, 302
free trade, 150, 316, 331, 346, 394
post-war, 331
and protectionism, 325
Free Trade Areas, 127, 338-9, 341, 343
Friedman, Milton, 81
Friends of the Earth, 436
Froogle, 378
FSA (Financial Services Authority) UK, 390–1
FTAA (Free Trade Area of the Americas), 341–3
FTSE, 389
Fuji, 336

G
Garland Call Centres, 230
Gates, Bill, 106–7
Gatorade, 131
GATT (General Agreement on Tariffs and Trade), 150, 265, 328, 331–2, 345, 347, 369, 449
GDP (gross domestic product), 68–9, 73, 76–8, 91
GE (General Electric), 15, 24, 145, 161, 406, 416–18
aerospace, 416–18
American icon, 416
and China, 418
and R&D, 417–18
GE Capital, 416–17
gender
inequality, 227–9
and work, 227–9
Générale des Eaux, 461
genetic modification (GM) 380–2
crops, 381–2
food, 381–2
patents, 381
genomics, 474
Germany, 8–9, 23, 69, 74, 77–9, 83, 89, 96, 119, 123, 145, 147, 161, 183, 188, 190, 193, 195–7, 214, 218, 227, 242, 244, 246, 250, 254–5, 266, 269–71, 322, 329, 357–9, 368, 372, 411, 433, 439–40, 459
capitalism, 110–12, 128, 409–10
and corporate governance, 410–11
economy, 111–12
and immigration, 218, 220
Mittelstand, 79
and patent applications, 368–9
pensions, 409–10
post-war economic development, 145–6
and takeovers, 409–10
taxation, 89
and trade unions, 411
unemployment, 78–9
unification, 78
Gillette, 17
Glasgow, 12
GlaxoSmithKline, 335, 474–7
and AIDS, 475–6
and Ranbaxy, 475–6
and R&D, 475
Glaxo Wellcome, 408
global
advertising, 130–2
brands, 130–2, 142, 144, 169–72, 378–9: and cultural differences, 170–2
business environment, 449–50
capital markets, 387–92, 399
commons, 426
company, myth, 161
competition, 315, 322–3, 346
corporate strategy, 159, 161
culture flows, 151
economy, 150–1, 346, 469–71
emissions, 427–8
environment, changing, 448–50
financial flows, 392–6
financial markets, 387–400
firm, 152–4
industries, 130–1
internet, 449
markets, 130–3, 159, 449
media, 449
networks, 151–2
politics, 268–9
retailers, 160–1
warming, 40, 335, 424, 427–8, 445
globalization, xxiv, xxv, 4–6, 46, 138–65, 205, 448, 450–1, 470–2
and business, 448–50, 460–8
and culture, 168–9, 168–70, 199–201
definition of, 138–41
development of, 138–50
and economic policy, 82
and entertainment industry, 170, 199–200
of the firm, 152–65
hyperglobalization, 138–9
vs. internationalization, 140–1, 148
and localization, 158–9
location theories, 152–4
and national diversity, 470–1
and pop music, 169–70, 200
process, 138–54
of production, 449, 454–5
of state power, 151
and technological innovation, 383–4
tranformationalist view of, 139
and transnational crime, 298–9
trends, 148–52
and the US, 138, 144–6, 148
and world trade, 346
GM (General Motors), 15, 45, 46, 145, 155, 157, 159, 161, 177, 216, 362–3, 380, 438
and Fiat, 307, 309
New United Motors Company, 157
GM Daewoo, 362–4
GNI (gross national income), 67–9, 91
gold standard (1870s-1914), 393–4
Google, 378–9, 388
shares, 379
government, 237–8
democratic, 235–6, 248–9, 252–62, 268
functions of, 259
governments
and banks, 81–2
and business, 235–41, 245–6, 250–2, 260, 264–6, 372–3
and the economy, 81–2, 127, 140, 150
and education, 358–61
and national security, 242–5
and power, 138–40
and technological innovation, 357–61
government, systems of, 246–63
coalition, 262
hybrid, 262, 273
parliamentary, 260–2, 273
presidential, 259, 262, 273
government trade policy, 324–30
import quotas, 328–30
local content requirements, 328
and national advantage, 319–20, 325–6
non-tariff barriers, 328–30
state subsidies, 328–30
tariffs, 328–30
VER (voluntary export restraint), 328–30
see for example Fiat 307–9
Grand Metropolitan, 406–7
Great Depression (1929-1930), 80, 109, 331
Greece, 8, 69, 90, 123, 183, 193, 242, 271, 357
green consumerism, 442–3, 445
greenhouse gas emissions 427–9, 438, 440; (2004), 427
see also Kyoto Protocol
Green Party/ies, 254, 256, 272
Greenpeace, 265–6, 436, 462
green products, 439
Greenspan, Alan, 82
grocery business, international expansion, 160–1
Guinness, 406–7
Gulf War, 244
G7, 266–7
G8, 266–7
G20, 335, 342

H
health and beauty products, 17
hedge funds, 396–7, 399
Helms-Burton Act, 327
Hewlett-Packard, 61
hierarchies, 14–16, 21–3
Hinduism, 180, 185–6, 208
HIV, see AIDS
Hofstede, Geert, 174, 191–4, 198, 202
theory of culture, 191–4
5 cultural dimensions, 191–4
Holcim AG, 162
holding company, 16
Honda, 19–20
Honduras, 381, 455
Hong Kong, 113–14, 143, 188, 322, 432
Hoover, 163
HRM, 6, 13, 21, 37, 51–6, 59, 63

international, 54–6
HSBC, 229–30
human poverty, 452, 456
human rights, 208, 244, 247–8, 266–8, 277, 301–5, 449, 460–1, 465–7, 471
Human Rights Act (1998), 303–4
Hungary, 119, 121–3, 125–6, 147, 174, 253, 262, 271, 451
    and foreign-owned companies, 411–12
Hussein, Saddam, 244, 268
hyperglobalization, 138–9, 470
Hyundai, 114–15, 363

I
IBM, 4–5, 147, 191, 373–4
IBRD (International Bank for Reconstruction and Development), 398
ICC (International Criminal Court), 301
Iceland, 322
ICI, 19
ICJ (International Court of Justice, the Hague), 300–1
ICT (information and communications technology), 373–6, 384
    and globalization 376
    and patent applications (2003), 368, 373–6
    see also computers; internet
IDA (International Development Association), 398
ideology, 246
IG Metall, 409
IKEA, and Russia, 119–20
ILO (International Labour Organization), 267, 337, 467–8
IMF (International Monetary Fund), 82, 139, 331, 333, 393–5, 397–9, 411–14, 449, 471
    and Africa, 458
    and Argentina, 398–400
    and Asian financial crisis, 402–5
    and debt relief, 413
    development, 393–4, 397–8
    monitoring, 397
Immelt, Jeffrey (GE), 416–17
immigration, 189–90, 215, 218–20, 236
    and Germany, 215
    illegal, 221
    and the UK, 189–90, 218
    and the US, 190
import
    quotas, 328–30, 455
    substitution, 325
imports/exports, 314–16
income
    distribution, 101
    elasticity, 99
    tax, 83

India, 68–9, 100, 132, 159, 178, 183, 186, 208, 218–19, 224, 242, 295, 320, 345, 359, 361, 368, 430, 433, 451–2
    and advertising, 132
    agriculture, 258
    call centres, 210, 229–30, 469
    caste system, 208
    coal, 432
    and coffee, 462
    democracy, 257–8
    emigrants, 219
    and FDI, 425
    and GM crops, 381
    greenhouse gas emissions, 427, 429
    and IT, 258, 320, 469
    and the law, 280
    patent applications, 368
    pharmaceuticals, 475–6
    software industry, 372–3, 380
individualism, 116–17, 169, 173, 187–8, 192, 198, 231, 249, 279, 450
Indonesia, 69, 113, 115–16, 142, 183, 190, 193, 218, 224, 241, 246, 248, 316, 402
    and Asian financial crisis, 401–5
    corruption, 404
    separatist movements, 404
    terrorism, 404
    tsunami, 404
industrial
    agglomeration, 152, 223
    restructuring, 155–9
    societies, 237
    structure, 70–1
industrialization, 70, 118, 140, 142–4, 154–6, 202, 206, 222–3, 263, 314, 325, 424–7, 444–5, 449
    and China, 142–4
    and the US, 144–5
Industrial Revolution, 222, 353–4, 425
industries, 103–5, 108–10
    and competition, 103–5, 122
    and environmental damage, 422–9, 431, 435
    manufacturing, 70, 73, 75–6, 91, 153–9
    nationalized, 10, 94–5, 108–9
    state-owned, 118
    see also public utilities: SOEs; TNCs
inflation, 71–2, 74, 81, 85, 91, 122, 124
innovation, 37, 59, 60–3, 351–64, 368, 474, 475
    core competences, 62
    cultural factors, 352–4, 359, 362
    and economic growth, 362

and first mover advantage, 318
    vs. invention, 351
    and Japan, 355–7
    and national systems, 357–62, 372, 384
    and patents, 364–71
    process, 351–5, 362
    and strategy, 61–3
    technical, 77
    and the UK, 353–5, 357
Intel, 62, 264–5
    and Costa Rica, 264–5
intellectual property, see IP
Interbrew SA, 162
    interest rates, 72, 79–80, 85–9, 91
international business, xxiii, 4–6, 33, 223
    black economy, 299
    and crime, 298–301, 305
    and cultural differences, 168–9, 192–200
    and dispute resolution, 291–2, 305
    and English language, 178, 196, 200–1
    environment, 138–48, 151–4, 157–65
    grey market, 299
    and language, 196
    and the law, 276, 283–4, 305
    and the internet, 238
    and negligence, 293
    and political risk, 245, 248, 266
    polycentrism, 168
    and product liability, 293–7
    post-war, 145–6
    and religion, 180–3, 187
    transactions, 276, 289–92, 305
    see also e-commerce
international
    competition policy, 336–7
    contracts, 290
International Covenant
    on Civil and Political Rights, 302
    on Economic, Social and Cultural Rights, 302
international finance, 387–419
    capital markets, 387–92
    and stability, 392–4
international financial institutions, 387–91
internationalization, 43, 54–6, 122, 140–4, 152–4
international law, 471
    and dispute resolution, 300
    harmonization of, 276, 291, 305
    reform of, 276
    private, 289–291, 295
    public, 299–300
    standardization, 285–6
international monetary system, development, 392

international trade theories, 313, 316–17, 347
    comparative advantage, 316–17, 322
    new, 318
    Porter's theory of competitive advantage, 318–22
    product life cycle theory, 323–4
internet, xxiv, 6, 7, 47, 101–2, 106–7, 159, 178–9, 200–1, 230, 375–9, 468–9, 472
    across cultures, 201
    advertising, 378
    based economy, 469
    and English, 178–9, 200–1
    global, 449, 469
    internationalization of, 379–80
    and older people, 217
    pharmacies, 476
    retailers, 6–7, 32–3, 47
    search engines, 378–9
    and security, 107, 378
    use (2002), 469; (2002/2003), 375; global (2004), 376
    see also e-commerce; Microsoft; Netscape; Windows
inventions, 351–3
    and China, 352
    and patents, 364–9
IP (intellectual property), 101–2, 292–3, 332, 351, 364–70, 476, 451
    and the law, 277
IPO (initial public offering), 388, 414
iPod, 59, 60–1
Iran, 239, 246, 316–17, 183–4
Iraq, 239, 244, 268, 300, 316, 183
Ireland, 40, 83, 96, 123–4, 162, 183, 271, 322
    tax, 40, 83
Islam, 180, 182–5, 352
    and fundamentalism, 183–4
Israel, 262
IT (information technology), 6, 11–12, 38, 43, 70, 95, 142, 156, 178, 223, 373–4, 468–9
    advances, 468–9, 472
    call centres, 210
    and English, 178
    India 208, 210, 320
Italy, 74–5, 123, 178, 214, 246, 254, 256, 266, 269–71, 308–9, 368
    and democracy, 309
    and Fiat, 307–9
    and pensions, 308
    and unemployment, 308
Iveco, 307

J
Jager, Durk, 17–18
Jamaica Agreement (1976), 394

Japan, 7, 12, 19–20, 46, 55, 69, 71, 74, 77, 96, 112–14, 116, 119, 128, 145, 149, 157–8, 160–1, 186–7, 191–3, 215, 224, 247, 256, 264, 266, 317, 319, 322, 325, 336, 344, 356–61, 368, 372, 459
  and capitalism, 112–13, 116, 173
  and car exports, 328
  and the company, 112–13; as family, 192
  and consumer electronics, 356–7, 361
  and credit cards, 207
  cultural identity, 173–4
  economy, 113
  and farm subsidies, 326
  and greenhouse gas emissions, 427, 429
  and innovation, 368
  and international business, 173
  kaizen, 157–8
  keiretsu, 112–13
  national culture, 173, 195
  national identity, 173–4, 195
  and nuclear power, 432–3
  patent applications, 368–9
  post-war economic development, 145–6
  religion, 186–7
  retail expansion into, 160–1
  reverse engineering, 371
  technological innovation, 356–61
  and TNCs, 195
Jobs, Steve, 60 see also Apple Computers
joint ventures, 9, 117–18, 123, 143, 153–4, 168, 195, 240, 279, 290, 309, 343, 370–1, 402
  and local partners, 153–4
  and trust, 195
Jordan, 184, 219, 247, 430
Judaism, 180, 185
judicial systems, 280–1, 284

K
kaizen, 157–8
keiretsu, 112–14
Kenya, 462
Kerkorian, Kirk, 196
Khan, Imran, 12 see also Picsel
Keynes, John Maynard, 81
Kia Motors, 363
Kleenex, 365
knowledge transfer, 350, 370–1
Kodak, 59, 336
Kondratieff waves, 354
Kosovo, 174
Kurds, 283
Kuwait, 218, 239, 244, 316
Kyoto Protocol (1997), 300, 428–9, 435, 440–1, 445
  ratification, 428

L
labour
  child, 466–7
  costs, 142–3, 155–7, 159
  forced, 208
  markets and migration, 220–23
  relations, 225–8, 232
  standards, 335–7
  see also trade unions
landfill, 441
language, 168–9, 172–9, 190, 201
  Chinese, 175
  and colonization, 176
  English, 175–8, 200–1; as a global, 178, 200–1
  and immigration, 176–7
  national, 173–6, 178
  native/local, 176, 196, 200–1
  Spanish, 175–7
languages, world's top ten, 175
Latin America, 251, 260, 264, 342, 372, 450, 453
  and child labour, 466–7
  and China, 342–3
  and FDI, 412
Latvia, 119, 123, 125–6, 271
law, 277–86, 464
  adjudication, 280–1
  civil, 277–85, 305
  and commercial liability, 285
  common, 281–2, 284–5
  competition, 277
  contract, 277, 291–2
  and contract liability, 285
  criminal, 278
  differences across cultures, 279–80
  employment, 277
  European Community, 286–7
law, international, 299–305, 449
  conventions, 277, 300–5
  and dispute resolution, 300
  public, 299–300
  treaties, 300–5
law
  Islamic Shari'a, 285
  legislation, 280–1
law merchant, 289
law
  precedents, 284–5
  private international, 289–291, 299
  and product liability, 285
  public, 277
  public international, 299–300
  statute, 284
LBO (leveraged buyout), 406–7
leaders, charismatic, 246
leadership, 198
Lee Kwan Yew, 188
legal liability, corporate, 278
legal systems
  national, 277, 279–85, 305
  non-Western, 285
  regional, 286–7
  supranational, 300

  see also EU
legislation, 280–1
legislative assemblies, 252–60
Levi Jeans, 169, 200, 287–8
Levi Strauss, 467
LG (electronics, South Korea), 114, 147
liability
  commercial, 285
  contract, 285
  corporate legal, 278
  limited, 10
  product, 293–7
  unlimited, 8, 9
libel, 293
liberalism, 236–7, 249
liberalization, 122, 128, 150–1, 401, 405, 409, 412, 450, 471 see for example the Czech Republic
Liberia, 239
Libya, 268, 316
life expectancy, 214
List, Friedrich, *National System of Political Economy*, 357
Lithuania, 119, 123, 125–6, 271
litigation, 291–2
lobby groups, 261
local content requirements, 328
location theories, 152–4
LTCM (Long Term Capital Management), 396–7, 399
Luxembourg, 123, 269, 271, 322
Lyonnaise des Eaux, 461

M
Maastricht Treaty (1992), 84, 86–7, 286
Macedonia, 174
macroeconomics, 66–9
MAI (Multilateral Agreement on Investment), 412
Majid, Anwar, 12 see also Picsel
Malaysia, 113, 115–16, 193, 210, 402
  and the Asian financial crisis, 405
Mali, 456, 459
  and call centres, 229
Malta, 123, 125–6, 271
management, 14–16, 21–2, 37, 51–2, 55, 155–6, 191–3, 198
  accounting, 56, 63
  Asian, 55
  financial, 56–8
  structures, 155–6
  styles, 55
managers, 25, 210
  executive bonuses, 410
  relationship orientation, 192–3
  executive remuneration, 476–7
M&A (merger and acquisition), 406–10, 414
  cross-border (2004), 408–9
  global, 408–9

  horizontal integration, 406
  vertical integration, 406
Mannesmann, 408–11
manufacturing, 38–9
  industries, 223, 225–6; changes in, 153–9
  international nature of 43
Mao Zedong, 117
market economy, 95–100, 126–7, 146, 188
  and competition, 97–100, 102, 108
  transitional, 117–27
  transition process, 121–7
  and Western values, 188
market forces, 316
marketing, 6, 13, 37, 43–51, 59, 63, 211, 215–17
  and consumers, 44–51, 59, 63
  and culture, 46–9, 63
  and ethics, 50–1
  mix (4Ps), 47, 63
  social, 51
  and sport, 48–9
  strategy, 211, 215–17
market
  research, 37, 44–5, 211
  structures, 102–6
markets, global and local, 159–61
Marks & Spencer, 11
Marxism-Leninism, 117
masculinity/femininity, 192–4
mass production, 154–9, 206, 223, 225, 354
  flexible (Japan), 157
Matsushita, 147
Mauritania, 459
Mauritius, 455
McDonald's, 5–6, 9, 48, 50, 169–72, 295
  and France, 171
  and globalization, 170
  and Japan, 170
  new image 2005, 171
  and Russia, 170
McDonnell Douglas, 336
MCI Worldcom, 408
media power, 308–9
mediation, 291, 305
Mercedes, 196–7, 329
merchandise
  exports, 1990-2002, 314
  world trade 2004, 315
MERCOSUR (Southern Common Market), 339, 341
mergers, 195–7, 406–11
  regulation, 411
  see also M&A
Metro, 160
Mexico, 69, 159, 177, 183, 190, 193, 218–19, 224, 238, 256, 264–5, 317, 341–2, 462, 468
  and FDI, 412
  low-cost labour, 142
MFN (most-favoured national principle), 331

and human rights, 331
Mickey Mouse, 26
microeconomics, 66–7
microelectronics, 373
microprocessors, 373–4
Microsoft, 46, 60–1, 106–7,
    143, 360, 374, 379
Middle East, the, xviii *see also*
    individual states
migration, 213–14, 217–24,
    232, 449
    international, 217–20
    push and pull, 217
    see also immigration
Mintzberg, H.,19–20
Mitchell, George, 27
MNCs (multinational
    corporations), 138, 141–2,
    158–9, 195–8 *see also* TNCs
Mobil, 407
    merger, 408
mobile phones, 98–100, 104,
    107, 409
    and safety, 99
    3G, 98–100
Moluccas, 404
money markets, 392, 396–7
    currency futures, 396
    derivatives, 396
    hedge funds, 396–7, 399
    speculation, 396
money supply, 85
monopolies, 102, 105–8, 127
Monsanto, 382
Moo-hyun, Roh, (South Korea),
    115
Morocco, 183–4, 247
motorbike market, 19–20
    success of Honda 50s, 19–20
motor industry, 105, 140,
    145–6, 154–9, 162, 195–7,
    216, 223, 252, 356
    anti-pollution requirements,
        307
    externalization, 159
    R&D, 356
    suppliers, 159, 223, 328,
        356, 372
    see also Fordism; mass
        production
Motorola, 100, 143
Mozambique, 459
multiculturalism, 189–90, 195
multicultural societies, 189–90,
    195, 202
Multifibre Arrangement, 455
music
    industry, 60–1
    on-line, 60–1
    technology, 60–1
Myanmar, 248, 335

N
NAFTA (North America Free
    Trade Agreement), 127, 151,
    193, 264, 339, 341–2
NASDAQ (National Association
    of Securities Dealers

Automated Quotations),
    388–9
national
    competitive advantage,
        318–21, 326, 411
    culture, 327
    differences, 448, 470–1
    identity, 173–4, 180, 190,
        195, 202, 206, 327, 340
    interests, 326, 334
    language, 173–6, 178
    security, 242–5, 259, 266
    unity, 262
nations, developing *see*
    developing countries
nations, rich and poor, gap,
    451–60, 470–71
nation-state/s, 172, 174, 202,
    206, 237–8, 241–2, 246–7,
    273, 470–2
    characteristics of, 195
    and international law,
        299–300
    and international trade
        policy, 324–30
    super culture, 196
    and trade, 346
NATO (North Atlantic Treaty
    Organization), 242–4
    members, 243
natural resource depletion,
    424–5, 430–1, 444–5
NBC, 416
negligence, and the law, 293–4
Nepal, 183, 455
Nestlé, 16, 195, 462
Néstor Kirchner, 399
Netherlands, The, 69, 123, 162,
    192–3, 269–71, 322, 368
Netscape Communications, 107
networking, 22
network organization, 22
    and social capital, 22
new economy, the, 468
News Corporation, 162
New United Motors Company,
    157
New York, 224, 244; and 9/11,
    244
New Zealand, 96, 252, 322,
    359
NGOs (Non-Government
    Organizations), 266–7
    and environmental
        protection, 424
Nice Treaty 2000, 269–70
Nigeria, 176, 239–40, 248,
    266, 295, 316
    and oil, 239–40
Nike, 24, 46, 48–9, 62, 143,
    169, 295, 467
Nissan, 140,173
Nokia, 99–101, 323
non-tariff barriers, 328–30
North Korea, 94, 114–15,
    114–15, 246–7, 257
Norway, 78, 183, 192, 317,
    322
    and aid, 459

labour costs, 78
NTL Inc, 162
nuclear power, 431–3, 435, 445
nutraceuticals, 216
NYSE (New York Stock
    Exchange) 388–90

O
Obasanjo, President, (Nigeria),
    239
obesity, 170–1
    and the US, 170–1
OECD (Organization for
    Economic Co-operation and
    Development), 467
Ohmae, Kenichi, *The Invisible
    Continent*, 199, 469
oil, 43, 66, 72–4, 105, 109,
    142, 145, 155, 184, 238–40,
    248, 316–17, 394, 451, 457
    and China, 317
    industry, mergers, 407–8
    and Nigeria, 239–40, 248
    and pollution, 433, 437
    prices, 43, 155, 317
    and terrorism, 317
    world reserves, 239
OLI paradigm, 152–4
oligopoly/ies, 102, 105, 151,
    155
online music, 60–1
online services, 377–9
OPEC (Organization of
    Petroleum Exporting
    Countries), 155, 316–18, 394
    and international investment,
        394
    members, 316–17
operations, 37–43, 63
    flexibility, 42
    international scope of, 43
    management, 38, 41–3
    speed, 41–3
    strategy, 38–43, 59; and
        performance, 41
    the transformation process,
        38–9, 63
    see also manufacturing;
        production; services
Orange, 409
organizational culture, 18, 21,
    51–6, 61–2
organization/s, 13
    and change, 17–18, 21–2,
        33
    classic global, 158
    complex, 162
    core competences, 62
    culture of, 18
    definition of, 13
    divisional structure, 14–16
        see for example GE, Fiat
    flexible, 470
    functional approach, 6,
        13–14
    functions of, 36–63
    international, 162
    matrix structure, 16–17
    multinational, 162

operational processes, 14
    restructuring, 18
    structure and strategy, 18–21
    supranational, 470–1
outsourcing, 71, 158, 230, 476
ownership, 209–10, 351
    company, 154
    of production, 153–4
    state, 128
Oxfam, 462

P
Page, Larry, 378–9
Pakistan, 455
Parmalat, 25–6, 57–8, 309
partnership, 7, 9, 11 *see also*
    firm; joint venture
patent law, 365–7
patents, 101–2, 152, 351–2,
    364–71, 381, 384, 474, 454,
    474–6
    and global markets, 367
PCs (personal computers), 374
    and internet use, 374
PCT (Patent Co-operation
    Treaty), 367
pensions, 214–15, 226
PepsiCo, 130–1
Peugeot-Citroën, 26
PEST analysis, 30–1, 34
Petroleos de Venezuela, 10, 11
Pfizer, 408, 454, 475
pharmaceutical industry, 335,
    337, 370, 406, 454, 474–7
    and AIDS, 475–6
    and India, 370
    and licensing, 475–6
    and patents, 474–6
    and prices, 475–6
Philippines, 113, 183, 402,
    380–1
Philips, 147, 162
Picsel Technologies, 6, 11, 12
Pierre Cardin, 455
Pirelli, 409
planned economy, 121–3, 127,
    128, 146
    and reform, 121–3, 128
pluralism, 236
Poland, 69, 74, 119, 121–3,
    125–6, 147, 174, 180, 183,
    225, 247, 252, 254, 256,
    262, 271, 451
political
    decision-making, 236–7, 259
    interdependence and
        integration, 449
    parties, 236, 256–60, 273
    pluralism, 248
    systems, 235–6, 246–8,
        258–60
    union, 338–9
pollution, 97, 307, 424–6,
    435–8, 445
    opportunity costs, 436
    transboundary, 431–4, 445
polycentrism, 168, 202
pop music, 200

population, 212–16, 221–3, 232
    ageing, 213–17, 232; and business, 215–17
    growth, 212, 221
    movement, 217–24
    world, 212–13
Porter, Michael, *Theory of Competitive Advantage*, 103, 318–21
Portugal, 123–4, 271
pouring rights, 130
poverty, 237–8, 452–7, 456
    human, 456
    income, 456
poverty trap, 231
power, 191–3, 235–6, 240–1, 246–7, 259
    distance (Hofstede), 191–4
    nuclear, 431–3, 435, 445
    and politics, 235–6, 241
    separation of, 259
    and the state, 138–9, 151
    structures, 151
PPP (purchasing power parity), 69
PR (proportional representation), 253–4, 256, 273
Pret A Manger, 171
price
    competition, 104–5
    elasticity, 98–9
private property, 101
privatization, 10, 108–11, 121–4, 128, 147, 258, 266, 388, 400, 407–8
Procter & Gamble (P&G), 17–18, 25
product/s 323
    characteristics, 104
    cost, 39–41
    dependability, 41–2
    design, 13, 38, 44, 55, 60
    development, 37–8, 44–5, 48–9, 59–61
    ethical, 50–1
    innovation, 44, 55, 59–62
    liability, and law, 277, 285, 293–7
    mass produced, 143, 155
    quality, 39, 41–2
    substitute, 104
    see also branding; segmentation
production, 14, 38–9, 94–8, 127, 223
    costs, 42–3, 98, 153, 157
    globalization of, 138–53
    and knowledge, 151, 157
    mass customization, 42
    ownership of, 94–7, 153–4
    see also mass production
property
    intellectual, 101–2, 277, 292–3
    law, 277
    ownership of, 101–2
    private, 101, 127
    rights, 152, 279, 451

prosperity, 457
protectionism, 324–5, 331, 333, 335, 346
Protestantism, 181–8
    and capitalism, 188
    Protestant work ethic, 187–8
Publicis Groupe SA, 162
public spending, 82–3, 91, 214
public utilities, 105, 108, 110

Q
Qatar, 316
Quaker Oats, 131
quality control, 157
quota restrictions, 346

R
race relations, 191
Ranbaxy, 475–6
R&D (research and development), 6, 14, 60, 147, 252, 350–62, 370–83, 406, 449
    cultural factors, 350, 352–4, 359, 362
    funding, 359–62
    and government expenditure, 359–62
    and patents, 364–70
Recep Tayyip Erdogan (Turkey), 283
recycling, 132, 436, 439, 441–2, 465
Reebok, 143
referendum, 254–6
refugees, 191, 218–20, 238–9
regional integration, 337–41
regionalism, 139, 151, 337–41, 346
    in Asia, 343
regionalization, 127–8
religion, 168–9, 172–4, 179–88, 201
    and power, 180
religions, major, 1900–2000, 180
Renault, 10, 140, 173, 309, 363
Republican Party, 260
reskilling, 229
retailers, global, 160–1
    strategy, 170
    virtual, 468
retirement, 214–15
reverse engineering, 371
Ricardo, David, 316
Ricoh, 143
Rio Declaration on Environment and Development (1992), 434–5, 445, 467
Roche Group, 162
Romania, 119, 125–6, 183, 283
Royal Dutch Shell, 240, 467
RPI (retail price index), 71–2
RPIX, 72
Rule of Law, 286
Russia, 100, 119–20, 146, 149, 183, 239, 242–3, 266, 317, 433, 451, 468

and coal, 432
and FDI, 412
and greenhouse gas emissions, 427
and the Kyoto Protocol, 428
and oil, 317
Rwanda, 300–1
    war crimes, 300–1
Ryanair, 39–41, 42

S
Saga Holidays, 215, 217
Samsung, 100–1, 252, 363
sanctions, 333
Saudi Arabia, 183–5, 218, 239, 242, 246–7, 285, 316–17
Schrempp, Jurgen, 409
science
    and invention, 352
    and protection of the environment, 424
    push and demand pull, 352
    student performance, 358–9
    and technology, 358–61
Scotland, 163, 247, 250, 255
Seat, 252
segmentation, 45, 63, 211
Seiyu, 160
self-employment, 8–9 see also sole traders
service industries 67, 70–1, 91, 210, 225, 344
    outsourcing, 71, 230
Shanghai, 224
Shanghai Automotive Industries, 363
share capital, 10
shareholder/s, 9–10, 15, 23, 24, 25–6, 28–9, 56, 108, 127, 140, 162, 210, 389, 392, 406, 411, 464–5
    Mannesmann's, 409, 411
    see also stockholders
shareholder value, 34
shares, 9–10, 15, 25, 387–90, 406
    trading, 389–90
Shell, 145, 295
Sherman Act (1890) (US), 106
Sierra Leone, 69, 268
Silicon Valley, 157
Singapore, 113–141, 143, 188, 322, 325, 372
Singer, 144
Singh, Manmohan, 258
Skoda, 147
slavery, 208
Slovakia, 252, 271
Slovak Republic, 119, 123, 125–6
Slovenia, 119, 123, 125–6, 174, 271
SMEs (small-to-medium size enterprises), 11, 26, 122, 142
    and globalization, 142
    and the internet, 380
Smith, Adam, *The Wealth of*

Nations, (1776), 81, 316, 353
SmithKline Beecham, 408, 474
social
    capital, 22
    change, 204–32
    class, 205, 209–11, 232
    democrats, 394
    justice, 109–10, 123
    market capitalism, 109–10
    mobility, 210–11
    responsibility, 460, 463–6, 471; corporate, 463–6, 471, 476
    services, 258
    stratification, 186, 204–5, 208–11, 232
    welfare, 78–9, 94, 101, 109–12, 114, 128, 231, 237
socialisation, 205
socialism, 94, 117 see also China; North Korea; Soviet Union
society
    ageing, 213–16
    capitalist, changes in, 205–6, 209–11, 213–16, 231–2
    civil, 236–7
    and international business, 205
    modern industrial, 205–6, 210–11, 213–16, 232
    types of 205–6, 208–10
SOEs (state-owned enterprises), 10, 94–5, 105, 108–10, 117–8, 121–2, 128, 146
    and pollution, 437
    and privatization, 407
software patents, 365–7
sole trader/s, 7–9, 11, 33
Solidarity, 122, 225
Somalia, 268
Sony, 200, 356–7
Sony Ericsson, 100–1, 143
Soros, George, 396–7
South Africa, 69, 176, 183, 238, 454, 475
    and AIDS, 475–6
South America, xx, 176, 183
    see also Latin America
Southcorp, 320–1
South Korea, 113–16, 143, 186, 191, 264, 325, 358–9, 362–4, 368, 402, 433
    and the Asian financial crisis, 401–3
    consumers, 363–4
    and credit cards, 207
    and Daewoo, 362–4
    and science education, 358–9
South Korea/North Korea, 114–15
Southwest Airlines, 39, 41
sovereignty, 240–2, 247–8, 268–9, 273, 340
Soviet Union (USSR), 94, 117, 119–21, 146, 173, 246, 431

economy, 117, 119–21
and technological innovation, 361
see also Russia
Spain, 8, 69, 74, 123, 178, 183, 244, 247, 250–2, 271, 433
and democracy, 250–2
sports drinks, 130–1
Sprint, 408
Sri Lanka, 186, 455
stakeholder/s, 24, 28–30, 210, 409, 411, 463–5
theory, 464–5
Standard Oil, 407
Starbucks, 461, 463
state/s, 237–8, 240–2, 246–7, 268–9, 273
and authority, 246–8
and defence, 242–6
federal system, 250
patrimonial, 246
subsidies, 328–30
transitional, 262–3
unitary system, 250
see also nation-states
steel, 73, 332–4
stock exchanges, 387–91, 414
and regulation, 390–1
stockholders, 10
Ston Forestal, 265
strategic
alliances, 370–1
change, 21
intent, 22–3
necessity, 326
thinking, 19–20
trade policy, 326
strategy, global corporate, 142, 151–2, 406–7
strikes, 225–6
subcontractors, 153, 158
subcultures, 206
subsidiaries, 158–9, 163, 341
subsidies, 458
suburbanization, 223
Sudan, 268
Suharto, President, Indonesia, 116, 190, 246, 403
suppliers, 223, 328, 464
supply and demand, 97 100, 102, 117, 152, 155–6
supply chain, 38
supranational institutions, 392, 470–1
sustainable consumption, 443–5
sustainable development, 424, 434–6, 443–4, 452, 462
Sweden, 87–9, 110, 123, 183, 192–3, 252–3, 271, 322, 359, 433
economic policy, 88
and the EU, 87–9
Switzerland, 162, 175, 195, 237, 322, 359, 368
SWOT analysis, 31–3, 34
Syria, 183–4

T
Taiwan, 113–14, 116, 143, 264, 322, 325
takeover, 406–11
cross-border, 408–9
hostile, 406–11
Tanzania, 459
tariffs, 333, 345–6, 451
tax
concessions, 83, 89
corporation, 84
taxation, 67, 82–4, 83–4 89, 91, 236
technological innovation, 349–84, 449–50
concepts and processes, 351–5
and government, 357–61
and scientific knowledge, 351–2
technological innovation theories, 352–5, 383–4
Porter, 353, 355, 383
product life cycle theory, 352, 355
Schumpeter's industrial waves theory, 353–5
technology, 56, 362–3
and change, 354
clean, 438, 440
and competitive advantage, 373
diffusion, 372
impact on business, 56 *see also* internet
and innovation, xxv, 6, 43, 59–60, 77, 349–84
knowledge transfer, 350, 370–1
licensing, 371
new, 468–9
revolution, 373 4
third-generation (3G), 98–100
transfer, 355, 370–2; channels, 370–1
transnationalization of, 150–1
telecommunications, 10, 11–12, 100, 108, 147, 162, 388
advances, 468
companies, 392; and bonds, 392
and 3G mobile phones, 392
territoriality, 238–9, 273
terrorism, 180, 184, 243–5, 251, 317, 416
Bali, 404
Jakarta, 404
9/11, 416
Tesco, 10, 39, 160–1, 287–8
and Japan, 160–1
vs. Levi Strauss, 287–8
TEU (Treaty of European Union 1992), 286
Texaco, 437
textiles, 252, 328, 330, 332, 343, 345, 455, 455–6
industry, China vs. India, 455

Thailand, 113, 186
and the Asian financial crisis, 405
banking crisis (1996), 401–2
Thatcher, Margaret, and monetary policy, 81
theme parks, 26
theocracy, 247
Thomson Corporation, 162
Timberland, 143
Time-Warner, 200
takeover, 406
TNCs (transnational corporations), 105, 136, 141–8, 151–4, 157–65, 195–8, 346, 449, 470–1
and Asian financial crisis, 402
and authoritarian states, 248
and developing countries, 425–6, 435; responsibility, 426, 435
and environmental management, 437
and FDI, 371–2
and global finance, 387, 406, 412, 414
and global standards, 466–7
and international trade, 318
licensing agreements, 153
and localization, 158–9, 162
local networks, 162–3
and M&A, 408–9
models, 162
'national champions', 411
and OECD, 467
and power, 411
regulation, 411–12
scope of, 141
and social responsibility, 460–8
subcontractors, 153, 158
subsidiaries, 158–9, 163
success of, 152–4
top ten (2002), 145
transnationality index, 162
Togo, 456
Tommy Hilfiger, 455
tort law, 291, 293–4, 305
cost of, 294
Toyota, 145, 147, 157, 309, 438
trade, 346
blocs, regional, 338–9, 346
in capital goods, 370–2
and developing countries, 344
embargo, 327
global, intra-firm, 151
sanctions, 327, 334
trade agreements, 346
bilateral, 346
regional (RTAs), 338–9, 346–7
and US globalization, 338–9
trade, international, 314–47
and developing countries, 344–5
and government policy, 324–30

growth of, 138–48, 164, 314
patterns, 316
regulation of, 330–37
and states, 324–30
theory of absolute advantage, 316
see also GATT; IMF; World Bank; WTO
trade liberalization, 312, 325, 329, 333–8, 346–7
the Doha Round, 334–6
and national interests, 334
and sanctions, 334 *see also* WTO
trademarks, 101, 153, 287, 292–3
trade policy, 324–35
environmental issues, 334–5, 345
and foreign policy, 327
labour standards, 335–7, 345
and national priorities, 324–7
strategic, 326
trade unions, 51, 53, 54, 110, 122, 155–7, 159, 225–7, 232, 258, 467
trading standards, 50
trading systems, world, 312, 315, 330–2
dumping, 332
evolution of, 330–2
fair practices, 331–2
most-favoured national principle (MFN), 331
transaction costs, 152
transitional democracies, 262–6, 273
and international business, 266
transition economies, 117–27, 128, 193, 206, 263–5, 398, 411, 450
and child labour, 466–7
and foreign capital, 411
and rule of law, 281
and technology, 411
transnationality, 162, 195, 200
transport
and communication, 159, 164, 350, 450
costs, 350
revolution, 222
Travelers, 408
treaties, 300–5
Treaty of Amsterdam, 106, 286
Treaty of Rome, 269, 271, 286, 292, 301, 340
Triad blocs, 149
TRIPS (Trade-related Aspects of Intellectual Property), 369–70
Trompenaars, Fons, 192–4, 198, 202
5 relationship orientations, 192–4
trust, 169, 195
tsunami, 404
TUC, 226–7
Tunisia, 455

Turkey, 8, 125–6, 219, 242, 270
  and democracy, 283
  and the EU, 283–4
  and FDI, 283–4
  financial crisis, 397
  and Kurdish language, 283
  and legal reform, 283
  separatism, 283
Turner & Newell, 296
TV ownership, worldwide, 199

U
UAE (United Arab Emirates), 184, 218, 239, 316
Uganda, 96, 459
  entrepreneurs, 96
UK, 8, 123, 192–3, 247, 250, 266, 322, 358–9
  ageing population, 215
  balance of payments, 75–6
  capitalism, 95, 101
  climate change levy, 440
  colonial expansion, 144
  Consumer Protection Act, 1987, 294
  and defence, 259, 359
  economic data, 80, 83
  economy, 69, 81–90, 101
  entrepreneurs, 96
  and the EU, 86–90
  fiscal policy, 82–3
  global competitiveness, 322–3
  greenhouse gas emissions, 439–41
  Human Rights Act, 1998, 303–4
  and immigration, 220
  labour government, 101
  Labour Party, 258–9
  military, 242–4
  north-south divide, 74–5, 101
  and nuclear power, 433
  Patents Act (1977), 365
  pensions, 214
  political system, 247, 250, 252–3, 256, 258–9, 260–1
  public spending, 82–3
  social class, 209–10
  socioeconomic classification scheme, 209
  and the UN, 269–71
  unemployment, 73–5
Ukraine, 120, 433
  and greenhouse gas emissions, 429
UN (United Nations), 237–8, 242, 244, 266–8, 289, 300–1
  Charter, 267–8
  Global Compact, 467–8
  and human poverty, 452
  ICC, 301
  ICJ, 300–1
  and international peace, 268
  member states, 238
  sanctions, 268, 300

Security Council, 267–8
UNCED (UN Conference on Environment and Development), 434
uncertainty avoidance (Hofstede), 191–4
UNCITRAL (UN Commission on International Trade Law), 289
unemployment, 71, 73–5, 91, 118, 122, 124, 237, 326
  Germany, 78–9
  and government, 71, 73, 75, 78–81
UNEP (UN Environment Programme), 434
UNIDROIT (International Institute for the Unification of Private International Law), 289–90
Unilever, 16, 467
Union Carbide, 295
UNISON, 226
United Biscuits, 406
Universal Studios, 416
urbanism, 221–5
urbanization, 221–5, 231–2, 424–6, 444–5
urban regeneration, 223–4
US, 8, 19–20, 45, 46, 58, 149, 161–2, 183, 190, 192–3, 195–7, 322, 358–9
  ageing population, 215
  agriculture, 343, 345
  automobile industry, 154–7
  and Cuba, 327
  and defence, 242–4, 359
  economy, 84, 86, 95
  entrepreneurs, 96
  FDI in, 148
  and financial reporting, 58
  and free trade, 342
  and GM crops, 381–2
  greenhouse gas emissions, 427, 429
  Hispanic population, 176–7
  and Kyoto Protocol, 428
  and law, 284
  military, 242–4, 260, 266
  and NAFTA, 341–2
  national identity, 195
  new trade theory, 359
  and nuclear power, 433
  and oil, 317
  Patent Office, 368
  political system, 250, 256, 260
  post-war expansion, 145, 154–6
  and protectionism, 333
  and steel, 332–3
  taxation, 86
  technological innovation, 355, 357, 368; and patents, 365–9
  tort litigation, 294–5
  trade deficit, 314
  trade legislation, 327

and world competitiveness, 322–3
  see also Coca-Cola; Fordism; TNCs

V
values, see cultural values
Venezuela, 10, 96, 238–9, 316
venture capital, 360
VER (voluntary export restraint), 328–30
Vernon, Raymond, International Product Life Cycle Theory, 323–4
Vienna Convention 1980 (CISG), 289–92
Vietnam, 143
  and coffee, 461–2
Virgin, 10, 11
Visteon, 159
Vodafone, 145, 408–11
  expansion, 409
  takeovers, 408–10
Volkswagen, 48, 147, 252, 309

W
Wales, 70, 73, 75, 247, 250, 255
  GDP, 73
Wal-Mart, 7, 17, 160-1
war crimes, trial, 300–1
Warner-Lambert, 408
war on terror, 244
water, 452–3
  Générale des Eaux, 461
  Lyonnaise des Eaux, 461
  management, 430–1
  privatization, 461
  world resources, 430–1
wealth, 94–5, 101, 127, 140, 184, 189, 206–7, 209–10, 239, 425
  accumulation of, 101, 127
  distribution of, 94
  inequalities, 224
weapons of mass destruction, 242
Weber, Alfred, 152
Weber, Max, 187–8
  Protestant work ethic, 187–8
Welch, Jack (GE), 416–17
welfare, social, 78–9, 94, 101, 109–12, 114
welfare state, 109, 127, 236–7, 258–9, 277
Wella, 17
Western values, 169, 173, 183–4, 187–8, 202
  vs. Asian values, 187–9
  and families, 231
Windows, 107, 379 see also Microsoft
wine exports, Australia, 320–1
WIPO (World Intellectual Property Organization), 367
women
  and government, 253
  and work, 210, 227–33; UK, 228–9

work
  changing nature of, 210, 229–32
  clerical, 210
  deskilling, 210
  and families, 230–3
  flexible, 228
  part-time, 228, 233
  and women, 210, 227–33
worker's rights, 465
working class, changes to, 209–11
working conditions, 454–5
workplace, Californian model, 157
World Bank, 331, 333, 392, 397–9, 411–14, 458, 471, 449
  and Africa, 458
  and AIDS, 454
  growth and change, 397–8
world, borderless, 469
world exports (2003), 345
world trade and globalization, 346
WTO (World Trade Organization), 118, 143, 150–1, 265, 315, 326, 331–8, 342, 345–7, 411, 449, 455, 476
  and China, 336, 344
  and consensus, 345
  and developing countries, 344–6
  and dispute settlement, 332–4, 345
  the Doha Round, 334–6, 476
  and GM crops, 382
World Wildlife Fund, 429, 467

X
Xerox, 27

Y
Yahoo!, 378–9
Yugoslav Federation, 119
Yugoslavia, 146, 174, 301

Z
Zaire, 176
Zapatero, José Luis Rodríguez (Spain), 251–2
Zen Buddhism, 186
Zimbabwe, 266